RIDING

MW00777405

To
Ted

Ride Safe, Ride Free

FR. Dave Barr
8/05/97

by

DAVID BARR

with

Mike Wourms

RIDING THE EDGE

Published by
Promotion Publishing
3368 Governor Drive, Suite 144
San Diego, Ca 92122
1 (800) 231-1776

@ 1995 Dave Barr

Cover design by Mitch Wourms
c/o C.S.N., 1959 Longs Hill Road
El Cajon, Ca. 92021
1 (800) 636-7276

ISBN # 1-887314-12-1

FOREWORD

Fasten your seat belts and hold on to your hats...Dave Barr is about to take you on a journey around the world! Before your incredible adventure is over, you'll ride through six continents, encounter countless cities, and meet dramatically different people from every corner of the world. When your experience is over, Dave hopes you will be encouraged to unwrap that secret dream you've stuck up on a shelf, take it down, dust it off, and decide to live your dream!

Riding the Edge is not a travel log - it is an **adventure** that dramatically changes in each of the seven stages. Each stage is a new exploit, a book within a book, and presents a new set of problems from the weather, to the roads, to the terrain, to the bureaucracy and the living conditions. For example, Stage One in Africa takes you from one riveting, humorous adventure after another, while Asia's Stage Five reveals interesting insights into the Chinese people and culture.

In every stage, you will meet a myriad of people along the way who cared enough to lend a helping hand to Dave as he traveled alone, without the logistical support of a central organization. You will be inspired as you discover how a journey to promote and heighten the awareness of the disabled, and their **abilities** rather than their disabilities, brings a whole new set of rules to world travel. Dave completed this 83,000 mile quest not to present himself as a hero, but to simply inspire others to live their dreams.

If the reader feels that world travel on a motorcycle is a simple, easy experience, then please, think again! According to Brend Tesch, the leading historian on round-the-world motorcycle travel, there have only been 70 people since the year 1912 to successfully circumnavigate the world on a motorcycle. It is an elite corps of riders who attempt to take on this planet on two wheels!   This is not the type of journey one decides to do "just for fun," as you will clearly see in the following pages.

Riding the Edge offers a wealth of information and experiences for readers of different interests, including motorcyclists, people who love adventure, people with disabilities, people who enjoy being encouraged and inspired, people who want to escape the rigors of daily life, and people contemplating an inter-continental journey - the hard way.

Mike Wourms

Note: For specific information on long distance motorcycle travel, contact Brend Tesch, Haus - Sonnenhof, Zur Fersicht # 18, D-52224 Zweifall, Germany, [Phone: 49-2402-75375].

DEDICATION

This book is dedicated to my late father, Preston Guy Barr, who throughout all the years of madness never failed to understand, giving freely of his love and support.

Also, to my mother, Lucille Barr, who lived this great adventure with the undying belief that I could go the distance!

TABLE OF CONTENTS

Chapter Fourteen (Continued)
Frozen Rivers, Faithful Friends, and Haunted Bunkers
Sumptuous Scenery, the Arctic Circle, and Reindeer Dangers
Living My Dream!
Radioactive Reindeer and the Biker Brotherhood

STAGE THREE: NORTH AMERICA

STAGE SEVEN: SOUTH EAST ASIA

Stage One: Africa

Chapter One

"I'm On My Way to Meet Jesus!"

August 29, 1981, 15:30: Every journey has a beginning, and mine started on this day in Southern Angola while on operations with the South African defense forces. On a scale of 1 to 10 for bad days, it rated about a 9.5 (with ten being death)!

The left-rear wheel of the light (non-armored) vehicle I was traveling in triggered an anti-tank mine, and 32 pounds (15 kilograms) of TNT erupted into a mighty explosion! Suddenly, I was launched - propelled through the air by the force of the unexpected blast.

Looking down at the truck from several feet above it, my first thought was "I'm on my way to meet Jesus!"

Fortunately, Jesus and I still have not met face to face.

As I floated above the truck, it exploded in flames. The raging fire and black smoke so engulfed the vehicle that it became a burning ball - the intense flames fed by the extra fuel we were carrying. I felt a surge of tremendous heat rise up to me, literally forcing my body even higher in mid air - away from the fiery force.

As suddenly as I shot up in the air, I fell back down to earth, crashing into the vehicle, landing exactly in my original launching spot.

But something was drastically wrong!

My legs were unnaturally twisted and tangled around my head, with my right boot pressed against my face.

I struggled to get out of the vehicle, but the fire surged all around and over me. I was burning to death as the fire sucked precious oxygen from my lungs.

The next thing I remember is being pulled out of the vehicle by Colonel Breytenbach, a true leader of men. In retrospect, I wonder if I would have returned that life-saving action for him - the vehicle was *shockingly hot*!

As Colonel Breytenbach lifted me out of the fire, quickly pulling me away, I saw the face of my friend, the driver of the vehicle, Lang Price, his glasses hanging off his ears below the chin, helping the Colonel pull me to safety.

They freed me from the fire and ran as fast as they could, dragging me away with them, knowing every second counted since the vehicle was loaded with C 4 plastic explosives and 50 caliber, heavy machine gun ammunition!

Suddenly, we heard and felt the force of an ear-shattering "Baloooom."

In an instant, I knew the vehicle was gone... and we were still here!

"Graham... Graham..." I called out, wanting assurance that Graham Gilmore, our radioman, was alive.

"Graham was blown out of the vehicle," Lang told me, "but he'll be okay."

Once I was reassured that all of us in the command vehicle were alive, I took note of my own right leg. I saw a mangled mess, with no blood flowing the burns had caused coagulation, stopping the bleeding. In my heart of hearts, I knew I would loose this leg.

Little did I know then that eventually both legs would go.

I spent the next 9 months and 18 days in one military hospital in Pretoria, South Africa.

The toll on my body was extreme: 20 major operations - four of them amputations:

1. The right foot went first when it started smelling bad.

2. The doctors wanted me to keep the right knee, but it would only have 30 percent movement. After a couple weeks of extremely painful irrigation treatments, and the knowledge that with a prosthesis I would have 50 percent or more movement (plus something you couldn't injure or hurt), I elected to chop off the knee.

3. A series of operations on the left foot and ankle left me with the ability to walk on the left leg with incredible pain. After consultation with medical authorities (most advising me to keep the leg), I asked the sixty-four dollar question: "Will I be able to ride my motorcycle again, or sky dive?" The looks of amazement on the doctors' faces was my answer, so I decided to amputate the left leg. First, they took the left foot, and two days later I had...

4. My fourth amputation - when they took my leg off below the knee.

Merry Christmas!

In addition to these disabilities, the accident also caused me to suffer total loss of hearing in my left ear (with a constant ring), and a partial loss in my right.

Severe burns covered my hands, arms and back.

Oh, yes, I am also colorblind.

What you see is what you get!

After 9 1/2 months of being patched, sliced, diced, and stitched, I returned to active duty on...

June 18, 1982: My first assignment was in the training team of 44 Parachute Brigade, under the leadership of the finest enlisted soldier that, in my opinion, the world has ever known - Sgt. Major Peter McCleese (*No Mean Soldier* is an excellent, best-selling biography that describes his amazing life). After six weeks, the team went up to Angola with a company of paratroopers we had been training.

I am no longer out walking in the bush. Any movements I make with the troops are on **armored** vehicles (not *light* ones), or helicopters. I'm getting smarter all the time. My new assignment was servicing machine guns and doing on-the-job training in the forward areas.

December, 1982: My contract was up, so I rotated back to Pretoria, South Africa, and separated from the South African army, heading home to the United States to be reunited with my mother and father, ending my military career, and beginning my life away from the death-gray world of the operational soldier.

I walked back into our house four years from the day that I had walked out, not knowing then that I was about to embark on an impossible, incredible, unbelievable journey to *The Ends Of The Earth*.

At the time, all I knew was that I was home, and that I was changed.

My parents knew my right leg was gone, but I didn't have the heart to tell them about the left one at the same time (though I believe they did suspect it). I'm just full of surprises! Some are better than others.

When my plane landed in Los Angeles, I took a taxi out to my home in West Covina.

"Let me off here," I instructed the cab driver, climbing out at a service station a few blocks from my house where I had worked as a young man. Entering their men's room, I cleaned up from the long trip, and put on a tie (I wanted to look good for Mom and Dad). I picked up my suitcase and all my gear, and started walking towards my house.

When I passed Jim and Dean Lorenzo's house (like a second set of parents to me), I thought about the steady stream of letter's I'd received from Dean while I was in the Marines, and I thought about the wonderful times their sons and I had enjoyed as carefree young men growing up together.

Further along, I sat down on a brick planter in front of the old folks home at the top of Siesta street - where my home was located.

"It's been four years to the day since I left home," I thought.

In my heart there was an emptiness, and yet, at the same time, an apprehension and an excitement. I looked around the street and seemingly nothing had changed. One neighbor was out trimming the hedge, kids were running around here and there, and the same roar of the freeway could be heard in the background.

West Covina was suburbia in middle-class America - and it had not changed one bit.

"Was the world I saw these last four years really out there?" I wondered, "Was it real? Was all the hatred, all the guns, the violence, was it all really there?"

I thought about places like Angola - "Was it a true reality of life?"

Four years ago, to the very day, I had stepped off the front porch of my family home and set out to those far away places, and now, I'm back on a planter, seventy-five yards from home, filled with elation, a heavy heart, and apprehension.

Elation - for coming home.

A heavy heart - for the people I've left behind.

And apprehension - at how my family would react to my loss of two legs. In my heart, I knew there would be no problem, but still, at the moment, it was an unknown factor.

I put my suitcase on my shoulder, got up from the planter, looked down at the sidewalk, and thought: "When I was a kid, I used to run around on a skateboard, up and down the sidewalk, when they were just building this old age home."

Then, I started towards my house (we had lived on Siesta since 1958).

I went to the door and knocked.

Mom opened the door, and immediately tears of joy flowed into her eyes. Through my own tears, I saw Dad behind her. All three of us hugged each other - and for several minutes we just held on, clutching desperately to the moment.

After a very touching reunion, late that night I made this final entry in my diary, closing out the last four years of my life:

> *It has been four years to the day since I started this diary. I have written one thousand, four hundred and eighty entries on two thousand and twenty-four pages. I have said a thousand prayers, looking for the moment when I could be reunited again with my Mother and Father. Thank God for the strength and power given me to come so far. Thus ends this diary.*

Next, I went out into the garage to have a reunion with something else - my old 1972 Harley Davidson I had owned for ten years at that time. I unwrapped it from its protective plastic, and after four years in storage, I began to reassemble it, putting on the front end and the rear wheel. Within a week, that old Harley was standing up on its wheels.

But how could I start it?

With my peg legs, my father and I realized I could never crank start it again.

And how could I brake on the right side with my mechanical knee?

Together, we devised a brake where my foot would sit on it all the time. We put an overload spring for the weight of the right leg. When the right stump pushes the leg, it depresses the overload spring that pushes the brake that stops the motorcycle.

It works... <u>MOST</u> of the time.

Dad and I then took the Harley down to our local dealer and asked him to install an electric starter (I should have done this years ago. It would have eliminated a lot of cursing and bitching on cold mornings).

A few days later he called and said, "Dave, your machine is ready. Do you really think you can ride this thing?"

"Well, I honestly don't know," I replied. "I've had a few sleepless nights thinking about it."

My friend, Blair Bushing, drove me down to the Harley Davidson dealer where my motorcycle was sitting outside the shop, ready to go. We wheeled it over to a parking lot next door and started it up.

I climbed on it for the first time in over 4 years, only now, both of us had changed!

The 1200 cc. motorcycle weighed about 590 pounds, unloaded, so it was a challenge to handle. As I put it into first gear, I started to ride around in the parking lot...very wobbly at first...doing donuts. Before I knew it, I was doing figure 8's! The smile on my face grew with my confidence, until I suddenly rode right out into the traffic and was gone, leaving the Harley Davidson dealer standing there clutching his unpaid bill with a very nervous-looking Blair, who got into the car to follow me home. (By the way, the dealer did get his money.)

I rode to the freeway and got on, just letting go with the throttle.

Before I knew it, I was rolling along at over 80 miles per hour!

These first few minutes were an absolute and utter joy. As I flew down the freeway, feeling totally free, I thought, "What a great privilege I have here. After all, life is a fragile thing, and good health is a privilege, not a right.

My thoughts flashed towards people with disabilities.

"Wouldn't it be something to share this simple accomplishment of riding a motorcycle as a double amputee with disabled people the world over?" My inner hope was that they might find a bit of inspiration from my example.

"Perhaps I could be a role model," I thought, "for those people who might someday suffer the loss of good health. Just as Douglas Badger had inspired me through the media, maybe I can do the same thing for others, even on a one-to-one basis. Perhaps I can give others something to look back on that will help them get back into the race."

Then my mind came back to my immediate surroundings of the crowded San Bernardino freeway.

"I'd better slow down because I am sure the California Highway Patrol is not going to share my enthusiasm."

January, 1983: That day the pilot light was lit.

Now, I only needed to feed the fire.

From that moment on, I thought and talked about making a trip around the world incessantly. My friends listened to my prattle as though I were insane, or had finally gone over the edge (in retrospect, maybe they were right)!

I started to pester people, looking for sponsors, but no one seemed to get very excited about my project.

"I have such a great idea," I thought. "Why can't others see it?"

After a year in the States, I determined it was time to return to South Africa where I planned to work, hoping to make a new life for myself.

But "the trip" was always in the back of my mind.

Having been a soldier most of my adult life, living from day to day as a civilian was not an easy adjustment. Somehow, to work just for a roof and a few possessions never made much sense to me. I believe we are here for a greater purpose: to follow our destiny, to live our life the way God would have us do it, which (at least in my case) never seems to be a safe, secure path.

In 1987, I took a good look around me, and at some of my friends. We were drinking and talking our lives away. I was never able to drink modestly... one was too many, fifteen were never enough. My drinking was often so bad that, as a drunk, I was truly an out-of-control idiot, tumbling and falling over furniture, slobbering words and phrases in futile attempts at conversations with fellow drunkards.

One Monday morning in August, I woke up with my tongue stuck to the roof of my mouth, my head pounding, very depressed. I could not remember how I got home, although I knew I had driven because the car was out front. It was at this moment that I realized my menace to my fellow man. "I have no right to drink because I can't control it," I thought to myself. "How could I possibly put somebody in my physical position, or worse, as a result of my drinking?"

From that day forward, bolstered and hounded by that revelation, I have not touched a drop of alcohol.

Almost immediately, that gave me more time and energy to devote to a world journey. Plans and schemes started forming in my head more solidly as my mind cleared.

The Search for Sponsors

Through the help of a friend, Monty Brett, I started to contact media people, using my sky diving (more about this later) and the motorcycle to attract their interest. As they interviewed me, I always ended up plugging my dream - a motorcycle trip around the world on a Harley.

Taking a Harley around the world is like taking a Cadillac off-road racing. My reasoning for taking the Harley Davidson was this:

"If I am to be an example for others, I must take the hard road." In the words of one of the greatest inventors in the world today, Dr. Nakama of Japan, 'Never do anything the easy way, you might miss something'."

In taking the Harley on such an endeavor, I would say to Dr. Nakama, if I ever met him, "I have missed nothing."

To further enhance my challenge, to my knowledge no one had ever attempted to ride around the world on a motorcycle as a double amputee!

I pestered any one who would listen, looking for possible sponsors, but nothing happened for another two years. Finally, Monty Brett, tiring of me pestering him, introduced me to a group of gentlemen, some of them ex-paratroopers who had done very well in business. Eventually, four men - Mike McWilliams, Mike Calender, Peter McCloy and Jurgen Schultz - decided that they would back me on an internal ride in South Africa/S.W. Africa (now Namibia) if I could come up with an appropriate charity to represent.

Now, I had to find a charity!

You'd think that would be easy, but when I appealed to several different charities, I discovered none of them wanted anything to do with me.

"Too dangerous."

"Too risky."

"Too much of a liability."

Too this, too that!

To my way of thinking, they all acted like a *bunch of scared chicken shits!*

Finally, I went to a Rotary meeting where I met Alex Thompson, a man who had dealings with the Leonard Cheshire Foundation, a world-wide organization for people with disabilities. Alex was interested in my project, and instructed me to go to a foundation home where I met two people who were to become very dear friends, Luke and Gary - quadriplegics.

Luke had an accident when he was swimming in the sea. As he was walking out of the water, a large wave hit him, knocked him down, and snapped his neck (don't turn your back on the sea); he has never moved again except in agony, from below the neck.

Gary was hurt in a motorcycle accident after he had a few too many beers, cutting short a career as a top-notch movie stunt man!

Both Gary and Luke expressed a desire to go sky diving, and I thought to myself, "How in the hell am I going to arrange this?"

I felt that if I could make their dream happen, perhaps the Cheshire Foundation would agree for me to make a trip in their name around the sub-continent.

I approached the proper authorities out at the drop zone, and received permission from the tandem master to make the jump. We brought Gary and Luke out to the airfield, and with the help of some fellow skydivers, we hooked them up to the tandem master - one at a time - for their individual jumps.

Luke went first, and his eyes radiated terror. Before he jumped, his head was bowed into his chest, and I could sense his anguish.

"Hey, Luke, what have you got to worry about?" I asked, trying to lighten him up. "If you bounce, you couldn't feel anything anyway!"

That brought a smile to his face.

When we put him into the plane, we had to be concerned about his head being down on his chest, since he might suffocate. But that worked out just fine.

We flew up to 9,000 feet, and, *for the first time in Southern Africa, to my knowledge, not one but eventually two quadriplegics were involved in a free-fall parachute jump!*

After these two very unique sky dives were made, a wealthy fellow who was jumping that same day gave us a check for R3,000 (about $1,500), and that money went to the Foundation.

The Cheshire Foundation appreciated the gift, and then agreed that I could make a motorcycle trip in their name.

When the word got out, money flowed into the account set up to receive funds from sponsors. I was to draw from this account, and then ride around Southern Africa. After the trip, it was agreed that I could overhaul my motorcycle with the excess money, and the remaining funds going to the Leonard Cheshire Foundation.

Preliminary Journey As An Amputee

October 17, 1989: With sweaty palms and contrived confidence, I started the Harley and rode out of the Cheshire Home with full fanfare and warm well wishes from the home's residents, especially from my friends, Luke, and Gary.

That day I rode to Bloemfontein, and the next day brought me into S.W. Africa (now Namibia), to the town of Keetmanshoop. I stayed at the home of two friends, Mel and Neda, as I prepared the motorcycle for its first real test - the attempt to cross the Namib Desert.

The next day I arrived in Bethanie - where pavement ends, and I turned up a dirt road that runs for 500 miles (about 800 kilometers) to Walvis Bay on the South Atlantic Coast. The ride up this dirt road was a treacherous one, with deep gravel, sand, and ruts.

The road is in fairly good condition for a vehicle with four wheels, but when you're riding on a fully loaded Harley Davidson (about 700 pounds), it can be treacherous! Normally, one crosses this type of road on something like a Japanese enduro which weighs far less.

On my first day on a dirt road, I got a little bit cocky, going too far in one day...about 300 miles (500 kilometers), averaging too fast a speed - about 50 miles per hour. When my tires dug into some deep gravel, the Harley wobbled and threw me off. I landed on my knees, then my elbows, then the motorcycle landed on me! It felt like a freight train as it came from behind and knocked me flat into the gravel and sand! Then, it went flipping along on its own, coming to rest on its kick stand, sitting on its wheels!

Never let it be said that the Harley Davidson Motor Company "don't make good kick stands!"

Flat on the ground in pain, the first thing I did was search for my heavy caliber revolver. There are lions in the Namib Desert, and there are the roaming Namas, a desert people who can also be hazardous to one's health.

When I located the revolver, I cleaned it out the best I could. It was hard to move! Incredible pain punished my pelvis and ribs. Later, I would learn that my pelvis and two ribs were cracked.

Holstering the revolver, I made myself somehow stand up and walk around, collecting the gear now spread out over an area of about 50 meters. Though I was delirious with pain, I had to keep myself moving, putting my belongings back on the motorcycle. My water bottle had been smashed, so I didn't have any water.

By this time, it was early afternoon in the Namib desert, and the 100 degree sun was merciless as it scorched my already scrapped and bruised body. In this mountainous (similar to Mojave desert) hotbox of scrub-brush and thorn bushes, I decided to seek protection in the small bit of shade that the motorcycle provided, and wait.

After about an hour and a half, a park ranger came along named John.

"Well, what's this?" John said, attempting humor which I didn't need at the time.

"This is what a motorcycle accident, looks like," I said sarcastically, trying my own hand at comedy.

"How are you?" he asked, seeing the seriousness of the scene.

"Well, not as good as you are," I replied.

"I can see that," he responded as he chuckled a bit. I would have laughed, too, I suppose, except it would have hurt too much.

"Give me about an hour. I'll go back to the ranger station and get a pickup truck we can use to carry your motorcycle. I'll bring some of the African rangers back with me to help get this machine up on the truck."

He left me a chair.

As John departed, I sat looking across the flats at some mountains, listening to the silence.

"I will carry on," I thought, "no matter what! I will not let this accident get me down." Then other words flashed through my mind. "Here it is, so early in the trip, and already this! There's so many people in Johannesburg who are wondering, if not almost betting on the fact that I won't make it across the desert."

That thought was depressing to me, but even more so was the notion that I might let the people at the Cheshire Home down, especially Gary and Luke, who had been so involved in the preparation and planning stages of this trip, right from the beginning.

They were <u>as much a part of it</u> as I was, and they were living it through me.

"If I fail," I thought, "I will be failing them."

About an hour later, the ranger came back. We loaded the motorcycle up - and it was in worse shape than I was...all the wiring was burned out, the left handlebar was smashed, the triple trees broke, the rims were bent - but the kick stand was okay!

That evening, Ranger John was teaching a bird course to some Rotarians in the area, and he took me to the meeting. Although it was painful to move, I thought, "If I just keep moving, I'll be okay, and won't stiffen up."

The pain was incredible!

Every now and again my hip made a "c-r-u-n-c-h" noise, and the act of sitting or standing brought stars to my eyes; laying down also hurt because of the cracked ribs.

One of the Rotarians we met that evening had an engineering works, and another knew automotive electronics, so I could see the beginning of something good. The next day, after taking the front wheel off the Harley, we put the whole machine into the back of a van and went on to Walvis Bay, about 100 miles away (160 kilometers), where I stayed at the hospital for the night. X-rays confirmed a crack in my hip where the buttock cheek bone is, and two cracked ribs.

"You'll need to stay here for a week," the doctor told me.

"Bull shit!" I replied, knowing I could not let anything stop this trip short of death.

The next morning, I left the hospital and caught a ride down to the engineering works. The owner assigned an old man named Shortie to work with me. He had ridden Harleys during World War II in North Africa and Italy as a dispatch rider, so we developed a rapport immediately. Together, we started working on the motorcycle.

Though I was in great pain, we worked for the next four days - from opening time to closing time (sometimes even later) - getting the motorcycle back in running condition. Luckily, the engine itself had not been damaged internally, and eventually the bike was ready to go again.

Everybody wished me well, and with a *great* pain in my ass and my ribs, I headed for Windhoek, about 260 miles (400 kilometers) away. Bounding along the road - through the desert, then the bushveld (grasslands with scattered shrubs or trees), I finally got off the dirt and arrived in Windhoek where I went to Power Guns to see Barry and Manford, old customers of mine from my days while employed at Used Gun Exchange. Manford took me out to his remote farm 55 miles (80 kilometers) down a dirt road, with no neighbors within 3 miles (5 kilometers), where I spent a very quiet weekend with his family.

That Monday, although I was still in excruciating pain, I had to push on. I headed out of Windhoek for Rundu, up in the Okavango area in the Northeastern part of Namibia. It took me two days to get up there and experience...

Another accident on a dirt road (I'm not having very much luck with dirt roads)!

I came off the thing in sand, and the pain - I was seeing stars and lights for minutes as I got up and stumbled around. I had to pay an African woman and her kids about 50 cents to help me pick the motorcycle up.

"Please don't tell my friends," I told her, "they will never let me live it down" (she didn't understand a word I said).

I spent the night at a hunting camp which was right below the Angolan border, turning around the next morning and heading back out in the direction of Grootfontein, and from Grootfontein to Tsumeb. Riding through the bushveld, the only vehicles I saw were from the U.N..

November 1: There was a camping area in Tsumeb where I spent the night. I sat looking at the clouds, thinking about my father, and some of his sayings he had for me through the years. A feeling of nostalgia swept over me.

The next morning, I moved on to Ondangwa, which is the base we operated out of when I was in the South African Defense Forces. I'm in my old stomping grounds, many years removed from the time, yet nothing had changed. There were still herds of goats, sheep, cows, and donkeys crossing and recrossing the road to drink out of the canal that runs along the western side of the road, creating a terrible traffic hazard. This area is known as the Operational area where the war had been going on with S.W.A.P.O. for the past 14 years. Many dead animals and wrecked vehicles are on the sides of the road.

I went on to Oshakati (where I had my first operation, eleven hours after we ran over the land mine), fueled up, had a cup of tea with the proprietor of the petrol station, then journeyed north 110 miles (180 km). There was a ridge climbing up off the road, looking into Angola. "I could get some good photos from there," I thought.

Once on the ridge, the realization struck me, "Now, how do I get off?"

There was no easy way.

So, I crashed my way down through the bushes, and was thrown off the motorcycle again on a very steep slope. Had I had gone over the nearby ledge, I would have continued rolling and flipping down the hillside about 150 meters. I managed to get the motorcycle up and climb on, but the slope was so great my right foot couldn't touch the ground. For stability, I put the trusty kick stand down and started it up, turning the handle bars 90 degrees.

I had to take off while it was still on its kick stand, so I revved up both the bike and my courage, then dropped the clutch. The motorcycle took off like a raped ape turning 90 degrees on the kick stand, my feet dragging behind me, my chest on the gas tank. With the motorcycle at an involuntary full throttle, I hit the sloping shoulder of the road, my legs already flying behind me, with only my hands desperately clutching the handle bars.

I flew over the narrow road, nearly hitting the rock wall on the far side of the road. When I finally stopped, I was exhausted, panting, dehydrated, shaking, but alive!

Incidentally, the pictures didn't come out!

Life's Mine Fields Continue

I pushed on to the border of Angola and S. W. Africa (Namibia) through a village supposedly held by S.W.A.P.O... the noise of my machine shocked the quiet village from their afternoon siesta. Animals, kids, and adults ran in all directions from the chaos my sudden arrival caused.

The REAL PROBLEM was my momentary visitation and return from the dam in Angola. As a white man in S.W.A.P.O.- held territory, I was viewed as an intruder from the Boer republic (meaning, South Africa). Returning from that dam in Angola, which was only a few hundred meters from the village, I came ROARING back through before the S.W.A.P.O. could get their rifles and start shooting at me!

The element of surprise worked!

I spent the night at a secure police camp, surrounded by a protective mine field, three white policemen and forty-five African officers. It was incredible to hear an animal wandering in the mine field - "BANG...bah, moo, heehaw"!

That would be the end animal's explorations!

At the camp, a drunk African policeman decided to shoot up the camp. In rather typical example of African justice, a South African police officer found the offender.

We then heard some loud yelling voices, and "S-M-A-C-K....u-h-h-h-h-h."

Justice had been served.

The South African policeman came back with the offender's rifle, giving it to one of the officers in charge.

November 3: The next morning, I elected not to travel with the convoy going back to Oashakotie. The police wouldn't be ready to move before 09:00.

"The road is straight and the visibility is good," I reasoned, "at least 100 meters on each side. The landscape is semi-desert, bushveld - and if I travel at a very high velocity, I should get past any ambushes that might be put in the road."

Mind you, this was during the run up to their elections, so there were many S.W.A.P.O. marauding in the area, trying to get votes.

06:00: Headed down the road about 70-75 miles per hour. "If they want to ambush me," I thought, "they'll have to run a herd of animals out on the road to slow me down, or they'll never get a clear shot."

Thankfully, I never encountered any hostile troops. On the entire, lonely 110 mile trip (180 km), I didn't see another vehicle (maybe no one else was silly enough to be on the road at that time of the morning).

When I pulled into the petrol station where I had fueled up the day before in Oshakati, the owner came out and said, "Dave, there's an announcement on the radio about your father. You need to call Mr. Don Hornsby in Johannesburg."

This was rural Africa, so it took a full half hour just to get a phone line through to Johannesburg. When I connected, Don told me that my father had passed away as a result of a heart attack.

With an incredibly shocked and burdened heart, I rode 600 more miles (1000 km) that day to get back to Windhoek, mechanically dodging herds of animals and various other road hazards, such as convoys of U.N. troop-carrying vehicles trying to monitor the cease fire.

Arriving in Windhoek, I took the motorcycle to my friends, Manford and Barry, at Power Guns, so they could watch my machine while I journeyed to the United States. I spent the night with the commander of the S. W. African parachute battalion, and the next day he took me to the airport where I flew back to Johannesburg for a one day stop over. One of my bosses, Dan Levine, at Used Gun Exchange, managed to exchange $5,000 for me, and Don Hornsby had my plane tickets ready. I paid my bills, thanked my friends for all they had done, then climbed on the plane and flew to London, and then on to Los Angeles, where I made it home in time, numb with grief, for my father's funeral.

I was home for 7 weeks, often sitting in the back yard in the cold nights thinking not only about the recrossing of the Namib Desert, but also of the world trip...praying to God for the power to carry on with this ride and see it through to the end. All the while, I am limping around quite badly, and did not tell my Mom about my accident. In her very grieved state, she didn't ask many questions, and I didn't volunteer many facts about why I was limping.

December 19, 1989: Seven weeks after I had arrived home, flew back to South Africa and arrived there on the 21st. On the 22nd, I flew to Windhoek. On the 23rd, I serviced the motorcycle, and, on Christmas Eve, I said good-bye to Barry, and resumed my journey around Southern Africa.

It was good that Christmas Eve morning to see the various African game animals out on the road in the early morning hours.

That first night found me back in the Namib Desert on the dirt track, isolated. Alone.

Unbearably hot.

The nearest person to me might have been 60 miles away.

The carburetor had been giving me trouble all day. In a temperature of about 115 degrees, I put a tarp over the motorcycle to shield me from the sun, and started pulling the carburetor and intake manifold off to find out why I was leaking air. I installed a new set of intake manifold bands while the engine was still fiery hot!

My repair completed by evening, I climbed one of the sand dunes and watched the magic sunset. Returning to camp, I opened my luscious Christmas Eve dinner - a can of baked beans and some bread.

The dusk gradually turned into night.

And desert silence.

There alone in that *Silent Night, Holy Night*, I began to really let down. With all the traveling to and from the U. S., the loss of my father, and the pressures and worries of trying to get the trip back on the road, it felt good to be totally alone. My sponsors still had no knowledge of my accident in the desert. If they had, I was sure they would pull their money out for fear of me hurting myself again.

Christmas Day: Another 200 miles in scorching 120°F heat (December is the height of summer in the Namib desert) down the dirt track, through the area where I had the accident. Believe me, I went through that day with a bit of anxiety in my heart, but strangely, it was a very good tonic to ride over that area again, totally on my own, for Christmas night.

Out in the middle of nowhere, I found water in an animal water tank, loaded up my canteen, put some water tablets in the disgusting green water, and kicked back to watch the sunset.

At last, no heat!

This is especially valued by me because of scar tissue, and because of the leather and plastic encasements attached to my prosthesis. My body has an extremely difficult time cooling - far more so than a normal person.

I ate my sumptuous Christmas dinner of another tin of beans and some stale bread as I enjoyed the dark and quiet of the Namib Desert, and the star-studded sky, wondering, "What is the future of this journey?"

From there, I rode back towards Keetmanshoop, staying with Mel and Neda. What a grand blessing to be on asphalt again! It felt like a magic carpet. After servicing my motorcycle, I was ready for the ride to the bottom tip of Africa.

Dignitaries and Baboons

It had been arranged for me to meet the mayor of Capetown, and to do a talk in a Cheshire home in the area. In Capetown, I met some motorcyclists who had taken a very keen interest in my trip after hearing me on a radio talk show, and had organized the meeting. That evening I gave my talk to the residents of a Cheshire home, encouraging them not to accept the constraints of society but to "live their dreams."

The next day I met the mayor of Capetown.

Out of Capetown, 75 miles (120 kilometers), I arrived at Cape Agulhas, where the Indian and the Atlantic Oceans meet - the bottom tip of Africa. I thought to myself, "What of the future? Would I ever see the North Cape at the top of Europe in the Arctic?"

Riding north up the majestic garden route along the Indian Ocean, to Durban, I met their mayor. I thought, "Man, who would have ever imagined that plain, ordinary Dave Barr would be meeting the mayors of two of the four major cities in South Africa?"

Leaving North out of Durban, the next stop is the Northeastern Transvaal, a province in the north of the country.

I usually search for out-of-the-way areas to make my camp, avoiding campgrounds when I can. To protect myself, I always carry a heavy caliber revolver, especially for old or wounded lions that can't hunt any longer.

One night while laying out in the darkness with a full moon, it was very quiet in the bush. As a precaution, I had packed gear under the bottom of the motorcycle so a lion could not reach under it and take a swipe at me. He had to come at me from my frontal view of 180 degrees.

Besides the lions, there were packs of hyenas in the area.

Midway through the night, I was awakened and startled by a leopard about 10 meters away from me, staring directly into my eyes! I grabbed my revolver and pointed it at him. As he was looking at me, I thought to myself, "Holy mackerel...nice kitty, nice kitty!!!"

The next 120 seconds seemed like 120 days.

Finally, the leopard decided that I wasn't anything good to eat, and shot off into a thicket. Out of the thicket came babbling baboons, screeching and running in all directions! Leopards regularly feed on baboons, so they were literally running and screaming and barking for their very lives.

Baboons can also be very vicious animals when they are provoked. Fortunately, although I had baboons within a few meters of me, none decided to attack.

Ultimately, the leopard ran out of the other side of the thicket with a dead baboon in his mouth. Dinner was served, and I'll guarantee it was far tastier than me.

By the time I arrived in Johannesburg, my machine was limping - the engine knocked, and the rear tire was going flat.

It was finished.

And no wonder!

It had been ridden 9,000 miles (14,500 kilometers) - and that was just a preview for what was to come!

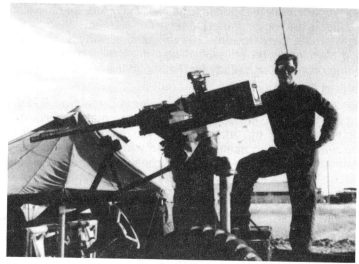

S.W. Africa: The vehicle that hit the land mine on August 29, 1981.
Dave is behind guns. A Long Journey Begins!

24

Chapter Two

Putting Muscle to the Dream

It was time to redo the whole motorcycle and prepare for a world attempt. I knew I wasn't going to find any more sponsors, so I did a major overhaul on the motorcycle by myself. In my "spare time," on the urging of Colonel Breytenbach, I wrote a draft for a book that was never published on my life as a soldier, called *Four Flags*. I did this with my friend, Luke Kotze. Every Thursday night and Sunday morning we had a ritual where I would sit and record, such as I am doing right now, and, in these recordings, I would tell him the stories of what was to be called, *Four Flags*.

To support myself, I worked full time at "Used Gun Exchange," starting my day there around 07:00, and usually finishing up around 17:00 in the evening. I also counseled with various accident victims and disabled people in the hospitals. Plus, I worked out an hour and one-half, five days a week. I received my gym subs for nothing because I opened the gym every morning at 05:00.

A hectic time, yes, but I had a mission: a world trip. My target date, set on New Year's Eve, 1989 at Colonel Breytenbach's house, was September 12, 1990.

I had 9 months and 12 days to get on with it.

Despite Monty Brett's attempts to get the media involved through interviews to help me secure sponsors, there were no takers.

From outside the paratrooper's circle, there was the late Jurgen Schultz and Don Hornsby. Jurgenz, an avid motorcyclist himself, set me up to speak to Concor Construction's middle management, and they paid me very well to do a rather poor job with a motivational speech.

My circle of friends never doubted that I could do the world trip, but I must confess, right up to the time I started, and right through the trip, I would never say anything so arrogant as "Don't worry, I'll go the distance." It was far too risky and too big an adventure to say such a silly thing.

By now, my Harley had 150,000 miles on it in total, so I sent the engine back to the United States to be rebuilt (the Harley Davidson man in South Africa had left the country, and the man who had taken over did not have enough experience to do an engine overhaul). Fully 95% of all the major mechanical problems I would experience upon this entire adventure would prove to be the result of improper or incompetent repair work done by various repairmen, and not due to the materials or workmanship of the Manufacturer. Sending the engine to the U.S. would later prove to be an expensive mistake.

I continued to work 10 hour days at "Used Gun Exchange" for Dan Levine and David Sheer. They knew my plans to leave, yet they gave me raises, and kept my job open for me while I was overseas for my dad's funeral for seven weeks, and during my trip around S.W. Africa/ Namibia. Their help made it possible for me to prepare for the world trip with steady income.

As the months passed, the pace picked up as I worked on my motorcycle, trying to get it ready. About a month before my scheduled departure, I presented Colonel Breytenbach with the draft of *Four Flags*.

In the last minute whirlwind of final preparations, I closed all of my personal affairs. Anything of value I owned was sold to help pay for the journey (the world attempt was not sponsored). I had paid for everything expect the motorcycle overhaul (which was paid for by the original Namib sponsors).

All my work on the Harley was done in Don Hornsby's garage; I don't know how I could have managed without his work facility.

September 8: Don gave me a going away party and invited all our friends, people who believed in me right from the start, and, I'm sure, some who probably didn't believe I could make it across Africa. If they had asked me then, "Dave, where should I put my money?," I would have been reluctant to tell them "Bet on me."

The party was not enjoyable for me. I like to celebrate when something is completed, not before the task starts. I kept thinking, "What if I fail and let all these people down? What would they think of me then? What about Luke, and all the residents at the Cheshire Home? They are living this through me."

The thought of failure created a cold, hard knot in the pit of my stomach, and it stayed there constantly throughout the trip. It would never let me fully rest.

September 11, 1990: Said good-bye to Luke. We parted with tears in our eyes. "You are my brother," he called out to me from his bed. Saying good-bye to Gary and the others was a bit easier, although still emotionally demanding.

The Day of Destiny...or Doom!

September 12, 1990, at 03:00: I awoke, opened my eyes, and started to live my dream, but there was no peace in my heart.

I woke up Don, Felicity and their sons. We all drove down to his garage in Denver, an industrial suburb in Johannesburg. Upon opening the garage doors and turning on the lights, I stared at the machine which, at that time, I had owned for 18 years. Now loaded, it seemed to be looking back at me, saying, "Okay, Dave, the time for talking and scheming is over. Today, your new destiny begins - the destiny that began with the land mine nine years and fourteen days ago."

I don't EVER want to feel what I felt that morning ever again.

The fear.

The feeling of ineptitude.

The uncertainty that overwhelmed me as I gazed upon the motorcycle.

My chest ached.

My heart pounded with adrenaline flowing through my veins. All my life I have heard that the world is a small place, and indeed that may be true when you sit down in the seat of a 747 jet and view it from 30,000 feet, but when you sit down on two small wheels and contemplate planet earth, it takes on a whole new and vivid dimension.

After filling up with gasoline, I gave Don, Felicity, and their boys, a big hug.

With fear in my heart, I hit the starter button.

"Don't get clever," Don said to me. "There are people here betting you won't make it."

These words of reality rang in my ears thousands of times over the next few years.

Don and his family followed me by car out onto the freeway, and as they exited the freeway to go home to the warmth and security of their normal environment (if South Africa can be called normal), we waved and shouted our love and affection for one another. I rode on into a very dark, cold morning, headed north to Tunis, 8,000 miles (13,000 kilometers) away, across the dark continent of Africa and on my way to destiny. Or disgrace.

Breakdowns, Baobabs, and Bureaucrats

Sunrise was magnificent over the wintry bushveld, so clear and bright with the promise of the new day. My last in South Africa.

The weight of the machine, fully loaded, was about 900 pounds. Foolishly, I had never test ridden the motorcycle fully loaded. My first discovery was that a bolt was cutting into my tire. Luckily, I felt the problem before it seriously damaged the tire. I

26

managed to get a hacksaw up inside the fender and cut the bolt down to a proper size, enabling me to carry on.

It was the first of *hundreds* of breakdowns!

As the day went forward, my first stop was in Pietersburg, where I had breakfast with the Cliffe family. Sadly enough, I was never to see Mrs. Cliffe again.

From there, on up through the Louie Treckhard area, over the mountains into the Northeastern Transvaal and, finally, in the heat of the day, I made the South African border. The motor had been noisy right along, and it did not give me any peace of mind. In fact, two days before I left South Africa I was still working on it. I had to do a valve job on an engine rebuilt in the United States because, to their shame, the motorcycle dealer who rebuilt the motor did not do a good job. Very sadly, they gave me something that cost me a lot of money but wasn't good quality work. The noise in the engine and low compression on the rear cylinder was just something I would have to ride with, hoping all the while that I could make it to England.

After clearing customs in South Africa, I went across the Limpopo River to the border post in Zimbabwe. I could take no photographs because the bridges are all designated as "military areas." Once across the Limpopo, and customs taken care of, I started out again across the Southern Zimbabwe bushveld.

Immediately, my gaze was transfixed on the beautiful, massive baobab trees. According to African legend, God, somehow offended, planted these trees upside down so the roots grow out! They are some of the most massive trees I have ever seen anywhere in the world. Some have been estimated at around 2,000 years or more of age, dating back before the time of Christ.

Once I crossed the border, there was virtually no traffic at all on the roads, reminding me of the old days when I was a soldier in the Rhodesian Defense Forces (I was not a mercenary, I was a professional soldier, serving in countries that I believed in, and taking an oath of allegiance to serve in the regular army. In all my service, I never earned more than $600 a month, so please, NEVER call me a mercenary). People who traveled out in these areas alone were an easy target for marauding bands of terrorist; smart people only traveled in convoys. Now, even with peace in the land, the traffic is still very negligible.

My first night was not spent out in the bushveld, but at a ranch that belonged to a family called the Caywoods. They were very nice people (typical of Rhodesians). They gave me a hot meal, a nice shower, and a warm bed for the night. I remember that night, as I lay back, still nervous about the entire journey, I heard ostriches out in the paddock (they are used as guards to keep out predators and unwanted guests). Somehow, their strange sounds said to me, "Your trip has <u>truly begun</u>."

Little did I know, at that time, how far my journey would take me. I had a vague mental picture of where I wanted to go, but, at this point, my main concern was just getting across the dark continent of Africa no matter what!

From there, we would see.

"If I don't make this first major hurdle," I reasoned, "I won't make it at all, so what's the use of too much detailed planning?"

Naively, I thought Africa would be my only major corker.

How wrong I was.

The next morning I was up early, got the motorcycle started, said good-bye to this lovely family, and left. Going down that mile or so of dirt road to the main highway, I nearly fell off the motorcycle in the sand.

"Holy mackerel," I thought to myself, "this thing has the maneuvering ability of a brick!"

All the old trials I had faced on awful bad asphalt roads and dusty, muddy dirt roads flashed through my memory and struck fear in my heart, plus I had no peace of mind about the engine or the mechanical side of the motorcycle.

That peace would elude me the entire trip.

Pushing north, I came to my first gasoline outpost for fuel. One of the Africans there said to me, "Well, when you come back by, bring me that jacket."

His comment sticks in my mind for some strange reason. Maybe it was the man himself - an informative fellow who clearly understood the situation for the average black man in Zimbabwe at the time - which wasn't very good.

Late that afternoon I came into Harare, the capital city of Zimbabwe, and immediately was struck with many familiar landmarks from ten years before when I was a soldier in what was then Zimbabwe, Rhodesia. I thought of my friend, Paul Hogan, who I had lived with whenever I was back from the bush, and the many other people I had served with in the Rhodesian Light Infantry. Many of them I hadn't thought of in ten years, and now, all of the sudden, I was back in the city that meant "R & R" to the soldiers. "R & R" means "rest and relaxation," but for us, it meant drinking, fighting and chasing women (the latter with little success in my case).

Memories flooded my mind.

I made my way to Mt. Pleasant to see Don Kiley, my old friend, and was given a very warm greeting at his house, and shown to a room. I met his mother, Jessie Kiley, and also his wife, Toots. Don and I had not seen each other in many years, so it was a festive few hours we enjoyed that evening getting to know one another again. Don is a very sensitive man, and I could tell he believed in me and the purpose of my trip.

That evening, I called down to South Africa to speak to Don Hornsby. He sounded quite nervous on the phone. "Dave, faction fighting is as bad as it ever was."

As he shared, I felt very guilty for having left my friends behind in a troubled land. I could only conclude that it was one more payment for deciding to live a dream.

Passports, Elephant Shit, and Blood

The next few days were "administrative."

I had to secure a new passport without any South African stamps in it. It was also necessary to get visas for various countries that lie in front of me, such as Burundi, Zambia, Zaire, and Central Africa. In the interim, while waiting for my passport, I met some of Don's friends. Their talk always centered around how fouled up the government was, and how many shortages there were. In fact, every day at a certain time, there would be an electrical black out. It was extremely difficult to get a phone line through to the other side of Harare, let alone the other side of the country!

During this time, I started exercising again, working on getting myself back into shape. In the past week or so I hadn't been doing any exercise. It was time to get back with it, for I would be doing a lot of heavy labor in the very near future.

I met some old friends from the skydiving club, Ken and Dot Purse. Ken was a soldier for many years in the Rhodesian army, and had served with the Special Air Service (SAS - the equivalent of our Delta Force). Both he and Dot were good friends, and qualified skydivers. We enjoyed a dinner at the Clover Gallax, a restaurant we used to frequent; it was a nostalgic evening.

Also, I worked on the motorcycle, always finding some little adjustment or maintenance work to be done here or there.

Questions were endless everywhere I went.

28

"Where are you going?"

"How long have you been on the road?"

"Where have you come from?"

"Why are you doing this?"

"Do you think you'll make it?"

"Are you crazy?" Sometimes I wondered.

Despite the fear and apprehension in my gut, I always put a brave face on things, looking people in the eye and saying, "Oh, I'm looking forward to the challenge of this adventure."

True, I was looking forward to the action, but there was very little I could say about the way I felt deep inside.

"No problem, Dave, you will make it." Hearing those words would just worry me all the more.

Don Hornsby and Jurgen Schultz said them. Their faith in me never wavered. Perhaps they could see something in me that I couldn't.

When I was filling out the application to get into Zambia, I noticed that all the lines had "Tipex" over old writing. They were using the application for a second time!

Ken and Dot enjoyed our conversations together, and laughed as we remembered the night Nick Carter and I went to jail on that Independence Day weekend over April 18-20, 1980. We had been out skydiving that day, and had consumed many beers before we went to town for dinner. On the way out, we got in trouble in front of a Zanu PF barracks which housed many ex-terrorists. These lunatics started chasing us with their AK-47s through the woods and around the residential areas. Nick, a tough SAS man, had to carry me (I was too drunk to run). By chance, we ran into a dog patrol which took us prisoners (undoubtedly for our own good), and hauled us off to jail. Had we not been arrested, we probably would have been found dead the next morning, our back sides full of AK-47 rounds.

In jail that weekend were many ex-terrorists who had been drunk and disorderly as well, but we were the only two white men among over 200 Africans, some of them Zanu PF terrorists, others just common criminals. Everywhere we went, we went back to back. At the time, we were both scared to death!

Ten years later, we could laugh about it.

The next day I learned that the oil refinery in Zambia had burned down, supposedly leaving no fuel in Zambia. This was a big worry, but it was also false information (when I arrived in Zambia, I had no problem finding gasoline).

I loaded up the Harley Davidson in preparation for leaving the next morning. I said good night and good-bye to Jessie Kiley, Don's mother, a lady who had fought in World War II, in North Africa, as a member of the nursing corps with the British army. She said something to me that would stay with me throughout the trip, ringing in my ears many a time when things got seemingly impossible: "Don't worry, boy, you'll do."

The next day, I started out at 05:00. Don Kiley and I shook hands, and I departed down the dark highway. My first stop was a gas station. Funny enough, it was the gas station in Kroi, where I had started my training in the Z/Rhodesian Defense Forces. Coming down through the Zambezi River Valley with my camera around my neck, I looked like a Japanese tourist. I wanted to take pictures of elephants crossing the road, but unfortunately, all I saw were baobab trees, the bushveld, the road ahead, and HUGE piles of elephant shit! They left these deposits of dung as they made their daily pilgrimage down to the Zambezi River to drink.

"If I hit a pile of elephant shit at 50 miles per hour," I thought, "I am going to come flying off this motorcycle and maybe eat a little something I don't want on the landing!"

Crossing the majestic and giant Zambezi River, once again I was not allowed to take photographs. The Zimbabwe authorities cleared me very quickly, but, in Zambia, I received my first major grilling by authorities. It took me two hours to clear Customs and Immigration.

Once moving again, in 100 degree heat, the countryside and bushveld was all burned out, and I didn't see any animals. Even the baobab trees looked miserable. Not long after entering Zambia, a police road block stopped me to check my passport and motorcycle documents. Roads, by the way, were rough and full of pot holes.

Later in the afternoon, my motorcycle was sputtering from fuel starvation. I stopped, and took out the fuel filter I had put in. That took care of the problem. Then, on into Lusaka where I found what was known as the Carousel Shopping Center - half completed like everything else. In that center, I found a sporting goods dealer who was a friend of mine and customer from the Used Gun Exchange, George Damoris. George was so glad to see me that he turned the shop over to his brother-in-law, Webster, and took me home to meet his wife, Diana, a lovely black girl.

Webster, I came to find out, was her brother, and he always seemed to be a side kick, hanging around on the fringes. George had what they call an "instant family." For some reason, he and Diana couldn't have children, so they went out to a Kraawl (a small group of huts), found a couple of kids, paid off the parents, and took the kids back with them. Now, they are their kids. They adopted a boy and a girl this way.

BINGO! A family!

I spent a few days with George, doing work on the motorcycle, gathering information, and getting a visa for Uganda. I met one of George's friends, an influential man in the area, who was Greek. The Greeks in Lusaka seem to be the big money men, and they work hand in hand with the government. This friend called up north to Mpulungu, where I was headed, at the bottom of Lake Tanganyika, to someone who owned a garage there. Instantly, the man agreed to give me some assistance in doing a tire change.

George, Diana and I went out one night to a nice restaurant on top of the hotel and had a wonderful meal. Many embassy personnel were there. I noticed how distanced from them I felt myself to be; I didn't have anything more in common with them. I related more to men like George, expatriates who couldn't settle in their own country.

When we came back to George's house, he warned me to be very careful on my trip, and to try and avoid any need for medical attention at all costs...the hospitals were so bad.

"The wife of one of my workers had a broken leg, and when they took her to the hospital, she ended up dying that day," George told me. "The hospital she was in was in such a state that it smelled like a shithouse. The conditions in our hospitals are so bad you could end up coming out worse than the way you went in.

"Frankly," he continued, "one of my biggest worries I have is that if one of the members of our family is ever injured seriously in an accident or illness, I would have to take them all the way to Harare, or maybe even on to South Africa, to get proper medical attention."

Properly warned, the next morning I loaded up the motorcycle, vowing to be as cautious as possible. About five miles out on this new day, I came to the site of a massive accident where unrecognizable, wrecked vehicles and mutilated, mangled bodies lay on the road, the lives smashed out of them. I rode through a pool of blood. In some of the vehicles, the bodies were obviously near death.

As much as I wanted to, I could not dare to stop and offer my help because I had no idea how the crowd might react to a white foreigner in their midst in this time of deep crisis.

The motorcycle continued to give me many handling problems. I moved the saddle bags full of tools to the front handlebars, but it did not change the unyielding and difficult handing ability of my BRICK.

The people of Zambia were generally very friendly, kind and helpful, which was a great relief, since I had no experience with this part of Africa at all.

About every 300 miles I stopped for gasoline (I carried an extra 24 liters [5 gallons] on the motorcycle).

Trucks, Checkpoints, and Fisheries

September 25: The first time I dropped this motorcycle on the trip. When I pulled over to piss, and put the motorcycle down on its block and stand, the stand slipped off the block and over went the motorcycle.

BANG! Down!

I was just lucky there were locals around, and everybody pitched in to get the thing up. Loaded the way it is, and carrying the system I have on the back of it, the motorcycle is **very** top heavy, and it takes three or four people to get the thing in the upright position. When the Harley was up, everybody shook hands, and with the appropriate "Thank you very much" I was on my way.

Next, a strong head wind hit me. It is a very tiring and difficult thing to get through (although not the worst conditions I would face on this trip by any means). Head winds are doubly difficult because I don't have a windshield on the motorcycle; I would be falling off the thing fairly regularly in the near future, and to constantly pick up the fallen motorcycle would eventually end up breaking the windshield, if it hadn't already been broken in the fall.

The first night out of George's place in Lusaka, I stopped at a rest house, and the questions began again. I quickly learned that I must have one story and stick with it. You never know who is questioning you. It could be a government employee, or just a friendly, inquisitive fellow. Whatever the case, I stuck to one story all the time. I never, never said anything about South Africa, and was constantly on my guard for trick questions.

Zambia, South Africa and her neighbors were very antagonistic toward one another then (not the peace we have today). On the other hand, Zimbabwe, Zambia and countries north used to trade with South Africa (a fact little known).

At this rest house, the smell of wood smoke from cooking fires triggered many memories of my time in the bushveld as a soldier, both in the South African and the Z/Rhodesian army. In many country areas, there are no trees - they have all been cut down for cooking fuel, or to build roundivaals (thatch huts).

Time passes swiftly on a trip like this, the miles literally flying under the wheels. One day, even though the roads were bad, with good weather, I made 420 miles beating along on that old machine. Although there wasn't much traffic, there were still great dangers. The big trucks take up all the road, and they won't give! Missing them on the motorcycle is usually accomplished with only inches to spare.

The food in the rest houses is usually terrible. I was constantly picking stones out of the rice and beans. And the meat...well, who knows the origin? My rule: if it doesn't smell bad, go ahead and take a chance. Up at 5:20 a.m., do my exercises, load the motorcycle, and have a little something to eat.

<u>There is absolutely nothing to eat on the road</u>! For Westerners, it is hard to realize that you can travel for great distances and never pass another vehicle, or a place to eat.

The first moment of a new day is always exciting. When I get moving on to whatever will be my destination by day's end, the juices start to flow, especially when I am out on the highway and the motorcycle is running reasonably well (very rare). I especially enjoy the wonderful sunrises from the back of the motorcycle (as seen through the rear view mirror). On the road, I get a sense of freedom that most people will <u>never</u> really know.

I ran into my first military checkpoint. The army, though they were kind, had no military bearing, were dirty and sloppy. They didn't ask me for any bribes, but, as always, they were amazed and pointed to my legs. When I would lift my pant legs up and show them my two artificial limbs, their eyes would just about pop out of their heads! Sometimes, they would shake my hand and wish me well.

Outside Kasama, I was stopped by drunk police. These guys worried me a bit more than the army did, but, in the end, they waved me on.

Finally, I made it to Mpulungu, a fishing town at the bottom or southern tip of Lake Tanganyika. I visited the fisheries where the kapenta fish are spread like a silver carpet all over the ground. I rode down a path between these fields of kapenta fish (a small fish from Lake Tanganyika that is dried out and eaten for protein).

I navigated my way down a very rough dirt road full of rocks and holes to a camping area along the edge of Lake Tanganyika, back up in the woods. There I met Denouse, who was a storehouse of information. He picked up information coming from the north - Tanzania, Burundi, Rwanda, Uganda, and Zaire, and also knew many details about Zimbabwe in the south. We shared our information. He asked me questions about the road up, the situation with the army, and the police. Then, I asked him about information to the north, about what to expect.

The next day I rode back over to the fisheries, and, on a dirt floor, sat down with an African fellow named Moses. I took out my tools, jacked up the back end of the motorcycle, and pulled off the rear wheel of the machine to change my tire. I carried a spare rear tire, a retread made into a knobby tire, for the road ahead (which I was led to believe was mostly dirt and mud). Next, I serviced the motorcycle, changing the oil and filter and other odd-ball bits of maintenance. Moses was a big help. Any tool I needed but didn't personally carry (I brought 75-100 pounds of tools, parts, and oil), he would produce for me.

By the end of the day, I was finished. I said good-bye to Moses, and climbed up a cliff behind the fisheries to find Dimitri, the owner of the place, and tell him thank you. The working staff inside the fishery stopped to watch me climb that cliff...this crazy man with artificial legs. When I got to the top of the cliff, Dimitri looked at me, and his mouth dropped down as he asked, "How in the hell did you get up here?"

"I came up the same way everybody else does," I replied.

He was amazed. I told Dimitri, "Thank you very much for your time and your help." We shook hands, then he watched and laughed like the rest of the African laborers as I made my way down the very, very steep hill, falling a number of times. Since I was already dirty and greasy from working on the dirt floor all day, I figured a little bit more couldn't hurt.

Each fall provided great humor to all these fellows (but it wasn't done meanly).

When I arrived at the bottom, the staff was all standing there with deep respect in their eyes, and humorous smiles on their faces.

I rode back over to the camp were Denouse was cooking. There was also a tour truck full of Australians who were also headed north. These trucks come and go across the continent of Africa - from Harare, Zimbabwe, all the way to London, and vice-versa.

As Denouse and I talked through the evening, the Australians partied down, feeling secure and happy about their trip across Africa.

"Why can't I feel that same type of security?" I wondered.

In my gut, there was still a nagging apprehension about what was to come, and most of that apprehension concerned whether the motorcycle would break down on me.

Crossing the Equator the First Time
October, 1990, Uganda; Hot and Wet

The Mud Pits of Zaire; October, 1990.
These pits were sometimes 4 meters deep (12 ft.)!

Zaire, Central Africa Republic, Cameroon. October-November, 1990
Throughout Equatorial Africa, I encountered dirt-mud roads.

Chapter Three

My Luxurious Boat Cruise and Other Misadventures!

The next morning, I was off to what is called "Cozy Enterprises," where, of course, officials were late in starting the day. So, I sat and talked with the locals who called me "comrade," a custom in the area. Before long, morning had passed and it was lunch time. I went to this dirty, dingy place - like many along my route - and ordered a plate of eggs. The guy who was serving them started giving me a hard time because I was an American. A month ago, in late September/early October, 1990, the Americans had put an embargo on the Iraqis before the Gulf War. He objected to that action, and was the first real anti-American I had met on the trip.

About mid afternoon, I was told to go down to the dock where I met some people from the tour truck. One of the New Zealanders asked me if I could chase after their tour truck, which was going to go through Tanzania while the group went up to Lake Tanganyika on the boat.

One of the tourists, a man named Rod, had left his passport on the truck. I believe it is the duty of one traveler to help another wherever possible, so I unloaded my motorcycle, told Rod to watch my gear, and I screamed back through Mpulungu out of town for a good ten miles. Finally, up ahead, I caught and stopped the truck. The driver, the assistant driver and I then went to the back of the rig where the gear was stored and spent the next half-hour searching for Rod's passport.

No luck. It was not there.

I then got on the motorcycle and raced back to Mpulungu, worried I would miss the ship myself. My heart was pounding. "If Rod is called to the ship," I wondered, "will he leave my gear on the dock unattended?"

If I missed that boat, it would mean another 6 days in Mpulungu.

Arriving back at the docks, I found the ship had not yet sailed, and my gear was secure. Then Rod came up to me, saying, "I'm sorry, Dave. I'm sorry."

"What are you sorry about?" I asked him. "We couldn't find your passport."

"I know," he replied. "I found it in my bag at the bottom in a place where I didn't expect to find it. When I looked through the bag again, alas, I came up with the document."

That crisis over, I went down to the dock and the motorcycle was loaded onto the ship, called "The Lemba," a vessel of pre World War 1 construction! It was a sweaty, miserable job for myself and eight others to lift the Harley over the side of the ship and down onto the deck without damaging anything. By the time we were done, my stumps were killing me, but I still had to completely unload the motorcycle and carry the saddle bags and other equipment up two stories! It took three trips up and down ladders, with all the equipment, to store my gear in a dingy little hole in the wall which was to be my cabin for the next few days.

Once in the room, I thought to myself, "Okay, it was a bit of a sweaty job getting the motorcycle on deck, and carting all of my gear to the room, but now that I am getting settled in, we should be soon putting off and heading up Lake Tanganyika. How nice it will be! Three days on Lake Tanganyika to rest and get ready to head for Burundi and points north. This will be like a cruise! It should be a very relaxing time. I'll just read, relax, and enjoy the sunrise and sunset."

Wrong!

It was about 17:00 in the afternoon when the ship cast off and gathered way. As we moved out and away from port, we weren't moving more than an hour or so when

I see these long boats coming along side of us with hundreds of passengers on them...plus their cargo. These people are all screaming and shouting and hollering. The crew threw lines overboard, and these new hoards of people started jumping from the long boats to the side of the ship! It struck me as downright bizarre that new passengers and cargo were loaded this way. Only later, near the end of the trip, would I understand the reason for this crazy behavior.

Even for those very athletic and quick, the process was difficult. When the waves rose, they had to jump from their long boat and grab the guard rail of our vessel, pulling themselves over the rail and onto the deck. If they missed the rail, they hit the side of the ship...SMACK, and fell into the water, hoping not to be crushed by the long boats. Sad as it sounds, this became an endless source of amusement for those hearty souls who made it the first time.

Children were a different problem. The kids can't jump across on their own, so the mother hollered to somebody already on the ship, hoping against hope that if that someone is not drunk, he or she could catch the kid!

"One...two...three...uhhhhhhh," across they go.

Funny enough, I never saw any children miss the set of waiting arms and end up in the drink.

These long boats carried a cargo of rope, bags of sugar, and bags of kapenta fish. After the passengers were off loaded onto the ship, all of this cargo was loaded by rope hoist. Before long, the whole deck forward of the bridge structure rose all the way up level to the bridge - more than twenty feet. The motorcycle was difficult to see since it was in the front left portion of the bow.

People and cargo were crammed everywhere!

Then the party began.

There seemed to be a endless supply of beer being consumed, dope being smoked, combined with radios blaring. Every hour or two, the ship would again repeat the process with more passengers attempting to jump across from long boats.

More people.

More tossed kids.

More cargo.

As we moved up Lake Tanganyika, I asked a crew member, "How many people do you think we have taken on?"

"Oh, about 2,000," he replied.

The vessel became a floating block of black humanity. Every time long boats would come along side, the people would move to the side of the ship and it would start listing about ten degrees. Many times I thought, "This crazy bucket is going to capsize!"

With so many people on board, I became increasingly worried about my motorcycle. "What if somebody stole the oil cap or my gas cap or some other vital part of the machine?" I wondered. "If anything is stolen, where am I going to get parts for it in Bujumbura, Burundi?"

The nearest Harley shop was either in Europe or South Africa.

Rod had given me a pack of Winston cigarettes, so I went to the only figure of authority I saw on the ship. The guy had corporal stripes and was carrying a pistol. I said, "Messier, ci vous plait? Securita, para moto," in my best broken French.

He turned around and replied, "Non problem, messier."

I took the pack of cigarettes out and gave them to him. About ten minutes later, I saw some fellow sitting hang-dog next to the motorcycle. Now, I don't know what this guy did to be shanghaied into guarding my motorcycle, but for the next three days and nights, there he was, sitting next to it! I never saw him eat or drink or go to relieve himself. Amazingly, for the price of one pack of cigarettes, I made it to Bujumbura, Burundi, with nothing missing from my motorcycle!

Rod and I dubbed our boat "The Good Ship Lemba" after a British Rugby song which is very risqué. We called it that because there was a constant babble of voices, music and people partying 24 hours a day. The toilets were plugged up, and people were shitting on the deck. As I walked along, I had to be very careful not to step in it and slip. Not being the steadiest person on my feet, it was really difficult for me not to step on somebody when I had to go back to the back of the ship to the dining room (slop house is more accurate). Inevitably, my unfeeling rubber feet would crush an unsuspecting person's fingers or toes of someone sleeping on the deck.

A screech of agony always would ensue.

The atrocity of the food surpassed all standards of slop! One night we had a dish we dubbed "rubber chicken" because it was as tough as shoe leather. Once, I chipped a tooth from the stones in the rice.

Ah, yes, what a wonderful, relaxing experience my luxury cruise turned out to be!!!

In my cabin, people looked in all the time during daylight hours, since there were no curtains.

To complete the experience, I met my first corrupt official, a man named Mantuki. He was a little weasel of a character, with snake eyes and buck teeth.

"Do you have a Tanzaniyan stamp in your passport?" he asked me one day.

"No," I replied, getting the sinking feeling that I was going to be held up in yet another Customs problem.

"Well," he replied, "this visa is $25 to put in your passport. Without it, you will have to be put off on one of the long boats."

Now, I don't know if he had the power to keep his promise or not, but I didn't want to push my luck (the thought of me jumping across to a long boat was worth the money). As I reluctantly gave shithead the $25, Mantuki put a stamp in my passport. While smiling on the outside, I thought, "You smelly little prick, you'll get yours someday!"

I couldn't have entered Tanzania with a clean passport issued in Zimbabwe, because the Tanzania authorities feel that, if you have a clean passport, like I did, you came from South Africa. In my case, it would have been very true.

As we moved into the second day, the stench of the ship increased to unbearable... a floating shit house full of humanity. Yet, more long boats came along side, off loading cargo and passengers. The only humor to this dismal affair was watching the occasional poor soul misjudge the wave and hit the side of the ship, then plummet, screaming, into the water. You might be thinking, "You're callous, Dave. How could you laugh at somebody else's misfortune like that?"

Well, the Africans laugh at the pain themselves, so why shouldn't I? Often I laugh at my own pain, so why not laugh at somebody else's? Humor is humor.

For the whole evening of the third day and early morning hours of the fourth, we had been disembarking people and cargo. On the morning of the fourth day, before dawn, the last of the long boats came on and took off the rest of the cargo and the last of the passengers. Then the decks were washed and cleaned, so by the time we put into Bujumbura, Southern Burundi, no one was left on the ship except myself and the crew, which suddenly signaled to me that the passengers and cargo we had taken from the long boats... were **ALL** black market!

Now I had to once again complete the laborious task of moving all my bags and tools down to the motorcycle. Upon arriving in port, it was a walk of over one kilometer to Customs and Immigrations. The Customs and Immigration people were very kind, moving me through quickly, but they said I had to find another office when I off loaded the motorcycle to pay some kind of a duty.

I walked back to the ship and off loaded the motorcycle. Once the machine was off and all loaded up again, I started up and moved around to Customs and Immigration, looking for the office to pay the duty. I couldn't find it, but I did find myself going through the gate and out of the port. I was free, and without paying their duty. "Ha, ha, I got you," I thought.

The town of Bujumbura was not a large place. Like most cities in Africa, it offers run down streets full of pot holes. (Later, I would discover that it was a veritable paradise compared to some of the population centers I would visit to the north.) I found a cheap hotel that had security for the motorcycle. As I was riding it around in back of the hotel, I fell off. How embarrassing. Some of the porters laughingly helped pick the motorcycle up and move it to the front of my room.

I caught a cab and went to the Rwandan embassy where I filled out the forms and turned them in with the fee required for the visa. Once this was all taken care of, I planned to go back to the hotel and relax. On the way back to the hotel, the cab driver says to me, "That will be 300 francs."

Now, I am not sure what the exchange rate was at that time, but his fee was FAR more than the ride was worth, so I told him to "Fuck off," and gave him 150 francs instead. If there is anything I can't stand as a traveler, it is being ripped off because I am a foreigner in another person's land.

Finally back at the hotel, I luxuriated in a very blessed, wonderful shower. It had been four days since I had been able to wash myself properly, so clear, clean running water was very welcome!

I changed money at black market rates (far better than the banks) with the lady who ran the restaurant. Then, time for dinner...more rubber chicken. I will never again curse Colonel Sanders for his meals!

I ended that day at 20:30 in the evening and thought to myself, "Well, tomorrow, north again toward Europe."

Bananas, Bob Marley, and Ping Pong

Up at 04:30 after a restless night's sleep...normal for me before I push off on a major part of the journey. Get up, load the motorcycle, do pushups, say a prayer and start down the road, looking for a gas station.

More crowds. Probably 40 Africans standing around, staring at me. Never did I feel any animosity from them, although it was difficult to feel comfortable with their stares. Since the border to Rwanda was only a few hours ahead, I changed just enough money to pay off the hotel and fill up the motorcycle. I came up 60 francs short of what I needed to pay. I started to drain the gasoline out, when everybody around me said, "Non, messieur, non, non." These spectators started taking change out of their pockets and paid the 60 francs.

"What a kind and very touching gesture," I thought.

After shaking hands with these benefactors, I moved on with a good feeling to the outskirts of town which was all shanties, smelling of cooking fires, rotting garbage, and diesel exhausts. Kids and animals were running amuck, out in the road full of holes. It was in this gloriously trashy setting that my first really close encounter took place.

As I was passing a parked truck at about 30 miles per hour, out of nowhere, from the front of the truck appears an African with a load of bananas, still on the branch, on his head! I managed to maneuver the motorcycle slightly so as not to hit the truck and also miss him, going between them. I don't know how my head did not hit the branch full of bananas the man was carrying. I guess I just ducked, but I honestly don't remember doing it. I passed him, missing him by a fraction of an inch, and missing the bananas...I don't know how I missed them at all. My heart was in my throat, but I just carried on up the road. "Good God, what would happen to me," I wondered, "if I ever hit somebody here in a place like this? That would be the end of everything."

I'd like to talk a bit about the roads that run through Northern Zambia and Burundi. They were very rough, with lots of holes, and of course, there were the trucks, especially the big ones that get in the middle of the road and simply won't give, no matter who you are!

Size and might makes right. <u>You</u> must get out of their way!

When I was confronted with these situations, I always had to hope that there was no hole or mud or other obstacle on the side of the road that might cause the motorcycle to be pushed in the direction of the truck, or over the steep shoulder. On the highways, everything is a war of nerves. When I had to give way to pass these guys, I often only had a few inches between me and a major disaster.

Blind, tight corners were another suspense-filled nightmare as I followed the "Yellow Brick Road."

And of course, there was the heat. It is hotter than a firecracker out there. At this point, I was probably at most 190 miles from the equator.

The countryside is very mountainous, with winding roads and rain-forested areas...at least where the fields are not being cultivated for bananas. Coming through the numerous small villages, I had to be constantly very careful of kids darting out on the road, or animals which are left to run free.

And, there is always the smell of cooking fires.

At 10:00, I made the border of Burundi, Rwanda, and everybody in Customs was on tea break, so I sat there for nearly half an hour, talking to a fellow. The man had Bob Marley type hair, was very dirty, and he had a disability - legs shrunk from polio.

We spoke for about ten minutes.

He told me about the politics and problems in Burundi, and warned me to "be very careful up ahead in Rwanda." My Bob Marley look-alike spoke these musings more as a mystic than a reporter.

As I listened, my legs felt like lead... Fear permeated my body.

Perhaps it was the near miss with the African fellow carrying bananas, coupled with two "near misses" with large trucks. The thought of even greater dangers up ahead caused me to wonder. As the trip wore on, these hazards became just part of a normal day, but in the initial stages of my trip, everything was bothering me, especially my absence of peace due to the lack of dependability of my motorcycle's most recent overhaul.

Finally, I cleared Customs and Immigration on the Burundi side, and crossed over to Rwanda where authorities cleared me quite quickly. When I was ready to head out, some jerk came over to me and said, "Open up the cabinet on the back of your motorcycle."

He wasn't wearing a uniform of any kind, so I told him to "Go get stuffed. What I have in my cabinet is none of your business." Up walked a guard with an AK47 in his hand. He pointed at the box. The gun was not pointed at me, but obviously that was the next step. So, I opened the box and this monkey now begins to paw through my things. I wanted to wring his neck! "How dare you invade my privacy," I thought. Later, I found out that fighting had started up around Kigali, and the insurgents had come in from Uganda, so there was plenty of trouble in the country at the time. No wonder the guards were so cautious.

The roads in Rwanda were excellent. I only hit a few muddy stretches. The highway seemed new, and the rain I encountered in the afternoon felt good. On the outskirts of Kigali, army personnel stopped me and checked my passport, then let me go. Further north, I was stopped a few more times. One soldier was actually quite belligerent and nasty. Looking at his rifle, I noticed that the gas plug which makes the whole rifle operate was missing. His general state of military bearing was far from impressive. "If this is the Rwandan army," I thought to myself, "these guys haven't got a chance if they are facing a determined enemy."

Now the rain came down in torrents - the first major rain of the trip. It felt good, since I was rapidly approaching the equator where the temperature is up around 42 degrees Celsius (over 100 Fahrenheit). Moving northward, I stopped only to add fuel from my spare gas cans.

Arriving at the border in the late afternoon, on the Rwandan side I received quite an interrogation as to why I was going into Uganda. I stuck to my story: "I am on an around-the-world trip for the disabled." I never deviated from that, since they send you to different huts, and then get together afterwards and compare notes to see if there are any inconsistencies.

On the Ugandan side of the border, the authorities did the same thing. I endured major interrogations in a number of different rooms.

"How much money are you carrying?"

"Where are you going?"

"What is the purpose of your trip?"

I never tell the truth about how much money I've got. When you're filling out Customs and Immigration papers, you've got to put down a certain amount. The thing is not to change money except as a minimal amount with the authorities - whatever else you need, change on the black market for the better rate.

That evening I arrived in Kabale, and got directions to All Saints Church where I hoped to stay. The roads deteriorated to muddy pot holes. In Rwanda and Burundi, I had been driving on the right side of the road like we do in the United States and other parts of the world. In Uganda, they drive on the left side of the road (this first dawned on me just before a potential head on collision with a bus!).

At All Saints Church, I humbly requested to spend the night, but there were no more rooms. However, the Christian attitude was one to be admired. They allowed me to share the ping pong table with a fellow who was a Boy Scoutmaster and a minister of a church. There were no flush toilets, and the toilets stunk badly. No electricity. It was a very dirty place, indeed.

Nevertheless, they were very kind and understanding, especially for my motorcycle. They allowed me to move the ping pong table over near the window so I could listen for possible thieves.

During the night, the Boy Scoutmaster and I had quite a conversation about the different problems in Uganda, and about the lack of money for the Boy Scouts to go to the different functions.

The next morning, I was up early, got the motorcycle loaded, but didn't have the money I needed to pay the church for lodging. Breakfast was beans and rice, the same as dinner had been. At the table, another minister was writing letters, and he asked me about the fighting I saw in Rwanda the day before.

I made a quick run into town, changed money, then came back out to pay the church for lodging. Then I left Kabale behind, and headed in what I thought was the direction of the Zaire border. However, I took a wrong turn and went 60 miles (100 kilometers) out of my way. Asking directions is virtually impossible. Even though Uganda is an English-speaking country, English is the secondary language, and people didn't seem to understand my brand of English. Road markings are less than desirable. Real bad roads and long stretches of rough dirt roads full of rocks were becoming more and more common. Road crews were out trying to repair them and keep them in shape, but it seemed they were fighting a losing battle.

At one point, the road was so full of holes that I road 10 miles an hour for about 40 miles; it was impossible to go any faster. Then I hit an *incredible* torrential downpour of rain that soaked me to the bone. The only saving grace from that storm was that it cooled down the engine a bit. The clutch was so hot that it was extremely difficult to pull in and out of first and second gear.

Little did I know that Zaire would all be in first and second gear.

Equators, Beans and Tea

October 3: I rode across the equator for the first time with the motorcycle, stopping to photograph the machine, take a short break, then push on towards the border. Late in the afternoon, I came to the border post and there went through another major grilling by Customs, police, army and whoever else wanted their questions answered.

After clearing Customs and satisfying these people that I wasn't a spy, or in their country for any subversive activity, I asked them, "Can I spend the night here with the police? There are bandits all about, and I would feel much safer with the men with guns." This puffed up their egos a little bit, and they answered, "Fine, you can sleep over here in an open garage."

Of course, the normal crowd was in attendance, but the crowd I drew was kind of unique as it was primarily the families of policemen and army personnel. Their wives and kids all gathered around as I unloaded the motorcycle in the carport. One policeman who had given me quite a going-over came up in a much more amicable manner and gave me a warning about Zaire.

"You will really be in for it with the roads. They are nothing like the good roads we have in Uganda."

"If Zaire is worse than Uganda," I thought to myself, "it is very bad."

That was an understatement.

For months and months before I started the trip, I kept getting warnings from people who had traveled through Zaire. One diary I read told about a family who had actually traveled through Zaire needing a specially-equipped vehicle to handle the roads, so I knew I was in for a real rough ride. It didn't do my peace of mind any good that the night before I entered Zaire I had to listen to this guy tell me how bad it was going to be.

That evening, a full moon came up over the jungle, and I'll never forget it as long as I live. The moonlight silently sculptured a silhouette on the tops of all the exotic trees and vegetation.

A policeman named James sat down next to me. We talked of our homes, and I told him about my background of coming from West Covina in the greater Los Angeles area. He asked me the cost of the homes, and when I told him, he says, "Ahhh, this is too much. It is ridiculous. I am building a home now, and I figure this home, when it is finished, will cost me the sum of about 200 American dollars! Then, I can move my new wife into the home. Is it not better here in Uganda?"

"James, for you," I thought to myself, "I am sure it is better here in Uganda."

We spoke about the politics of Uganda, and about some of the happenings in the world around us. I could see from our conversation that the news media in Uganda was weak in reporting world events. At the end of our conversation, James stood up, shouldering his AK47, and said, "Dave, my friend, I will pray for you." We shook hands, and he turned and walked away into the night.

"What a touching gesture," I thought, beginning to revise my views of officialdom in countries like Uganda. James, the policeman who had grilled me earlier, when away from his official functions, was very kind. I appreciated their showing me that they were more like people I could identify with, as opposed to the grinding, intimidating officials we so often expect.

My luscious dinner that night was half a tin of beans and a cup of tea. I lay down on the ground of this open carport - my first night on the ground. There were to be many, many more before my trip was over. My thoughts about Zaire produced nothing in my heart but absolute fear. "How could my huge, lumbering motorcycle get through the roads of Zaire?" I wondered, as if all that was behind me had only been child's play.

After sunrise, which was fairly late, I was ready to start up and go. There was a big crowd waiting for me as I rode out of the police camp. I saw my friend James off in the back of the crowd, and we waved. Our eyes caught one another and I thought to myself, "Please, James, do pray for me in the next couple of weeks. I am sure I'm going to need it."

I rode over a horribly rough road for about 2 1/2 miles (4 kilometers), through the no-man's land to the Zairian border. I waited there for over an hour while those arrogant pricks drank tea before they came to perform their Customs and Immigration duties.

Zaire, C.A.R.-Cameroon, October-November 1990; Taken by Bruno Piet.
I nearly drowned in road conditions similar to this.

Chapter Four

Zaire's Truth to Zem Stories!

The gate went up, and ALL the stories I'd heard about Zaire became truth to me in very vivid colors!

In the first 5 minutes I came flying off the motorcycle in deep mud at about 10 miles per hour. I was stuck under the motorcycle for about 5 minutes until a couple of bicyclists pulled up behind me. They managed to get the motorcycle up enough so that I could crawl out, then the three of us got the motorcycle up. We pushed it a bit to get it out of this particular little mud stretch.

No more than 20 meters down the road, I went down into the mud again. By this time, I was covered from head to toe in black, stinking mud, and I'm thinking, "Oh, my God, is this what it's going to be like all the way to Central Africa? Will I ever make it?" The distance was over 700 ridden miles!

The same two guys helped me pick up the Harley a second time, asking me if I was drunk. "Non whiskey, messieurs," I replied.

There was no way around this mud. I looked for dry areas, but they just didn't exist. The rain forest was coming up on both sides of the road, so there was absolutely no scenery...just the road and the wall sides of the rain forest.

I moved down the road again, another mile this time, thinking that maybe I had encountered a particularly bad stretch, and that it was now over. Then bingo - more mud, and down again. I stayed stuck for about 20 minutes until I was rescued by another couple on bicycles (not the same two, luckily enough). It's good to change these people every now and again, as I imagine they get tired of diving into the mud themselves, getting their already-ragged clothes dirty just to pick up this dirty, muddy, *heavy* motorcycle. Of course, most people were willing to help, especially when they saw I had a disability.

The heat was tremendous. I usually traveled at about 10 miles per hour in second gear. When these guys helped me get it up, they had that look, "Please, would you give us something?," so I gave them each a ball-point pen.

In our Western culture, you might say, "Dave, you are a cheap bastard."

But I had to be careful. Out alone in this strange land, if I gave them money, it would be very risky. You simply never know what they might get into their heads. The best thing to do was to give them ball-point pens. In fact, going through villages, they would often come out in droves, all chanting something, with hands outstretched, palms up. I later found out they were chanting, "BIC, book, BIC, book," meaning they were asking me for either pens or school books.

I fell off the motorcycle at least ten more times in the next few miles!

I was going nowhere fast.

Then, I met the Zairian truckers - men who drive big 5 and 10 ton semi and heavy trucks for a living over these mud tracks. They've got to be the toughest truck drivers in the world for what they go through to get from point A to point B. I saw a lot of ancient, beat up, old Flats, Mcroodes, Peugeots, and Magaris. Once, the driver of one of these old rigs had to stop and help me after I had been pinned under my motorcycle for about 15 minutes with leaking gas all over me.

What a combination...mud, sweat and gasoline!

"Don't light a cigarette next to me," I told the driver, "or we'll **both** go up!"

This particular helper wasn't an African driver, although I don't quite know how to place him. He and his partner spoke a funny language which wasn't French. They were very helpful, shook my hand, and wanted nothing from me at all. I fell off a few more times during the next couple of hours, but I was making a bit of progress. My main concern was the motor, which was running ***extremely hot*** with the low speed and the build up of mud on the front cylinder.

I had to stop for breaks frequently. By this time, I was weak with hunger from all the exertion. On this one particular break, I had another tantalizing dinner of half a tin of beans and some bread; that restored my strength.

I also did something that was kind of interesting. Many people often ask me, "Dave, when did you give your first public address about the journey?" Until reading my own diaries, I really wouldn't have been able to tell them. But, I found while looking through the diaries that, on this particular day, I started talking to an imaginary audience that was off in the rain forest, telling them, "Ladies and gentlemen, think about the words 'endeavor,' 'struggle,' and 'Living your Dreams'." I was already rehearsing, trying to come up with a great opening for a speech to anyone in the future who might listen. So now, when someone asks, "Dave, where did you give your first really incredible talk on the journey?," I tell them, "I gave it in the rain forest of Zaire. My audience consisted of monkeys, birds and other exotic animals who would stare in puzzlement upon this crazy man who was waving his arms and speaking to nothing in particular."

After my break, I got on the motorcycle and started up again, bouncing on ridiculous roads covered with rocks. I drove in first gear on top of the rocks, constantly hearing the bottom of the motorcycle being beaten by them. I've already bent the front rim, and the front forks were hammering up and down constantly (bottoming, or topping out).

The holes were as much as two feet deep, and usually in a series so steady that I could not maneuver around them. I usually made one or two holes before I was hurtled off of the motorcycle.

Then there's the mud ruts the width of a set of dual truck tires. Once I got down in these, if the mud had dried a little bit, I had a chance. If they were still soft, sooner or later I was going to go down. The motorcycle, as you can see from pictures in the middle of the book, is loaded up high, making it top heavy and very unyielding. That's why I rarely managed to get through a rut without coming off. Nothing can be wider than a set of dual tires, or it is torn off of the motorcycle by the walls of the rut.

More dangerous were the eroded roads that had been reduced to little, narrow ledges. On either side there was usually a two- or three-foot drop.

Then, around 4 or 5 o'clock each day, the rain came down, sometimes so torrential that it was hard to breathe. It's like being in a shower because it's so hot; steam rises from the various surfaces, like a cow pissing on a flat rock.

This stretch of road presented me with my first real nasty bridge in equatorial Africa. It was very narrow, planks were missing, and nails and bolts stuck up in the air, inviting my tires to hit them. To negotiate this was very risky.

There are also some bridges that don't have any sides, and some that just have a metal structure. If you hit the structure, you're going to hurt yourself just as bad as if you fall off the bridge altogether!

The motorcycle was banging along so hard at times, I was afraid I was going to break an axle.

Towards the end of the day, about 17:00 in the afternoon, I come to the first real town in Zaire - Beni. Upon entering the town over the rough, rocky main street, in first gear, I saw a bunch of Africans sitting on the side of the road. Raising my hand,

I screamed, "Yahhhhhh, I made it!" They all jumped up and started dancing around, shouting and screaming themselves. It was an amazing thing to see. I didn't realize I was able, with my fervent sigh of relief and feeling of victory, to invoke such a passionate response from my erstwhile audience.

The next order of the day was to find a place to sleep that night and clean up - I was mud from head to toe. I found a "hotel" which was no more than a broken down rat and cockroach infested group of rooms. I didn't feel like sleeping in the room, so the proprietor and I pushed the motorcycle into the courtyard where I placed my sleeping bag and gear out next to it.

I washed up out of a bucket, watching the water turn to mud rather quickly. As the night settled in, I realized Zaire was going to be quite a challenge. The entire day, traveling from about 8:30 a.m. until 5 p.m., I had ridden less than 50 miles (80 km)!

Dinner was a very sumptuous, big plate of eggs and chips, blended in the local tomato sauce; it looked like red water with lumps in it.

Laying down next to my Harley in the courtyard, trying to sleep, people kept walking in and out, making noise all night. It turns out my location was right next to a busy beer hall. Eventually, through sheer exhaustion, I dozed off, ending a very hard, long day.

Many more were to come.

The Worst is Yet to Come!

In the morning, same routine: load the motorcycle, push it outside the compound, and head for the nearest petrol station where gasoline was a dollar a liter ($4 a gallon), pumped by hand. Next, I found a garage which allowed me to change my front tire from a semi-knobby to a full-knobby (I carried both with me). The spokes also required tightening in the front wheel. The garage proprietor, a young man named Phillip, was very well spoken in English.

"Where did you learn to speak English?" I asked, amazed at his fluency.

"I spent a year at university in Texas," he replied. "I enjoyed the United States, but this is my home. My family has owned this business for quite a while. There was a grander time when the Belgians ran the country, but now, it has gone badly down hill."

"Why are the roads so bad here, Phillip?" I asked, stretching my shock-pounded body to limber up a bit.

"Well, it's a problem. The private business community has wanted to pave a road from Kisangani for years, but President Mabutu of Zaire will not let them. He's afraid that we would gain popularity."

"What a horrible little man to create this situation," I thought to myself.

There's just so little for his people because transportation is so difficult. Plus, the poor roads knock up the cost of transporting goods into these areas by double - triple, who knows? The roads were so bad that the repairs to the vehicles must be incredibly expensive... when you can get the parts in this very remote area.

"We get most of our gasoline from Uganda," Phillip told me. "That's why it is so CHEAP here in Beni!"

Where the Ugandans got the gas is anybody's idea.

Then Phillip asked me a rather obvious question.

"What do you think of our roads since coming from the Ugandan border to here?"

"Cripes, I have never in my life ridden over such terrible roads," I immediately replied. "I came off my motorcycle maybe 18-20 times in just one day."

"Dave, just grit your teeth," he told me, shaking his head, "because what's ahead of you between here and Kisangani is far worse!"

I thought to myself, "Oh, my. God help me!"

Then Phillip made a very kind gesture. He said, "Follow me after I have finished with the changing of the tire over to my family store. There, I'd like you to take whatever you want as far as food and provisions, no charge of course."

At the store, I selected four tins of beans (there's no accounting for my taste!). Pasta or rice would be smashed, or made wet from the constant rain.

"Is that all you want?" he asked.

"That's all I can carry, Phillip," I replied. "Weight is of the utmost importance, and I am already somewhere around 900 pounds. I am very grateful for your generosity, but this is all I can take."

Besides, I knew four tins of beans could take me a long way.

I wasn't out of town five minutes when I started seeing the mud was red - not the black mud I had been in the day before, but it stinks just as much. There were many little villages I went through, constructed of thatch and mud. When I saw mud in the road, or a road totally covered by water, I'd ride up through people's so-called front yards - in between and around, dodging kids, chickens, pigs, goats and whatever else they had, to come back on a spot of the road that was dry. A couple of times, I still hit mud and down I went.

The villagers were very kind. They would come out and pick the motorcycle up. They noticed I had a disability, so they seldom wanted anything in return but a handshake. When it appeared they wanted something, I would pass out the ball-point pens (I carried about 300).

Late that morning I hit the first of the big mud pits, 3 to 4 meters deep and up to 100 meters long. This particular one was about 30 meters long. They got to be depressing very quickly. I'd ride maybe one mile, or maybe ten, then hit another one.

You cannot get around them, you must go through them since there's rain forest on both sides of the road.

So, I rode into them, and fell off the motorcycle almost immediately. The bottoms of these pits would be a foot, sometimes more, deep of mud and slush. Each time I fell, the villagers would descend upon me like locusts - only not in a mean or savage way. They would take the baggage off the motorcycle and carry it to hard, dry ground. These kind people never stole anything from me (they could have very easily).

The next step was to start pushing or plowing the motorcycle across these mud pits. During the pushing and pulling, the wheels freeze up in the wheel well because of mud, so the machine literally needs to be plowed through this mire. Of course, I always made an effort to try and help these guys push the motorcycle, but I was never very confident how much my feeble efforts helped. Usually, it took about a dozen people to do the pushing, with many more around, shouting encouragement as "sidewalk supervisors." Later, I discovered rescuing people and machines from the mud pits was a major part of a village's revenue.

Imagine the scene.

One white man and twelve Africans sloshing in a mud pit, sweating and stinking from our own particular brands of smell. My smell is gasoline, sweat and mud, and theirs is body odor and mud. Sometimes, the locals just tell me, "Stay out of the way" in sign language, and they push. I try to make my way across these things as best I can, but there were a couple of times that it was so bad they actually had to pick me up and carry me!

Once on the other side on hard, dry ground, it's time to load up and make the big payoff. By now, half the village is surrounding the motorcycle, and they are all shouting and hollering at a deafening pitch, hands outstretched. I start passing out ball-point pens to the faces I recognize (one thing I had to do was remember the faces of those who helped, because, Lord forbid, I give a pen to somebody who didn't help and forget somebody who did).

It is hard to imagine, as a Westerner, that any road conditions anywhere in the world could ever be this bad.

Although I felt nothing but "good vibes" coming from the villagers I encountered, I found they had a different attitude towards the people on the tour trucks (overland tours). I discovered that the locals resent these tourists because they look down from their trucks, dressed in their designer-type casual wear, with their cameras photographing them like monkeys. I could understand the villager's animosity.

Once, before I understood this, I was seen talking to a tour truck full of people, and without knowing it, turned my own good situation to bad. As soon as they left on their way, I made about another 500 meters and went down again in the mud and water.

This time, the attitude of the help was different!

A man who had helped me before jumped in and tried to help me again, but a woman was grabbing him, trying to pull him away. I sensed she was shouting for him to make me give him money, so I took out 500 Zaires from my shirt pocket that I kept for emergencies - that's about 50 cents - and put it in this guy's hand. He and another fellow then jumped in and we got the motorcycle up, pushing it out. This scene felt increasing ugly since the woman was still shouting, ranting and hollering. I immediately started up my motorcycle, told this kind fellow, who was obviously going to have a lot of trouble with his wife later that night, "Merci," and got on my way.

After about a mile of progress, I came off the motorcycle again in water and mud and was pinned underneath it for a good 10-15 minutes. Slowly, I sank into the mud. I thought to myself, "If someone doesn't come along soon, I could *drown* under this bastard thing."

Time kept going, and I kept sinking.

When my face was just barely out of the water, a couple of bicyclists came along. To my very great relief, they were not from the last village. They were able to get the thing off of me enough so I could scoot out from underneath it.

It took all three of us to upright the motorcycle, but we still couldn't move it out of the mud until more people came. We waited patiently for more people to come and eventually they did. Of course, the payoff once again was ball-point pens, handshakes and great big, "Merci, messieurs."

Body and Machine Breakdowns

After the motorcycle has been down in mud and water, I always turn the engine over carefully with the crank start lever to force water out gently from the cylinders. Once I've done that, it usually starts right up, blows water out of the exhaust, coughs it out of the carburetor and runs, to my very great relief.

On this same day I broke the front brake hand lever. Now, I could only grasp the remaining part of the lever with two fingers, a big problem when slipping and sliding along muddy roads or when going downhill on what is left of the top of a rut. When you move down a hill, you need to brake both the front and rear brakes. Now, it was virtually impossible to get the thing to stop while pulling on this shortened lever.

In these deep mud ruts, my right knee would sometimes hit the side of the mud wall. When it did, the whole motorcycle would come to a sudden stop as my knee sank into the wall, the socket of my right leg rammed right up into the hip, cutting and bruising it terribly. Great pain accompanied this delightful experience.

After awhile, my battered right leg began making bizarre grinding noises in the knee joint. The socket in the left leg, which has a leather liner in it, started to swell, putting incredible pressure on the stump. And, it was hard to keep my shoes on. As I got into this mud, it tended to suck them right off my feet (pegs).

To say the least, life was such a joy!

I had to take the front crash bar off - or what was left of it - and throw it away as it had been bent and broken away from its mountings. Now I faced an even more difficult problem. When the motorcycle fell, it was even more difficult to get it back upright.

I'm battling the heat, the pain in my stumps, my back and arms and everything else are sore, and, though I am in very good physical condition, nothing can prepare me for being bounced up and off my seat constantly since I can't stand on the foot pegs. If it weren't for the kidney belt I was wearing, I am sure my back would not have lasted a half hour. As it was, my good physical condition enabled me to keep going without any great pain in my back.

The main pain I have is a big pain in the ASS from constantly being thrown off my seat!

My back shock absorbers were really taking a beating. One time I touched them and discovered they were too hot to handle, as were the front fork tubes which were constantly going up and down all day, and the oil had blown out of the front fork seals.

Every time I saw the mile odometer click, I thought, "C'mon, click another mile!" Every passing mile was a feeling of accomplishment and joy, bringing me nearer to the end of all of this misery.

Now I turned west, heading across Africa instead of north. I lost count of the number of times I fell off the motorcycle. One particular time, I saw a series of holes to be conquered, when suddenly, the motorcycle was careening off into the jungle, leaving me along the way.

"Oh, my God, what if there is a snake in here or something?" I thought. If there had been, it would have been "poor snake" as he would have been flattened by the motorcycle. Coming out of the bushes like some muddy monster out of the *Creature from the Black Lagoon*, I got to the motorcycle. Locals were standing and looking at this strange man standing there in their midst, dripping mud and water. Motioning to them to give me a hand, we picked up the Harley and pushed it through a series of holes.

More ball-point pens, handshakes and mercis.

Then, on my way again.

Late in the afternoon, the rain started pouring down, killing any further possibility of travel, so I pulled along side the road, slipping and sliding, just managing to keep the motorcycle up.

"Well, that's it for today," I thought.

It's about 17:30 in the evening, and the mosquitoes are swarming around me as I struggle to eat my half a tin of beans and cook some tea. A truck passes me and gets stuck in the mud ahead, causing other trucks to back up along the road. I could hear the driver all through the night, revving his engine, trying to get out of the mud unsuccessfully. I rolled out my sleeping bag on the side of this so-called road in the mud and laid down about 19:30, trying to go to sleep while fighting the mosquitoes.

Of course, other wonderful and relaxing happenings occurred that night. Besides listening to passengers shouting and hollering to one another for God knows what reasons, there was a herd of cows that came walking through my camp. I grabbed everything that was stationary on the ground that was not up on the motorcycle, attempting to protect it, all the while hoping the cows would not step on me. Fortunately, they managed to navigate around me and the motorcycle with only minor brushes. As they paraded through, I thought, "Please, don't knock this horrible thing over on me! I'll never get it up!"

The next morning brought even more challenges!

I got up feeling tired and strained, although I can't imagine why.

Then, of course, I had the usual crowd of people standing around me. The heat started to mount, yet people still stayed, laughing and carrying on about my presence. One person even handed me a small bag of peanuts and bread. "How very kind," I thought as I ate my peanuts and bread in front of all the other laughing, staring characters. Tired, and tired of being a spectacle, I thought to myself, "Please, just go away. Leave me alone."

In their land, I have become the monkey; they are the tourists.

Some truckers came over who couldn't speak any English, but a couple of them spoke French. Between my speaking a few words of French I learned from the dictionary I carried with me, they assured me the road was better ahead. I thought to myself, "Well, we'll see, because I've heard that before."

At 11:30, <u>finally</u>, they got the stuck truck out of the mud, and told us we could go forward. As I hit the mud, everybody starts plowing and pulling my motorcycle through the two foot deep mire, when who should arrive on the scene but another motorcyclist.

We looked at each other in amazement - two lonely white boys out in darkest Africa. As it was, there was no time to talk or exchange greetings as we were pushing and plowing my motorcycle through the mud. I noticed that this fellow was on an XR 500 Honda, and he too had to be assisted in getting it through the mud. Out the other side, off I go, as he is just starting through the obstacle course of mud and misery.

After a mile or so, I stop and sit down in the dirt to repair a broken strap on my right leg. I am fishing through my bag for a piece of leather string when along comes this other fellow on a motorcycle. He stops, and we look at each other. He is French, and, obviously, we don't understand each other.

"I'm David," I said, introducing myself.

"Ahhh, I'm Bruno Piet from St. Quinton in France," he replies in a puffed up manner. He noticed what I needed, and pulls out a piece of leather string from his bag. We shake hands, and he's on his way; I'm alone again, repairing my right leg so I can get up and get going.

The road is better now, and that lifts my spirits. But, I also wonder, "How long will it last?"

Stopped at Kamanda for gas, and discovered that the price is negotiated on a piece of paper with no particular spoken words. We agree on $1.50 a liter ($6 a gallon), and what I bought smelled more like kerosene.

"Holy mackerel," I thought, "how is this going to run in the Harley?"

Fortunately, my machine has very low compression pistons, so it will burn virtually anything. I filled up, then paid the bill. A big crowd gathered around, watching me take out my money. "What an easy target I would make," I thought, breathing a sigh of relief only after getting back on the road.

"Onward and upward we go!" I thought, my spirits being a little bit better despite the mud. The combination of better roads and a motorcycle running okay encouraged me.

However, I was soon to discover that life could, and would get worse.

Battling the Mud!
Zaire, C.A.R.-Cameroon,
October-November, 1990

Chapter Five

Pygmies, Crocodiles, and a Lost Leg

The motorcycle had to be stopped about every ten miles. With screwdriver in hand, I then started to pick out all the mud off the front cylinder and air fins. Sometimes I couldn't see the front of the motor at all. The chain guard was torn off from mud. The starter motor relay went bad from water damage (within days, I changed two). From then on, a screw driver was used to short across the solenoid and start the engine. I used that technique all the way to London!

Bounding along throughout the day, I only fell a couple of times - a record for me. At the end of the day, the inevitable rain started again, so I located a Kraawl (a small group of huts along the side of the road). At one of the thatched huts, I spoke to the man in charge, making the sign of "sleep," and he nodded. Of course, more people gathered around while I tried to do needed repairs on the motorcycle: opening up the primary, cleaning out the mud, then sealing it up with silicon seal and a piece of an old inner tube. Mind you, it's got a belt drive in it which is something that really saved the day later.

When I settled back in the late evening, the crowd of about 12 people living in the huts all went on their way. I heated up my tasty half tin of beans and made my tea, listening to the music of the jungle. One particular little animal was quite a screamer, although I don't know what kind it was. It made these loud sounds - "Ahhhhh! Ahhhhhhh! Ahhhhhhhhhhh!" This went on constantly; the thing is screaming in hysterics throughout the night. I thought to myself, "What a tired little animal this one surely must be by the next morning!" There were also different bird sounds.

Looking up at the moon through the rain forest trees, I experienced an amazing sense of peace and tranquillity. I fell into the "sleep of the dead," exhausted from the distance I'd covered that day - probably a total of about 40 miles.

Before dawn, I loaded up the motorcycle. I wanted to get a photograph of this small village, but I couldn't get the people to pose for me without giving them something. I felt I couldn't give them my pens, as I needed them for people who were actually helping me. So, no picture.

Not long out of the village I fell off the motorcycle in holes full of water, landing in the nearby bushes, praying no snake was waiting for me. Now, I lay in mud and sweat, waiting for people to come along.

I hadn't been in third gear in days! My average speed was between 10 and 15 miles an hour. At 15 miles an hour, over terrain like this, I was actually going very fast. I was still getting thrown off the motorcycle very regularly but, though I was bruised, I usually was not hurt too badly thanks to the mud cushioning the blow.

Of course, I had an abundance of scrapes here and there, particularly cuts on the hands, not only from working on the motorcycle but from being thrown off the thing. I wore no gloves when riding because when they are full of mud, they slip off the handlebars. I had to grab the handlebars with a death grip just to be able to attempt to control the Harley. Also, I did not wear my glasses any longer because it was easier to see without them. However, there's a price for that. The dirt in my eyes sometimes felt like sandpaper under the eyelids.

In the late afternoon I entered **Epulu, home of the pygmies**. I had been seeing these little people on the road occasionally as I rode along. They have small pot bellies and paint themselves white. Most carry little bows and arrows. Inevitably, they have this great long pipe they're smoking. I don't know what they smoke, but they sure seem happy as they wave at me.

Epulu was a very nice camp, and it had toilets!

If you wanted a shower, you went to the river.

"Be careful of crocodiles," advised a local. They explained that "Just last week a tourist was taken by crocs." I never saw a single crocodile, but I did pass on the river.

Instead, I took my legs and my dirty clothes off and I gave them to an African fellow who stood next to me, staring in amazement. He took my stuff and started to wash them while I got on some rocks and gave myself a much-needed bath. I then put on my clean clothes, which were wet and mildewed (the only thing I was ever able to keep reasonably dry was my diary). With wet, mud-free clothes on, I felt like a new man.

I took the primary cover off my Harley and cleaned it. When I did that, I was messing around with the starter and didn't watch myself and got my finger caught in the starter drive gear, grinding it right over the clutch hub. It was fortunate that the shaft wasn't anchored properly. My finger just went through the thing, cutting, not crushing it. In great pain, I danced around like a banshee. It was stupid of me to fail to disconnect the battery.

A German fellow came up to me while I was dancing around with my bleeding finger. He started complaining about the Africans up ahead who were begging, shouting and hollering at him. Seemingly oblivious to my pain, the man told me the police and other officials were trying to get bribes, making life generally miserable. To this point, I hadn't encountered any really bad officials, other than the one, Mantuki, the little prick on the Good Ship Lemba.

After cleaning my hands off and putting a band-aid on my "social" finger (my middle digit), I took a walk to the village up ahead, about a kilometer away, and sat at what passed for a restaurant. It had a few wooden benches under a few dirty tables. Flies were everywhere, especially over my bowl of beans, which was my dinner.

In the evening, I tried to go to sleep, but the mosquitoes seemed to love me. The repellent I was using didn't work. So, I closed my day listening to the buzzing sound of the mosquitoes and the rushing of the river. "I've come 63 miles today," I thought. "Pretty fair going considering the road and terrain that I've had to traverse."

At 02:30 in the morning, the beans hit. It was everything I could do to get my legs on and walk/stumble across the campgrounds to the toilet. After getting back to my sleeping bag, I took myself apart again and laid back to listen to the night animals until the dawn.

Sardines and a cup of tea for breakfast, then on my way to Kisangani.

The road out of Epulu was a very pleasant change. There was one time during the day that I actually got the thing into third gear up to about 30 miles per hour, believe it or not! For the most part, though, it was still first and second gear. I only came off the motorcycle a few times during the whole day, so that made it a *very* good day covering 80 miles (130 kilometers).

Towards the middle of the afternoon, I came to a town called Meduza, a village of thatched huts where mud passed for main street, with a few derelict brick buildings with no glass in the windows. This is a MAJOR village; a small village would be a few thatched huts. There I asked for "Essauns" meaning "gasoline." I was directed to a hut where a man came out. I used my pen to write down numbers as we negotiated a price - $2 a liter ($8 a gallon), a horrible cost for this terrible gasoline.

Jerry cans were produced, and with a siphon hose (an Oklahoma credit card), we proceeded to fill the gas tanks.

Of course, when we were finished, this guy put my pen in his pocket.

"Swell," I thought.

By this time, a crowd of several hundred people gathered around, but they were very quiet. The atmosphere was more of menace than festivity.

Most of the time, merchants want American dollars if they can get them. I didn't have near the Zaires I needed to fill up the gas tanks, plus both of my gas cans. So, I tried to work out a price for a dollar exchange rate.

"Non, non," replied the merchant. He didn't want dollars at all.

"Great," I thought.

So, I counted out my Zaires; I had 31,000 Zaires for the gasoline. The gas itself came to more than what I had in Zaires, so we took gasoline out. When he found out that I still didn't have enough money, having miscounted the Zaires, the crowd went "Uhhhhhhhh."

The heat that afternoon was oppressive, the smell from the crowd was threatening, and the fumes from the gas added an odor of menace to the air. The crowd closed in, virtually bearing down on me as I was bent over the motorcycle, recounting my Zaires.

Again, the crowd growled "Uhhhhhhhh."

"What now?" I thought, feeling very apprehensive about my future.

We had to take out even more gasoline. When he took out an extra half liter, I thought, "Well, that's fine. What's his time worth? Just keep your mouth shut, Dave."

I was now ready to get on the motorcycle when the man speaks up again.

"Non, messieur, non."

"What now?" I wondered.

I waited in suspense while the man walked off with his Jerry cans. A few minutes later, he came back and gave me change for the extra half liter of gasoline that he had taken.

"Judas Priest," I thought, "you just never know!"

Not wanting to stay in this highly-charged atmosphere one more second than necessary, I got on the motorcycle, shook the man's hand, said "Merci beau coups" and took off, getting the hell out of Meduza as quickly as I could.

The Legless "Devil"

Not long out of Meduza, more bad roads. The first part of the bad road was ruts with mud in them which I hit at about 20 miles an hour - too fast for that terrain. The motorcycle caught the middle of the rut and the front wheel went up and hurled me off like a sack of potatoes through the air for about 15 feet. Luckily, I landed in mud without rocks. I was able to right the motorcycle myself, believe it or not, but the rear carrier was dented up pretty badly, which irritated me.

It wasn't a kilometer before I hit yet another long mud rut. I was going through it, thinking to myself, "Hey, I'm going to make it. I'm going to make it all the way this time!." It was during this feeling of triumphant joy, at accomplishing the impossible, that towards the end of the rut my left leg got caught between the mud wall and the motorcycle, tearing the leg right off me. I reached up and grabbed my stump, rolling off the motorcycle to protect the stump. It would have created a real problem to poke the bone through the bottom of the stump out here. In that short instant, a million possible negative scenarios about impossible medical care and filthy hospitals flashed through my mind.

Laying there in the mud, I looked up to see a couple of Africans on the mud wall. One is going, "Ohhh, ahhhh!" They are talking to one another in very loud sounds. I could only imagine they were saying, "Look at this man, he's torn his leg off!"

It had been a lousy day to that point, so to brighten it up, I scooted back through the mud to where the leg lay, opened up the caliper on the top and got my stump down inside the socket and closed it all up. When I stood up, that was too much for these guys.

"Uh-yeee-uhhhh!" they were exclaiming, yelling, shouting and pointing. Before I knew it, they ran off into the jungle.

Luckily, the motorcycle had fallen against the mud wall, so it was fairly easy for me to upright. I managed to get it started, and I was off and on my way again before these natives returned, probably with spears or bows, to kill this white "tockolash" (devil).

Among the other fun-filled adventures along the super highway of Northern Zaire, there was the vegetation tunnels that grow right over the road. You cannot see anything inside these tunnels which are sometimes 50 to 60 meters long. You might see the other end, but you don't know if, in the middle of it all, there's a hole, water, rocks or mud.

And you must pass through them.

The headlight is useless, and besides, by this time, mine is not working.

So, in through these tunnels I go - blind.

Well, this one particular time I hit mud in the tunnel and went down, managing to keep myself from getting caught underneath the motorcycle. It was starting to PISS down rain while I sat there for over an hour in the mud, inside this dark tunnel, trying to keep my spirits up and not get depressed. Precious gasoline is leaking out of the motorcycle, and I know there's not <u>near</u> enough fuel left to get to Kisangani.

Trying to keep my spirits up, I slowed my heart rate down, and said a prayer for strength. As I prayed, a feeling came over me that it didn't matter how bad things got. If I didn't damage the motorcycle, I would make it. An hour or so later, a truck came along. He couldn't get around me, and thankfully, I managed to catch his attention before he drove over me!

The driver and some of his passengers pulled the motorcycle up and we pushed it out of this tunnel. I got going again, but was soon down, and the same truck came along and repeated the process. This went on for quite a while - me going a kilometer or so, another set of mud ruts, and down I'd go. The last time, the driver said, "There's a village up ahead. Please pull off there so we can get past you."

The road improved a bit in this last 6 miles (10 kilometers), and I made the little village. The truck driver was in very poor humor by about the third time he had to stop and get his people to pick the motorcycle up. A lot of times when a truck driver sees a set of ruts that are full of mud and water, he likes to get a flying run at them and just plow through to the other side. Having me down in the mud spoiled that strategy, so I can't blame him for being irritated.

There's just no way around me.

After helping me, now the driver has to manipulate the mud pit himself, and since he has lost momentum, he usually gets stuck, forcing his passengers to get out and push the truck! Every time there is straining and groaning, straining and groaning until the thing is out of the mud. Then they go a mile and find me laying down in the mud again. So, when the truck finally passed me at the village, it was easy to understand why all the passengers were waving and rather jubilant that this crazy foreigner was out of their hair once and for all!

At the bridge I met an old man, and gave him ten Zaires for a place to sleep. Since it was raining, and too slippery to ride, some people in the village helped me push the motorcycle off the road.

Did I say village?

It was really just a few huts huddled together out in the middle of the rain forest with about 12 people living there.

After an hour, they lost interest in me and went about their own business, and I went about mine, settling down to my succulent meal of half a tin of beans, some bread, and a cup of tea.

Another truck stopped in front of the village, and one of the drivers spoke reasonable English. "There's bad bridges and marshes ahead," he told me.

I didn't sleep very well that night.

BIC's, Bridges and Barley

Awake about 05:15. The morning is clear and bright as I load the motorcycle and eat my other half tin of beans. I hadn't moved 500 meters out of the village when I hit mud and went down.

Another great start to a new and wonderful day!

I had to wait quite a while until someone came along. They lifted my motorcycle up and I dispensed "thank you's" and ball-point pens.

My next encounter was with an official some miles up the road. A policeman stopped me and said, "Messieur, a Memoui (souvenir)?"

I handed him a BIC pen, full of mud.

As I traveled through the villages, the kids and adults would stand with their hands out and holler, "BIC, book, BIC, book, BIC, book." Sometimes it sounded like a swarm of bees.

The villages had no electricity or running water, but sometimes when I would stop, kids would come up and feel my water bottles. If they felt empty, they would take them and fill them up at the village well. I often feared they would unintentionally give me contaminated water, so I silently prayed when they returned the water bottles to me. It would have been very impolite of me to put water purification tablets in the water in front of them, and I didn't want to hurt their feelings.

I was hitting more and more very narrow bridges with no sides, with boards missing, or with nails sticking up. They were difficult to cross without getting a flat tire, breaking a rim, or, Lord forbid, going over the edge into whatever it spanned. I broke another spoke on the front wheel, and tightening the spokes was something I was doing almost on a daily basis. By this time, the rear rim was bent by something I had hit.

One particular time, I went down outside a Zairian Army camp. The soldiers came out, pointing their rifles at me as I was stuck under the motorcycle in the mud.

"Cies vous plait, messieur pettie Aid," I said, meaning, "Give me some help here" in a very strong manner. The sergeant looked at me like I was some kind of a fool for challenging his authority. Nevertheless, he turned around to the rest of his men and told them to put down their rifles. Then, they got down into the mud with me and lifted the motorcycle up, pushing it out of the mud.

When they saw I had a disability, the sergeant says, "Problem, messieur?," and I answered "Oui." I lifted up my pant legs and showed them; their mouths all dropped open; the sergeant hollered at his troops, and they did a very surprising thing - they all stood to attention and saluted! I shook their hands, and the last man I greeted spoke to me in broken English, saying, "God go with you" (I'm sure the average tourist would not have gotten that treatment).

Early that afternoon, I came across a rain forest clearing station where they were removing lumber. I met a Frenchman named Jiles who was kind enough to give me 10 liters (2 1/2 gallons) of gasoline at no charge. I was able, with this 10 liters, to make it to Kisangani.

On down the road, I tumbled, bounced and banged along, falling off regularly on the "Wondrous Conditions Autobahn of Zaire."

Suddenly, my motor is revving up, but there is no power.

"Start working, boy," I said out loud.

It didn't.

I stopped and opened up the primary to discover that the drive belt was broken because of the rocks and mud forced into it. I started cleaning out the primary, and taking off what was left of the outer primary cover. In the middle of this job, along came a vehicle with a priest in it, and he gave me a fresh loaf of bread and wished me God's blessings, which I bloody well needed by this time! I gratefully ate the bread with dirty, greasy hands; it was the first fresh bread I had in days.

Then, back to work changing the belt. It took about an hour, and all the time I was trying to race the soon-coming, always faithful afternoon rain. The clouds were building up with water, and were ready to dump it on earth, right smack on the spot where I was working, turning the road into another quagmire of mud.

Off again, I finally had a mud victory! I actually maneuvered my motorcycle through some mud ruts without smashing my knee into a mud wall or getting my left leg ripped off!

Just before I arrived in the next village, the rains started and my motorcycle flew out from underneath me. The villagers came out to help me pick it up and moved me over between some of their huts, next to a whole line of road construction equipment.

A big crowd gathers as I try to eat my dinner. Somebody brings me a bowl of hot rice, with barley mixed in it, and I sit gratefully eating the first hot food I've had since I left Epulu.

By this time, it is dark and the crowd has lost interest, leaving me alone to put my wet, soggy, muddy body into my wet, soggy sleeping bag.

Every day seems to start with something diabolical, and this one is no different.

When I awoke early in the morning, I needed to go to the toilet, so I motioned to an old African fellow who understood my needs and led me way back into the rain forest. I stumbled and fell going up this hill that was still slick with mud, only to discover that the toilet was just a hole in the ground.

"Don't fall in, Dave," I told myself. "God forbid!"

Then, it was back to work on the motorcycle. I took the primary off and patched it up again with more rubber inner tube and silicone sealer. "How long will it hold?" I wondered. "Five minutes?"

With a big crowd in attendance, cheering "Bon Voyage," I left the village and the road construction equipment that was just sitting, sinking into the mud.

My next stop: Kisangani, which is the major city in the north of Zaire on the Zaire river.

Chapter Six

Shrinking Stumps and Big Barges

The road was better than it had been in days.

Banging and bouncing along, I started to pass through more and more villages. Finally, at about 9 o'clock, I hit **blessed, beautiful pavement**! Oh, it was rougher than a corn cob, but to me, it was beautiful! I was actually able to speed up and shift into third gear, going along at 35 miles an hour, dodging goats, donkeys, chickens, pigs, kids, people, horses, and hand-drawn carts.

As I moved along through this maze, it felt like flying at 100 miles an hour!

The wonderful paved road continued for the next 10 kilometers (6 miles), all the way into Kisangani. I located a place my friend, Jiles, told me to go to - a garage called Cafco. There I met Julio, the boss (a Portuguese fellow). I told Julio my Harley needed a steam cleaning, so he took out his power washer, and the motorcycle was given a bath for the first time since leaving South Africa. The aluminum was already corroded by the red mud that had been on it ever since leaving Beni, 700 miles (1150 km) ago.

I was given a helper named Prosper to assist me in my repairs. By the looks of Prosper, if he had prospered any more, he would have been dead.

We welded up my carrier box, and beat out most of the dents so the doors would close properly.

Next, I repaired the front brake lever. It was heli-arced.

The primary was repaired with a sheet-steel plate by putting a patch over the big area at the bottom that had been torn open.

When the work was finished, Julio would take no money.

Next, I received directions to the Olympic Hotel which has a camping area within the hotel that looked like the Garden of Eden. I was pumped up with pride as I rode in on my newly repaired, freshly bathed Harley Davidson. The other travelers from Europe, Australia, and places about really took notice when I came in on my machine. They must have been thinking, "What is that stupid bastard doing on a Harley in Zaire?"

They came over, shook my hand, and told me, "We've never seen a single Harley in Africa before." I thought to myself, "That's because no one is stupid enough to try Africa on a Harley."

There were always black market hawkers hanging around the tourist hotels, and a few of them tried to sell me a book on phrases in French. They quoted me their price, when a fellow named Peter, an Australian who had been across Africa a few times, came over and took up the negotiations.

"These guys are trying to rip you off," he told me. A very heated argument ensued between the two traders and the two travelers. Just about when it seemed destined to escalate into violence, the traders backed off.

As I mentioned earlier, the one thing I cannot stand is being ripped off because I am a foreigner. You can charge me a fair price and I'll pay it, but please, don't ever try to rip me off!

The next priority: a shower, usually a difficult challenge for me. I managed to find a chair with no seat on it, and placed it in the shower stall. I turn on the water, then sit on the chair. I take my legs off in the stall. My legs get soaking wet as they sit in the corner, but that makes no difference since they're wet all the time anyway. This place is like an open sewer in the corner of this shower stall, and it stinks.

As I shower, I realize that I have lost quite a bit of weight since I left Johannesburg - maybe as much as ten pounds. That weight loss creates pain in my stumps because, as the stump shrinks the socket becomes too big to fit the stump.

I parked my motorcycle under an awning that used to be a big stage area for the hotel in grander days. Many years ago, Kisangani obviously enjoyed quite a grand and lovely lifestyle, but now, sadly enough, it is just plain run down. About midnight, it starts to rain; it just pours and pours. Every one out in the open camping area got flooded, whether they had waterproof tents or not. Everyone under the awning got fleas and mosquitoes.

Road Warrior, Road Weary

It has been one month on the road.

One month living my dream.

In one month, my dream has turned into a nightmare.

Of course, no one forced me to make this trip. If it was a nightmare, it is because I created it by deciding to ride this PIG of a motorcycle, loaded down with gear, instead of riding a more appropriate enduro which weighs less than half of my Harley.

In my first month, I had covered about 3500 miles (5000 kilometers) since leaving Johannesburg...averaging about 113 miles (180 kilometers) per day!

Later that day, Bruno Piet rides in and parks next to me. We smile at one another with a strong sense of pride and accomplishment.

An African fellow named Eugene came up to us and said, "Are you guys going to need petrol?"

"Yes, sure," we answered. We put Eugene on the back of Bruno's motorcycle, and went into town where I saw the only petrol pump working in the whole country! There was a long line of cars backed up around the block, and, on the other side of the petrol pump people stood with Jerry cans. Now, don't ask me how Eugene did it (he must be a master con artist among his own people), but he managed to talk the responsible people into letting Bruno and I jump the long line and fill up our gas tanks. Of course, we gladly paid a small amount as a tip when we finished. People were shaking our hands, saying "Bon Voyage," and "Welcome to Zaire." I was amazed at the good atmosphere around this pump. Frankly, in the U.S. people would have been shooting each other.

Back at the Olympic Hotel and camping area, I gave away all of my jackets, except a thin one. In the hot weather, I just don't need the jackets; they are extra weight, especially being wet all the time. It was just not worth keeping them. Unfortunately, one of the jackets I gave away to a couple of New Zealanders was a Navy foul weather jacket that I'd had for 16 years. It was a present from my mother and father on my 22nd birthday in 1974, and it really hurt me to give it up.

But, one must survive, and one cannot survive with things you don't need out on the road.

I also gave away my ten pound jack, reasoning, "If I have a flat tire, that's no problem. If I need to lift the motorcycle up for something, that's no problem Africans will always come along, and they'll happily help me lift the motorcycle up, put it on blocks."

For them, this is great fun. The ball-point pen is a bonus!

We went out looking for a river boat to take us down the Zaire River, and Eugene took us to one boat that said, "We'll take you up the river for nothing, but all the stevedores and our crew are on strike. We won't be going anywhere before Tuesday

58

(four days away), and only if the strike is settled."

We located another boat with an African captain and crew that appeared to be a motorized barge with a helm at the back, up in a wheel house, with two non-motorized barges strapped along the sides. This captain said he would take us for 35,000 Zaires (about $42.00).

The catch: he's leaving that afternoon!

We **rush** back to town, load up with food, and got ourselves ready to move that afternoon. We paid Eugene for his assistance, then went to the bank for more money, then went back to the barge and paid the captain.

Next, we had to negotiate a price to get the motorcycles loaded onto the boat. Once that price was negotiated, I shouted at the African stevedores, "Strong Men," holding my arm up, flexing my muscles. All the Africans jumped up and yelled in unison something in French, obviously trying to reassure me that they could all do the job.

Rolling motorcycles down planks across the water onto the barge was a worry. Bruno's motorcycle, of course, went quite easy. Mine, however, even unloaded, still had the box and the carry system on the back; the total package: almost 800 pounds. However, the Africans manipulated the task with little trouble.

When the motorcycles were loaded, we waited for an hour before finally casting off down the Zaire River.

The barge was called the "Kinzazie," and the captain was a jolly, big ole' fellow. The crew was very pleasant to both Bruno and I. There were over 100 African passengers on the boat, plus the cargo, plus one policeman. My own mood was rather jovial since I hadn't fallen off the motorcycle now for 2 days (of course, we hadn't gone anywhere).

As we go down the Zaire River, we are often met by dugouts - logs the Africans hallow out, then stand up in, propelling them with long poles that reach the bottom of the shallow river. The Zaire River is as much as a kilometer wide in some places, and it has islands in the middle of it. It is quite a beautiful and majestic body of water, unchanged by time or man for the most part, lined on both sides with rain forest.

From a distance, we can also see little villages, storybook beautiful, unchanged by anything we know in the Western World.

On the negative side, the heat is sweltering!

The toilet and shower stall are both together. One can go to take a shower, and, if you are not careful, you'll come out smelling worse than you did when you went in. By the way, this one toilet and shower services the entire barge.

Our first night out, we watched a very beautiful sunset. One of the most impressive parts about sunset on the Zaire River is that it marks the time when the flies do a shift change with the mosquitoes. There's about a 1/2 hour grace period from the two parasites.

We put into one of the islands for the night, and shut down. For awhile, there was peace, then they kicked in the generator on the back of the barge.

"Klunk, klunk, klunk," was the nocturnal sound we listened to all night long. Bruno and I talked, and I discovered he'd spent six years in the French Marines, so he too was a military man. He told me that he had just divorced his wife, and put his motorcycle on a plane to Nairobi where he immediately got mugged and robbed of rings, money, and other valuables he was carrying. "My life as a free man," he told me, "had started on the left foot."

I shared a bit about my own service in the American Marines and Vietnam.

We heard thunder, and knew a rain storm was coming in around midnight. Putting my legs back on, Bruno and I gathered our gear under cover as the winds came up and started to whip things about. Once all of our possessions were covered, we managed to climb under a tarp. An African fellow, spotting us under the tarp, weaseled in right between us just as it started pouring rain.

When I wear my legs, I cannot lay very long without having incredible pain in my stumps. So, I spent the rest of the night cold, wet, and miserable. Obviously, I didn't get any sleep.

The next morning, the rain eased off and we were on our way again. Though it was quite cool during the first part of the morning, the heat, eventually started building up. We "enjoyed" our normal tinned food, breakfast and lunch, but in the evening we had a bit of a treat. A long boat came along side selling, for a few cents, catfish and bananas. That night, Bruno and I really enjoyed a nice meal.

The next day, we docked at a small port. Now, the people in these places are in no hurry to do any work, so we waited around for an hour before anyone so much as made a sign to start unloading the barge. After washing some clothes, I read a book while melting in the dead heat.

At Bumba, we're supposed to disembark, and it is always going through my mind, "What horrors will we encounter in the next phase of Zaire?"

Bruno managed to get more catfish. He sure loves his comforts, and he does know how to cook. Much of the weight he carries is for better living on the road, where most of the weight I carry is tools, spare parts, oil and extra gasoline. Bruno doesn't seem to be bothered by these kind of things, and lives a lot more comfortable life than I do.

At the end of a day's ride, he looks relaxed, I looked haggard.

October 15th: We come into Bumba, where we were supposed to unload. After about an hour of hem and hawing, voices started to escalate, and the situation started to get real mean. The price to off load the motorcycles was to be 3,000 Zaires ($3.50).

It wasn't us that agreed on this price, it was some of the crew. It was also the crew, and the Stevedores, who were about to have a major brawl (probably over who was going to receive the lion's share of the 3,000 Zaires). Now, to unload Bruno's motorcycle is not much of a problem. Mine, however, is definitely difficult. The motorcycle had to be taken across two other barges, then up a very steep slope. Once up on top the slope, it then had to be pushed to the Customs Office.

Finally, the debate was settled, the motorcycles were off loaded, and we packed up our gear and took off through the streets of Bumba, looking for our way out.

Back to Muddy Normal

Sure enough, we hit mud and down I went.

We lifted the motorcycle up, and I rode about 100 or so meters, then zap, down again in the mud again.

Now I'm in a very foul mood. I just left the boat and already I'm falling in mud when there's still another 300 miles (500 kilometers) to go to get out of the country.

FINALLY, we get out of Bumba, and we're moving along fairly well when I notice a noise in the primary - almost a grinding - is increasing. We stop, and I take the clutch out and examine the bearings. They look a bit dry, so I asked Bruno to go to the next town and see if he can locate some grease. He comes back in about 1/2 an hour with the grease...and some bananas. I gratefully ate one of the bananas, then put some extra grease on the bearings.

Away we go.

Next, I developed a noise in the lower end of the motor.

The road to Yacoma was no good. Five miles up that road I had fallen off many times in deep mud and water. Bruno and I were covered from head to toe with mud. I really must hand it to my friend, Bruno. If I fell down in the mud, he'd get down in the mud with me. I really don't know what I would have done without him. His spirit was great, and he always had a smile on his face.

"Missieur, what are you doing in the mud?" he'd ask.

It is hard to explain to you how much I appreciated his help and company. Without ever complaining, he'd help get my motorcycle up and off we'd go again.

We decided to go back and catch the main road to Lisala, which was more mileage than we had planned. The road was slightly better, but I still fell off very regularly as we trundled along. On the last kilometer before Le Salla, I fell off a few times because we had to climb a very steep hill. One time, I went down in mud and water and Bruno could just barely get the motorcycle off me so I could get out from underneath it.

The new road obstacle was sand. We had been hitting mud, holes, and rocks right along, but now we also had to contend with sand. On our first major stretch of sand, Bruno and I are both tearing through it as best we can, when, simultaneously, Bruno on one side of the rut and me on the other, we both go down (he's on an enduro bike with knobby tires). I break open the primary on a rock, it fills up with sand, and the belt is broken.

I only have one spare belt left. "Lord forbid that I should break it," I thought. "If it goes, I just won't be going anywhere."

After an hour, I cleaned out the primary, put in the new belt, got everything back together, sealed up the primary with more inner tube and silicone sealer, which only holds for a few minutes, then off we go.

Both of us fell regularly in this deep sand.

And of course, we were still contending with the mud.

Bruno, with his knobby tires, gets through the mud fairly well; for myself, it was a different situation.

I broke my front brake lever again when I was coming down an eroded hill on a path a little over a foot wide and fairly slick. I couldn't use my brakes, and heading towards me is a truck, coming across the bridge. He was coming across, and he was not going to stop.

On either side of the road, the drop was easily a good couple of feet. I raced to make it to the bottom, and was just able to turn, but not enough. I was clipped by this asshole, and flew off the motorcycle over the front. It came charging after me like a maddened rhino into the rain forest.

I'm very, very lucky that when the motorcycle actually hit me, the force of it's movement was slowed by the thick vegetation I had crashed into. I was scratched, bruised, but otherwise okay. I was also grateful that there were no snakes hanging in the vines to make my life even more miserable.

Bruno gots off his motorcycle and, as usual, he's laughing.

"David, David, Sava, Sava," "Are you Okay?"

"Oui, Oui."

Fortunately, locals were near, and they managed to man handle my motorcycle out. Later, I tried to explain to Bruno that all I saw in those last few moments were the driver's eyes, wide with fear. They looked like saucers in his head, and he was grinning a death's head smile as we collided with each other. I looked at the motorcycle and fortunately, it was just the box and the fuel carriage can that had been damaged. No serious problems.

The truck driver just kept going; maybe he didn't have any brakes (common with these trucks). I believe Mercedes, Peugeot, and Fiat ought to come and do some excellent commercials showing the things their trucks are going through. It's not just that they are going through terrible conditions, but if it's a 5 ton truck, they'll be carrying 7 or 8 tons and then passengers on top of that.

These trucks look like a regular, giant rolling circus.

The Friendly Foreigners Forge Ahead!

When Bruno and I go through a village, we are always waving, "Bon Jour, Misseiur, Bon Jour," being kind to the people. After all, one never knows when you might fall off the motorcycle in the mud in the middle of the village and need their help.

Well, this rainy day we were getting to the end of the village, and starting to go up a hill when the rain came down and turned the road into a quagmire. This particular village was led by a religious leader who came out and surveyed the scene. Bruno helped get the motorcycle off me, then villagers pitched in and got it up.

"Let me have a try at it" Bruno said.

"Okay, go" I replied.

Bruno gets on the Harley, but doesn't make it 50 meters before it is laying on him, burning his right leg with the exhaust. He was screaming and flailing around like a trapped rat, hollering.

"That's one thing I don't have to worry about," I thought as I rushed over to help. "If the exhaust gets on my leg, there's no problem."

The villagers got the hot exhaust off of him, and he came over to me saying "David, Misseiur, vioux moto," meaning "It's your motorcycle."

Indeed it was, for better or worse.

The organized crowd started pushing my motorcycle up a very steep hill, a little over a kilometer. As they went up, the wheels stopped turning, so they were forced to plow this big, heavy machine through the mud with all the gear. Two helpers grabbed me by the arms to help me through the mud. Honestly, I felt I could have made it, but these fellows insisted. All the way up the hill, one was saying to me, "God, Bless, God bless." He had a little cross in his hand and he was holding my hand, trying to impart human contact and compassion to me.

I was deeply touched by his gesture.

About half way up the hill, the village at the top of the hill came down and took over from the village at the bottom of the hill. The new villagers now were pushing my motorcycle up. I wanted to give the down hill villagers something since they had spent the last half hour pushing and dragging my motorcycle with Herculean effort, plowing it virtually through the mud, but they refused.

"No, non, non, Misseiur," the head elder replied.

The new villagers plowed and pushed the Harley through the mud, and I got two more helpers. After slowly advancing through six to eight inches of mud, the motorcycle was finally at the top of the hill, resting in front of the Head Man's hut. Bruno and I were invited inside and given a bucket of water to clean ourselves, then served some rice with barley in it (which went down very, very well, indeed).

Bruno had quite a conversation in French with the village Head Man, and we presented him with a bit of money on the sly. About 20:30, we decided to call it a day, and so we both laid down in what was the path to his front room, with people peering in from every corner. Before I went to sleep I asked, "Do you think our motorcycles will be secure?"

"No problem," they assured me.

That night, when I awoke and looked out the window, there was a guard standing next to our motorcycles with a lantern in his hand. Now that's hospitality!

In the early morning, when I went out to chip the mud from the wheel wells, a small boy pestered me for a screwdriver. I gave him one, and we both chipped the mud out from under the fenders so the wheels would turn freely.

To a large crowd of well-wishers, Bruno and I rode away to shouting, yelling and waving. It felt so festive...like watching the Queen Mary pull away from port with all the spectators waving and shouting to the passengers, "Bon Voyage, Messieurs." What incredible fanfare from this humble village in the middle of nowhere in Zaire.

Note the refueling can on top of carrier.
Alone on the PIST in the Sahara Desert, Niger
December, 1990.

Riding the Sahara at Sunset, Niger.
Photographed by: Spaniards.
December, 1990.

Battling the Sahara, Algeria.
José and Estaban are behind the motorcycle pushing and eating sand.
December, 1990.

Chapter Seven

Mud Pits from Hell

Two miles from the village fanfare, my front tire went flat. I pulled over, studied the tire, and when I couldn't see any nails, I thought, "This looks like a job for *Tire Weld.*" I put the *Tire Weld* in the tire, and we took off.

Another mile or so down the road, the tire went flat again.

This time, I used my air compressor to inflate it, rode another mile or so, and the tire went flat **again**, just as I entered a small village where I luckily found a man who could fix flats. We lifted the motorcycle up and put it on blocks, then I took the tire off and the tube out. I tried to fix the tube with glue, but there was too much moisture in the air, so I put in a new inner tube. The other fellow tried to fix the old tube with his glue, but he too found it too sweaty from the air's moisture.

With a new tube, we took off again...to more trouble.

Within a few miles, I'm down in the sand. Bruno came racing along, parked his motorcycle on hard ground, then came back and helped me.

We were soon off again.

Another mile or so, and we are deep inside the rain forest, and I am deep down in mud. Bruno laughs as we get the motorcycle up, but I'm afraid my sense of humor is waning. Once we resume, I realize that I had failed to turn the gasoline back on (I turn if off when I fall so excess gas doesn't get down in the carburetor).

The motor ran out of gas and down I went again.

Then, the course smoothes out. We just fight the normal battles - mud, hills, ruts, and general misery for about the next 100 kilometers. Suddenly, we are confronted with a massive hill...complete with mud ruts and holes. Fortunately, a group of locals volunteers come forward to push Bruno and I through the holes and ruts and a new element, TAR!

At the top of the hill, one of the first things that comes into our vision is President Mabutu's palace, overlooking the Zaire River.

"You fat, horrible pig," I thought to myself. "You live in a palace like this when the rest of your country doesn't even have a paved road across it. You are a terrible, terrible little man."

We learned there was a campground down another terrible road on the other side of the town of Lisala. We journeyed there and set up camp. The pleasant proprietor of the little campground volunteered to fix us lunch.

"Oh, great," we thought, until he served us chicken...very rubbery chicken...the kind that can take your teeth out if you try to pull it apart. Then there was "rice with rocks,"...so you had to be careful how hard you chewed.

The mosquitoes and the parasites buzzed their warm greetings to us as we prepared for the night and our evening shower.

We learned that the roads ahead were heavily flooded, and that maybe one or two trucks a week are getting through from Businga. We were advised not to go on, especially since the starter on my Harley was acting up again. So bad were the reports that Bruno and I discussed trying to locate a truck or even a plane to take us up to Businga or Gbadolite.

That evening, we settled in with a pleasant campfire, cooking our own dinner (better than rubber chicken). As Bruno crawled into his tent for the evening, and I lay under the stars, rain began, soaking me completely.

"David, come inside the tent," Bruno suggested. Quickly I took him up on his

65

invitation, but the tent too was soaking wet (still better than being directly in the rain).

On the bright side of this night, the mosquitoes stopped eating us!

The next day, we rode into town where we discovered that there might be some trucks out later. We also went to one of the offices for a Belgian logging company up in the rain forest to inquire about any flights. We learned a couple of military flights were scheduled.

A man name Gee accompanied Bruno down to the airport to ask about these planes. When they returned, they said: "No, there are no flights up to Gbadolite. We'll just have to go push on at this point."

"Is it fair to keep going on?" I wondered to myself. "How could I keep holding Bruno back?" These questions nagged at me.

"The roads ahead have many flooded areas," Gee reported, "and your motorcycles would certainly have to be carried across them." My Harley was so heavy, I didn't know how plausible that scenario was.

Back to the campground, where we have dinner. My motorcycle has been starting hard all day. I've checked the points and other problem areas, but can find nothing wrong. It's just starting hard. I fixed my primary, as best I could, with more used inner tube rubber and silicone sealant. The inner and outer parts of the primary are smashed in very badly.

The next day we investigate our options more in town, and return to camp that night for more rain in the tent. Gee gave us really a nice meal this day, with **real** potatoes, carrots, meat, and coffee (nothing tasted like rubber).

The next day, Gee heard that there was a flight coming in, so we went back to the airport to check it out.

There is a flight, but their polite reply was, "No dice, we can't give you a lift." So, we are back to waiting to discover if there are any trucks going toward Businga.

In town, I noticed one thing about the advertising in Zaire: it's painted on the walls. One of the most popular advertisements is for a particular kind of beer. The ad has a character named "Ton-Ton" popping the lids of the beer bottles, and shows the beer flowing over from the bottle into his mouth. A crowd is depicted below him, anxiously waiting for him to throw them some of the beer he's got in boxes around him. The message: for a good time, follow Ton-Ton's example.

Wherever we go, a crowd seems to gather around, standing and looking, joking and carrying on. I always try to communicate in a few words of English, or in my broken French.

"There's a truck in the afternoon," Bruno reports. We decide I'll go on that truck, and Bruno will ride out the following day.

For Better...or Worse?

We put my motorcycle on the back of the 5 ton Magaris truck, and depart about 16:00 that afternoon. After about 30 kilometers, a bearing on the engine cooling air fan goes bad. The driver, named Michael, looks at it, but he doesn't have the proper tools to repair the problem.

"You need tools?" I asked him in my broken French, finding it hard to believe he had none.

"Oui," he replies.

So, we go to the back of the truck, get some of my tools, and pull the fan off, locating the bad bearing.

"Non Problem," he says, and I think, "Great, he's got a bearing!"

Michael opens his kit, but all the bearings are the wrong size.

66

Time to call it a night, so Michael's passengers - about 30 of us who were on the back of the truck - tried to find a place to sleep. I lay my gear down, take my legs off, and stare at the stars as I listen to the babble of voices all around me. "It is amazing how you can have people all around you," I thought, "and still feel this alone and isolated."

Up at 04:30, I put myself together before anybody else is up. When I go to put my sleeping bag back on the motorcycle, I noticed a man standing on the back of my Harley.

When I shouted at him to "get off," which he did, a woman started giving me a hard time. She reached out at me and I slapped her hand away. Once she got the message that I wasn't to be messed with, they backed off.

Michael heard the commotion, and he told them, "I have no tools. This man is a big help to us getting going. Leave him alone." After that, attitudes towards me changed.

There was a little motorcycle on top the truck that belonged to one of the passengers. We got it down, and Michael asked the owner to ride back to Lisla and bring back the proper sized bearing (giving him a sample). The man couldn't get the motorcycle to start, so I pulled the spark plug off and cleaned it, then the fellow was on his way.

"What in the Hell have I got myself into?" I thought. "These last 30 kilometers haven't been as bad as some of the areas that I've come through by myself. Maybe I should just try to push on by myself."

Then I thought, "These people need my help right now to get them going. I've received a lot of help from people in Zaire. Now, it is my turn to give something back."

The day goes by, and Bruno comes past. I was working on the motorcycle, cleaning out the inside and putting new rubber pieces on the holes of the primary. We chatted a bit and then he was on his way.

I'll miss him.

One of the passengers kept trying to force liquor on me. "No, I don't drink," I kept telling him. On the other side of the "camp," there was quite a party going on.

Late in the afternoon, a kind woman brings me a big bowl of rice and some bananas. We are all short of water, and when a man went to get some, he took one of my water bottles with him. Apparently it was quite a walk to where the water was.

In the meantime, I sat, thinking and reading.

"I will not get depressed over this miserable situation," I said to myself. "Even though I'm hot, dirty and don't seem to be going any where right now." If there's anything I hate, it is inactivity, just sitting around. It drives me nuts! In our current location, there's nothing much to see or do. The rain forest surrounds both sides of the road, except for the little bit of cleared area where we sleep. Most people are outside in the sun, hot and miserable. Some are laying down underneath the truck. The babble of voices is everywhere.

Finally, late in the afternoon, the little moped comes back with the bearing...used, but it will fit. Michael and I start assembling the blower, put the bearing in, then tighten everything up, adjusting the fan belt. By this time, Michael, one of the party participants on the other side of camp, is now drunk!

As we repaired the truck, my confidence in my choice of vehicles nose-dived. I noticed that the suspension was shot, and four wheel nuts are missing off of one tire (the others all have wheel nuts missing, just not four!). This truck is a legendary "African Special." It also has no starter, so we must stop on a downhill slope, or the truck has to be pushed by the passengers to get it to started.

Michael was a skilled driver, so he needed only a small push to hit the clutch and "Bang," it would turn over. This day, as he climbed behind the wheel, his drunken expression seemed to say, "We're going to make up some time now." There are 3 passengers in front with Michael, and they are passing a bottle of terrible smelling stuff back and forth. The reek of alcohol is tremendous, and, combined with the heat coming from the engine, it is enough to make the less hardy throw up.

But somehow, Michael handled it very nicely.

Late that night, we came to one of the flooded areas, and down we went into about five feet of water; it was gushing into the inside of the truck. "There's no way I would have gotten through this on my Harley without someone carrying both me and my machine," I thought.

Michael's philosophy for manipulating mud is to hit the mire at a high rate of speed. Once the truck whacks the water, the passengers are thrown around and out. Some are hollering from up on top of the truck, and others are splashing in the mud and water. Mud is inside the cab, covering the windshields, and oozing into the back.

"How can Michael even see where's he's going," I wonder. "Perhaps, he's just been through these things so many times that he just points and prays."

Finally, with much grinding, groaning, slipping and sliding, out the other side we go.

At first, I thought I understood Michael to say we were going to travel non-stop to Businga, so when we stopped at 23:00 in a village, it was a double delight (since by now Michael seems very unstable from booze). Everybody climbs down off the truck. My motorcycle, fortunately, has gear packed all around it and on top of it, so nobody is standing or sitting on it. In this little village, we all take out sleeping gear for the night.

When I inspect the motorcycle, it is covered with baggage and bananas.

A bank teller on the trip, a fellow named Jerome, saw the book I had been reading, and asked me, "Could you please give me that book when you are done?" I did, and he radiated happiness since there was nothing available to read in English anywhere. Even though he also spoke French, he said "There's not much to read in French, here, either."

The next morning, after going about twenty kilometers, we had a fuel problem...the motor started cutting out. Since they don't carry any extra fuel filters, here's what took place. Michael took off the fuel filter housing, handing the fuel filters to a young kid who starts blowing into them, getting diesel fuel all over his face, hands and shirt! This kid blows into them for about 20 minutes, and then empties all the fuel from the fuel cups. The kid then wipes the filters off with his 'T' shirt, puts the semi-dry fuel filters back into the cups, puts that assembly back on the mounting of the engine, and away we go.

The truck worked fine!

If I understood them correctly, I believe the young kid was some sort of a mechanic/apprentice on the truck.

We went about 5 more kilometers when we came to a stalled truck from the same company as Michael's employer. We stopped for twenty minutes to try and help them, but were unsuccessful. So, we take on twenty more passengers! That brings us up to about fifty people.

We're off again. The truck is FULL of people and I'm OUT of patience!

As we start to go, an African fellow walks up to the cab and signals for me to "Get out of the front seat." I politely tell him to "go fuck yourself," and an argument ensues. Michael settled the argument by telling the man to "Shut Up," and then allowed him to sit in the front seat...on somebody else's lap!

Now, we are 5 people in the cab.

FINALLY, we arrive at Businga late that day. We go across the bridge over the river, and I notice that, at one time, Businga must have been a very splendid little town in the country.

When we arrive at our camp, Michael stops his truck, gets out, and orders the passengers to unload the motorcycle (which they did). Once it was on the ground, I made a motion to get on it, and he said, "Non, Non, Messieur." Michael had the passengers push it all the way down into the camping area, where, to my great relief, I happily joined up again with my friend, Bruno. We shook hands and had a bit of a reunion.

I bade farewell to Michael, my friend, driver, and alcoholic. He wobbled off on very uncertain legs to his truck. As we parted, he said to me, "David, when you can't walk, DRIVE." As he walked away, I thought that "The Lord indeed does work in mysterious ways. I might have made it through these last 70 miles (120 kilometers) on my motorcycle, but if I had done it alone, I would have never been able to lend a helping hand to Michael and his crew of fifty passengers. Without my tools, they could have been stuck for days."

Broken Brakes, Faulty Starter, and a Ripoff River Crossing

Washing out of a bucket, I cleaned off some of the mud, then I began to work on my motorcycle. I tried to repair the rear brake, as it wasn't taking very well. Since I could only get 2 fingers on the broken front brake, I virtually have **no brakes**.

In the evening, Bruno cooked up some beans, then we laid back under a huge canopy of thatch with open sides. We put our sleeping bags on benches, sleeping off the ground. A fireplace was going in the middle of this huge thatch canopy. Naturally, rain started, and it rained right on through the night.

The next day, because of the night's rain, Bruno and I decided to stay at the camp and let the roads dry out. After spending most of the day reading books, we climbed onto Bruno's motorcycle and went to town...through all the pot holes, the mud and mush, to a little restaurant Bruno found before I arrived. There, we had a meal. Two fellows whom Bruno had met previously came over and started talking with us. At the end of the evening, I paid the bill for the lot of us, but as we walked out, the two fellows discovered what had happened, and they paid me back. They wouldn't take the dinner for nothing. I thought that was very commendable and honest, especially since I knew they had little money.

The next morning, we made the usual preparations to depart, but the Harley wouldn't start - the battery was down. Bruno tries and tries to start it for the next 20 minutes, until he's sweatin' blood.

"Hey, just leave it sit for a few minutes" I told him, and then I cleared out the cylinders. This time, it starts right up. We ride out of camp and down the awaiting road of floods, mud, rocks, and ruts.

I kept the motorcycle up for 6 miles, until I hit a hole with about a foot and a half of water in it. The "hole" was about 8 meters across - the entire width of the road. I didn't make it out the other side. Bruno came back, laughing as usual, at me in the mud. My own sense of humor was not in the best of condition by this time. He gets the motorcycle up, I climb out from underneath it, and we both lift the machine up on its wheels and push it out of the water.

Twenty miles down the road, again I go down, shouting and hollering in my sarcastic best voice, "Boy, how great these roads are!" We're always hearing about "how good the road is" up ahead from fellow travelers, but it's always false optimism. The one time I put my motorcycle on the truck, the road was bad, but not as bad as it had been made out to be.

No road reports are believable anymore!

A little bit later we stopped because I felt a drag on the motorcycle. Upon examination, the rear brake was dragging, so I had to release it before I burned up the wheel cylinder.

On we pushed another 30 miles; it took us two full hours, in second gear all the time. The good news: not once did I come off the Harley!

Then, we stopped for a bit of a break.

After our break, we hit a good dirt road and I was actually able to put the motorcycle into 3rd gear. No kidding! We rode along in 3rd gear for a few miles, and then we hit pavement - very good pavement. Now, I pushed the motorcycle and put it in 4th gear for the first time in over 1000 miles in the country of Zaire.

I am flying along in absolute excitement, knowing that I'm going too fast because of the goats, donkeys, and other animals out on the road. I couldn't contain myself. I just had to give it a burst until I got into Gbadolite proper, the town where Mabutu was raised. It seemed to be in a little better condition than most of the other towns we saw in the rest of Zaire.

We located the maintenance yard of Safco Company where we were told I could probably fix my brake lever. We took the lever off, and they made a brace for the broken piece by taking a piece of steel and drilling two holes in one side of the brake lever and two holes in the other. Next, they bolted this piece of steel on to give it a bit of flex, and, at the same time, hold it together. The idea worked well for quite awhile.

We met a fellow there named Daniel who invited us to come and spend the night at his house. We followed him over to his place and met his wife, an African woman named Flo, who was a very gracious hostess. There, we enjoyed a REAL shower in hot water. To us, this was something.... we were just over the moon! The amount of dirt coming off was amazing. Later, we enjoyed a dinner of spaghetti that was quickly devoured by all.

Later that evening, Bruno went with Daniel to a bit of a party, and I went out to their thatched patio, threw out my sleeping bag where the motorcycles were, and went to sleep. At 02:30 a.m. the rain woke me up.

"What will the roads be like up ahead," I wondered. "My God, help me. It is still 100 kilometers to go before we get to where we can cross into Central Africa."

Up at 04:00, we loaded our motorcycles.

"Would you like coffee?," Daniel offered.

We did, and took an hour to drink coffee and talk. I'm not used to the coffee, I was really wired up! When we hit the road, we finally located some gasoline out of Jerry cans on the black market (none of the beautiful new petrol stations were operating - no gas!). Then, we changed our money.

On our way out of Gbadolie, we enjoy a nice paved road as we head for the border of Central Africa. Then, the pavement ends, and we revert back to the customary old dirt roads (not as bad as some others we've seen). We were given incorrect directions, and ended up going up a dirt track, on our way to nowhere. When we checked our directions, we were told, "Non, messieur, you are going the wrong way."

70

We turned around.

Coming back, we encountered a soldier in the road with his rifle, standing in front of some type of outpost. I sensed danger, so I we turned around, and sure enough, that fellow start chasing us with rifle in hand. He didn't shoot (maybe he didn't have any bullets).

Finally, we arrive at the river that separates Central Africa from Zaire.

Customs and Immigration takes us two hours.

When we ask the price for taking a boat to the other side, nobody seems to know what to tell us. When a boat finally comes, and after we load the motorcycles on in the late afternoon, we discover the charge is $60.00 for the two motorcycles and us - $30.00 per motorcycle and person. We had violated the Golden Rule: always negotiate the price before committing yourself.

What a rip off!

Of course, by this time the motorcycles were already loaded, so there was nothing we could do about it.

We ended up paying the thieves.

Chapter Eight

Central Africa - the Challenges Continue!

We rolled off the boat to an abandoned farming area where we stopped for the evening and set up camp. Then, we located the Customs and Immigration Post, which was closed. We were told that we could go into the town and do any shopping we needed to do, so Bruno went to town and bought food for us to eat that night. When he came back, we cooked a dinner of noodles and pilchards (a small fish, like a herring), then sat back with a cup of tea to watch the sunset over the Lee River.

Normally, I wouldn't give pilchards to my dog, but my eating standards had fallen so drastically by this time that I actually enjoyed the dinner!

We went to sleep about 21:00 and, you guessed it, in the middle of the night it started to rain...just long enough to get us good and wet. The next morning, Bruno took my passport and the papers on my motorcycle and went up to the Customs office. We were cleared into the country within fifteen minutes!

Amazing.

Customs without commotion or chaos! None of the hassles we had experienced in other countries.

Could this be a good omen?

We went into town to a crude petrol station in the African style; petrol came out of a hand pump from a tank in the ground, and the gas was more plentiful and much cheaper than in Zaire. We filled up completely, including my extra 6 gallons (24 liters). Then, we were off.

Yes, we encountered more pot holes, and some areas with water across the entire road. Fortunately, the roads were built with a bed of sand underneath, so I had no problem getting across lengths of road up to 20 and 30 meters, even with a foot or more of deep water covering it.

What a joy!

We were making good time, and I wasn't falling off my motorcycle every five minutes.

About 10 kilometers from the border crossing, I hit a massive hole where a truck was stuck and I fell over and hit the truck. We lifted the motorcycle up out of the hole, and managed to get going again. After 15 miles, I'd only fallen off once.

Will wonders never cease!

We hit a very rough, hard dirt road, full of pot holes and rocks - it's the main road going to Kouango, and Bangui, our goal. Fortunately, there were no big deep holes or whole systems of large mud pits, or long rutted areas. The going was rough, but good enough so I could get my Harley into 3rd gear (no shit), and keep it there, averaging about 25 to 30 mph (or 40 to 45 kph) , which is really big time for us right now! Or, for me anyway. Bruno could go much faster, but he's kind enough to stay at my speed.

Central African countryside has more farming than Zaire, and is very open. I can see through miles of countryside into the mountains off in the distance. There's no cooped up, cramped feelings like you experience when riding through the rain forests of Zaire, with tall trees on both sides of the road, and you can see ONLY in front or behind.

Out of Kouango, we turned west and headed for Bangui, bouncing and banging along right into the afternoon; we stopped and purchased fuel at a place called Banberri.

After getting fuel for the motorcycles, we fueled ourselves with some hot bread. Bruno wanted to push on, but with the sunlight flashing so strongly in our faces, I really didn't want to risk it. Then, I thought, "Bruno's been putting up with me for quite awhile, helping me out all the time. The least I can do is reciprocate and bend a bit."

So, we pushed on, westward, for about fifty miles (80 km).

I had three very close calls riding into the sun, the worst being a VERY close encounter with a truck coming out of a dark tunnel of overgrown vegetation. The sun blinded my eyes. As I entered the tunnel, I could see nothing, and we nearly collided - head on! He did not have his headlights on, naturally, so it was only by the grace of God that I survived that incident.

Late in the afternoon we entered Grimari, where I managed to hit some mud and fall. By this time, I'm tired and in a bad humor. Bruno and some locals help me get the motorcycle up, and as I'm moving away, I realized that I left my gloves on the ground. I turned around to get them, only to discover that a band of children had picked them up and were running in my direction to bring them to me.

That little act of kindness from those young people meant a lot.

We located a church in Grimari willing to let us stay there. As we ride into the church grounds, a crowd of African children gather around us, standing, watching, shouting and performing for attention. In this chaotic atmosphere, I start work on my motorcycle to get prepared for the next day. I'm having a problem with the battery terminal, and the foot brake is giving me difficulty again, dragging, so I'm easing off of it a little bit more.

Late in the afternoon, it rains very hard, driving the circle of gawking kids back to their homes.

Bruno and I cooked dinner inside a classroom that a nun had shown us. I washed our two metal bowls, two spoons and two cups; then we sat back and cooked some tea and waited to go to bed. That night, as we slept out in the veranda, it rained continuously.

I thought to myself, "What state will these bloody roads be in tomorrow?" as the little raindrops plunked into the ever-growing puddles around me.

The next morning, the kids were all back, standing there, watching, along with the nuns. One of the sisters told Bruno, "You should wait for at least a few hours before you leave to give the roads time to dry. Besides, they don't like people driving on the roads directly after a rain as it makes them an even bigger mess than they already are."

About 08:30, we decided to push on, anxious to get away from the gawking kids, and ready to take our chances out on the road.

For about the first 30 miles, it was very touch and go. Many times the back end of the cycle started to come out from underneath me, but I managed - with great effort - to regain control. The roads in Central Africa are unique in that they are sometimes grit or gravel under the mud to help save you from losing traction altogether and going down...a product from a more prosperous day.

I must constantly monitor speed. Some areas in the road are covered with water for as much as 15 to 20 meters, and I ride through them not knowing if there are hidden holes or rocks. Despite these challenges, Central Africa's roads are 100% better than Zaire's.

Animal Obstacles and Obstinate Timing Chains

Cows cover one side of the road to the other.

We can't just follow behind these bovine behinds forever, so we actually start pushing our way through the herd. Bruno plows first, yelling and hollering, beeping his horn to entice these stupid bastards to move. I'm following right on his tail. When we switched, and it was my turn to holler and beep, I'll never know how I managed to stay on my motorcycle...but I did!

In the villages of Central Africa, the people seemed less aggressive in asking for a BIC pen or a school book. I appreciated that.

Another main difference in this country was the speed of the taxis, usually a Toyota or a Datsun van. They are built to hold about 15 people, but they often have as many as 20 - 25 people hanging out of the windows and holding onto the railings. These vehicles are also stuffed with goats or pigs, and are bursting with baggage on the roof tops. The drivers fly down these horrible dirt roads on down hill sides as fast as 60 mph (95 km) - so fast they cannot stop for an emergency. If you see one coming, get off the road - as far and as fast as you can! If a taxi hurtles out of control, or blows a tire, or if one of his wheels comes off because of missing wheel nuts, you want to avoid getting flattened.

Remember, these guys can't stop!

I've also seen bigger buses, such as Renaults and Mercedes, that hold about 30 people, coming down the road at much too fast a speed to be safe, with windows always broken out of them, and roof racks loaded to bursting with bicycles, food, animals, and even a child or two sitting up there.

At 11:30 we enter Sibut and hit the tarmac. I was actually able to push the motorcycle up to 50 mph and put it in 4th gear...no kidding! Missing pot holes in the paved road as best we could, it was much better than the dirt.

The danger coming through villages is trying to avoid goats, dogs, pigs, chickens, and donkeys. There were many times I nearly hit goats and sheep out on the road.

When you ride on the tarmac, you watch for pot holes and other unexpected road hazards, like buses coming the other way in your lane, trying to avoid the same pot holes. It's your responsibility to stay away from them and not get hit. Believe me, bus drivers are not looking out for you!

Late in the afternoon, we came into Bangui, the capital of the Central African Republic. At the outskirts of the city, Bruno and I stopped to register at a Police Station when a tour truck suddenly appears. I spot Dave and Mary, and return a book loaned to me by one of their passengers. We waved them on and wished them well, then went over and took care of all of our business.

We stayed at the 7 Kilometer Campground that night. If it hadn't have been for Bruno, I would have never found the place. We went through a market where the people were all out on the sides of the road, shouting and hollering. Quite unnerving. We moved through a maze of carts, donkeys, various other animals, and tens of thousands of people.

That night, to celebrate our safe arrival, we ate a restaurant at the campground. The food is both bad and expensive (the last time we celebrated this way).

We set up camp, enjoy a nice *cold* shower, then lay back to relax. I was trying to sleep outside the tent, swatting mosquitoes, when a tour truck came in, waking every body up until about 21:00. Finally, all settled down, and I could once again sleep.

Bruno had been upset that afternoon because his motorcycle had started running quite poorly. His frame broke in the back section where you sit and mount your gear, although it was still serviceable. Though the Harley is somewhat heavy and unwieldy to ride in mud and sand, it is extremely heavy duty in its construction being well built to handle major amounts of abuse and punishment. The next morning, Bruno rides into town to check on our visas. He returns about midday, reporting that he found the Nigerian Embassy.

"I'll need your passport," he says, and off he goes once again, taking care of the formalities for us both. When he came back late that afternoon, he's on foot.

"What the hell is going on?," I wonder.

"My Moto quit on me," Bruno reported. "I located a little garage over on the far side of Bangui where they will let me work on it, but I had to leave the machine there. I'll be back later in the evening."

Bruno then left again to go to the garage to work on the Moto. When he didn't show by 20:00 that night, I located the driver of one of the tour trucks, requesting that we go into town searching for Bruno.

We drove all over Bangui, but we couldn't find him. I'm starting to feel apprehensive. "If he's in any trouble," I thought, "then I want to make an effort to find and help him such as he's helped me."

The search ended without results.

We went back to the campground in the tour truck, a converted old British Army Bedford with beefed up suspension. Most tour trucks are 2 1/2 ton Bedfords with 4 wheel drive, and they usually tow a trailer behind them with cooking gear, extra food, and passengers' baggage. These trucks carry from 10 to 15 passengers in the back, each paying about 2,000 pounds Sterling (at that time, about $3,500) to go from London to Zimbabwe, or from Zimbabwe to London.

When we returned to the campground, Phillip served me a wonderful meal out of the kitchen of his tour truck. He was the first guide ever kind enough to feed me some of the meat, spaghetti and luscious foods the tour people are eating (anything's better than Pilchards).

The following morning when I awoke, I noticed Philip gazing at my motorcycle, and I realized that he was a Harley Davidson fan by the look in his eye. "Would you like to take a ride on the Harley Davidson through town?" I asked him as a kind of a thank you for his assistance the previous night. His eyes lit up as he readily jumped on the back and we took off to the airport and back - about 12 miles.

Phillip was so excited. Afterwards, he took photos and we talked a bit. To my great relief, we were only briefly back at the campground when Bruno rolls in. He's very disappointed with his Moto because he can't get it to run right.

"Well, let's go and work on it," I said.

I knew only too well how he was feeling. His morale was very low. I put him on the back of my motorcycle, and to the garage of Jeane Martoux we go where we pull out his motor and start working on it. We take the cylinder head off and discover two burnt valves that we grind by hand.

Later that morning, I rode over to the Nigerian Embassy to pick up our passports. The Nigerians called out the Nigerian Ambassador who shook my hand and gave me the visa...for free! He also asked me to forward a letter for him from Nigeria. "The mail service in this area of the world is less than dependable," he said to me.

I return to help Bruno with his motorcycle. We put the motor back in and it starts right up!

Later that afternoon, we go to the offices of DHL. We called France about the primary belts I needed for my Harley. They tell me they will not know anything until tomorrow.

By now, I'm afraid I'm going to lose my friend, Bruno; he's talking about moving on since his motorcycle seems to be running pretty good now. Later, we all went to a cafe and sat and talked. When Bruno tried to start up his motorcycle, it would not start. He worked on it for about 5 minutes, and finally it ran again, but by the time we hit Jeane's it was missing again, and coughing.

We pull the engine out once again, this time finding the real problem. His timing chain had stretched, and was skipping the teeth on the timing gear. We rode my motorcycle back to the camp ground, with Bruno in a very low state of mind.

The next day, Bruno goes with me to the DHL office where I am told "It's no dice. The Harley Davidson shop in France can't help you." Bruno makes calls from there to see about getting a timing chain sent out for his Moto.

Later that afternoon, I ride to the American Embassy and meet a fellow named Bret from the Embassy's Security; he tells me to speak to Lisa in Citizen Services.

Lisa gave me a phone book. She told me to come back later in the afternoon and she would take me over to the phone exchange (centralized phone booths for tourists where long-distance rates could run as high as $10 per minute).

At 13:00, we went over to the phone exchange. There, I called New York and spoke to a Harley Davidson dealer who told me, "I can't help you, but you might call another shop."

I called an after-market dealer, and the man told me, "I can get you 3 belts and an idler bearing in roughly 5 days, but I'll need a check for $593.00 to cover it."

When I hung up, I called Mom.

November 1, 1990: "Hello, mom, this is your son." We exchanged a few pleasantries, and we reminded each other of this very special day... precisely one year from the day my father had passed away. I wished her well, and much love.

Then, I explained my problem and popped the question: *"HELP*, I need money! Could you please send an Express Mail check for $593.00 out of my account to this address for motorcycle parts?"

Of course, she was only too happy to comply.

Corruption, Exploitation, Violence...and Other Road Hazards

For the next five days, I could only wait.

As it turned out, Bruno needed to wait five days for his parts as well, so he found himself a place to stay away from the campground, leaving the tent for me (Thank God! It rained almost every night). Of course, the rain goes through the tent, so in the morning I always get out of my wet sleeping bad and put on wet legs with wet stump sockets and wet pants.

Everyone does their laundry in a sink in the shower. Everyday, I wash a shirt and a pair of underpants. I change my stump socks every other day, and my pants every 3rd or 4th day, depending on how filthy they get. When I wash, I hang my clothes up immediately, yet it takes almost a full day to get them dry because of the tremendous humidity. *If* they do dry, it usually rains that night, and bingo, they're soaking wet again.

Bangui is a very run down Capital City, and its people seemed on edge when we arrived due to an attempted military coup which had failed quite miserably due to the assistance of the French Foreign Legion Base at Bouar that had helped squash the rebellion.

The uprising was staged to kick the President out of power. Because the President was still in power, many locals were irritable towards foreigners (the most likely scapegoats for their pent up aggressions).

At the camp one day, passports were stolen from a tour truck, right out of the front seat of the truck! Now, theft in the campgrounds was something that went on regularly. One had to watch one's gear, or ask somebody to watch it. Often I would look after one of the tour trucks' equipment in the evening while they went into town to have dinner or to shop. I had nothing better to do.

When I was away during the day, I always asked somebody to keep an eye on my few possessions.

About an hour after the passports were stolen, an African declared, "We have found some passports, but they will cost you 15,000 Franks apiece ($55) to return them."

What a scam. Much hollering and shouting ensued.

Personally, I have no compassion for people who exploit others, especially in situations like this. In the gas stations, one must be careful that they always ring off the previous amount of gasoline from the meters before they start pumping gas. If you don't watch, they will try to scam you into paying more.

Another danger at gas stations can sometimes be the crowds. Once, while I was fueling up, the crowd became very aggressive; I ended up shoving someone away from me. I remember taking off very rapidly, just as they were trying to grab some things off the motorcycle. I felt very lucky not to have fallen in the rush to get out of there!

When I had to visit or travel through the 7 Kilometer Market Place, about 2 kilometers (1 1/2 miles) long, I would always attract a crowd of young African fellows who would start chasing me, shouting and hollering. The way the market was positioned, I had no choice but to pass through it. I would just wave my hand very humbly, doing my best to stay ahead of the pursuing mob, trying not to run over any animals, kids or people. To maneuver around, I dodged huge pot holes, an occasional truck, and many donkey-drawn carts, making it out the other side and taking off before these characters caught me (I was sure they intended to do me a number). Bangui has a very poor reputation for violence and muggings against tourists.

Out the other side of the market, I would go about my business of the day. When I would reapproach the market, I pulled in my clutch and glide up so no one could hear me. Then, I would start into the market place as quickly as I could, once again picking up this crowd of young Africans chasing me. I didn't know what they wanted, and I didn't want to find out!

One day, when I was moving through the market place, waving, saying "Bonsieur, messieurs," "Good day, Good day, Sirs," trying to stay ahead of the mob, two donkey carts stopped in front of me and decided to talk. I couldn't get around them, and the mob was closing in quickly from behind. Before I knew it, they were throwing their arms around me, trying to shake my hand and saying, "Bon Moto, messier," meaning "good motorcycle." I was beside myself with relief. They had never seen a Harley Davidson before.

From that time on, we were friends. When I would go through the market, they wouldn't chase me any more. Instead, they would just wave to me. Even the Army people, as I would pass their barracks, would be out there and wave to me. They no longer bothered to stop and check my passport or hassle me; I was becoming a regular face around the area (too regular).

After a few more days of working on the motorcycle, I found a bad bearing in the rear wheel, and repacked and replaced one of the front wheel bearings. I also serviced all the clutch and starter areas, and changed the oil - 120 weight, Aero Oil. I don't know what the actual weight was by automotive standards, but it was thick and seemed to work well in the motorcycle (it wouldn't be the last time I used aircraft oil).

November 6, 1990: After five days, I go down to the Air Freight Terminal to get my parts, but there's no package!

I'm very upset!

I stop in to see Bruno every now and again to see how he is doing, and he appears quite satisfied with life. In fact, he was talking about taking a job there in Central Africa, but it would be two months before he started (Well, we'll see. He's just thinking of it). The plan was still for both of us to go forward to France (if he got his parts in time and if I got my parts in time).

One day, Lisa came to visit me at the campground with a Gunnery Sergeant from the Marine Guard at the Embassy, Gunny Rowland. He invited me to attend the Marine Ball on November 10th as the oldest Marine in their area. I readily accepted the invitation, thinking about the good food that would certainly be served, and knowing that it would be a great interlude and positive alternative to wasting time waiting for parts.

The next night, I fully loaded up the motorcycle (I could not leave my tools, etc., behind at the campground) and I rode across Bangui to the Embassy where I met up with Gunny Rowland, who took me to a very nice house provided for him and his wife, Laurie.

We have cold showers at the campground. Here, I was able to take a *hot* shower! I took my legs off and climbed right down in the hot shower. It was great! I got a haircut as well, and was beginning to look like a human.

November 10, 1990: During the ceremony that evening, the Gunnery hands the oldest Marine (me) a plate of cake; the oldest Marine takes a bite and then hands the cake to the youngest Marine, who also takes a bite.

I messed up.

When I was told to pass the cake, I did. But, when Gunny went to shake my hand, I handed him the fork. He had this strange look on his face, "Why you stupid bastard, how could you do that?" I also had a look on my face that expressed "It's not hard for me," since I was never a ceremonial soldier.

I met Ambassador Simpson that night, and the other Marines. They all treated me very well.

After a very lovely dinner with *real* roast beef and all the greens and potatoes I could eat, I was in "hog heaven." Then, I was taken over to Brett's home (one of the men who worked in the Embassy). We sat and chatted for about half an hour before we went on to the Marine house where they were having an "after ceremony" party. The Marines and I talked off and on right through the evening. It was finally, at about 03:00 a.m., that Gunny Rowland, his wife and myself all walked back to his house. I went to sleep in a nice soft bed for the first time in weeks (I hadn't slept on anything but the ground).

Friends, Faxes, Packages and Taxes

The next days were spent in minor maintenance on the motorcycle while waiting for my package to come in. I was starting to get depressed. I just wanted to get on my way and go. I kept my spirits up by meeting different people in the campground. One of them was a follow named Luther, from Germany.

Luther was a very interesting guy who had spent 3 years in Konya, working to build a machine shop and teaching people machine work. He said he was able to teach only one person. He had to build the machine shop himself.

"All they want to do is just sit around on their ass and let everybody else do the work for them," he told me. "I only met one person who wanted to learn something and raise himself up. All the rest were just a lot of useless bastards." Luther felt that all the money dumped into Kenya and the other countries in Africa was useless; he felt that no one should give them a penny.

"They aren't worth it, because they don't want to help themselves," he said.

Most of my days were spent running back and forth to the Airport, hoping to receive my package. I could have moved on, but I had only the remaining belt in the primary . If that belt broke, I'd really be stuck. While I was in "civilization" (if you want to call it that), I figured it was worth the time to get extra belts and an idler bearing.

Another interesting person I met there, through changing money, was Dr. Hdieh. He and his wife invited me over for lunch. I met their daughter and son-in-law, who were Christians working to help blind children learn Braille. Dr. Hdieh was of the Bahia faith. He and his wife had been persecuted and run out of Iran 30 years ago.

"Anybody of the Bahia faith that stayed, or couldn't get out in time, had been killed," he told me. He never went back to Iran, and settled in Central Africa. Dr. Hdieh had a reputation as an excellent dentist, and was quite kind to me. His wife always gave me a very good exchange rate on Traveler's Checks, which was a big plus in her favor.

Whenever a tour truck left our campground on its way to Zaire or points north, I would wave to the people as they were driving out to the main road that led out of town. As I did, an empty, desolate feeling would rise up inside me, asking, "When will I be going?" The last time I experienced that emptiness was in the South African hospital after the accident that took my legs. All my buddies were getting out of the South African Army, preparing to go home to their families for the holidays, and I was stuck, stranded, and immobile, feeling useless.

On another evening, while sleeping in my tent, about 23:30 two Danish boys came to my tent and told me, "We have had our cooking gear stolen. You should check on your stuff and see if its all there."

When I checked out behind my tent, sure enough, my stove, my cooking bowl and one of my spare tires were gone. Upset as I was, I realized that I had become slack in my security, and had left stuff out when it should have been put away. I put my remaining possessions in front of the tent, then went back to bed, trying to get some sleep for the rest of the night over the noise of what sounded like voodoo ceremonies going on in the adjacent woods behind the campgrounds, sometimes from midnight until the early hours of the morning. I never found out what the drums and wailing were all about.

In the mornings, I did push-ups for exercise, trying to keep myself in some semblance of good shape for the rough ride to come. There was still another 300 miles (500 kilometers) of dirt road... just to get out of Central Africa!

Then, of course, there was Cameroon, more dirt and mud as well.

November 14th, 1990: Bruno had received his parts from France, and started to reassemble his engine. He was in a pretty good mood as we spoke about our future plans - whether we would continue to travel together. It appeared he would go on with me to Cameroon and points North.

Later that day, I went to the airport and saw a Customs inspector.

"No package," he said.

I blew up... went wild.

Finally, a man came up to me and asked, "Problem, Messier?"

"Oui," I replied with absolute disdain. "I want my package!"

Days of frustration poured out in my ranting and raving. "I've waited far too long for this stupid package, and there has been no fax for me at the Embassy concerning any delays. I've heard nothing!"

This man took me to another office, and low and behold, there were my parts!

I couldn't believe it. Then he really shocked me.

"Messier will need to pay 9,000 Franks ($30) tax for us to release this package," he told me.

I responded in my typical, calm manner.

"Bull Shit, I'm not going to pay it," I responded in my typical tactful and diplomatic manner. Then, I left the man's office in a huff.

I raced over to Jeane's Garage and told him the story since he had a friend in Customs. Jeane called his friend and made an appointment. We went over there and he did some fast talking.

My package was delivered...with me paying a minimal tax!

Now that I had my parts, it was decided that on Friday Bruno and I would go north.

The next day was spent in preparations. I rode around and saw Jeane and thanked him for all of his help. Then I went to Dr. Hdieh and his wife and thanked them for all their kindness; I exchanged some more money. Next, I fueled up and went to the Embassy where I received a fax saying "The parts were sent on the 12th of November."

I read that fax, thinking very loving thoughts. "Well, no shit, you sent it late and didn't fax me about it. Thank you very much, fellas, for helping a fellow American!"

Finally, back to the campground to get ready for the trip out of Bangui and Central Africa.

November 16: Got up, did 200 push-ups, loaded the motorcycle, and by 04:30 I was on my way across Bangui to wake up Bruno. Once I arrived, he told me, "Ah, I must go to a dentist. My tooth hurts. I'll meet you at the border."

His dentist appointment was at 08:00.

"He'll be able to catch up with me quite easily," I thought as I bade him good-bye and gave him his motorcycle helmet. I kept the tent on the back of my motorcycle and rode away. Very sadly, although I didn't know it then, this was the last time I would see my friend and benefactor, Bruno Piet.

Alone Again

After stops at a couple of police road blocks on the way out of Bangui, and then another one about 5 miles outside of Bangui, I was on my way West, headed for the border of Central Africa and Cameroon. At the main gate in and out of Bangui, my passport was stamped for the last time.

Finally, I was the road... with thick fog, making it quite dangerous, since animals wander all over these roads. I had to put my glasses up on my forehead because the mist was so bad I could not see out of them. I hit a number of very deep pot holes, and broke another spoke in the front wheel. To be safe, I rode in first and second gear most of the time. As dawn came, the fog eventually cleared, and I was able to get up into third gear.

Just short of 100 miles (160 km.) out of Bangui, I went onto dirt road again. The dirt was the best I had seen so far in Africa; I was able to maintain speeds of 40 to 45 mph - probably too fast to avoid anything that might jump out in front of me, but I just didn't seem to care. My adrenaline was pumping, and I was finally moving!

I made my first fuel stop, then rode another 100 miles (160 km) without stopping.

In Bouar, I filled up all three tanks and was able to carry on from there. Of course, the asshole behind the petrol pump tried to cheat me out of 400 Central African Francs (CFA), but I wouldn't have any part of it, and became quite boisterous. Perhaps my shouting wasn't the wisest thing to do, as quite a crowd gathered around me - and they didn't seem friendly to this foreigner challenging one of their own, even though the man was a pig and a thief!

When I went to buy bread for my lunch, the vender wanted so much for it that I thought, "Piss on this. He can shove his bread up his ass." I went to another store when I bought the bread at a fair price.

In Bouar, there's a big French Foreign Legion Base. "What an asshole of a place to be stationed in," I thought to myself. "I'd hate to have duty in a place like this."

I rode over 300 miles (500 km) that day, and by late afternoon, I had made it to the border. Police, Customs and Immigration all cleared me through quickly. I rode another 500 meters and came to the border of Cameroon. There I showed my documents, and the official said, "Wait." Within a half hour, more officials came and I cleared Customs and Immigration, riding into Cameroon proper. I had left Central Africa behind!

Chapter Nine

Cameroon - Zaire with Termites!

The first acceptable place I found to sleep was a Catholic Mission, knowing that Bruno would go to the same place. When I asked permission from a fellow named Dereck to stay the night, I was relieved to hear the words, "Indeed, you can," since I was very tired from my first day on the road in about two weeks.

They gave me a room without any electricity or running water, but we did have a nice dinner with Dereck and a French girl that was there doing volunteer work, but neither of them spoke any English, so communication was, as usual, difficult.

I was worried about my friend, Bruno, since he hadn't caught up to me. My main concern was that he had not met with any ill fortune... the roads are so dangerous.

My first morning in Cameroon, I got up at 04:30 and loaded the motorcycle, and did my pushups to get my blood flowing. Dereck came out and motioned, "Follow me." We had breakfast where I was served some bread, very good cheese (the first in a couple of months!), and hot coffee. After breakfast, I bid good-bye to my friend, started the motorcycle up and rode out.

At the outskirts of town, more police officials wanted to check all my gear, going slowly, as if waiting for a bribe. They were saying that this and that was wrong with my motorcycle. Trying to stop their con game, I showed them a letter from the American Embassy in Zimbabwe, reading that "Dave Barr is riding around the world on behalf of the disabled."

Then, I showed them my legs.

As one of the police inspectors was reading my papers in his broken English, I commented, "You are very intelligent to be able to read French and English, and still speak your own language, too."

This seemed to satisfy his ego, and he finally allowed me to pass without paying a bride.

About a mile up the road, I spotted mud and ruts approaching.

"My gosh, doesn't this look all but too familiar...like ZAIRE," I thought to myself. As soon as I hit the mud and ruts, down I went.

A couple of fellows came out of their house, which was right by the ruts, and within 10 minutes we lifted the motorcycle up and out of that particular rut. They were very happy when I gave them a couple of BIC pens from my endless supply before going on my way.

The next few hours saw me through more mud and ruts; I regularly fell off the motorcycle. My spirit was sinking deeper than the mud ruts and pot holes. I had sincerely hoped I had put all this hassle of almost-impassable roads behind me, yet here I was, battling ridiculous "roads" all over again... with at least another 200 kilometers before the map showed me hitting paved road.

So, I just kept plugging.

And falling.

And falling.

And falling.

Once I was pinned under my motorcycle with it leaking gasoline all over me, waiting 30 minutes until a truck came along.

With rain forests on both my left and right sides, it felt and looked exactly like Zaire. No scenery; just rain forest. I only saw the sun when it was directly overhead, on top of me.

83

The horrible, frightful and dangerous vegetation tunnels were back.

Finally, I came to Meiganga where I was stopped by the police for inspection. "The road is better ahead," they told me.

"Sure," I thought sarcastically to myself, knowing I'd heard that song somewhere before.

When stopped in Cameroon by the police or army, I was told to mention the Cameroon Football Team which had won the World Cup. That distracted them; they would get all excited and proud, shouting, "Cameroon Number 1." Then, they would become more friendly, appreciating the fact that I knew they had won the World Cup soccer match. That little bit of interest in their country made them feel good.

After that, they would normally wave me on.

The road was better; I was actually able to get into 3rd gear. The Harley had been taking a beating, and there were still many pot holes that couldn't be avoided on the dirt road. My front rim bent even further, although it was still serviceable, though quite shaky. After about 35 miles (50 kilometers), it started raining again. I tried to keep going, s-l-o-w-l-y and e-a-s-i-l-y. At one point, I stopped because I was slipping so badly.

A pickup truck with two Africans in it came along and stopped; they gave me a bag of peanuts. We shook hands, and they went on their way.

"What good will," I thought.

Some days I meet pleasant people, and on others, thieving bastards. It seems to balance out. Attitude helps. If I smile, most of the time I'll get a smile back.

The rain quits. I sit another hour, waiting for the road to soak in the water. For the rest of the day, I bounce on through the pot holes and the mud, but I manage to stay upright. Wonders will never cease!

Finally, I enter Ngaoundéré in the late afternoon.

Body and Machine: Holding Off Self-Destruction

Cannot find any camp ground, so go to another Catholic Mission where I get a cheap room for about $1.50. I walked downtown for dinner - very expensive. I walked back about 1 1/2 kilometers, and by this time, my right knee is really damaged. The metal bushings in the hinge piece that allows the lower part of the leg to swing are gone, and it is flopping to the left and right as I move forward, making a horrible noise. Just walking and standing upright on it gives me trouble.

"It's got to hold up until I can get to London and get something done about it," I think to myself.

"I hope it holds up" is also my feeling about the motorcycle. There's a banging sound in the lower end, and it is running rough.

I must keep going.

In Zaire, I said to myself, "No matter how many times a day I fall off this bastard thing, as long as the motorcycle doesn't break, I will keep going." So far, with a variety of parts, patience, and persistence - I am making it, but I still don't have any peace of mind about the motorcycle.

Now, my own mechanical parts are starting to self-destruct!

After dinner, I take a shower and plop on my bed, exhausted. My back is killing me, but if it wasn't for the kidney belt that's solid leather, my back would have given out long before this.

I'm still worried about Bruno, since the amount of close calls I've had on these roads are absolutely countless.

On the plus side, riding on these roads at times can be pure adrenaline.

Concentration must be total, or tragedy is assured every single time I hit a big hole or a quagmire of mud. I must constantly avoid oncoming vehicles that totally ignore me. And, there is always the dodging of animals, both in villages and out on the road.

I fall asleep that night with the wonderful thought that I had made it onto pavement... **Blessed Pavement**!

Yesterday, I traveled as much as 400 miles (600 kilometers) on dirt roads (**good** dirt roads). 900 kilometers is a long way on dirt in two days. Not bad for the old dog.

The next morning, fairly refreshed, I loaded the motorcycle and went to breakfast. I talked with a man named Franco, from Italy. As we finished breakfast, I felt him push something into my pocket. I pulled out $5,000 CFA (about $25.00 American dollars). I tried to refuse him, but I knew his feelings would be hurt, so I graciously accepted it. We talked a bit more, and I was very touched by this gesture of sensitivity that he showed towards me, and for the reasons I was doing the trip. It was also good to speak to somebody, even in broken English. It had been days since my last English conversation!

I stopped for petrol and some brake fluid; the front brake was starting to leak now.

"I must keep it working until Europe," I thought. Bangui was half-way across Africa, so I am on the down hill side.

The asphalt was very, very good!

Like floating on a magic carpet with no shock absorbers!

As I traveled on this black velvet, I remember thinking, "This is the best road since 2,000 miles (3500 km) ago in Rwanda."

Periodically, I was stopped by the police, but they never hassled me for a bribe.

The last city in Cameroon was Garoua; out of there, I hit a very bad dirt road: sandy, full of holes, rocks and a number of dry river beds. About half-way through these roads, I cleared Customs and Immigration. The remaining distance to Nigeria was 25 miles (40 km.).

The heat was over 100 degrees (38 c)!

On the Nigerian border, the Captain of Police grilled me for half an hour about why I was coming through, and about my trip for the disabled. I practiced my Golden Rule, staying with my patent story.

"I'm riding around the world trip on behalf of the disabled," I told him. I especially watched for any trick questions relating to South Africa. After he finished interrogating me, he sent me to about six different huts where I was asked the same questions again.

The same answers were given.

Then, all the questioners compared notes, and finally signaled me on. Next, I had to declare my finances, since you must have a specific amount of money to enter Nigeria.

Then, on to another lovely asphalt road! Of course, asphalt roads were still full of pot holes, so I had to be on my toes (if that's possible for me).

In the few hours, I was stopped six more times by police! I was becoming very irritated with this.

"Why the hell did they let me into the country if I'm being stopped so many times?" I wondered.

Same crazy questions, same patent answers.

Nigeria - Nice People, Cheap Gas, Pesky Termites

After receiving bad directions and getting lost, then unlost, I finally arrive in Yola, my first major city in Nigeria. I ask for directions to the Mission by stopping a car displaying a "News/TV" sign on it, and by asking the man inside, "Where is the nearest Mission?"

"Follow me," he replied, and led me right to my destination where I met the Bishop.

"You can stay here for free," he told me.

That was great news.

After a good shower and a close look at my deteriorating machine, I went to a lounge and sat talking for the next hour and a half to different African priests. Dinner was served at 19:45. It was with great appetite that I ate the sumptuous fare that these priests had prepared for all of us. After dinner, I excused myself and went back to my room and closed my day about 20:30.

I awoke at 05:00 to the eerie sound of "the Holy" being called to prayer (when I say "the Holy" I am referring to Muslims here) by the wailing of the local Muslim clergy. The last time I heard this eerie, early morning sound was as a soldier in Israel, out in the West Bank.

By 07:00, I had the motorcycle loaded and ready. Fr. Charles came out and said, "Come on in and have some breakfast." After breakfast, he said, "Just wait until 08:00 and I will arrange for a car to take you to a bank where you can change some money."

When I was taken to the manager of the bank, he made the money exchange for my traveler's checks without charging me a commission. "That was a very nice gesture," I thought. "I seem to be meeting a lot of nice people lately."

Back at the church, I said "good-bye" to Fr. Charles and Fr. Good Will (yes, that's his real name!). The first place I went was to the service station to fill up all my fuel tanks. There must have been 100 people around me when I pulled in.

The bill came to $2.00!

That's the cheapest petrol I have seen anywhere in Africa, or anywhere in the world. I took on 9 gallons (36 liters) of fuel, so that figures to about $.22 cents a gallon! And, it is good quality - 98 Octane! My motorcycle now started running like a striped assed ape.

In every town I was in, I had to ask directions to the next town because signs were never clearly marked on the roads. The roads were asphalt and quite passable, but there was still considerable danger trying to avoid oncoming buses or trucks. These drivers believe it is your responsibility to get out of their way - period. Sometimes there is no shoulder to turn off onto because it has been eroded away, so one must plan ahead when one sees a bus or truck in the distance.

Constant vigilance is the key - one must be aware of what's unfolding on the road at ALL times - or else you could get very hurt. The conditions reminded me of Cameroon where the road was not so bad, but the oncoming vehicles often would occupy my lanes, completely ignoring the motorcycle. There were many wrecked vehicles along the side the road; whenever they had a wreck, they'd strip the vehicle and just leave it sit as a grim reminder of how things don't always go the way we want.

The terrain was very bushveld and open, as compared to the confinement of Cameroon. Funny enough, the landscape reminded me of Zimbabwe. As I came through the small villages, the smell of cooking fires often lured me to stop and get some food.

I was stopped only one time this day by the police outside of Darazo.

The heat is terrible - about 115 degrees (44 c). The Harley Davidson seems to be handling it okay. I stop in Kar to buy food for dinner and breakfast...two small loaves of bread and a bag of peanuts. The lady that got the bread for me was very nice. Although I probably had a 100 people suddenly surrounding me at the store, I didn't feel tense; these Nigerians seem to be an easy going lot. (This is not the case in the southern part of the country. The locals there are known to be very belligerent.)

I encountered two road blocks today, both Army. At one of the road blocks, the man made me quite nervous as he drunk, and delighted in waving his rifle around. One accidental discharge and there could easily be one dead Dave Barr!

In the late afternoon, in the middle of nowhere, I pulled off the road back into the bush about 1 mile (1 1/2 kilometer), out of sight for security and privacy. I shut the machine down, laid out my tarp, and began to work on the motorcycle, getting it ready for the next day's ride. I had just ridden a little over 300 miles (500 kilometers) - not bad after starting at 10:00 a.m. After I ate my dinner of peanuts, beans and bread (it is safer to eat peanuts for protein than meat), I leaned back to watch the sunset, very relaxed, with a feeling of peace (very rare). As the dark gathered, I took my legs off and closed the day.

Midway through the peaceful night, I turned on my side and heard this noise...like a rustle under the tarp. I thought to myself, "What's that? There must be scorpions galore under this tarp, or perhaps on top of it."

Grabbing my flashlight, I looked on the tarp, but I could see nothing on top. I slammed my hand down on the tarp and heard the rustling noise again. With a tingle of fear and adrenaline up my spine, I took a shoe off of one of the legs, stuck the flashlight in my mouth, and lifted up the tarp. I was prepared to start beating these invaders before they jumped up on top of the mat and started to sting me.

Well, what do you think I saw under the mat?

Termites...by the thousands!

The only explanation I could think of was that the ground was warm, so when I put the tarp down, the heat coming up created condensation. "The termites came out of their holes to get a drink," I thought.

There termite mounds were all around the area. I thought, "If they don't bother me, I won't bother them." I put the tarp back down and went back to sleep. For the rest of that very beautiful moon-lit night, those termites left me alone. The next morning, they were gone, probably searching for a less troublesome source of moisture.

More bread and peanuts for breakfast, then load up and get on my way. As I moved out onto the road and gathered speed, I had one of those really good feelings about the day.

The BIG Dipper, BOGUS Insurance, and BORDER Thieves

But how often are feelings wrong?

I hadn't traveled too far, maybe only ten miles (16 km), and my speed was up to about 50 or 55 mph. Suddenly, there was this huge deep dip in front of me. The motorcycle left the ground and then hit the bottom of the dip. When it did, it bottomed right out, sending me slamming into the tank and onto the seat. Then I came up the other side, on a very steep climb; I jumped a small bridge that was in front of me, and once again, came off the seat, flying through the air. All I could do was clutch onto my handlebars - my legs were dangling out somewhere behind me.

When the motorcycle came down, I slammed on top of the tank, once again, barely managing to control the motorcycle. I had to pull over and get my wind and my heart beat under control. By now, I could feel blood pounding in my ears from super adrenaline. At times like this, I wouldn't mind smoking a cigarette and having a drink. It just shows how one cannot relax for a moment. If one starts to sit back and say, "Hey, isn't this Africa beautiful today? Man, the road's good, and everything just seems to be going my," then bingo, you get nailed!

I'm doing quite well along the road to Kano until an oncoming bus moves over into my lane and I get run off the road. Fortunately, this road had shoulders. Once in Kano, a major city in the north of Nigeria, I asked directions to the Central Hotel's Tourists Campground. When I arrived, I discovered many tour trucks there; one truck was going north, and their guide told me, "There are some problems with the Algerians in the Visa process. Apparently, one of their crown princes was thrown out of Britain on an expired Visa, so as a retaliation, they are now making it difficult for tourists in their own country."

While setting up camp, I met a man named Mohammed who took me into town; he also gave me some Visa forms for Niger. In town, we caught a taxi to the Niger Embassy; they took my passport and said, "Come back tomorrow."

On the way back to camp, I stopped and bought a small cooking stove (since Cameroon I had been eating cold food). I cooked up some noodles with peanuts in them; the meal was quite tasty, but the mosquitoes were so bad that I had to put up Bruno's tent for refuge.

The next morning I was up early and heated the left overs from last night's dinner. At 8:00 a.m., Mohammed had a friend who couldn't speak English go to town with me to try and find a reputable camera repair shop. I had tried to get my camera repaired in another place, but the service people I encountered invariably wanted to charge too much money, so I said, "To heck with them."

On our trip to town, we got screwed on the taxi fare. The guy paid for it as I was pretty upset, and let him know about it. Our trip failed to produce results.

Later that same day, two young fellows, one named Bangcoli and the other was named Sonny, came by to see me. I told them about my broken camera. "No problem," they said, "let's go into town."

So, we did.

They located an honest merchant who looked at it and discovered dead batteries were my only problem. I had put new batteries in only a couple days before. I didn't trust this camera, and when I got to London, I discovered my instincts were right - fully 60% of all my photographs were ruined!

Bangcoli and Sonny did a lot of the bargaining for me in the town market place so I wouldn't get ripped off; I was very grateful to them as they brought me around to the back areas of the town where I could find better deals on the various items I needed.

The next morning at 04:30, I got up, heated "left-overs" for breakfast, did my pushups, broke down my tent, loaded up the motorcycle, had a cup of tea, relaxed a minute or two, then cranked up just after 05:00. As people woke up to the sound of the Harley, I waved farewell to them and rode out the campground and out of Kano in the gathering dawn. Through the villages on the outskirts of Kano, I waved to people and they enthusiastically waved back.

The terrain started to become far sparser, with less trees, more open space, and more arid land. I fueled up in Katsina, the last town before I would cross the border to Niger. When I hit the border, it only took half an hour to clear Customs to leave Nigeria, and then I rode up the road to the Customs and Immigration post of Niger.

As I was going through the typical formalities, one of the policemen said, "You must buy $50.00 worth of insurance to go through Niger."

"But Messier," I humbly replied, "I already have insurance that I bought for Niger and Algeria while I was in Kano, Nigeria." The policy I purchased was bogus insurance, just a phony form, and it had cost me $10.00. But, I knew I needed something. Now, I didn't want to end up paying another $50.00 for more BOGUS insurance. The policeman started getting angry, so I tried to be humble and reason with him.

He'd have no part of reason.

He started throwing papers through the air, ranting and raving, dancing around like a demented Jackel. "If you won't buy insurance," he screamed, "go back Nigeria!"

I then approached a sergeant, and humbly tried to explain that I was traveling around the world for the disabled. He looked down at my legs as I lifted up my pants, and says, "Oui!"

He then turns around to the raving clown and tells him, "Shut up."

Finally, my customs and immigration paper work processed quickly, and I didn't have to buy the bogus insurance. The sergeant then instructed his men to line up and salute me. I took great pleasure especially in seeing the little prick who had been throwing the wobbly now standing to attention, deeply embarrassed by his enforced homage. If ever a black man could have been red, it was this guy. He was as red as a fully-ripe beet.

Entering Niger, after these hassles, was a big relief.

At Maradi, just over the border, I went to one bank where I wanted to exchange some money. A huge crowd gathered, which made me nervous, since other travelers had warned me that Niger was "a big den of thieves." A well-dressed, well-spoken man came to me and said, "I'll look after your motorcycle while you go into the bank." I accepted his offer, and went into try and exchange money. No dice - they didn't accept traveler's checks. So, the man took me to another bank with a security area for the motorcycle. I was able to change my money there, thanked this kind gentleman, and went on my way.

Maradi is in the Sahara Desert, and getting out of town was a problem. I became turned around in the city, and ended up going through an ancient market place. I hailed a cab driver and asked him, in French, "How do I get out of Maradi?" He kindly led me to the outskirts of town without charging me any money.

The roads in Niger were excellent, the best I'd seen in Africa to this point. There's almost no traffic on them, so there's a lot less thrills. I was even able to look around and observe the desert terrain! For some, a desert is a bleak and miserable place, but for me, the beauty is the openness and the solitude.

I fueled up in a town in the middle of nowhere. A great crowd of kids gathered, most of them naked, running around, laughing and happy about this bizarre traveler in their midst.

Next, I came across camels, often called "the ships of the desert," but miserable and disgusting beasts in my opinion.

Outside a small village, I came upon a young European woman with a motorcycle. "Is all well with you?" I asked, and she replied, "Yes, all is well, thank you," in an American accent. "I live in the village and work for the Peace Corps," she explained. We only spoke for a few minutes and then I was on my way towards

Agadéz, but it felt soooooo good to speak to someone in English!

I missed my turn off and ended up in Birni-N'Konni, so I turned around and went backwards 7 miles - not too bad. Heading north again towards Agadéz, I'm still on very good roads. When I stopped at a small village to buy some bread, children came up to me, took my water bottles, and enthusiastically went off to fill them up for me.

I rode on for another 10 miles to get away from any civilization (I saw no cars or people the entire distance). Then I rode a mile off the main road, back into the desert, where I couldn't be seen by any one. A few unattended camels were my only company. Feeling this was a secure spot, I stopped the motorcycle, unloaded it, put down my bed roll, had my dinner and laid back to enjoy the beautiful sunset and dusk - my first in the Sahara. I'd covered 400 miles (600 kilometers) this day, so that heightened my enjoyment of the clear night sky and absolutely magnificent stars. I was so enthralled I can't actually remember when I was lured to sleep in the tranquil quiet of that Sahara night.

The Unparalleled Sahara Desert

On the road north to Agadéz, the desert became more bleak. I have seen deserts all over the world - the Negev, Judean, Sinai, Namib, Mojave - but I could never imagine the size and magnitude of the Sahara Desert... it's like another world.

After traveling north for a number of hours, I stopped to refuel out of one of my gas cans when, in the distance, I saw a camel caravan. The camels were tied nose to tail and they stretched back for at least two miles! There was one camel rider for every 5 or 6 camels. I could see the tiny profiles of kids running alongside the camels, goats and sheep. Unfortunately, they were too far away to photograph, but the sight was spellbinding. "Men and camels have been traversing this desert since time immortal," I thought. For the moment, it seemed I was witnessing a tradition both timeless and mystical.

Back to reality.

Another police check.

By the time I stopped, I almost fell off the motorcycle because my rear brake was not working well at all; somehow, I managed to keep the thing upright. As the policeman started asking me the same old questions, I thought, "You little prick, you're looking for a bribe, aren't you?"

He didn't get one from me. I acted stupid, saying, "Don't understand" in French. Eventually, he waved me on with a look of disgust on his face.

Outside Agadéz, I was stopped by the police again.

"You need to go into the town and sign the register," I was told.

I did, and once those formalities were finished, I rode on to the Esale Campground where I made my camp, relaxing with a cup of tea. There I spoke to a couple of German fellows known as "commercial tourists" - the first people I ever met who were selling vehicles they had driven across the Sahara Desert. They told me they were having trouble finding a market for one vehicle, and were negotiating for another.

The next morning, after my push ups in the dirt, I started repairing the motorcycle in the early morning light. I took off the outer primary and found another big hole in it. I cleaned out everything, then went over to a tour truck, secured some silicone sealant, and with a piece of an inner tube, patched up the hole. Other maintenance that day included some welding on the back box and the crash bar on the right side in the rear.

Next, I washed some clothes.

"I'll make a trip into town," I thought, "and find the Peace Corps." The young Peace Corps girl I had met on the road said they were having a Thanksgiving dinner that evening. I located the Peace Corps house, and spoke to a young lady named Celeste.

"Yeah, we are having dinner here," she replied. "It costs 2,000 CFA (about $8)."

I was willing to pay the money since I was just desperate for some English-speaking company, and committed to coming back that evening.

Back at the campground, I took a nice cold shower (as there never was hot water) and relaxed by reading the rest of the afternoon (something I was to do more often in this place). In the evening, about 18:00, I started back to the Peace Corps house for one heck of a Thanksgiving dinner. They were all good, clean kids, doing a great job for other people, but the generation gap was tremendous. I couldn't really identify with them. Our age differences, ideologies, and experience levels in life were drastically different.

About 22:00, I excused myself and rode back to the campground in the pitch black of night. My headlight was only working intermittently, so I was lucky not to hit any animals or other obstacles out on the road. Just as I settled in at camp for the night, a group of French tourists arrived, making much noise and merriment, pitching their camp right next to mine.

So much for my night's sleep!

The following days at the campground were spent working on the motorcycle, getting it ready for the next grueling section of the trip - through the Sahara Desert. I spoke to Dean (an American) and Susan (Dutch), who were driving across the Sahara together, all the way back to Holland. We took time to become friends through many long conversations.

Agadéz is NOT a cheap or convenient place to live! Once, when I tried to change money, I couldn't locate the bank.

"The bank closed two months ago," I was told. An African fellow agreed to sit on the back of my motorcycle and show me around. We found a hotel that changed $70 of my money... at an exorbitant exchange rate!

"It stinks," I thought. "Locals are always after the tourist buck."

The Algerian Embassy had a reputation for a "nose in the air," arrogant attitude; apparently, the workers were that way with everyone! People sitting outside the Embassy constantly complained about the Embassy staffs' attitudes.

One time when Dean, Susan and myself went to the Algerian Consulate, we sat for an hour before they finally asked us in. The head man at this consulate was named Ali Baba (believe it or not), and a more nasty little cretin you won't find anywhere. Apparently, his mean disposition filtered down to his staff who virtually *interrogated* me as to why I needed a Visa.

"I'm on an around-the-world trip for disabled people," I explained to them, showing them my legs. I never knew what they were really thinking, and the interpreter involved in these interrogations seemed almost useless. I had no idea what he was telling the officials, but the treatment they gave all of us foreigners seemed unbelievably rude .

"Why wouldn't they just willingly let people into their country who were bringing in money to help their beleaguered economy?"

The Algerian economy was suffering. The Americans were in the Gulf War, and there were problems with the embargo of Iraq. I was told that Algeria was "pro Iraq" and anti-American (maybe I was lucky just to get into the country). With the issuance of my Visa in doubt, the thought of being stymied and refused permission to travel through Algeria was absolutely shocking to me.

I didn't know what I would do if the Visa were denied.

Luckily, later that day I was told I would receive my Visa on Thursday; Dean and Susan also received theirs with no wait. That put us all in a good mood!

Back at the campground, Dean and Susan (armed with their Visas) came over about 13:00 to say "good-bye," and to take some photographs of me and the motorcycle, then they went their way. I looked across the campground and once again experience that old empty feeling of being left behind. I'll never get used to it. To this day, when I see people getting ready to go away, I have the same empty feeling.

That night, I cooked a tin of beans with my noodles, trying to give myself a treat and raise my spirits. Because it was dark, I didn't have to worry about flies when I ate. Flies were a real and incessant problem during the day; at night, they changed guard with the pesky and blood-thirsty mosquitoes.

The next few days are spent passing time, waiting for Thursday and my visa to come so I could head north to Algeria. Utmost in my mind was the "PIST," a stretch of land 420 miles (730 km.) from Arlit (Arhli), in northern Niger, where there is no road at all! I'd heard many horror stories from others about the "Hogar Route" (the PIST). I understood that the catastrophic stories associated with this "non-road" made it a tangible threat to my completing the trip.

November 29: I went back to the Algerian Consulate where the infamous Ali Baba told me to "Come in" after I waited an hour outside. He then asked for my passport, and 2,220 Franks ($10); I gave them to him, and he said, "Come back at 12:30 to receive your Visa."

I left the embassy, going back to the campground to change oil on the Harley Davidson, using the last of the 120 weight aircraft oil I purchased in Central Africa (I had taken about 10 extra liters with me).

Then, back to the embassy to receive the most difficult Visa to date to secure (At this point in the trip! Asia would prove to be far more difficult.). Thankfully, the Visa was waiting...and there were no further problems!

Returning to the campground, I met a Dutch fellow named Harry, who had bicycled all the way across the Sahara from Holland. His bicycle weighed 130 kilograms (about 275 pounds). I've never seen a bicycle so loaded down. We had dinner together, then bade each other good night at 20:30. I laid back thinking about Harry's related experiences about crossing the PIST on his bicycle. Finally, I drifted off that night, knowing that tomorrow I could finally start heading north again to Europe.

Up at 04:30 the next morning, I did my exercises, got the motorcycle loaded, said a prayer asking God to watch over me through this day, and started out of the campground about 06:00. One more police check, then on my way, accompanied by a glorious morning sunrise over the Sahara. The magnificent, big red ball seemed to grow out of the desert in the distance.

Enthralling. Powerful. Majestic.

It's impossible to put into words what I saw and felt - that soaring sense of freedom that occurs when nature and motorcycle both seem to be at their best (which is rare for my motorcycle).

"On good road!!!" I thought to myself. "What can stop me now?"

I tried NOT to think much about the PIST.

Chapter Ten

The PIST - the Ultimate Challenge

Arlit (Arhli) was about 120 miles (200 km.) up the road, and there was virtually nothing along the way except good tar road and beautiful desert. In Arlit (Arhli), with the help of a small boy, squeezed on the back of my motorcycle, we located a camping area just north of the town.

I was looking for anyone "going north" who could take some of the gear off the motorcycle to lighten the load on the PIST - the weight of the machine was over 800 pounds. Someone suggested that I go to a certain bar and restaurant in town were travelers often gathered. It sounded like a good idea to me, so I rode back to Arlit (Arhli) proper, attracting a huge crowd around the motorcycle at this bar.

"Don't worry, I'll look after the motorcycle" someone volunteered in French (with me only half understanding these conversations). The man looked trustworthy, so I said "O.K." and went upstairs to discover a group of people who owned the 4 wheel drive vehicles parked outside.

"Is anyone here going North?" I asked.

"No, we're all headed South," came the reply.

Disappointed, I went back to my motorcycle where a tremendous crowd was congregating, actually causing a traffic problem. The pressure and pushing of so many people was starting to get on my nerves. I met a fellow named Sullaman who suggested, "Let's put the motorcycle back in the parking area of the hotel over there. They have a guard." It seemed like a good idea, so we pushed the machine back to an enclosed parking area, about 250 meters away.

Entering the hotel, I waited for the next 3 hours for a vehicle, anything that looked foreign that might be going north. My idea was to stop and ask them, "If you are heading North, can I accompany you?"

It is very unwise to try to cover this stretch of desert by yourself. If you are hurt, or suffer a major breakdown, there's a good chance that you will die (or, so I have heard). The rule of thumb for the PIST seems to be - "Travel with somebody else." For the next three hours, a crowd surrounds me, some trying to sell me souvenirs, some offering a manicure, others trying to sell me coffee. I wanted to shout, "Get the fuck away from me! Leave me alone!"

They were like flies.

Finally, about 17:00, I went back to the parking lot and started working on the motorcycle. While I was working on it, a hotel official told me, "You'll have to pay 2500 CFA (about $15) to have the motorcycle stay in the parking lot."

"Fuck off!," I told him. Another person trying to rip off a foreigner. For me, it was too much. I loaded the motorcycle up and left, riding back out to the camping area.

My excitement rose a bit when I noticed a couple of new trucks.

"Which way you headed?" I asked.

Naturally, they were heading south. It seems I'm always trying to swim up stream or ride against the wind, out of tune with every one else.

Unloading the motorcycle, I tried to relax, bothered by a sinking feeling in my stomach that I wouldn't be able to find my way north with any companions.

"I might have to try this bugger on my own," I thought.

The standard practice of motorcycles crossing the PIST is to marry up with a vehicle that will carry all their gear and the motorcycle run on the markers, doing the navigation. The vehicle carrying the gear can pick an easier course, with the motorcycle some distance away, carefully watching the direction they go. If the vehicle becomes stuck, then the motorcycle goes over and helps the vehicle. A marriage of convenience, if you like.

That night as I lay back, swatting mosquitoes and listening to people in the campground bargain over vehicles that had come south that day, I thought "I'll just keep my fingers crossed. Hopefully, I'll find someone going north tomorrow."

Flat Tires and Flat Out of Luck!

Up at 05:00, I loaded up the motorcycle and started up, waking all those loud mouths from the previous night, then riding out of the campground. About 10 kilometers (6 miles) into the desert, to a vantage point where I could see vehicles in route either north or south, I had trouble with the motorcycle.

"I'll just sit here and wait to see if any vehicles heading north will come my way," I thought, while I worked on the motorcycle. It wasn't long before a vehicle came by and stopped. An Austrian fellow, named Haans, who was traveling south, stopped to offer me assistance (by this time I had cured the problem).

Before Haans went on his way, he gave me some tinned food that he didn't need any longer. He planned to sell the vehicle he had driven from France, then fly back to France and buy another one, repeating the process. It served as a bit of an adventure vacation, and an opportunity to make money at the same time. These people were known as "commercial tourists."

I sat all day watching the horizon for any vehicles going north.

No luck.

Nothing going north.

In the late-afternoon, I decided to go back to the campground. On the way back, I got a flat rear tire. I stopped to have a look, but could not find any nails in it. So, I took out my air compressor and started pumping it up. It held air, believe it or not. I got on it and went back to town and found the so-called "truck park." There I negotiated a price of $50.00 (the best I could do) to carry my gear, but the truck was leaving in about an hour, and I was very uncomfortable about the appearance of the fellow driving the truck.

"If I drop the motorcycle in the desert," I thought, "this fellow looks like the type who would just drive off and leave me alone, hauling off everything I own on the back of the truck."

That idea was not very encouraging.

"Who knows, maybe he's only going to the border of Niger/Algeria," I tell myself, trying to look on the bright side.

Ultimately, I pass on the idea of going on with this Niger vehicle.

So, the search continues.

In town, I met an African lad who spoke English reasonably well; I put him on the back of the motorcycle and went to a hotel he knew about where he felt someone might be heading north. We got there, but could find no one. "I have a friend who will be going north, but he first has to get a Visa," the lad told me.

"Over the weekend, that's not very likely," I thought.

I thanked the boy, then rode back out to the campground. While talking to someone, he said, "Look at your tire. It's going flat."

Sure enough, it was.

As I started to work on it, some Swiss campers came over and said, "Let's bring it to our camp and fix the tire, then you can have dinner with us."

Glad for the help and company, I accepted.

We brought the motorcycle over, and using their jack, pulled the rear tire off and broke it down. I located the puncture in the tube and fixed it. The tube was actually kinked; I'd never seen anything like it before. The kink created the hole. After patching the hole, every one was in a very jubilant mood as we ate our spaghetti dinner. The Swiss had just crossed the PIST with no major problems except a couple of flat tires on their Mercedes van. They used my air compressor to blow up one of their tires that they had just repaired. Three of the party were on motorcycles, and one drove the van. They didn't know each other before the trip, but had met in Tamanrasset, Algeria, and went on together. The motorcycles were able to help the van when it got stuck in sand pits.

These people seemed to be very devout Christians.

"Why don't you try making it just to the border by yourself?" Reichardt said. "At the border, you are very likely to find some Germans, French or Italians. They make adventure trips down from Tamanrasset, to the border, then back with back-up vehicles."

That seemed like a good idea, since Reichardt felt I had a pretty fair chance of making it to the border. The idea appealed to me. I slept in their camp that night, thinking I would give it a bash on my own in the morning to the border...a distance of about 150 miles.

Up early, I have breakfast, and load the Harley Davidson. I say "good-bye" to these very kind people and ride out in the direction of the PIST as the sun comes up fully in the dawn.

Bouncing, Banging, and Bottoms

There's no sense of freedom in my heart as I look out into the desert, sensing nothing but fear of isolation out there on this motorcycle. I keep heading north, and soon the hard ground gives away to soft sand. To keep from sinking in the sand, I must maintain a speed of about 50 mph (80 kph) at ALL times!

The motorcycle is in a constant fishtail. On the horizon, I could only see more rolling flats of sand, and sometimes, hard ground. Now, when I hit the hard ground, I've got to keep the motorcycle at about 45 mph (72 km), so I'm bouncing and banging along, constantly being thrown off the seat. My right foot keeps slipping off the rear brake; I'm constantly putting it back on, taking my right hand off of the handlebar (making things even more difficult).

Another challenge: when you spot an obstacle, you must start maneuvering away from that obstacle a good 200 meters before you get to it. The machine is working under you constantly. You must not tighten up, yet you must hold firmly to the handlebars to keep the front wheel from being seized by different ruts you encounter. Eventually, you *carefully* maneuver yourself away from any obstruction. Any sudden moves will result in disaster.

When I spot the skeletons of old vehicles that didn't make the grade, I think, "There's not too many second chances in a place like this." These wrecked vehicles are grim reminders of failed crossings. Pushing on, I just manage to keep the motorcycle upright. Numerous times, I nearly come off.

"How in the heck would I pick this thing up out here on my own?" I wonder.

Moving forward, I was shocked how fast the miles went by - I looked and discovered that I had already gone about 40 miles (60 km)... and, hard to believe, I was still upright on this sand. I passed some vehicles going south and waved, feeling pride, even exhilaration in my heart. They stuck their heads out of the vehicles and couldn't believe what they were seeing - an old Harley Davidson out in the Sahara. Or, perhaps they were thinking, "You simple idiot, riding out here on that!!!" Even as I enthusiastically waved, I had to keep a real sharp eye on what is in front of me, and where I was going, so I didn't fall off and get stuck in the sand.

A few more miles up the road, I felt my back end sinking. I managed to look back and see a flat tire.

"Judas Priest!," I thought. Things like this just get my goat. "Why," I wondered, "when I have a problem, is it always a recurring problem?"

When I stopped, it became clear the only thing I could do was put air into the tire. I did, and it went flat again.

Now, I was going to have to wait.

"Why don't you get your jack out and jack the thing up?" you might wonder.

I don't have a jack; I gave it away in Zaire.

"Who needs a jack," I reasoned. "Why carry the extra weight? Whenever I've got a flat tire, it's just a matter of lifting the motorcycle up, putting blocks under it, taking the wheel out, fixing the problem, and putting the wheel back."

In Africa, there are always crowds to help. They won't leave, no matter how long you're there. They'll lift the motorcycle up, whatever I need, for a few ball-point pens and friendly hand shakes.

Out in the Sahara, that is not the way. I wasn't able to find a jack in Arlit (Arhli) or Agadéz (maybe I didn't look hard enough), foolishly reasoning, "Since there are no nails or broken glass to cause flats out on the PIST, I really won't need a jack."

Good thinking, Dave! What a genius.

When all was said and done, I had **seven** flat tires in four days.

So, I'm stuck in the Sahara without a jack.

What next?

Well, I just sit and wait, trying not to get depressed. No brain, no pain.

An hour passes.

Finally, I see some vehicles off in the distance! I flash them with my mirror and they change direction, coming to a stop next to me. This big fat Algerian fellow, in flowing white robes, gets out of the car and comes over and puts his hands on my shoulders.

"Oh please, don't crush me, don't kill me," I think to myself.

He looks me sternly in the face and says, "Messieur, are you out of your FUCKING mind being out here alone?"

Timidly, I thought to myself, "Maybe I am out of my mind," as I tried to explain to him in my feeble French that I couldn't find any vehicles going north.

Out came the jack I needed. We got the Harley up, I pulled the rear tire off, broke it down, and sure enough, the tube was kinked again. I couldn't believe it!

Because I didn't want to hold these fellows up any longer than was absolutely necessary, I put in my spare tube and filled the tire up completely with air. Riding on a hard tire is going to make the rest of this trip even more difficult.

Once we had the tube in and the tire on, and everything filled with air, we let it sit for a few minutes to see if it leaked; I kept checking the tire pressure...it seemed okay.

When it was time for the Algerians to go, He gave me a big hug and said, "Allah go with you." (The Algerians were without a doubt the finest people I met in all of Africa.) They went their direction and I went mine, only now, with a full inflated tire, I was really battling through the sand.

The rear shock absorbers are completely shot, not doing their job at all. The rear tire is constantly being rammed into the fender, and when it hits the fender, it bucks me off of the seat. I desperately clutch on to the handlebars as my ass flies in the air.

Of course, there's the recurring problem of my right foot being bounced of the brake peddle. This is a constant irritation, and quite dangerous, as well.

On for another 20 or so miles down the PIST, bouncing and banging along, at times flailing through the air. I came to the edge of a dune (not being aware at the time I was riding on a dune), and suddenly there was nothing underneath me!

Launching Pads, Sand Torpedoes, and Toureg Terrorists

As if coming off a launching pad, I was flying through the air, the engine screaming. Then, the motorcycle started falling earth ward. (The cardinal rule here is: never suddenly let off the throttle. If you do, the motorcycle will come to an immediate stop, but YOU WON'T!!!)

Of course, I let off the throttle.

As soon as the motorcycle touched down in the sand, it just burrowed right in, and I flew off, becoming a human sand torpedo! I don't know how far I flew... maybe as much as 10 meters... before I came to a halt with a mouth full of sand. I got up meaner than a snake, looking back at the motorcycle, sitting up on its wheels in the sand, looking at me as if to say, "You Fool!, you let off the throttle, didn't you?"

Now, I sit and wait down in a sand depression.

A good hour goes by before some Toureg children (nomads living in the desert) come over the hill and stare at me. I show my friendship by giving them some balls of fried dough (intended to be my lunch). At that point, I didn't have much of an appetite anyway - you can imagine why.

"Go on kids, beat it!" I thought, not really wanting any company.

After awhile, they went.

An hour or so later, over the hill comes a couple of adult Touregs on camels. Now, these guys have broad swords mounted on their backs, and large knives clearly visible on them.

"Oh boy, here we go," I thought. I slowly took my can of CS gas that I carry with me at all times for protection, and put it in my pocket. I had already moved the baggage off the motorcycle to hard ground, about 100 meters away.

The camels kneel down and they get off, looking like a couple of characters out of an Omar Sharif movie - with black flowing robes, faces veiled, and swords and knives on them. They came over to the motorcycle, but no words were spoken. We all just started pushing and shoving and digging for the next thirty minutes, trying to dig this bastard machine out of the sand and onto hard ground.

When we were finished, the two men made the sign of money.

"I knew these bastards wouldn't settle for ball-point pens," taking out every bit of Niger money I had - about $3.50. I gave it to them, fully understanding that $3.50 is a lot of money to these characters.

Apparently, it wasn't enough!

One of them grabbed my jacket, and I thought, "That's IT!!!"

I'd had these people up to my ears here in Niger, so I grabbed the jacket back.

One grabbed something else, and I grabbed it from him.

Next, I strap my possessions down underneath the bungie cords on the motorcycle, having already loaded my saddlebags and the heavy stuff. Knowing the danger, I never turn my back on them, and keep the CS Gas canister in my hand all the time.

Whatever they grabbed, I grabbed it back from them and put it onto the back of the machine.

After awhile, there was nothing left to grab.

We stood within a few feet of each other in a Mexican standoff at high noon. I prepared to spray them as I waited for them to go for a knife or a sword. Frankly, they looked bewildered, as if they were wondering, "Why is this fool out here in the middle of nowhere, alone, and not intimidated by us?"

They apparently thought better of pulling a knife or sword. Had they've done that, I would have gassed them and their camels (I've had too many negative experiences with camels when I lived in Israel, years before).

I got on the motorcycle as they moved off towards their camels. I started up and got going. When I was safely out of knife throwing range, I gave them a proper thank you with my finger in the air!

20 more miles of bouncing and banging along before I come to a hill. On my way up the hill in the sand, I'm thinking, "Hey, I'm doing pretty good. This is what an enduro rider must feel like, only enduro bikes don't weigh 800 pounds."

Moving up the hill, B-A-N-G, the motorcycle hits something buried in the sand.

The front end flies up.

I was forced down onto the gas tank, then down into the rocks we went.

The motorcycle was just sitting there, not all the way over on its side. I got up, made sure nothing was broken on me, then went over and managed to fully upright the beast.

The front wheel was flat.

"Today just ain't my day," I thought. "Things just aren't working out the way I would like them to."

I took out my diary and wrote. Then I took a therapeutic walk on the ridge, thinking I would watch the sunset before spending the night in this isolated place. In the distance, I see a Volkswagen van. I watch. "If he keeps going the direction he is headed," I think, "he'll end up in a sand pit."

He does, and it did.

I walked down to the stuck vehicle where two Frenchmen are hollering and shouting at each other.

"Bonseur, messieur," I said.

They both were very startled as they turned around, wondering where this apparition appeared from. I asked them if I could help, but in the end, my help wasn't needed. They put metal slats under the van, and were then able to get the vehicle out of the sand pit. I noticed one of them had a Harley Davidson T-shirt on.

I described my problem, and they came over to my motorcycle on the other side of the ridge. When they saw it, one started hollering, "Viva, Harley Davidson, Messier." He takes out a bottle of Champagne, breaks the cork, and offers everybody a drink (this was very touching and typical of the French; they have a lot of class). I only wish I had a picture of us...toasting Champagne to a wreck of a motorcycle in the middle of the Sahara.

Out comes the jack and we fix the flat.

Unfortunately, I broke a strap on my right leg. When these fellows first realized that both my logs are gone, they start shaking their heads, babbling to each other in French, looking at one another, obviously wondering how in the hell I got out here. When I told them "I came from South Africa," they shook their heads even more.

About this time, my luck changed. We saw a 4 wheel drive vehicle going north and we managed to hail him down. 100 meters either way and he would have missed us. He drove over to us, and the vehicle contained three Spaniards: the leader's name was Bonie, and there was Jose and Estaban.

When I explained my problem, they agreed to help, telling me that "It gets much worse in Algeria."

"Wonderful," I thought. "That news will help me sleep soundly tonight!"

They agreed to haul my baggage, and refused my offer to pay them. All extra baggage was loaded onto their vehicle. Little did they know what they were getting themselves into. I bade my French friends "good-bye," and carried on northward with my new Spanish benefactors.

Laughing All the Way to Algeria - Ha Ha.

My assignment was to run the markers, where the sand is more rutted. They would be off in the distance, watching me, going over easier ground.

We rode the rest of the afternoon, bouncing and banging along. A couple of times, I went down. They'd stop, coming along laughing and cackling. The reason for their laughter? When I hit a bump, they'd see my ass fly up to the top of the box in the back (a good foot or so off the seat) and then come down. They just thought this was the funniest thing!

We pushed on, right into the evening, as they were trying to make the border that night so we could get through the border formalities quickly in the morning.

It wasn't to be.

I got another flat front tire, so we set up camp.

I pulled the front tire off (they had a jack - no shit), and as we opened it up, we realized that the valve stem had completely pulled away from the tube. My heart just sank (my spare tube had already been damaged beyond repair). "What a day it's been," I thought. "What next?" Immediately, I began to think that I was going to have to ride on the bare rim.

Estephan was a mechanic who owned his own garage; he was in charge of the maintenance of the vehicle. Jose was the cook, and Bonie appeared to be the leader, and possibly the vehicle owner; he spoke English.

Estephan put his hand up, as if to say, "Don't worry, Dave. Just have a bit of confidence in me."

He then cleaned up the hole in the tube, and burnt all the rubber away from the metal valve stem. He then managed to get the valve stem, with a washer over the top of it, down inside the tube. He then put another washer on top of the tube over the other washer and valve stem. He put glue and a large patch over the valve stem and washer. Next, he put a small washer on top of the patch, and then he threaded a nut down on top of it all and tightened it down. Of course, he had glue on the washers as well.

When we were all done, we pumped air into the tube and it held air!

Next, we put the tube into the tire; to our great relief, it didn't leak.

Unbelievable! This was something we would never attempt to do in the West. Then, I put the wheel back on the motorcycle. By this time, it was late, and dinner was served.

These fellows must have feared starvation - they probably had a 100 pounds of food in the back with them. They had tinned vegetables, meat, and many delicacies - things I hadn't seen for days.

We had a proper gourmet meal.

After dinner, they crawled away into a tent. That amazed me. There was a full moon out, and they were missing it! I took my sleeping bag and went a distance away so I couldn't hear them snoring or farting. I put out my bag and laid down, exhausted, weary to the very bone. When I was laying back, I looked out into the desert - the sand was totally white under the moon. All other things, be it a bush or an outcropping of rock, was totally black, as if these things were lit by the most gigantic black light in the universe.

Amazing.

Awesome.

As tired as I was, it was actually hard to sleep with such incredible beauty and silence. The solitude was magnificent. "These poor guys are missing all this, sleeping in a tent."

The next morning I awoke before dawn and got myself together, packed my sleeping bag, and looked in awe at the open, empty desert. I thought, "What incredible beauty. Wouldn't it be something to come across this in another manner so you can enjoy it?"

After sunrise, the others started to get up. We had a cup of tea and packed up the vehicle. To my great relief, the front tire on the motorcycle was still holding air.

Soon we were on our way. I had trouble in the sand, but as long as it stayed level, or was fairly flat ground, I could control the motorcycle. Funny enough, it felt so much easier to ride with none of the gear on the back. It was like being on the back of a Tinker Toy. All I had was the box and the tools inside it, plus my extra gasoline (one of my cans was now empty). Without the extra weight, the motorcycle was a lot easier to ride.

In about 30 kilometers, we arrived at Asamacka, on the Niger side of the border, and cleared customs in about 45 minutes (Don't ask me how Bonie managed to do that.)

I had broken a rubber grommet holding my oil tank, so I was able to work on that while Bonie took all my papers and took care of customs. We had to negotiate our way out in the soft sand of Asamacka (very difficult for me) without running over any people.

On the Algerian side of the border, we were another hour clearing Customs and Immigration. The officials were cheerful, yet far more professional than the ones in Niger. "If these men are representative of the Algerian people," I thought to myself, also thinking of the Algerians who had helped me out earlier, "then this is going to be one fine country." My trip would ultimately prove that the Algerian people were some of the kindest people in all of Africa.

Chapter Eleven

Algerian Volcanoes, a Mangled Machine, and the End of the PIST

I fell just once on the Algerian border - in deep sand - in a rut. Jose and Estephan got behind the motorcycle, pushing it, while I gunned the motor; they ate a lot of sand. This was all done in a very good spirit of camaraderie. "I don't know what I would do without these guys," I thought.

They were a god-send, to be sure.

Even with four wheel drive and balloon tires, they also got stuck twice on the border.

On we went into a little town called In Guezzam where we managed to find and buy gasoline... how they get it there is anyone's guess.

In the afternoon, we were on our way north. In Niger, the markers are usually a tire, a barrel, or a wrecked vehicle, but in Algeria there are proper eight foot markers. Though they are white, they have a red tip on top (that doesn't do me much good - I'm color blind!). But, for the most part I do pretty good at navigating the markers. The motorcycle is in a constant fishtail, as usual, with my continuing problem of my foot falling off of the brake.

The three Spaniards are off in the distance, following me from a mile or so behind and to the side.

One particular time I was riding along not paying close attention to the markers. Suddenly, I looked up and nearly panicked, my heart in my throat, discovering they were now off in a different direction.

I had turned almost 90 degrees away from them!

Very gently, in a gradual manner, I eased my way back on course through the soft sand. Given another few minutes, we might have been irrevocably lost out there, no longer able to see the markers. I don't think my Spanish friends realized how close we had come to being lost - possibly forever.

I have heard tales that the desert claims about eighty people a year. Don't know how true it is, but this I know for sure - the Sahara is the biggest, most intimidating dessert I have ever seen anywhere in the world.

My tires do not hold. About sixty miles from the border, I have another flat. When my friends catch up with me, I tell them, "Listen, I am holding you guys up. Just take my gear off and I'll carry on, on my own, somehow (being the martyr that I am)."

Bonie laughed and said, "Nonsense. We're together, and that's that."

I deeply appreciate how these men took their time to help me out. I must be very straight forward. I believe that if it wasn't for their help, the chances are that I would not have made it on my own.

We get the tire apart, and, to my very great relief, it isn't a valve; in fact, we can't find a hole at all. We are taking quite a beating, and I notice that I have another spoke - my fourth - out in the front wheel.

Next, we enter into a mountainous area where I como off the motorcycle regularly (every few minutes it seems). A couple of times we actually lose each other in the rock formations while looking for the best way to go. In the mountains, it is rare you see a marker - they are so difficult to find.

The rock formations are just magnificent! Many times these formations jettison up a hundred stories into sky. The formations are usually composed of black volcanic rock, with sharp edges; sometimes you can see places where sand has accumulated in pockets on them, creating an absolutely, incredibly beautiful scene of black and white.

On we go, me still falling off the motorcycle, them still getting stuck. Toward the end of the day, I was moving along a small trail, stupid with fatigue, when All of the sudden there was nothing underneath me but air.

I dropped for ten-feet, cartwheeling with the motorcycle, down a sand embankment. It was a miracle that the machine didn't land on me and kill me. Fortunately, the fall didn't break anything.

When the Spaniards came around (they had been below me, moving along on another trail when I became air borne off the top of the embankment), they shook their heads, not believing what they had witnessed. With more cackles and laughter, everybody was smiling as we got the motorcycle up and resumed our route.

Other rock formations looked like lost cities or great black-rock castles on another planet - petrified cities. It was amazing to see the black of the rock against the beige/white sand.

One time, I came off the motorcycle and smashed flat the front muffler on rocks; we had to stick a screwdriver up inside it to open it up a bit, allowing the exhaust to pass through unheeded. The primary received another big hole in its side, and the bottom of the inner primary is gone, along with the lower part of the outside of the outer primary. When the motorcycle is stuck in sand, I can see sand pouring out of the primary. I wonder, "How is it even running the way it is?"

It is a mystery to me that I am able to keep going at all. It amazes me that the electric starter and bendix drive inside the primary are still functioning!

Many times when I fall on the right side, the air filter and housing get sand forced into it. When I open it up, I notice the intake of the carburetor has inhaled great amounts of sand. I think to myself, "The pistons must be getting ground down to nubs."

Yet, it all seems to keep going... with no lack of power.

The back tire is banging into the fender, throwing me up in the air. To say the least, over these four days, the wedding tackle took a real pounding. What torture for both machine and rider! Rocks hitting the under carriage of the motorcycle, the front end banging and clanging to the point where the front lower forks are hot to the touch. There's four broken spokes on the front wheel (its all bent up), my rear rim is bent, and the motorcycle in general is a mess. I think to myself, "I just hope the machine makes it to Tamanrasset where there is a campground and facilities where I can work on this thing and get it ready for the next stage of the trip across the rest of the Sahara and Africa."

Towards sunset, I hit a rock embankment and fly over the handlebars. I must have flown twenty feet before landing. Once again, there's just no explanation why I didn't break something.

Jose and Estephan have been working like animals during the day, helping me pick the motorcycle up, pushing it out of deep sand onto hard ground. Many times, because I must gun the engine, these guys pick up a face full of sand! The spirit of these fellows is excellent; they never frown, complain, or act like they were disgusted with me or the motorcycle for creating such havoc in their lives.

Dinner was my favorite time of day as these fellows know how to travel and eat in style. We sit around and laugh, making lighthearted comments about the day's events. These nights were my reward for having made it through another horrifying day. I loved to walk out of earshot and listen to the quiet, gaze up at the moon and the black light scenery of the desert, enjoying the solitude and the magic of the Sahara night.

I hardly slept that night...just kind of levitated and relaxed; still, I felt rested in the morning. Our days are very long - starting early in the morning, and ending just before total dusk. These guys are in a hurry to get across the desert. Sometimes I wish we would take a little more time to appreciate the Sahara, but they're wanting to get back to Spain and their normal way of life as quickly as possible.

The next morning I was up early, put myself together, looked the motorcycle over and fixed a couple of things. By 06:00 we were off, them pushing me out of the sand. I hadn't gone 500 meters when I went down in deep sand.

Good morning.

I couldn't seem to maneuver or get any speed going in the miles of deep sand interlaced with rocks. During the morning, I must have went down twenty times or more! Each time, their vehicle would pull up behind me, sometimes with me stuck underneath the motorcycle. They would then lift it up off me, start it, and push it out of the sand. It was frustrating and physically very demanding for all concerned!

When riding, even if it is on the sand flat at fifty or fifty-five miles an hour, one must have total concentration. If your mind deviates - even for the smallest time - you'll hit something, or end up being flung off the motorcycle. If you are badly hurt in a place like this, I can assure you, the chances of making it back to civilization are very slim (it's a couple of hundred miles in either direction).

If I break an arm or anything else, are these guys going to be able to ride the motorcycle back? No, I don't think so. They would be putting themselves at unnecessary risk, plus, they are not qualified to ride something as big as the HAUG on the street, let alone in the Sahara.

What about a major breakdown, and if the motorcycle can't go on? There are two choices: remain with the motorcycle, or abandon it (the desert is littered with abandoned vehicles). I try to keep my mind off of these very grim scenarios. It is, as always, all or nothing.

Now we are hitting corrugations - washboard effects on the desert surface. They are the biggest I have ever seen, so my front wheel is bouncing in every direction, banging back and forth, up and down, the lower part of the front end being hammered into the upper fork tubes. My teeth are banging away; it is hard for me to get my vision to focus. I just try to skip across these washboard surfaces as quickly and safely as possible.

On the afternoon of the 4th day, we hit harder ground where there is a dirt track. We follow the dirt track for about 6 miles (10 kilometers), when we come upon **blessed asphalt**...we knew that we had made it to the end of the PIST!

Soon we would be in Tamanrasset.

Damaged Machine, Dead Batteries, and Deep Canyons

The asphalt, though very rough, was beautiful.

No more SAND!

We rode along this blessing for about another 20 miles (32 kilometers) until we came into Tamanrassot, a small city out in the middle of nowhere in the southern part of Algeria. We located the campground and set up camp. I went right to work on the motorcycle. The exhaust needed welding; I opened the primary, cleaned it out, and regreased the starter bendix drive; it is a wonder that the primary belt was still intact.

Many tourists came over to our camping area, photographing the Harley, asking

103

me questions. I quickly advised all who would listen **NOT** to cross the Sahara on a Harley Davidson! I felt quite a bit of pride, somewhat puffed up by all the attention; it was necessary to remind myself that had it not been for the Spaniards, I doubt very much if I would have gotten that far.

18:00: Took an ice-cold shower; there's no hot water at this facility - naturally! We drive over to a local hotel in their vehicle and had a nice meal (my treat... the least I could do for these fellows; I knew they were not going to take any money from me). We laughed about the adventures and misadventures we encountered coming over the PIST (we had covered over 450 miles [750 kilometers] in four days).

That night, as I climbed in my sleeping bag next to the motorcycle, I thought, "I don't *ever* want to see sand, dirt or mud roads ever again as long as I live! If its in this lifetime, it's too soon!" (Unfortunately, my future was to bring thousands more miles of sand, dirt, and mud roads.) I know the rest of the way to Tunis is all pavement, so I naively think, "Perhaps the hardest part of the trip is out of the way. Maybe it might even be possible for me now to just relax and enjoy some of the scenery."

At three the next morning, I was attacked by diarrhea, and spent the rest of the night putting myself together and then undoing myself again as I ran back and forth to the toilet.

06:00: The Spaniards get up and start packing; we had tea and cookies.

"I will miss them. They have been true friends and benefactors to me in this journey." We all shook hands, exchanged addresses, and then they drove off. I felt that very sad, empty feeling inside of me when I feel I'm losing good friends forever.

Alone again, I ride my motorcycle into town to locate a bank where I can change money (it is obligatory to change $100.00 while in Algeria). Once that was done, I go back to a garage and ask, "Do you do welding?"

"No problem," they reply.

The front exhaust pipe and carrying box needed to be rewelded. Both jobs took about two and one-half hours. When finished, the welder told me, "That will be 600 dinars ($20)."

I was aghast at such a price in a place where the average wage was just a few dollars a day or less. I got him down to five hundred dinar, but he would not take any less. In all my excitement about making it back to civilization, I had made a stupid mistake and ignored the golden rule - always ask the price first!

I relearned an expensive lesson.

The rest of the afternoon was spent in the campground meeting other people. One couple I met had a 1954 Royal Infield with a sidecar; they were going to attempt to cross the Sahara. "Good luck to you," I thought, "anything is possible." But truthfully, I didn't think they could do it. My deep-down thought was, "Good luck to you because you are going to work your ass off trying to get this under-powered thing across the PIST."

On the plus side, they picked the right month - the temperatures were hovering around 90 - 95 degrees. In the summer, when it was 125 degrees, they would burn a piston. The same is true on the Harley Davidson - that's why I opted to cross equatorial Africa during the rainy season... a cooler Sahara.

I had a late lunch/early dinner in the restaurant at the campground - camel meat and potatoes. Camel meat tastes and has the texture of the beast itself - bad and tough.

Many cars cross the desert, including the Mercedes, but the greatest car of all for desert crossings is the French Peugeot. Why? Because it durable and simple (in my opinion). Peugeot is the one most in demand in Niger of all the vehicles coming south, driven to Arlit (Arhli) for sale. The desert crossing is the only way to get vehicles into Niger.

As I lay back next to the motorcycle and close my day, I think, "Tomorrow... northward to Europe."

The next morning, I meet a couple of Australian fellows who were standing next to me, observing what I was doing. When I tried to start the motorcycle I discovered the battery was dead - and was to be an endless worry for the rest of Africa.

"Do you have a jumper cables?" I humbly asked.

Fortunately, they did.

We put cables on and jump-started the machine. Then, I reloaded it, shook hands with my rescuers, and took off, praying that the battery... not the alternator... was bad. At the first petrol station I came to, I left the motor running as I took on 32 liters of fuel (good quality, and quite cheap compared to Niger and some other places in Africa).

For the next 23 miles (forty kilometers), the road was very rough, full of pot holes, so I kept the motorcycle in second gear much of the time. I had to be on my toes (stumps, if you prefer) all the time, paying close attention to my speed. Sometimes, I'd come into an area where the whole road was full of potholes for stretches up to 100 meters. If I hit these things at a high speed, I would break something. The last thing I wanted to do was blow the front tire with its delicate tube in it.

There are stretches of dirt road full of deep corrugations that shake me so violently that I can't see straight and my teeth chatter.

Late in the morning, the motorcycle starts dragging. Pulling over, I discover that the rear brake is locking up again, smoking badly. "Bloody hell, will there ever be any let up of the problems with this BASTARD motorcycle?" I wonder in disgust! My main hope is that I haven't burned up the seals on the wheel cylinder. To make it possible to carry on, I take half an hour to let it cool, then back the adjustment all the way off the brake. The only reason I can see for the failure is that when the brake is applied, the master cylinder is hanging up because it is full of sand and doesn't return the way it should, causing the rear brake to drag.

"I'll have to take care of it when I get to Europe," I think.

Of course, I'd also have to fix the front break lever (most of the PIST had been conquered with a broken front break lever from one of my *numerous* falls).

As I rode, I saw massive sand dunes rising hundreds of feet in the air, often taller than city buildings. The distinctive rock formations were sometimes beautiful, sometimes majestic, and always awe-inspiring. I was growing to appreciate the vastness of the desert.

When I stop to put in more fuel, there is a dead desert silence.

No vehicles.

No motorcycle engine.

Nothing.

Just the road, the motorcycle, and me... thousands of miles from home in the middle of the Sahara Desert!

Stopped in the town of Arak at a camping area. Not knowing whether or not the motorcycle would start in the morning, I felt it best to be where I could jump start it if necessary. An Arab fellow approached me at the campground with an unusual comment: "George Bush?" he asked.

"Non George Bush," I replied quickly.

The fellow seemed to relax. We shook hands, and he brought me some bread while I worked on my motorcycle. Next, my new friend started heating a big tub of water, then he motioned and said, "Douche," meaning "Have wash."

During the dinner he made for us, we watched a magnificent sunset, and then, for about an hour afterwards, we spoke about the Gulf War with me using my broken French and well-worn dictionary.

His kindness and hospitality were simple, but from the heart. He wouldn't take any money from me for staying in his campground, although that night I was his only customer. When I did lay down to go to sleep, he brought out a mattress for me to lay on in the dirt. It was with a very warm feeling of friendship that I closed the day.

Up early the next morning, I did my pushups, and had my breakfast (leftovers from the night before). Once loaded up, it was time to break the stillness of the morning by starting the motorcycle. By seven o'clock, the sun started coming up in the canyon... it was amazingly beautiful!

Blues and pinks turning from twilight to day light.

December 7, 1990: My friend and benefactor came out, we shook hands and said "Avoue." Knowing I didn't have enough gasoline to make it to the next town because the gas station that was supposed to be in Arak didn't exist, I expected to run dry during the morning, deciding to go just as far as I could. There was enough fuel for a 100 miles (160 km.) or so. Then, we will see what happens.

Before me was open country and some of the most beautiful sand dunes I have ever seen. The biggest hazard a person can encounter while traveling on the road in this part of the Sahara is the dune coming across the road. There are usually signs up saying "Sable," meaning "sand" or "danger" in French (I'm not sure which).

Sometimes, the road is clear, and sometimes a dune covers the road... so absolute attention is required. If the dune is covering the road, you hit the throttle, keeping the speed up on the motorcycle. That way, when you hit the ruts in it, you have a better chance of keeping control until you hit the tarmac again.

And, above all else, don't wander off into the desert! There are no markers to show you which way back to civilization.

The road north was good through these great, deep canyons, very beautiful in the early morning as the sun came down on the dunes, so red and clear. It was one of those times when a person gets a true feeling of freedom, of being part of a great adventure.

My first destination was In Salah, but I didn't have enough petrol to make it. After about 100 miles (160 km.), I ran out of fuel.

I waited.

It wasn't too long before some French people came by in their Peugeots. These "commercial tourists" were going to attempt to take their Peugeots across the Sahara to Arlit (Arhli) or Agadze to sell them, make a profit, then fly back to France. They kindly gave me ten liters of fuel and refused my money. However, they did take some photographs of this very funny looking motorcycle and the even funnier looking man.

11:30 a.m.: Rolled into In Salah and took on a full fuel load, then headed on to El Goléa. After only a few miles, the motorcycle started missing badly due to a condenser problem. I had to keep it down under a certain rpm to prevent it missing.

More open desert, and very beautiful blue and black mountains in the distance rising up out of the desert floor like great monoliths reaching into the sky. About 17:00, I arrived in El Goléa, where the weather had turned very cold. Sand had been blowing across the road all afternoon, and the realization now struck me on this afternoon that I had crossed into the northern Sahara's winter.

Evil Eye, Frozen Ass, and Hand Cranks

In El Goléa, I saw a group Algerian women walking along the street. All of them were completely covered in black except for one eye which I call "the evil eye." These women view the world out of this one eye... the rest of them is completely covered! It is said that after their wedding day, the only place they will ever know is their husband's house, and an occasional small walk to the market place. "What a miserable existence!" I think as they pass.

Locate a campground, pull in, and start to work cleaning out the spark plugs and the points. I examine my fuel bowl just to make sure there's no dirt in the carburetor. As I perform these maintenance tasks, in pull four Peugeots with German commercial tourists. They come over to look at the motorcycle.

We chat, and then they invite me to dinner (they didn't have to ask twice!). As we chatted, the women cooked up a beautiful spaghetti dinner which was eaten with great relish. About 20:30, after a cup of hot tea, I crawled into my sleeping bag.

In cold weather, I usually wore my space jacket for warmth - but it had fallen apart during that very day. I had given my heavier jacket away in Zaire to lighten my load. Tonight, all I could muster was a light wind breaker and sweatshirt. As I fell asleep, I remember thinking, "This is Pearl Harbor Day."

03:00: Roosters wake me very early; couldn't get back to sleep. Their stupid crowing always reminds me that the time of peace and tranquillity are over, and that the struggles of a new day are about to begin.

Got up, did my pushups, made a cup of tea, and sat quietly in the early morning until just after 08:00 (when the Germans finally got up). I didn't feel right in starting up the motorcycle and waking them, especially after all their kindness and hospitality the night before. Had it not been for that hospitality, I can assure that I would not have hesitated to start up.

When I tried to start up, there was no power. So much for evil thoughts.

Upon investigation, I found that my negative terminal on the battery was broken.

"Good Morning! It's gonna be a great day," I thought to myself sarcastically. It took another half hour to fix the problem and get rolling.

The desert is freezing cold this morning... the coldest day of the journey. I'm freezing my ass off! Plus, the wind is blowing sand into the air, and when it hits, it hurts! I have my face covered with a bandanna to shelter me from the penetrating sandstorm.

I came upon a Japanese motorcyclist; the poor fellow was having mechanical problems, so I tried to help him. "I'm heading back to France," he told me. "My motorcycle is running, but it just won't go very fast." I examined his motorcycle, but could not spot anything wrong. As I rode away, with both of us waiving, I felt very sorry for him. "Was there anything else I could have done for him?" I wondered to myself. Maybe wrongly, I went on anyway, knowing he would get through the desert - albeit very slowly.

As the miles drift by, it is getting colder and colder. Oh how I longed for the warmth of my space jacket now!

Heading north, I finally arrive in Ghardaia where I go to a service station and ask the all important question: "Excuse me, sir, can you tell me where I can buy a jacket in this town?"

No one understood my English. By now, I'm at the point of total frustration because of this language problem I've been battling for a couple of months. Language barriers make it almost impossible to get anything done. It is so frustrating and difficult to describe to the reader how I feel when this occurs continually.

Riding about town, I run into a man on a motor scooter who guided me over to a campground where I met a fellow who could speak a bit of English - a Burber named Arabei. I told Arabei I was looking to buy a jacket and some other warm clothing, and he replied, "I will look into it."

In the campground I also met a Swiss couple, Jerry, and Valeri. We talked for a bit, and then they said those magic words - "Why don't you join us for dinner tonight?" I never say no to these invitations... anything is better than my cooking!

Since I have spent much of my military time in the bush, it was fairly easy for me to fall back into the mold of living rough, probably much easier than for the average person. But even for me, in the midst of the freezing weather, it felt extra good to get a *hot* shower - my first since I was in Central Africa the night of the Marine Corps ball (you remember, I was the dummy with the cake and the dirty fork!). It is only when you don't have luxuries that you really miss them.

Arabei lived in this campground in a little pup tent; everything he had in the world was here with him. Yet, he unselfishly and happily gave me some old clothes, a sweater and a cap - the cap I still have to this day, and a few other odds and ends. When I went to pay him, he said, "No, you insult me. Please, you take."

As we became better acquainted, Arabei shared with me the problems the Burbers were having with the Moslem Algerians. "We get the worse jobs, or get passed over so they can have the jobs. Life is very difficult for us." He paused, as if to hold back the pain, then continued. "I spent two years in the Army, and was qualified to be an Officer, but was not allowed to because I am a Burber."

As a fellow military man, I felt very sorry for Arabei. Yet, he held no bitterness towards the Moslems, or the world. He was just a fellow who wanted to make a living and live a normal life... somewhere besides in a pup tent.

Ghardaia is an Arab city, so the first thing I hear early in the morning is the holy being called to pray. It is an eerie wailing sound, something that can send shivers up one's spine if one doesn't know what is being chanted.

I got up, packed the motorcycle, and when the others arose, I said "Good-Bye" to them and went to start up.

Nothing.

The battery terminal had again come away. I had to push it up to make contact with a piece of rubber, but it wasn't going to work any longer. So Jerry volunteered, "We can fix this." He put tape around the corner of the battery, and then took the terminal and stuck it back on to the place where it broke off, then fixed the battery negative lead to that, filling it all in with a resin, that, when hard, would hold it in place.

We then sat for a couple of hours drinking coffee and eating bread, waiting for the resin to set. When it did, we put the battery back in the motorcycle. We hit the starter, and it went "Wom, Wom," but the motor didn't turn over. I opened up the primary, and sure enough, I had broken another primary belt! "It was a good thing I waited all that time in Bangui, Central Africa, to get those extra belts sent over to me," I thought. By the time I had the belt changed it was early afternoon, so I decided to spent the rest of the day at the camp, wanting to change my oil, but nothing was open during this time of day... it was prayer time.

After 16:00, Jerry and I went into town in a taxi. We purchased some oil, came back, drained the old oil out and put in the new. "There," I thought, "that should take me to England."

That night I had another wonderful dinner fixed by Valerie and enjoyed by me and a few others at the campground. We had a jolly good time, trying to understand our French and English, back and forth, with camaraderie shared as only travelers can.

Jerry and Valerie had their Volkswagen van fixed up very nicely, but encountered problems in Algeria the week before when their windows were smashed out by protesters. To this point in my journey, I had not seen anything like this destructiveness. Throughout my travels, I practice trying to look like I do not have a lot of money (it's easy when you're broke!) - no designer clothes, no chrome on the motorcycle. I do a very good job at looking poor so as not to attract negative attention. If you look like you have a lot of money, or appear to be a wealthy foreigner, especially in a country as poor as Algeria (with a high unemployment rate), the residents tend to become mean to strangers who look like they have everything. In fact, when you comparatively examine our lives with someone like Arabie, we *do* have everything!

The next morning, my battery was dead again!

Now I know I have a real problem.

We managed to put the jumper leads on from Jerry's van and start the motorcycle up, then load it while the engine warmed up. We all said "good-bye," took some photos, then I rode out... alone again, feeling that old emptiness closing in on me.

During the early part of the day, the battery seemed to be taking a charge, so I concluded that my charging system must be okay, and that the battery is the problem.

But that did not solve my headaches on this particular day.

Going through the small town of El Alia, my front tire went flat again. I rode it, rough though it was, to a little battery shop. There the locals gathered as I took the front wheel off, pulled the tube out, and determined that the valve stem was leaking. I didn't quite know what to do with this; I was surprised it had lasted as long as it did (Estephan had done a very good job. During the crossing of the PIST, I had seven flat tires - two rear, five front - and none attributable to make-shift valve repair...it had lasted approximately 1500 miles).

One fellow standing in the crowd, a man who seemed to be a leader, said, "You can leave your motorcycle here. You don't need to worry about it. Come with me."

He motioned me into his car and took me to a tiny tire shop where the owner, to my very great wonderment, managed to repair the tube again! By now it was full of patches, and the valve stem had been taken out and repaired twice. I was just amazed at what these people could do with so little.

The fellow with the car took me back to my motorcycle and I put the tube in and on to the tire. Then he said in French, "Please come to my house for lunch." In my heart, all I really wanted to do was just to get going. But to have said no would have insulted him, so I followed him over through the little back alleys of clay, adobe buildings - not at all like the normal cement and cinder block houses I had seen in other parts of my journey. We parked and went inside his house; everything was clean and neat. We sat down on a rug and had a very nice lunch. There were some amazing Arab tapestries on the wall, and this fellow even had a television! "This man is obviously somebody important," I thought to myself. "Only the important and the wealthy can afford such niceties in this country."

After we were done, and enjoying coffee, his brother came along and ate all the leftovers.

When we parted, I rode out of town and arrived in Touggourt about 16:30. I began my usual search for a campground, but with no luck. Now irate, I was also aggravated by the fact that I knew my battery would be dead in the morning from sitting overnight.

With my mood completely soured, I finally found a cheap hotel called "The Oasis" (a dive by any other name) and checked in.

I had to remove every bit of my gear off the motorcycle and bring it into my room for security; then, I worked on the motorcycle for about an hour. My day ended about 19:30 after a shower - without lights - believe it or not!

The next morning started out rough. I was up early, heated my leftovers from the night before for my breakfast, then loaded up the motorcycle. As I was pushing it towards the front gate, I lost balance and it fell over. By this time, I was in a rage. I turned around, grabbed the excess gear that was packed around the box, pulled it all off, and then, just out of shear meanness (I don't know how else I could have done it), I picked up the machine and managed to get it up on it's wheels.

Then, I reloaded it.

When I am ready to start it - you know the routine by now - the battery is dead. Back to hand cranking. By this time, even though it is freezing cold, all of my jackets are off as I work myself into a virtual frenzy until suddenly it starts.

Burdddddddddddd.

The motor is running at idle. I reach up very slowly, as if sneaking up on the throttle, then grab it and rev it high.

Rmmmmmmmmmmmmm, Rmmmmmmmmmmmmm.

"Please don't quit!" I think, exhausted and by now sweating blood.

When I got the idle to settle down and rev to a point where I knew it wouldn't just pop and quit on me, I reloaded the entire machine, got on it and finally left the hotel behind.

I don't like staying in these dollar or two per night hotels because if I have any major problems, such as starting my motorcycle, I would rather be in a campground where there might be some people with jumper cables (I never saw jumper cables in Algeria or Tunis unless possessed by a foreigner).

As I am riding out of the town, I think to myself, "Well, this day is off on another positive note. The Dave Barr Flying Circus is on the road!"

Snow, Stares, Stairs, and Soaked

I made good time for about the first 115 miles (185 km.), stopping, to fuel up out of one of the cans. Then, on to Biskra, a very modern, European-looking city with concrete buildings and high rise apartments - things I hadn't seen yet. As I rode through Biskra and out the other side of town, the terrain truly changed.

"I have exited the Sahara!" I thought, silently rejoicing.

I rode over a mountain pass, and as I came down the other side, sure enough it started snowing. On a journey like this, it seems that when you finish with one set of problems, you immediately get a new set. I had left the Sahara with its high winds, facial sand blasting, and mechanical problems on the motorcycle, and then bingo... over one mountain pass into snow and horrible head winds blowing the stuff into my face! Fortunately, my ears are not freezing too badly because I have Arabie's cap on (to this day, I still have that cap. Wherever its really cold, I put it on and say, "Come on, Arabie, let's go."). Other than my ears, the rest of me is freezing and I'm now soaked to the bone.

I can't see very well as I ride through the snow, the headwinds, and the freezing cold. The snow stuck to my glasses; I was constantly riding with one finger over the lenses, acting as a wiper to keep the snow off. I made good time despite all of this.

The terrain became scrub brush, looking much like San Bernardino, in California. As I approached a small town called Ain M'lila, I felt my front end get wishy/washy; the tire was going flat again. Since my speed was about 55 mph, I held on for dear life. There was a van close behind me, so I tried to cautiously motion him around me while I fought to hold on to the handlebars without falling off the motorcycle. There was no shoulder at this point in the road, and my vision was increasingly limited by the snow sticking to my glasses. I managed to wrestle the thing off the road, onto a narrow, very steep shoulder that suddenly appeared with a deep drop.

This immediate challenge demanded every skill I had to keep the motorcycle from falling down, going over the steep shoulder, or losing control and ending up back out on the pavement, causing an accident (where I would surely come off second best). Finally, I somehow managed to bring the machine to a stop.

The two fellows I had been cautioning pulled in right behind me and asked, "Is there a problem?"

"No shit there's a problem!" I thought. "I've always got a fucking problem."

My answer was much more civil, "Yes, there's a problem. Do you folks have a jack?"

They did, so we lifted up the front of the motorcycle and I took the wheel off. They took the wheel, told me to wait, then drove on into Ain M'lila. For the next half-hour, I sat in the freezing wind and falling snow.

When they came back, they said, "Your tube is finished."

Of course, I didn't have another tube, so they went back to Ain M'lila, bringing back the owner of a garage... with all his sons... in a Peugeot pickup. It took all five of us to lift the motorcycle with no front wheel and put it on the back of the pickup. I sat in the back with the motorcycle while they took me to their little tire shop in the outskirts of Ain M'lila.

"Tomorrow solution," the father told me, suggesting I go to a hotel. The two fellows who befriended me took me about 21 miles (34 kilometers) to the closest cheap hotel. When they let me off, I offered to pay them for their help, but they didn't want anything to do with it. For the most part, I found this to be the attitude all across Algeria.

After checking into the hotel, I endured many people staring at this bizarre and dirty looking foreigner who walked funny, and whose right leg made a horrible grinding noise as I walked. My joints were all worn out - both in the ankle and the knee on the right leg. As I was climbing up the stairs with my soaked saddlebags on my shoulders, I managed to fall down with everybody looking at me.

I get so sick of the stares when I fall.

I cooked dinner in my room, ate and read awhile, then laid back to try and count the blessings of the day. It was hard to discover them. I had ridden about 280 miles (400 kilometers) in freezing cold and snow. I told myself, "That's really pretty good mileage for all the bad weather and hassles of the day."

The next morning, I ate my dinner leftovers, went downstairs in a foul mood, and caught the porter sleeping. After rudely waking him up, he got me some coffee and a crescent roll. Then I walked out of the hotel with all my gear on my shoulders, out to the main road, standing for about a half hour in the freezing rain before finally catching a taxi to take me the 21 miles (34 km) back to Ain M'lila and the garage. The trip only cost me about three dollars (an excellent rate, mainly because the gas in Algeria was very cheap.)

The garage was opened at seven thirty by the father with his four sons. They told

111

me, "Sit down and wait." Dib Nabil, one of the sons, got into a truck and took off looking for a tube. About ten o'clock we had coffee and a very sweet cake with atomic energy in it. After that, I was revving - ready to work, but with nothing to do. Dib came back about noontime, reporting "no luck" in his search to finding an inner tube (I knew he wouldn't find one in this town).

After a big sandwich, Dib and I drove into Constantine to continue the search for a tube, but again, no luck. Then Dib suddenly hit the top of his head with his hand, as if he just received a brainstorm. We left the 3-ton Fiat truck and took a taxi down to the local gendarmaine (Police Station). Dib did some fast talking to these fellows who weren't noted for being a real benevolent bunch of characters. We were brought in front of a high ranking officer who spoke a little bit of English.

"I cannot find an inner tube for my Harley Davidson anywhere," I told him. "Can you help me?"

Within thirty minutes, his assistants brought me two 19" BMW wide profile tubes that they use in their police motorcycles. "Thank you" very much," I said, not knowing if these would work. "Will these fit into a 21 inch, narrow profile tire?" I wondered to myself, thankful for any port in the storm.

The policemen refused my money.

We took a cab back to where Dib had parked the 3 ton truck, then drove it Ain M'lila, about 25 miles (40 km.) away. Upon arriving, we forced the tube into the tire, and although it had a couple of lumps in it, it still seemed to hold air.

By now, it was almost dark. It had been snowing all day; the weather was miserable. I decided to go back to the hotel, so Dib drove me the 21 miles (34 km.) back to the hotel where I spent another night.

Up early the next morning, I was greeted by the sound of the wind howling outside. "Oh great," I thought, "very soon I'll be out in that cold, wet weather." I caught one cab into town, then another to Ain M'lila. At the garage, I loaded up the motorcycle. When I went to pay the father in French Francs (not dinars, since they are desperate for foreign currency), he said, "Non, messier," with his four sons standing behind him.

"Please, messier, take the money, you deserve it," I insisted, wanting to pay him for the all their kindness and help.

"Non, messier," he repeated again. "Por Allah," he said, meaning, "For Allah" (their God). "Go in peace."

Later, I learned that Algerians consider strangers coming into their midst a reincarnation of Mohammed, returned to earth. They are given three days to prove differently. Since I never spent more than two days with any group of Algerians, I never found out what happens when they discover you aren't Mohammed!

While riding, right from the start, I had a wobble in the front end of the motorcycle, so I had to hold on tight with both hands. The wobble was caused by the 19" tube bunched up inside the 21" tire. The motorcycle has problems with stability, especially around corners.

On this very cold, miserably wet morning I said "good-bye" to these very fine men and rode in the direction of Tunis. Since I did not have a rain jacket, I was getting soaked and freezing my ass off. Naturally, in the Dave Barr tradition of making a hard trip impossible, I took a wrong turn and ended up in road construction for miles and miles (with plenty of mud in the construction area!).

I journeyed about one hundred miles on my corrected course before I needed gasoline. After fueling up, the thing wouldn't start again.

The battery was dead.

In my best French, I asked some of the gas station customers if anyone had jumper cables. Despite my clearest, "Kables, kables, messier?," they did not comprehend what I was saying, shaking their heads to indicate they did not understand.

Finally, a fellow came up to me and asked me in French, "Problem, messier?" I explained my jumper cable situation the best I could, and he replied, "Come with me."

Naturally, I was not excited about leaving my motorcycle, but not to come with him would have been an insult. He seemed to know what I was thinking, since he replied in French, "Don't worry about the motorcycle."

We went to a garage and found a piece of loose cable (mind you, I have not seen a jumper cable anywhere in Niger or Algeria unless it was owned by a foreigner!). We went back to the motorcycle with the cable. I then stripped off the ends, cut the cable in half, took a borrowed battery and hooked it up - the motorcycle started right away!

I thanked this very kind man for his help, and he asked me, "Do you have money for food?"

"Yes," I replied, "enough to get to the border." Then he said, "No, that's not enough. Here are 50 Dinars. Make sure you get something to eat." Then, with a handshake, we parted company, and I carried on.

Rare Jumper Cables and Wobbly Rides

The road went from bad to worse.

Rain turned to snow and mud (fortunately, gravel was underneath the mud, so I didn't fall off).

Upon entering the town of Souk Ahras, the gendarmaine advised me not to try and make the border that night, but to just go and get a room. I went to a local garage and asked the owner if the motorcycle could sleep inside his garage for the night. "Yes," he replied, "but you will have to wait outside until after five o'clock when I close."

"Do you have any jumper cables?

"No, and frankly, I don't know where you can pick up any," the man named Bill replied.

Bill directed me to a very cheap hotel that only cost about $1.50 a night. I unloaded my motorcycle and carried all my gear over to the hotel where I checked in, went upstairs to my room, then laid back, soaking wet, freezing, panting, out of breath, my stumps killing me from carrying gear up stairs. It was a miserable room, with one light bulb hanging from the ceiling. At times like this, it is hard to keep up my morale.

16:30: I go down to the motorcycle. Somebody comes out of the cafe and gives me a cup of coffee and won't take any money for it. At five o'clock, Bill motions me over with the motorcycle and we move it safely inside the garage.

I went to buy some bread, but the fellow would not take any money. A little bit later, I have something to eat in one of the many "hole in the wall" eating houses: Eggs, a bagel, and a bowl of chickpea soup. When I finished, this fellow would not take any money either! For all the problems that I encountered, this special treatment from these perfect strangers - people who are poor themselves, and appreciate what I am doing - says to me, "KEEP GOING NO MATTER WHAT."

I only made 132 miles (211 km) this day.

That night, while having dinner, I talked with the proprietor of the restaurant about religion and about America. Of course, I never mentioned my time living in South

Africa, nor did I bring up Saddam Hussein and the problems in Iraq. Funny enough, except for the "George Bush" comment in the southern part of the Sahara, I never had any problems or felt any animosity toward me for being an American.

The next morning, I went down to the garage and I waited about twenty minutes for them to open up. After loading my motorcycle, IT WOULD NOT START! No shit.

And, there were no jumper cables.

"Maybe you can try another garage," Bill advised. I did, but they also had no jumper cables. This was especially fun since it was raining hard... and I was getting soaked.

Next, I decided to try and push the thing. There was a bit of a downhill slope from the garage, so downhill we went.

It didn't start.

Some street kids got involved, pushing me to another place where it was downhill - this time it started! I offered these kids some money, but they wouldn't take it.

I was just out of town, fighting snow on the road, when my worse fears came true after about ten miles. Up in these mountains there is ice on the roads, and the gendarmaines there said, "You have to turn around and go back. This road to Tunis is closed, and there is no other way."

Of course, the language barrier made any discussion impossible. And so, in this miserable weather, I turn around and I head back to Souk Ahras.

Just out of town, the motor starts to run real bad, then finally quits. I manage to roll it downhill near a place that is supposed to be a garage; a fellow helps me push it inside. We put the battery on a charge, and I open up the points plate and have a look, turning my back to go get something out of my tool box. One fellow near the motor takes out a wrench and goes for the bolt that holds the advance mechanism in; it is a little, thin bolt with a big head. "If he gets that wrench on it, he is going to break it," I thought, "and I am really going to be in trouble."

I shout "Non, non."

It was that close. He actually had the wrench on the head, ready to apply torque. Quickly, he pulled his hand away.

"Thank you," I said, greatly relieved, "but please, leave that alone."

The engine had been running terrible, "Probably because the battery was bad and not making good contact," I reasoned. We cleaned the terminals as best we could, charged up the battery, and eventually got the motorcycle to start up.

It seemed to run a little better.

Saying good-bye to these good Samaritans who would take no money for their services, I rode out.

A good distance out of town, near the Algerian border, I stopped to fuel up, letting the engine run. Once at the Algerian border, the police told me to shut the motorcycle off.

"The battery is no good," I told him.

"Shut it off regardless," they replied.

So, I shut down the motorcycle and went into their office to take care of the formalities. Afterwards, when the motorcycle would not re-start, the police pushed the thing and it started right up. Looking back as I rode out, I waived to the police and screamed "Viva Algeria." They all held up their hands, hollered and waived back. "I'm leaving behind me a fine country and a very fine people."

On I went for a few miles, and approached the Tunisian border. The difference between the Algerians and the Tunisians is like night and day. The Tunisian customs and immigrations cleared me with no problem. They too told me I had to shut my motorcycle off, but when I asked for a push, they said "No, you can roll the motorcycle downhill, back towards Algeria."

This was courting disaster, but there was nothing else I could do. Rolling it down the hill, it would not start. A fellow walking back to Algeria from Tunis volunteered to help push it back to the top of the hill, a good 200 meters. I paid this guy what change I had in my pocket, and he was very happy. "The Tunisians are not like the Algerians," he told me. "They are not very nice at all" (I was soon to find this out). "The custom's official actually told me NOT to help you."

When I started pushing it out of the customs station towards a gas station that was about 150 meters away, a custom's official (not any of the ones I had dealt with) came out and helped me push it to the gas station. The owner of the gas station, Mohammed, said he would charge the battery, but that the motorcycle would have to stay outside. "It will be safe," he told me, "because I sleep just inside. It will be next to my window."

Now I must find a place to change some money, and locate a flop house for the night; the place I found was only a dollar. Then, I had some dinner (chicken, not rubberized!). That evening as I laid back in a room with six beds in it (but nobody in there with me), I thought, "What will tomorrow bring?"

The city of Tunis was 120 miles away (210 kilometers), and it had been another lousy but interesting day. The hospitality was great on the Algerian side, but the Tunisians certainly had a few lessons to learn about courtesy. I had literally pushed the motorcycle into Tunisia.

The following day I got up, had something to eat, then went down to Mohammed's petrol station where we put the battery back into the motorcycle. I tried to start it. Deader than a mackerel.

Next, I tried to explain to Mohammed that I wanted jumper cables.

No dice - they didn't have any, and had no knowledge of them.

What next?

I tried to hand crank it.

No go.

One of the Arab fellows watching this farce tried his hand at starting it... it doesn't fire at all. No backfire. Nothing.

Next, I walked all over town for several hours, trying to locate jumper cables. There is no such thing in this town or anywhere - either in Algeria or here. It is amazing. Two countries without even one set of jumper cables!

The last alternative was to put the motorcycle in the back of a pickup and haul it across to Tunis and the harbor. I ask everybody that comes into Mohammed's if they want to be paid to put the motorcycle in the back of their vehicle and take it to Tunis. Finally, a fellow named Armar says "Yes, I'll do it. Wait here until I come back. I've got some business to take care of."

When Armar returns in his Peugeot pickup, we load the motorcycle up into the back and take off down the road in a truck that was four wheels mounted on junk. The front wheel was shaking and shimmering; "Here we go again," I thought. "Another bright adventure on the back of a truck."

On the way to Tunis, I didn't really have a great look at the countryside as I was feeling a bit crest fallen with a motorcycle in the back of the truck that wouldn't start or run. As we moved on, I noticed a military cemetery from World War II and I thought to myself, "Here they rest, thousands of miles from their homes, all alone, nobody to come and visit their graves. They're just here - by themselves."

115

Armar had agreed on a certain price, and when we arrived at the docks, he took me right to where I would have to go to load the motorcycle onto the ferry. Armar and his friend and I off loaded the motorcycle, nearly breaking our backs.

When the time for payment came, he didn't want Tunisian money, he wanted French Francs. That was fine with me, but I didn't have the correct amount of change. We argued back and forth; Armar and his friend tried to crowd me and I would just push them back away, very gently, so as not to invoke anger.

The argument escalating, getting much more heated. If there's anything I don't like, it is being cheated by people in a foreign country. The difference between the Tunisians and Algerians was illustrated here; these two guys had turned into a couple of assholes, and I wasn't going to take their shit.

Another person heard the argument and came over, getting involved. He maintained that they should give me what I wanted for change. They gave him the change, and he gave it to me. The two men then got into the truck, started up and drove away. As I examined the amount of change he gave me, I discovered they had shorted me by about $5.00.

To double the irony, before I was able to check the change, and before they got into the vehicle to drive off, these two men had the gall to ask me for another dinar so they could get something to eat.

"Fuck you," I thought.

That was how our short relationship ended. Of course, I got stung in the end. "I hope your wheels fall of on the way back," I thought lovingly as Armar drove off.

On the bright side, we cleared the border and drove about 50 kilometers. The sun came out and had stayed out all the way to the city of Tunis. Although it was still freezing cold, at least there was sun.

Later that afternoon, somebody who worked at the port came up to me and asked, "What are you going to do...wait two days next to the motorcycle for a ship to come?"

"I don't know," I replied.

"Well," he said "we can try to pull it to a garage, and then you can spend sometime at a cheap hotel and wait."

That sounded better than sleeping on cold cement here at the port.

We tried to pull the motorcycle (with a car), but as soon as I put it into gear, it slid and down I went, bang, at about 20 miles an hour. The motorcycle wasn't damaged, but I was a little bruised. We called it a day, and I realized that the machine was never going to work trying to start it that way.

I tried to start it by hand, but no go, even though the points seemed in order. The battery was just so dead that there was no way I was going to get it to go.

That depressing night was spent at the port, next to the motorcycle. The following morning, custom officials told me, "You will have to move the motorcycle." They radiated a negative, surly attitude - absolutely arrogant assholes.

It was going to be at least another day before the boat for Marseilles arrived, and in the midst of the waiting, I'm never sure about what is being said to me. The language barrier is so disheartening at times, no, ALL of the time!

My mood is as foul as the weather. The rain and wind make it miserable, especially at night when I try to huddle between my baggage as a shelter from the wind.

"Things could be worse," I thought, but I'm not sure I meant it. After all, the circumstances were a bit bleak. I'm stuck in Tunis, heading for Europe, but my motorcycle doesn't run!

On the plus side, I have come a long way, and made it NEAR the top of Africa. Unfortunately, I couldn't ride the last mile across Africa to get to the port (we can't have everything).

My 2nd day at port, the ship finally came in and everybody debarked. The following morning, it was time to load. Of course, the motorcycle still wouldn't start, so as all the cars lined up, I pushed the motorcycle. As the cars moved forward, I moved. Once I cleared the gate to customs and immigrations, a fellow came behind me to help push. Of course, he leaned the motorcycle over too far, and down it went. We struggled to pick it up, then push it all the way to customs and immigrations. After clearing customs, I went and changed some money.

Next, I've got to get the motorcycle on the ship, and it ain't going to be with me riding on it. Another Tunisian fellow gets behind me, and we start pushing the beast up the ramp, me sweating blood by this time. My stumps are in agony pushing up the ramp. Finally inside the ship, I secure it. My helper starts to walk off before I can pay him. I called after him, and gave him all the change in my pocket - a couple of dinars - money well earned. It was refreshing to find somebody in Tunis who was kind, and not just after a quick buck.

During the trip, I have lost about fifteen pounds, which causes my stumps to piston up and down; the knee and the ankle joint on the right leg are shot. So, it is an effort to walk, and to especially carry things. On the boat, the climb up two flights of stairs to my room was horrible.

As the ship pulled out, I met a German fellow named Attila, who had his hair all shaved off, maybe trying to look like the mystical figure, Attila the Hun. Attila introduced me to Urnst and another German fellow; they all traveling together. We had a nice conversation, then they left me alone with my thoughts on the fantail of the boat where I watched the coast of Africa pulling away.

"Oh dear God, how did I make it across all of that?" I wondered. My mind flashed all the miles, the apprehension, the fear, the pain, the problems with the road, the people, the motorcycle, the weather. In a flood of emotion, I said a prayer of thanks for the strength and help that had been given me while transversing the continent of Africa.

In the distance I could see the city of Bizerte, one place I did not visit (I felt truly crest fallen about that). On the lighter side, I thought, *"I'm probably the first man in the world to ever traverse the continent of Africa, from Cape Agullas, to Tunis City, on a Harley Davidson."*

Later that day, Urnst, Stephen, Attila and I all got together up on the deck of the ferry. In sharing my problem of the non-starting motorcycle, and my need to find a Harley Davidson shop, Stephen said, "I know of a Harley Davidson shop in Marseilles." They told me they had jumper cables with them, so we could try to start it that way when we arrived in Marseilles.

Could my luck be changing?

We met in the fantail of the ship that evening. With my little gas cooker, I cooked up a nice meal for dinner, avoiding the costly cafeteria of the ship. We talked, and I learned that Urnst was a Discotheque Owner and Stephen was a Physicist - very intelligent company. I never came to understand how Attila got his money, although he looked like he could be a bouncer in Urnst's disco.

10:30: Closed my day on the Mediterranean Ocean, leaving Africa behind.

The next morning, I got up very early and went to the fantail of the ship. There was no one around. In the solitude, I took my late father's shirt off which I had worn every single day of the journey across Africa. It was literally a rag, and as I took it off, I thought of the miles put behind me, across the continent of Africa.

Symbolically, I threw the shirt over the back of the ship and into the ocean.

Stage one was over.

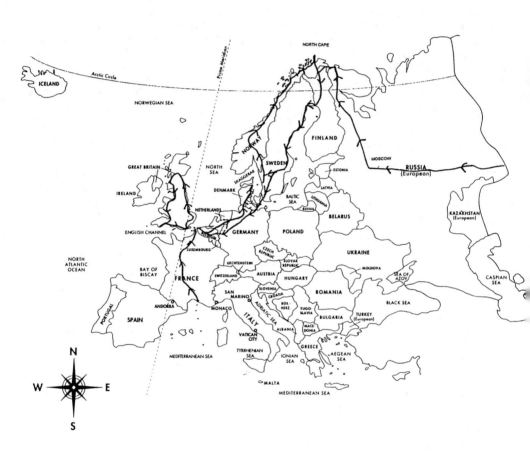

Stage Two: Europe

Chapter Twelve

Changing Continents, Changing Problems

11:00: We put into the port of Marseilles!

It was bitterly cold, but not snowing or raining.

Pushing the motorcycle off the ramp, we jumped into my new friends Range Rover and went to clear customs and immigration. The radio in the rover blared out Rock 'n Roll.

What a great way to signal I was now in Europe!

"Give me that old time rock and roll..." and other songs with similar lyrics sent my toes... I mean pegs... a tapping!

After leaving customs, we drove back as close as we could to the motorcycle, but still had to push it three quarters of a mile back to their vehicle. After hooking up the jumper leads, we couldn't get the thing to turn over. With the help of the jumper cables, and then kick starting, it finally turned over and started up... will wonders never cease?

Stephan climbed on his enduro bike and led the way across Marseilles to the Harley Davidson shop. Stephan went in and spoke to the owner in French, a man named Philip. When Philip saw the motorcycle, he said to me in broken English, "Messier, what have you done to this Harley Davidson? It looks terrible!"

"Well, I have just come from Johannesburg on it," I replied, trying to sound as casual as I could, as if I had just returned from a little ride across the entire continent of Africa! He ranted and raved about the bike for a few more minutes, but once he settled down, he began to understand the enormity of what this motorcycle had endured.

"Well, let's wheel it inside," Philip told me.

It was too late to start working on the motorcycle, so Philip gave me directions to a cheap hotel (which wasn't so cheap). I stopped at a number of little flop houses along the way, and they all wanted thirty to forty dollars for one night! By now, my stumps were killing me; after walking a couple of kilometers with my saddlebags on my shoulder, I almost felt like I couldn't go on. Finally, I didn't feel like arguing about rates anymore, so I just took a small room.

Out of Africa

That evening I called Mom; it was good to hear her voice.

"Mom, I've made it to Europe okay, and Africa is behind me!" I told her with great excitement and relief. She was very glad to hear that; we wished each other our love, and hung up.

Now, time for food. I painfully walk down the street and locate a pizza shop where I ate a piece of pizza, a cupcake and drink a cup of coffee. When I tried to pay, the man would not accept my money (Once again, the Algerians proved to be a very kind people.)

The next morning, after a bad nights sleep, I go downstairs and consume a couple of little pieces of bread and a cup of coffee. I was under the assumption breakfast was "on the house," but instead they charged twenty francs for it.

"You pack of thieves," I thought.

119

After leaving the robber's den, I walked back across Marseilles to the Harley Davidson shop which opened at nine o'clock. I started work on the motorcycle, changing my front tire and tube. Philip gave me a used battery for nothing. I fixed a few other minor things. At the end of the day, Philip only charged me 200 Francs for the tire and tube.

Four spokes were out on the front wheel. Philip couldn't believe how beat up the machine was. He told me, "I have too much work to be able to do anything this big at the moment."

"I understand," I told him, wheeling the motorcycle outside. As a "thank you" for letting me work on my machine, I bought the repair shop some cake and other goodies - after all, Christmas was just a few days away.

A fellow who was going in my direction offered to show me the way out of Marseilles. As I went to start up, sure enough, the stubborn bastard wouldn't. Philip retrieved a jumper battery and some jumper cables; we put them on, and it started.

"You've got to run the thing for at least a couple of hours to get the battery up to snuff," he told me.

I followed this fellow out of town, and at the north end of Marseilles, we waived at each other. On my own once again, moving ahead, it was freezing cold with a light snow. After about 110 miles (176 km.), I pulled off the highway and fueled up. The motorcycle did start again, though just a bit hard because the starter itself was bad, pulling too much voltage off the battery.

Snow is every where, but fortunately, there is no ice. I locate a garage to house the motorcycle for the night, then secure a horrible little room to stay in. It had no shower, so I cleaned up in the sink, then and went down for a cheap dinner of pasta and bread. Most of the crowd eating here were truck drivers, and they created a festive mood - like a banquet - lots of eating, laughing, joking and wine. These truck-driving strangers acted more like long-lost brothers at a big family reunion.

I went back to my room, laid back and closed my day after a bit of reading. "I wonder if the motorcycle will start tomorrow?" I asked myself. "Hope it does."

5:30: Awoke to the howling wind outside, wondering:
1. Will the motorcycle start? and
2. How cold is it going to be outside?

Got up, ate a crescent roll, drank coffee, took my gear down to the garage and the motorcycle, rolled the motorcycle out, loaded it, and then pushed the starter button.

AH... it started right up!

The starter motor is burning out, so it will only turn for about 7 seconds. If the motorcycle doesn't start in that time, the battery is dead.

I let the machine warm up while I prepare myself to travel in the snow. Although warmly dressed, as I start, I'm freezing my ass off.

Because of the ice, it was not advisable to ride on surface streets, so I took the toll freeway - expensive, but free of ice. Traveling north through Lyon, after about a hundred plus miles, I stopped for gasoline for the first time, hoping the battery would be fully recharged. The motorcycle had been running very poorly (What else is new?). After getting gas, I pulled over in the snow, sat down in a parking lot, took the carburetor apart and discovered traces of water. Next, I checked the points and the timing, then tried to start it again.

It wouldn't start.

The battery had run down.

Next, I checked the points and the timing to see if they are firing. I retarded the spark a little, then tried to start it again.

Uurrrrrr, urrrrrr - it muttered ever so slowly until it fired, to my great relief! I drove back onto the freeway and rode another 100 miles or so before I came to a town called Courtney. The price quoted at the first hotel I checked was too high for my budget. I found a cheaper place, but it had no vacancies. The female proprietor said "No" with a look on her face that seemed to suggest, "We don't want your kind around here." Just as I was feeling a bit down hearted from this rejection, a man who had been sitting in a parking lot with a whole bunch of children in his charge came up to me and said, "Problem messier?"

"Wee, non hotel. I don't know where I'm going to spend the night. I've got to get this motorcycle out of the miserable rain."

"Wait for me," he said.

Although Maurice did not speak English, I somehow understood his message as he walked the children to a nearby bus stop. I started to turn my motorcycle around, but slipped in the mud and the whole thing fell over. A young woman passing by gave me a hand uprighting the machine. She was a big strong girl, or the two of us couldn't have done it.

Meet a nasty person, meet a good person.

Seems to be a rule of the road throughout my entire trip.

It's also a good lesson in life.

Maurice came back to my motorcycle, and said, "Follow me to my car."

For about ten miles I followed him down a very narrow country lane to a little village - no idea of its name. We put the motorcycle away in a garage of a house that was about four hundred years old, and carried some of my gear inside where I met Maurice's wife, Angela, and their daughter, Julie.

The family seemed very close, with much love shared between them. Their home was modern and clean, yet it presented a rustic, antique air. Angela prepared a very lovely but simple dinner. Afterwards, we had coffee and conversation - the best we could with a dictionary between us! Their kindness and hospitality was wonderful.

Maurice was a teacher of music, and very proud of his brother, an international sports photographer; he showed me magazines with his brother's photos in them.

That evening after a shower, I laid back in the stillness of this old country home, virtually untouched by the madness of big city noise and the modern world.

"What will tomorrow bring?" I wondered.

Certainly not relief.

Riding alone, I often speak to imaginary future audiences, describing my adventures. At this point in my life, I've only spoken to a few disabled groups, so it seemed good to practice for what I hoped would be plenty of public speaking engagements when I arrived in England. In my rehearsals, I often nodded my head, or bobbed it up and down as if to give the feeling and emotion of the accomplishment of crossing Africa. It also helped to keep me from freezing my ass off!

When driving by me, people must have looked at this crazy foreigner, with a funny look in his eye, on a beaten-up, horrible-looking Harley Davidson motorcycle, and said to themselves, "That man looks like he has gone out of his mind He's even talking to himself!"

Chuckling to myself at these thoughts, I fell asleep, knowing tomorrow would be another day on the road in the constantly changing and challenging weather.

December 21: 06:00: I heard Morris practicing at his piano - very quietly, with his daughter, Julie, sitting next to him. I will never forget the love and warmth of that scene, shared by the daughter and father. Angela was up so she made us all coffee (we drank out of a bowl, which is very usual in France).

07:30: Started working on the motorcycle. Pulled the condenser out and took carburetor apart. Put in another condenser and a new accelerator pump. It started right up! Will wonders never cease? Two days in a row! Next, I put on my gear - a rain jacket and gloves I bought in Marseilles (One of my best deals in clothing; I never buy new clothing, but always shop in the second hand stores).

December 21: Good-byes were given, with a "Joy Noel" ("Merry Christmas") to little Julie, since Christmas was only four days away. With warm feelings, I rode off into the cold rain and wind on my way north.

The Paris traffic was terrible!

What a mess!

For mile after mile I cut in and out of lanes in a rain so heavy it felt like a cow peeing on a flat rock - and I was the rock! The rear brake on my motorcycle is almost nonexistent, and the front brake is not working well either. I move forward through this maze, getting lost and turned around, riding for miles this way, then that way, until I finally see a road sign that points me in a direction leading me out of the snarl and mess of Paris.

My next stop was Saint Quentin, miles off the main freeway, but the hometown of my friend, Bruno Piet. I felt it very important to return his tent, and hoped to learn what he was doing now - whether living in France, or if he had returned from Central Africa.

At a gas station, the owner kindly helped me look up "Piet" in the phone book - he wasn't listed. I remembered that Bruno had on his petrol tank a sticker saying "Saint Quentin, Sarazzen Honda." It turned out that Sarazzen Honda was within walking distance, so I left my motorcycle at the petrol station and walked in the rain down to Honda shop.

In a combination of poor French and English, I tried to explain to the owner of the shop that Bruno Piet's tent was in my possession and I wanted to give it back to him.

"Ah, Bruno Piet in Africa," he told me.

"Yes, that's the man," I replied, leaving him the tent; unfortunately, he did not have Bruno's address. My only hope is that one day Bruno will come back and this man will return his tent as a show of my appreciation for his help and comradeship while traveling through half of Zaire and Central Africa.

Bruno was a great guy, someone I'll never forget.

It was still raining like nobody's business as I left Saint Quentin on my way toward Calais. Off the highway at Cambrai, I found a cheap motel (about $15 dollars at the time); a petrol station was willing to lock up the Harley Davidson (it is vital to keep the thing inside at night, or it won't start the next morning). The day's ride covered only about two hundred miles because of visibility limitations - it doesn't get light enough to ride until about 08:30, and darkness sets in very quickly.

On top of the rain and short day, I was slowed by a miserable gray tint - sort of a mist - as I rode through the countryside of France. That tint made the World War I cemeteries along the way seem like especially grim reminders of a violent past. "I hope we never see the likes of a world war again," I thought as I climbed into bed that night, closing my day.

December 22: The next morning I was up early and went over to the gas station. As usual, it was raining and very cold. When they opened the garage, I got the motorcycle out, and - what do you know! - it started for the third morning in a row (it had ran good all day yesterday). In a very lighthearted mood, I think, "With any luck and nothing going wrong, I'll make it to Dover, England this day."

As I left Cambrai on my way north to Calais, I fought a headwind and rain. There would be no let up even for the final mile. I placed a T-shirt over most of my face to keep the rain from hitting it directly. Mind you, rain at 55 miles per hour is like being hit in the face with thousands of flying needles! Once, the headwind and rain lifted the T-shirt up over my eyes, and I couldn't see where I was going, grappling crazily at the top of my helmet, trying to get this thing down before I ran off the road.

That's not something I want to experience again!

Upon arriving in Calais, signs all through the city guided me down to the ferries to cross the English Channel to Dover. At the dock, one miserable custom's official rudely told me, "Move your motorcycle." I did, but was so upset at his manner that I walked right up to his face and asked, "Is that all, you asshole?"

Lucky for me, he didn't speak English, or if he did, he didn't acknowledge my question, but just gave me a mean look. Then I bought my ticket, loaded the motorcycle on the ferry, and was guided to the location where motorcycles were placed and tied down.

As the ferry pulled out and away from the mainland of Europe on its way to Dover, I breathed a sigh of relief. It felt sooo good to hear people all around speaking English. This ferry trip symbolized my relief that the many months of struggling to get across Africa were finally over. I had struggled with roads, different cultures, unfamiliar languages, horrendous weather and treacherous terrain... and now, this was the culmination.

Suddenly, as the crossing came to an end, in the distance loomed the white cliffs of Dover. What an incredibly beautiful scene those cliffs presented! I could only imagine how the aviators of World War II must have felt after coming back from a mission and spotting those white cliffs - what relief and joy would well up in their hearts. That same feeling was also in my heart on this day.

When the ferry docked, it felt like being home.

Good old blighty.

Christmas Cheer, Beer, and the New Year

I found a place to stay that night, expensive by my standards, but the cheapest bed and breakfast I could find. After my shower, got my clothes washed and had dinner with the family who owned the place. That night, in bed, I quietly and peacefully reflected on the past three months and ten days since I had left South Africa. Finally, it came home to me that **the first major struggle of this incredible journey around the world was over.**

The next morning, my first real day in England, I read a book in bed until called for 8:30 breakfast. At the table, I met an obnoxious Irishman "on the dole," meaning he was receiving money from the British government to live. This man was full of hatred and bitterness against the British government. "How dare you bite the hand that feeds you," I thought to myself. I did not get along well with that man.

During the rest of the day I decided to just relax and enjoy the comfort and warmth of this home. Late in the afternoon, I went downtown and bought a couple of things for my dinner. When I returned, Peter Morpuss, a man I had not seen for four years, was on the phone; I gave him directions to the house. When he arrived, we embraced each other, and that hug made up for a lot of lost time.

We went downtown to dinner, where I asked Peter, "Do you know of any work in the area? I've got to earn some money to keep me going while I find a place to put my motorcycle so I can do the major repairs it needs."

Peter looked distressed. "Dave, work is difficult to come by," he told me. "Even menial stuff. Britain's unemployment rate is quite high, you know."

No sooner had I finished one set of problems when I faced another challenge. Guess that's the story of this whole trip.

Exit the Sahara with snow storms, rain and bad weather, and enter into England with a new set of challenges for the next six months as I prepare to head north to the Arctic. Find work - find a place to store the motorcycle and do major repairs on it - that's my new challenges.

Peter promised me he would call soon with any news.

Christmas Eve: Up at 07:00, thinking about what needs to be done in the coming days. Even though the weather was miserable and gray, the spirit of Christmas seemed everywhere, but definitely different from in the United States where the entire country gets hit with a crazy "buy-buy-buy" frenzy. Here they had managed to preserve a unique spirit of Christmas.

Mrs. Borner, the head of the bed and breakfast, invited me to have Christmas dinner with them. "Thank you very much," I replied, accepting her invitation, spending the afternoon helping her peel all the vegetables to make preparations for the dinner.

I called Paul Whitehead, an old Army buddy from South Africa, and told him of my situation. "Dave, I may be able to help, and even find a place for you and the Harley Davidson."

"I hope so!" was my enthusiastic reply.

Christmas Eve, 22:00: Charlie Borner, the son of the couple who owned the bed and breakfast, said, "Dave, come along with me. I'm going to a pub for a bit of Christmas cheer."

"That sounds like a very good idea to me" I replied, so off we went in his M.G. motorcar (which he handled with a great amount of skill). We went to the other side of Dover where Charlie picked up a friend, and from there we went to a place called "The Hare and Hound Pub" out in the countryside. This old British Pub had a unique family atmosphere, very cozy and warm, and lots of beautiful British girls, most of whom seemed to know Charlie (he appeared to be quite a lady's man). During the evening we enjoyed a few cigars together, and talked with many people. As I shared about my adventure, a strong sense of accomplishment started to sink in. "Yes, I have just finished coming all the way across from Africa to Dover on a motorcycle," I tell my next listener, realizing the culture shock of these last 100 days was tremendous.

Christmas Day, 01:00: When the pub closed, we took the M.G. to the house of Charlie's friend, and dropped him off. Charlie then took me to an incredible vantage point looking down into Dover Harbor. The lights and ships in the Harbor sparkled like a gigantic Christmas tree! I'll never forget that sight, that special moment as the cold, clean-swelling wind blew through us.

That night I remembered last year's Christmas Eve dinner - a can of beans while watching the sunset and then the stars in the Namib desert, totally alone.

The next few days were spent working on the motorcycle and writing a nine-page report about the journey across Africa.

Paul Whitehead and Graham Gilmore, both Army buddies of mine, came down from London. Paul said, "Dave, you can stay with my parents. The motorcycle would be secure in their garage."

That was great news, and so was Graham's.

"I might be able to find you some work in the security business," he explained.

How quickly things can change!

After our visit, I tried to get my Carnett Passage stamped (the travel document for the motorcycle), but was unable to do so down at the port. This was very distressing because I knew that the people who issued it through the Automobile Association in London would give me a hard time with the refund without the stamp.

I repaired my right leg by putting a new set of belts on it. The only way to get the belts undone was with a grinder. The bolts and nuts that held everything together were all rusted. Charlie helped me with a grinder we brought into the house. Once the repair was completed, it was a little easier for me to walk. My hosts still seemed amazed that I was able to make it across Africa in the condition my motorcycle and me were in.

Saturday, December 29: Early in the morning, I carried my things downstairs. The weather was rainy (usual), and the wind was blowing (normal). After I loaded the motorcycle, Charlie helped me move it out front. The family took some photos of me, and I bade these fine people "Good-bye." Amazingly, the motorcycle started easily, and I rode off through the rest of Dover into the British countryside. Though it was raining, miserable, gray and gloomy, the British countryside was awesome, even breathtaking. Ancient stone walls marked property boundaries of meticulously manicured old farms, adorned with ancient old Victorian structures steeped in history and tradition.

As I made it to the motorway, heading for London, the rain got worse and worse. It was impossible to see anything but the highway in front of me. At the Heston turnoff, on the M 4, I made my way to a gas station where I called Paul, leaving a message to "come and pick me up." Later in the afternoon, Paul arrived and I followed him in the rain to his apartment in the Acton area (West London). We moved my stuff inside, but the motorcycle (much to my dismay) had to sit outside with no particular security at all.

It was good talking about the old times in the army with Paul, who was still serving as a medic in the S.A.S. (equivalent of Delta Force in the U.S.) reserves. Paul had been invaluable in his help in finding me a place to live with his folks, and also in helping to solve other problems.

New Year's Eve: I moved over to Ernie and Mary's place (Paul's mother and father). Ernie and I hit it off immediately, and we always seemed to have a good rapport. We spent most of the day watching videos until about 17:30 when Paul picked me up and took a group of us over to a Chinese restaurant, then on to a pub for the rest of the evening (it was New Year's Eve!). Being the dull bastard that I am, I drank orange juice. At the stroke of midnight, the bells of London rang out - it was an incredible, amazing sound. As if on cue, within fifteen minutes after the bells, everybody started to leave the pub, destined for other locations.

Back in the quiet of my room I thought, "This has been such an incredible year, one of the busiest of my life." I almost hurt reliving the memories: I rode six thousand miles in January on my last trip, then overhauled the Harley Davidson preparing for this journey; wrote my first book, *Four Flags* (not yet published); started my world-wide journey on September 12th, probably one of the most tense, fearful mornings of my life; rode eighty-five hundred plus miles to arrive at this bed in England; had days that stretched from 03:30 until late in the South African evening; and finally, a flurry of memories pounded my mind about the trials and tribulations of the great overland journey from Africa to England.

No wonder I said a prayer of thanks to God in heaven for the strength He gave me to accomplish and complete this last year - still alive. As I reflected upon God's gift of life, I also remembered that it was twenty years ago today that I was cited for valor while flying a medivac mission in the Quason Mountains at night - December 31, 1970, in Viet Nam.

With these thoughts, I not only closed the day, I closed the year.

The Quest for Sponsorships, Jobs and a Healthy Machine

My main priority now was to find work, so I bought some "new" second hand clothes to make a good impression on an interview.

On January 3, Graham Gilmore came by to tell me, "Dave, I have a friend who wants to have a bit of an interview with you about some security work at night."

We walked down to the train station, switching trains one time. I mention the trains because often there is much walking involved to get to the station. We got off at Earl's Court, then walked to the offices of Securatron where I interviewed with a fellow named Nash. "There should be about three days worth of work," Nash told me, "and it will pay about forty pounds a night."

The amount seemed like excellent money to me, so I said, "Fine, you can call me anytime."

The other thing I had been checking out was places for the motorcycle to be worked on. I had gone to the main Harley dealer in London, but his labor rates were thirty five pounds an hour. (The United States was in recession, and the power of the dollar was down, so thirty five pounds figured to about $75.00 an hour - absolutely inconceivable!). He didn't seem at all interested in letting me work on my own, even though I explained to him my peculiar set of problems: lack of money, what I was doing and why I was doing it.

I never heard anything more from him.

At another place I found a more sympathetic ear, but still no action or commitment on their part to let me work on the thing in their shop (I admit that's a bit of a cheek, but in my situation, I could not afford to pay other people's labor).

At the third shop Paul took me to, it was closed, we could see one Harley Davidson through the window among the Japanese motorcycles. I made a mental note to try "Tigercycles in Action" another time (little did I know that I would have a long relationship with this shop and it's very peculiar owners).

My biggest concern right now was to find a job and start making some money. At the rate I was spending money on just living expenses, I would soon be broke. My room at Mary and Ernie's was sixty pounds sterling a week (a very good rate for London, especially since it included food). I felt fortunate about my arrangements, but the reality was still there: an outflow of cash with nothing coming in. Since I planned on spending six months in England, waiting for the weather to thaw in the arctic before I started moving north, I needed to do something in a hurry.

January 4: After breakfast, I rode to Tigercycles in Acton where I met Tigger, a man of about three hundred and twenty pounds (23 stone). We talked about the trip and my needs concerning the motorcycle. Tigger, a biker himself, had a truly sympathetic ear as I explained about the knock in the engine, and the need to rebuild of upper end of the engine (never was right). He listened to the thing, and said, "Dave, it sounds like it might need a major overhaul."

That's not what I wanted to hear at all.

"I have some work to finish, and I've got to clear it with my partner, but if you can wait about three weeks before you bring the motorcycle in, I'll let you work on it in our garage."

What a great relief!

Now I had a place to start repairs on the motorcycle in preparation for the next stage of the trip.

That evening in bed I thought to myself, "Why I am doing this trip? I tell everybody it is for the disabled worldwide, but am I doing it for them, or for me and my own selfish reasons? Or both?" In trying to be honest with myself, I concluded that "Yes, I am doing it for the disabled...and for myself."

The first evening at my new "so called" job, I took a couple of buses across town, and then took a good walk to the Marble Arch Apartments. There I was greeted by the supervisor who was going to show me around.

"You are to do three tours of the premises each hour, with ten clock checks. You will alternate these tours with your fellow security guard."

As we walked, there were numerous stairs to climb and long passages to go through. That's no problem - except for the noise I make. My right leg was grinding and clanking (especially noisy in the hallways late at night). The shift started at 22:00 and ended at 08:00. Every other hour I made the three tours up and down stairs, inside and outside.

In the morning, after work, I went to the bus ticketing station and bought a day pass, only to be told by the girl who sold it to me that "This pass is not good until nine thirty."

Bloody hell - there's always a catch. Upset with this news, and in great pain from being up and down stairs all night, I went back and sat on a bench for the next hour and a half in the freezing cold, waiting for my day pass to become valid so I could take a bus to Victoria Station. Once there, I had almost a mile walk down to Maunsel Street to the offices of Cheshire Foundation International where I met Mr. Tony Talbot. We talked about what I could do for the Foundation, and we agreed that I would make a three week media and speaking tour to raise the Foundation's profile in the local areas. I also agreed to speak at night to the residents, staff and family in the various homes to try and be an example for motivation of the residents to do more for themselves. At the end of this meeting, I marveled to myself that the son-of-a-bitch had not even offered me a cup of tea.

In my miserable walk back to Victoria Station, I can assure you I was in no mood to be trifled with - the pain was tremendous. Caught the Number 11 bus back to West Kensington, then walked to Mary and Ernie's apartment where I finally had the very blissful moment of pulling off my legs... the pain flowed out of my stumps into the atmosphere around me.

What a great relief!

January 9, 1991: Slept three hours, then got up, made my dinner, and was on my way back to the Marble Arch Apartments. Once again, a night up and down stairs, pushing time clocks throughout the place, grinding and clanging along the hallways (a few heads came out to query what all the noise was about?).

The topic of the day is the embargo the Americans and the United Nations have on Iraq. The line in the sand had been drawn: Iraq has been told, "Get out of Kuwait by January 15... or else." As of this day, Iraq is not giving an inch, so all are very apprehensive about what is going to happen in the short term future.

The next night at work, I had a good talk with an Iraqi fellow who said, "I cannot go back to Iraq without being put into prison for not answering the call to Jihad (Holy War) against the infidels of the West." He told me, "Suddam Hussein is crazy. His only interests are in the twisted goals of Suddam Hussein. He couldn't care less about his people, and he's not a real popular person in Iraq."

It was refreshing to speak to this fellow and discover that there are reasonable people in the world (as contrasted to the ones shown on television, raising their fists in anger, screaming "Jihad, Jihad").

When my photographs were developed that I took coming across Africa, to my great disappointment the majority of them had been ruined by the camera. The lens had somehow blurred, and the photos were indistinguishable as to what or where they were taken.

Imagine the anguish!

One chance at this once-in-a-lifetime journey, and this so called camera, sponsored by Nikon, gave me nothing but problems on the Namib trip. They swore up and down it had been fixed... but look what it had done.

I could never capture those moments again.

The next morning I took the one kilometer walk to the ticketing booth where I got a bus ticket, then on to Victoria Station where I stood for half an hour waiting for another bus to Fulham to catch another bus to Kensington. On my way home, I went to the Post Office where I stumbled on something, fell and tore a hole in the nice pants I had bought. I cannot tell you how angry that made me, but it is also why I do not buy brand new clothes.

Three hours sleep, then I made my way on the maze of buses and subways over to the offices of Securatron where I collected my check. Nash told me, "There will be no work for you on Monday and Tuesday, and very possibly, no work until the weekend." In my heart, I believe I was being told to piss off because of all the noise my right leg was making. How it worked at all was a wonder - all the bushings and bearings in the knee broke down long ago.

For the next few days, I worked on the motorcycle. I removed the box system off the back of the motorcycle and threw it away... it was junk by this time.

Graham Gilmore, the radioman who was in the vehicle when we blew up, came by one afternoon and we took a train down near Big Bend Tower, walked past the War Rooms to Piccadilly Circus, then all the way down to Oxford Circus, passing Trafalgar Square along the way.

London is so steeped in history - its incredible!

My thoughts in bed are about the trip. I'm also wondering what will happen with the Cheshire Foundation as they arrange this media and speaking tour? I've had a hard time connecting with Tony Talbot. Of course, I also wonder how I am going to get the motorcycle working, and finally, what will I do for work? Though there was a promise of work in the future from the security company, it seemed a very shallow one indeed.

Nothing seems to be going right for me right now.

On the sixteenth, in the morning, I watched the news and all the arguments going on in parliament... debates for and against a NATO strike on Iraq. Later in the day, I called Dave Bramley at Tigercycle in Acton and he told me, "Go ahead and bring the motorcycle over, Dave."

I had it there in a hour.

First, a good steam clean was in order. The motorcycle was filthy dirty - it hadn't been cleaned since Zaire. Next, I started taking it apart, starting with the gas tank and cylinder heads. When we took the cylinder heads off, we saw the pistons were very sloppy. We thought this was the noise we heard in the lower end, since sound travels in these motors. "What a big relief it would be to not have to split the cases."

Little did I know!

As the day progressed, I took apart other things to get them ready for repair and servicing.

16:30: Received a telephone call from Mary Delaslo saying, "Dave, I'm trying to find you a sponsor."

"Well done Mary," I thought, "what a good lady. Maybe things are looking up for me. At least they are going in a positive direction with the motorcycle - things are finally getting done."

At dinner there was a news flash - the war in the Gulf had started, and was dubbed *Operation: Desert Storm*. This would be the main news in the weeks to come.

The next days were spent repairing the motorcycle. I discovered the starter motor was completely burnt out. When everything was done to it that could be done for the moment, we put the motorcycle on Dave and Tigger's service van and hauled it over to Mary and Ernie's place to be stored.

Underworld, Under the Weather, and Under Funded

Tigger drove the van; he's a hard guy to figure. He's like a great, silent bear (Dave calls him a fat pig). He doesn't speak much, but has many moods. Tigger was very quiet and thoughtful, sometimes sitting on the chair in their filthy, dark office, like a great, fat, evil lord with his beard going out in all directions and his thoughtful, penetrating eyes and long hair, always contemplating something. He seemed to have his finger in many other pies besides the motorcycle shop, but what they were, I don't know.

Dave Bramley was my height, and built more conservatively. We talked, joked and laughed in the shop. Dave is the master of low humor with his round face, pointed chin, sharp nose, and brown hair.

Apparently Tigger and Dave met each other in jail, and started a friendship that was to stand for many years. These fellows had a more or less "mutt and Jeff" relationship with each other, with a dash of the "heckle and jekyl" mentality. They were constantly digging at each other as I would watch in amazement.

Now that the motorcycle was back at the house because of space problems, I would not see these fellows for a week or so. Their shop was a tiny place that had been a motorcycle shop since 1906. The working area was covered over with corrugated fiberglass, and when it rains (very often) the roof leaks! The maintenance area was no bigger than an average living room, yet three little lifts were crammed in that space for work on customers machines.

Lately, I'm wasting a lot of time.

My problems are small compared to the news - eight Scud missiles were fired on Tel Aviv and Haifa. Lord help us all if the Israelis get drawn into all this fight. The whole Middle East could go up in a major war (I'm sure that's what Saddam Hussein wants).

One afternoon, I had the pleasure of meeting Jeremy McWilliams, the brother of Mike McWilliams, one of the original sponsors on the Namib trip. He and his friend, a lawyer, came up with some ideas that might help me find sponsors through charities that might help me if I help them. It sounded good, so they agreed to put together a proposal for me to use.

Whenever out and about taking care of other business, I would always stop at various places to ask about jobs. I asked a limousine company and a cab company if they needed somebody to wash and polish cars. I looked at ads in the paper for dispatch riders on little Hondas. "No," they told me, "you don't have enough experience riding around London. I spoke to a another man who told me "My insurance would not cover you because of your disability."

Everywhere I turned seemed to be another dead-end.

I found a job with the Civic Trust. Me and two others were taken to a place where we were to sell these memberships at twenty five pounds each. On the way over, we were guided by a black fellow, a Xhosa from South Africa, named Keith. He told me, "I'm in exile as a member of the Pan African Congress."

"Why are you in exile?" I asked. "For planting bombs in shopping centers and train stations? For killing civilians?"

He evaded my question, and instead came back with some political bullshit. The idea of selling trusts for such a "leader" disgusted me. When we arrived at the Cheswick Shopping Center, and I watched his methods of trying to sell these trusts to people, I didn't like him at all. I bade him and the others "good-bye" and walked off, thinking, "Man, that just wasn't my bag of worms!"

The good news for the day: Tigger told me my parts would be here in about a week. The bad news: Israel had been hit again by missiles, and everybody feared for the future. A MAJOR war in the Middle East was brewing.

I met again with the Cheshire Foundation, and was shown a proposed itinerary throughout the UK. Tony Talbot, as usual, was very standoffish, and does not give much in negotiations. Least of all, a cup of tea.

"Well, now for accommodations, maybe I can call Mrs. Breytenbach and see if you could stay with her relatives," Tony said, reading the instant dissatisfaction on my face. "Is there something wrong?"

"Yes," I answered. "I am not prepared to do the tour that way."

"Well, what do you mean you are not prepared?"

"I am not going to stay with the relatives of people I don't even know," I explained. "If you want me to do this, I'm very happy to, but I would like to stay in the homes themselves."

"I'll see what I can do," was Tony's monotone reply, seemingly irritated that I didn't immediately comply to his idea. Once again, he didn't even offer me a bloody cup of tea. Fuck you, Tony!

Jeremy McWilliams called. "Dave, I've just finished a letter that I want to send to various charities. Hopefully it will encourage them to sponsor you."

"That's fine," I replied. "Good for you, Jeremy."

Tigger called and said, "We're ready to move the motorcycle back over to the shop." That same day, we again loaded the motorcycle into the van and took it back down to the shop to start the assembly on it the next day.

In those next few days, it felt good to be working on the machine again! We reassembled the motor. I pulled the rear wheel off and the brake linings were in pieces; they needed to be relined.

At least we were moving ahead.

We went to the Harley Davidson shop and came back with £ 127.00 ($250.00) worth of parts for various other things that needed to be fixed. I secured a used primary and exhaust from the Harley Davidson after market shop that was owned by a chapter of the Hells Angels in London. Makes you wonder where they located their used parts, doesn't it?

I called South Africa and asked a friend of mine, a captain at South African Airways, about bringing a leg up to me - one I had rebuilt some time back and had kept in reserve. He agreed to do this in the next few weeks. My right leg, bad as it was, was continuing to get worse.

My ride back from Acton usually involves two buses and a good wait along the way. But the traffic in London, at that time of day, is impossible. Though it is only a couple of miles as the crow flies, it can take up to an hour and a half sometimes to get back to Ernie and Mary's.

Sometimes I poke around at the old Bromton Cemetery. Emma Parker, the lady responsible for getting women the right to vote in England, was buried there. So were the Foey Brothers, famous comedians who had performed many years ago in the United States. There were other famous and dignified people, including the Cunard Family, and Admiral Fremantle. There was a World War I section with thousands of soldiers buried in it.

In the catacombs, you could actually look inside and see the caskets on top of one another. Also inside were bronze bells and angels - the incredible architecture was amazing to me. Catacombs, headstones, family crypts and monuments were everywhere. Often, through iron bar doors, I could view the caskets stacked on one another.

One of the more amazing graves was that of a motorcyclist - Percy E. Lambert, the man who set the one hundred mile an hour mark on a motorcycle in 1913. He was later killed that same year trying to break his own record. Rest in peace, Percy.

I met with David Malloms, an ex-colonel in tanks, who was one of the most positive people I had met in the Cheshire Foundation. One of the first things he did was give me a cup of tea. Tony Talbot had seemingly vanished. David introduced me to Stuart Lory, the editor of *Charity Magazine*. We had a nice pub lunch, then returned to the office where we talked for over an hour. David was a man with whom I could communicate, and was extremely positive about what I wanted to do for this upcoming tour in the U.K..

"The wheels are in motion, David," he confidently told me. "Good things are going to happen."

Since I hate suspense, this was good news to me. I felt it important that this trip be used for something in a positive direction for the disabled, and not just for the glorification of myself and the Harley Davidson Motor Company.

"We will try to look for sponsors for your worldwide trip," David also told me. "This will help your continuing work with the Cheshire Foundation."

"Thank you," I replied "but I want you to know that I seek no reward in working for the Cheshire Foundation. **My main desire in this journey around the world is to perhaps inspire people with disabilities to live their dreams and do more for themselves.**"

Engine of Destruction, plus the Gulf and Pub Wars

The next few days, from morning until dark, I worked on the motorcycle in this dingy little shop. Even snow would leak in through the roof, so it was bitterly cold. Dave and I just pushed on.

"This guy has worked in these conditions for years," I think to myself. "He reminds me of myself, and some of the places on my trip where I had sat down and worked on the motorcycle in the snow, sand and mud. Compared to some of those places, I guess this isn't too bad after all. At least the atmosphere is always one of laughter and lurid humor."

I'll never forget David's shit-eating, evil grin when he would come up with some horrible joke, and I'll never forget how he would throw things around in the shop when he got angry. At those moments, I would just try to make myself scarce and stay out of throwing range.

My motorcycle was nicknamed "the engine of destruction" because it had often fallen, knocking other motorcycles off their racks. Luckily, the things it hit were themselves in a terrible state of disrepair.

Much of the business Dave and Tigger received came from dispatch riders - probably the hardest motorcycle riders I have seen anywhere in the world. These men ride upwards of a thousand miles a week in the crowded streets of London, dodging between the lanes of cars. The only people who might know London better than the dispatch riders are the cabbies. What these dispatch riders do to make their money is incredible.

The snow on the London streets is not a problem for cars because the cars wear a path in the snow, but snow is a problem for me, especially if it is packed hard. I slip on it quite often, and fall down, usually ruining my pants and making me madder than a snake. Inevitably these falls are in front of other people who rush over to "help the cripple," making the cripple even angrier. These incidents never deter me from going where I want to go and doing what I want to do.

While assembling the motor, we discover that the cylinder head is cracked - apparently the result of something that happened when the mechanics rebuilt it in the United States. The transmission had water in it which couldn't be drained out; the drain plug was stripped. These people back in the U.S.A. took a great deal of money from me to do a terrible job. They should all be ashamed of themselves. "These dopes do not deserve to call themselves a Harley Davidson dealer at all" I thought to myself.

We were able to repair the rear cylinder head to keep going - that was a big relief. If I had to buy a new cylinder head, I'd be sunk - the costs would have been phenomenal!

February 8: I go to the motorcycle shop and work all day with Tigger, putting things back together. We were able to start the motorcycle, and it sounded pretty good all and all. Tigger and I were very pleased about that!

Got a call from Mrs. Cornwell from Bandstead Mobility Center. She told me they were interested in my project and wanted to meet with me. Since this was the only disabled organization to call me, I agreed. It was frustrating to know that Jeremy had sent his letters out to various charities all over the country, and so far this was the first feedback I received.

It was time to settle up with Dave and Tigger for all the parts and help they had given me. First of all, they refused to charge me anything for their extensive labor. They had provided much-needed expertise, especially in some very sensitive assembly areas. Dave had built a new carrying rack for the back of the machine that was greatly improved from my old one; everything would be carried in saddlebags.

To pay for parts, I changed eleven hundred American dollars and gave them seven hundred pounds. We aren't finished yet; I know I'll have to give them more before the machine is finally done.

When I finished paying them, they ask, "Dave would you be interested in working for us for £ 20.00 a day?"

They didn't have to ask twice!

At last I had a job.

During this time, my left leg is acting up because a bearing on the caliper has gone bad. The stump is always sore.

I received a package from the Queen Elizabeth Disability Foundation saying that "they were hopeful to be using me to raise money for their cause." It was not clear if they understood that I would need their financial sponsorship, in return, to do whatever they required me to do for them.

Other news of the day: 250 people had been killed in a bunker in Baghdad from a missile. This releases much antiwar sentiment in the country (with the media's help).

I thought to myself, "Hussein can do anything he wants and nothing much is said, but we hit a bunker with civilians inside (beyond our control) and everyone starts getting upset at the allies."

As a soldier, I know civilians unfortunately get caught in the middle of wars. However, there was no reason for civilians to be in a command bunker that was sending out radio signals. On our monitors, that bunker was a legitimate military target. It wasn't our fault that Hussein put those people in harm's way.

I met with Ted Lawrence, head of the British Amputee Servicemen's League, and told him of my trip, putting myself at his disposal to counsel any amputees that may be coming back from the Gulf War. He said that my services may well be needed if we stay much longer in the Gulf.

Travel in London can be extremely difficult. On this particular day, I caught my first bus across town to the Liverpool Street Train Station. It took one hour, followed by another hour of standing and waiting for the next train that would take me to Chatwell Heath. After my meeting with Ted Lawrence, he took me back to the train station to catch another train back to Liverpool Street. From Liverpool Street, I took an underground subway to Shepherds Bush, then walked about a kilometer to catch another bus to the motorcycle shop where Tigger and Dave told me they would bring the motorcycle over that evening. Next, two more buses with a long wait in between them, then a walk to the apartment.

This was a very common day... hopping buses and subways, and walking distances sometimes up to a kilometer between them. My stumps feel the strain; the right leg continues to grind along, making it difficult for me walk and making me a spectacle in the public eye. In my mind I'd often tell myself, "All of this is for a purpose as I work towards the next step in the trip."

About this time, Tigger knew of a pub that needed security since there was dope dealing going on. There were many undesirables that the owners did not want in the pub anymore. "Dave, if you will work behind the counter washing glasses and keeping an eye out," they told me, "we will pay you £ 50.00 a night." Dave would bring in their Rottweiler dogs; who knows how much he was making. It was just one of his many scams. However, since fifty pounds is a lot of money, I agreed.

During my first night on pub security, the police raided the place because of a fight. Tigger tossed the two fighters out of the pub, and the police were down there again. This tension-filled situation was instigated by some black thugs in the area who didn't like us being in the pub, knowing that we were watching out for their dope dealings.

The pub closed at 23:00. Then I made the long trip back across London. When I got into bed, it was 01:45.

What a day.

The next day I worked all day at the shop, then worked the pub at night. Fortunately, the pub was quiet, so I made my fifty pounds without any great worry of violence.

Sunday, February 17th: Started up the motorcycle, only to be greeted by one hell of a valve noise (I was very worried about this). I rode about seven miles, and ended up coming back. I replaced the lifter to try and fix the valve noise.

No dice.

Smoke was everywhere.

Upon investigation, it turned out the rocker arm shafts were not tight enough, so they were moving and leaking, causing all the noise. After repairs, the noise disappeared; I'm very pleased about that. With the motorcycle repaired, I then

133

decided to take it for an extensive test drive, manipulating my way through the back streets until I came to the M 4 Motorway where I rode for about sixty miles in the freezing cold (ideal weather to break in the upper end of a Harley Davidson) with no problems.

That maiden voyage for the repaired motorcycle was encouraging.

For the next few days, I worked both at the motorcycle shop and at the pub at night, where one of the fellows helping us was a guy named Wolf, the Sergeant at Arms for the London Hells Angels. He was a good deterrent to violence since he was a big man like Tigger, only not as fat. With these two huge men patrolling the scene, problems at the pub started to decrease.

I wrote an article for *Combat and Survival* magazines, and they actually paid me for writing it (one of the few that did)! A fellow named Duncan Brewer came by and took all my transcripts for the article, and also took some photographs, paying me £ 250 pounds for the photographs.

I had a meeting with the Queen Elizabeth Foundation, and everything went quite well until I mentioned that I would need some financial sponsorship to enable me to help them out on a worldwide venture - maybe a few cents a mile just to help cover my expenses. That didn't go over very well, and I never heard from them again. They must have felt I was independently wealthy.

The bombing war in the Gulf was still in full swing - big headlines in the daily newspapers, television and radio.

February 24th: Rolled the motorcycle out, thinking about taking a ride on that Sunday morning. It was very cold, but no snow on the ground. Sure enough, the battery was dead!

"No matter what I do with this damn thing, there's just no let up."

I pushed it back inside.

Turning on the television, the news stated that the ground war had started. "I hope it goes quickly, with as few casualties as possible."

I am feeling as gray inside as the weather is outside. I am not depressed, but I hate sitting and waiting for the Cheshire tour to start. Then, I must wait until May before it is reasonable for me to start on my way towards the North Cape, which is well above the arctic circle.

The war in the Gulf seems to be going well for the allies. Of course, there were exceptions. We heard about the odd American or British plane being shot down, and twenty-seven Americans who were killed by a scud missile. But the saddest thing, of course, was the nine British soldiers who were killed by an A10 American pilot who mistook them for an Iraqi vehicle. Unfortunately, this happens in war. When I was in Viet Nam, I remember accidentally shooting a group of Koreans while doing close air support at night.

Working in the shop I made a mistake on a machine, and Dave had to redo it. Frankly, it is a regular occurrence. Despite my general knowledge of motorcycles, I do not have any real mechanical ability or training. I especially hated working on the newer Japanese motorcycles because they are not as simple and straight forward as the older Harley Davidsons.

At the Coach and Horses Pub that evening, we were thin on security. Tigger wasn't with us, so that just left Dave and I in the pub, plus Dave's two Rottweilers in the back. A group of blacks in one corner of the pub started in on me, threatening to "cut me up." I turned around and came back at them very strongly; I just can't stand yapping mouths. They didn't have enough nerve for a one on one confrontation, but would rather wait like jackals until their prey is outnumbered.

134

The threats and gestures continued whenever I was behind the bar. Towards closing time, an Arab in their group gets up and starts hollering and shouting at me, then hauls off and takes a swing. I grab a heavy ashtray and whack him hard, forcing him to fly backwards.

In the midst of the chaos, suddenly, it was TIGGER to the rescue!

Where he came from I don't know.

All of the sudden there's this huge mountain of flesh rushing through the place like a cyclone, throwing people out as if they were defenseless sacks of potatoes. I have never seen a fat man move so fast and yet be so violently graceful in all my life. It was a great relief for me that Tigger showed up because I was sure in my heart that the pack of dogs would have been on me within moments of the trouble starting.

The police seemed to arrive almost simultaneously. The truth is, they had their eye on the pub because of all the drug dealing going on. They grabbed the Arab, and we all went down to the police station. There Tigger and I gave our statements; we didn't finish till about 03:00. By the time I climbed into bed, it was 04:00...a long day indeed.

February 29: The day started up at 07:00, with me again catching my two buses down to the motorcycle shop to work all day with Dave. A couple of fellows from another motorcycle club came by, and together we all took the van down to the Coach and Horses Pub, an hour's drive across London. We took our respective stations, and a new onslaught of rude comments started right through the evening. Finally, I got into a face to face argument with one pig who claimed he was going to "cut me up."

"Hey, get out of here," I told him, "and don't come back until you can act like a human being."

He didn't like being referred to as a non-human, but in the end he didn't do anything. Ultimately, the police on patrol came in and removed the man physically from the place. The other two fellows from the motorcycle club didn't do anything about this confrontation. I can only hope that if we had come to fisticuffs that they would have stuck with me (the loud-mouth was a very big fellow). Looking at some of these guys and the lives they lead - drugs, booze and the pub - they seem to have no hope. They live on the dole, nonproductive and barely existing as human beings. What a miserable, depressing way to live!

We received a call from a fellow in another pub claiming that Tigger was also looking after *The Spotted Cow*, a pub a few blocks away. The man said, "The bad crowd that has been hanging around your pub is now turning up at my place, and I'm not at all happy about that! But, I'm calling to let you know that it sounds like they are scheming to come down later in the night and give you fellows a real hard time."

"Will you give us a call if you see them leave?" I asked him, and he assured me he would. My thinking was that we could call the police before they arrived. Sure enough, within thirty minutes Lance gave me a call saying "They're on their way," and five minutes later the pack of jackals enter into our pub.

New threats.

Noise level increases.

My own mouth started up as well - I had no tolerance for these disgusting, "so-called" human beings. As if on cue, the police showed up and hustled them all out of the pub; they were surprised, shocked, and extremely angry by the police's quick - almost magical - response. After that, we sounded the bell, cleared the pub, completed our evening routine, then headed home.

The streets are quiet, and there are no traffic jams. The drive along the Thames River, and going over the lighted bridges that span the Thames, is an exciting contrast from the bustle of the daytime London. A giant city - asleep. There's also an overwhelming sense of history that runs through the myriad of old Victorian buildings we pass - homes where families have often lived for centuries. As we drive along, I keep telling myself, "That's £ 50.00 more in my pocket. I've done it again tonight. There's just no end to what I'll do to keep this trip on the road."

The same day that we were combating the local thugs in the pub in South London, the Iraqis had given up their thuggery and surrendered. The war in the Gulf was over, but in the aftermath Kuwait oil fields were burning - the wake of the fire's destruction was incredible.

At work the next day, Tigger informed me that the pub manager and his wife had just packed up and left town, leaving us without a night job. Though I'm relieved about not going to the pub at night, I am more concerned about the £ 50.00 a night I have just lost - money much needed.

Tigger, Dave and Dave at "Tiger Cycles."
Acton, West London
January - April 1991

Chapter Thirteen

Snowtime, Showtime, and Low Time

Sunday is usually my day to get out and ride the motorcycle. It was running a bit better now, but the lower end of the motorcycle becomes quite noisy after warming up. I am very worried about it, but can't find any metal in the oil, so I decide to just continue the way it is. It never seems to be 100%.

While traveling through the English countryside (always a joy), I was met with bright blue skies and brilliant green fields filled with cows or sheep. The stone borders of the different farms seemed to frame the picturesque old farm houses, barns and out buildings. Little villages, some unchanged for centuries, frequent the country roads, making traveling through England like traveling back through history.

Mary Delaslo had approached various people looking for sponsorship, but nothing had come up. In fairness, Levi Straus had offered some free Jeans.

"Keep em fellows."

Meanwhile, my work in the motorcycle shop continued, covering everything from picking up dog shit, to cleaning out the drains we pissed in (the toilet was up stairs, so we couldn't be bothered walking all the way up), to sweeping the shop floor. In the morning, we moved the motorcycles out of the shop (because it was so small) to the far side of the street on the sidewalk. I also fixed tires and other minor servicing. Very basic work, and I never had any real proficiency at it. Many times Dave came along and had to say, "No, we've got to do this again." He never lost his patience with me (a wonder!).

There was more laughter than cursing in this little house of fun.

Ruins, Raids, and Robbers

The motorcycle shop was at the bottom of a three story house, inside a block of businesses and flats. They were all connected. Dave claimed a ghost lived there - an old lady who had died many years before in the bathtub. Tigger and I never saw the ghost, but Dave swore there was one around (a good ghost). Up in the rooftop were pigeons that nested in the attic, constantly cooing. One unoccupied bedroom on the top floor was full of pigeon shit.

The next level down contained a bedroom and a bit of a stove - a real mess from a previous occupant who had the manners of a pig. The level just above the shop was Dave's apartment, containing a bedroom, a little kitchen and a shower in the kitchen. Definitely not luxury living.

Finally, in the motorcycle shop you had the two Rottweillers - Jess and Rocky. Rocky was the biggest, with the temperament of a junk yard dog. Funny enough, the two dogs got along. Jess was unpredictable; one day she might let you pet her, the next she'd eat your hand.

Luckily, I got along with both dogs. They were trained as alarm and watch dogs for the downstairs, and they lived in the office, keeping it in a constant state of chaos and upheaval. In the mornings as I moved motorcycles around, I had to be very careful not to stop in a huge pile of dog shit and slip or fall.

While Tigger's wasn't a glorious place to work, and while the working conditions were not the best, my job had stopped the outflow of my money, and Dave and Tigger were interesting characters.

One day Tigger came to the shop on a slightly used Harley Davidson, grinning from ear to ear. He already owned a 1983 Harley Davidson, the Evolution, but now he had this new one - a softtail. Tigger was delighted with his new toy, purchased at a price of £ 5000.00 ($9,500.00). After showing it to us, he rode to his place in Lewisham where he parked it outside. The next morning when he came out - you know it - the bike was gone!

For the next few days, Tigger was one tiger to absolutely avoid.

March 12: As Dave and I were opening the shop, the police moved in and closed the doors right behind us! Four of them immediately started a search of the place, but wouldn't tell us what they were looking for. Perhaps they were trying to find some stolen parts or motorcycles.

"What are you looking for?" I asked.

"We can't say" was their simple reply.

For ninety minutes they looked through the shop. When they came to my jacket, they found my can of mace gas and, as a result, they made me take a trip down to the police station. Tigger came in with two other police behind him. They had raided his house, and brought him down to open his safe. When the police finished comparing notes, they decided to take us down to the "Ealing" police station (the scene reminded me of the Monty Python movie, *Life Beyond Ealing).* In the car with two policemen, we talked about politics, crime and race. It was as if we were just a group of guys going out for a pub lunch...only I was going to jail.

At the station, they cleared Dave and Tigger but put me into a holding cell. On the wall graffiti read, "Crime does pay but don't get caught," and "It will only be a short while and they will let you out." After about ninety minutes, they did. I was very glad, since jail was clearly a place where I'd go crazy if I had to spend any length of time.

When they brought me in front of the desk sergeant, he said, "Well what do we have here? The low plains Drifter?" Everyone in the station burst out in laughter. Even I laughed at the British sense of humor. Once I was booked, he told me, "Don't ever carry a can of mace again."

"Sergeant, that stuff is very expensive," I replied. "Why don't you let me send it home to my mother."

"I can't do that," he replied.

"Well, what am supposed to do to protect myself?"

"In England, you are not supposed to protect yourself," he replied, almost ashamed of the fact.

"Well, criminals have rights in the United States," I thought to myself, "but they have even more rights in England." Somehow it just does not make sense to me that I am not allowed to protect myself with whatever force I deem necessary. It shows how twisted "civilized" society has become.

On the way back to the motorcycle shop, I realized that there was life beyond Ealing. At home, I thought about Tigger - things weren't going so well for him, either. First, his motorcycle was stolen, and now the police. What next? Well, at least he wasn't booked!

They also raided George's apartment across the street. George was a middle-aged, balding pervert who used to come in and talk about all his porn movies, and braggod about the girls he had over to his apartment. He was the sort of slimy fellow that most likely only viewed the porn movies, and his only girls were his right or left hands. He constantly complained and hollered that "life is against me." He had never been out of Acton except for twelve years in prison after he shot someone in a nightclub (In England, civilians are not allowed to own guns, so only the criminals have them!).

Other types that used to frequent the motorcycle shop were drunks and drug addicts - the choice population of Acton. They'd come in and brag about what great motorcyclist they used to be. Blab, blab, blab. If Dave was there, he would tell them to leave, and they'd usually go; Tigger would just throw them out - he had zero tolerance for that type of "biker."

Steve Rose called to say that "All was on in Huddersfield for the 12th of April," and gave me the number of the Barnsley Warrior Motor Cycle Club, and of a painter called "Trotsky" who wanted to paint the gas tanks on my motorcycle. The Barnsley Warriors Motor Cycle Club were the first motorcycle club in the world to lend me a helping hand - people who took time to care about what I was doing and why I was doing it.

The days went by working in the shop, waiting for the time to get on the road again. Though the work was unpleasant, Dave could, with his constant farting, be even more unpleasant. His passing of gas seemed to be an endless source of a amusement.

While we were working, the dogs were kept inside the office. Whenever someone would enter the shop, they'd both start barking until Dave shouted, "Shut up you fucking dogs!" Then he'd go to the front and take care of the customer who, by this time, was probably wondering if he or she had come to the right place.

April 11: My last day at work. The routine was the same, except at the end of the day Dave paid me. We would see each other again when I finished the Cheshire foundation tour in 3 weeks.

That evening was spent preparing the motorcycle for the trip up to Huddersfield. I paid Mary and Ernie off, and said my "good-byes," knowing I'd be leaving early the next morning.

The night was a restless one due to the anticipation of the ride out of London.

Tours, T-shirts, and Temperatures

April 12: Up at 05:30 and on my way.

The weather had been fairly good for the past week, but this morning it was gloomy. After getting on to the freeway, it started to rain. Situation normal. Despite the weather, the traffic flowed well, and I made good time. Huddersfield was 200 miles (320 km.) north of London, and I made it there in 5 1/2 hours.

At the Chamber of Commerce, they called Steve Rose. When he arrived, we did a newspaper interview, and then he took me over to the Huddersfield Hotel - over 200 years old. Royalty had stayed there in the distant past, and despite its age, it seemed to be a cozy place.

Steve had arranged for the Barnsley Warriors to meet us at Trotsky's paint shop about 10 miles (16 km) away. Traveling there, I felt a strange vibration in the rear wheel. After meeting the Barnsley Warriors, I checked the rear wheel and discovered much movement in it. I pulled it off, but first removed the gas tanks and front fender so that Trotsky could start working on them.

When the rear wheel was off, we saw that one of the bearings had worn out the hub it rests in. This was a major problem! Trotsky said, "There's an engineering shop across the alley." We took the wheel over to them, and I explained how important it was to have this problem solved by tomorrow morning.

It was Friday afternoon.

"We'll see what we can do," they told me.

"The first long ride out on this pig and it is already giving me major shit."

We all agreed to meet the next morning.

Steve then suggested we go over to a pub that had been taking a special collection for the local Cheshire home. We had a lunch, and there I met a good looking young woman with the same birthday as mine - April 12th - TODAY! We all chatted, then went back to the hotel where I cleaned up, relaxed a bit, and in the evening Steve returned for what is known as a "pub crawl."

Now understand, I'm a very boring guy, and don't drink anymore. Nevertheless, we visited several crowded pubs, endured the noise, and ended up in the one I had been in that afternoon. There I met the birthday girl again. We talked, and I started to think there might be a chance for a short term romance here, when, wouldn't you know it, in walks her old boy friend, and the ass end falls out of my seduction plans. Oh well, I'm on a motorcycle adventure, not a love ride!

The next morning, Steve was at the hotel and we drove in his wreck of a car to Trotsky's. Trotsky had spent most of the evening doing a great paint job to the tanks and fender. He had painted a globe, with a rider, on the right tank. The left tank had "around the world" on it. There was also a list of the names of the countries I had traveled through painted on the right tank (I was most proud of this).

Now, for the rear wheel.

The engineers had worked for a few hours and were able to build up the inside of the housing so that the bearing fit nicely. They wanted £ 60.00 ($115.00) for the job - money well spent since they saved the day.

After assembling the motorcycle, we went to the *Royal Swan* pub where the newspaper people were waiting, along with some of the residents of the Beachwood Cheshire home. The motorcycle was carried up the steps into the pub, and in a short ceremony the fund-raising money was handed over to the Cheshire home residents. We had a toast, then lifted the greasy dirty motorcycle the hell out of the pub.

We took the motorcycle to the hotel, and I cleaned up for a party that was being thrown by the Barnsley Warriors. At the party, it didn't take long for things to get in full swing. What a sight! It was all bikers... both Harley riders and people with Japanese motorcycles. Actually, there was only one person in the club who had a Harley - Rob Murphy. I later discovered that most the members of this club were masters at building custom Japanese motorcycles.

As the party progressed and booze flowed, I choked on cigarette smoke. Even though I am deaf in one ear, and have only partial hearing in the other, the music was so loud that my good ear was going numb. During one pause in the music, Rob called me forward and bestowed upon me a B.W. T-shirt.

What a great honor!

I pledged to them that I would wear it to the North Cape (in fact, I wore it to many other unique places the world over). Before the evening was over, as I was dancing with one of the lovely ladies, I felt something slipped into my pocket. When I checked later, I found that they had put the cost of the rear wheel repair into my pocket. What a great sense of brotherhood this group had shared with me.

Very late in the evening, after saying "good-bye" to all, I took a cab back to the hotel. The next day was spent relaxing and reading. I also scoured information on the Harley Davidson Super Rally to be held in Honderfoss, Norway, in May.

The next morning, with the rubbish collectors watching, I started up and rode away, thinking how thankful I was to God for the opportunities given to me.

The sky was gloomy and the highway was crowded, so it was hard to appreciate the countryside. The sun found one gap in the clouds, and her rays beamed out as I headed north. **The dark blue North Sea seemed so incredible. "This adds**

another ocean that I have had the privilege to see from the back of the motorcycle."

By midday, I enter Edinburgh and immediately become horribly lost. After asking directions at least six times, I finally located Mayfield Cheshire home where I was greeted by the lady in charge.

Alister, the Harley Davidson dealer in town, came by to greet me and give me some Harley Davidson T-shirts. Believe it or not, this was the first time that a proper Harley dealer had even taken notice of the trip!

After dinner, I set up for my slide show - the first one of my life; I was very nervous. We started at 19:00, and despite my nervousness, the retelling of the journey from South Africa seemed to go rather well. Everyone stayed for the entire show - about ninety minutes.

The next morning, Alister and a few fellows from the Harley Davidson dealership rode up to escort me out of Edinburgh. They led me out of town to the A68 highway. Before we parted, Alister asked, "Dave, is there anything else we can do?"

"Yes," I replied, "could you please call the factory and speak to the head of Public Relations International?"

He said he would. I hoped to be able to set up an appointment with the Harley management team when I arrived in the U.S.A..

I shivered along through the countryside, in and out of snow flurries and ice-cold winds, somehow managing to get myself lost, riding an unnecessary extra twenty miles. My humor was lower than the temperature.

When I climbed on my bike to leave, I thought, "Please, please don't break down on me."

This day I was to meet the chairman of the Durham County Council, Mr. Mick Terrins. Yes, I needed to wear a jacket and tie, and then cover it with my rain gear since there was still snow coming down. At the Durham County Council's offices, Mick Terrins, chairman of the council, greeted me, and turned out to be quite an interesting 81 year old fellow. He had worked fifty years underground in the coal mines, so he was a man's man who clearly understood the problems of the working people. Despite his age, he climbed on the back of my motorcycle to pose for the photographers.

"I hope I can keep from puking all over everyone," I thought as I met the other councilmen and councilwomen for lunch. Since they all had drinks, they reminded me of what Dave and Tigger would say to me when we talked about parliament - "Everybody is soused all the time, and that's how they run Britain." I had a bit of a chuckle to myself over that one. But please, do not misunderstand. This crowd really appeared to be very sober.

After lunch, I conducted a radio interview by telephone. Chairman Terrins then presented me a tie, a book with the history of Durham County, and a specially cut wine glass for my mother. What a warm and touching gesture.

Next, onto Marsk by the sea, where I was warmly greeted by the matron of the home, Connie Turner. I worked on the motorcycle for awhile, then pushed it over to the garage and lockup area about fifty meters away. I had just completed that task when a reporter and photographer asked me, "Dave, could you move the motorcycle back out so we can take pictures?"

Naturally.

With flu and fever, I brought the bike out and then put it back again. After that, it was time to get ready to do my talk and slide show that evening to an audience of about fifty people. I was impressed how the matron had called the local motorcycle club and asked them if they would like to attend the show.

A dozen bikers were in attendance, and it felt good to have other bikers in the audience. Had a bit of trouble with the old fellow who was changing my slides for me. He would miss slides because he was shaking so badly. Although he was doing the best he could, it put me on the spot. Oh well, you can't win them all! At least he was trying.

The next morning, as I was getting ready to leave, a reporter and photographer show up, asking for a story and pictures, and requesting that I ride the motorcycle around for them. When I was getting ready to leave again, another car pulls up requesting a radio interview for a local station in Cleveland.

After "good-byes," I hit the road to the Spofforth Cheshire Home in Weatherby - in the freezing snow. The snow forced me to keep one hand off the handlebars just to keep my glasses clear. My index finger became a wiper.

Next, the motorcycle started to run rough when the headlight was on. "There must be something wrong with charging system."

It never seems to end.

When I arrived in the Weatherby area, I eventually find the home, and am greeted by a gentleman named Phillip, who had served thirty seven years in the British Armed Forces, including a tour in Korea. He had been promoted from an enlisted man to a wing commander - the equivalent of a colonel by the time he retired. We talked off and on for the next couple of hours about military service, and about the various military conflicts happening throughout the world.

"Dave, is there anything I can do for you?" he asked me.

"Well, I have been having a problem with my motorcycle's charging system. Is there someone you know who can help? I think it is an electrical problem, and my battery is starting to die."

"I'll look into it and see what I can do. I have a friend who is a bit of motorcycle buff. I'll speak to him."

That night, in bed, the flu and fever still were attacking - I shook, shivered and sweated throughout the night.

Sources of Inspiration - and Perspiration

The next morning brought another very rough and disappointing day. Supposedly, I was to rest and take it easy on the weekends, but that was not the case.

Phillip called his neighbor, an aerodynamics engineer, to check the charging system. He discovered that the starter solenoid I had bought new in London a couple of months before had gone bad. We called the Harley Davidson dealer about forty miles away and he had the part, so off Phillip and I go to get it.

With new solenoid in hand, at a price of twenty five pounds sterling, we head back and I install the part. Next, since the battery is still down, we take it over to a battery shop and recharge it.

In bed, I read a very touching letter from a woman named Carol Williams who had taken in my talk and slide show at the Marsk Cheshire Home. She told me how much I had touched her and her husband's life. He had a bad motorcycle accident and a badly damaged ankle that was never right. She told me that my talk motivated them to live their future dreams. Letters like this one, and ones in the future, would help me keep going when I started to question my reasons for doing the trip. Although I never thought about quitting, there were times when I questioned my own reasons for the trip. Often, I'd ask myself, "Am I just doing this for myself, for my own selfish motives, and for the glorification of the Harley Davidson motorcycle? Why do I care about Harley Davidson anyway? To this time, they have not seen fit to lend me a helping hand or even answer my letters."

As I turned out the lights and said my evening prayer, I thought to myself, "Today is the 20th of April. What is the significance of the 20th of April?" The date kept ringing in my head until it hit me like a bell tolling. Twenty-one years ago today I left the United States to serve my country in Viet Nam.

During my talk and slide show, for over an hour I suffered unbearable misery from this flu. I was sweaty, shaky, and my back was killing me as I told my audience about the trip across Africa. When I asked, "Are there any questions?," I secretly prayed there would be none.

There were.

Afterwards, I staggered upstairs. It had been one hell of a day.

That night greeted me with more sweating and shaking. A nurse came in said, "Dave, your temperature is around 104." Later that evening, she checked it again, and it was down to about 100.

What a restful weekend!

The next morning I was off down the road again. Cold as it was, it seemed like magic riding through this countryside with patches of snow on the green pastures. The forested areas and agriculture all blended to make the landscape a kaleidoscope of shades of green against the bright blue sky. Even though I was still sick, just feeling the cold air, the sun and the beauty of the countryside all combined to make me feel better.

The next morning was one of the most touching in the entire trip as all the residents and staff gathered to see me off, waving and shaking hands with me before I rode out into the English countryside.

The 40 mile trip to Honorfeld Cheshire Home near Birmingham, a big industrial center, went quickly.

The outstanding resident in this home was Vincent, who had a bad heart and was a paraplegic. Vincent seemed deeply pensive in his ideas about his immediate surroundings, and about the world around him.

The talk and slide show went fairly well; the children in the audience pushed me to a new level of creativeness, trying to hold their quickly-diverted attention. After the show, I collected my slides and went upstairs where the nurse brought me some cocoa to soothe my shakes and sweating.

I got up to a gray, overcast and rainy day still feeling terrible. Victor led me out of town, and waved to me from his van as I sped down the highway. In Stockport I got lost, and pulled off the road to check my map and to relieve myself (I had to piss so bad it was coming out my ears).

When I re-started the motorcycle, it gave me a hard start. "What now?" I thought, feeling sick. "It's raining out, and now this thing has a dead battery again." Anyway, it barely started, and as I went down the road I realized it needed gas.

Pull into a Stockport petrol station for fuel.

Once again, it barely started. With a very depressed feeling inside, I rode out into the traffic. At a major intersection, sitting between cars, the engine died.

The machine would not start. The battery was dead.

With cars moving all around me, I climb off the thing, put the kickstand up, and pushed it across this big intersection to a safe place, away from traffic, about one hundred yards away.

Now, I'm soaking with sweat and rain. Finally, a man named John comes up to me and says, "If we can back this thing around the corner, I've got a buddy who has an apartment there who may be able to help you."

"The battery's dead," I told him.

"He has a charger," John replied.

So, we backed the motorcycle around the corner where I met Paul, a Harley Davidson fan who put the battery on charge. It turns out Paul has a Harley all in pieces in his apartment - I was among fellow bikers! They called another friend, an auto electrician, who came over and checked out the alternator and charging system.

"The alternator is not putting out," he told me.

"Great, that's a very big job!" I thought to myself. As a temporary solution, we went to an automotive shop where I bought a battery charger and put it away in my bag. I called Irene at the Green Gables home and explained, "I'll be a bit late."

After charging the battery, I start the motorcycle up and thank these very kind people for their help. Shaky, miserable, headachey and sweaty from fever, I rode out into the light rain.

My next destination - the Hovenden House Cheshire Home, a beautiful estate in the country in an area where Robin Hood and his band of merry men had lived many centuries before. I received a phone call from Diana Charleton, the marketing manager of the Harley Davidson Motor Company - U.K. Boy, my head really perked up then! "Harley Davidson is finally taking notice of my trip, what do you know."

"Hello Dave, what are you doing?" she asked. I explained about the around the world trip, and told her how I'd come all the way across Africa, and of the work I was doing for the Cheshire Foundation and the disabled.

"That sounds wonderful," she replied. "What can we do for you?"

"Well, I have a bad alternator, can you do anything about that?"

"I'm sorry," she replied, "I can't help you there."

"Well," I replied, "how about thirty thousand dollars to do the rest of the trip?"

"I am VERY sorry about that," she immediately answered. "I definitely cannot help you."

Of course, I knew these answers would be forthcoming. On a more realistic note, I asked her to phone and write the public relations and marketing people of Harley Davidson in Milwaulkee.

She promised to do that, and told me, "I speak to them at least once a week."

I was trying to establish a groundwork so that when I contacted the Milwaulkee office once I arrived in the US, I would be able to get some kind of an audience with them.

That evening, starting to feel physically better, I gave one of my best talks and slide shows to about seventy people (all the residents, staff and families were in attendance). At the end of the show, Mr. Wilson, head of the home, shook my hand and thanked me. One of the nurses jumped up and presented me with a Bic Click ball-point pen - like I used to give out to people who had given me a hand. We all laughed.

The next day, I headed towards the Park House Cheshire Hotel for the disabled, located in the Sandringham area. As I rode down a narrow country lane, the trees had grown over the top of the road. The sun filtered down through the green leaves and branches, causing an amazing effect. The woods were quite thick with underbrush, and I could envision lords and ladies bounding out through the woods dressed up in costumes of yesteryear, following a pack of hunting hounds who were hot on the scent of a fox. It was as if the spirits of the past, of a time long gone, were all around me and I could feel their restless energy as I passed through the forest.

I rode along the wall of Queen Elizabeth's Sandringham Summer Estate to Park House, another historic home going back many hundreds of years. The Queen gave it to Lord Leonard Cheshire for the Cheshire Foundation. Lord Cheshire turned it into a hotel for the disabled; **to my knowledge, this was the only hotel in the world that catered to people with disabilities of any kind** - blindness, paraplegia, quadriplegia, muscular sclerosis, muscular dystrophy, you name it. People with massive disabilities could relax in a different and entertaining surrounding, away from the daily life of the regimented Cheshire Homes. It was also a place where residents from different homes could meet to discuss problems and ideas.

I was shown to a beautiful room where I settled in before meeting with the reporters and photographers. When I was asked to wheel out the motorcycle, I became a bit irritated by one photographer who kept saying, "Let me help you push it. Let me help you with that."

"Please, leave it alone. It's better if I do it myself," I explained.

After media interviews, I rode over to a World War I monument right outside the gates of the Sandringham Estate. The monument had six sides on it, and contained the names of men who had died in the 1914 - 1918 Great War. Often, there was more than one name from the same family (there were at least three different sets of double names). I was shocked at the amount of suffering within these families, and thought to myself, "After all the suffering of this so called 'war to end all wars,' it wasn't twenty years later and we did it again."

That afternoon I presented my talk and slide show to the most miserable audience I'd had on this trip. There were fifteen people, most of whom went to sleep and fidgeted; no staff was in attendance, and there was absolutely no interest.

At the hotel, I met Michael, wounded in the war in Ireland. He had been shot in the head, and lost all ability to use his arms. His talk was sporadic, repetitive and difficult for him. His injury sentenced him to a wheelchair for the rest of his life. Michael's one delight was to yell "Yabba Dabba Do" "Yabba Dabba Do" incessantly, to the point of becoming maddening. "You'd do well with Fred Flintstone," I thought.

Most of the people in these homes have never been in a war, never rode a motorcycle, and were struck down by fate, generally in the prime of their lives, disabled through disease, sickness, or accidents. It is always a grim reminder to me, and should be to anyone else who encounters the disabled, how fortunate we are to be able to look after ourselves, whether we have a disability or not.

Another house with special memories on this trip was the Seven Rivers Cheshire Home where I visited an old church dating back to the 1330's. There was a list of all the pastors who had presided over the church from the time it was established. I was amazed at the small stairwells within the church that went up into the steeple. These stairwells were far too small for anyone nowadays to climb except for a small child.

Plaques on the walls commemorated folks who had died in foreign lands. Many of them were personnel of the Royal Navy, or in the Army. By each name, it described whether they were killed in action or killed by an accident. I especially felt for those killed by accident or sickness while serving abroad, but not really in the line of duty...more a victim of circumstances. Being a soldier myself, I know every man dreads dying from a sickness or an accident while on active duty in a war zone. To fall fighting for one's country is a far more preferable death (if there is such a thing as a preferable death).

I met a young boy named David who served in the Sea Cadets. While walking out on the perimeter of the home where they had a lake, David came up to me and started asking me all kinds of questions, and telling me about the Sea Cadets. I sensed immediately that he was a very sensitive young man. He wanted my address, so we walked back to my room where I gave it to him and told him he could write to me. He gave me a big hug and walked away with a tear in his eye.

Later at the show, David's mother was there, and told me how much her son had been touched by my presence. I pulled out my Buck fishing knife that had the marlin spike on it for opening knots, and gave it to her to give to him (he was unable to attend the talk). "He can use this in the Sea Cadets," I explained to her.

The next morning, it took me two hours to go eighty miles in the terrible weather on the back roads because I couldn't use my headlights (remember my charging problem?) while traveling to the Anthill Cheshire Home - a "purpose built" Cheshire Home. Anthill had no history, but was specifically built for the disabled, and had a big occupational therapy area.

As I relaxed later that day in this place, I came to realize that a purpose home was not one I particularly cared for. There were buzzers going off all hours of the day and night (difficult to sleep), and there was very little peace and quiet with trolleys going down the hallway rattling. Anthill brought back some very unpleasant memories of one military hospital in Pretoria, South Africa.

06:00: I awoke to buzzers going off and rain outside my window.

"God bless their suffering souls," I thought as I rode out into the rain. In my eagerness to get away from that hospital atmosphere, I suddenly realized that I had forgot to put on my rain pants, soaking my whole lower body and flooding out the sockets of the legs!

Another home visited on this trip was the Le Court Cheshire Home where I met a fellow named Tony Reynolds, the Head of the British Racing Car Driver's Society for the Disabled. He was in a wheelchair because his bones were fusing together. Tony drove racing cars with hand controls, and passed all the tests required to show competence (Tony was not a resident of the home).

Jane, a reporter from the local radio station, did an interview and, no shit, she insisted on recording the sound of the motorcycle. So I drug the bloody thing out of the garage where it had been charging it's battery and started it up for her.

Next, members of the Disabled Motorcycle Association arrived with their President, Andy Brown, or "Bandit" as he was known, introducing himself and the rest of the members. Each member of the club had a disability, ranging from paraplegics to amputees, mostly from motorcycle accidents. They immediately made me a member of the National Association for Disabled Motorcyclists of Britain - quite an honor.

The next morning I arrived at the Arnold House Cheshire Home, my last stop on the tour. Tony Tabot, from the main office in London, was in attendance at one of the better talks I was to give.

Afterwards, I climbed into bed and closed my day, knowing that my work for the Chochiro Foundation, at least for now, was over. The tour had taken me to 16 Homes throughout England and Scotland.

Chapter Fourteen

Suspense, Starters and a Super Rally

May 3, 1991: Without much pomp and ado, I rode back to the M-25 and then to the M-4 and into Hammersmith and made my way over to the Tiger Cycles in Acton (West London) where I was greeted by the dank smell of dog shit, urine, oil, and gasoline. When the two dogs barked, Dave shouted, "Shut up you fucking dogs."

I knew I was home.

We unloaded the motorcycle and put it away without the worry of reporters coming and asking me to lug it out again. During breakfast, it was decided that I go down to live on a friend of Tigger's boat. I felt it would be better than going back to West Kensington where things were pretty crowded, and I didn't want to add to it.

We took what I needed out to the Thames River and put my stuff aboard. They left, saying, "We'll be back in the evening."

"Oh boy," I thought, "we're in for a big night."

The rest of the day I just kicked back and relaxed, enjoying the quiet and solitude of the boat.

I truly needed a break.

About 19:00, big ole Tigger and Dave stick their heads into the window, and the nocturnal activities begin! We walk down to a place called *The Magpie and Crown Pub.* There was a jolly crowd in attendance that Saturday night. Everybody was raising hell and having a good time, boozing it up. When the pub closed, we walked back to the boat, then decided I would drive us into town (since I had not been drinking any alcohol) and we would get something to eat.

Driving Tigger's Land Rover is an exercise in ambidexterity since it has a clutch (I need both hands and arms to manipulate it). Tigger and I are in the front, and we have drunk spitting Dave in the back. Dave keeps grabbing my head and knocking it forward, trying to pull my baseball cap over my eyes as I manipulate the very narrow back streets in London.

Tigger is a fast driver even when he's sober; he keeps me in constant suspense as to whether he is going to hit a car parked along the side of the road. When he is going to pass somebody, he never slows down, and usually passes with only inches to spare on each side of the vehicle.

Now, it is my turn to try and drive these narrow streets, passing oncoming drivers probably as full of booze as my own cargo. Spitting Dave is still grabbing at me, making a general "ASS" of himself while trying to get us all killed.

We stop at a hamburger stand and order. While waiting for our order, Dave decides to dance with me. Shit Head is so drunk that he falls back and I go down on him. We are rolling around in the dirt, both of us trying with little success to get up. This incident completely ruins my only clean clothes. Dave is cackling like a idiot while Tigger sits there looking at us like we are a couple of dumb bastards. Funny enough, I felt like a dumb bastard rolling around with spitting Dave. All the time the general public is walking by as if nothing is going on.

After eating our hamburgers and dusting ourselves off, we still had to drive the few miles back to the docks where the boat is moored. Dave is once again in the back seat, grabbing my head and shaking it.

Finally, the obstacle course completed, I park the vehicle near the boat. Tigger immediately grabs his sleeping bag, and I have mine. We heard Dave wandering around on the upper level of the boat, whining to himself, "I want something warm to sleep with or I'm going to get cold." In the end, he threw his jacket over himself, and probably shook and shivered through the rest of the night (Suffer, you bastard!).

The next day I awoke to Tigger's snoring - sounded like a huge beached whale. Dave was back to moaning, complaining about the cold. I made tea for the lot of us, and we all sat and laughed about last night's adventures.

After they left, I read a book for the rest of the day, contemplating all the excitement and pressure of these past few weeks on the road: the public speaking, the media interviews, meeting new people, mechanical problems, and being constantly on the move.

Now, it all came to sudden stop.

I also thought about all the things I needed to do to get ready for my attempt to ride to the North Cape - the top of Europe. Of course, my biggest challenge was to repair the motorcycle and get the charging system working.

The next day I made a few phone calls at the marina pay phone. I studied my maps, looking for the best route to take from here to Belgium, and then on to Denmark, Sweden and Norway. The trip calculated out at about 5,000 miles (8,000 km.). My main concerns were the weather in the Arctic, and the condition and reliability of the motorcycle.

The Lord of Compassion

Tuesday, May 7th: An eventful day.

After coffee with Dave at the motorcycle shop, I put on a suit and tie and pulled out the motorcycle. My battery had been charged up the night before, so the machine was ready to head into the heart of the terrible London traffic - not something I relished. Since traffic seems to average about six miles per hour, I often cut between the lanes - not big lanes like in the United States, but very narrow lanes, increasing the danger. It is "white knuckle" riding all the way down to Victoria Station, then to the Strand in the heart of London to Maunsel Street where the Leonard Cheshire Foundation is located.

Tony Talbot greeted me, and we took some pictures. At about noon, Lord Group Captain, Leonard Cheshire, Victoria Cross - arrived (Victoria Cross is the same as our medal of honor). We shook hands and took photos with the motorcycle, then went inside where we had a little cheese and wine party in my honor. Lord Cheshire and I sat and spoke to one another for about twenty minutes, almost oblivious to the crowd around us. He was a tall, thin man with balding hair, and had deep-set, sensitive and penetrating eyes on a very thin face.

If I ever was close to a living saint, it would be this man. Of all the people I met on this trip around the world, without hesitation I'd say that Group Captain, Lord Leonard Cheshire was the most incredible and impressive person I met.

One thing he said that was to shape the destiny of this journey.

"Would you be willing to go through China to our home there in Kunming, and on to the home in Moscow?"

"Indeed I would," I answered. If he had asked ask me to ride to the North Pole, somehow I would have attempted to do it!

After the luncheon, I returned to the motorcycle shop where I took off my suit and tie and put the motorcycle up on the rack. I pulled the primary apart and found that the alternator had been torn right off it's mountings on the side of the crank case. Tigger and I could not understand how or why something like this had happened.

The next day Tigger and I continued working on the motorcycle, still looking for the noise and banging in the lower end. We pulled off the rear cylinder head, but didn't find anything wrong.

"Maybe there's a piston banging around," I thought, but there wasn't.

My evenings were peaceful and pleasant, sleeping on the boat. My dinners usually consisted of scrambled eggs and beans on bread. It might not sound very appetizing to you, but after a full day's work, it was the only meal I had the energy to fix.

The next day, Dave said, "Let's start on the Harley again." We fit the rear cylinder head back on, and adjusted the push rods. Then we put in the carb and intake manifold. Tigger lent us a hand with that. By now, it was 20:00, and time to go home.

On my walk to the bus stop, I had back pain and my stumps were killing me. No wonder - I'm on my feet ninety percent of the time during the day. Naturally, the bus had standing room only. At the next bus stop I wait, then catch the bus down to the next one, then walk down to the marina, a little over a kilometer. By the time I hit the boat, I was in horrible pain!

Unfortunately, I still had to cook my dinner before I could experience the blissful relief of taking my legs off and laying back to let the pain flow out of my stumps.

Friday, May 10th: Hit the motorcycle shop earlier than usual and woke Dave up. He was pissed off because I was earlier than normal. You'd think I was the police banging on the door. After he settled down, I started more repairs on the Harley Davidson. About 09:30, I was ready to start it up - it seemed to run okay, but I won't know for sure until out on the highway and can get the engine real good and hot.

The rest of the day I did various jobs for Dave, and at five thirty I started on the Harley again, first taking the rear wheel off and breaking down the rear tire, fitting a new tire on the back. This was a big job.

Dave didn't like the looks of the spokes in the front wheel, so he took the front wheel off and replaced all the spokes. By about 19:30, Peter Morpuss arrived, followed shortly after by Graham Gilmore. We all went over to Paul's parent's place in West Kensington, then on to a pub where we had fish and chips.

Peter and I spent the night on the boat where he shared the frustrations of his job, and the headaches he was facing working twelve to sixteen hour days in the hotel. Though he had a career and I didn't, I felt sorry for him, realizing my worries sometimes are quite small and petty compared to earning a living in the hard world of industry. Compared to working a regular job, I'll take any adventure or hazardous way of life.

The next morning as we parted, I realized what a dear friend Peter was - my "best friend" from the South African Army, truly a sidekick, a confidant, a good man and a good soldier. We have experienced much together, including my miserable cooking when we were in the army.

Back at the shop, I put the wheel on the Harley and snug up all the bolts and nuts on the machine, taking it off the rack. In the late afternoon, I started loading up the motorcycle only to notice it had a flat rear tire.

I could have screamed I was so angry!

I unloaded the motorcycle, jacked it up, take the wheel off, and break it down to find out why a brand new tire and tube had gone flat. The answer: I put a hole in it while mounting it the first time.

Replaced the tube, said "good-bye" to Dave and Tigger for the last time before my journey. I owed so much to these fellows. Who knows how much more time and money I would have spent in England without their help?

Back at the docks, the care taker helped me put the motorcycle in a secure shed. Then, I made my way down to the boat, knowing there'd be no sleep this night. I read until about nine-thirty, then thought about my challenge tomorrow as I embarked on the road towards the North Cape. I closed the day with the normal apprehension and excitement in my heart before another big quest.

This day would be my last in England for several weeks.

On to the Cape!

May 12: 05:47: Sunday morning, and it was exceptionally quiet as I took the long walk up the docks, painfully climbing to the top of the hill where I took the motorcycle out of the shed, loaded it up, and got ready to break the morning quiet with the sound of my engine starting.

Varoooom.

That sound is exhilarating!

After warming up the motor, and listening carefully as I always do, it is time to head out to the M-4 motorway, then to the M-25 (the ring motorway around London), heading South towards Dover. The day is a bright sunny one, so it's with a very light-hearted feeling I rode. Once off the M-25, it is easy to appreciate the beautiful English countryside.

Suddenly, it dawns on me... "I am on the move, I'm really on the move again! All this sitting, waiting, working and apprehension has a payoff - this day, the next portion of the trip begins."

I think about the trials and tribulations I've faced from the day I left Johannesburg to head to the North Cape, but nothing could dampen the excitement of being on the move again.

Exhilarating.

Wonderful.

The bright sun, the green fields, the great road conditions made my heart pitter patter with excitement. In Dover, I called the Borner Family to say "hello" and inform them that I was doing well. I thanked them again for their kindness and hospitality while I was a boarder with them.

At the ferry offices it cost me forty pounds sterling to take a boat across the Zeebrugge into Belgium. I rode the motorcycle onto the boat and strapped it all down, then went up and bought myself a lunch (a big treat for me). When I was going through the line, one of the cooks said "Take all you want as far as vegetables and stuff like this."

"All right," I thought, thinking I was in hog heaven. But, when I come to the cashier, I was two pounds fifty short. As I was searching for more money, the cashier said, "There's no one around. Don't worry about it. Just go on through." It seemed my good feelings were rubbing off onto other people (it won't last).

As the ferry pulled out at about eleven-thirty, I walked around a bit on the bow, looking across the English Channel as we made our way toward Zeebrugge in Belgium. When the ship put into port at Zeebrugge, I unstrapped my motorcycle and found my way out to the M-49 heading north for Holland. After about eighty miles, I crossed the Dutch border and stopped for fuel and directions to the next camping area. "There's one real close," I was told, so I made my way over and checked in.

While setting up camp, two young boys came over to gawk at the motorcycle and unsuccessfully asked me questions (they spoke only Dutch and I spoke only English). We tried to communicate by sign language as they touched and looked at the motorcycle in amazement. I imagined them saying, "Can you believe he actually rides this piece of junk?"

After a typical dinner of beans and pasta, I closed the day at 21:30 by crawling into my little tent that Dave had given me - the end of my first day back on the road.

The next morning my breakfast consisted of heated leftovers from the night before (sound like my journey across Africa?). Some habits die hard. Anything to save a buck - money is always a big worry. There's never been much of it in my life, and my meager supply is steadily dwindling.

I hit the starter button and the roar of the engine announces the start of a new day. As it warms up, I put on my kidney belt, then my jacket on over that, moving out of the campground into the surrounding countryside, then on to a major highway going towards Nijmegen and Arnhem. Heading towards those cities, I remembered from reading a book called *A Bridge Too Far* that two big battles in World War II were fought by British paratroopers in these areas.

The road in Holland is very good, moving through lowlands and swampy areas (not swamps, just very wet pasture lands, quite soggy). Unlike England, there are no rock borders from one farm to the next. Instead, they have fences much like we have in the United States (in my opinion, not nearly as beautiful as England). Every so often I'd see a giant, massive windmill. Like most other people, I imagined the windmills in Holland to be small, dainty, quaint little affairs, but the ones I saw along the highway on this day were massive four story structures with huge propellers - most impressive.

About 14:30 I crossed the border into Germany.

The terrain changed quickly!

Now I was riding in rolling hills with forested lands - much more like North America. As I pressed on through the rain, I found a campground and decided to spend the evening (I'd ridden over three hundred miles that day).

I went into the local store and bought a few things for my dinner, but forgot to buy sugar and tea. Ever since I was in the South African hospital after the land mine accident, I've have had a major problem with my short term retention. It just seems to be getting worse.

I had my dinner in the miserable rain. When I took off my legs, my left stump was in terrible pain. Looking down at it, I noticed a pussy discharge coming out of two sores.

That's not good news.

To try and stop the problem, I cleaned the sores and covered them up with elastoplast tape.

02:00: Woke up, but could do nothing but lay in bed until 06:00 when I heated up my soggy noodles for breakfast, packed the motorcycle, then headed for Hamburg.

It rained right through Hamburg, and the traffic was terrible. The German countryside, though beautiful, is very crowded. The autobahns themselves are magnificent highways, and one always knows when one is getting close to a major city in Germany because the traffic starts backing up for miles, making it necessary to cut between the lanes.

I fueled up and met my first group of Harley people going North; we exchanged a few pleasant words.

Shortly after that, I crossed the German border into Denmark, fighting the rain and head winds all the time. In the Danish countryside, things were more modern looking compared to England. Denmark is much more like Germany - rolling hills, but less wooded areas.

As I made my way North, sometimes the main highway went down to one lane in each direction (not a dual carriageway). The cities were all clean and neat, and people often would smile and wave as I went by.

The cost of gasoline was shocking! Germany ran about $4.25 a gallon; I was amazed people were able to own a car at those prices. Further, the cost of oil in Germany and Denmark was $8.00 per liter (quart).

Heading north, the wind was a gale force, pushing me all over the road. I had a few close shaves. Look at a map and you will notice that Denmark is virtually a peninsula between the Baltic Sea and the North Sea - hence the strong winds.

On my next stop, I asked a young girl directions to the closest campground in the area. As she was talking, I glanced down at a magazine on the counter in front of us and saw a very explicit photo that graphically displayed the lower part of the female anatomy. She saw that I saw the magazine. We both smiled, but frankly, mine was more a smile of embarrassment than anything else.

My camp was far away from anyone else - very isolated. My tent could not stand in this howling wind. I prayed it didn't start raining as well. Finally, I crawled into the sleeping bag at 20:00, though it was still light, just to avoid the wind.

The next morning, the winds continued, promising a miserable and rainy day as I rode through Ålborg on up to Fredericshavn where I purchased a ticket on the ferry to go across to Götenborg. While waiting for the ferry, one fellow who spoke very good English told me, "It's still frozen and extremely cold in the north. Ice is on the roads. I don't know if you can make it to the North Cape. Why not try later? Maybe June."

His report put me in a very low mood as I stood waiting for the ferry in gray, cloudy and rainy weather.

13:00: The ferry arrived, opened up it's bow, and all outgoing traffic unloaded, heading to their destinations. The motorcyclists rode on, secured their bikes, then went up on deck. From the front of the ferry, I watched the waves crash under the bow of the ship from a sheltered area.

"Doesn't this rotten weather ever let up?" I wondered. "It is starting to put me in a very low state of morale." It reminded me of the Cheshire tour throughout England and Scotland where I rarely experienced any sunshine.

As we started to come into Götenborg port, I went down to unstrap the motorcycle and put on my rain gear when I felt something in the sleeve of my jacket - an allen key that had been missing. Finding the tool felt like an omen from God to cheer me up. It enabled me to switch my mirror (in Europe they drive on the right side, so car and motorcycle mirrors are positioned differently). With a light heart, I rolled out of the ship, went through customs quite quickly, and moved on North through the rest of Sweden.

The E-6 single lane highway wound through the mountains and deep gorges. I rode over a bridge several hundred feet high and realized that below was a giant Fjord (a canyon full of sea water) with magnificent, steep cliff walls. The countryside displayed numerous pine trees, but the terrain was very rocky. If the sun would come out, this place might seem like paradise

At the Norwegian border, while attempting to negotiate the custom's area, I fell over. A truck driver came and helped me upright the motorcycle. I said "thank you" and got out of there in a hurry, embarrassed, my tail between my pegs.

The engine of the Harley Davidson is hammering away as usual; the noise is in the lower end, I'm just hoping it will get me through this trip and back to England where I can do something to repair it.

Norwegian drivers don't seem to be in any hurry to get anywhere. They are slow, very careful drivers, and easy to pass on the well-maintained roads. As I entered a camping area in the late afternoon, an old man who ran the place said, "No, I don't want any money. Just go and camp any where you want."

What a nice gesture.

My mileage this day was just over two hundred miles, all in high winds and rain. There's over 2000 miles (3200 km.) to get to the North Cape. That night, again unable to erect the tent because of the winds, I slept in a green pasture, enjoying the gathering dark.

On the bright side, the rain stopped!

May 16: The next morning, while still in my sleeping bag, the old man brought me a cup of coffee. When he saw my legs propped up against the side of the motorcycle his eyes seemed to shoot out of his head. Trembling hands offered me the coffee.

"Thank you very much, sir" I said. He stared at me, looked at my legs, and walked off!

"Imagine that," I thought, "coffee in bed out in the wilderness. What a great way to start the day!"

Parties, Prizes, Salamis and a Super Rally

My next major stop was Oslo where it was rainy and miserable. On up the E-6 highway I continued until I came to Lillehammer, then asked directions to Honderfoss - the host city of the Harley Davidson Super Rally this year.

"Carry on another six kilometers," I was told, "and you come to a massive campground along a beautiful river with woods and trees - that's it." When I found it, I noticed a railroad track bordering the camp. During the next four days, no one seemed to notice the passing trains during the non-stop partying and music.

At registration, the desk fellow asked, "Where are you coming from?"

"South Africa," I reply.

"You have come from South Africa on that old Shovel Head?" he asked, somewhat amazed.

"Yes I have," I answered.

"Then you win. You win."

"I win? I win?" My spirits soared.

"What have I won?" I asked.

"The long distance award," he proudly replied. "No one has ever traveled overland from South Africa to this place for this rally here in Norway. You are definitely are going to win the long distance award. Congratulations. Now, your entrance fee will be $35.00."

I nearly shit my pants!

"That's a lot of money to me," I thought, "but its probably worth it. What the hell - I won." If I hadn't "won," I am sure I would have said, "Hey, forget it fellows" and just carried on. I envisioned that winning the long distance award probably meant there would be money, perhaps a trophy, and certainly a kiss from a pretty girl. All I needed to do to receive my reward was endure the noise and halibalu until the 20th. And so, with a very lighthearted feeling (everyone loves a winner), I went into the campground looking for a place to camp.

I found a campsite with some American fellows who were Army people. I met a fellow named Dan, who was retired from the U.S. Army, and a big fellow named John, married to a woman still in the Army (John had been out for years). I pitched my tent next to theirs, and we quickly became friends. John weighed over 300 pounds and sported a mohawk haircut. Dan, a retired warrant officer, had served in Viet Nam as a pathfinder, so the three of us had much in common. Dan's son, young Scott, sat and listened to all our lies and bullshit as we talked about the good ole days when we were "Young, dumb, and full of cum."

Some Norwegians from the camp office asked me, "Dave, would mind doing a newspaper interview?"

"No, not at all," I replied. "I'll be here for the next three days like everybody else, so if you want to call the newspaper that's fine with me."

They seemed so excited that I had come overland from South Africa to this meeting. "Oh boy, am I really in for it - this is going to be one hell of a prize." After all, I had traveled further than any of the other 2,500 Harley Davidson riders at the site.

To make matters better, the magnificent sun was finally out, the winds died down, and it didn't rain for the next three days. "Wonderful," I thought, "maybe the weather is getting better as the summer approaches."

Dan and John let me use their Coleman stove to cook my meals - it was so much more efficient than my small gas cooker.

Lillehammer was far enough North that it didn't get dark until about 24:30 at night, and the noise level at the meeting seemed always just short of ear-bursting. "The further North you go," I was told, "the longer the days will get until eventually there will be light twenty four hours a day." I had heard of these areas all my life, but to actually be going into them is another thing, and really got me excited.

On the second day of the rally, I did a long interview, riding the motorcycle and photographing for a national Norwegian newspaper. Later, a television crew came and interviewed me.

Our camp was next to a group of Swiss people who were very good at speaking English. Mike, the one guy in the crowd who couldn't speak English, was a virtual giant, about six foot seven. This huge fellow was also going to the North Cape.

"Maybe we should team up together," I suggested.

Mike was all for the idea. Even though he didn't speak much English, we knew that wouldn't bother us at all. "With this Goliath by my side," I thought, "I'll never have to worry about anybody trying to get nasty with me." I hadn't had any traveling companions since the Spanish fellows going across the Sahara Desert, so I liked the idea of traveling with somebody again. He also had a newer evolution Harley Davidson, so there should be no problem with break downs for him.

The bands seemed to play in endless shifts almost 24 hours a day. During the rare moments of band breaks, they piped in *loud* music! The drink of the day was moonshine - much cheaper than normal liquor. A glass of beer in a small glass was $5.00. But Norwegians made moonshine for much less. The government turns a blind eye to the homemade moonshine if you don't sell it. At the camp, they were selling it, and, if you drank a certain copious amount, you won a free cup. A pint of Johnny Walker Scotch would cost about $25.00 - shockingly expensive, just as the gasoline for $4.50 a gallon or more, or a can of beans for about $1.20. A crummy little hamburger and french fries cost about $8.00 at this meeting (and everywhere else).

I noticed there were few new Harley Davidsons here. Most Europeans rode older models, delighting in fixing up and repairing the old machines - like riding a piece of history.

John was a factory-trained mechanic, taking his course in Milwaukee. He volunteered to look at my motorcycle, so I took it out and rode about ten miles to get it good and hot, then John took it for a ride. He looked funny riding around on the thing with his mohawk haircut and huge belly.

"It sounds like your lower end is giving you trouble," he told me. "Those high pitched pounding and tinkling sounds are coming from the bottom end of the motor."

My spirits start to drop. "If the engine has to be gone through in Europe," I thought, "it will cost me a fortune."

I felt slightly better when he said, "It should make it back to England or the United States where you can do something about it a lot cheaper."

I made a decision to just keep going with the machine until it falls apart I'm determined only two things are going to stop this trip: 1. If I run out of money, and 2. A major accident cripples or kills me.

Mike learned a Norwegian word - "Fricken" - which means girls, and the fricken at this super rally were absolutely beautiful. They came from all over northern Europe, but mostly, from Scandinavia.

"Tomorrow I'm going to kiss one of these lovelies in the awards ceremony," I thought.

May 19th: The music was blaring as I was asked by the organizers of the rally to bring my motorcycle up to the main tent where they started giving out the awards. The announcer would say, "This award goes to the best custom paint job," "This award is for the best custom motorcycle," "This next award is for the best classic motorcycle." Some winners received money, others a trophy and a kiss from the pretty girl. I thought, "Hey, I'm really in the pink here."

Finally, they came to my award. "This year's long distance award is won by Dave Barr - a man who has traveled overland from South Africa." As I walked forward to accept my award, the pretty girl disappeared, and the presenter hands me a polished stone!

No money.

No kiss.

No trophy.

Just a lousy ten-pound polished stone?

My heart nearly hit the floor. I was flabbergasted.

"How could you people do this to me?" I thought. Bravely, I stuck out my hand and shook this man's hand and valiantly tried to smile, hiding my feelings of horrible disappointment.

The perpetual party resumed immediately after the awards. I walked back to my camping area feeling hangdog. Dan and John knew how disappointed I was, so Dan volunteered to take the rock back to Germany and post it home to my mother for me.

The next day the party and music died.

People nursing their hangovers now faced the reality of riding back to their homes and the normal routines with throbbing heads and queasy stomachs. I noticed that some people were throwing out salamis, big packets of bacon, and other absolute delicacies.

They looked upon me with amazement written all over their faces as this wild looking, crazy American started going through the trash cans grabbing salamis, sausages and bacon that they had the gall to throw out! Eventually, I had about thirty pounds of extra weight in my saddlebags - REAL FOOD. There finally was an upside to these 3 days of party and noise. With about $100.00 worth of new goodies in my saddlebags, and with a satisfied smile, I finished loading the motorcycle.

Frozen Rivers, Faithful Friends, and Haunted Bunkers

After the rally ended, Mike and I rode on, hoping to continue our string of three days of magic weather.

No such luck.

Immediately upon hitting the road, we experienced an icy cold head wind; we were in a snow storm! I had a spare helmet with a face shield on it, but since the snow stuck to the shield, it needed to be constantly wiped. Mike was riding with one hand as well, using a finger to clear his glasses.

On our stops, we noticed that the rivers were frozen, although there was no problem with ice on the roads; the Norwegians put something on the road surface that prevents icing.

We approached the outskirts of Trondheim, about ten miles out of town, and asked directions to a fellow's house we had met at the rally named Roar Spica. Roar's wife had a brand new Harley Davidson Evolution with a sidecar, and Roar rode a 1938 Indian with an eighty-eight cubic inch motor.

"The Indian runs along fine at ninety kilometers an hour," Roar told us. He welcomed us into his home, so we put the motorcycles away in the garage, then went upstairs to shower and get cleaned up.

At our meal, the conversation always came back to Indians or Harley Davidsons. I discovered that they paid $2,000.00 every six months for motorcycle insurance - and that is supposedly a discounted rate for people riding Harley Davidsons! What an inconceivable amount of money - just for insurance! Roar told me, "If you are in an accident and anything happens, you are taken care of and looked after very nicely for the rest of your life." People here pay incredibly high taxes for their medical system.

The Scandinavians were nice people, but they seemed to enjoy being looked after from the cradle to the grave. Their sense of personal responsibility is far less than what we have in the United States.

07:30: After breakfast, the motor won't turn over - the battery is dead.

"Will it never let up?"

Roar gave me a jump start, and we followed him into Trondheim where he led us to the Rams Motorcycle club. They were only too willing to help, so we rolled our bikes downstairs to a basement work shop that was part of their facility.

The check of the charging system verified that the alternator wasn't working. I now knew what that pinging noise was - the alternator had ripped from the wall of the crankcase again. I hesitated to do anything with it because I knew that there was something even more major wrong with the lower end. As a temporary solution, we bought another battery charger - the exact same kind I had left behind in England.

The downstairs workshop was a massive cellar about 50 meters long with huge oak pillars holding up the ceiling. The Rams told us, "At one time this was an interrogation bunker for the Gestapo during World War II. We also have a resident ghost here who throws things occasionally around the work shop."

"Oh boy!" I thought to myself when I was told we would sleep here - with the ghost!

Mike elected to sleep up stairs.

I preferred the quiet of downstairs, away from the noise and drinking on the next floor. Being a non-drinker, I was ready to go to bed a lot earlier than the others.

Sumptuous Scenery, the Arctic Circle, and Reindeer Dangers

May 22: In a land where the sun shines almost 20 hours a day, we leisurely get up and resume our quest for the North Cape. That's one sentence Mike could say in English: "Ya, Dave, we go North Cape!"

Out of Trondheim, we move up into the highlands where there was still a lot of snow on the ground. The scenery became more and more beautiful as we headed North. The road itself was rough, and had many dips due to large rocks pushing up from down below the surface of the pavement, caused by extremely cold conditions that they have for at least half the year.

We stopped to photograph the frozen lakes and rivers still under ice.

Absolutely magnificent!

Perhaps the most beautiful spot in the world.

At our camping area that night we meet a Swiss couple traveling by car. We chatted with them as they put up their tent, preparing to freeze their asses off (same as us). We cooked our dinner and all ate together. It's great being a traveler on the road, meeting other people. Even though our lives only brush against one another for a short moment in time, there's always something special we take away from these magical encounters.

Mike decided to stay in a room so he could wash some clothes. I wasn't bothered. I took my battery out and put it on charge.

We had covered over 300 miles that day, and flashes of the roads, the terrain, and the people we saw shot through my mind as I closed this day.

May 23: Not knowing if he understood me, I told Mike, "Today, my friend, we are going to cross the Arctic Circle."

He just looked at me and nodded his head.

We pulled onto the road, moving through very forested areas, and along magic fjords. The sea flowed inland, and there were deep cliffs and snow covered mountains in the distance. We traveled over long, high bridges that transverse very deep, sheer rock gorges. Sometimes we go to higher elevations through the trees and an occasional small tunnel. Eventually we encounter what I called "ice palaces" - long stretches of road, sometimes up to 50 miles, where there are few trees, and the rocks and sides of the road are covered with snow, sometimes up to four feet high!

All morning long we rode in snow flurries.

Suddenly, about 11:15, we arrived at the Arctic Circle!

The snow behind the monument was piled up about two feet deep. We rolled our motorcycles next to the monument and took photographs in the bitter cold - about 10° minus Celsius. We went into the pavilion that they had next to the monument to enjoy a nice hot cup of coffee and a cigarette. Mike and I were both excited about crossing into the Arctic, and I was most put out by the enormous cost of one cup of coffee - $3.50!

This spot has real history. Many famous people have posed in front of this monument. A few years later one person told me, "That bare spot between where it says 'Polar Circle' used to be a swastika. German officers used to stand and pose there for photographs during World War II. The swastika was rubbed out after the war."

But the monument remained.

When we'd climb off the motorcycles, Mike would stamp his feet and say, "Ya, Dave, cold!"

I wasn't having any problems with cold feet.

There's an upside to everything!

I loved to have a bit of fun with the Norwegians, notoriously slow drivers. When we would overtake them in a snowstorm, they would be all bundled up in their cars, pointing down to my feet as if saying to each other, "Look at that guy! He's wearing a pair of tennis shoes with no socks out there in that snow."

Little did they know!

When Mike then passed them with a frozen look of pain and misery on his face, they must have become confused all over again.

That night we made it to Narvik; Mike wanted to get a room, but they were too expensive even for him. So, we traveled further up the road, another 15 kilometers or so, crossing a couple of very high bridges over the fjords down below us. What an absolutely magical ride that day. Even though it had been snowing and miserable along the way, we had crossed the Arctic Circle, the fjords, rode through massive, long ice palaces, and been through several tunnels!

We had a system when it came to tunnels. Since my headlight only worked sporadically, as a tunnel approached, Mike would go ahead with a golden ring of light around him. I would follow this man in the center of the golden ring. His shape and motorcycle appeared as a black silhouetted knight on a thundering dark form with a golden ring around him. Back into the sunshine on the far side of the tunnel, the spell of the magic moment would be broken.

We found a campground where I removed the battery and put it on charge, oiled my chain, and adjusted it. Mike went to take a shower, but I wasn't about to because I would have had to sit on the floor - there was no chair to sit on, and it was a freezing cold arctic night!

The next morning, I got up about 6:30, put myself together, and went over to wake up Mike. When I would say "Morgen, Mike," he would fart in answer to me. If he farted, I knew that he was ready to get up and start his day!

You see, we didn't need to speak the same language!

We stopped a number of times this day to take photographs - one special one from high on a mountain. Mike walked in snow about 2½ feet deep to the side of a mountain looking down on the motorcycles and a massive fjord to the west of us. The water was dark blue, and with the snow coming down to the water's edge, the location radiated startling color contrasts.

We moved ever northward and started to spot reindeer, especially worrisome in tunnel territory because we'd never see a reindeer if he bolted out in front of us. A number of times Mike and I saw as many as 50 to 80 reindeer at one time. In one sense, they were a marvel, and provided a deep sense of being in touch with nature. In another sense, a collision with these lovely creatures could kill us and them.

Other dangers included roads with sheer cliffs on one side and high hillsides on the other.

We entered Alta, the home of the Bunkers' Motorcycle Club, reputed to be the most northern motorcycle club in the world. They are about 400 miles (600 km) north of the Arctic Circle by road. We managed to find their club house, but no one was home. We didn't feel it was proper to just put up our tents, so we went into town and made a few phone calls (one dollar for a local call!). Both times we didn't get the person we were looking for, and at a buck a call, we said, "The hell with that!"

We located a camping area, put up our tents, and managed to use their stove and facilities for nothing. They wanted 10 crowns ($2) just to use the heat they had there.

"Kiss my ass" I thought, reasoning that we were already paying enough for the campground. We had to stay in campgrounds because the motorcycle battery needed to be charged on my machine every evening.

Tomorrow we will go on the North Cape, the very top of Europe.

Living My Dream!

May 25: I woke early with a sense of excitement - we were so close to the North Cape - a place I had been dreaming about for the past few years. As I hooked the battery back up, I dropped a nut down in the grass and spent the next thirty minutes looking for that special nut that secures the battery strap.

Mike awoke with his usual fart which mingled nicely with my grumbling. He helped me search for the nut, and we finally found it.

We rode about 100 miles and came down into the bottom of a beautiful fjord were we bought tickets to catch the ferry across to the North Cape Island. While waiting to depart, I met a beautiful American woman named Sally from Berkeley, California. "I'm working as the hotel manager at a hotel on the North Cape Island for the next few weeks," she explained. I also discovered she spoke fluent Norwegian. "What an amazing woman," I thought. Looking over at Mike, he had that "Got Fricken" look in his eyes.

The ferry was a 40 minute ride across to North Cape Island. Sally made the trip especially pleasant as we now saw the fjords from a different view. Before, we saw them from up high on mountain passes from over the tops of bridges, spanning one side of a fjord to another. Now, we saw them from down on the water, and it was just wonderful!

When we got to the North Cape Island, I reluctantly bid Sally good-bye and we rode off on our merry way, getting fuel and a few things for the night.

Climbing over a mountain pass of black rock, ice, and snow, we are pleasantly surprised to discover sun on the other side. **Late in the afternoon, we come upon the North Cape monument.** We went to a line of rocks that were about 50 meters from the monument itself, and looked on in awe. We'd see the Arctic Ocean off and on during our ride up this 20 mile (32 km) dirt road, but now we could see it clearly.

We waited for other people to clear away from the monument, and then we moved our motorcycles up to it and took some photographs. We were clowning around, giving the finger to anybody who might see this picture another time. I have since used this photo in many of my slide shows.

Mike wanted to wander through the museum, but I declined. They wanted 90 crowns ($15) for that tour!

There was a fence at the monument so you wouldn't fall the 1200 feet down to the Arctic Ocean's edge. I spoke to some German people, telling them that "I'd come from the bottom tip of Africa to the North Cape."

"Congratulations," they told me.

It was a very warm feeling.

Mike and I tried to communicate with each other how great it was to be at the North Cape. All of the sudden Mike appears a little uneasy and says, "Dave, Cape Agullus."

"Yeah," I thought, "all the way from the bottom tip of Africa."

He starts pumping my hand. Belatedly, it's sinking in, how difficult it was to get from the bottom tip of Africa to the top of Europe.

This time, I was with a friend

Back on December 27, 1989, I had been at Cape Agullus, very alone and wondering apprehensively at what I would go through to arrive at this point and moment. The German couple broke out bread, cheese and beans to celebrate my accomplishment, and we had a sumptuous meal. Sharing this moment with others was very special.

We took some photographs of the sun reflecting off the Arctic ocean. Within a month's time the sun will be rotating up in the sky for 24 hours a day and never go down. At this time, the sun is not really going down, but is hovering just above the ocean, sending out a reflection of gold. I thought to myself, "What a blessing to see so many oceans from the motorcycle through the grace of God."

Sleeping at the North Cape is forbidden; no tents are allowed. However, we were determined to put our bags down right at the North Cape just below the monument. **For this one night we will sleep on top of Europe, 500 miles (800 km) north of the Arctic Circle.**

The temperature fell below zero centigrade that night, and it started snowing. The next morning, we asked the biggest question of every day: Will or won't these motorcycles start?

Mikes, no problem.

Mine did not get a charge last night, so we were anxious.

It started!

When the engines were warm enough, we began the lovely, slow ride down to the ferry in time to cross to Kalfjord. When I saw an American fellow on the ferry who was drunk and very lonely, making a general tit of himself, I thought about how lonely I sometimes get on this trip. I said a silent "thank you" prayer to God for giving me the strength to handle that loneliness without booze.

Norway has a small population of approximately 4,000,000 people, so the highways are not crowded. Reindeer are more frequent than cars. After traveling most of the day, we elected to stay in Karasjok, a city on the Finish/Norwegian border, sleeping on the Norwegian side.

About 22:00 a "Fricken" appeared out of nowhere. Mike jumped up and was looking at this poor girl goggle-eyed (easy Mike). She was a beautiful Norwegian girl who walked over to us and says, "What are you doing here?"

"Well, we're camping here, it's a campground isn't it?" I replied.

"Oh, okay," she said, charging us a minimum amount of $5.00 to stay in the cheapest camp yet in Scandinavia. I believe the girl just gave us a break because we had such a motley appearance.

Tomorrow we move into Finland through Lapland.

Lapland was green and beautiful, but quite flat. The road was in far better condition than it was in Norway, so we made very good time. Lapland had reindeers too, and Mike loved to stop, get off the motorcycle and sneak through the woods behind them. He looked like a giant hunter from another world with his helmet on, and no rifle, armed with only his little camera, all dressed in black leathers, sneaking up in vain on these reindeer. When he'd get in range for a photo, they'd all jump and run off. Mike would then utter some small curse at being discovered again.

When we passed over the border, the customs people didn't smile. They didn't speak. Mike and I kind of laughed at their rudeness. Naturally, they didn't like that either, but frankly, I get tired of people looking down their noses on us because we're on a motorcycles.

We cashed some travelers checks and were charged $4 for the privilege. Everything is very expensive, especially gasoline.

We moved south to Tornio, located on the Swedish border at the top of the Gulf of Botenviken (the Baltic Sea), veering to the right into Sweden, leaving Finland, Lapland and all its happy people behind. I found the Laplanders very handsome, lovely people, quite large in size, but almost unable to smile - very dour. When I shared this observation with the people in Sweden, they said "Ah, the Fins are all like that. A very boring lot."

Radioactive Reindeer and the Biker Brotherhood

The Swedes joked that all the reindeer had electric eyes due to the Churnoble nuclear disaster. Perhaps the lack of humor in Lapland is because reindeer are a major economy - they sell the fur and meat for bread. Who wants to buy contaminated, radioactive reindeer?

We moved down the coast of the Gulf of the northern Baltic and found a little campground with the sea right below us about 20 meters. The owner liked bikers, and let us use the cooking facility for nothing, charging us only about $4 to camp.

Because of the great road conditions, we had covered over 400 miles (600 km) today! The next day was also to be a good one as we rode over bridges and marshes, and along small country roads that followed the shoreline of the Baltic Sea through pine forests. The scenery was so green, and the weather was downright warm compared to where we had come from. There was no snow on the ground, and the lakes and rivers were free of ice.

When Mike came alongside me hollering "Get off the highway," it meant he had to take a piss. Once, on a road outside a small town called Luleå in Sweden, a car pulls up as we're finishing our business. A man walks over and introduces himself as Tommy.

"Do you have a problem?" he asks. "I'm from the Aurora Choppers Motorcycle Club. Would you like to work on your bikes or have a shower and a cold beer? If so, follow me to our club house."

It was too early to stop for the day; I wanted to keep moving, but Mike looked like he wanted to shower, so we both nodded our heads in agreement and followed this fellow to a three story house out in the countryside. Tommy introduced us to a few of the fellows in the club, one being the club president, Kenta Olsson. Kenta and I hit it off right from the moment we met. I described my problem with the noise coming from the lower end, and he said, "Let me ride the motorcycle."

He took it for a ride, and when he came back, he said "It sounds like the lower end. Pull the inner primary out of it and we can get a better look."

Reluctantly, I agreed to attempt this difficult job.

Mike was inside the house getting cleaned up. The lucky bastard almost never had to work on his motorcycle - just adjust the chain occasionally. The Evolutions are far more dependable than older ones such as mine.

I pull the primary apart in about an hour's time. When I pull the magnetic rotor over the alternator, what do I see but the alternator is all torn away from the crank case and in pieces inside the rotor housing. With great disappointment, Kenta looks at it and says, "I'll order you another one."

"That's the second alternator that has been torn off it's mountings," I explain.

"Well, you still need to order another one."

After cleaning up the parts, we enjoyed a good dinner of chili con carne and beans made by Doris, one of the members wives. I was just amazed at how kind these people were opening up their home and work shop. Later in the evening, when the members left, they let Mike and I stay in the house.

The next day was spent in performing odd jobs on the motorcycle in the club's comprehensive machine shop. During the winter, they kept their Harleys in special bays at the club. Their bikes reflected an amazing amount of self engineering. Instead of buying a part from a store at an enormous price, they would make the part themselves and do a better job than the factory part.

The paint jobs on their machines were also unique. Kenta's was very plain, just one color, but it was the runner of the crowd - it put out more horsepower and really

161

got down the road. Kenta took me over to another motorcycle club's work shop, the Labbigaskogens, meaning "Wolves in the Forest" which reminded me of the story of Goldilocks, and not bad-ass bikers. After introducing myself and explaining my mission, I was able to get a couple of parts I needed to carry on. Mike went with us, but was quiet, being very self conscious of his English (this is unfortunate because he's always the odd man out).

The next day I met Latta, Kenta's wife; they had planned to take a motorcycle ride on Kenta's chopper. When they returned, Kenta had my alternator with him! The next step was to mount the alternator into the wall of the engine - which HE did since I don't have any real great mechanical ability. I just know enough to keep my machine wired together. Drilling and tapping small holes into an engine block is definitely not my forte.

When the motorcycle is back together, we start it up. It sounds all right when it's cold, but not when it is hot. I took it for a ride around Luleå, and when I came back that clunking was there again. Another fellow took it out and came back saying, "I can't hear anything."

Kenta said, "I can't either," but I knew it was still there. When I start to pay Kenta for the alternator and other parts, he refuses my money. "No, Dave, we don't want any money for this. The club wants to sponsor your repairs."

"Come on," I replied, "you put me up here and have been very kind to me. You should take this money."

"No, we don't want it. This is what the brotherhood is all about."

In the midst of this, Mike decided to go on his own way. Since he couldn't communicate, I believe he felt as though he were wasting time. Mike and I gave each other a great hug (I felt I was hugging a big, friendly bear).

We still write to each other.

June 1: Swedish coffee is about the strongest coffee I have found anywhere in the world. It just wires you up. What I usually do is put a little in the bottom of my cup and fill it up with hot water that I boiled, then drink. These guys just drink it straight - cup after cup. It's amazing that they don't explode with all the energy they take in.

Bosie, a club member, volunteered to lead me out of town. When I stopped to fuel up, he wouldn't allow me to pay for it. We rode out to the main highway and there, after a few miles, he waved to me and took the off ramp.

"It is always difficult to say good-bye to friends," I think. "It leaves me with an empty feeling, riding away from people who have cared enough to help."

As I leave behind the friendship, security and warmth, I'm greeted by a rainstorm.

After about 20 miles, I hear that clunking in the lower end of the motor.

I felt sick inside. "Will I ever be able to get rid of this problem?" Despite the clunk, I continue on for 250 miles (400 km) through lovely wooded country side, interrupted only by farms, or a lake, ultimately ending up at a hillside campground. There, in the rain I ate my dinner, set up camp, and lay back in the evening night, acutely aware that once again I was on my own.

Chapter Fifteen

A New Leg and Old Friends

Just outside Örebro, I stopped for petrol and asked the lady behind the counter if she knew of any motorcycle clubs that would have a workshop. She said she did, and made a few phone calls for directions. Following these directions, I ultimately located a bunch of bikers sitting around their clubhouse drinking beer and chit-chatting with each other. I introduced myself and told them of my loud clunk down in the lower end of my motorcycle.

"No problem," they responded. "Wheel the motorcycle in."

They fed me a nice cup of very strong coffee which left me wired - boy was I ready to work! We had difficulty getting the primary apart, but once we had it down we could see that it was just barely touching the alternator again. We took the magnetic rotor to a small machine shop in the country and the guy turned the inside of the rotor down on a lathe. We brought it back and put it together.

It was now very late - too dark to go further. I'd already covered about 300 miles (500 km).

Lousy Weather, Shithawks, and Failing Film

Within a half an hour, the rain started and would stay with me for the next 200 miles (320 km) - all the way to Götteburg where I became confused and lost in the traffic. I almost had an accident before I found the ferry terminal where I had to wait, soaking wet in the cold, for 2½ hours for them to open their ticket office. Many people who walked by me and my dripping puddle of water would give me a look of disgust and disdain.

"You horrible little people," I thought to myself. "What do you know about being on the road? All your life has been in secure, warm places. You don't know the meaning of an adventure." I judged them by their judgments of me.

Finally, I was able to buy my ticket and go inside, leaving the puddle. "I hope they slip and bust their asses!"

It was another four hours through a rough sea with rain coming down before we put into Frederikshavn, right at the top of Denmark.

Since it was still raining, I found a camping area and closed my day.

The next morning, everything I own is wet from my leaking tent. Rolled up my wet sleeping bag, now weighing about four times its normal weight, and started up and off down the road. With the howling wind, the freezing cold, and the rain, I was having a lot of trouble, especially when passing a truck where I'd fight the slip stream off the front of the vehicle. Sometimes I could actually feel my rear wheels start to slip out from underneath me. The bald spot over 1/2 the rear tire becomes even more dangerous in these conditions. I would constantly fight to stay on the motorcycle, especially around even gentle curves. Very scary... a white knuckle riding experience requiring total concentration.

"Well, the weather has been steadily lousy for the past 270 km here in Denmark," I thought to myself, "the same as it was the last time I was here."

I decide to go to Esbjerg and take a ferry across to England, making my way on down to London. Upon arriving at Esbjerg, I put my motorcycle behind the customs office, walked about a half kilometer to the ticketing office, and purchased a ticket.

When I went back, there were people lining up to get ready to go onto the ferry. I noticed a 1909 Morris car in mint condition, and spoke with the proud owner. He had been to an antique car rally in Norway.

I also met a fellow named Paul who bought motorcycles in the United States and then would ship them to various destinations in Europe. We had our dinner together, cooking it outside on the deck. It cost us a pittance compared to eating in the dining room, which would cost an arm or a leg! HA, HA.

After dinner, I found an open door leading to a set of cabins that were empty. I had the entire cabin to myself, and closed my day alone.

Later, a crew member came along, stuck his head inside, and asked me "What are you doing?"

"I didn't see anybody here, so I figured it would be okay."

"Don't worry about it," he replied, "I understand."

He'd seen my leg sitting in the corner, so I had a whole cabin to myself that night.

The next morning was actually bright and clear - believe it or not! I went up on deck and had coffee and a cigarette, then went down into the hold of the ship and loaded the motorcycle, getting ready to move.

Once through customs and immigration I was on the road, 110 miles away from Acton and the motorcycle shop. After about 1/2 hour on the road, and true to form, it started raining, wind began blowing, and I was absolutely miserable.

Welcome back to England.

I rode directly to the motorcycle shop where Dave, Tigger and I had a wonderful reunion. It was great to see these two shitbirds. Dave said I could stay at the shop, and offered me a spot on the top floor - the room full of the pigeon shit.

"Fine," I replied, "any port in the storm."

I only had a few days until I was slated to have the motorcycle ready to move to Felixtowe where it would be put on a ship to Baltimore. The evening was spent with Dave and Tigger telling them about all the different adventures I'd had on the road. They really appreciated my stories.

I awoke the next day to the pigeons cooing up in the attic. By the time I left the room and went downstairs to start coffee for the morning, I was cooing, too - to wake Dave up!

We had a good laugh.

During the morning I performed various tasks around the shop. It was as if I hadn't gone anywhere physically, but had just finished a four and a half thousand mile dream. With so much still going through my mind, I couldn't seem to get my act together in the shop. I knew it was starting to irritate Dave. Late in the day, I broke a valve cover trying to get a bolt out of it on a motorcycle. I just couldn't seem to do anything right. Thankfully, Dave was understanding about the whole thing and he took care of the problem.

After work, I went upstairs with a vacuum cleaner and a broom and cleaned up all the pigeon shit on the floor near the window, and tried to cover up the hole in the attic where they were defecating all over the floor. The dust was terrible, and the sound of pigeons flapping around everywhere was depressing.

The next morning I again awoke to the sound of pigeons - Dave calls them shithawks.

I called Don Hornsby in South Africa and was given very bad news about what was going on in the country - faction fighting, violence and bombs. When I hung up the phone, I felt no peace of mind for my friends and what they were suffering.

The shipping company that was to send the motorcycle to the United States called and said that due to an unloading problem, they might not be able to send it. That really upset me.

"Why can't I depend on anything? Every time I get near a boat there is some type of problem."

I got more bad news that day. All of my film, both slide and regular, taken while going to the North Cape was bad. My heart dropped right down to my shoes. I had no visual record of anything I had just come through. All the snow, the cold, the frozen lakes, the beautiful ice palaces, the wonderful forests, and the fjords vanished in an instant.

I called my friend Mike in Switzerland and asked him, "Please send me copies of all the photographs and slides you can spare."

He did, and that saved the day.

It was during this particular time that I got most depressed. "How are people to believe what I've done if they can't see a photograph?"

I spent the next two days relaxing on the boat, reflecting back on the past three weeks of hard riding.

The U.S. Bound Barnsley Warrior

Monday, June 10, 1991: All my gear that was to ship with the motorcycle from Felixtowe to Baltimore had to be sorted out and loaded up. As I started to leave, MORE BLOODY RAIN! The traffic was terrible, of course, all the way out to M-4. Once I turned on the M-25, a massive ring freeway around London, it rained even worse; the traffic was backed up for miles.

Turning north to Felixtowe, the traffic lets up a bit and I no longer need to cut down between the lanes. I made it into Felixtowe, about 120 miles (200 km). Finding my way down to docks by asking directions, I paid for the transportation of the motorcycle to the United States. I had to show the foreman how to start it.

"You can't ride it to the docks - that's against union rules."

I left the motorcycle in their care and just hoped for the best, taking out about 40 pounds worth of tools and gear that had to go back with me to London. The driver from the shipping company took me to the train station where I ultimately caught two trains back to London, then I caught a subway to Shepherd's Bush. Climbing out of the subway to a bus station at Shepherd's Bush, and a bus came back to the motorcycle shop. Once I was back at the shop, I was bushed from the constant up and down on my feet for hours, carrying this load of tools and other gear that would stay with me all the way to the United States. I wasn't willing to trust my whole set of motorcycle tools to the shipping company. It would have been too expensive to have to replace these tools.

It was with incredible relief that I lay back, taking off my legs that night.

Awaking to the sound of pigeons, I go down and wake Dave up by my own cooing, the sound of the London SHIT HAWK. Dave comes out and says "Isn't this wonderful? A house and motorcycle shop combined into one? We brush our teeth and shave in the same sink we wash the dishes in. The shower's in the kitchen. Man, this is really low maintenance," Dave shouts.

The dogs bark.

"SHUT UP YOU FUCKING DOGS!"

Dave goes on to remind me that as men approaching middle age, we have managed to avoid the accumulation of material things in our lives." "In essence," he says, "WE HAVE FUCK ALL to show for all our years."

I dress up in a jacket and tie and catch two buses down to Victoria Station. From there I walked on to Maunsel Street, a little over one mile, to attend a meeting with David Mallom. David presented me with some photos of my meeting with Group Captain Lord Leonard Cheshire. He also provided me with some of the newspaper articles concerning the Cheshire tour - thirty reports in all. "David, I believe this is only a small bit of what was accomplished from this trip," he told me.

Friday, June 14: The leg I was wearing was just rubbish. It was grinding badly, and I knew the axle was going to break on it at any time. The leg that was being sent up had been overhauled by Barford Jones, so my fortunes were changing.

Peter Uys, a man staying at the same Portland Hotel where the crew and pilots of the South African Airways put up at night when they lay over, called to tell me, "I have your rebuilt leg. Come and get it."

"Indeed I will," I replied, catching the bus out to Marble Arch where I was greeted by a short fellow who had been a helicopter pilot in the Rhodesian war. Peter had also flown "helos" up in Angola, and we discovered we had friends in common from the good old days. Now, he was a commercial copilot on a 747.

To bring me my leg, he cut down on his normal luggage and instead placed my leg in a big suitcase by bending the leg at the knee. At customs, nobody checked him. Can you imagine the problems he could have had?

"What's this?"

"Well, it's a leg, sir."

"I can see it's a bloody leg. Who does it belong to? Surely not to you."

This leg would serve me faithfully for the next two years before being destroyed in an accident.

The fit was fairly comfortable, but the leg made quite a banging noise at the knee due to its design - very antiquated. When I took a step, it went "CLACK." Of course, it also had a squeak, but it didn't grind, and the hinge mechanism on the knee moved freely without any problem.

"Well, this new leg is quite handy," I thought to myself later that night. "I feel so much more versatile, almost as if I could run and fly instead of forcing the joints to operate. The foot and ankle joint work instead of just hanging down, catching on things. The only draw back - it is noisy as hell!"

I received an invitation to the Barnsley Warriors annual motorcycle show on June 16. I offered to do a raffle and split the money with them. "Well see," they told me. "This would be a great time to see many wonderful people again," I reasoned as I accepted their invitation.

At Barnsley, I was by greeted by Steve Rose, Rob Meyers, and others members of the Barnsley Warriors who took me to Neil and Sharon's home. Steve and I talked at quite good length as he was preparing to join the French Foreign Legion. Tactfully, I told him, "You're out of your blooming mind, Steve. What are you doing?" The Foreign Legion is not fighting any where. You'd just be wasting your time."

At Dave and Sandra's house, Sean, one of the members, got to talking about ghosts. "Listen, don't be alarmed if you see a ghost in this house," Dave and Sandra said. "This house is over 150 years old. We've seen a ghost here. It's not a bad ghost. It's never hurt anybody."

"Right. Fine. Thank you," I reply.

Sean claimed he was a bit of a clairvoyant.

"Give me something, and I'll tell you its history," he told me.

I gave him the belt I was wearing. He took it and held it for the next ten minutes while we carried on a conversation about other things. Eventually he started to talk.

"This belt belonged to your father, and I feel a great pain in my chest. Your father died of a heart attack, didn't he?"

"Yes," I replied.

166

"That's about all I can tell you."

I had not mentioned to any of these fellows that my father had died of a heart attack, or that the belt ever belonged to him.

The next day was the Barnsley Warriors annual motorcycle show down at the soccer field located near a sports pub. Once there, we all pitched in and started working to mark different areas for different classes of motorcycles. Categories ranged from the old antique motorcycles to custom choppers and super street specials. Tents were erected on various locations for refreshments.

About 10 o'clock people started to arrive. By mid-afternoon, there were between 75 and 80 motorcycles on display, and the crowd grew to between 700 - 800 people. Trotsky, the fellow who had painted my motorcycle, was there as one of the judges. Unfortunately for him, many of the motorcycles entered in the show had paint jobs he had created - the best, in my opinion.

Towards the end of the day, Rob Murphy, club chairman, announced the raffle winners, and the winners of different classes of motorcycles. Finally, I was asked to say a few words about my accomplishments to the crowd.

Later, a couple of girls came up to me with tears in their eyes. "Well, isn't that incredible," I marveled. Maybe they were drunk. These two girls had been very touched by my sharing, although I really don't know what profound message I had shared besides saying "Thank you very much to the Barnsley Warriors for helping to keep the journey on the road."

Afterwards, we all pitched in and cleaned up the playing field, packing all the equipment away.

Prison Tales and Final Endings

During our conversations, I learned that the chairman of the motorcycle club, Rob Murphy, had served seven years for armed robbery at a bus station. He apparently came in with a shot gun, held the place up, and grabbed the money bag and ran off. When he checked the money bag later, he discovered a pair of old tennis shoes (they didn't fit), and an old transistor radio that didn't work. Rob's "major heist" was a source of endless amusement among his fellow bikers.

After he was released from prison, his next "big caper" was to steal a case of SPAM - believe it or not! When the police determined he was the thief, they surrounded his house. Now, knowing Rob had a previous ARMED robbery conviction, the police were very cautious. They called out to him, and he came out with his hands up! Next, they went into his house and searched until they retrieved the case of SPAM.

Rob went back to jail.

At the pub, we were all holding our sides, just rolling with laughter as these tales of "meaty crime" were shared by some of the other members.

At the end of the evening, Rob pressed something into my hand and said "This is from the Barnsley Warriors. It is the profits from our annual motorcycle show. We all want you to have it."

This gift amounted to 200 pounds. In London a few days later, when I purchased my plane ticket, it came to 198 pounds 98 pence. So, my trip across the Atlantic ocean was courtesy of the Barnsley Warriors. They were the first motorcycle club in the world to pitch in and lend me a helping hand, to say "Dave, we believe in you and what you're doing and why you're doing it." I will always be deeply touched by their kindness. I am adamant about this: the only reason I was able to accomplish what I did was because of the help I received from people like the Barnsley warriors.

Sean, the untrained medium, walked up to me and pressed a medallion into my hand. "This is a scale from a dragon's back. It's handmade in China. Wear it always, and it will protect you."

"Thank you," I said. Then, I whispered into his ear, "Continue to develop your gift and learn to help others with it." He nodded his head.

The next morning Neil and Sharon took me in their little car down to the bus station where we met with many members of the club who had gathered to see me off. There were tears in the girls' eyes, and I must admit there was a tear in my own.

When I arrived back at the motorcycle shop, Dave and I had dinner, watched T.V., and closed the day.

That night, as I rested in my pigeon shit loft, I realized that this was one of my last nights in England. I thought about how much I would miss Dave and Tigger, and our laughter and low humor. Then, I thought to myself, "On the other hand, I'm glad to be getting out of here. I'm sure this place is going to get raided again!"

The next morning was the last time I would wake up to pigeons cooing.

During the day, we all continued our patter of laughs, comments, and low humor. Always cackling, but there was an undercurrent of sadness.

Late in the day, Peter Morpuss arrived to take me with him that night. Dave and Tigger walked me out to the car, and we all hugged each other. I tried to thank them for all they had done, but words failed me in my feeble attempt.

My heart was definitely hurting.

"Dave, just do it," they told me. "Go all the way."

I turned my back to hide my tears, and as we drove off, I could hear the dogs bark as Dave entered the shop, screaming at the top of his lungs, "SHUT UP YOU FUCKING DOGS!"

That last night in England my mind wandered over the last seven months and all the incredible things that had taken place - the people, the miles, the weather, the wondrous sights - how fortunate I have been!

My mind drifted back to Dave, standing in his corner of their dirty, smelly dingy little office, moving back and forth in a small space while he smokes a joint and laughs with Tigger, sitting across the office in his corner as the mean, fat lord, with his Harley Davidson cap on, and his beard going in all directions on his face. His inscrutable blue-gray eyes stare off in the distance, contemplating some future evil scheme. I will always remember these two. Without them, and all they did for me, I don't know what I would have done with my time in London.

The next morning, Peter took me down to Gatwick airport.

Once the bags were checked in, we looked at one another and embraced. Our relationship goes back to the time when we met each other in the recruiting office in January, 1981. It is difficult to say good-bye to Peter, not knowing when we'll next see one another again.

I entered the departure lounge and waited for the call to board the plane. As the wheels of that plane left British soil, Stage Two of the journey was complete.

Barnsley Yorkshire England, Some of the Barnsley Warrior
The President on the right, Rob Murphy April 1991

Cheshire Home During Promotion of April - May 1991 England

Meeting The Founder Lord Groupe Captain Leonard Cheshire Victoria Cross
London, England May 1991

First Crossing of The Arctic Circle
May 23, 1991, Norway.

At The Top of Europe "The North Cape" with Mike Merkel
May 25, 1991, Norway.

Stage Three: North America

Chapter Sixteen

Historical Roads on My Rag-Tag Dream

As the plane took off, and England fell away underneath me, I realized that Stage Two of this journey was over.

Stage Three - North America - was about to begin.

In Baltimore, I was greeted by my friend Lang Price, the driver of the vehicle that we blew up in on August 29, 1981. We hugged, retrieved my baggage, then drove to his place in Maryland, a beautiful little cottage out in the woods, away from everyone, totally silent except for birds chirping and the wind whispering through the trees.

After getting my gear squared away, Lang took me to his girl friend, Erin's, house in Bethesda. She was a student nurse, and an impressive, strong-willed woman who could hold her own with Lang - himself quite a handful! We enjoyed a lovely dinner out on the veranda of her two story house overlooking suburbia. Since we had not seen each other in six years, Lang and I especially enjoyed telling stories about our time in the army together.

While in Maryland, the most impressive sight I saw was "The Wall" in honor of Vietnam Veterans in Washington, D.C. I had heard about it for years. The Vietnam Veterans' Memorial was built by private funds (not by taxpayer dollars).

I'll never forget that rainy day as I looked up the name of Leo Beach, one of the first crew chiefs I flew with in Vietnam. When I found his name on the wall, I felt a very heavy heart for all those who had been killed in the war.

It seemed so useless - so senseless in the end!

On our way to the wall, I noticed a Vietnamese woman selling umbrellas to the tourists. As we walked away, I became very angry about her being there.

"Take it easy," Lang cautioned me.

When I noticed a Park Ranger, I approached him and requested, "Would you have that woman removed?" Unable to stop at that, I continued, "The Vietnamese didn't have the balls to fight for their country the way they should have - they let us do it for them. Now, they don't have a country and they're here trying to peddle umbrellas at our monument."

"How dare her!" I thought to myself. "Damn gooks, anyway."

The Park Ranger removed the Vietnamese woman I felt had defiled the place.

Memories of 1981

Suddenly, my thoughts were shaken.

An accident happened right in front of us!

Lang pulled in behind the wrecked car, got out of his vehicle, ran over, had a quick look, ran back, put on his fireman's helmet and took out his medical kit (Lang is a volunteer Fire Department paramedic).

Two young boys, about 22 years old, were standing alongside the road - they had been the driver and passenger. A young woman was in the back of the car. Lang gently took her out, put her on the ground, and started to work on her. The top of her head was split open, and her face was bashed. While Lang was going through his emergency medical procedures, I photographed the scene (NOT the young woman...that would have been totally depressing).

173

The paramedics arrived.

"I'm very reluctant to leave the young woman in their hands," he told me, "they aren't up to standard." Lang's standards are very high. With some reluctance, we returned to our car and as we drove away, I said a prayer for the young woman that "God's will be done." I rolled a couple of cigarettes, and Lang and I smoked in silence as we drove home, deep into our own thoughts of the accident and "The Wall."

The accident triggered some memories of the land mine explosion Lang and I experienced back in 1981. Just the idea of the two of us once again near possible death made me feel very pensive. I walked around the forest that afternoon praying for that young woman, thinking, "If she is to live, she will. If not, not."

Her head injury was massive. Lang came out after a bit and told me, "I called the hospital. The girl was pronounced dead on arrival."

For the next few hours, we talked about the wall, God's will, our own brush with fate in 1981, and the young woman. We discussed what we have been through together... the armies, the violence, the hatred, and the misery we'd seen in this world. We spoke of the young woman, barely twenty-two years old - in a spilt second, BANG, her life was over. Yet, here we were that night, standing in the moonlight, allowed by God to carry on to whatever our destiny may be.

The Trials Begin Again!

June 25: The motorcycle was to arrive in Baltimore, so we drove down to the port. The shipping agent's office told us where to find the ship. When they opened the cargo door, the Captain let me go in and I spotted the motorcycle strapped to the wall. I immediately noticed that the dummy who rode the motorcycle onto the ship in Felixtowe failed to disconnect one of my battery wires (the battery was dead, flat down all the way). I felt fortunate that no fires had started.

I rolled the motorcycle off the ship and down to the dock where Lang was parked. He had jumper cables, and fortunately it started right up. I was instructed to ride it over to the customs dock, and then parked the motorcycle, walking over to the custom's office.

"Well, where's the motorcycle?" asked the custom's agent. "I haven't inspected it on the ship yet."

"Well, it's now over at the customs clearing shed," I replied.

"How did it get there?"

"I rode it over."

The man went wild, cursing the stevedores for letting us take it away.

"Come and inspect it," I told him. "I haven't done anything with it," I continued, just trying to keep my cool and not get upset.

"You will have to wait for a few hours."

"Right," we thought, "we'll just go on into Baltimore."

During our break, we took in some sights, had a lovely lunch, saw the USS Constitution and a World War II submarine. We went through this fascinating vessel, and it was amazing to me how the crew lived in such tight quarters.

Later, the custom's officer signed off the motorcycle, but was very irritated by the whole exercise.

Out of the dock, it felt good to take the 45 mile ride to Lang's place with the wind mixing with the warm sun on my face. When I arrived, I vainly put the battery on charge, knowing in my heart that it was really no good (thank you, idiots at Felixtowe).

The next day Lang and I rode down to the Rockville Harley Davidson dealer where I sat with a salesman named Brook, showing him the photos from the trip. He seemed impressed, but people act like they are all the time. "I'll have to talk with the owner of the shop," he told me, "to see if he will give you some kind of discount on parts."

I bought my battery, and we rode back through the lush green country side.

The next day, back at the Harley Davidson dealer, Brook said, "Dave, there's good news. The dealer will give you a discount on all the parts you buy. Also, he has contacted the factory, and they want to speak to you."

This was very good news indeed! I was finally getting somewhere with the Harley Davidson Motor Company (or so I thought).

While at the shop, the rear crash bar needed welding, so we wheeled the motorcycle up to the work shop where one of the mechanics did a very good job of welding it. He charged me $10 for the five minute job, and seemed to have an attitude problem. He was the first person I encountered in the United States who was negative about the trip... as if it had offended him.

I then bought $210 worth of parts (after my $122 discount), and drove back to Lang's where work began. First, a new starter drive gear to put in. Next, the rear tire had to be broken down, and replaced with a new one. Rear wheel bearings had to installed (the right ones, I might add), and new mirrors put on.

The days had not been so hot since my time traveling across the Southern Sahara. Europe was snow and rain, and now I'm in very hot weather again, making it far more difficult for me to do physical work.

Oh well, you can't have it all.

Another day, Lang and I visited the Battlefield of Manassas, down Highway 185. We walked through the battlefield where I was amazed to see the open ground where the troops clashed with one another, and then see the forested areas from which they ambushed and attacked. Was it bravery or stupidity that motivated these men to keep going on and on at each other the way they did? Whatever the case, the carnage must have been incredible.

Many times the armies would shift sites, leaving their dead on the battlefield, never coming back for them, the corpses rotting for months or longer. When someone would finally come to bury them, they often found only skeletons. Many times they didn't know whether they were burying Union or Confederate soldiers. Lang and I were shocked - we'd never read about these horrors in any of our history books!

June 29: Time to leave. I went down to the fire station with Lang where we met Erin and her twin daughters, took some photographs, and said our good-byes. As I rode out, Erin and her two twins, Jennifer and Abby, were all standing there giving me the finger! This picture will be forever imprinted in my mind.

Lang led me to Highway 495 where I was on my way across the United States, stopping in Norfolk, Virginia, to see some relatives.

After a few days with my relatives, on July 2, at 03:30, I left my Aunt Marie and Mary Alice standing in the street and rode off in the direction of the long tunnel out of Norfolk, Virginia. The tunnel was all lit up but had no traffic, so it amplified the pounding of the engine. Very quickly, I was on the open road, making it through Richmond before the rush hour traffic.

It was another hot, oppressive day, but I made great time, hitting Milton, West Virginia, at about 13:30 in the afternoon. I thought, "That's far enough for the day."

Pulling into a camping area, the lady there said, "It will be $13 to camp here for the night."

"Go fly a kite," I said. "I ain't paying $13 to pitch a tent."

I hadn't noticed any place where I could slip off the road and not be seen, but the lady was kind enough to guide me to a Ranger's Station where I could spend the night for a lot less money.

"Yes. C'mon in. Just go and set up camp. We'll catch up with you later," the kind ranger told me. I pitched my tent (still wet and mildewed from Denmark) under a tree and spent the rest of the afternoon working on the motorcycle. Next, I opened a tantalizing can of chili con carne for dinner. Ah, the luxuries of life on the road are never ending!

I'd covered 470 miles of road today, and the motorcycle had performed well for the most part, with the lower end of the engine was still clanging away.

I must just carry on.

Electric Shocks and Failing Voltage!

I woke up in the middle of the night with electric shocks going through my right stump. They kept coming all night, about every 30 seconds. I felt headachy, as if I had a fever. When I tried to eat last night's leftovers in the morning, the chili tasted like shit. As I left about 06:00, I realized that the rangers had never collected any money from me. Now that's what I call a good discount!

This day's highway took me through the Bluegrass country of Kentucky - as grand and beautiful as you see in the movies. Coming into Louisville, I crossed a bridge that goes over the Ohio River into Indiana. As I was going over that bridge I thought of my Grampa Carter, who used to tell me, when I was a boy, about how he would swim across the Ohio River as a kid. As I rode across, it was as if I could see him down in the river, splashing along, a young man - free and alive.

I had been sick all morning with the flu - headache, fever, my nose running, and nausea (sounds like a cold commercial!). My right stump still suffered from electric shocks about every 30 seconds.

In Henryville, there was a relatively deserted State Park, so I established my camp and laid back to shake and shiver with a big bottle of water which I refilled about three times during the day. In the afternoon, a Park Ranger came and told me, "You are going to have to move. This is for horse camping only."

Now mind you, there was nobody else in the whole place! I couldn't believe this cretin's attitude. Anyway, I pleaded with him in my sick and feverish state until he saw my point of view.

"Well, if people come in we're going to have to ask you to move," he told me, as if to protect himself from any problems later.

"Fair enough," I said, "if they come in I'll move."

Finally, during the night my fever broke, and I was able to get a bit of sleep. Such is life on the road.

At a service station the next morning, the rain started coming down very hard so I changed to my rain gear. After fueling up I went to start the motorcycle, only to hear, "Errrrr, errrrr."

The machine was very difficult start.

"Oh no, not again!" I thought, wondering if the alternator was once again going bad. I rode on up to Indianapolis, where I located Erin's sister's house where Lang and Erin were vacationing. The lovely home was over 100 years old, and the huge property had a big, green lawn and old oak trees. It reminded me of how the entire area must have looked one hundred years ago.

"As beautiful as it is here," Lang told me, "it's real miserable in the winter when snow comes and the temperature gets low."

As the day wore on, I was once again getting sick - my fever rising, nausea increasing. Next, my motorcycle brakes started locking up. Of course, each time I tried to start the thing, I heard that familiar "Errrrr" before it finally kicked over. When we arrived in Fort Wayne, Indiana, some of Lang's friends put the machine away because I was too sick to do it, going directly to bed.

When I woke up, I put a new voltage rectifier on the thing, but it still started very hard. Further testing revealed it wasn't the voltage rectifier but the alternator that was bad. You can imagine the deeply depressed feeling I had as Lang and I went down to buy yet another battery charger. From now on, I'll be stopping at campgrounds so I can charge my battery at night.

I tried to contact someone at the Harley Davidson Motor Company to set up an appointment, but with no success.

After three days, although still sick, I said my good-byes and headed for Gary, Indiana, then Chicago, Illinois, taking the 249, the ring road around Chicago, stopping what seemed like every five minutes to throw thirty cents into a toll basket. "You bunch of schisters!"

Once clear of Chicago, I tried to make a phone call to Milwaukee - only fifty miles away. The call cost me $2.05. I couldn't believe it! What incredible gall these people have charging that much money! At Harley Davidson Company Motor Company, I wasn't able to get through to Dan Klemencic, the person I was trying to contact.

On to Racine, Wisconsin, where I located a campground off of the road. The fellow running the place said, "You can stay anywhere." In this massive campground, I found a secluded place off in the woods that had an electrical outlet so I could charge my battery. Ralph, the old man who ran the campground, had a tracheotomy, and I could tell by talking with him that he was very lonely. He identified with me because I had a disability.

"Why don't you and I go and have a hamburger? Do you feel like one?" Ralph asked.

"Sure," I replied.

We went to the McDonald's about five miles up the road in his old Cadillac. Ralph tried to communicate, coughing and wheezing through his tracheotomy. "Caused by smoking," he explained. "Had cancer... heart attack as well. Used to drive a truck." He told me his family had done him bad, taking all the money he earned while driving trucks. His wife and kids no longer spoke to him. My heart really went out to this old fella.

Back at the campground, we chatted a while longer. I asked him if he had served in W.W.II, and he said "Yes," showing me a picture of himself as a young man in the Navy. I thought "What has your life been for, you poor old fellow? You don't have any family, and you live in a little trailer in a campground. What a sad way to spend your golden years."

When I checked my battery that afternoon, I discovered some kids had been playing near it and knocked it over - all the acid had spilt on the ground.

"Well, let's go and get some acid," Ralph said, and took me to the nearest Harley Davidson dealer where we filled it up, hoping no damage had been done.

The Evolutions Meet the Old Dog

The next morning, I received a phone call from Dan Klemencic of the Harley Davidson Motor Company, second in charge of public relations in the United States.

Dan suggested, "Let's get together on July 12. I'll try and have Catherine Tinkie, our international marketing and public relations manager, in the meeting with us, but I can't guarantee anything because she is out of the country a lot."

Today, I'm on the main highway heading north towards Milwaukee. On my way I pass the Harley Davidson factory and was quite impressed by the sight of "Mother" - where they build the engines and transmissions.

Next, on to Menasha where I called Dick and Mary Hendricks, friends of mine, getting directions to their place. After I rode up, Dick put my motorcycle in their garage, then we all chatted and had a lovely dinner. Dick showed me some of his photographs of when he rode Harley Davidsons, of hill climbing and enduro riding with old knuckleheads, flatheads, and panheads, with machines dating back to the '30s and '40s. I was very impressed! Dick told me, "It feels good to have a Harley Davidson in the garage again."

The next few days were spent working on the motorcycle, putting in a new primary belt, and other odd repairs while waiting for my July 12 meeting with Harley Davidson.

July 12: I got up at 05:15, cleaned up, put on a suit and a tie I borrowed from Dick. Of course, my "best" shoes were raggedly old tennis shoes that were falling apart, and Dick's shoes were too small. No matter how hard I tried to dress up, I still looked like a sack of shit tied in the middle! After getting all ready, I very gingerly rolled the motorcycle out of the garage, trying hard not to get any grease on Dick's pants.

I cranked up the motorcycle and headed back down to Milwaukee - about one-hundred miles away. About a third of the way into the ride, it started to rain! I pulled over and put on my rain gear, trying to protect Dick's suit, and hoping there was no grease inside the rain jacket.

Next, the police pulled me over in the rain, saying "You're not running your headlight."

"I have a problem with the charging system," I told them.

They were very polite to me, but insisted that I put the light on anyway.

"I understand," I replied, turning it on for a short distance until they were out of sight. I remember how the police looked at me so funny. I guess that they don't see many Harley bikers out in the rain with a suit and tie on.

At the factory, I pulled in under a canopy. There were other motorcycles there - all shiny, new evolutions - all looking very good. My old dog was quite a sight next to them, dripping as much oil as water.

Off came the rain gear, always trying to stay away from anything greasy. I walked over to an office in the factory to wait for Dan Klemencic to arrive. As usual, I was early, and had a good wait. Fortunately, it was in a section of the factory where they had a display of different engines.

When Dan Klemencic came in very casually dressed, he asked me, "Why don't we go on the tour around the factory? It will show you how we make parts, but I won't be able to show you where we assemble the engines and transmissions for security reasons."

That made sense to me.

All the time we were on the tour I was sweating my ass off in the damned suit! Dan commented that "You didn't need to dress so formally," he was in Levi's and a sport shirt. Other bikers at the factory looked at me as if I were an alien.

At tour's end, I met Catherine Tinkie, who asked me, "Well, Dave, what can we do for you, and what are you doing?"

I explained my journey, and the reasons for it. Then I asked the all-important question, "Would you like to help sponsor my trip?"

"No, we can't help you there," she responded.

Without hesitation, I volunteered another possibility.

"Well, I need an engine overhaul. Can they help me there?"

"We don't sponsor anything like this," she replied. "We just don't sponsor anyone."

Now, my heart was sinking.

"Well, I've had many potential sponsors ask me, 'Why should we put anything into this trip when the Harley Davidson Motor Company won't help you out?'"

She looked at Dan, and I could tell he had a sense of appreciation for the adventure I was on, and cared about my purpose. Earlier, he had been very attentive to my sharing as we toured the factory.

Not one to give up, I continued.

"Catherine, I need to rebuild this motor because there's something wrong in the lower end that keeps tearing up the charging system. I think the engine will make it to Alaska, and that's where I would like to do the overhaul. The weather there is nice and cold - a perfect place to break it in."

"How much will that cost?" she asked, showing some interest for the first time.

"About $2,500" I replied.

"I don't know," she said, shaking her head.

"I will discuss it with some other people," Dan interjected.

I knew I had an ally in this man.

"The reason I must do an overhaul is due to bad work done in a dealership here in the U.S. where I sent the motor to be overhauled from South Africa before I started the trip," I piped up. Then, I suggested, "What if I give you the motorcycle at the end of the ride - to go into the 'Hall of Fame'?" I asked.

"That might be an idea," Dan replied. "I'll see what I can do. Give me a call on Monday."

After the meeting, Catherine went on her way, and Dan walked me outside, treating me to a lunch off one of the catering trucks (they go all out for a visiting dignitary!). We then took some photos of the motorcycle in front of the factory. After I shook Dan's hand, off came my suit and tie, on went the rain gear, and I drove out the driveway, leaving all the beautiful, shiny motorcycles behind.

As I rode home, I thought, "If they give me money for the overhaul, in the end, my motorcycle will go to their Hall of Fame which they're planning to build. Basically, what I have done is sold my motorcycle for $2,500 IF they accept my offer."

Mighty Rivers, Huge Mountains, and The Continental Divide

July 16: On the road again. It was my Mother's birthday, so I called home at 04:00 to say "Good morning, and Happy Birthday, Mom" before I rode away from that beautiful home on the shores of Lake Winnebago, heading west on Highway 21 out of Oshkosh. Soon, I crossed the Mississippi River.

What a mighty river It Is indeed!

Once across the Mississippi into Minnesota, my speedometer cable broke, although it only had 18,000 miles on it. I drove another hundred miles to a small town called Sherborn where I found a nice little campground some distance from the highway. The proprietor put me out on a little finger of land with water on both sides where I could have my own privacy. I hooked up my battery and was relaxing when the son-in-law of the proprietor came up to me.

"I heard you're having trouble," he said. "I ride a Harley myself. Maybe I can help."

"I broke my speedometer cable," I replied. He excused himself to make a phone call, then came back and told me, "There's a shop about 20 miles down the road that has a speedometer cable. If you want to go with me, we can get it." We hopped into Barry's pick up truck and drove to the small shop that had the speedometer cable.

At sunset, the wind was blowing so severely that I couldn't light my gas cooker - cold beans and bread for dinner - a fitting reward for the 340 miles of roads covered this day.

The next morning I left camp, tackling a very strong headwind. The weather just never seems to cooperate with me. Nevertheless, each day I start out with a feeling of freedom and of anticipation for the day's events. This is especially true in the United States where the roads are so good.

Rolling into South Dakota, I treated myself to a $2 hot breakfast special - I figured I owed myself something. Late in the day, I found a remote campground about midway through the state, put the battery on charge, and started to relax since there's not much to do on the motorcycle this day. The proprietor let me stay here for only $4, and threw in a pen as part of the bargain!

I closed the day swatting mosquitoes.

I woke up the next day to a furiously blowing wind and did my pushups - 135 each in three separate sets. Sometimes I wonder why I try to keep up with the exercising in such lousy weather conditions. On the highway, the high winds blew me and the motorcycle all over the place. It was much more than a headwind - it hit me sometimes from the side, then, if I'd come up between hills, I'd get blasted from another direction. Naturally, this was complicated even further as the large trucks swished by, changing the wind patterns yet again!

As I traveled through Rapid City, I remember thinking, "I wonder how my meeting will work out with Dan Klemencic at the Sturgis Rally?"

Entering Wyoming, the landscape was beautiful - ranch country, green and hilly. The mountains were covered with trees, whereas South Dakota had been a plains state, although still green and beautiful. I especially enjoyed this scenic part of the trip until my motorcycle engine started sputtering and coughing. I wondered what the hell was going on now.

Next, a policeman pulled me over and said, "You are riding with your headlight off. I've got to give you a warning. You are now on the computer. If we catch you again, you will be given a ticket."

I turned it on for the policeman, then turned it off again when he left a few minutes later. "From now on, I'll turn it on every time I come into a town," I thought.

In the Greenhorn Mountains the scenery was absolutely magnificent! I don't know how high the elevation was, but there was a power loss on the motor, forcing me to run in third gear to get over the passes. The scene was so beautiful - the trees, the mountains, the cool air, and the good winding road.

I stopped in a little town near the bottom of the mountains on the western side. I met a man I had passed on the interstate who had taken some video footage of me from his car. He asked, "Can I shoot some more video of you here at camp?"

Of course, I said "Yes," speaking for a few minutes into his camera.

He offered me $20 for my time, but I refused the money.

As we departed, I gave him my address and phone number in case he knew someone who might want to sponsor part of my trip. Nothing ever came from it.

From the time I left South Dakota until I crossed into Wyoming, I traveled 340 miles. Tomorrow, with any luck, I'll make it into Pocatella, Idaho.

I got up at 04:30, did my pushups, and started the motorcycle by 05:30. I rode out and down into the lower canyon country when the sun came up over my back - it was absolutely magnificent! I was headed west and south, so it wasn't glaring down in my face as **I crossed the Continental Divide!**

Later, the countryside changed from canyons to desert and then back to mountains. As I came into Jackson, Wyoming, the snow-capped Grand Teton Mountain Range was off to my right. What an incredible site - some of the most beautiful country I had seen in America!

Out of Jackson, I climbed over a mountain pass at 9,650 feet elevation. The motorcycle was back in third gear grunting along.

Coming down the mountain, I crossed into the flat lands of Idaho, going through Idaho Falls, then about another fifty miles to Pocatello, where I called Paul Ban, Lang Price's Dutch uncle.

Paul gave me directions to his house, and I was there in five minutes.

Repairs to My Bike, My Leg, and My Ego (Water-Ski Mania)

Paul was a handsome, tall fellow who looked about thirty-eight, but in fact was fifty-two years old. He smoke and drank, but was a man who seemed to take everything in stride. His wife, Jackie, nicknamed "Chicken" (No, I don't know why!), was a lovely girl who looked younger than her 30 years. I hit it off immediately with both of them since they were long-range motorcycle riders. Paul had ridden all over the United States on an old Harley Davidson.

After settling in, Paul took me to the local motorcycle shop, an after-market Harley dealer, where we met the owner, George Linford, who told me, "Dave, you can come in and use anything in the shop anytime you want to."

Very kind of you, George.

Of course, when I do screw up, I always seem to do it in front of a crowd. On my way out of the shop, I fell over on the motorcycle and landed in the gravel. I managed to get the motorcycle up, while the group looked on in wonder at this icon of a world traveler. In an attempt to make light and cover my embarrassment, I boasted, "Ladies and gentlemen, this is all just part of my party tricks."

Afterwards, I slink away with Paul.

I decide to stay with Paul and Jackie until we all head for the motorcycle rally in Sturgis, South Dakota, where I'll get some kind of answer out of Harley Davidson as to whether they will give me the money to overhaul the motor.

After a very long day of traveling - over 400 miles - at 24:30 I laid back in the bungalow of a friend of theirs that was away for the next couple of weeks and closed my day.

During the next few days, I worked on my motorcycle, putting a new alternator in and doing other basic maintenance work, including installing the new right handlebar.

During this time, I did two television interviews, and one for a radio station. It was great living a few blocks away in my own private cottage, not under foot at Paul and Jackie's.

We visited an Idaho Bar where bikers liked to meet - a western-type bar. Bikers around here seemed to like to wear cowboy boots.

"Well, this is out west," I thought.

At this bar, I gave a short five-minute talk to try and create a bit of interest for the talk and slide show I was to give on Sunday, July 28. The local motorcycle club was there, as was the A.B.A.T.E chapter (a group representing biker's rights and education). Everybody was saying, "We'll see you on Sunday."

Social life for the bikers here was pretty good. When talking about the general population of Idaho, they'd say, "It's them and us," meaning "It is the Mormons and anybody who is not Mormon."

Once I was walking along in town and a belt broke on my right leg. I held it by hand as I walked, but was still a good mile from the cottage. I located an alley where I could sit down out of sight and take the leg off. I pulled out a couple of tools that were in the bag I carry, and put another belt on. What a sight it would have made if somebody had come by and seen me sitting there, like an old hobo, with my leg totally off!

A few days later, I got a phone call from Jeff Hampstein at the H and H Dive and Travel School, asking me, "Dave, would you like to come out and do some scuba diving in our tank?"

I thought that would be fun, so I readily agreed.

Jeff was a very unique person, about my height but quite stocky. He was an ex-Vietnam Veteran. His "pool" was not a pool, but a HUGE indoor tank - twenty-six feet deep.

"How did you manage to build it?" I asked him.

"Well, I couldn't locate explosives, so drilled holes in the rock and dirt and filled them with black powder. When it blew up, I'd just lift out the debris in buckets until I was down twenty-six feet (it was about 50 meters long). He completed the entire project pretty much by himself!

I sat in a class with a couple of others who were there training; later, we took our gear to the tank deck and suited up. To my surprise, there were bright, brilliant-colored fish in the tank; some quite big. They would even eat food out of your hand!

The next day, Jeff invited me to do some water skiing with the CW Hog Foundation, riding in the boat as the tow rope observer. "Sure," I said, and the next thing I knew we were hooking up Jeff's boat and driving over to American Falls where we met a number of disabled people. We launched his 18 foot, 120 horsepower boat into the lake, and it hit a top speed of 45 mph in no time. Jeff had a ski designed for a quadriplegic, and people with lesser disabilities. We must have been quite a rag-tag group!

There were amputees, and a fellow named Tom - a paraplegic disabled in the US Army when a tank hit him, causing spinal damage from just below the shoulder blades on down. I rode as observer, and we went around the lake time and again with this specially made ski with a disabled person on it.

At the end of the day, Jeff asked me, "Would you like to drive the boat while I ski?"

Now it had been some years since I had driven a boat, but I'm always game for anything. "Let's give it a bash."

After throwing the rope to the skier (Jeff), Tom, the paraplegic, was going to be the observer. Jeff shouts, "Hit it," and away we go.

I am sitting up on the back of the driver's seat; there is a walk through between the driver and passenger seats. As I make a hard right turn, trying to swing Jeff out, I slide over to the empty partition, and flew to the back of the boat. I thought I was going right over the back, but my backside came crashing into the back of the boat at the transom.

Now, the boat has turned a full 180 degrees and is actually starting back towards Jeff, who has dropped the rope and raised his arms, going down as deep as he can so the boat would not run him down. I was struggling against the power of the motor to get my right leg, which was in front of me, back around behind me so that I could crawl towards the controls and shut the motor off. Tom sat there with the white face of stark terror in his big, saucer-sized eyes.

Finally forcing my right leg behind me, I crawled against the centrifugal force to the back of the seats where I was able to eventually grab the controls and shut down the motor.

To my very great relief, I hadn't run over Jeff. Luckily, the tow rope didn't get caught up in the props. When I drove over to Jeff, he was bobbing, white-faced, in the water.

"Jeff, do you want to go for a ski ride?" I asked. He laughed and smiled and said, "Let's go for another turn."

I am very pleased he did that. I would have felt badly if he had said, "No, I would just as soon get in the boat and drive it back my self."

Sturgis or Bust...Pure Motorcycle Mania!

August 1: Paul, Chicken, myself and a couple of others were ready to head out for Sturgis. Greg drove behind us and was going to do some filming. About an hour out of Pocatello, I started having power problems again. My throttle cable wire had come lose; it only took a few minutes to sort it out.

The security of traveling with a group was nice, but it also had drawbacks. For one, we were always stopping so someone could piss, so there's very little continuity in our ride.

Yellowstone Park was beautiful, indeed, but so crowded that you really had to watch the traffic. Stop and go, stop and go, like Los Angeles at rush hour. When someone would spot an animal, all the cars would stop and the tourists would shout, "Oh look, there's a moose." Out would come the cameras.

Then "Oh, look, there's the Old Faithful Glacier."

More stops and photographs.

It was as if these people had never seen any wildlife or trees in their lives!

In the park we picked up three new bikers - Casey, Barbara and Russell, who camped with us that night. Of course, my motorcycle was having trouble again - the motor was missing at high rpm. Sure enough, upon inspection I discovered that the points were burnt badly. I could not understand why, but put another set in, along with a condenser.

The next morning, all the way into Cody, Wyoming, my motorcycle ran like a champ. We stopped at a gas station where we met a couple named Gene and Donna on a big Harley Davidson Dresser.

Now, we were six bikes.

Later that day we rode over the Big Horn Mountains which just seemed to go up and up, magic and wondrous, full of green pine trees and rock formations. Going down the other side of the mountains, I had trouble with my rear brake sticking again - it gets hot and seizes up.

On we went for another hour, stopping in Sheridan, Wyoming, so some welding could be done on Casey's old Harley. We camped about 50 miles from Sheridan, cooking tins of beans for our dinner.

My motorcycle was breaking down fairly regularly; my starter failed later in the day. I discovered a wire off the relay, and fixed that, but then it started cutting out at high rpm again. Of course, I still had that big noise in the lower end of the motor, so there's absolutely no peace of mind about what I am riding.

Finally, we arrived in Sturgis!

We elected to stay at a campground called Bear Butte Creek, five miles out of town. On the ride in, I never saw so many Harley Davidsons in all my life! Bikers camping on top of one another. The only experience even close for me was the Harley Davidson Super Rally in Norway. The unique rumble of the Harley Davidson motors incessantly permeates the festive countryside where perpetual parties and non-stop bands seem to be always bombarding the senses.

Around midnight, I try to sleep (every party needs a pooper).

The next day Barb, Russell and I rode into Sturgis to put my name down on the attendance list from different countries, and to see if I could recognize any other names. I was hoping to qualify for the long distance award.

"It would be a nice feather in my bonnet," I thought, "to have that award from both the European Rally and from one of the biggest motorcycle rallies in the world - the Black Hills Rally of Sturgis. Who knows - this time I might even get a kiss from a pretty lady!"

Main street was solid motorcycles. They were parked facing one another in the middle of the street, in two rows down for blocks. They were parked against the curbs. No cars were allowed to go down main street. We found the main office and signed in from South Africa so that for anybody coming from that country would see where I was staying and we might get together.

In speaking to one of the officials about the long distance award, he tells me, "Well, the guy responsible for that hasn't showed up."

"So what does that mean?" I ask rather irritated. "Are you not going to have a long distance award after fifty years because this one year someone doesn't show up?"

It appeared that this was the case.

No official wanted to take responsibility.

"Hell, I'll even put up the money for a plaque," I told one official. "I've come all the way from South Africa. I'd like a fair shot at this long distance award."

My offer fell on deaf ears. I honestly think this man didn't believe I had come from South Africa by road (except for the oceans).

On the way back to camp, we made a grocery stop. It was absolutely astounding - unbelievable - breath-taking how many motorcycles were coming into town! Imagine the largest gathering of people you have ever witnessed - and then mount each of them on a Harley, and you have some idea what I saw.

It was only 08:30 in the morning, and we were headed away from the rally - thank God! Going into town, the line was stop and go for about one mile!

Inconceivable!

"What a great way to burn up a motor," I thought, watching the snails pace towards Sturgis. We rode back to the campground and spent the rest of the day doing absolutely nothing, listening to the buzz and humm of the Harleys all around us.

Celebrity and Sponsorship Chasing

On the third day, Gene and Donna were going to head home, so we decided to go to Waldrug to see Z-Z Top, a rock band. Greg, the video producer, was to be there, and he wanted my motorcycle photographed and filmed next to Z-Z Top. He told me, "There's a chance you might meet Willie G. Davidson (the son of

184

the founding father of Harley Davidson), and be able to speak to him about your trip."

"Maybe he would want to get involved," I thought wistfully.

The three of us took off quite early in the morning, and headed east 75 miles to Walldrug, where Gene and Donna said their "good-byes" and headed off back to Minnesota (I never saw them again).

Greg Lick and his crew came in. He said, "Hello," and told us, "We'll be meeting with Z-Z Top at the end of town closest to the highway." We rode up there, and were greeted by the incredible scene of the two magical looking Harley's of Z-Z Top next to an old, perfectly customized classic car. Next to all of this was the big Harley Davidson semi-tractor and trailer.

I pulled my motorcycle up to their two motorcycles which were sitting in front of the car much in the manner of an escort. We photographed and filmed amidst the crowds with everybody cackling about my motorcycle sitting next to the Z-Z Top machines.

My motorcycle must have looked like a pig with lipstick.

When Willie G. Davidson appeared on the scene, Greg Lick introduced him to me.

"Hi, how are you?" he said.

Greg briefly told him about my journey, and he replied, "Very good. Keep up the good work." We shook hands, and then he was swarmed by many others vying for his attention.

Naturally, I took a tremendous number of photos with both of my cameras, and others took plenty more for me. Unfortunately, I didn't check on how much film I had in my cameras, and later found out that **I didn't have any film** in either one. I didn't get any photographs of this entire time!

Thankfully, I do have the memory from the video Greg Lick took, showing me meeting Willie G. Davidson, the Icon and savior of the Harley Davidson Motorcycle Company.

Next, I drove towards Rapid City where I was to meet with Dan Klemencic at the local convention center. After amenities, I asked the all-important question.

"Have you received any clearance on that $2,500 we talked about for my motorcycle overhaul?"

"Yes, we did," he told me. "We will send a letter to the Anchorage Harley Davidson notifying them of your coming, and instructing them to meet your needs. The letter will advise what the company is prepared to do on your behalf."

"That's great news," I replied, thinking especially about that perpetual noise in my engine. "Thank you very much! Are there any papers I need to sign?"

"No, there are no papers to sign. Just get there and they will know about you."

When I rode back to the campground it was well into the evening, so everybody was already getting drunk out of their minds, listening to blaring loud music from perpotual nameless bands. About midnight, I tried to resign from the rest of the astronauts and fall asleep, but the rumble and dust from the Harley's and the increasing decibels from the band permeated every pore of my body.

While others seemed to have no worries or concerns, I stared at the roof of my tent and thought about my motorcycle. It had run along fairly well today, but it still was missing at high rpms. If I keep it under 3000 rpms, it seems to run all right. There's no apparent reason for this behavior. I took the carburetor apart, and the points didn't look too bad. By now, I had put in two condensers.

"Oh Yeah! How Did You Ride Across the Ocean?"

The next day, I met with Bob, one of the rally organizers, and showed him pictures of my journey from South Africa through Europe into the United States.

"Dave, I'm sorry there's no long distance award this year," he told me.

I was disappointed. Clearly, no one had come this far.

"We could send you a certificate of merit," he told me.

"No, that's okay," I replied, appreciating that he was at least trying to make some amends because some nameless official had fallen down on the job and not taken responsibility for his position.

Outside, Barbara and Russell asked me the results of the meeting.

"There will be no long distance award this year, and that's that."

My comment caught the ear of another official who asked, "Where did you come from?"

"I've come overland from South Africa."

"Well, how did you ride your motorcycle across the Ocean?" this man asked sarcastically.

I was amazed at his stupidity.

"You don't ride across the Ocean," I said, aggravated by his ignorance. Then I opened up. "You're so smart you can't even run a rally. When someone doesn't show up, there's no one willing to step up and take responsibility for the vacant position! And you have the nerve to ask me about riding across the ocean?"

I really vented on this fellow.

Later, I decided to ride up to Mt. Rushmore to take some photographs of the four presidents. It started to rain and it became very foggy. At the base of the mountain, I had a bit of luck because the clouds cleared long enough for me to get a photograph of the motorcycle with Mt. Rushmore in the background. I gazed upon the four presidents on Mt. Rushmore with awe, not only for who they were, but for the incredible man that created them from the face of the mountain. He must have been one hell of a guy with a chisel!

Next, I journeyed to the convention center for what I thought was to be another meeting with Dan Klemencic, only to discover he had to go back to Milwaukee.

I rode back to the campground, woefully dreading the thought of another night with all the noise of parties and bands. "Thankfully, tomorrow I'll be on my way to Alaska."

Before I left the convention center, I called the Cheshire home In Saskatchewan and asked them, "Would you like me to detour (it would have been 700 miles) up to your home to do a talk and slide show?"

The told me that the head of the home was away, and would be back in a few days. Upon her return, they would have her call London to secure references. Later, I called her again, and she explained, "No, I've been back for two weeks, but I've been too busy to call London. Frankly, I don't know where we would put you."

"Don't worry about that," I replied, "I can sleep out on the grounds."

"Oh, no, we couldn't do that," she immediately responded.

The woman sounded so apathetic to the idea of my visit that I just told her outright, "Lady, please, it is all right. I just won't be bothering to come by."

Amazing to me, hers was an attitude I encountered right through North America. To this day, I honestly do not know what the problem is.

Do I make disabled people uncomfortable because I aggressively press on with my life despite my handicap?

Do I intimidate them because I ride a Harley?

Or, is it because I am a person with a disability who is trying on his own to set an example for other people with disabilities to live their dream and break society's established ideas of how we should live and act?

Is it somehow offensive to their egos that a person with a disability dares to be out there challenging them?

I honestly do not know the answers.

But tomorrow, I'm on my way to Alaska, and I can leave the world of politics and social amenities behind!

North To Alaska - One Sputter at a Time!

The next morning I feel great joy at getting out of this noisy, crowded place and on the road to Prudhoe Bay - 5000 miles (8000 km) away.

It was overcast going through Sturgis, but as I progressed, the sun came out... it was a beautiful day.

In Wyoming, while getting fuel, I met five other bikers who said to me, "Would you like to tag along with us?"

"I don't know if I will be able to keep up. I'm having engine problems," I told them.

"If you can, you are very welcome."

We rode together for about five minutes, they quite a bit ahead of me. Soon, a situation developed where two of us were passing a truck together (something you shouldn't do) when my motorcycle started cutting out. Hurriedly, I signaled the guy to go ahead so he wouldn't get hit by the oncoming vehicle. I lagged back and went behind the vehicle.

That was the last I saw of them as I poked and prodded along on my miserable machine that ran like a tired old mongrel!

In Bozeman, Montana, just outside the township, I saw a Harley Davidson sign and pulled into the shop, meeting John, the owner. "My machine is constantly cutting out," I told him, "and it seems to be getting worse."

"It could be a number of things, but it is a bit too late to do anything on it now. Would you like to spend the night in the yard?"

"Yes, that's very kind of you," I replied.

"We will look at it in the morning. I'll let you do your own work if you want to," he continued.

So, I settled in the yard behind the shop.

About 20:00, John walked back up from his house (a couple hundred meters down a dirt lane) with a nice big steak dinner with salad and potato for me! I was overwhelmed by this kindness. What a treat!

The next morning I pulled the exhaust off, and the rear brake lever, then taking the cam cover off to see if we could find anything wrong inside. "Things look pretty good here," John said. "Maybe the springs for the advance system are weak."

"I'll try anything," I thought. "I've just got to stop the missing."

I cleaned up the points which I could see were bad again, and put in yet another condenser. I put all of this back together by about 11:00, and was on my way up a very long grade towards Butte, Montana, a beautiful, beautiful ride when the motorcycle starts cutting out again!

Everything that could be checked had been checked. Everything seemed to be in good condition, and yet I still couldn't get it right.

Coming down the far side of the pass, I used the rear brakes a lot, and they started to seize up and get very hot. I pulled over to let them cool down.

Is there no end to this shit?

About eight miles south of the Canadian border, I called it a day, locating a rest area where I bought some beans and bread for my dinner. After eating, I spent an hour trying to find the problem; the points were burnt again. I cleaned them, hoping something else was wrong.

Once again, the condenser failed; I have now changed three condensers.

That night, I thought about how my old motorcycle was taking me back in time, to the journeys of travelers fifty years ago, when transcontinental trips on the bikes of their day were even more mechanically treacherous than mine.

The next morning was a beautiful dawn, and I felt very good since the machine seemed to be running along smoothly. At the border, the Canadian custom agents, efficient little pricks, grilled me with questions for about thirty minutes, even running a computer check on me.

"Do you have any drunk driving offenses?" they asked.

"Yes, I had two careless driving offenses, the result of too much to drink." I was sure that answer would keep me out of the country. I thought to myself, "Well, you bunch of bloody assholes. How dare you keep me out of your country when most international drug dealers and terrorist use Canadian passports."

I couldn't believe my luck! All they could see was the motorcycle and drew the conclusion that I was a shitbird. "You horrible little men!" I thought. Perhaps I would have felt differently, but these JERKS had a real attitude problem.

Finally, much to my surprise, they allowed me to carry on.

"See, I told you I'm one of the good guys," I said to an agent who just looked away as I passed him.

In Lethbridge, I found a Harley Davidson shop and once again changed the points and condenser. I took the carburetor apart, working with the mechanic all morning, even doing a compression check - it was excellent. These mechanics only charged me $50 for labor - a big discount.

For 20 miles the motorcycle ran fine, but when I encountered a bit of rain, sure enough, the engine started cutting out again.

My heart just sank. What is wrong with this machine?

Why does such a simple motorcycle have a problem that nobody can figure out?

What is wrong with all of these Harley Davidson Mechanics?

I stopped at a campground just north of Calgary, traveling only about 180 miles that day. The Indian fellow in charge would take no money.

"Just enjoy the evening and leave everything clean," he told me.

I met a motorcyclist there who was talking about returning to Wisconsin. He had a month's vacation, and had planned to go up to Alaska.

"I hear the road is rough going up the Alaskan/Canadian highway, and there's been a lot of rain lately. I just don't know."

After he learned of my trip from South Africa, he seemed amazed. He spoke to his wife, and they decided they would attempt to carry on. I never saw them again since they had a big touring Kawasaki with a trailer on the back; they'd have no problems traveling along at 70 miles per hour.

I had problems just moving forward!

The next morning, the cutting out got worse; finally, I pulled in under a bridge in a driving rain. I took the point cover off, and the points were burnt up again! I put in yet another condenser, and cleaned up the points as best I could, resuming the ride in a most negative mood.

And what do you know?

Inexplicably, the motorcycle ran fine.

I rode about 180 miles that day through flat lands towards Edmonton without any major trouble! Whoopee!

That night, I bought a can of beans ($1.39). I was already shocked by the cost of gasoline - two and a half times as expensive as in the U.S. - and measured by the liter. Then, when I went to buy a pack of cigarettes, I nearly shit a gold brick! They wanted $6.00 Canadian for a pack of cigarettes! I was so shocked that I didn't buy the cigarettes, even though I only had a few left. "No smoking while I'm in Canada," I thought.

I arrived at my campground about 15:30, very early for me to be stopping, but it had been raining all day. Besides, I needed to buy new points and a condenser for the motorcycle the next day.

After a sodden, wet night, I rode to the Harley Davidson shop where I bought more points and condensers. When I told them of my problem, they said "It's hard to believe you can put in four condensers consecutively and have the same problem." I agreed.

Out of Edmonton on Highway 43, it was very wooded, hilly, and beautiful. My only stops were every 100 or so miles for gasoline. The motorcycle was running okay, making good time.

Crashes, Cowboys, Moonshine Terry and Fish to the Rescue!

In Grand Pierre, I hit some unmarked road construction where a section of the road was cut out. While trying to get back onto good pavement, the motorcycle hit about a three inch sharp ridge at a wrong angle, whipping it around. All I could do was hold onto the handlebars. At about 35 miles per hour, I hit a deeper, dugout section of the road, and then the curb... head on!

My front forks bent back into the motor.

I felt myself being propelled forward while clutching my handlebars.

A light post was coming straight toward my face.

"Oh, no," I thought in an instant, sensing this is one of those times when the hand of God was there. Miraculously, I never touched that pole. Didn't get a scratch on me. Wasn't even bruised.

Just shook up.

As I climbed off the motorcycle, I remember thinking, "I just cannot seem to get through a single day without some depressing shit happening to me."

I also said a quick prayer of thanks for my deliverance.

I spotted a biker on an old Harley like mine coming through this area earlier, and we had waved. Now, that same guy was again coming down the road. I flagged him down, he stopped, looked at the damaged motorcycle, and introduced himself as "Fish."

"Don't talk to anyone," he tells me. "I'll be back in about 10 minutes. I know you haven't got insurance, and you can get in big trouble in Canada."

Fish left, then came back shortly with a fellow in a pickup truck. Moonshine Terry sported a wild looking red beard, and was owner of Moonshine Welders. Between the three of us, we put the Harley up on the truck and got the hell out of there before any police could come by.

In ten minutes we were gone - I had no time to get shook up or even think about the accident.

At Terry's shop, we took the front end apart. "We can get the tubes straightened out," they told me, "and it shouldn't take too long." We banged out the front rim which had dented itself in once again; it has never been true since Africa.

That evening, I met Terry's wife, Anita, and she did a "grocery" on Terry's command, cooking us a wonderful dinner while I took a very welcome shower and climbed into clean clothes. After dinner, Terry took me to the little motorcycle shop in town.

Now, none of these guys had big new Evolution Harley motorcycles. Not this bunch! They all rode old shovelheads and pans - old Harley Davidsons, the same as mine. We poor boys could identify with each other.

Fish was full of tattoos, and Terry, even though short, was the boss - nobody disputed his word. Later that evening, we went to a bar where bikers used to go, and I saw many drunken Indians sitting around, face down on the tables, sleeping it off.

"We put up with them Indians," Terry explained. "This is one of the few places they can come and drink. They don't bother anybody, even though they are drunk and sloppy at times. The cowboys around here (pronounce that 'Caw boys') don't like the bikers, so there's trouble between us at times. We put up with the Indians, so if the 'Caw boys' want to give us a hard time, they've got to deal with the Indians too. That evens up the odds."

That night, I was amazed to remember that I had ridden more than 300 miles, experienced an accident, took apart the front end of the motorcycle, eaten a good hot dinner, had a shower, met all kinds of different people - from bikers to drunk Indians - and now, was in a warm soft bed instead of in a morgue.

Each day is a reminder of our fragile future.

The next morning, Moonshine and I continued to work on the front end. We tore the tubes down and took them into a repair shop that we thought could straighten them out.

"No, we can't straighten them. We're afraid they would break apart."

"I have a pair of front forks," Terry said, "We can see if they fit."

Terry's forks were standard length, and mine which were 4 inches longer for more ground clearance from rocks and other obstacles.

The fork tubes fit. So, we put everything back together and the motorcycle was sitting ready at about 13:00.

We had lunch at a striptease joint. I ordered a hamburger and some french fries, but it was rather difficult eating my lunch while watching a completely nude girl twist around on the floor in a very enticing manner. After the performance (oh, I mean, my lunch), we went back to the shop where I loaded up the motorcycle, leaving Moonshine Terry, Fish and the boys behind.

I rode about 70 miles until I found a state camping area off in the woods where there were only two other campers. **The following morning I crossed into British Columbia**, one of the most beautiful provinces in all of Canada, where I headed northwest out of Dawson Creek on the Alaskan/Canadian Highway (affectionately known as the Alcan Highway).

On the Alcan I met my first "oil road" - a mixture of tar, rocks and oil, blended together to withstand the severe winters. There were gravel patches in these narrow roads, and though they were well marked in advance, it still was a bit exciting to hit the gravel, especially on a corner when there was an oncoming vehicle.

I journeyed through Fort St. John all the way up and over to Summit Lake, quite high in altitude, then down the other side to Laird Creek. I had been over mountains, along rivers and streams, and seen wildlife along the road. I was especially excited when I saw mountain sheep.

In Laird Creek I bought some bread and put fuel in the motorcycle. The store clerk was in a terrible disposition; the few dark, wild hairs growing out of her chin shook when she talked; she must have been a monster to live with.

"Is there a book exchange in town?" I asked.

Now mind you, the town was only a few buildings along the highway.

"Next door," the hairy chin answered.

Sure enough, I was able to exchange a couple of books I had already read for a couple of others in their small library. "Maybe my luck is looking up," I thought, wondering what were the odds of finding a book exchange in such a small town.

That night at my camp it was very calm and peaceful, with a light breeze blowing through the tall pine trees. Suddenly, I saw a beam of light streaking across the sky, as if shot from a laser.

"Holy mackerel, am I seeing my first UFO?" I thought. "After years of hearing about these things, and seeing countless accounts of sightings on T.V., I'm actually seeing one up in the sky!"

This incredible beam of light burst open across the whole moonless night horizon, consisting of various colors and shapes. My mind was bombarded with the different images and shapes formed by these swirling lights.

Finally, I realized I was witnessing the Northern Lights!

Believe me, no man could ever devise a light show so incredible.

I laid there very quiet, with the wind in the trees, the smell of pine needles in my nose, looking at this kaleidoscope of magnificent colors for half an hour - then it all doubled back up into the beam, and the beam was suddenly gone. Forever.

The next morning, after a couple of peanut butter sandwiches, I hit the cold, clear, magnificent road. About five miles down the road, my motor continued revving, but I lost power.

Now what?

As I pulled over, I discovered that my drive chain had dropped off the motorcycle. I walked back a couple of hundred meters and picked the broken chain up from the highway. Normally, a broken chain is not a problem, since I always carry extra master links. But, in this case I managed to run over the chain with my rear wheel, bending it.

It was no longer serviceable.

For the next two hours, many people passed, but none stopped.

Finally, a big Ford pickup truck with a welding unit on it slowed up, and a fellow named Adrian asked, "Can I help you?"

"Indeed you can," I answered. "I need to get back to civilization and find out about getting a new chain for my motorcycle."

"I don't see a problem there," he answered, "but I can't put you onto this truck. However, I could tow you."

The word "tow" did not thrill me. I was reminded of a rather grim scene in the Port of Tunis when a fellow tried to tow me to start my motorcycle and both of us ended up getting thrown at about 20 miles per hour.

But, it appeared I had no choice in this matter, so we wrapped a rope around the handlebars, and we rigged it so I could let go of the rope and it would disconnect. For the next five miles, Adrian towed me back to the campground. A couple of times I nearly veered into oncoming lanes of traffic; one time I had to let go of the rope, forcing Adrian to back up so we could try again. Twice I lost my balance and nearly came off the motorcycle.

All in all, it was a frightening ride.

Normally, towing a motorcycle is not that difficult, but with my legs I do not have the same kind of balance as the average person, especially starting out, and going around corners. We could only go about 15 miles an hour, so going five miles to the campground was a major undertaking.

After we put the motorcycle away, Adrian said, "Why not come with me to my shop in Laird Creek?"

I accepted, hopped into his truck, and we went to see his gigantic shop full of welding equipment. Adrian did industrial welding along the Alcan Highway for the maintenance of the highway, and for various installations along it. Since there's no electricity coming from a central location, people here have their own generators.

We ordered a motorcycle chain from a Yamaha shop in Fort St. John, and they said, "It will be delivered in the late afternoon on Greyhound bus."

Since it was only midmorning, I asked Adrian, "How can I help you?"

"Well, you can give Gene a hand around the shop. Maybe do a bit of cleanup." So, while waiting for the chain, I cleaned up the shop and helped Gene weld some stuff on to his work truck.

Yesterday, things had gone very well. I had ridden four hundred miles. Today - shit. I cannot seem to get a positive rhythm forward for more than a day at a time without problems.

Near the end of the day, the Greyhound bus came through, and my chain was on it. I paid Adrian the $80.00 for a standard chain (not a roller chain). Things are very expensive in Canada.

Gene took me back to the campground where I installed and adjusted the chain, now ready to move forward in the morning. At 23:00 I closed my day. It doesn't get properly dark until just after 23:00.

Bugs, Batteries, and Borders

The next morning I was off at about 06:00, hitting various forms of large insects constantly. I clean my glasses about every two hours, and then "Blap," my vision is gone again until the next cleaning. My biggest danger in this area - besides the rough roads and the gravel patches - is hitting wild animals, some quite large.

Towards northern British Colombia and the Yukon border, I was low on gas. Spying a little settlement off in the woods, I pulled in, hoping they might have a gas station. I was smack dab in the middle of an Indian reservation. I went up to a double-wide mobile home, knocked on the door, and asked the young fellow who answered, "Would you happen to have any extra gasoline? I am running short and I need about a gallon to get into the Yukon territory where there is a town just over the border on the map."

The young man went and asked his father, who told me, "I have it if you don't mind using gas I have mixed for the chainsaw."

"Absolutely not," I replied. "Any port in a storm will do."

I knew the mixture would smoke a bit, but it wouldn't hurt the engine. I put in five liters, then paid the fellow. As we talked, I learned they were located on the historic old Yukon Trail. We took some photos and shook hands.

I stopped to take another photograph at the border where a big sign read, **"Welcome to the Yukon Territory."**

Chapter Seventeen

Puttering My Way to Prudhoe Bay

My first town in the Yukon was of a reasonable size, so I purchased a full tank of gasoline. The road was good for a short distance, then became increasingly rough. The wind was blowing, but the day was bright and clear. "I'd hate to be on these roads in a terrible rain or snow storm," I thought to myself.

At my next stop, I met another Harley rider on a full dresser - an older one like mine. He introduced himself as Spencer Zogg, saying, "I know who you are. I keep hearing about you. I heard about you at Sturgis - the fellow with no legs who is riding up to Prudhoe Bay."

"Is attempting to ride," I corrected.

"What do you know," he continued, "isn't it something that we should meet up with each other?"

"Maybe all my little set backs were geared to bring Spencer and me together," I thought to myself.

"Well, how about we go on together and maybe have a night or two on the road?" I suggested.

"That is a great idea," he replied.

We rode together the rest of the day, and found a campground just outside of Whitehorse. For $5.00, the owner let both of us pitch our tents and shower. We cooked dinner, then I showed Spencer some photographs of my trip.

Spencer looked like a weight lifter. He smoked his pipe all the time, and had big, thick glasses and light colored, dishwater blonde hair. He had ridden through 48 of the United States, and was now making Alaska his 49th. He had crossed every province in Canada and Mexico as well - all on his old shovelhead. That made Spencer a different kind of biker - not a weekend warrior.

Spencer was also a poet.

I closed this day with fond memories, realizing I had covered 460 miles without too much effort.

We stopped at the Harley Davidson dealer in Whitehorse the next morning because Spencer wanted to change the oil in his motorcycle. From there, we rode on through the Yukon, around the bends and corners and over the rough roads.

The country was magnificent - beautiful! We saw marsh land in the low areas, and mountains, forest and rocky formations in the high areas. I particularly enjoyed the clean smell of pine in the higher altitudes.

At our next gas stop, when I went to re-start the motorcycle, it gave a hard start...I knew I was in trouble again!

My heart sank down through my knees.

The charging system had once again gone bad.

Spencer pushed my motorcycle and we got it started, riding on to a bigger service station/garage complex. The owner put my battery on a quick charge for an hour, then charged me $5.35.

"Well you prick," I thought.

I met a few people like this dick head on the Alcan Highway, usually older. The younger people, under 40, seemed friendly, but the older people just seemed to be a miserable lot who didn't like bikers.

Ah, Alaska - the Arctic Circle and Cold Foot!

Our next stop was the Alaskan/Canadian border where we crossed out of Canada into what seemed to be a "no man's land" - very rough road and a sign saying,

"Welcome to Alaska." For Spencer this was a very great moment because he was crossing into his 49th state - something few bikers have ever done. We took photographs, then he opened a little flask of whiskey and we took a drink.

"I have made it" he declared.

"Congratulations, and good for you" I responded.

We went on to the custom's house where we met an efficacious little fat prick of a custom's officer who proceeds to give us a hard time. I started to get verbal with him when Spencer put his hand up as if to say, "Take it easy."

"Who are you to look down on us," I thought. "You are a horrible little man who probably has done nothing in your life, or you wouldn't show such a horrible attitude towards your fellow man!"

Alaska greeted us with beautiful roads, very smooth compared to the Canadian side. Also, there were electric power lines to every small settlement, village and business along the way.

We also smelled smoke in the wind. When we came to our first high area, we discovered there was a major forest fire raging.

The overall beauty of the Alaskan countryside makes the rest of Canada and the United States look like a landfill. Normally, I am very partial to the beauty of the desert, but there's nothing to compare to the green and beautiful countryside of Alaska - it is second to absolutely nothing anywhere in the world!

In Northway, about 40 miles inside the border, we met a fellow from Great Britain named Iver who gladly put my battery on charge for the night. After fueling up, Spencer went to start his machine so he could ride it around the side of the building where we were going to sleep that night.

His motorcycle wouldn't start either!

His battery was dead!

We both looked at each other, knowing we had a new bonding. Not only were we both long distance travelers, but now we both had the same type of charging problem on the same day. We put both the batteries on charge.

Spencer also keeps a journal, but he speaks into a tape recorder. It seems a lot easier, and if I did it, I might even be more expressive in my thoughts about what I am doing, and the countryside around me.

That evening, as we set up camp, I couldn't help thinking, "This Northway is a very, very cold place, befitting of its name."

The next day, the weather changed, becoming rainy off and on. Our motorcycles seem to be going well for both of us, so we made good time, stopping only for fuel and coffee to ward of the cold. When we hit Fairbanks, we had already covered about 300 miles. There, we located the local Harley Davidson shop which, being Sunday, was not open.

We waited to see if anyone would come by. After about an hour, a guy walks through the parking lot, and I asked him, "Is there a biker bar around here?"

"There sure is," he replied. "Just go down the street and you will see a sign saying *Frank's Place*. That's where all the bikers hang out."

We went to *Frank's Place*, immediately meeting a big strapping fellow named Kurt, drunk out of his mind. "If you need a place to stay, I have a place that will be safe to house your motorcycles. You can work on them the next day. I've got schooling in motorcycle maintenance of Harley Davidsons."

We agreed to go with him and spend the night at his house.

"Kurt, I'll be pushing on to Prudhoe Bay tomorrow morning," I told him, "so I'll need another battery."

I was not taking the primary off again to replace the alternator just to go up to Prudhoe Bay and back and ruin it again. That would be the 4th alternator I've put into this thing. There would be no more!

"Kurt, is there anyone who could help me with a battery for a couple of days?"

He spoke to one of his friends who volunteered his battery. "It has a pretty good charge on it," he told me. When I told him "Thank you" and offered to pay for it, he said, "No, just bring the battery back."

"I'll do that in the next few days," I told him, not knowing how long it would take to get to Prudhoe Bay.

Spence and I followed Kurt's car through pouring down rain for 13 miles back the way we had come...to a place called the North Pole. Kurt worked in a garage just the other side of a giant Santa Claus! Honest. We stashed the motorcycles away in the garage, put both batteries on charge, and took a short drive to Kurt's house where we met his lovely wife, Katrina, who worked in a local nightclub. We also met a woman named Joy who looked like a good mate for Tigger - a 300 pounder.

The next morning as I started to leave, Katrina gave me the hostel number of her brother who worked up in Prudhoe Bay on the pipeline as a welder.

"Thanks," I thought. "Maybe I can find a place to get a free night."

Before I left, I stripped the bike of anything that was not absolutely necessary. No extra clothes. I just took my tent, tools, oil and I borrowed a 5 gallon gasoline can.

"Dave, you've got the 1,000 yard stare," Spencer observed as I readied for departure.

I'd been staring off in the distance trying to anticipate what the next few days would bring on the so-called Hull Road or James Dalton Highway.

"Yeah, you're right," I answered. "I'm getting my tunnel vision. Everything is becoming focused on what is ahead and the things I will face going up that Hull Road into the Arctic."

As Spencer shook my hand, I departed for **Prudhoe Bay, the most northern point of the North American continent that can be reached by road.**

After about 30 miles, I stopped at Fox and got fuel and a cup of coffee.

"Where you headed?" some faceless people asked.

"Prudhoe Bay."

The nameless people all smiled at each other, looking at me as if I were a gibbering idiot. Quite frankly, at times like this, I felt like a gibbering idiot!

"You're going to need a permit to go up there...you can only go so far. The authorities don't like any one without official business going above Cold Foot."

"Well, we'll see," I replied. "I've come up all the way from Africa, and I'll be damned if I'm going to stop now because of some petty official or permit."

Out of Fox, the dirt road deteriorated into very small pot holes that were very closely spaced together; they really jarred you when you hit them.

Unfortunately, the gravel on the road was not very deep. While in third gear, probably at about 30 miles an hour coming around a fairly gentle bend, the motorcycle slid on the shallow gravel and slick road with mud on it. I hit a meridian, losing control. The force threw me toward the edge of the road, close to a long drop. The dirt pushed up on the road's edge by a road grader deflected me enough to stay on the road.

This was a very, very close one indeed.

Next, I encountered a mountain range that seemed to go up and up. I don't know what the elevation was because there were no signs posted along the way. I slowed down, staying out of third gear when possible. Only on the straight roads would I put the machine into higher gear.

As I hit the top and started winding down the other side, I remember thinking, "Which is more dangerous? The ride up, or the ride down?"

At the base of the mountain range, there was a long, high bridge to take me over the Yukon River. As I traveled this bridge, I took a few photographs and thought of Jack London's book, *Call of the Wild*, about this area. For a few minutes, I was transported back to my childhood days.

Finally, I experienced my second crossing of the Arctic Circle!
More photographs.

A German fellow in a van, coming back, introduced himself as Norbert Hine.

"Do you mind if I take some photographs?" he asked in his heavy accent.

"Of course not," I replied, "you're very welcome."

We talked for about twenty minutes while he took notes.

"Dave, I'm a free lance journalist and photographer in Munich, Germany," he told me. This chance encounter was the start of a relationship that has lasted until this very day. Because of an article he later wrote, I was invited to appear on television in a trip to Germany, then on another in January, 1995. Norbert proved to be one of those rare and unique individuals truly concerned about the trip and the reason I was doing it.

And, he could understand and recognize an adventure when he saw one.

I moved on up the line to Cold Foot, covering about 300 miles that day - 260 plus of them on the dirt. I was tired, starting to lose my edge. I remembered my bad accident in the Namib desert, and determined to spend the night at Cold Foot.

Cold Foot was the place where you were supposed to secure a permit to proceed any further. However, the knowledge was not substantiated by any facts I could uncover. Most of the vehicles I had seen on this road were big, three axle drive diesels. One trucker I spoke with told me, "I only get six trips up to Prudhoe and back - roughly 6,500 miles (10,000 km) out of a set of tires."

The Hull road's main purpose was to be a service road for the Alaskan oil pipe line.

At the Arctic Circle, the sun doesn't go down until just after midnight, but I was able to bed down inside my bag and fall asleep after reflecting on the day and the things I'd seen, both good and bad. I especially enjoyed the moose and caribou, and the black bear along side the road.

It's great to see this wildlife in North America.

Caribou, Check Post Cops, and Rock-Throwing Trucks

August 20: This was the day I planned to make it to the top!

In the morning, thick frost froze everything; the temperature had to be down to 20 degrees F or less. Drinking hot coffee to warm up, I forced down my semi-frozen peanut butter sandwich.

After thoroughly warming up my motorcycle, I pulled out on the road, holding tightly to the handle bars as a feeling of adventure unfolded. Shots of adrenaline were pumping through my veins. Despite the cold, I'm very thankful the sun is out.

A sign shortly out of Cold Foot said: "Next Services 244 miles." That reference was obviously to Prudhoe Bay and Dead Horse Camp.

As I moved down the road, suddenly I was engulfed in a dust cloud, but I couldn't see the truck. The closer I came to it, the more difficult it was for me to see. Only after I almost ran into it did I realize how close we were. I had to jump out into the oncoming lane, not knowing if anything was coming because I couldn't see around the monster in front of me.

Dust blows almost all the way across to the other side of the road, so it is always a risk to move out and around these trucks. Fortunately, this one was only going 20 miles an hour because he was going uphill on a winding road. I managed to get around this guy and a couple of others during the course of the morning.

Russian roulette on the road.

Right over the top of the Brooks Range, I came to a check post where a man looks at me on my motorcycle and says, "You can't get up here."

"I can," I reply in my great voice of confidence. "I'm going around the world from bottom to top. You better let me pass. I'm not going back," I said firmly but respectfully.

He looked at me kind of funny. I guess he could see the wild, very determined look on my face.

"Well, be careful," he tells me. "You didn't see me, right?"

"Right, I didn't see you," I answered. "You're not here. You're a ghost. Goodbye."

I was immediately on way before anybody else could pop up and give me trouble. Also, I didn't want any of the trucks to catch up to me.

Next, on to open tundra (green, beautiful marshlands) for miles and miles. This vegetation grows right on top the water, and freezes most of the year. There are patches of hard ground out in the marsh land, islands in a sea of green. The smell is crisp and beautiful. The sun was out, so it was just an absolutely magnificent scene.

The road started getting very rough - not in the sense that it was unkept, but that it was covered with what is affectionately called "Alaskan pea gravel" - small rocks. The motorcycle and I shook very hard for the next 130 miles; my vision blurred. Even at 35 miles an hour my teeth rattled.

Off in the distance every now and again I'd see a big, brown cloud of dust - my signal that another truck was on its way! When they passed, they showered me with gravel and rock. I especially enjoyed the projectiles that pummeled my knuckles. My head light was cracked from one of these passings. When the wonderful time would inevitably come when the truck would pass, I'd duck my head down as close to the dashboard as I could, listening to the colossal noise of rock, wind and truck tires flying past me. I'd always say a quiet little prayer that I didn't hit anything as we pass, knowing full well that one of these bigger rocks would kill me if it hit just right.

The only real danger on the road besides these big truck were the herds of caribou which would just pop up on the road. I could usually see them coming, running along the road, before they decided it would be great fun to jump out in front of me. I had to be very careful.

A few times, I almost went down on this rough road in patches of gravel. My street tires, both front and rear, made this part of the adventure even more difficult.

When I stopped once to pour in gasoline from my reserve can, the world suddenly seemed amazingly quiet. I had not experienced this sort of silence since I was in the Sahara.

By the time I spotted Dead Horse Camp in the distance in Prudhoe Bay, my body was aching; it had been pounded and beaten by the Alaskan pea gravel so tremendously that it seemed a miracle that I ever made it. I still couldn't focus on the speedometer - the dial was a blur.

A great sense of relief set in.

I made it!

Dead Horse camp was 300 miles (500 km.) north of the Arctic circle.

When I pulled in for gas, the pumps were housed inside a shack so that they wouldn't freeze.

I went to the hostel where Katrina's brother, Ken, would be.

"He's out working," the guard told me. "But listen, you look as if you could use a hot cup of coffee and something to eat. There's a snack bar on the second floor. It won't cost anything. Help yourself to some coffee and sandwiches."

"Thank you," I said, thinking, "What a very kind man. Now I'll go pig out so I won't have to buy anything to eat tonight." All the while, I wondered, "Where am I going to sleep tonight?" I knew things would get mighty cold, down to 15 degrees, or maybe zero.

As I was grabbing a couple of nice roast beef and chicken sandwiches, and a cup of coffee, a fellow was staring at me in amazement. The mud on my face and jacket made me appear as a food-starved wild man munching away with great gusto.

"Hello," he said, "What are you doing?" he asked me.

I explained my motorcycle ride around the world, and that Prudhoe Bay was one of my target areas.

"How can I drive right up to the ocean?" I asked him.

"Only by going through the ARCO compound," he replied.

That didn't sound like good news to me.

"I'm David Sanderson," he told me. "Perhaps I can help you."

"That would be great," I replied. "Dave, what do you do here?"

"I'm a helicopter mechanic and crew chief for the Evergreen whale survey."

"Oh yeah?" I said very enthusiastically, "I was a helicopter mechanic and crew chief while serving in the Marines."

"That's where I started working on helicopters, too."

Now we had an immediate rapport.

"When you finish with your sandwiches, we've got a company pickup downstairs. If you'll follow me over to the gates, we'll see if we can get you through. I'll file responsibility for you."

"Great!"

Back outside, it was below freezing; all the water in the puddles was frozen solid. Mind you, it's August 20, and it's mid-afternoon! I had to take my battery out and put in the extra battery I was carrying. As other men came in off their shifts, and saw the motorcycle, they made various comments, some complimentary, some suggesting lunacy.

I appreciated most of the comments, but in my mind, I kept thinking, "I've still got to ride back down the same damn road."

I followed Dave over to the ARCO gates where the guards stopped us. David spent 45 minutes trying to get us permission to go on.

Nobody in authority wanted to take responsibility.

So, we turned around and went back to Dead Horse Camp. I saw a sign reading "Dead Horse Camp, Prudhoe National Forest." It seemed humorous, since there weren't any trees within miles. We pulled the motorcycle in behind that sign as a good land mark, and I looked south, trying to grasp the enormity of the next part of my journey - to the bottom tip of South America in Terra del Fuego.

Making it to the top of Prudhoe Bay brought me very little joy, although I was proud of the accomplishment. What occupied my thoughts most was the return trip back of 540 miles (860 km). Somehow, I had to do it without wrecking the motorcycle or killing myself. Then, I will rejoice.

"Listen, I've got a plan," David said. "We'll take your motorcycle over to the helicopter hangars where we can put the batteries on charge, and you can come into the hostel from the back. I've got an extra bed in my room. You can sleep there and get a shower. Food is served in a buffet, so we can eat it back in our rooms. I'll go and get your dinner - that way you won't have to pay for any of this. It's over $100 a night if you want to spend any time up here, and the motorcycle would be stuck outside. The temperature could get down to zero, and lower."

The idea sounded great to me!

We drove back to the Evergreen hangars where they had big Huey twin engine helicopters. We put the batteries on charge, went to the hotel, and I had a very welcome shower. The mud and the dirt just flowed off of me!

Dave and I had a deep discussions that night about religion, life, time, and mortality. When I'm riding on the edge - flirting with death - my moods and conversations become more serious. We discussed television ads that perpetrated the idea that you can live forever if you buy this or that product.

But mortality and time are always working against us.

The next morning, we went to the hangar to fetch the motorcycle and the charged batteries. I put the spare battery in my saddle bag, loaded up, and with a big hug to this very kind person, took off, never to see him again.

Welcome To Alaska
August 16, 1991

Second Crossing of The Arctic Circle
August 19, 1991 Alaska

Dead Horse Camp/Prudhoe Bay
300 miles north of The Arctic Circle
End of Hull Road
August 20, 1991 Alaska

Chapter Eighteen

Anything But Downhill!

The freshly watered dirt road splattered mud immediately all over me. So much for being clean!

Through the tundra, over the Alaskan pea gravel, I was once again being pelted by gigantic trucks showering me with stone, dust and noise. About 150 miles down the tundra, moving at a good pace (around 50 mph), my vision was so blurred I didn't notice my oil light until the motor started rattling and making noises. I immediately shut the ignition off and coasted to a halt, wondering what in the hell was going on.

Closer inspection revealed the entire front of the motor was covered in oil.

"Holly mackerel," I surmised, "one of these trucks has thrown a rock and it's busted a hole in my crankcase."

My heart was sinking quickly.

"My God, not now. Not so close to getting to Anchorage. To lose the motor now is unthinkable!"

Looking closer, I realized that one of the oil lines going to the oil cooler had a big chunk missing out of it. Obviously, this was the problem. Breathing a little bit of relief, I next needed to determine whether the engine had seized up.

I took out some extra oil hose from my saddle bags and replaced the oil line. Then, I took the extra oil I carry and put my two quarts in. By this time, a grader driver pulled up and added two more quarts of oil from his machine.

I manually turned the motor over until there was a oil return back into the tank. Putting the spark plugs back in, I started the thing up. What do you know? No noise at all! The grader driver smiled at me, held up his thumbs in victory, put his big machine in gear and was off down the road.

Through the tundra and back over the Brooks range of mountains again, I came to the check post. The fellow there looked relieved that I made it back, and that he wasn't going to get into any trouble.

Down the other side, my vision was blurring, teeth were rattling, and my body was racked with pain as I carried on right to the entrance of Cold Foot, very grateful I made the 265 miles back down from Prudhoe Bay in one piece.

Now, one final rough stretch to go.

At the local store and restaurant near my camp, the owner was so amazed at what I was doing that he said, "You just help yourself to a free dinner tonight. I'll tell them that you'll be coming in." I thanked him very dearly because a hot meal like that was infinitely more welcome than my normal tin of beans.

At dinner I met a miner named Joe who was interested in my adventure.

"I'm not doing anything," he said, "can I come out and chat with you a while longer?"

"Sure. I'm just going out to my camp. I'm near a little table. I'll show you some pictures."

When Joe arrived at my camp, he told me, "We killed a grizzly bear here a week or so ago."

"I hope you killed him, and he's still not wandering around mad somewhere."

Joe enjoyed the photos, and told me some of the history of gold mining in the area.

"They still pan for gold in the rivers up in these areas. They live very extreme and hard lives." Joe himself could not straighten up from a lifetime of being bent over rocks. Before Joe left, he took from his truck a fisherman's yellow rain suit and gave it to me. I explained to him that I couldn't use the raincoat since I had one from France, but the rain paints were ideal (mine were full of holes). His had heavy duty suspenders, and I knew I'd be a lot warmer wearing them. After this very kind gift, Joe went his way and I closed my day.

A Two-Wheeler to Anchorage!

The next morning, everything frozen again, very cold, I got up and forced down a peanut butter sandwich which was like glue in my mouth. Warmed by a cup of hot coffee, it was time to go.

Early in my ride, I got up too much speed and almost went over a ledge that would have definitely been the end of me. The last words Don Hornsby spoke to me on that fateful morning, almost a year ago, were: "Don't get clever."

His words rang true in my mind again and again.

"Slow up, Dave. Don't get clever."

Soon, I'm crossing the Arctic Circle again. In fact, I crossed it and didn't even know it. The weather was so bad, with clouds and mist and the visibility so low that I didn't actually see the Arctic Circle sign as I passed by. My focus was on the road ahead of me, and any trucks that might come by.

Over the Yukon River which could not be seen because of the heavy mist. Years later, I would show a picture of the Yukon River to Russians and they would all go "Da! Jack London!" referring to his book, *Call of the Wild*, apparently required reading in Russian schools.

Over the second mountain range, as I came closer to Fox and the treasured asphalt, a construction crew was out working on filling in holes on the dirt road. I blasted past them at about 45 miles an hour; they looked up, saw the motorcycle, and waved enthusiastically. With great pride, I returned the wave. It was a very joyful moment because I realized I was about to hit the asphalt, completing my quest to get to the top and back.

As the bike hit asphalt, I stopped for a moment of prayer and thanks that I had made the round trip without damaging myself or the motorcycle in any severe way. Now the achievement starts to hit me. **I had just ridden almost 1,100 miles in four days on rough dirt road!**

At Fox, the lady behind the gasoline counter just smiled and said, "Well done" when she saw me covered in mud, smiling like a possum eating shit. Only now did the rain start to pour down. Man, that was close.

Now on to Fairbanks and *Frank's Bar* to return my borrowed battery. Riding in the rain, I wondered, "How would the trip to Prudhoe Bay have been if it had been in a heavy rain, or a snow storm? Surely I would have fallen off the motorcycle on some of those mountain passes."

It sent a chill up my back to think about how it could have been.

When I arrived at Jess' Garage, everybody shook my hand, saying "Well done! You made it!"

I felt like the conquering hero. I made it to the top of Alaska. All along, I was saying to that motorcycle, "C'mon ole dog. Just get me there. Just get me back. Your day will come. When we get to Anchorage, anything you need, you will get."

With God's grace, I'd hit Anchorage the next day.

Spencer Zogg called me at the garage to tell me that he had stopped at the Anchorage Harley Davidson, letting them know I was coming.

"We have received a letter from the Harley Davidson Motorcycle Company telling of Dave's coming," they told him. Spencer described the problem we were both having with our alternators... his had been torn off the wall of the crank case just like mine.

That night at Kirk's house we had a lovely, quiet evening, celebrating with steaks for having gone to the top.

The next morning we were up early. It was raining out and miserable, but that didn't change my good mood. After some coffee and breakfast we went down to the shop where Jess gave me a solid brass ZIPPO lighter with a marine corps emblem on it (he'd been in the Marines as well).

"You deserve this more than I do," he said. I was very touched by this kind gesture.

Today is beautiful, even though overcast. The mountains are topped with snow, reaching off in the distance into the sky over 10,000 feet, covered with green, forested lands and spotted by rivers along the road. The smell of pine and rain in the air made everything even nicer.

I'm pushing along faster than normal because I'm not worried much about the motorcycle anymore. It's going to get really fixed once and for all!

About 105 miles (165 km.) out of Fairbanks, I run out of gasoline. I can't believe it! I'm out of gas! What the heck is going on here? This thing should go as much as 120 miles on three gallons. This is unbelievable.

When I stopped, a car pulls up next to me with two fellows in it who ask, "Can we help?"

"Yes, I need some gasoline," I replied.

"OK. Wait here. There's a place down the road about five miles."

While I was waiting, another car pulled up with a man and a woman inside. The man introduced himself as "Cat Man," a member of the Vietnam Veterans' Motorcycle Club; he served in Vietnam about the same time I did, in the infantry. During our conversation, he handed me a cigarette, and I couldn't resist because of my high mood. It was wonderful to smoke that cigarette!

My friends soon returned with gasoline, and I was on my way, stopping to fuel up down the road... and buy a pack of cigarettes. I'm thinking to myself, "What the heck, I'm enjoying life here in the next week or so."

I pushed on through magnificently beautiful country, but after about 105 miles I switched to my reserve and the motorcycle ran out of fuel again. It is inconceivable that the thing is getting such bad gas mileage! Although I'm going a bit faster, it shouldn't use that much more gas.

I was dumbfounded.

Within a few minutes, Cat Man and his woman pull in behind me again, laughing hysterically. I'm incredibly embarrassed.

Repeat performance.

Within half an hour, they return with gas. I put the fuel in and was on my way, thanking them very much for helping me out... again!

I was within about 100 miles of Anchorage when I fueled up and got directions to Vance Avenue where Debbie and Carter Cole live. I'd planned to stay with them a few days.

The next morning we took the motorcycle down to the Anchorage Harley Davidson shop where I met Barry Matteson, the owner. He was surprised to see I wasn't in a wheel chair. Then, he was even more surprised to see that the Harley Davidson was a two-wheeler.

"I thought you'd be in a three-wheeler or a side car," he told me.

Frankly, this is something that will probably irritate me forever. People hear of me and immediately think I'm crippled and can't get around on a two-wheel machine, or assume I need a wheel chair just because I've got two peg legs.

Barry told me, "You can stay in the shop if you'd like, and you're welcome to work with Lee, my head mechanic, on preparing the motorcycle for the rest of the run. I'm going to contact Dan Klemencic at the factory just to confirm all the arrangements. But don't worry, I do have his letter."

Repair and Restoration; Man and Motorcycle

Carter Cole took me down to the Disabled Foundation where I met a fellow named Les Meissner, who wanted me to give a talk and slide show to other disabled people in the Anchorage area. He said, "I'll set everything up. I think we can get a room at the National Alaskan Bank. I'll let you know more in the upcoming week."

Carter then dropped me off at the Harley Davidson shop where Barry showed me my lovely little room on the second story over the shop. I was really impressed with the room, not quite sure how to act after sleeping on the road so long. "I'll have to be very careful of dirty hands in a place like this," I thought to myself.

The first thing Lee and I did was wash the motorcycle to remove all the oil from the broken oil line, and to clean out the dirt from the road to Prudhoe Bay. The motorcycle hadn't been washed since London!

Some media people came to the shop for an interview and photographs. We put the motorcycle up on the stand and I acted as if I was working on it for the photographer.

After they were gone, Lee and I went ahead in earnest. By the end of the day the entire motorcycle was in pieces. Lee found that the swing arm axle was no good, the bearings were no good, the shock absorbers were shot, the hydraulics and shoes on the rear brakes were ruined, and the front brake was in bad need of repair.

Plus, there were numerous other problems.

And that's before we started looking at the motor!

It looks like it's going to be a long, hard road to get this thing right.

While we worked on the motorcycle, a girl named Barbara kept popping in all the time.

"Why don't you have some dinner with me tonight," she said. "I'll cook it."

"Better than beans," I thought, and readily accepted.

Barbara looked after the apartments upstairs. Barry uses the rooms when friends or visitors come in from out of town. The rooms are called "Hog Heaven." They are a side business to his main business, the shop.

I spoke to Barry about giving a talk for the Harley owners group and the Vietnam Veterans Motorcycle Club in Anchorage, to which he enthusiastically replied, "A good idea!"

"Hopefully," I admitted selfishly, "I will find somebody who will want to sponsor my trip."

I had no thought of speaking for money, however. At this time in my life I was not at a level of public speaking good enough to be charging folks for my talk. It was just a pleasure to stand in front of others and pass on a message of encouragement that perhaps they could use at sometime in their lives when things weren't going so well. Besides, I enjoyed sharing a great adventure.

By the end of the day, Barry said, "Everything's set. You will be speaking on the 8th of September, a Sunday morning, at *The Sourdough Mining Company*, a big bar and eating area."

204

We discovered what the big noise in the lower end was - the cone the crankshaft goes through, that contains the Timkin bearings, had vibrated lose from the case (something that doesn't often happen, but when it does, it creates a noise). That why the alternators mounted on the crank case wall were being torn up.

Lee wanted to find an engineer to fix the crank cases. This was good news to me because you can't buy new crank cases from Harley Davidson, and the crank cases on the after market sell for over $500.00.

K.D. Clark, an old army friend of mine, was now a prison warden in Anchorage. We hadn't seen each other in almost 10 years. We spoke on the phone, and agreed to meet that evening, August 29.

About 18:00, K.D. walked in the shop, dressed in shorts, pot bellied, with bird legs and little spindly arms. K.D. was always like that, even when we were in the army. Despite his appearance, I never saw him fail to perform any of the many incredible physical feats put in front of us. He was one tough soldier. K.D. had been an infantryman in the Marine Corps for 10 years, and served two tours in Vietnam, fighting through the Tet offensive. He had a long military history in the Marines, the Rhodesian Army and the South African Army. I was proud to call him a friend and a comrade in arms.

K.D. looked shocked at me when I told him "I've quit drinking." No wonder. The last time he saw me I was drunk out of my mind. I reminded him how it had been 10 years to the very day - August 29 - that we'd run over the land mine. It felt symbolic that I'd be with one of my old friends who actually was on that operation in one of the vehicles when our's hit the land mine, blowing us up. K.D. just laughed about the whole thing saying "Well, if you can't take a joke you shouldn't have joined."

Typical black humor.

K.D. was a man never given to any emotion. He always used to say, "I have military acquaintances but no friends." Maybe that's just the legacy of a man who has seen too many of his friends killed in action over the years.

When he dropped me off that night, we swore we'd get together in the next few days. We never did.

That night in bed, wild emotions ran through my veins. Ten years ago, at 15:30 in the afternoon, my life changed in a split second. Though I didn't know it at the time, this trip, and the purpose of my new destiny had begun with the fiery flash of that land mine.

During the next few days, we continued to work on the bike, picking up the crankcases that had been sent away to an engineer. Before I paid him, I asked, "Are you sure this is going to hold?"

"Yeah, no problem," he answered.

"Are you absolutely sure?" I questioned again. Personally, I didn't like the looks of the job.

"It should be no problem," he told me. "I build racing engines. They are under tremendous pressures - so I know what I'm doing."

Next, we started to reassemble the motor.

With the depressing smell of ribs and steaks frying across the street at the local restaurant, I continued to save money by eating my chili con carne and beans for dinner, and peanut butter sandwiches for breakfast and lunch.

September 1: I stopped smoking again, wondering all the while how long it's going to last.

Shows and No Shows

September 5th: That evening Carter Cole came to pick me up and take me to the National Bank of Alaska where I set up my equipment. Les Meissner was there, Carter and Debbie, plus Barbara from the shop (she volunteered to take me back). Believe it or not, the talk and slide show was given for three able bodied people and one disabled person... yet the disabled people in the community all knew about it.

The apathy was unbelievable.

Though I personally was not hurt, it was disappointing that they didn't want to hear about a real adventure. Les was equally astonished, himself an avid wheel-chair racer.

"I hope the talk I give for the Harley Owners Group and the Vietnam Veterans is better attended than this," I thought.

The next day while I was working, Moe, one of the employees at the shop, handed me a white envelope containing $100.

"Who gave this to you?" I asked.

"I don't know," he replied. "We just found it sitting on the counter with your name on it." In my heart, I believe K.D. had somehow slipped into the shop, left the $100, and walked out. Years later, I learned that he lost his job in Anchorage, and then went on a wild spree all over the world. Old army comrades spotted him here and there. Eventually, he dropped out of sight altogether for over one year.

September 7: When the motorcycle was all back together, Lee started it up. We couldn't hear any noise in the lower end - wonderful! The machine sounded nice and tight. I was very pleased by the whole experience which took 11 days from the time we started working on it to the time it was ready to go for its first ride.

I took off and went through Anchorage, and after less than 5 miles, the son of a bitch quit on me. I couldn't believe it. I got off and thought, "What have I done? Seized a piston? What is going on?"

Lee told me he had set the engine up exceptionally tight, but this was ridiculous.

Upon examination, I noticed that the fuel filter was empty; I speculated that perhaps the fuel wasn't flowing enough to go through the fuel filter. Funny enough, every time I put a new fuel filter on, there has been trouble. I remembered the last time was in Zambia, and I ended up having to take it off.

I removed the fuel filter, and carried on with no more problems.

September 8: This Sunday morning I got up, put on Barry's suit, and rode to my slide show with Barbara following me on her Knuckle Head (an old Harley built between 1936 and 1947). She had built the motorcycle up herself, and was a very interesting, tough girl. She had worked with her first husband as a fisherman. When I discovered she'd built that old Knuckle Head by herself, my respect rose higher. Also, she was quite an accomplished pianist.

We rode in a rain storm to the *Sourdough Mining Company Bar and Grill* where I set up the slide projector, the screen, and my map up on the wall with my route. There was a luncheon before my show, and about 100 people arrived! It was standing room only!

After Barry Matteson introduced me, I shared my talk - why I was doing the ride, and my experiences through Africa and Europe (didn't say much about the United States). At the end of the show, I was pleasantly surprised at the warm reception.

Everybody was clapping and carrying on!

Barry asked people to settle down, then awarded me a check for $500 from the Harley Owners Group of Anchorage. I was shocked. It was beyond my belief. I had never been paid anything to speak publicly!

After the meeting, I put on my rain gear and rode about 60 miles in the heavy rain around Anchorage, using my solitude to enjoy the moments I had just experienced. In one suburb, quite close to downtown, I noticed a moose in someone's front yard eating from one of the trees. Nobody was bothering him either.

Back at the shop, I went upstairs, undressed and tried to relax. Before giving a talk, I'm always anxious. Now, I am letting down, but there's still some butterflies in my stomach. It is just so important to me that I give the people who come to listen something good to take away with them.

In the next few days, it was important to put break-in mileage on the engine, which I did. Once I rode out along Cook's Bay to Portage Glacier. While riding, I'd always stop to look at this incredible glacier. Most of the riding was done in the rain.

The cold helped the engine break in. One morning when I started the motorcycle up, I spotted oil coming out of the base of the front gasket.

"What now?" I thought.

Lee looked at it and said, "Well, the front cylinder has to come off. We're going to have to plug up that oil vein in the crank case."

"Why can't things just be right the first time?" I thought to myself with some anger about the whole process, though it was not Lee's fault.

Within an hour, the front cylinder came off, and the hole was plugged up with a special compound that had to sit overnight.

The next day we put the front cylinder back on.

I met a man named Don Hillingas, and we chatted about my trip.

"How much will it take for you to get down to the Los Angeles area?" he asked.

Sensing where his question was headed, I politely informed him "I'm not really looking for donations. I'm hoping instead to locate a sponsor. I'd like to be able to do something for the money I receive."

Don then invited me to come to his pick up truck where he wrote me out a check for $500. I tried to talk him out of it.

"Please, take this," he said. "I will look for sponsors for you. I have contacts in Asia, and perhaps I can do something that will help you out with them."

I received a phone call from Spencer Zogg who arrived home in late August after hitting snow up in the summit of British Columbia. "The longer it takes me to get going," I think, "the more snow and ice I'm going to encounter on the road and moving south back towards the lower 48."

September 10: I received a request to speak at the Jesse Lee School for abused young people in their teens. Joyce O'Connor gave me directions to the school.

The next day I borrowed Barry's Rambler and drove to the school where I spoke for about forty-five minutes. Joyce later dedicated a corner of her classroom, calling it "The Dave Barr Odyssey." She put up a map and some photographs so the kids oould personally follow my trip as it progressed. Joyce used the trip for the precise purpose I intended, and I was very proud to be a part of a plan to motivate others to do better in life.

September 12: Time to leave. Barry gave me a big hug and said "Dave, you're riding for all of us." I was very touched by that. He expressed the feelings in my heart I was unable to say.

Exactly one year ago I was saying good-bye to Don Homsby and family in South Africa.

Chapter Nineteen

On Wings of Eagles

I rode out into traffic with deep feelings, but high emotions didn't get me very far. Ran out of gas in Palmer.

So much for high emotions interfering with what you're doing. I walked over to a local rail yard and spotted some men loading a train with ore.

"Does anyone here have a gallon of gas I can buy?" I asked.

"Sure," one of them replies, "no problem."

I received the gas, walked to the bike, then rode on and filled up in Palmer.

Out of Anchorage, a woman in a taxi leaned out her window to say "Hello, I've read about you in the newspaper."

It felt funny to be recognized.

I traveled towards Tok, 300 miles away, climbing mountains, and watching the sun gleam out over a glacier. It was magnificent to see the brilliant white of the great glacier off in the distance from a spot high on a mountain across the valley.

Another time, in the late afternoon, while riding through a valley, the sun came out and a rainbow went from one side of the valley across to the other - seemingly stretching several miles. It was the most magnificent rainbow I have ever seen, reminding me of God's promise to man that He'd never destroy the earth again with water.

I rode into Tok, right near the Canadian border, and purchased fuel, provisions and found a campground. I'd ridden at least 350 miles, and for the first time I can remember in many moons, my motorcycle didn't need any attention!

That night it was bitterly cold, below freezing.

In the morning, there was a heavy sheet of ice on everything, yet the motorcycle started right up, although I noticed it was leaking gasoline out of the carburetor. Once on the road, it stopped.

When I stopped for gas once inside Canada, I noticed that on the front of the motor the base gasket started to seep oil again. I was so angry I could shout! Nevertheless, I continued on, managing to get to White Horse where I found a state campground. They didn't have any prices posted, so I thought, "It must be like Alberta - a state camping area where you don't pay."

I found a place next to a creek, and it wasn't long before a Ranger comes along and asks for $8.00.

"You don't even have prices posted," I protested, very upset. "You've got a lot of gall not telling us how much you charge so we can decide whether we want to stay here or not."

The ranger just shrugged her shoulders, and reluctantly I paid.

A little squirrel was running around, trying to get into my bread on the campsite table I shooed him away. This must have been a STATE campground squirrel because later he was on the bread again, only this time he shit on my dinner. "You little bastard!" I shouted, chasing him off. He probably ran to spend the rest of the evening with the Rangers.

The next morning I made good time towards the British Colombia border, crossing into British Columbia where I noticed some birds along the road eating a kill.

One of the birds was different.

The bulk of the birds flew off in their various directions, but one with a huge wing span of over six feet flew along side the road. I gently drew along side of him, and looked into his eyes, realizing I was looking into the eyes of a bald eagle, no more than a few meters away from me!

I slowed down to about 25-30 miles an hour, and we looked into one another's eyes. I thought to myself, "How many motorcycles riding along have ever had the experience of riding next to a bald eagle, the mascot of freedom in the western world?"

As we looked into one another's eyes, that feeling of freedom ran through my veins.

After a few hundred meters, the eagle seemed bored and contemptuous of this small, inconsequential human riding along on his dirty old machine. He soared up into the sky, up over the forest, never for me to see him again.

The Bearded Lady's Sister, Red Ron, and Generous Strangers

As I pulled into a small town for gasoline, I encountered a nasty lady who had a striking resemblance to the lady who sold me bread in Laird Creek. I needed to cash a traveler's check, which she did, charging me 5% for the service! That really upset me, and I told her, "I think your attitude is really very low class."

She looked at me as if to say, "Who are you to tell me anything?"

I was glad to get on my motorcycle and ride out of Asshole Junction, leaving the bearded lady's sister behind. Later, I discovered that they were indeed related!

I found a campground where the owner let me stay for nothing, asking only that I "come in and put your signature on one of the walls." When I walked inside his restaurant, I was amazed to see signatures of people from all over the planet. I signed my spot, "Dave Barr, Around The World For The Disabled."

The next day, as I'm ready to leave, I notice a flat front tire.

The day is off to a roaring good start!

With help, I pushed the motorcycle over to a compressor and put air in the tire, hoping for a slow leak. "If I can make it to Fort St. John," I reason, I'll be OK. I can fix the tire at the motorcycle shop."

20 miles down the road the tire goes flat again.

I was really angry. I managed to pull off the road near a puddle of water (I'm going to need water to find the leak). Jacking up the motorcycle, I took the wheel off and broke the tire down.

Suddenly, my back is hit by a huge gust of wind and the "swooosh" of a passing truck. The powerful force of that lumbering truck knocked my motorcycle off the jack.

No sooner did this happen when lo and behold, Big John and Red Ron appear on the scene with their girlfriend. These two big Yukon boys jump out, pick up the motorcycle and set it on a log - even before introductions take place!

"We've been down to Laird Creek for a wedding, now we're going back home to White Horse." Both men rode Harleys.

Using the puddle of water to find the hole, I fixed the tire, then used my little compressor to inflate it. I shook hands with Big John and Red Ron, who stuck $20 in my hand, saying, "Good on you, guy. You just keep going. Maybe this will help you go just that little bit farther." Their gesture of kindness was very touching.

Later that day I decided to change oil at a small town service station run by a young girl named Kim; she told me she rode a Harley Davidson Sportster. As I examined the oil, it was a relief not to find any metal in the oil or the filter.

The next morning, I was reminded how even the baser things we take for granted sometimes become major challenges on the road.

When I got up, before I left camp I needed to take a crap. Since I wasn't staying at a campground, there were no facilities, so I wandered into the forest where I slipped and fell in mud. I completed my business of answering the call of nature, then slip-slided on all fours out of this quagmire I'd gotten myself into - cloaked in mud - back to the motorcycle.

The day had barely started and already I was greasy, muddy and ornery!

Things got better later that day when I was waved over by an elderly man and his wife in a van. The man says, "Are you Dave Barr?"

"Yes, I am."

"Well, we read about you in Anchorage and saw you on the television. We think what you're doing is just incredible, and we'd like to be just a little part of the trip."

He then stuck $20 in my jacket pocket. I was taken aback by this very kind gesture, thanking him as I rode on down the road.

That night, after covering almost 450 miles, I pulled in behind what appeared to be an old, unused rodeo stadium. I went down a hill on a good dirt path to a place right on beautiful Lake Lac La Hache, my camp overlooking the water. It was the kind of scene you dream about.

The following morning, for the first time in six days, I didn't put on my rain gear! The morning was cool, but not freezing, and the going was good until I hit miles of road construction where I had to cut between lanes. This signaled I was getting closer to a major metropolis - in this case, Vancouver. I was amazed - I hadn't seen traffic this bad for a long time - perhaps since Chicago.

I was shocked at the amount of traffic going across from Canada into the United States. It was backed up. My machine couldn't just idle with the traffic, so I went to the head of the line. When I motioned to a lady to please let me in, she said "No."

I cut in front of her anyway.

When I went up front, the Customs officer asked me, "Why did you cut in front?"

"Ma'am, it's an air cooled motor," I answered. "I can't let the thing overheat. It's just been overhauled." She was very understanding, and said she would tell the lady behind me.

"Do you have anything to declare?"

"No."

"Thank you," and I was on my way. I certainly appreciated her attitude over the shithead Spencer and I had encountered going into Alaska.

Back in the good old United States, I celebrated by having a cigarette!

What a great feeling! People never talk about that today. Smokers are treated like people infested with the plague. I don't think it's right, even though I'm a non-smoker for over four years. No matter what anyone says, that first cigarette just tastes fantastic... especially with a cup of coffee!

Reunions, Repairs, and Mysterious Reactions

I made my way on down to Tacoma to Fort Lewis where the M.P. at the entrance gate let me call my friend, Mike Lanskov. I managed to get a hold of him and told him "Mike, I'm at the front gate." When he tried to get permission for me to ride the motorcycle on base, the M.P. asked for my proof of insurance.

I handed him the bogus insurance papers I had bought in Nigeria the year before. The official looking document was worth nothing, but the M.P. waived me on while Mike struggled not to laugh.

I knew Mike from both Rhodesia and South Africa, but now he was a staff sergeant, looking very fit in his uniform. At Mike's room I meet Richard Molson! What a reunion! I had not seen either man in over ten years! The last time I saw Richard was at one military hospital in Pretoria, South Africa. Richard had lost an eye to shrapnel on operations in Angola. Before he went home in December of 1981, Richard had taken an old Tower musket from Angola back to my Mom and Dad and gave it to them personally.

The next day, Mike took me out on his 15 foot open boat with a 25 horse power Mercury to Puget Sound where we placed a couple of crab pots in various places. We felt very small in this little boat as HUGE cabin cruisers and motorized yachts floated by. We laughed to ourselves at what we had and what they had.

At the end of the day, we had a pot full of crabs, and that evening we ate crab and shark meat caught that day!

Mike and I talked of many experiences from our past; Mike is the epitome of a professional soldier.

I entered California on September 26.

It was quite beautiful in northern California and over a mountain range I had a spectacular view down into a valley of the ranches dotted with clumps of trees. When I got on Interstate 5, the scenery stopped and the heat began. I'm down to wearing one thin jacket to keep the sun from burning my arms.

About 100 miles out of San Francisco, I spot a biker on a Harley Davidson on the side of the road. I pull over and ask, "Do you need any assistance?"

"Yes, I'm out of gas," he replied.

"Well, that's no problem." I took the hose off of my gas tank to the carburetor and drained a couple of liters of gasoline out to get him going. We rode together to a service station. After being helped so much, it felt good to be able to help another.

I had just turned off in the direction of San Francisco from Hwy. 5 onto Hwy. 580 when back end started getting wishy washy underneath me, fishtailing.

I had a flat tire at 60 mph!

Somehow, I managed to wrestle the motorcycle onto the shoulder of the road without falling. After about five minutes, a California Highway Patrolman drove up behind me and asks, "Is there anything I can help you with?"

"Yes," I answered, "could you please call the phone number of a friend I know who has a pick up truck? His name is Richard Molson."

"Sure," he replied, and I gave him the phone number.

The CHP officer came back to tell me he had contacted Richard, and the man was on his way. 45 minutes later, Rich arrives for our second reunion! Now, we've got to figure out how to get this big motorcycle on his little Toyota pick up.

As luck would have it, a pick up truck pulls up and a big strapping fellow named George gets out, saying, "It looks like you guys need a ramp."

We did.

"No problem," he says, and out of the back of his truck he produces a nice long motorcycle ramp. Even with the ramp, it took all three of us (with George doing most of the work) to get the bike on. Once the task was completed, George says, "Just keep the ramp and bring it to this address tomorrow."

We thanked him.

At Rich's house, I put a new tube in the tire, then put the tire back on the rim. We took the wheel down to a service station to get the bead to set on the tire. When that was done, we put the tire back on. As we rolled the motorcycle off the ramp, I'll be a son of a bitch if the front tire was now flat!

It was late. We decided to leave this new problem until tomorrow.

Rich and I talked for awhile, and he told me he was in college as an English literature major. What a transformation! From a foul-mouthed soldier in Africa to a man of great vocabulary in America!

About 22:30 we went to bed. It was difficult sleeping knowing that I would arrive home tomorrow and once again see my dear old Mom.

The next morning, I was up quite early. I tried to wake Rich up, and he displayed some of that new vocabulary by telling me to "fuck off." After these early-morning pleasantries were exchanged, I persisted until he finally got up.

After going to the automotive shop, we bought a tin of tire weld - that was to be a big mistake! Years ago, you didn't look at a label to find out what type of tire weld you were buying. Tire weld was tire weld. It seals small punctures.

We took this concoction back and I inflated my tire; it held perfect. We waited 40 minutes to make sure it would be all right; it was.

Out again on Interstate 5, I decided to stop and get some gas. Pulling into the gas station, I noticed a flat front tire again.

It just never seems to end!

I pushed the motorcycle over to some shade since it was extremely hot, around 100 degrees, and started to fix the tire, noticing a patch had come off the tube.

"That's strange," I thought, cleaning up the spot and putting on a new patch.

After about another 30 miles, another flat.

By now, I'm really acid.

I jack up the motorcycle, take the front wheel off again, break it down, and notice that TWO patches have come off. What the heck is going on here? Was it a reaction to the tire weld?

I decided to drain as much of the tire weld out of the tube as possible, and put on two new patches, checking the others to make sure they're holding. A couple of shots with my little electric compressor, and off I go again, the heat and sun bearing down on me.

After 40-50 miles, still another flat tire. By this time, I'm jumping up and down, screaming and shouting as though tripping out on drugs, breaking into a catatonic rage.

I dug into my tool kit, took out the jack, and lifted the motorcycle up as big diesel trucks roared past, causing the motorcycle to waver back and forth on its stand. I'm expecting it to fall at any moment. In the midst of this marvelous experience, I drink my last bit of water.

Tire fixed, I ride another 50 miles or so and start to relax, thinking, "Maybe I've got it this time."

The son of a bitch went flat again.

Now I'm numb, just managing to wrestle the thing off the road without being run over by a truck. Mind you, this fully loaded machine still weighs in the neighborhood of 800 pounds.

Jack out, tire off, break it down, tube out, wipe excess tire weld.

All four patches are off this time!

Replace all four patches, air it up, put it back on the motorcycle, get going.

Later that afternoon, I stopped at a Standard Station, asking, "Do you have any patches? I'm running low," and it was still about 150 miles to mom's house.

"Well, we don't have any more patches. Check across the street," they told me.

I walked across the street.

No, they didn't have any.

I walked to the next one.

No, they didn't have any.

I spotted a tire shop.

No, they didn't have any patches that would help me.

A young Mexican lad filling up his car overhears my need, and says, ""Hey, MON, you need some patches? I can get some for you."

I said "Thank you," and followed him to a makeshift garage where there were half a dozen Mexicans all working on various cars on a dirt floor covered with oil. He went into a little shack where they kept their tools, and came out with tire patches and some glue. I paid him, saying "Gracias, muchos gracias, amigo."

By this time it was starting to get dark, and the sunset was wonderful, a small reward for a very rough day of 4 flat tires on the front wheel, and 6 since yesterday afternoon. After riding another 70 miles, I finally came to the turn off that one would take me to Lake Isabella and then to Bodfish where my Mother lives.

I decided against riding up this very dangerous, steep, winding road along the Kern River with an unpredictable tire. So, I pulled into a restaurant that had a big parking lot, called Mom, and told her I would arrive home tomorrow morning.

After a hamburger, I pushed the motorcycle out to the back of the parking lot near a couple of trees. There, I put out my tarp and sleeping bag, lit up a cigarette, and stared at the stars with the noise of Interstate 5 in the distance.

What a day!

Quite early the next morning, I quickly rode the 75 miles to Mom's place up the Kern Canyon. As I traversed that final stretch of road up the hill on the side of the mountain where she lives, in the small town of Bodfish, I came around the corner to her street.

Immediately I see her.

She was outside, opening the gate, with my cousin Mindy, her little daughter Emily, and her husband all standing there! What a touching scene - it will imprint itself in my mind forever.

I shut the motorcycle off. By this time, Mom was at my side. We gave each other a big hug, and tears of joy flowed from our eyes.

Indeed, I had come home on my motorcycle all the way from Africa.

September 29, 1991: home.

What a warm word.

As I went back to fetch some of my bags off the motorcycle after that very touching reunion, the son of a bitch front wheel was flat again.

"Fuck it for the time being," I declared. "I ain't gonna work on it."

That night, after everybody had gone to bed, I went outside and sat on the bench, looking at the mountain. The night sky was so clear and bright, with so many stars, in my Mother's little hometown of Bodfish. I thought about the miles, the trials and triumphs, and the people I had met to this point in my journey.

The reflections staggered me.

About one-third of my journey - approximately 30,000 miles - was now complete!

214

Chapter Twenty

My Empty, Sinking Sponsor Ship

I installed a NEW tube, vowing to NEVER again use tire weld! A man at a local motorcycle shop explained, "There's tire weld for tubeless tires, and tire weld for inner tubes. If you put the one in an inner tube that's intended for a tubeless tire, it will eat the patches off."

No shit. I had a 50-50 chance to get it right, and the law of averages worked against me.

Bakersfield television wanted to interview me, and I suggested we meet "in front of the Harley Davidson dealer in town." I called the owner, and he agreed. Why not? It's free publicity!

I rode down the next day and met the owner of the Harley shop; he seemed extremely disinterested in my trip, never even asking one question!

"The media people called," he told me, "and they'll be an hour and a half late."

I wandered around like a lost fart for the next hour and a half.

When the media did arrive, I met with Kurt Rivera and he gave me a 2½ minute piece on prime time that night. At the end of the interview, I asked the Harley store owner, "Would you like me to give a talk and slide show to the local Harley Owners Group?"

He looked at me with total disinterest.

Finally, he said, "We'll, I have to speak to the president of HOG and I'll let you know." When I called him a week later, he told me, "Naw, we're not really interested. We'd rather have our normal BBQ."

That attitude seemed to follow me throughout California. On the 2½ minute news story which aired three times over the next three days in prime time, I gave a telephone number that people could call to schedule talks and slide shows - at no charge - for disabled groups.

I didn't get one phone call.

One of my biggest frustrations was trying to find the money to carry on the rest of the trip. I faithfully approached various organizations - people I had been referred to - with the consistent result - no interest.

Mom told all of her friends about my upcoming talk and slide show at the Elk's Lodge, and they all said, "You bet. We'll be there." In fact, when the day came, only six people showed up (but they were a very good audience).

It was a funny show, since I was using a very ancient projector, my mother put in each slide manually. As she inserted the slide, I'd be talking. If she thought it was time to change the slide, she just changed it, whether I told her to or not.

"You've talked about that long enough," she'd tell me.

I was thankful Mom wasn't operating the slide projector when I was giving a major talk to a big crowd of people.

While home, I needed to try and earn some money. One of my friends from Pocatello, Jeff Hampstein, suggested I try to find ostrich feathers to serve as dusters for computers. I called my friend, Peter Manderson, in South Africa, and asked him to check into ostrich feathers - ostrich eggs - anything pertaining to an ostrich that we could use to make some money.

This was typical of the crazy schemes I tried.

In the end, it all came to naught because the South African government imposed a ban on ostriches.

I keep trying to locate a sponsor, or a way to make money to finance my trip around the world. In my mind, there are only two things which could stop me from making the rest of this trip: 1. a major accident that further disables or kills me, and 2. I run out of money.

Other than those two things, there's no compromise.

All or nothing.

The trip has become my life from the first time I rode the motorcycle with my disability.

As I push forward towards Mexico, Central and South America, I am determined to accomplish this dream.

Although I've sometimes been down, I've never considered stopping.

I've already gone across Africa, to the top of Europe, and to the top of North America. Perhaps I could stop now and save face, but I started this thing to finish it. It's over when it's over.

Sometimes at night I'd sit out in my backyard, looking up at the stars, meditating. I remembered one night sitting out there on that very sad trip home for my father's funeral. I was insecure and worried, yet determined to pursue my dream. Now, my future consisted of Mexico, Central and South America. It was as though I had accomplished nothing. I shuddered to look forward, and was staggered when I looked back.

Cousin Orvil and Captain Hook

One of my more memorable experiences while at home with my mother was a plane ride with my great cousin, Orvil, one of the older boys in the aviation field; he started flying biplanes in 1933! In World War II, he flew DC3's during the D-day operation.

Since he was 75 years old, I asked him, "How do you keep requalifying for your licenses?"

"Oh" he said, "I don't have a license."

"What do you mean you don't have a license?" I asked, not believing my ears.

"Hell, I haven't requalified for a license in years. I stopped logging at 12,000 hours."

"How long ago was that?"

"Oh, about 20 years ago."

Orvil owned a little tail dragger, single engine airplane built in 1953. He took me out to the airfield and we took off in this thing.

While in the air, I learned that Orvil had emphysema so bad that he could hardly breathe during the best of times, let alone in the high altitudes. As we soared heavenward, I worried about him passing out at the controls and bringing us abruptly earthward. I know I couldn't land the damn thing.

Cousin Orvil had also been quite an accomplished motorcyclist in his day, and was a genuine thrill-seeker. We talked while we were flying, and he told me, "I'll never get used to the thrill of a light aircraft lifting off the runway. It always excites me and gets my adrenaline going."

"I can relate," I thought, remembering the way I feel every morning when I first get on the motorcycle and head out on the open road.

Another special adventure started with a call from an old skydiving buddy, Al Krueger, aka "Captain Hook." Al had an arm off at the elbow, yet had been a three time world champion skydiver. He was organizing a "pieces of eight" skydive (eight people or more with amputations) and he was going to call the team, "Twenty percent off."

216

"Yes, I am interested," I told Al, and agreed to be available in November over the weekend of the 9th and 10th. To prepare for the jumps, I called my friend in South Africa, Peter Mannerson, and asked him to send my gear over.

I'm given use of a pickup truck, and my cousin Al Garris of Big Al's Paint and Body helps me fix the mechanical problems and clean up the paint job. Al was to be instrumental at the end of the trip in helping me get another vehicle, and in booking me some talks and slide shows which made money for me. He also volunteered to try and find me sponsors. I appreciated his attitude towards what I was trying to accomplish.

There's trouble in South Africa. Israel peace talks with the PLO are in a stalemate. There's mass murders in a Texas restaurant.

The world turns.

I spoke with Keith Ball, the editor of *Easy Rider* magazine, and showed him a map of my trip and some photos. I briefly explained the journey, the ground that had been covered, and asked, "Would you be interested in doing an article?"

"Yes," he answered, and assigned me a writer named Clay Sharage, a man I cottoned to immediately. We went to Clay's office and set a time for me to come and do a major interview.

"Will there be any sort of payment to me?" I asked.

"No, I am afraid not," he answered.

Clay also wanted to put me in touch with Ace and Laurie Martin, two other world travelers. I had read a couple of articles in *Easy Rider* that Ace had done, and I agreed they would be good people to meet. Clay passed their phone number on to me.

The Rotarians Society in Kernville asked if I would give a brief talk with a few slides after their monthly dinner. I agreed, and spoke to a mixed audience - one half fell asleep, and the other half sat enthralled.

I spoke with Bob Nevolla, referred to me by the Disabled Biker's Association in England. Bob explained "The disabled motorcycle association in the United States has simply been a dud, yet the English have taken the idea and made it flourish."

"What do you think is different about us in America?" I asked.

"Well, the image right now is of the corporate biker - a big play thing - a status symbol."

How true Bob's observation is I honestly don't know. It seems to me there's many more ordinary people riding motorcycles today than when I first started riding.

I met a rider from the Van Nuys Harley owner's group who invited me to something called "The Love Run."

November 1: The day my father passed away. That night I sat under the stars thinking about a phone call I had just received from Pinky in South Africa telling me that Pat, an old motorcycle riding friend and drinking buddy, had been killed in a motorcycle accident. Pat was the father of 5.

One year ago I had been sitting under a tree in Tsumeb in Southwest Africa, Namibia, thinking about my father.

To attend the Love Run, we rode down to Glendale Boulevard to get into the lineup. These guys took off at such a high rate of speed that I couldn't keep up with them on my old shovelhead without damaging the engine. I just poked along at 60 miles per hour.

The event seemed more like a fashion show. 95% of all the motorcycles were newer, bright shiny machines loaded with accessories. The registration fee was $40, and I didn't have that much love in my pocket. They didn't seem very interested in my offer of a $10.00 donation.

We went back to the motorcycles and waited because we couldn't move until the whole crowd started moving. The fashion show ended at 10:00, and now we could roll. I don't think I've ever heard a den of Harley Davidson engines rumbling and thundering that way. Even louder than Sturgis!

As we entered the freeway, I noticed many of the exits were blocked, and people on overpasses were waiving at this incredible procession of motorcycles cruising along. When we got to the Hwy. 14 cutoff, I split away from the multitude.

So much for the Love Run.

The next day I rode to the offices of *Easy Rider* in Aguaro Hills where I met with Clay and we did a major interview for what was to be a short article. They took a few of my pictures from my Africa adventure, and Clay took me to lunch.

Sky-Dive Mania

The following weekend I went out to Perris, California, to practice skydiving. I signed a ten-page release form, initialing every page. After that, they make me speak into a video camera, saying "I will not sue you if anything goes wrong and I am maimed or disabled or killed."

When I first started skydiving in June, 1973, you signed a piece of paper with information that basically said that if you were killed or hurt, they would notify your family. You paid your money, you took your chances.

The next day, Al Frezbee, a friend of 18 years, and Tony Dell, another friend, made jumps with me from about 13,000 feet. It was absolutely wonderful to get out and air the bones. The buildup is so exciting.

The final directions are given to the pilot - left, right, you feel the plane moving. You look out the door, down so far.

Finally, Al gives the signal to cut back on the engines and we line up on the door. "Ready, set, go!"

Once you cross the threshold of the plane, you enter into a void of speed, sound, light and scenery. Al and Tony form their two man, and I fly down to be the third person.

This is the first jump I've made since South Africa. We raced through the sky at terminal velocity, about 125 miles per hour (200 km.), looking at one another. Al's beard goes upward around his face; Tony Dell sticks his tongue out; we all pull in together and gave each other a big kiss - a moment in the sky shared with friends!

What a beautiful experience.

At 3,000 feet we turn 180 degrees and track away from each other, looking around to make sure we are clear...then pull the pilot chutes out, and deploy the main chutes.

Suddenly, we stop going 125 miles (200 km.) an hour, and slow to about 6 miles an hour in three seconds.

Out of the speed, sound and adrenaline, you experience a world serenely flying under your main canopy, turning to the left and to the right, maneuvering around, feeling the beauty of the world below as you sail so easily above it.

Finally, you land back down on the ground.

For me, landing is always a bit of a chock because I have no give in my right leg. The pegs I am wearing are legs made years ago just for sky diving. They make me about six inches shorter that I normally am. The right leg is just a socket with a steel peg and three braces on it. It weighs about 13 pounds, and is held on with belts. The left leg is a socket with a caliper above holding it on, with a rubber foot and no shoe. I'm shorter than normal because it is easier on my back when I land.

On the ground, everything comes to a dead stop. Then, you gather up the parachute and everybody meets, smiling at one another, replaying the things that happened on the jump.

Any jump you walk away from is a good jump.

Between the 8th and the 9th, ten amputee jumpers, myself included, made seven skydives. My biggest problem was entering the formation. We would crowd up in the doorway just after the last few adjustments to the course were made, and the pilot was given the command to throttle back, then "ready, set, go" and out the door we would plunge into the sky. There was a sequence that we all had to enter for our formation, and everybody had their own particular slot. I constantly had trouble because my legs threw me out of balance, tending to hit the formation too hard, thus disrupting it.

Remember, the formation was all amputees - everybody missing an arm or a leg (in my case, two legs). We are fragile flying machines with the aerodynamics of a brick. Living junkyards falling through the sky. When our formation goes out of control, there's people with prosthetics banging and crashing into each other. The dangers are much higher than a normal skydive since we are made of metal and hard plastic, hurtling through space at speeds over 100 miles per hour!

In the end, after seven skydives, we didn't make the grade and get the eight man formation we wanted.

Time To Begin Again!

The restarting of the journey draws ever closer!

The old butterflies of anticipation start anew in my stomach.

On November 24 and 25, I was to meet and ride with Ace and Laurie Martin. I rode north about 300 miles (500 km.) to an off ramp that Ace and Laurie told me about.

There, we greeted each other and started a friendship that has lasted to this very day. About 10 minutes later, Richard Molson appeared; he rode with his head turned a little to one side to make the best use of his one and only good eye.

Richard has arrived.

For the next two days we talk of many things. Ace has traveled through 50 countries, and has ridden to LaPaz in Bolivia, the highest city in the world, at around 18,000 feet. He was in first gear for two days going up a mud road, nearly being forced over the edge constantly by buses and trucks coming down.

Ace also has been across the northern Sahara, and to the North Cape. He has met the Bunker's Motorcycle Club, and stayed with the Aurora Choppers as well. There were many people we knew in common.

Ace's Harley Davidson looks like a huge two-wheeled bus with a massive carrier on the back and a very intricate gear exchange system. It weighs 1400 pounds unloaded, so when you put the two of them on it, and all their gear, they are probably up around 1700 or 1800 pounds!

I don't know how the machine handles it all.

After two days of Ace and I swapping sea stories, poor Richard's head was about ready to burst. But before we split up, Ace, Laurie and I formed a new motorcycle club called the Long Rangers. He was Long Ranger One, I was Long Ranger Two, and Laurie, the secretary.

By the time we arrived back home, I had ridden over 520 miles.

David Mallams of the Cheshire Foundation London called, saying I would have to do my own Visas for the Peoples Republic of China and for Russia. This was not good news because if one doesn't have an organization helping you, it is sometimes impossible to get into a socialist country.

The work is never done on the motorcycle. Of course I had to replace the battery. Then I had trouble with the rear master cylinder hanging up; I needed a new master cylinder. Within a month, the new master cylinder started leaking, and I had to replace that master cylinder with another master cylinder.

Christmas was to be very warm, spent with friends. Orvil came over, and Jim Buckley, an old skydiving friend, who lives in Ridgecrest and works for the Navy doing survival systems for the space shuttle. Rich Molson rode down from San Francisco. Mom cooked a wonderful turkey dinner for us all.

New Years Eve was a quiet time for Mother and I at home. After I watched television for a while, I went outside and sat in the night looking up at the stars and watching the mountains behind my mom's place, listening to the quiet, thinking about the future, the new year and all the adventures that would soon start to unfold. The feeling in my heart was that it was going to be a very full year indeed.

At midnight, I prayed for the strength and guidance to get through the new year.

The next few days were spent in preparation.

On January 7th, I had my last night sitting outside in the cold, looking at the stars, enjoying the peace and quiet, contemplating the future, saying my prayers, and looking up at the mountains. I thought to myself "Will I ever get the chance to sit and do this again?"

The next day I took the short 120 mile (198 km.) ride down to Mindy's. For the next few days I will operate out of Mindy's, doing various things, running around seeing people and saying good-bye.

On January 12th I was to attend the wedding of Patty Foxcroft, a friend of mine from South Africa. He was marrying an English girl in Santa Monica, a nurse. He asked me to attend the wedding, and then said, "Will you be my best man?" I agreed, and he gave me the ring.

Back in South Africa, Don Hornsby asked me to buy them a wedding present they would never forget. So, I labeled each one of the items before I put them into the box with a member of the Hornsby family's name: Don's mother, Freda; wife, Felicity; their two boys, Garath and Gerrad. After wrapping these gifts up, I took them to the wedding.

After the wedding, we sat in a lovely reception at a very posh hotel on the beach. All of the nursing friends were there from her hospital, and her mother, a very conservative lady, had flown all the way out from England. Susan herself was English, and appeared to be a very conservative girl.

I tried to get away before they opened the presents, saying, "Patty, I am sorry but I have got to get away before the traffic hits."

My real reason, of course, was that I didn't want to be around when they opened up their gifts from the Hornsbys!

I got the hell out of there, and once back at Mindy's, I called Don to tell him that all went well, that they loved the gifts given in the Hornsby name - sex aides such as rubbers with Roosters heads on them, whip cream with a very suggestive picture on the aerosol can, and other various disgusting items, unmentionable in a book.

I can only imagine the look on Patty and Susan's face when they opened their gifts in front of all their friends and her mother and saw these wonderful things that Don had sent them - a gift that they will never forget!

I had done my duty. I just didn't want to be around to see the look of GRATEFULNESS on their faces.

January 14: I awoke at 03:00 to resume the journey. I laid there until just after 05:00, then loaded up the motorcycle. I remember opening the doors and looking at it as I had a little over a year ago, feeling that nauseating fear in the pit of my stomach.

There was also the hurt of leaving my mother behind once again.

I said a few last words to Mom as I was letting the motor warm up, the temperature was ice cold, there was snow on the ground, the wind was howling as it usually is in the high desert at this time of year.

I gave my dear old mother a last hug and a kiss. I could see she was being brave and fighting the tears in her eyes; there were tears in mine also. I straddled the motorcycle and rode away down the dirt road. I looked back and there was mom standing at the back of the house waving to me as I waved to her, until the house was no longer in sight. The pain in my heart was great.

Saying hello is such a wonderful thing, but the good-bye is such a painful, hurtful thing; one always leads to the other. It is with this pain in my heart and tears freezing ON my cheeks that I hit the main highway. As I gathered speed and felt the pound of the machine underneath me, it overcame the feeling of sorrow, replacing it with one of joy and the excitement of **adventure** that lay ahead.

It was with these emotions that I rode on through the icy desert.

The next evening was spent with a friend of mine, Keith Hendricks, an old skydiving buddy. Keith had been through more in Vietnam than any other person that I had known. He was quite a man, a friend, and one hell of a skydiver in his day with over 3,000 jumps to his credit.

On the morning of January 16th, we were up just after 4:00 am. Nancy, Keith's wife, made us a big breakfast. I went out and got the motorcycle loaded. Keith and I gave each other a big hug. I kissed Nancy and started the machine up; when it was warm, and I rode away from my friends. I started heading south towards the border of Mexico. The ride is quite a long one, well over 150 miles, from Phoenix, where Keith lived to Nogales on the border. Moving down the Interstate towards the border, I saw the sun rising just to the south side of Mt. Superstition as I got onto the Freeway.

At Nogales on both sides of the border I was waved through without any formalities. When I had crossed that border into Mexico I had truly finished Stage 3 of this journey.

Stage Four: South America

Chapter Twenty-One

Trash, Potholes, and the Pacific Ocean

When I crossed the Mexican border, Stage 3 of this journey was truly finished, and Stage 4 started.

In the first small town I entered, the narrow street had no stop light that I can recall, and the traffic was heavy. Further south, about ten miles into Mexico, I stopped for an insurance check, then continued down a double-laned road.

In the United States, every thing was orderly, neat and clean. The first Mexican countryside I saw was dotted with gray-brown scrub brush, and loads of trash along the road. It was unbelievable. I was shocked how trashy it was!

Welcome back to the Third World, Dave.

I moved along an increasing narrow road full of potholes. The miserable looking scrub brush stayed with me all the way to Hermosillo where I found a camping area for an almost sleepless night, thanks to a yapping dog off in the distance.

The next day, my ride was near the Pacific Coast with many open areas and few services along the way. Somehow I managed to miscalculate the distances, and ended up on gas reserve out in the middle of nowhere. I pulled into a restaurant and asked one of the patrons in my broken Spanish for some gasoline.

"Muy bueno," he replied, fetching a can out of the back of his car. After he put one gallon in my tank, I offered to pay the man, but he replied, "No, senior." His generosity left me with a good feeling.

Except for the well-maintained, double-laned toll road, the narrow Mexican roads breed potholes! They shoulders often had steep drop-offs down the side of steep embankments. Truck traffic abounds, and due to oncoming traffic, it is difficult to get around them. I'm often in first and second gear, poking along, with sand, dust and small stones tossed into my face. Mexican trucks seldom have mud flaps, so I was constantly assaulted with small stones. Once, I dodged a large piece of brick thrown back at me; it had been caught between a set of dual tires.

Passing is difficult because you must have an avenue open enough to get around the trucks.

Plus, you'd better look behind you as well. I mean, way back! There might be somebody coming down the road at 80 or 100 miles per hour, passing the whole line of traffic. A sudden move on your part and you'd get flattened. I had a couple close calls because I didn't look far enough back.

When I crossed into Mexico, I was struck by all the memorials along the road for people who had been killed in road accidents. Sometimes, I'd see a single cross; at other places, especially at corners, I'd see as many as twelve to fifteen! I'd shudder to think what had occurred on these corners. Were these many individual accidents, or was it one big bus accident? I'd see these memorials all the way down to the bottom tip of South America, and then not again until Russia. I often prayed that my name would not end up on one of those white crosses.

Mud was a major problem after a rain. The villages along the highway seldom had paved roads, so the mud would flow onto the highway, making it extremely slick. Driving behind a truck, they'd kick up this mud and my glasses would immediately be coated with brown slop. I'd be blinded until I used my finger as a wiper to clear off enough mud to let me see again.

Stage four was becoming a war of nerves since wrecks started to appear quite frequently. I saw two very grizzly ones in one day that backed up traffic for miles. I'd play chicken on a regular basis, skipping down onto the oncoming lane and then pulling back in whenever I saw oncoming traffic. All in a day's work for me.

After being spoiled by obedient drivers who followed the rules of the road in America, now I'm back in the Third World - and the only rule seems to be, "Don't get killed!"

Once crossing over the Tropic of Cancer, it was like turning off a switch. Immediately, the weather got hot! When I stopped to photograph the sign saying "Tropic of Cancer," I took off my heavy jacket and put on my thin jacket, then carried on.

Small town traffic was an adventure. Sometimes it would back up for a mile or so with one narrow, little street right through town, often a quagmire of mud. Luckily, the mud often had gravel underneath it so I could get traction. I'd ride on these roads with my feet down, holding on to the clutch - in and out constantly. The clutch got hot as hell, and the hotter it gets the more difficult it is to pull.

At the small town of Aca Poneta, I tried to find a place suitable to spend the night, and ended up going out of town. I made it just out of town and I see a little slip road. As I pull off the road just the other side of a tall bridge, I hit gravel and down I go... what do you know - my first spill of stage 4!

As I started to unload the motorcycle, I hear a voice behind me say, "Senor, Senor." The Mexican fellow standing there helped me lift the motorcycle up and I guided it down to a spot down below, just out of sight of the road, where he then helped me turn it around. Next, I unloaded and put up the tent.

"Agua, senor, por favor?" I asked him, handing him my water bottles. Off he went, probably down to the river, to fill them up for me. When he returned with the filled bottles, I pointed at all the scars on his chest and stomach. In reply, he made like a dog being ravished. "Boy oh boy, you must have had a hard time recovering from that," I thought, then settled in to a miserable night of mosquitoes and heat.

The following day I located an airport, and with great language difficulties made inquiries, trying to communicate that I wanted aircraft oil. Once I was understood, I bought six quarts and asked, "Where could I change it?" They pointed to a fence in a field that had a little footpath along it. So, I rode along the path, stopped, and changed the oil out there in the field.

In the last three days I had ridden nine hundred plus miles. I could hear a noise in the bottom of the motor, and oil had started to seep out of the base gasket of the front cylinder again. "Will my reoccurring problems ever cease? Will I ever have any peace of mind?"

Electric Man, Speed Bumps and Buzzards

I don't know how many close calls I had on the roads through Mexico, but there's one that will always stick out in my mind as I bounced and banged down pothole highway. I'm usually too close to the vehicles in front of me to see the bone-jarring holes coming up, so I just keep hitting them - some quite big! This particular time I went out into the oncoming lane to pass a bus. I saw a truck oncoming, although I calculated I had plenty of time to get around the bus. About midway into passing the bus, my motorcycle suddenly has a loss of power, bogging down. Time started dwindling into mili-seconds of eternity. I quickly spotted that a spark plug wire on the right cylinder had come off. While reaching down to grab the spark plug and wire together, I became a human conductor! The motorcycle quickly picked up power and speed, with me just managing to clear the bus as the truck whizzed by, simultaneously catching me in the wind stream from both of them.

I wondered what the truck driver must have thought.

"Was this crazy gringo motorcyclist with electric eyes playing chicken?"

My eyes must have been glowing from the voltage running through my body to keep the motorcycle running.

Continuing down the road only until I could find a spot where I could get off safely, I shut the motor down, then walked around in a bit of a daze, shaking from both the electricity and the enormity of the close call. After gathering my composure, I put the spark plug wire back on the rear cylinder properly, started up and got on my way. Of course, I was going to have to pass that damn bus once again, but hopefully under better circumstances.

After five days, I entered the major city of Guadalajara, where I hastened to get through the city traffic safely, and then back on the road again. Major cities hold no interest for me unless I have a purpose for my destination.

January 21,1992: On my way through some flooded roads and towns. Fortunately, most of my time was up on a toll road, so I was able to make good headway. The Mexican authorities have done a very good job with these toll roads, although they are expensive - almost as much as France.

Later that day I encountered a beautiful view of the Pacific Ocean! The next few hundred miles seemed to flow right along the Pacific on Highway 200. This ride reminded me of rides I frequently took many years before in California along the beach fronts of Sunset Beach, Seal Beach, Huntington Beach, Newport, and Balboa, drinking beer at different bars along the way, and socializing with other bikers. Now I was many years removed, and thousands of miles away, reminiscing.

Dead animals frequently littered the road; I saw buzzards for the first time since Africa. I'd frequently encounter people from the villages in the rivers and streams washing their clothes (no electricity in many of the villages). The water seemed quite clear and unpolluted.

Riding into Plaza Azul that evening, my odometer indicated 325 miles for the day.

Appearing fairly regularly, especially in the villages, are "lambodas" (speed bumps) with a little sign saying "Pedigro" - danger. I had to keep the motorcycle in first and second gear to go slow enough so as not to jar me and the bike to pieces. But sometimes, out in the open country, I'd encounter a little obscure village of thatched huts. Suddenly, there's a lamboda! I'd then have to do everything humanly possible just to avoid hitting it and come flying off the motorcycle at 50 miles an hour.

The deeper I go into Mexico, the greener and more scenic it becomes.

In Acapulco, I made a wrong turn, missing the loop road around it, and ended up going right through the city. The traffic poked along, and stop lights of very long duration helped emphasize the 100 degree heat.

It had to be!

My motor was getting hotter and hotter. At one intersection, as I was sitting there, it started to ping; I had to shut if off, knowing I was seizing up my pistons. Then, I pushed my motorcycle over to the side of the road and let the thing cool off for about an hour. I turned the motor over periodically with the crank start, then asked the shop vendors "How can I get out of town without going through anymore traffic?" They very kindly gave me a way out.

I still experience a nauseating, sick feeling in my stomach when I think, "If that motor had seized up, I don't know what I would have done."

225

The negative scenarios were infinite.

After the motor cooled, I started up and shot through traffic very quickly, up a steep hill, then out on the ring road that goes north around the city. By the end of the day, another 320 miles had been covered.

The first village where I asked directions to a possible camping area was very hostile, so I just kept on moving. I'd been warned repeatedly NOT to sleep out on my own in Mexico. "Dave, it can be very dangerous!" everyone told me.

At the next small village, I asked the gas station owner if I could sleep back in his garage; he agreed. When I rode into the place, I noticed that the whole front was cluttered with discarded oil cans and trash; an absolute horrible mess! Parking the motorcycle inside so I was out of view of everybody else, I placed my gear out on the cement floor where I ate my beans and some tortillas, closing my day at about 20:00. Because of a bar at the far end of the service station, I had to put up with noise until about 23:00.

Finally, things settled down and I went to sleep.

The following day I arrived in Puerto Escondido, once again amazed at the wall to wall rubbish. I'd see it out in the countryside too. Sometimes, I'd be riding along the road with just the normal amount of rubbish when All of the sudden I'd see a huge trash bag thrown out of a car - bursting open. The government did not seem to have any program to address this trash problem.

In Salina Cruz, I decided to take a very cheap room, without air conditioning, for a few dollars. It felt good to have a secure place that night to sleep.

Wind-Blown Biker Sucks Diesel Fumes

The next morning, I didn't get very far in an area known as "the wind" - the thinnest area of Mexico between the Pacific and the Caribbean. While riding along, leaning over at a very steep and dangerous angle, the gusting wind was creating a control problem for me and the motorcycle. It kept wanting to veer into the oncoming lane when the gale force wind let off a little bit. I saw a vehicle do a U-turn in the road ahead of me, and had to slow down. When I did, the wind blew me right off the motorcycle and onto the shoulder.

Down I went. The son of a bitch that made that illegal U-turn never even bothered to stop.

Two people along the road came over and helped me get the motorcycle up onto the highway. Realizing that this wind was too powerful to buck, I doubled back a mile or so to a hotel, paid a couple dollars, put the motorcycle into a compound, then took all my gear up to my room and relaxed a minute, catching my breath.

Next, I checked out the motorcycle. I still had the knocking noise in the motor, and had no clue what it was. I could only hope it didn't get worse. It seems as if the engineer in Alaska didn't do his job as promised. My hope is that the thing will get me through South America before I have to do anything about it.

The wind was blowing so hard it would not allow my right leg to swing back to its proper position. If I got in another wrong angle to the wind, it would virtually knock me over from behind. I decided to sit up in my room and read, hoping the wind would die down a bit in the morning.

At the hotel, I met some Americans who were going down to Guatemala to do some hang gliding. I spoke to the fellow leading this little expedition in a very bizarre vehicle full of different hang gliders, and parts for hang gliders.

"Do you mind if I go along with you tomorrow if the wind is up?" I ask.

I planned to take the gear off of the back of the motorcycle, making it less wind resistant, and follow these guys down the road.

"That would be fine, no problem," he told me.

Of course, when I travel with other people, I often do not get away as early in the morning as I would like. I had to wait for these guys to get themselves ready, and for them to stop at a restaurant and eat. By the time we were actually going, it was after 10:00. Definitely not my style.

We made good time through the day - temperature over a 100 degrees. With the motorcycle unloaded, I encountered no troubles with the wind. I only had a bit of a lean as the wind gusted for the next 75 to 100 miles (120 - 160 km) out of Salina Cruz.

In this very tropical area, bananas were the crop of choice. Where they weren't being grown, the scenery reminded me much of the rain forests.

In Tapachula, my guide had some friends in the hang gliding world that he called from a downtown square, and was told to "go down to Madera" about 20 miles away, where we met him at a restaurant and beer hall. I sat with them while they drank their beers and told stories about hang gliding which reminded me of my parachuting days. Late that evening, Richard joined us. He belonged to a wealthy family that farmed mangos in the area, and he took us to his villa on the sea. What a magic place it was indeed!

After a good nights sleep, I loaded up, waited for the others to get up so I could say good-bye, then headed out for the Mexican-Guatemalan border - about 20 miles away.

I had no problems **crossing from Mexico into Guatemala**, but once on the Guatemalan side I had about six offices to go through. I'd pay a little here, a little there - before you know it I had paid $20.00! Of course, I always had to demand the change - they never voluntarily gave it back! I gave my change to a boy who watched my motorcycle.

My plan for today was to make it to the border of Honduras and spend the night there. Down the road about 50 miles (80 km), I took a wrong turn and ended up going another 60 miles (100 km) out of my way. Things were not working out according to plan.

The weather in Guatemala is very, very hot - near a 100 degrees most of the time, with tremendous humidity. The countryside is sugar cane farming. The farms reminded me of the sugar cane estates in the Durban area where we used to go many years ago for the New Year's holiday.

Outside of Guatemala City, I stopped to ask directions from a man carrying a bundle of wood on his back, a machete strapped to his hip. The guy looked at me, dropped the bundle of wood, and took off back into the woods - gone. I can only imagine what I must have looked like to this fellow.

Once in Guatemala City, I was lost totally. Asking directions, I got sent this way, that way, and finally, after about an hour and a half, I made my way out of the city and onto open road again.

In Guatemala, I breathed a lot of diesel fumes. In Mexico, most trucks have their smoke stacks straight up - not so in Guatemala. They don't use as many big semi-tractors and trailers (this may explain the better roads). Instead of putting the smoke stacks straight up, they put them right out the side, so I got blasted with diesel fumes, right in the face, every time I passed a truck. They don't use the lean burning diesel we use in the United States; it's an oily, greasy diesel fuel. The fumes are very black, as were my lungs and face by the end of the day.

The drivers are aggressive, and the roadside memorials are plentiful, especially in the mountainous areas with winding roads. In a small village where I was buying petrol, a fellow told me, "We've been having problems with banditos. We just had a shooting, and the police were involved."

I needed a place to sleep, so I thought, "Why not go to the police station? Even though they had a rather seamy reputation with the locals, maybe they will treat me a little better. I certainly won't have any problems with bandits there - unless the police are the bandits."

I located a policeman and requested, in my broken Spanish, if I could sleep at the police station. "Si, and campomenta policia," he replied, pointing down the road to a police camp. When I pulled in at the camp, I showed them a note that this policeman had given me. They pointed to an area between two wrecked cars. I went over there and put my tent up trying to stay out of everybody's way.

The Guatemalans are a friendly people, and that attitude seemed to carry right through Central America. When I would wave to people when passing along the road, they would always wave back and smile.

The next morning, I crossed over a very steep mountain range, and down the other side **I came to the Honduran/Guatemalan Border**. Once again, I went from window to window, paying a little money here and there, and it is up to $20.00 again.

Honduras roads change radically. I had to be very careful of big potholes, especially in the mountainous areas with winding corners and steep ledges with no rails. It would be easy to go off if I had to do a fast maneuver to avoid a pothole, and lost control.

I survived, making fairly good time.

Upon arriving in San Pedro, I called Roatán Island and the Ramero Dive and Yacht Club, speaking to a fellow named Mike.

"I had missed the boat headed for Roatán Island due to the problems with wind in Mexico. What can I do?"

I had been invited to be the guest of Ramero and Connie, owners of the Dive and Yacht Club. I was instructed to ride another 60 miles on a horrible road full of trucks and terrible drivers, eventually arriving at Puerto Cortéz.

By this time, I had traveled 300 miles (500 km) that day. Now, I had to find a way out to the Island of Roatán. A fellow at a Texaco Service Station named Georgie Rodriguez spoke very good English, and told me, "You can put your tent up behind the service station. It's a big yard with some old wrecked trucks on it, but you can stay there as long as you like. Tomorrow, I'll help you find a boat heading down to Roatán Island."

The offer was appreciated, but the truck yard wasn't a good place to get rest. It was a 24-hour service station, with noise all night long!

The next morning, I met one of the petrol attendants named Virgalo - he struck me as exceptional. The attendants used to spark the girls as they would walk by; the girls themselves would always turn their heads and coyly smile back. After awhile I dubbed Virgalo as "gigolo." These fellows had nothing much in the way of material goods or money, but they were very kind. In the morning when I would sit with them, they'd always bring me something to eat. In the afternoon, I'd reciprocate by sharing my lunch with them.

An old black man that was around the station told me, "I'm originally from Texas, and spent 26 years at sea as a baker in the Merchant Navy. Had to quit because of this bum leg." He had a little basket on the front of his bicycle full of cakes and other homemade baked goods. I'd buy some of these goodies and pass them out to my friends with some Coke. Often, they'd feed me many of their local dishes they brought from home.

Georgie took me down to the Port a couple of times, and eventually we found a banana boat called the "Juanita" which was going to the island. It looked like a real bucket! The captain told me, "I'll not be leaving tonight, but I'll be going tomorrow night. You are welcome to come along."

"Why don't you come out to a little town out on the other side of the bay," Georgie said, "and we will have dinner out."

Great idea.

We went to a very ethnic restaurant, picked a fish out from a tank, and as they cooked it up, Georgie told me more about himself. "I'm in business because my father would not allow me to join the Army or the Navy." Georgie was 28 years old, and a very successful young businessman.

"Why couldn't you go in the Army?"

"My dad claimed there was no future. My dad was a very honorable man, and he wanted to instill the same values in me. He didn't want me to be corrupted. He made me go to school and get my education, then helped me get the service station I have today. Now, I have a wife and children, and a good business. Frankly, I am glad I did what my father wanted."

We had a lovely dinner; don't know what type it was, but it was the best fish I've ever had. Georgie then took me to the dream house he was having built overlooking a bay near the port. His own little piece of heaven.

I worked on the motorcycle all the next day, steam washing it with Georgie's big steam cleaning machine. Then I reset the points and performed other general maintenance. By afternoon I was ready to go.

Banana Boat Bath

I rode down to the port where, in the early evening, I met the banana boat (their main cargo actually WAS bananas). Five black stevedores man-handled the motorcycle down onto the ship and tied it down, and I located a place where I could stay close to the motorcycle, glad not to be over the engine room where everybody else was; later, I learned that was the preferable place to be!

We departed about 22:00, and I'm still thinking, "Why is everybody back over the engine room? What's the sense of being crowded together around that noise and heat? Heck, since there's nobody up on the bow, I'm going to take my sleeping bag up there to relax."

I did.

Stars clustered in the clear, bright sky, and I just relaxed and started to sleep. Suddenly, we hit a decent-sized swell, and I thought, "That's really not a problem. I can handle that."

Within an hour of hitting that swell, a large wave came right over the top of that bow and crashed down on me. There was water all over the deck and me. Instantly, I was soaking wet! From that time until dawn, we were in a rough sea with water coming over the bow. I actually floated in about six inches of water, sliding back and forth on the deck. Yes indeed, I had found a good place.

"You know," I thought to myself, "I have yet to have a pleasant experience on a boat." I thought back to the Limba in Lake Tanganyika, and also the trip down the Zaire River.

Sunrise brought a much calmer sea. Things were beautiful again. I put on my wet legs, taking my wet sleeping bag and laying it out on top of a stack of lumber that was near the bow.

229

We passed some beautiful small islands that looked like something out of a South Sea adventure story - palm trees, blue sky, the dark blue ocean, and picturesque waves lapping the white sandy beaches. It was just magic.

"Well, I am enjoying all of this," I thought, "without being on one of those pesky cruise ships where tourist stuff themselves with food and luxuries." Of course, I was deluding myself. I would have loved to be on a cruise ship instead of this banana bucket!

The people who had wisely stayed by the warm engine in the back of the boat now surfaced. I chatted with the ones who could speak a bit of English about the general situation in Honduras and Roatán Island. How sad it was to think of all the work the people put in each day to live in poverty, without hope.

That morning we put into a little port on the Island of Roatán. The dock was broken down wooden planks built out into the water.

"I don't trust my motorcycle being rolled out on that," I thought to myself, wondering also if the pick-up trucks on the "Juanita" could make it.

Once a large portion of the bananas were off loaded, one of the trucks was man-handled off the boat by brute force. Next, they lifted the motorcycle off and put it down on the other side. I got on, waived good-bye to the Captain, and rode off in the direction of Ramero's Dive and Yacht Club.

After about five miles, I came to the club where markers on a very well kept dirt road led me to a two-story A-Frame building. Attached to the A-Frame area of the resort was a concrete, two-story building with individual rooms such as you would find in a motel. There was an office and dining room in the tropical resort - all very ethnic. A resident snake (obviously not poisonous) lived up in the rafters, and every now and again you would see him. Everything in the A-Frame was made out of wood, even the floor. The view showed a lagoon that acted as the harbor and docking area for the dive boats and various yachts.

The hostess showed me to my room on the ground floor. I moved the motorcycle around next to the room, and unloaded it. A couple of laborers suggested we take it "down to the docks and give it a good wash to get all the salt water brine off of it."

"That sounds like a good idea to me," I replied.

Then came a wonderful shower for Dave Barr as I prepared to meet Connie - Ramero's wife. She runs the place in his absence. When the diving boat came in, I met Mike Winchell. During my stay, Mike would show me the basics of scuba diving, and allow me to go on a couple of the dives with him.

Scuba Diver with Stumps

The next day was spent in the swimming pool doing different drills that Mike Winchell gave me. He also taught me the nomenclature of the equipment I would be using. As a final preparation, he had me dive down in the deep end of the pool.

The next day was to be the diving day!

The day started early for the instructors as they had to move about 40 bottles of air out to the diving boat. We all pitched in and made short work of a heavy task. Once out on the diving boat, the divers get themselves into their scuba equipment while the boat puts out to sea. This particular day we were going to a place called "The Wall."

When the time came, I took my legs off, strapped everything on, then scooted to the back of the boat and fell over the side. I will never forget what it felt like - another world, a new dimension of water, silence and tranquillity. The water was extremely clear, with a view up to 100 meters. We dove down to about 30 feet exploring the ocean bed, Mike pointing out the different plants and fish that could cause harm. What a magic world! What joy to scoop around in the sand and glide through the water.

I had a bit of a problem with my stumps staying behind me. They kept wanting to come around underneath me, and it was as if I were swimming along forward in a sitting position. I didn't quite know what to do with all this. We adjusted the air vest occasionally, but didn't get any better results. Later, we discovered I needed less of a weight belt.

Mike took me to the edge of "The Wall" and I looked off into a great, vast, blue void; time and space seemed infinite as I stared down the ledge at the various plants growing on the side of the wall. Absolutely captivating! So many different types of fish swimming about - in schools or individually. Incredible!

Once back on the boat, full of excitement, I took my equipment off and put my legs back on. When all the other divers came up, and we stowed everything away, we journeyed back to the resort for lunch, once again helping to carry in the oxygen bottles.

The next day's dive was also something very incredible. We dove down to a sunken tanker and a downed aircraft. I could have swam around the ship forever. I wanted to go into the bridge and down into the hole, but Mike motioned "No!" Instructor knows best.

Next, we swam over a downed DC-3 - being a skydiver and paratrooper, this aircraft had very particular meaning to me. At 30 feet deep, I explored the cockpit as best I could from outside; there was a hatch on top that one could look down through. Swimming around to the main cargo door, I sat there, thinking "How many skydives have I made out of a DC-3 just like this?"

Probably over 150. I have jumped as high as 22,000 feet out of DC-3 and as low as 400 - at night. Sitting underwater in that doorway, I visualized the horizon and imagined the buildup of excitement in the aircraft as it nears the jump run. I saw myself making final adjustments, then eventually hearing, "Ready, set, go," stepping out into the void of the sky. A tinge of sadness hit me as I sat in the DC-3 knowing it would no longer fly across the horizons of the world, but would rest permanently in its watery grave, providing a home for fish.

That evening, Mike gave a karate demonstration to the assembled guests at the resort. It was really amazing to watch him. Mike was a fourth Dan black belt, and at the demonstration, it was clear he was NOT a man to end up fighting.

The following day presented a series of problems for me to solve before leaving the island. Ramero had cleared me on to the "Alexandria Express" which was in even worse condition than the "Juanita." "It doesn't matter," I thought to myself, "I've got to get moving."

Get Me Out of Here!

I was shown the way down to a different docking area where there were some warehouses, and the motorcycle was put into a shed. After waiting around all afternoon, they told me, "We are not going this evening as planned. Instead, we will go tomorrow morning because the weather will be better."

After locking the motorcycle inside the shed, I found a place to sleep on the boat - a dirty, filthy, stinking mess. My sleep was disturbed by the blaring music from a nearby discotheque, and by attempting to swat the swarms of mosquitoes that didn't seem to notice my insect repellent. What a wonderful night! Early in the morning, the crew - who had been partying at the discotheque - returned to the boat... drunk and noisy.

The next morning the captain told me, "We will not be leaving today as the weather is not right."

"Fuck this," I thought.

I could tell the captain did not particularly want me around, and I didn't like his attitude either, so I decided to pack up and go back to the resort and see what were my other options. When Ramero heard my report, he became very upset, saying, "There is no problem out on the ocean. I do not understand what the their problem is."

Next, Ramero tried to book me on a twin-engine jet aircraft that comes in once a day. The motorcycle had to be unloaded and weighed; to do this, we had to pick it up about two feet to place it on a wagon. Then, the wagon was pulled over to the scales, which, as luck would have it, didn't work.

When the plane arrived and I saw the cargo door, I realized there was no way we were going to load the motorcycle in there. So, after all this hassle and an entire afternoon at the airport waiting for this plane, hassling with customs, the police, the weigh master and the airline, we had to take the motorcycle off the wagon, reloaded it, then ride back to the resort.

By this time I am turning up like a bad penny, and the resort was full. There was no place for me to stay so they put me in Mike's room. Mike did not seem very pleased with that (later I found out he had a girl he had been sparking, and she was very likely to visit him that night).

I felt like a spare dick at a wedding!

I left Mike, and took my stuff very quietly over to a service room that was being refurbished. That night at dinner, I told Mike what I had done. He obviously felt bad, but not bad enough to cancel his date with this girl! After dinner, I snuck off and went back to my room, sleeping on the concrete floor, feeling like odd man out.

The next day I was told that, "The 'Juanita' is back. It will be leaving in the evening. Would you consider going back on the 'Juanita'?"

"Sure I'll go back on the 'Juanita'," I quickly volunteered, anxious and ready to hit the road again. I found my way back to the dock late that afternoon, but could spot none of the crew. I sat next to the motorcycle for several hours waiting for someone to come along. Eventually, a little dog showed up to keep me company. I put my sleeping bag on a cement slab and laid down, trying to get some sleep.

At 22:00, the crew shows up, roaring drunk. They loaded up some stuff set out on the beach, lashed it down, then manhandled my motorcycle back aboard. When they managed to get it on without a catastrophe, I figured I could relax a bit. I collapsed into a deep sleep, and it became apparent we were going nowhere this night. Laying back down with the dog next to me, it starts raining; we get soaked. I could hear the very heavens scoffing. "On behalf of the crew, the pouring rain and generally turbulent weather, God would like to welcome Dave Barr back to the 'Juanita' for his next exciting boat ride across the Caribbean."

That morning at sunrise we set "sail" on our thirteen hour trip. But, before we set out, an old American named Captain Jack came aboard. "That's my dog that's been hanging around," he told me. As we talked, I discovered that this character had been a carrier plane pilot during World War II, and also flew during Korean war. He spent 25 years in the Navy, and retired as a Commander. He told me, "I married a Bolivian woman, but fell out of favor with her and her family while living in Bolivia. At one point, I had the police chasing me, so I shanghaied a helicopter and flew it into Brazil, then journeyed across Brazil on foot."

232

His stories were amazing and incredible (I could tell I was dealing with someone who was telling the truth). He had lived many adventures in his life. "I wonder how Captain Jack fit in with those resort people?" I thought to myself. "He probably didn't, nor did I," I mused, answering my own question.

At Puerto Cortéz, there was a bit of sadness as I bid good-bye to Captain Jack and his trusty dog. Back at the service station, I started to pitch my tent when the men said, "Don't put it there. We're expecting rain."

Like a jackass, I ignored their warnings and pitched my tent anyway.

That was to be a huge mistake!

About 03:00 in the morning, rain started coming down so hard it flooded the tent, and once again I was literally afloat in water. There was nothing I could do but just get up, put on wet legs, wet clothes, get my rain gear on, load the motorcycle (sitting in about six inches of water) while I waited out the storm. The downpour was tremendous (on the plus side, no mosquitoes).

Another Close One

That next morning, I was off. After riding only about 15 miles down the horrible road leading to Puerto San Pedro, dodging trucks, potholes, water puddles, and mud, trying to see through the blinding rain, suddenly it stops! When the rain stopped, my mood improved incredibly as my clothes started to dry out.

In Tegucigalpa, the capital city of Honduras, I noticed my old oil leak out of the front cylinder was back. "Nothing I can do about it now," I would have to just to push on.

Out of Tegucigalpa I nearly had an accident; it was one of those special times when there was no real explanation for me not being hit by the car. I pulled out in front of the driver because I simply didn't see his vehicle.

Somehow, he missed me.

How, I honestly don't know.

Bridge over The Panama Canal
Linking North and South America
February 13, 1992

Making of right steel foot
Porto Ordaze, Venezuela March 1992

Chapter Twenty-Two

Bribes, Borders, and Breakdowns

I made it to the border that evening, going from toll window to window, paying a little here, a little there, then crossing over to the Nicaraguan border. Once again, pay here, pay there - before I knew it, I had paid out $45.00.

The Nicaraguans took the cake for tolls and taxes, and it wasn't from corruption because they gave me receipts at each window. They just taxed you to bankruptcy! There was a road tax, a vehicle tax, a tax for everything you could think of coming into their country. If there was a way to monitor it, they probably would have had a shit tax as well!

The motorcycle carburetor had been giving me problems, flooding out during the day; I took it apart and fixed it. When that was done, I went over to what looked like a little cantina to buy some bread. The woman disappeared, and was gone for quite awhile. I couldn't understand why it was taking so long to get the bread until she returned with two cooked meals. That misunderstanding cost me $4.00. I'd eat one for dinner, and one for breakfast.

The Nicaraguan authorities gave me permission to sleep on the border, so I put my tent up on a grassy area at the far end of the officials' buildings. I sat there eating my dinner as a crowd gathered, looking at me and the motorcycle. Although they were not mean, and tried to communicate the best they could, I would have appreciated a bit of privacy with my dinner.

In Managua, when I became lost, it was no problem asking people for directions; they seemed very pleasant in this city. From Managua, I carried on south to the Costa Rican border which I made that afternoon.

In Costa Rica, after clearing Customs and Immigration on the Nicaraguan side, I went across the border. The Costa Ricans didn't charge me major money to get in. Instead, they were on their lunch break and just sat there eating their sandwiches, letting everybody else sit and wait. Afterwards, the woman who had been sitting wouldn't even talk to me for an hour. Finally, some other fellow came along and got me through the formalities.

Once in Costa Rica, I spotted some travelers along the rode and asked them if there were any camping areas. "About 30 miles down the road," they said.

The countryside changed drastically from the dry, scrub brush of Nicaragua to the green hillsides covered with vegetation in Costa Rica. Road conditions were good, so it didn't take me hardly anytime to get to the state campground right on the coast, about 3 miles (5 km.) from the main road. It was quite beautiful. Although they didn't have any lights, they did have public facilities, varied vegetation, birds everywhere, no traffic noise, and lots of people camping - all foreigners from various places in the world.

The next morning I was on the highway quite early. There was no traffic, and the people seemed to be far better drivers than any I'd seen since the United States.

In San Jose, a big city, I got lost, and signaled two dispatch riders, motioning them to help. I sometimes get a feeling about people in places like this. My six senses told me these two young fellows would be a good bet to get me through San Jose and out the other side.

They were. After a series of complicated street maneuvers, we arrived at a sign saying "Panama." Despite the time and effort it took to lead me to this spot, they wouldn't take anything for the help they had rendered.

After riding up some mountains and a very steep pass up and up over the top, the down side presented an amazing view of the lush green wooded country which flowed south along a winding road and river. When I entered a small town, I noticed a Red Cross building with a big empty lot next to the ambulance station.

"Would it be possible for me to spend the night in that empty lot?" I asked.

"Fine. No problem," they replied.

When I was setting up, I drew a small crowd. One of the medics from the ambulance station brought me a welcome cup of tea, they invited me to come inside and wash up. That night I thought about the 330 miles (525 km) I had covered, about the near miss in the mountains with a semi-tractor and trailer - how I had nearly went underneath him as I tried to miss a pothole and he came around a corner in my lane. "Daily occurrences," I thought. "I can't let this stuff get on my nerves, or it's the end of the road," I told myself.

Never Waive Without Stopping

I will forever dislike roosters because it's their cockadoodledo that's the first thing to disturb my sleep each morning, declaring, "Wake up, Dave. A new day of trials and tribulations is about to begin." Sometimes, they start so early that it is still several hours before the sun is up enough to let me get going. Up at 05:00 this particular morning, I knew I was in trouble - it was already getting hot as I rode through very tropical area on a dirt road for quite a few miles. After about 50 miles (80 km), **the Panamanian border appeared**, and I rapidly made it through customs/immigrations on both sides.

When I went to a bank with some travelers checks to exchange for the local currency, they gave me back American dollars!

"What is this? I want Panamanian money," I explained, a bit aggravated.

"Si, senior," they replied, "it is Panamanian money."

I was shocked that the Panamanians used American dollars. That certainly made things a lot easier for me.

After clearing all the formalities, I rode for about 5 miles (8 km), and was stopped by police who checked my papers.

"Do you have any maps of Panama City?" I asked.

"Yes. No problem," they replied, and gave me a map, helping me spot where I wanted to go. Very kind of them!

I hit another police roadblock about 80 miles (140 km) up the road. A policeman came out and looked as though he was waiving to me; I waived back, and kept going. This was to prove to be a mistake!

10 miles (16 km) later, they had a roadblock out just for me! The officer was hollering in Spanish, so it was difficult to make out what he was saying. Later, I came to understand that I should have stopped at the other roadblock. The officer at this roadblock was going to write me ticket, but I pleaded, "Por favor, senor."

Then he indicated he wanted a bribe. Again, I said "Por favor, senor," in my broken Spanish, trying to convince him that it had all been a misunderstanding. In the end, I passed through without paying a bribe or a fine.

As I approached Panama City on the north side of the bridge that spans the canal, a fellow passed me with a girl on the back of a Sportster. I waived frantically to him, so he turned around and caught up with me. He introduced himself as Darius Knowlton, and told me he was stationed at Howard Air Force Base.

"I'm on my way to Albrook Air Force Base to find the clubhouse of the Road Knights Motorcycle Club. I understand that foreign travelers can stay there."

"That's right," Darius agreed, "if you can find people to let you in."
This news gave me a bit of a worry.
"Follow me," Darius said.

A Rare Ride Into History

We rode over the bridge over the Panama Canal. While high up on that bridge, it struck me that **this part of the journey (the North American Continent) had taken me from the Atlantic to the Pacific, from the Prudhoe Bay/ Dead Horse Camp in the Arctic (Alaska), all the way to the bottom crossing of the Panama Canal, from North America to South America.**

February 13, 1992: What a view I had while going over the bridge! It seemed a couple of hundred feet high as I looked down to the east at the inlet to Panama Canal, and to the west out in the Pacific Ocean. It was one of those very rare moments of the trip where I realized that something really wonderful had been accomplished. These moments are short lived.

Darius took me to Albrook Air Force Base where we discovered the Road Knights were not at their clubhouse. We tried to find somebody who could help us. We went to the MP's office where Darius worked, but no one had any information.

"Why don't you spend the night in my room?" Darius suggested.

"Great," I replied, thankful and relieved to have a place for the night.

"In my days on a Marine Base," I thought, "this could never have happened - security was too tight." I followed Darius back over the bridge to Howard Air Force Base, then to the barracks where he lived in an individual room.

For security, we had to take every bit of gear off of my motorcycle! I gave him the lighter stuff and carried the heavy saddlebags myself. I wasn't trying to be a hero. They were just so full of grease and dirt that I didn't want him to ruin his clothes. We carried equipment up three flights of stairs, then down a long corridor to his room. By the end of this routine, my stumps were killing me! We had to make two trips to get it totally unloaded. The heat and humidity made the situation worse for me. I was sweating blood.

Once done, Darius said "Dave, you smell like the southbound end of a northbound mule. There's a shower in the back of the room." Darius was right. I hadn't had a shower since I left Ramero's Resort on Roatán Island six days earlier.

Next, now dressed in nice clean clothes, we ordered a Shakey's Pizza - believe it or not - right in the middle of Panama. Amazing.

After Pizza, I tried to call the phone numbers I had for the Road Knights, but had no luck. "Don't worry about it for the rest of the evening," Darius suggested. "We can work out something tomorrow."

Darius was a heavy set, big fellow and with a mean attitude - he'd been an MP for 12 years in the Air Force. "I am a short timer," he declared. "Because of the rift, I decided to get out of the Air Force early," he told me.

Darius became extremely irritable while riding, cursing at this person or that person, threatening to "knock their blocks off," constantly giving them the finger. Of course, he was big enough to back up his running criticisms. I'm glad he took a shine to me as a friend in the motorcycle brotherhood. With a strong feeling of friendship and kindness, we closed our day about 23:00 in his crowded room. "Don't know what I would have done without Darius," I thought as I fell asleep.

The next day I again tried to find somebody in responsibility with the Road Knights. As generous as Darius was, I knew he couldn't take too much more of this. I needed the Road Knights to help make this the staging area for the next part of the journey as I secured visas, took care of repairs, and arranged to transport the motorcycle to the Mainland of South America.

Finally, I contacted Danny Cooper who said, "I'll meet you tomorrow at the club's facility at Albrook."

That evening, I rode on the back of Darius' Sportster to an Army Base where I met Ski, and his wife, Dawn. Ski was in an infantry outfit, and his wife was on a woman's softball team. Boy could she swing that bat! I've never seen anything like it. Since we were all Americans, it felt like a touch of home on a Saturday evening - everybody drinking beer, laughing, having a good time. At the ball game, they were even selling hot dogs, hamburgers and cokes.

The next morning I moved all of my gear back downstairs. What took two of us two trips going up took me six trips alone. My left stump especially was causing me a great amount of pain.

When Darius got up, he met me downstairs. When we were ready to go, somehow my right foot caught under the foot peg, my knee bent, and down I went, motorcycle on top of me. Darius comes over with a look of disgust on his face and starts to pick up the motorcycle. I am angry at myself, and horribly, horribly embarrassed. To add shit to the pile, my front break lever for the hand brake was broken.

When we arrived at Albrook Air Force Base, we met Danny Cooper, U.S. Army retired. "Welcome aboard," he said, showing me the clubhouse and where I could throw my bags. Fortunately, the clubhouse had air conditioning - very welcome in the tremendous heat.

Once I moved in, everybody was kind enough to leave me alone to relax. The nights were extremely hot, but that didn't keep me from a first good nights sleep in quite a while.

Sore Stump and Darin Gap Lumps

The next day I grind off some of the inner socket of my left leg to help relieve some of the pressure where my open, puss-filled sore is bleeding on the inside of the stump. I also placed a collect call home to my Mom to say "hello" and to let her know that I've made it to Panama City.

I caught a taxi into Panama City, a crowded, dirty place, with very narrow streets, going to the Colombian Embassy where I learned that a visa wasn't required. Next, I walked down a block or so to the Venezuelan Embassy; they told me, "Return in two days to pick up your passport and visa."

Back at Albrook Air Force Base, I sat in the air conditioned lounge reading from a big log about people who had shot or attempted to shoot the "Darin Gap," a stretch of land about 90 miles (150 km) outside the south part of Panama City. It is a dirt track that finally becomes just a dirt path.

There are no bridges spanning the many rivers, or a proper road into Columbia. So, when you want to cross a river or stream, you have to negotiate a price with the Indians to put the motorcycle and all your gear up on pontoons. The cheapest account that I read about was by a fellow on a BMW in 1986 - he got across for $871.00. As you can imagine, they have you by the balls in a situation like this. I decided to try and find an alternative way to get into Columbia.

During the evening, I spoke to John St. Williams about my dilemma of attempting to shoot the "Darin Gap." "Dave, I don't think there's much hope of finding a ship or a banana boat over to Columbia. People have tried, but as far as I know, they never make it."

238

Some stories in the log confirmed this.

"Let's try the airlines," John suggested. "Tomorrow morning, let's go over to the airport and snoop around and see what we can come up with."

It sounded a like a grand idea to me.

The next day we drove to Tocuma Airport and found our way to American Airlines. "No, we don't fly motorcycles on that route," they told us, "but you might try Lasca airline."

We went to Lasca airline, and talked to the freight side of their operation.

"No problems with motorcycles," they told us. "It will cost you 47 cents a kilogram." That was incredibly cheap, so I made reservations. The only small hitch - I had to sign a waiver in case there was any damage done to the motorcycle. My ticket was about $125.00 to fly to Barranquilla, Columbia. I dated my departure for a week later to give my left stump much-needed time to heal.

That evening, a medic came by and looked at my stump, giving me some antibiotics, bandages and salve, plus some anti-malarial tablets! "This stuff is more valuable than mosquito repellent," he told me, referring to the tablets.

The Sagi and Omer Saga

At the Road Knights Clubhouse, there were two motorcyclists who just arrived: Sagi and Omer. Once I discovered they were from Israel, we started a conversation in Hebrew. Despite our age difference (they were much younger), we struck up an immediate friendship. I had no problems relating to them, and they didn't seem to have much problem relating to me.

We had dinner together, and we all slept out on the concrete that night since it was too hot to sleep in the rooms.

Thankfully, the sore on my left stump is starting to heal. During the day, when no one is around, I try to spend as much time as possible with the leg off to ease the irritation.

The next day, Sagi and Omer went to find a contact person who could speak to them about sailing their motorcycles to Venezuela. They had spent the entire day running around and getting messed about; their "contact" kept dodging them.

"How are you getting across, Dave?" they asked me. When I told them, and explained how cheap it was, they both said, "We'd like to go on the plane too." Since we were talking about going the same direction down through Brazil, we decided we would all go on together - there's security in numbers.

A couple of more days went by with everybody doing the final preparations for the journey. When it was time for us to leave for Tocuma Airport, John and Darius came by in a van and followed us to the airport.

At Lasca Airlines, we prepared our motorcycles by taking the oil out. I did not take the battery water out of mine, but instead tied off the overflow tube, making sure everything was sealed up. Once the motorcycles were weighed and measured, they were placed on their sides on a pallet and strapped down.

It cost $320.00 for me and my motorcycle together to fly to Barranquilla, Columbia. Sagi and Omer's cost were slightly more because the dimensions of the Yamaha motorcycles were actually bigger than the Harley Davidson. We all were very pleased with the price.

John and Darius took us around to the front of the building to check in at the ticket counter. Then, I said "good-bye" to John St. Williams and Darius Knolton, two people very instrumental in giving me a hand in finding both my way into Panama and my way out.

The bag I've got to carry to the plane weighs approximately 100 LBS. Sagi and Omer helped me get it on my back, and then I carried it up to the check in counter. When the bag was placed on the scales, the girl looked at it and just shrugged, like "Who cares?" She let the overweight bag go through.

After completing Customs, we climbed on the plane and headed from Panama, across the Caribbean to Barranquilla, Columbia in fifty-five minutes.

Upon landing in Barranquilla, we had to claim our baggage (mind you, mine weighs a ton), carried it to a long line for Customs and Immigration where I put it down and drug it as we moved forward. It took over an hour to get through the formalities! When we moved to the front of the building to catch a taxi cab over to the air freight terminal, nobody seemed to know the location of the Lasca Air Freight terminal.

Sagi and Omer kept telling me, "Don't speak to anyone. Everybody is a thief!"

Suddenly, next to me stood a lovely young woman. I had the feeling she was not a thief. "My name is Rebecca," she told me. "I know where the air freight terminal is for Lasca." She gave us directions, and we hailed a taxi, loading our gear into the back, heading for the terminal.

At the freight terminal, we asked, "Can we sleep on the cement slab out in front of your building?"

"No problem," we were told.

In front of a crowd of onlookers, we sat up our "camp" in this really dirty, miserable place. The crowd just stood there watching us cook our dinner. To save dishes, we all eat out of the same bowl - a normal ritual for us when we ate together on the road. About 01:00, the crowd finally drifted off and we could relax and go to sleep, swatting mosquitoes in the torrid heat.

Up about 04:30, the crowd was back, and I had to put my legs on in front of everybody. When the officials arrived to open up the hangar, we took our paperwork inside and completed their regulations. Now, we were told to go into town to an address they gave us.

The Diabolical Day Meets Rescuing Rebecca

One fellow at the hangar kindly arranged for a car to take us into town. One of the first sights that shocked us was the large portion of automobiles from the 50's era. Our own car was a 1955 Chevrolet with a V8 motor. Our driver drove as though possessed, passing and winding his way through the traffic as if he was on a motorbike! We just sat back and held on for dear life until we arrived at the designated building. "I'll wait for you," he told us.

The next eight hours were downright diabolical.

We went from room to room, up and down stairs, as much as eight floors. Every person we talked to pestered us for more money to "speed up the process." Sagi, a good Jewish boy, wasn't about to pay any extra to get through this mire of bureaucracy. Of course, since I had lived in Israel for almost four years, two of which were spent in the paratroopers, I wasn't about to pay either. We gave each other mutual support on that miserable day.

One man told me, "I need to see the registration for your motorcycle."

"I don't have it," I replied. "It's with the motorcycle."

"Go get it," he demanded.

So, I had to go downstairs and ask our man who was still waiting in the car to take me all the way back to the airport to fetch my registration. I was fuming - mad at the man for insisting to see it, and mad at myself for having forgot it. We hurried back at breakneck speed, only to find out it was lunch time from 12:00 until 14:00! So, Sagi and I sat on a bench just waiting, giving each other moral support.

At 14:00, the diabolical process began again. To this office for papers, to that office for papers. Out of all the places in the world I have traveled, I have never had so much paperwork given to me to import my motorcycle. By the end of the day, about 15:30, Rebecca (from the airport) showed up and helped us get all our paperwork resolved. I realized now that she was in customs! Then, she disappeared again; we still had about an hour's worth of work to do.

At almost 17:00, we arrived back at the Lasca Air Freight terminal, only to have some more papers signed. It turns out that it was Rebecca who was supposed to sign them off, so she had gone to the airport office, anticipating our return. She inspected the motorcycles, signed our paperwork off, and after ten hours of running around and being prodded for bribes, it finally came to an end - thanks to Rebecca's help.

We wasted no time putting oil in the motorcycles and getting them prepared to ride. We put gasoline in them, paid everybody - the driver only cost us $15.00 for the whole day! That was money well spent.

I bade farewell to Rebecca, and we were off; it didn't take us long to get out of that trashy, horrible city of Barranquilla. What a miserable place! It had the trash of Mexico, but the roads were worse - often broken completely in half! A canal ran through the city that was solid trash; I knew it was a channel because there were bulldozers in the canal trying to remove the rubbish. What a horrible, messy job. It stunk to high heaven.

Open Roads and Quiet Sabbaths

On the open highway, the road was rough and full of trucks and buses, but it still felt like a godsend after ten days of no riding. It was good to be on the road and done with all the bureaucracy for a bit. We were all silently hoping that Venezuela and Brazil were not the same.

About a half hour before dark, we found a little trail going off back into an area of bushes and trees. We rode back there and found a farm house where we asked the woman, "Do you mind if we sleep on your property?"

She nodded her approval, so we rode back to a lake right behind us and set up camp. The lady and what looked like her sister, with a bunch of kids, come to watch us as we were cooking our dinner. They were very friendly, so we shared our big bowl of coffee with them and took some photographs. About 20:30, they bid us "Buenos noches" and walked back to their humble dwelling; we settled back to swat mosquitoes for the rest of the night.

The next day reminded me of Africa - problems from morning to dark.

The road was rough and hard going. The countryside was sandy and miserable looking, very swampy, a lot of patches of water. As we rode, we were stopped periodically by Army or police. One time they asked for a bribe so I gave the guy a ball point pin; he seemed happy with that.

In the mid afternoon, All of the sudden my front end started wobbling horribly. I pulled over to discover that the top of the fork tube had come undone. Its unbelievable. I'd never seen anything like this before. Along with Sagi and Omer, we were able to get the cap back down into the tube and tighten it up. After about another mile, I noticed there still was a funny feeling in the front end. Once again I stopped, this time to learn that the lower triple tree had broken - that's what caused the original problem. I had to re-tighten the top fork cap as well.

At the first town we came into, we located a man who welded up the triple tree. We thought that would take care of the problem. We rode until late afternoon when **we arrived at the Venezuelan border**; we crossed into Venezuela very quickly with no Customs/Immigration problems.

About an hour into Venezuela, I feel the front end starting to wobble again! The cap was starting to unscrew, and the front triple tree is broken again. I limp into the next little town at extremely low speed - very dangerous, because the traffic behind me is coming at high speed, and is very aggressive in trying to get around me.

We are directed to the town welder with equipment that looked like it was just a big pile of junk. However, he did a good job on welding the triple tree. At the same time, I noticed that one of the screws holding the whole clutch lever assembly onto the handle bar had broken; so he also welded something on top of the broken screw to allow me to take it out and replace it. What good ingenuity!

By now, it was late and we were tired. We found a slip road and rode back a mile or so to find a very quiet place to put up our tents and relax for another evening under the stars.

A routine was starting to develop as we traveled together, especially with Sagi and me. We liked to rest in front of my tent in the evening with our tea and talk about different political problems, both in Israel and throughout the world. His insight was incredible for a man only twenty-three. We found it very easy to talk. He often tried to speak to me in English, and sometimes did fairly well. At other times, I would speak to him only in Hebrew. Since I had not spoke it since leaving South Africa, it felt good to sharpen it again.

Sagi and Omer like to stop about every fifty miles and smoke a cigarette - takes about ten minutes each time! Since the road is fairly rough, we also stop about every 100 or so miles for gasoline.

These two characters like to argue, especially in the early morning. One starts to talk about some inconsequential little thing, and immediately the other will argue with it. They reminded me of my time in the Israeli Army where everyone seemed to wake up irritable and miserable. Of course, these feuds never had any malice attached to them - just arguments for the sake of argument.

One morning, after traveling about 10 miles, my motor starts missing. I pull over and determine the carburetor is flooding out. "What else can go wrong?" I think to myself. I clean the carburetor out, make a minor adjustment to the float level, and we're off again - it seemed to hold.

In Barquisimeto, we go from bank to bank to bank, trying to find a place to change travelers checks - to no avail! Finally, we do a deal on the black market to get our cash.

Traffic is horrible. We cut between lanes when we can, and the rest of the time we just idle along. At these slow speeds, I'm worried about burning a piston. Even out of town the traffic just poked along this single lane road, backing up for miles. We endure a routine of passing, more passing, and ducking in and out of lanes as oncoming traffic approaches. Finally, we see a stream off in the distance, just outside the town of Alaregua. We take a road down to it, and camp there for the night after covering about 250 miles that day.

We bathed in the stream, especially appreciating that we didn't have any problem with mosquitoes. We had a candlelight dinner that night, since it was our first Sabbath together on the road - Friday evening to Saturday evening, the day of rest for Jews (though we agreed not to rest the next day if the weather was right). With candles glowing, the warm and pleasant atmosphere that evening transported me back to my time in Israel. Omer chanted the Sabbath prayer on this last day of February.

The making of the right foot
Porto Ordaze, Venezuela March 1992

My Hotel on the Road in the Amazon region
March 1992 Brazil

Typical Bridge on Transamazonias
March 1992 Brazil

Polícia Militar
Escort Platoon
São Paulo, Brazil
April 1992
(Note: Zulato stands directly behind me.)

Chapter Twenty-Three

Crumbling Hotels and a Broken Foot

March 1, 1992: This day we would cover many miles on the rough, narrow road with plenty of trees along the farmlands. We were stopped by police periodically as we traveled through Venezuela. Today, one of the police asked me for a bribe.

"No senor, por favor," I said. "My little money is for my world trip for the disabled."

He looked at my legs and said, "Oh, I am sorry, senor."

"Senor, estada persona grande," I declared, calling him a "great person." This puffed up his chest, and he was very happy with that answer.

Sagi and Omer didn't pay any bribes either.

Periodically, I had to stop to tighten my front fork tube, usually going another 50 miles or so before the next cigarette break. This day we actually went 91 miles at one time! At a gas station, my front fork tube cap was right out. "If it comes apart at high speed," I think to myself, "it will be curtains for Dave Barr." After the welding job, the lower triple tree no longer clamps the fork tube properly - a most dangerous situation. I'm constantly watching the top cap on the fork tube.

Late in the day we enter Cuidad Bolivar where we locate a cheap hotel, literally crumbling away, and for $2.00 we secured a room that smelled like shit. The walls were crumbling, and moisture from the ceiling dripped down on us. What a dump!

I worked the rest of the afternoon on the motorcycle, and then washed clothes and took a shower. Sagi and Omer went to try and find the Brazilian Consulate; after some discouragement, they learned it was no longer in Cuidad Bolivar as it was supposed to be according to the book we had on South America.

During the evening, I spoke as best I could to the owners of the hotel about some of the things we had seen along the road. Of course, the dictionary was in constant use since they spoke little English, and I spoke less Spanish. They told me the carnival period had started for the Brazilians living in Cuidad Bolivar.

"I wonder if the Brazilian Embassy (now located in Puerto Ordez) will be closed these next few days," I thought to myself. "I certainly hope not!"

The next morning we headed for Puerto Ordez, which was the prettiest city I saw anywhere in South America, all the way down to Rio de Janeiro. It was amazingly clean, with well kept, good roads and very modern buildings. They had waterfalls next to the road, and a huge river that flowed out to the ocean. What a refreshing change of scenery. The people were very friendly as well. When we located the Brazilian Consulate, our worst fears were realized - it was closed for another two days for the carnival holiday.

Needing a place to spend the next few nights, we located a big open field outside of town with a lot of scrub brush, a couple of miles off the main highway. We spent the rest of the afternoon there, and all the next day relaxing, talking about various things, and doing a bit of work on the motorcycles.

Unplanned Breakage

After carnival, we rode back to the Brazilian Embassy in Puerto Ordez. As I was pushing my motorcycle into a parking space, my right foot broke in half and my ankle came apart. "What is going on?" I thought, beginning to think that anything that could go wrong would go wrong. In all my trip planning, my right foot breaking and my ankle coming apart were never really anticipated. I carried extra straps just in case I broke a strap on the belt that holds my leg on, but the thought of the foot being broken off was something that hadn't even occurred to me!

I asked around, trying to find a place in town where they had orthotics and prosthetics. Finally, I found a man who made artificial limbs. When I explained my situation to him, he seemed very disinterested, and told me, "I don't have any spare feet. I suppose I can order you one, but it will be very expensive."

That put me off right there.

As I stood outside this man's shop, trying to figure out what to do, a lady who had overhead my conversation with Sagi and Omer came up to us and said, "There's a welding shop down the street and around the corner. Perhaps you can go there and maybe they can do something."

That sounded like a good idea.

While looking for the welding shop, I was coming out of a parking area and through a dip when suddenly I had to make a stop in the middle of the dip. The dip was a drain for water, and my feet couldn't touch the ground. As the motorcycle leaned too far to the left, down it went. There were a couple of young fellows standing there cackling about the whole thing; I really got upset. My adrenaline kicked in, and I took that fully loaded motorcycle and picked it up, moved it, and put the kick stand down; to this day, I can't believe I did it! I then headed towards these two young assholes and they took off running, not wanting anything to do with this crazy man who has no right foot and walks cockeyed since one leg is about three inches out of balance. As I made progress towards them, they made even faster progress away from me. I didn't catch them, and that's probably just as well. I wanted to ring their necks. At that moment, I felt like the hunch back of Notre Dame - gone out of control.

I finally located the welding shop in a back alley. I tried to explain what I needed, but they just couldn't conceive of what I was trying to explain. Naturally, they spoke no English. Finally, they told me to sit down and motioned for me to wait. While waiting, they served me tea and some fresh baked bread.

After about half an hour, a fellow named Richard Brant shows up, and he speaks English. I told him my problem, to which he said, "Perhaps we can figure something out." He then spoke to the welders, and they nodded their heads and started taking some measurements.

In the end, they took a piece of pipe, welded it to a flat plate with half an inch of metal sticking down from each end of the plate, comprising the toe and the heal of my "foot." On top of the piece of pipe they welded the bottom of the ankle joint, then bolted it on to the leg.

Presto, I had a steel foot weighing about five pounds!

Though it was ugly, it proved to be more practical in gravel, sand, mud, and dirt than a regular rubber foot. It could dig in and get traction where my other foot could not. Not to mention - this thing will never break! To top off this adventure, the welders would take no money for all their help.

Armed with my new foot, I went back to the Brazilian Embassy where Sagi and Omer were completing the process of securing their visas. We left there during the rush hour, and at one point Sagi ran into Omer. Omer had to make a quick stop and Sagi hit him. Luckily enough, there was no damage done to men or motorcycles. They hollered and shouted at each other as Israelis will do, but without any venom. Once the shouting match was over, we were on our way again.

A little farther out of town, Sagi was looking to one side when a bus made a sudden stop. He just missed rear-ending him. We all held our breath when this was happening and thanked our lucky stars - and God.

About 15 miles out of town we spotted a rock quarry in the distance. We rode back into the quarry where we couldn't be seen and made camp for the night. As we talked that night, Omer told me he planned to farm in the Moshav, just like his father. Sagi said, "I want to be a veterinary doctor, but I'm worried about passing entrance exams at Hebrew University in Jerusalem."

The following day, roads are rough, but very negotiable at 50 miles per hour. We road in mountainous areas and beautiful rain forests that leads to a strikingly mighty plateau that stretched for miles and miles; at the far side of this majestic plateau we saw a lovely river.

Turning onto a dirt road, I hit a dip and was thrown off of the motorcycle. Sagi and Omer came up behind and we uprighted the bike in no time. We decided to stop at a campsite which - believe it or not - had a thatch roof on it.

The Unbelievable Flat Tire Tale

At the camp, Sagi discovers he has a rear flat tire, and his tire-changing tools left something to be desired. We took out my tire tools and broke the tire down, getting the tube out and fixing it, then putting it back together. When he started to use his compressor, the air line burst; it was a little foot operated piece of junk. So, we used my electric compressor to get the tire up on the bead, but we could never get the bead to seat (it was good enough so we could ride on it).

We took a ride down to the river with me on the back of Sagi's bike. When we went through a sand pit, Sagi hesitated on the throttle and both of us were launched in the air at about 20 miles an hour. Fortunately, it was soft sand, so we just had a good laugh about it. Down at the river they jumped into the stream, and I took my legs off and climbed on the rocks to take a very welcome bath - our first in four days!

The next morning we hit a police check outside of Santa Elena that held us up for a half hour. In Santa Elena, we secured provisions and then headed for the border. Just outside of Santa Elena, again we were pulled over by the police for about 25 minutes. They all wanted pictures with us.

Our next stop was border Customs and Immigration where they wanted some permit that we didn't have. We had no idea what it was that we should have secured back at the border when we entered from Columbia, but they acted like it was very important. For a moment, we were not sure whether we would be allowed to pass. Finally, they let us move on. Perhaps they too were looking for bribes, and when they determined none were forthcoming, they let us pass. Who knows? One thing for sure - we were all sick of the Venezuelan police.

At the Brazilian border we were cleared quite quickly, with no hassle.

In Brazil, a new set of problems start. At the border, the pavement stops and you start "the Trans Amazons," 800 miles (1300 km) of dirt, rock, corrugations, mud, and holes down to Manaus, on the bank of the Rio Negro River. This ride was to be absolutely diabolical! It would take us six days to get to Manaus, with trials and tribulations all along the way.

The road runs directly south, and it wasn't 2 miles out of the border town when we hit powdered dirt. Omer's dust blinded me and Sagi. How do you see through a blanket of powdered dirt? It was worse than the densest fog you can imagine, except that it stuck to our sweaty faces and wet clothes.

After a long patch of winding road and coming down steep grades, we finally hit hard dirt and were able to carry on at about 40 miles per hour. We suddenly noticed that Sagi was missing, and stopped. About ten minutes later, he comes down the road, telling us he had "fallen off my bike in the dust."

We decided to slow down to 35 miles per hour.

That didn't last very long. Once we got moving, Sagi and I were back up to 50 miles per hour since the road turned good for about 5 miles. I glanced back in my mirror and saw both men stopped. Riding back, I discover Sagi again had a flat rear tire. Repeat last tire patching procedure. After about fifteen more miles, Sagi had yet another flat. One of the older patches had come off.

Since it was getting late, we decided to camp and fix the tire the next morning. But Sagi was beside himself. "Leave it 'til tomorrow," we told him, but Sagi was a stubborn ass. He insisted on fixing it that night, and we helped him where we could.

We put more air into Sagi's tire from my compressor, planning to locate a large compressor in the village in the morning.

That night our dinner conversation focused on the lousy, difficult day with the police authorities and bad roads. Now, we were heading for Manaus with over 700 miles of surprises ahead of us.

No relief the next day. Rain greeted us in the early morning, so we knew the dusty road would now be converted to mud and rock. Before going very far, we stopped at a village where we located a commercial compressor to put air into Sagi's rear tire, getting the bead to seat.

After about four miles, Sagi now has a front flat! When we inspected the damage, we discovered the tire itself had a chunk missing, so he had to replace the tire with the spare he was carrying. After about another five miles, the front tire goes flat again, and Sagi is thrown off of the motorcycle.

By now, Sagi's patience has vanished; it has become a depressing situation for all of us. No matter what happens, the idea to quit or to leave a rider behind never comes into our heads. Sagi and Omer have been together most of their lives on the Moshov, and for myself, I was not going on without them.

This was to be a wise decision on my part.

In examining the flat, we decide the patch came off because of the rain. Now, the rain had stopped, so we dried it out and patched it properly.

We rode another six miles and I had to stop - a bolt had come out of one of my front disk brake calipers. I replaced the bolt, and we were on the way again.

Next, we stop because a nut had come undone on another caliper bolt and it had come out. This time we went back and located the bolt that Sagi had seen bouncing a long the road. We secured it this time - with loctite.

The motorcycles were complaining about the horrendous roads the only way they could - by breaking. These horribly rough roads were full of washboards, caked mud fallen from trucks, rocks, and huge potholes that were bone jarring. We eventually came into the miserable town of Boa Vista meaning "good view" (the name was the only good thing about it). We located a welding shop where repairs were done on the front end of my motorcycle.

We asked directions whenever we could.

"Senor, por favor, direction, Manaus."

"Si, si, esta direction," they answered, pointing down the road. Before we knew it, we were out of Boa Vista.

The weather was cloudy and overcast, and to our detriment, we never checked the compass. We carried on through the afternoon, and all of us fell at least once in mud. In the late afternoon, we located a place to set up camp.

I told Sagi and Omer, "Hey fellows don't worry about rain. I feel like it will be a dry night." They took my advice and didn't bother to put up a tent.

About 23:00 it starts pissing rain down on us. Well, I opened my big mouth didn't I? By the time we scrambled to get our tents up, our bodies, sleeping bags, and gear were all soaked!

Usually I'm up about 05:30, finish my diary, then listen to the sounds of the morning, watching the day turn from gray dawn to sunshine. It is a beautiful, peaceful time to mentally prepare for the trials and tribulations inevitably ahead during the day. About 06:30, Sagi and Omer start their usual argument over coffee. We eat a basic breakfast of beans or peanut butter on bread. Hey, this is an adventure, not a party!!

On this particular morning, Sagi looks down and starts hollering, "Ugh." He has another flat tire! He's dancing around, hopping mad; the rear tire had gone flat overnight. Repeat the same procedure. By now, we are professional tire changers. "I'm just glad it's not my Harley having all these flats," I think to myself.

Just barely out of the camping site, I hit a bad section of muddy road and go down. Omer jumps off his machine, and between the two of us we get mine up and we're on our way. This day has started out to be a good one!

We ride for an hour, coming into the small village of Bonfin, looking for a compressor to get the bead to seat down on Sagi's rear wheel. We asked directions here and there, and finally find a compressor; after about fifteen minutes of trying, we get the thing to seat.

"Senor, direction Manaus quando kilometers la gasolina?" "In the direction of Manaus, senor, how many kilometers do we have to go before we come to gasoline?"

We had seen no gasoline in the village.

"Manaus, Senor?" he replied.

"Si, Manaus" I responded.

"Manaus," he says again, backing away from me with a funny, bewildered look in his eye.

"Si, Manaus, Manaus!" I thought, "What is this guy, a simpleton?"

Then, very humbly, he says, "Senor, you are on the Guinea border."

My jaw dropped open. "Guinea?"

"Si, senor, Guinea. You are on the Guinea border."

By now, Sagi and Omer sense something is not right. "What's the problem, Dave?" they ask. I then told them in Hebrew what the man said. They looked at each other, and then at me, and all at once our morale dropped lower than whale shit in the ocean. This fellow informed us we now had to go backwards 80 miles (130 kilometers) to Boa Vista, then go south. There was no other road to Manaus except out of Boa Vista. Boa Vista had 3 entrances or exits, and apparently we had come in one and went out the wrong one.

The three "geniuses" of world travel bid farewell to this fellow and started the ride back, slip-siding through mud, banging over the holes and rocks. We had traveled 160 miles (260 kilometers) for absolutely nothing, and wasted a full day.

In Boa Vista, we needed gasoline but nothing was open. Finally, a truck driver said "There's a petrol station down the road." When we seemed confused as to his directions, he said, "Follow me." We followed his big truck to an open gas station and fueled up. At the station, we met a fellow who said, "I'll show you how to get out of town." We followed him to just south of Boa Vista where we encountered a nice, paved road which went on for some 60 miles (100 kilometers), all the way to the next town. Manaus was still 600 miles away.

After about 20 miles (35 km), **Sagi had another flat rear tire - number eight!** By now he is numb, wandering around, his hands on his head pulling his hair, wondering "What's next?" How well I know the feeling.

THE WORLD

Regular tire drill. Repair tire. Inflate tire. Look for compressor to seat the bead.

We found a little place by a gentle stream to stop that evening. During the night, I heard something outside of my tent. As I looked out, there was a dog making himself comfortable on my rain suit. He looked at me as if to say, "This is my bed for the night," and laid down, falling asleep.

In the morning, I looked at the dog, he looked at me, scratched a flea and walked off. "Good morning, thank you, and good-bye."

Zaire Re-visited, Front Forks Re-welded

That morning, we were not able to shift out of second gear as we rode on the mud, holes, rocks, and ruts - much like Zaire. I came off the motorcycle, and was glad Sagi and Omer were there to help pick it up. There were long stretches under construction, so in the rain these areas were just mud. Trucks came down through these areas extra fast, hoping the momentum would carry them through. We tried to stay out of their way, but still had a few very close calls.

At Carcaro, we were able to find bread - no kidding! This was the first we'd seen in Brazil.

My rear exhaust is smoking... a big worry.

Ten miles down the road we come to a river where we have to wait a few minutes for a barge. Once across, we moved south when I felt the front end wobbling very badly; the weld on the lower triple tree has broken again. We continue another 6 miles, and it is everything I can do to hold onto this thing, even barely creeping along at 10 miles an hour. I appreciated Sagi and Omer waiting for me as they could have moved along much faster on their purpose-built motorcycles.

I saw some huts off in the rain forest and rode up a little mud road into a compound. As I climbed off the motorcycle, a leopard suddenly appears, walking in my direction. My eyes must have been as big as saucers as I looked at this thing. A man runs off the porch, grabs the leopard, says something to it, then grabs a chain and put a leash around his neck, gently coaxing it back to the porch.

In Portuguese, he tells me, "I let the cat go free at night. He takes care of any Indians around here who try to steal from me." A real watch cat.

I showed the man my lower triple tree on the front forks, and he replied, "No problems, senor." We wheeled the motorcycle over to a welding shack, obviously some type of maintenance station for something. He then cut away all the old weld and re-welded it, then welded plate steel around the thing in a box on the sides of the new weld to make it strong. He worked about 2 hours, yet I had to force money on him. He finally accepted the equivalent of $7.00 - money well spent. It didn't break again.

In the late afternoon, when we were all down on reserve, we finally found gasoline at $2.55 a gallon; it had that old smell of paraffin in it such as is used in Africa. It was dispensed out of jerry cans.

While getting gas, I noticed my rear exhaust pipe was wet, and that oil was coming through the exhaust. This really worried me, as it indicated a bad rear cylinder. My heart just sunk down to my knees. What now?

That wasn't all. Later, my rear brake pedal broke off. I managed to retrieve the pedal, but I had to carry on without any rear brakes because my foot is no longer sitting in the stirrup. My unfeeling foot is constantly slipping off the peg, just to add to my overall discomfort and feeling of gloom. Is there just no end to the problems?

That night, we locate a camp where we can't be easily seen from the road. We hide all our valuables after dark in the bushes, since we've heard many stories about bandits on this road, and trouble with Indians. Though we had a bit of security in our numbers, we didn't want to take any unnecessary chances.

One time when we were moving along, we stopped to check where we were by asking an Indian who was walking along the road. I didn't get two words out of my mouth when the guy breaks into a run, holding his bow and arrow in one hand and a blow gun in the other, his little ass working back and forth with a leather sarong holding his genitals, flapping in the breeze. Maybe he was related to the sugar cane cutter in Guatemala.

We came to a small truck stop where the police had a road block up, saying "You men cannot pass." The truck stop didn't look inviting at all, and neither did the people. "The bridge is down and the road has washed out," we were told, so Sagi and Omer cooked up a story.

"Listen, Dave, go show them your legs. Tell them that if we have to wait, we want to go down to the river and wash."

I went over to the policeman and started to talk him as he looked down at my legs. I lifted up my pant legs and said, "Por favor, senor" and made a gesture of wanting to wash down at the river ("Rio" in Portuguese). He nodded, lifting up the gate. We rode about another 10 miles (16 km) until we came to a big line of trucks that had been parked there for a couple of days, the drivers sitting in groups playing cards, cooking, and chatting.

At the construction area we saw them building a make-shift bridge. Fortunately, they immediately waived us across. We headed down the river bank that had been gorged out, me slip-sliding along. I hit the bridge at about 15 miles per hour and the motorcycle straightened out, barely managing to go up and over the bridge, then slide down the other side. I gave it the throttle and managed to get up on top with the rear wheel fishtailing around. How I made it, I do not know. Everybody was standing up on top watching this incredible performance, hollering, shouting, and raising their hands, waiving. I felt like the king of the mountain as we continued down the road, knowing it was not great skill but shear luck that I didn't come off the motorcycle and make an ass of myself.

The bridges we pass in this section of the Amazon display signs saying "Cholera." Obviously, they mean "Don't drink the water." In one mud area, the motorcycle turned 180 degrees with me still on it before we both went down. Sagi and Omer were both laughing their heads off; "I'm glad they still have their sense of humor," I think. My own sense of humor is rapidly evaporating.

March 10, 1992: We cross the equator in the rain and mud. I came off the bike again at about 15 miles per hour, but it still hurt plenty.

Armed Amazon Indians and Mud Fights

We set up our camp, and Sagi and Omer said "We're going to walk down and bring back water from the stream we just crossed." They leave, and as I am sitting alone, out of the jungle comes an Indian. He looks at me and I look at him, both of us surprised. I try to explain to him in broken Portuguese, "We just want to spend night here. Leave in morning." Then, I offered to shake his hand.

Picture this. The fellow is staring at me, wearing just a loin cloth, armed with a bow and arrow, a blow gun, and a shotgun over his back. He nods his head, we shake hands, and he walks right off back into the jungle - never to be seen again. When I told Sagi and Omer about the incident, their eyes grew wide, them thinking that perhaps by tomorrow our heads would be impaled on stakes.

"I don't think there's anything to worry about," I told them.

"Yeah, like we didn't have to worry about rain the other night!" they replied.

The next morning, the day started out with me hitting a mud slick and going down at about 15 miles an hour again. I broke a belt holding on my right leg, and I tore a hole in the primary of the motorcycle. I changed the belt on my right leg, then opened up the primary. It was full of rocks and mud that had done damage to the belt.

After only a few more miles, I hit mud again. This unique mud was red in color, and had grit and a bit of gravel under it. You could get traction, but the mud would be thrown all over. The big problem was glasses getting muddy and blinding our vision. Sometimes, we get our speed up to 30 miles per hour and then, All of the sudden, the mud would have no support underneath it, and down we'd go.

Once, at about 25 miles per hour, the motorcycle threw me over to the right and then it landed on me; the axle bolt knocked a hole in the top of my helmet. When the motorcycle hit me, I had my hands clinched so my fingers wouldn't get caught in the chain or spokes. The motor raced and roared, blowing smoke. Then it finally died. Fortunately, nothing broke inside the engine.

Another time that day, I fell and the motorcycle landed on me again. By this time, I was pretty bruised, but felt fortunate that no major damage had been done to man or machine. I continued to practice the mind set I maintained in Africa: "As long as its not broken and I'm not broken, we'll just carry on."

March 10, 1992: We crossed the equator - my second crossing (only heading south this time).

Later that day I went down again and broke part of my clutch lever. Although it is now very short, it is still serviceable, so I carry on. In another fall, I broke the brake mount for the front brake; it was hanging loose. Luckily, we had some duct tape and were able to tape it up enough to hold.

We continued on. After another fall, my oil tank mounting rubbers were broken; I stuffed a piece of rubber inner tube under the oil tank. The mounting rubber grommets on the battery side also broke, so I replaced them with the last of my rubber mounts.

Ushuaia. Most Southern city in the World.
May 21, 1992 Argentina, Tierra Del Fuego

Chapter Twenty-Four

Deteriorating Bikes and Dispositions

"Get to Manaus" - that's the thought that drives us.

The sun is out and very, very hot.

At one point, I was negotiating a rutted area when a truck appears behind me. I happened to look over my shoulder and spot him coming at me at about 30 miles an hour faster than I was going. "What does this idiot intend to do?" I wonder. "It looks like he's going to hit me."

I managed to speed up enough to get out to a little wider area, then turn into the embankment. Luckily, it was mud so nothing was damaged. I was once again thrown off the motorcycle while shithead continued on down the road.

My right front fork tube brakes open, and it takes all three of us to get it back together. About 3 miles later, it breaks again. The threads are stripped - a pretty grim scenario. We manage to get it back in.

Now, a big bus comes barreling up at us, wildly honking his horn. There is a downed tree across the road, and he can't get around us without hitting some of the branches. The three of us stood our ground, saying, "Fuck off. Go around us."

The people in this area do not seem to be very nice.

Once we got the thing back together, I rode in first gear for miles and miles until we hit blessed pavement once again just as we entered the city of Manaus on the bank of the Rio Negro River. What a wonderful place to finally be!

We ask directions to a hotel that's supposed to have a campground. Once we arrive, we learn there's no campground; it's a tourist trap, very expensive. We met a young fellow named Jay who told us, "I can take you to a campground."

We followed Jay across town to another place. I liked the looks of it, but Sagi and Omer didn't. So Jay says, "Come to my house."

We decide to follow him back across Manaus, trusting our "good feelings" about this young fellow. We arrived at a shabby little apartment building, not a "favella" (ghetto), but very close to it. By U.S. standards, Jay's apartment block was a tenement built in a ghetto.

Sagi and Omer's motorcycles went up on the landing next to Jay's apartment. "We will use the laundry room for yours," he tells me. We unloaded the motorcycle and let it sit in the street until it was time to close the building. Other tenants in the building would help keep an eye on it. There was a strong community spirit in this very poor neighborhood.

The next thing was a shower! We hadn't encountered any bathing facilities in the Trans Amazonas. After six days in the heat and mud without a shower, even our "cold water" shower was wonderful!

Jay spoke very little English, but we tried to communicate with the dictionary. We somehow got along, and immensely appreciated his invaluable help.

The next day he took me over to a motorcycle shop where they said, "Yes, you can work on your motorcycle here." They allowed me to repair numerous little problems, and they welded my rear brake pedal back on for me. I put the last of my rubber mountings on the battery box, patched up the primary, repaired the starter (I'd been using a screwdriver on the solenoid terminals since the starter button burned out).

Next, I took the motorcycle to a car wash with a power washer, and with the help of a Brazilian boy, spent an hour washing it down and cleaning it up. With a clean motorcycle, repaired and running better, especially after I changed the rear spark plug, I went back to Jay's house. I know the bike will continue to deteriorate, but I hope to make it at least to Bahia, Salvador, where I have friends I met in South Africa.

The following day Jay took us to the docks where we negotiated prices for ourselves and the motorcycles to be floated down the Amazon River to Belém on the Atlantic coast, directly east. Without Jay's help, we certainly would have paid more. He gave us a good recommendation, so the people in charge gave us very reasonable prices.

To thank him, we took Jay out to a much-deserved dinner. He was a very lovable fellow, not a real macho guy, very easy to get along with.

That night on television they were showing a variety show where the women were stripping down to their panties. If they failed to answer a question correctly, off came an article of clothing. These women were flashing their breasts. It was extremely entertaining to watch, far better than "The Price is Right.".

Sleeping at Jay's house was difficult. There was a dog who barked all night, and roosters who would start to crow about 02:00 in the morning. And yes, the couch I slept on was full of fleas and cockroaches. Not luxury living, but it was the thought that counted. Jay freely opened his door to us and just couldn't do enough to help.

The Battle of Boats Continues

We were scheduled to ship in the afternoon of the next day. So after gathering all our things together, we said good-bye to the residents of the tenement building. They were all waiving; some shook our hands.

Jay led us down to the port. Along the way, the houses were built on stilts over the river, using it as their personal sewer. It stank of pollution and surely was a breeding ground for disease. These people live in conditions that are hard to imagine for those of us in Western nations.

The motorcycles were loaded onto the ship by rope (not a rope hoist). The crew threw rope over the guide rails of the upper stories of the boat, then let it down into the boat. That method worked fine for the Yamahas, but a fully loaded Harley Davidson was a bit difficult. The two guys holding the rope on the other side nearly ended up flying up over the rail themselves.

Once on board, they were rolled to the back of the ship, right over the top of the engine room. Boards with open gaps in them were all that separated us from the engine room below. This was our home for the next two days. With the engines running underneath us, it was virtually impossible to carry on a conversation.

As people loaded onto the boat, we said good-bye to our friend and benefactor, Jay. We gave him a big hug; he had a tear in his eye. We couldn't help feeling compassion in our heart. We were going on to our future, and he was to remain forever condemned to a very small life in Manaus, his dreams never realized. My heart went out to him.

The boat full of people looked like a colored jungle with all the hammocks hanging from the ceiling; they made it very difficult to walk about. Hammocks and wall to wall people, plus each traveler's personal possessions are on the deck. With only a steel foot for traction, I slipped all over the place.

I went up on the bow to get away from the hammering of the engine. As the boat put out into the Rio Negro River with black water, the roar from the engines was deafening! For the first few hours we took shifts watching over the motorcycles. Finally, Sagi and Omer ended up in the back, and told me, "If you want to sleep up front on the bow, go ahead." I grabbed my sleeping bag and tarp and went up to the bow and tried to relax. In the middle of the evening I got up and looked over the bow. I could see we were moving from dark water into muddy brown water. The Rio Negro was flowing into the Amazon River! What an amazing thing! I would have loved to have seen this in the daytime.

The next morning I went to relieve Sagi and Omer so they could go up forward for a while. When the bell rang for breakfast, we agreed to go in relays. A line formed that was quite long for the one scoop of sugared hominy they put in your bowl, plus coffee. You sit down, eat, get up and make room for the next group of people. This goes on until everybody is fed.

Once I saw them drag a side of beef down a dock where we had stopped to let passengers off. Here comes the crew dragging this side of beef onto the deck of the ship and to the back where they hang it up. When they got out into the river where the water was a little cleaner, they threw water all over it, then put a tub underneath it and cut pieces of meat off, then filled the tub with beans, rice, and cooked all this up. When the dinner bell rings, it says to me, "Come and get it before we throw it out." All the boat water comes from the river, and all the boat toilets empty into the river. There's nothing to flush - it just goes back into the river.

Are you getting hungry?

Not surprisingly, Omer was sick by this time, his stomach bothering him; he was running a fever. All of our heads hurt from the engine noise.

At times on the journey, the Amazon was so wide we couldn't see either shore! I've crossed the Mississippi, the Limpopo, the Zambezi River, and the Orange River, but I've never seen anything that even in a small way compares with the mighty Amazon. There were swells on that river that felt like being on the ocean.

A thief was caught on the boat, and justice was rapidly served. He was beaten, then taken to the forward part of the ship and locked into one of the storage rooms with all his gear until we put into port.

That evening, I was thinking, "I wonder how much different this trip would have been had I not decided to ride a Harley Davidson." My old, already beaten up Harley simply was not the best choice to take on rough roads for 800 miles at a time. A specific-purpose bike would have been much easier, and probably would have eliminated 95% of my problems.

Then I reflected back on my reasons I was doing this trip - for people with disabilities who were traveling their own, hard road. The bastard motorcycle just made my hard road harder.

At one port, we took on a dog that was tied up near to where we were. The poor, miserable mutt was constantly barking. Yap, yap, yap, yap, yap, yap, all day and all night. Fortunately, he was barely audible over the engines, but he was still very irritating.

My luck with boats continues.

We put in at Santurm where we watched everybody else disembark and walk to another ship that was between us and the dock. When everybody was off, a man said, "Senor, you are supposed to go to this other ship." We hurriedly grabbed our gear, loaded the motorcycles, and rolled them over to the side of the other ship. They had to be lifted up and over by hand!

After everything was stored on the other ship, we had fifteen crewmen sticking out their hands. Sagi and Omer told them "get lost." At times, they are a couple of unfeeling bastards.

Once we were transferred to the other ship and the motorcycles were latched down, we found a small place for the three of us right up against a bulkhead towards the front of the ship, away from the engines! After two days of those motors, our ears would be ringing for a week.

The best part of the new boat - no dog!

The worst part about this trip is never quite understanding what is going on. Just when we think we've got something figured out, we discover we don't. For example, when we asked if we only took one boat down the river, they said, "Si, Si." Of course, that wasn't right, so we almost missed the other ship. Now, our new ship puts out of the little port and heads down the river. There was much shouting and excitement as the ship pulls away.

A fellow named Louis appears on the scene, and he becomes our mouth piece. Sagi and Omer don't have too much desire to fraternize with the Brazilians, so they more or less keep to themselves, but I like to learn about people - what they think, what they do, etc. Louis and I joined up and everywhere I went he went. He constantly asked me questions in his broken English. Between his English and the dictionary, we were actually able to communicate. He often would help translate for the crowds of people the best he could. When stuck for a word, he would go to the dictionary, never trying to guess.

I kept slipping around on deck because of my steel foot. Eventually I put a boot on over it, which made the right leg too long, and far more difficult to walk because I had to lift my hip farther to swing the right leg.

Louis was also a bit of a guitarist. At night, people would gather around and sing Brazilian songs; sometimes they'd try an American one. After about an hour, one of the crew would usually put an end to it so he and others could climb in their hammocks and go to sleep. "No more music," he would say, and that was that. There's always a spoil sport at every party.

The swell was going inland, yet the current was flowing out - incredible.

We started into a series of channels (massive deltas). Lord knows how they navigated through the night; we did get stuck on a sandbar once for about ten minutes.

"Boat beggars" would paddle out to us in their little canoes, enticing passengers to throw things down to them. The object of this game was to catch whatever was thrown without falling into the water. Anything can be thrown. A can of beans, a bottle of beer; if it hits a beggar on the head and crowns him, with the possible result of drowning, that doesn't matter. The game is to try and get whatever you throw into the boat. In many cases they succeeded. Then, everybody would pat the thrower on the back, cheer, and maybe hand him a bottle of beer as the hero of the moment. After the circus, the boat beggars left with their new loot.

Little houses, usually on stilts, would come right down to the river. I was amazed to see television antennas on the roofs of these primitive huts. Of course, we saw many other river boats and steamers plying up and down the river, along with barges of various sizes and types being pushed by a big tug boat. We saw fisherman eking out a living out of the river.

In the middle of the night, if I wanted to have a piss, it meant putting my legs on to navigate through the maze of junk and hammocks to the back of the boat and the toilets. "I'll be glad," I think to myself, "when we get to Belém and can get on the road again."

Land Ho!

The following morning Belém came into sight. We knew we were close when the dwellings along the river became more numerous, and traffic along the river increased. We could see the mouth of the Delta, and the Atlantic Ocean beyond. **We had now crossed from the Pacific side in Panama around from the Caribbean all the way to the Atlantic.** It felt fantastic to see the different oceans in the world.

When we docked, the motorcycles were lifted over onto the dock. When we started to ride out the gate, a man said "No, you can't go. You need a piece of paper." He wrote down a building number for us, and we had to go back and find that building number.

"You need to have an inspector look at the motorcycles," we were told.

He wasn't in. After about an hour, he shows up and looks at the motorcycles, signing the papers. Now, he wants 7300 cruzeros - about $7.00. We all went nuts. "What is this for?" we shout. "We've already gone through customs."

Had I been on my own, I probably would have avoided the argument and paid the price. But not Sagi and Omer. They put up an argument. In the end, the inspector settled on half that amount, and we paid it. We call it "collective bargaining with the Civil Service."

In Belém, we ran around in circles trying to find our way out of town. When we finally hit the open road, it greeted us with plenty of potholes. In some stretches, we got our speed up, then a sudden burst of big potholes would appear for a stretch a 100 meters or more. We had to slow down and go around them whenever possible with great care.

Rain also greeted us on our first day back on the road.

In the latter part of the afternoon, we came to a farm house, looking for a place to camp that would be out of sight. A fellow pulled up in a vehicle and asked, "What are you doing."

"We are looking for a place to sleep," we answered in broken Portuguese.

"Come with me," he said. I have a service station and you can sleep in the open space next to it."

We followed him down the road a few more miles, parking the motorcycles under a big tree next to a pig pen! Of course, we attracted the usual crowd of onlookers who stood and gawked at us.

"Beat it," the service station owner told them. We very much appreciated that.

I started working on the motorcycle again, changing the points and condenser; the points were all burned up from another bad condenser. The oil is down again, yet I'd put in two quarts (2 liters) at Belém. I went over to the service station and got another liter of oil; it looks as though I'm using a liter (quart) every 100 miles - a very, very bad ratio. The rear exhaust is wet with oil, a sign the motor is failing. None of this does much for my dwindling peace of mind.

The following day we battled bad roads. When I say "bad roads," I mean HUGE systems of potholes - sometimes the pavement is gone for 200 meters. We move slowly but steadily, stopping every 50 miles for Sagi and Omer's cigarette break, and every 100 miles to fuel up and for me put in another quart (liter) of oil.

That evening at camp, Sagi and Omer went down the road to find a place to fill up all of our water bottles. While they were gone, three Indians came down to our camp, dressed in rags. I tried to tell them what we were doing, but I don't know how much they understood. They were friendly enough; after a few minutes, we shook hands and they were on their way.

This day we had gone 280 miles; at least we were covering ground! That night, Omer and Sagi were talking about selling their motorcycles and going home (they were homesick). Sagi said, "I might go back via New York and work for a couple of months before I take my entrance exams to the University in Jerusalem."

We spoke that night about the army reserve. "I know I'll be called up for a period of time in the reserves when I return to Israel, especially with the problems on the West Bank. Israel is much like our trip - the problems never seem to end."

I readily identified with Sagi's comments. When I served in the Israeli Army, we patrolled in the West Bank, and found it to be one of the most hateful places in the entire world!

The Legless Wonder Rides the Mechanical Mess

The next morning at about 04:00 I awake to the smell of gasoline. I scoot over to the motorcycle, and sure enough, the carburetor is leaking gas. "I had shut the fuel off," I think to myself, "so there must be a bit of debris in the fuel valve." I jiggled that valve and it stopped.

As we headed down the road, late in the morning we come to Teresina where we needed to change travelers checks and purchase oil. At the service station, a crowd gathered around me - more than 80 people, and growing... flowing into the street! When I motioned that I needed to go, the crowd motioned back that I stay, not with malice, but they were just interested in this strange looking man and his motorcycle. My main concern was Sagi and Omer coming back and not seeing me, since I was now hidden in this massive crowd.

After about fifteen minutes, a television crew pulls up to do a short interview. I couldn't believe it! Somebody had called the local television station and probably said, "There's a funny looking foreigner here riding a funny looking motorcycle - you've got to see this."

After the interview, I moved to a service station across the street, with much of the same crowd following after me. I waited almost an hour, and began to think that Sagi and Omer missed seeing me, and decided to push off on their own. "That would be a terrible way to end our relationship," I thought.

Luckily, they did show up, and said, "We've been all around the city trying to find a bank who will change traveler's checks. We just wanted to come by and let you know not to worry." Then, off they went again.

Another hour went by of standing in this tremendous heat, staring at faces staring at me. This crowd was getting on my nerve!

Finally, Sagi and Omer return and we got the hell out of Dodge city. "Oh, how nice it was to be moving, even on the horrible messed up roads!"

We moved south about another 150 miles through the rest of the afternoon and found a service station with a big, open field where we put up our tents. The owner of the service station did not seem to mind. We bought a few provisions and actually found some bread there. I pulled out the rear spark plug - it was all fouled, and gave it to a young fellow as a sample. He went to get another spark plug for me. My brand new points are burned, a sign the condenser is out yet again, and needs to be replaced. Of course, my motorcycle has used about three quarts (liters) of oil during the day. Since we had traveled about 250 miles, it is now burning more than a quart of oil every 100 miles.

The following morning the battery is dead. Good morning. What next? We pushed the loaded motorcycle over to the service station area and jump start the motorcycle. We rode about 50 miles (80 km), and the machine is cutting out every now and again. Eventually, it won't run at all because the battery is that dead.

In the next town, I tried to locate a charger while Omer and Sagi took care of some other business. As I went from store to store, I had to push the motorcycle.

260

Once again, a crowd gathered and followed me everywhere. When I finally did find a battery shop, my stumps were aching from having to push the motorcycle in the heat. The owner told me to "bring the bike in the shop," so we pushed it up a slight ramp, then put it on charge. The crowd comes into the shop right behind me. I thought to myself, "Please tell these people to just go away and leave me alone."

After an hour, the battery was up enough for me to go. But, instead of wasting energy on the electric starter, Sagi came over and kick started the motorcycle. It started right up. Using this method, we could perhaps get a couple of days out of a battery charge.

On we go down the road, hitting police military or federal highway police checks regularly. They were polite, and neat in appearance, with very professional attitudes. We were never asked for a bribe, and always put on our way quite quickly.

The lambodas have returned! We go through towns and can't pick up any speed, staying in second gear because of the lambodas. If the town is three or four miles long, we've got to slow right down and go over these things again and again, sometimes every fifteen meters. It is unbelievable! In a town such as Teresina, we might have to go over these lambodas for half an hour getting to the other side. They are often more sharp than curved, and can be painful to go over repeatedly.

The road deteriorates from bad to worse, full of potholes. It is rare to hit a good long stretch of road where there are no serious potholes. During one of these bad stretches, the top cap of my front fork tube popped open again. Sagi and Omer stopped, and it took the three of us to get the spring pressed back down inside the tube.

After a few miles, it pops open again because the threads are striped out. I ride along with this tube being held only by the lower triple tree. Now, this may be a bore to most readers, but anybody who is a motorcycle rider will know what I am talking about. The front end is wobbling all over the place, so I've got to keep it at about ten miles per hour. How I made it to town without the lower, already-welded triple tree breaking again, God only knows.

We opened up the other side fork cap and lift it off, taking the springs out of the front end altogether, removing tension from the top of the fork tube. Then, we put back together the fork tubes, compressed within themselves to their lowest point; It was actually almost on a rake downward.

We move forward again, me with no springs on the front end; it bottoms out all the time! Bang, bang, banging along the road, I especially dread any rough area - it is **bone jarring,** especially on my hands! Plus, the rear shock absorbers are gone, so the back end is just floating along. Every time the rear tire hits the fender, it knocks me off my seat like a bucking horse.

Oh what a wonderful day! The motorcycle is using more than a liter of oil every 100 miles, I don't have any springs in the front end which is ready to fall apart at any moment, there's no rear shock absorbers, and the charging system is gone! "How much longer can I keep going this way? The thing is to just to keep moving on in the right direction. I've had more trouble with this motorcycle in the last ten days than I have had in the past 20 years.

Contrasting Encounters of "Tranquil" Times

We encounter many different attitudes along the road. In one town, Omer wanted to try to call home to Israel on his birthday, but we couldn't find an operating telephone. When we sought assistance, the people we spoke with were very antagonistic.

Yet, 30 miles down the road, when we asked a fuel station if we could use their lot to camp, they responded, "Yes, by all means spend the night here." We see both extremes.

At one camp, the small crowd watching us kept saying, "Cobras, cobras," making like a snake on the ground. "We might have problems if we sleep here," we quickly determined. We were in a dark area, and apparently that's what snakes like. Showing great snake sense, we picked up our tents and moved to a lighted area.

In one crowd, two young girls took a shine to Sagi; one wrote him a note saying, "You are beautiful." "The poor girl," I thought, "she must be on drugs. What about me? I'm the real beauty!"

In the middle of the night, a truck pulled into our camp near the tire service area with a flat tire. He woke the service station owner, and the two of them started hammering and banging, with the sound of an air compressor completing the shrill symphony. So much for a quiet night.

The following morning, the guard on the premises, with an old Winchester rifle slung over his shoulder, said, "Tranquil, si."

"Tranquil your ass," I replied. "This place is more noisy than Grand Central Station!" Well, at least we avoided the snakes. To celebrate Omer's birthday, I bought a cake. Unfortunately, it was crawling with ants. We picked the ants off while singing, "Happy birthday, dear Omer"!

Sagi and I have developed a system for starting. I hold the motorcycle and the throttle, and he holds the handlebars, cranking the machine over manually. It seems to work.

Another joy of the road. If a truck is trying to miss a bunch of potholes, he will veer into your lane and run you off the road. Size makes might!

I know I am holding Sagi and Omer back, and would understand if they said to me, "Dave, we've got to go out on our own." I never heard those words, and deeply appreciated it. We mutually helped each other. We were more than friends - we were a team.

We went through Petrolina, an industrial town, and then on to Feira de Santana. The rain started to come down in torrents. Sagi and Omer wanted to stop; they don't like riding in the rain. We are getting close to Bahia, Salvador, which is our destination, and where I have a couple of friends - Americans I met in South Africa. "When I get there," I think, "I can make arrangements to repair the motorcycle."

Sadly, this will be the last stop for us as a team. We celebrated Omer's birthday again at our last dinner; I wondered if they were also celebrating finally getting rid of me.

I called my friends, Joe and Nancy, and they said, "We'll come out and pick you up." We were about 30 kilometers away from them.

March 21, 1992: the first day of Autumn. The days were longer when we came down south towards the Equator, and shorter when we moved south of the Equator - a good 1,500 to 2,000 miles as the crow flies.

That evening after our celebration dinner, Sagi and Omer decide that when they get to Rio they will sell their motorcycles. Sagi was going to go to New York to work, and Omer was going directly home.

The next morning, about 08:00, Joe and Nancy arrive. What a welcome sight! I had not seen these people for almost eight years from the time they had left South Africa. After our reunion, I introduced them to Sagi and Omer.

Joe insisted that Sagi and Omer join us for a few days at their place, out of the rain. I was very relieved about their offer. I hated to go off to "paradise" and leave these two friends who have been so good to me out on their own. Thanks Joe!

On our way to Joe's house, the rain came down so hard it was difficult to see Joe's pickup. After about 25 kilometers, my motorcycle stalled. We got the jumper cables out in the rain and started it up again. Their place had a step down back garden, and the entire property was walled. There were banana and mango trees. Joe and Nancy had made a tropical paradise for themselves. In the middle of Eden sat a swimming pool, a barbecue, and an open-air patio. The main house was very modern by any standards.

The first order of the day after getting the motorcycle parked was to shower and remove the grime and crud. We had been about eight days without a bath in torrid heat and humidity, sweating all the time. The shower was a luxury beyond compare! Next came a scrumptious meal served by Nancy. I experienced my first feeling of optimism in a long time.

9,000 miles had been traveled from the time I left my Mother standing outside in the snow, in California, on January 14, 1992, to this point in Bahia, Salvador. In the past month alone, with Sagi and Omer, we had covered over 4,000 very difficult miles. That night in bed I thought to myself, in the quiet of this secure, clean room on a bed with sheets, "What's my next step? How will I get the motorcycle repaired and get the adventure back on the road again?"

March 24: The day I say good-bye to Sagi and Omer after they spent two days at Joe and Nancy's. Omer just shook my hand with his helmet on and rode away. Sagi and I embraced and shook hands, but he couldn't look me in the eye. I'm sure there was a tear in his eye. It took everything I had to keep myself from shedding a tear. We had come through so much together; it was a unique relationship reserved for travelers. As Sagi and Omer rode out of the compound, they were gone from my sight forever.

Later, Joe told me they were still looking for a place to get the battery charged. Where in a major city do you get a small motorcycle battery charged? Doesn't seem like a major problem, but it puts me in a foul mood. That night, I think, "I spent $2,500 in Anchorage to get this motor ready for the rest of the trip (no reflection on the Harley dealer there), and here I was with an engine that was crap, and a dead battery with no place to get it charged!"

With Sagi and Omer gone, it just seemed my whole world of machine and men is crashing around me. That night was one of the lowest moments of my entire journey. I never thought about quitting, but believe me, I was depressed.

Joe and Nancy share that their situation is not good at work. They are having considerable trouble with the staff and directors of the company they work for. "We are nearing the end of our contract, and will be moving on in a couple of months." I felt I was putting undo pressure on them during a bad time in their lives.

We can't find a place to get the battery charged, let alone find a place for me to work on my motorcycle. Communication is extremely difficult. My depression grows deeper.

Finally, that night, I get a break during a telephone call from Mrs. Sandy Smith in São Paulo, Brazil [south about 1,000 miles (1,600 kilometers)]. I explained my problem to her, and she said, "Well, let me see what I can do. I'll call you back in a day or so."

The next day Sandy called to tell me about Wilson's Trucking, a company that owed her husband a favor. "Talk to them," she told me, "and see about transporting the motorcycle down there on a truck if you can't find a work shop."

I was not able to locate a work shop in Salvador, but I did eventually find a way to charge the battery. Whoopee!!

To move the motorcycle by truck I needed a permit. Joe's company kindly sent a pickup to the house with a woman driver named Susan who spoke very good English. She took me from place to place until we finally located the office responsible for issuing government invoices to move vehicles. I completed the forms, and was instructed to "come back this afternoon."

People in Salvador were constantly giving each other the finger and shouting insults. They seemed like a very surly lot.

That afternoon, I received my papers.

The following day, I moved the motorcycle and myself. Joe managed to get me a plane ticket to São Paulo, so I called Sandy Smith and told her, "The motorcycle will be arriving in four to seven days."

By now, I had been about nine days with Joe and Nancy. With my leaving, they could finally get on with their lives. I felt I had become a burden, although their attitude was always very positive towards me.

The next day a driver came to show me to the depot for Wilson's Trucking. I managed to start motorcycle after cleaning up the burned points. I then followed the driver out to Wilson's Trucking. Just as we drove up the street leading into their yard, the motorcycle started to run on one cylinder.

That was it; it had had it!

I met the driver, Mr. Rizzotto, who flamboyantly assured me, "I'll look after the motorcycle as if it were my own." We put the beast on the truck and I bid it good-bye. "See you in São Paulo."

Bahia Lapataia
End of Route 3, 2000 miles (3202 km) from B.A.
Bottom of South America

Chapter Twenty-Five

São Paulo's Marvelous Policia Militar!

That evening, after dinner, Joe and Nancy drove me to the airport. My bag weighed 110 Lbs (54 KG) - 80 lbs (38 KG) over limit. Fortunately, when the bag was put on the scales the girl behind the ticket counter was distracted, bitching at some young fellow. My bag got pushed into the system without me paying an exorbitant amount of money for being overweight.

At the departure lounge, I thanked Joe and Nancy their hospitality.

The two-hour flight to São Paulo on a Varig plane went smoothly; the service was excellent.

Arriving in São Paulo, I was greeted by Mrs. Sandy and Raymond Smith, British citizens who lived in Brazil for many years. Ray worked for a big English consortium, and Sandy assisted him wherever she could; she was also the head of the local Cheshire home.

We loaded my things into the boot of their car and drove across town past frequent favellas; I saw more in São Paulo in that half hour drive than I had seen anywhere. People "lived" under bridges in cardboard shacks. It was horrible. The Smith's apartment complex was 13 stories high. Their two story garden apartment was on the top floor, overlooking São Paulo. They settled me in their son's room; he was away at college in England. I had a good feeling about being in São Paulo - the weather was cool, and there were no mosquitoes! How I had longed over the past few months to get away from heat, humidity and bugs.

It seemed as though my wish had come true. That night, I enjoyed one of my deepest night's sleep in a very long time.

The following day, Sandy contacted Mr. Guilherme; he was the military and police Harley Davidson dealer in the São Paulo area. "I'll try and get a hold of some of my contacts and locate a place for you to work on the motorcycle," he told me. "In the meantime, hold tight."

Sandy took me to the Cheshire Home where I met the residents. I was enthralled by their jolly and happy attitude about life. Imagine it. These people were paraplegics - amputees - all with major disabilities. Yet, they were laughing and carrying on. I told them about my trip, then we all sat down to a meal.

One very lovely young girl named Elianna was a paraplegic due to polio. I thought to myself, "What would her life have been if she had been gifted with the use of her legs?" She was shockingly beautiful from the waist up. How cruel life can sometimes be to people. Yet, her attitude always reflected a smile and a laugh.

I also met Richard Stevens, a man who would play an important part in my time in São Paulo. He was an English businessman, and had lived in São Paulo area for many years. Richard was a dynamic character with a "go for it" attitude in business. He often served as a translator for the foundation.

Richard came back with us to Sandy and Ray's apartment, and we chatted during our dinner of bacon and eggs - a good English dinner. I excused myself fairly early since I was starting to feel sick. That night, I was constantly up and down with the shits.

The next day, Richard told me "I've spoken to the British International School Head Master, Nigal, and he would like you to give a talk to some of the kids if you are interested."

"Sure," I replied, "I'd be happy to if it would be of some use to the Cheshire Foundation."

Speeches, Barbecues, and the British

Richard took me over to the school where we enjoyed lunch with the graduating class of the school. I met Nigal, the Head Master, a young English fellow, and was surprised that he was only about 35 years old. During lunch I thought, "This man is paying me compliments? Little does he know that I'm a high school dropout."

That afternoon I was introduced to a very large class of kids between 11 and 13 years old. I spoke for about thirty minutes, pointing to my map of the world with my route on it, and to photos I had laid out on the table. After the talk, they asked questions, then examined the map and photos. Judging by their interest, I knew my journey had made an impact on their lives.

As we drove back across São Paulo, Richard asked me, "Would you like to speak to the Cultura?," the culture society for both British and Brazilians.

"Sure," I replied.

My motorcycle is not due to arrive until next Monday. When I called about the arrival date, the people I spoke with were very friendly. It is said that the people in São Paulo are a far friendlier, more intelligent bunch of people than up north; my personal experience seems to confirm this.

I met Richard's family: his wife Vicky, his sons Mark and Jason, and their adopted girl, Nina, a Brazilian. Richard's home was large, with many different plants. There were many rustic artifacts that had been turned into furniture, such as the table and the bar. Outside, they had hamsters, three parrots, and an ever-present dog. The place was a veritable zoo!

Richard asked Mark, "Would you help Dave with the motorcycle when it comes in?" and Mark jumped at the chance.

Sunday, Richard brought me down to the yacht club where I met Richard Flanagan, a design engineer for the General Motors Corporation in São Paulo. As we talked about motorcycles, Richard said "I used to go to high school with Willie G. Davidson, and we raced against each other on many occasions. He was very skilled, but I actually beat him a couple of times." "What a privilege to meet such a man as this," I thought.

As we were talking, it was suggested that I be used as a catalyst to encourage the Board of Directors of General Motors to donate a vehicle to the Cheshire Home. The plan was for me to give a motivational talk to their management group, and do some positive things in the media to help promote General Motor's image. In return, General Motors would give a van with a lift on it to the residents of the Cheshire home. Richard Flanagan was all for the idea, but unfortunately, as things developed, he wasn't able to get it past the Board of Directors.

Sunday was barbecue day at the Cheshire Home. Richard Stevens, his family, John Smallwood and his wife, Sandy Smith and her daughter, Xenia, who had just arrived from England, were there, joining the residents in cooking a big side of beef. A good time was had by these British expiates who speak Portuguese as well.

The home is situated in a favella, so the neighborhood is a rough one. Yet, the people from the favella come and sit on the veranda of the home with the residents in a cordial, community atmosphere.

Monday, we were up fairly early to go to Wilson Trucking in São Paulo. Of course, it is all the way across town and quite a long drive. We arrived just as they backed up the trailer to the dock. Upon inspection, I could see that everything had been looked after carefully by Mr. Rizzotto.

"Unfortunately, we do not have a pickup to deliver the bike for you immediately," they told me. "We should have something later this afternoon."

We then drive back across town and make final arrangements with John Thornton, an engineer, to house the motorcycle in his garage. While there, I met Bruno, a fellow motorcyclist. He was German, but born in Brazil.

Mark, Richard Steven's son, came over and took me to John Thornton's apartment in the late afternoon - a two story affair right near a big main boulevard in a horrible looking neighborhood. Wilson's Trucking delivered the bike to this address, and we off loaded the Harley Davidson, rolling it into the garage.

The following morning Mark picked me up and we beeped our way through the terrible traffic of São Paulo, even though it wasn't rush hour. São Paulo is the third largest city in the world.

When we arrived at John's, I went to work immediately, with young Mark's help. "Hold this. Hold that. Bring me this tool." First I took off the gas tank, then the cylinder heads and the cylinder barrels. The pistons looked okay, but were wearing more on one side than the other. Next, I needed to check out the alternator to find out why it wasn't charging, so I pulled the inner and outer primary off, all the clutch, and took off the alternator rotor. I was very relieved to see that the stator itself had not been hit or torn off at the wall again. I thought this was a miracle!

"The problem is probably with the volt pack," I thought.

Bruno came over later in the morning and took the volt pack to have it tested. It came back "no good." I then checked the play in the crank shaft and I could see when I grabbed the connecting rods and moved them that the whole crank shaft was moving. That made me sadly realize that what had been repaired by the "no problem" engineer in Anchorage was not repaired properly. It had all come loose, and I was going to have to split the cases of the motor.

At this point my spirits sunk to a very low point indeed.

I received a call from Giulherme; he gave me two choices as to where the motorcycle could go. "I have a friend with a motorcycle shop who could take the motorcycle in, but you would not be able to work on it."

"Forget it. I'm not interested," I told him.

"The next choice is the policia militar's escort platoon on the other side of São Paulo. I have one more inquiry to make and then I can let you know."

"That's where we'll go if we can," I replied.

About an hour later, he called and confirmed they would house the motorcycle and let me work on it. "In fact, they are willing to assign a man to help you."

"Lets get it over there," I enthusiastically replied.

Aladdin's Cave - My Magic Moments

Giulherme sent his man, Francisco, across town to pick me up with a trailer in which we shoved the motorcycle and all the different parts, heading over to the policia militar's garage where I met the boss, Captain Rooie, and his second in command, Lieutenant Dante. We rolled the motorcycle back to a special area just for motorcycles in the policia militar's escort platoon where Lieutenant Dante introduces me to Zulato.

No one here speaks any English, so all conversation is translated by young Mark. As I meet all these people, I'm trying to tell them how much I appreciate their letting me work on my motorcycle in their garage. Lieutenant Ricardo said, "I will have a car waiting for you every morning to take you across town to the garage."

Later that evening, I am to give a speech. A fellow named Chris from Ray's office picks me up and takes me on a hair raising ride. Chris could barely see over the steering wheel of his car, but drove hell bent for leather through the streets of

São Paulo to get to the British Club where we would have dinner with the Round Table Society.

There were two speakers that night - myself, and a child psychiatrist who, out of his own pocket, opened a home for children with Aids. What a touching, very special person. He spoke for about thirty minutes, we had dinner, then I spoke for about thirty minutes. I felt my talk and my journey paled compared to what this psychiatrist was doing for his fellow man.

After the talk, back in the car for another crazy ride with Sir Chris, the British Grand Prix driver. Once we arrived, I was literally shaking with relief to be done with this man and his driving. How he had driven this long without killing himself or someone else I don't know. "God protects drunks and fools."

The following night we went to a mock election for the British Parliament which was to take place in a few days. The mock election was at the cultura where I met many people, both British and Brazilian. There were a few Americans. At around 21:30, the election results were announced. The conservative party won the mock election. A cheer went up. The conservatives also won in England barely a day later.

The following morning the police car arrived at 06:30 am sharp and took me down to the maintenance station where Zulato and I went to work, taking it apart. We put it up on a work stand and lifted it up. We took off the front end, then the rear wheel. We dismantled part after part until only a bare frame was left sitting on the lift.

It was difficult getting any work done. Every time I turned around there was an officer who was attached to the depot, or just passing through, who wanted to hear about the journey. Nobody spoke English, so out came the dictionary. We would all shake hands, and after about 15 minutes, they would be on their way.

Later that same day, Zulato took me back to the store's department where they kept all the spare parts - there was a whole section for Harley Davidsons! It was indeed an Aladdin's cave of spare parts! I realized that whatever was wrong with that motorcycle, the parts were here to take care of the problem. What a sight for sore eyes!

Zulato said, "No problem, Davidey" - my name in Portuguese. Staring at that stockpile of parts, it was the first time in the last couple of weeks that I was starting to pull out of my depression.

We split the cases late that day and saw where the repair had come undone that was made in Anchorage. I remember asking the engineer who fixed it three times, "Are you sure this will this hold?"

Three times he answered, "Yes, no problem. It will hold."

Now, here I am thousands of miles away and it didn't hold. We were also very fortunate in that a few more miles and one of the screws would have come all the way out of the crank case and hit the flywheel (as it was, it had just touched the flywheel, leaving a bare, shiny spot on the top of it). If that would have happened, everything inside the engine would have been ruined.

That afternoon, a reporter shows up with a television crew for an interview. Of course, they filmed the bare frame of my motorcycle, the engine and whatever else was left sitting up on a bench in pieces. I talked them through the map, and also showed them some photos.

April 11: Ray and Sandy have a farm out in the country and go out to work it on weekends. On Sunday morning we drove out. Ray drove at break neck speeds, roaring down the freeway at a colossal velocity. We went up a narrow little country dirt road until we arrived at this very beautiful place on the side of the hill - about 100 acres.

When we arrived at the Siteau, I said, "Ray, you certainly have integrated yourself nicely into Brazilian society."

"How do you mean?"

" Well, you scared me to death from the time I climbed into the car."

We all had a good laugh.

That evening we caught the news and saw the motorcycle in pieces on the bench - that was the biggest joke of the day.

The next day was Sunday, April 12, my 40th birthday. Sandy said, "We're going to a barbecue over at the Smallwood's house."

"Perhaps I will just stay here and read and relax," I suggested.

"No, we'd like you to come with us," she answered. "You will meet some nice people, and you have nothing better to do."

I felt they were counting on me coming, so I reluctantly agreed.

We drove across town (Sandy drove - much saner!). We arrived at the Smallwood house, a lovely, walled place, where I met John and his wife, Bruno, John Thornton and a few other people. We had a great barbecue and chatted and joked. At the end of the festivities, they brought out a birthday cake with 40 candles on it. The penny dropped - this was a surprise party for me. A jolly good time was had by all, and they presented me with a huge mock check - about three feet across - for $125.00 with a map of the world stenciled behind it. I was deeply touched by all of this. I had told no one that this was my birthday.

They clamored for a speech, so I tried to express to them the reasons for my doing the trip. Their kind gesture to me, a virtual stranger, helped me know once again that I was doing the right thing, and that I must carry on no matter what.

Atomic Coffee and Staggering Schedules

The days to follow went something like this: Get up about 5:30, have coffee. At 6:30 the police vehicle arrives and drives about 30 minutes to get across town to the main maintenance depot. From there, I'd walk to the back of the depot. The police would be finishing their exercise period as Zulato and I would start working on the motorcycle - about 07:15.

They had coffee there all the time - very strong stuff. Atomic coffee. It would literally jag you up like doing speed.

After coffee, we'd go to work on the motorcycle. There was one particular time when we had the cylinder heads apart and they needed to be cleaned. Jackson, a very jolly fellow, had been in the policia militar for many years. Jackson decided to join Valdimar, who had been helping off and on with Zulato and me. They started lapping the valves in, making a clacking and banging noise almost like drums. Even though the unit is racially integrated, Jackson starts doing a very primitive African dance, and a big laugh was had by all.

The police are always digging each other, calling one fellow a "homo," or another a "commodore" - a lady's man. They enjoy all the macho games. This one fellow nicknamed "Arafat" by Zulato catches the brunt of many jokes. Arafat bragged about his beautiful wife, so the others started saying, "She's not only beautiful, but she's beautiful for everyone." Then they say, "If you want her photo, just go see Zulato." That joke always set poor Arafat in a fit. Then, another fellow would say, "Yes, his wife is beautiful, and she's got huge tits." This friendly banter went on every day. Only Arafat never seemed to enjoy it.

At the end of the day, my stumps are usually killing me since I've been standing all day. It is even difficult for me to walk the 100 meters from the escort platoon's

269

garage to the front garage to hail Lieutenant Ricardo so he can bring the car around. What a relief once in the car! My head feels like exploding from trying all day to understand others and to be understood. We have the dictionary - "booka" - between us, but it is so tedious searching for key words in every conversation.

Zulato is definitely a master mechanic, and knows how to work on a Harley Davidson. Although he doesn't have the special tools he needs, he simply improvises - that's how we got my cases apart.

At the end of this one day, and after enduring another hair raising ride with a young police driver, I get myself ready for Richard Stevens to pick me up and take me to the Cultura where I gave an hour and a half talk about the trip around the world to about 40 Brazilian women who are learning English. They ranged in age from about 18 to 40, and some were quite beautiful. After the class, they all lined up for a kiss! As they did, I thought, "Oh boy, wouldn't it be great to give a talk every night! Beats the hell out of a polished stone." That night made up for the kiss I didn't get at the Harley Davidson Super Rally of Europe when "I won" a rock instead of a trophy or a kiss.

One day, a group of people arrived from Belo Horizonte (a few hundred miles north of Sao Paulo). In the group was a Harley Davidson mechanic and the Harley Davidson dealer from Belo Horizonte. They came over to meet me, and I spent the next ninety minutes going through all my photographs and map with them. The dealer takes off his T-shirt and gives it to me, so I took off my old T-shirt and gave it to him. One of them said, "Davidey, God rides with you."

"You are absolutely right," I thought to myself, "If He wasn't with me on this trip, I wouldn't be here today."

The mechanic examined my crank cases, and declared one was beyond repair. My heart just hit the bottom. What now? To have crank cases imported from the United States would cost a fortune. With duty, they cost five times what they cost in the United States.

As they leave and I'm sitting there starting to feel depressed, Zulato walks into the room with a set of brand new early Shovel head crank cases! I didn't know what to think! We started to clean them up immediately, getting them ready for assembly.

In the middle of that job, I was interrupted by Mr. Guilherme himself, the police and military dealer. Although he had already helped me a lot, I had not yet met him. As we spoke, he introduced me to Louis, the Harley Davidson dealer in Rio De Janeiro. We talked for the next half an hour. It was good to finally meet Mr. Guilherme; I will be forever indebted to him for arranging to get into this garage. How he managed it, I don't know. I learned that he was the man who created the Amazonas motorcycle - made totally in Brazil, and using a Volkswagen engine for power. I saw a video on what the motorcycle could do, and it was amazing. Unfortunately, Mr. Guilherme made a few bad business deals with some Americans who cheated him, and lost the factory that produced the Amazonas.

After they left, a fellow from a magazine called *Doas Rohdas* - it means "Two Wheels" - appeared and interviewed me for about an hour. When he was finished, it was time to call it a day.

When traffic is heavy, it can take as much as an hour and a half to get back to the apartment. I usually arrive between 19:00 and 19:30, and am exhausted. As quickly as possible, I usually have dinner, get a shower, then climb into bed.

A new problem. I received a letter from Marilyn Dear in Hong Kong, a most impressive and unique lady I've known since I lived in South Africa. Marilyn speaks many languages, and is always in the upper echelon of business wherever she goes.

She had been interceding for me ever since January, trying to find a way for me to get into mainland China. Her letter was not optimistic. "To this date, David, I have not made any positive contacts that can help you get into China. The only way that I have discovered so far is for you to enter by escort, and that would be horribly expensive."

Richard Stevens was searching for a sponsor who would pay to fly the motorcycle from São Paulo to Hong Kong. He told me that without a sponsor it would cost upwards of $7,000 to fly the motorcycle to Hong Kong. That shocked me out of my leg sockets!

After the Easter Holiday, even though the shop was technically closed down, Zulato agreed to work with me. We were now starting the assembly phase. John Thornton also helped. Finally, the engine was assembled.

During lunch time, Zulato went somewhere for his lunch, and suddenly, seeming out of nowhere a lunch arrives (the kitchen where I normally take my meals with the officers was not open). Apparently, Lieutenant Ricardo had left money with someone to purchase me lunch everyday I was working. What a touching gesture. I hope and pray I live up to all these people's expectations, and do accomplish my goal of giving something to the disabled.

My days are very long and stressful. They usually start about 05:00 in the morning, and I meet the police car at 6:30. In light traffic, we get across town to Tapiula and the maintenance depot in about a half an hour. There, I start my day of working and of battling language barriers. That battle actually starts the second the car driver arrives. They always want to talk, and I can't understand their language. I just keep nodding my head as if in agreement until they try to pin me down on something...then we search through the dictionary (it can be downright dangerous when they try to find a word while they are driving!).

At the garage, after exercises and roll call, Zulato and I get started on the motorcycle. I'm interrupted regularly through the day to speak to different officials and conduct media interviews. We work as best we can until about 18:00 in the evening when I catch another car back to the apartment. In heavy traffic, the run back usually takes an hour and a half. The nicest part of the drive is sitting while the pain just seems to ooze out of my stumps.

On the freeways, I often spot these little motorcycles that come between the lanes, often five or six of them, one right behind the other with only inches separating them, racing along at 30 to 40 miles per hour between the lanes of stopped cars. If any car made a quick lane change, or had a door open, these drivers would crash into each other like dominos.

At the apartment, I clean up, eat, and sometimes then go out again to speak. It seems there's always something. It is very rare that I get into bed before 22:00 or 23:00.

One time, after speaking at Cultura, one of the English teachers took me to a dinner at a Polish couples apartment; fifteen of her students were there, and we spoke about the journey. We had a nice pizza dinner. A woman named Malasandy was there, and she seemed to want to get to know me better. She was a very attractive blond-haired gal. Unfortunately, there was just no time to spare for such socializing; the story of my life.

John Thornton had taken my cylinder heads to be reconditioned, and called on this day to say, "David, they weren't able to complete the work as scheduled. It might be as late as Monday."

Winter is Waiting!

I nearly went over the moon with frustration. There's such an urgency inside of me to just get this thing done! Every day I wait here is a day that it is going to get colder down in Patagonia and Tierra del Fuego, only 650 miles from Antarctica; it is already winter time there.

I was told that the president of a Harley Davidson club wanted to see me, and might be able to do something about the heads. So, Zulato and I drove over to his address. When I explained our situation, he said, "No problem," then made a phone call to an engine reconditioning shop not far away. They said, "Yes, we will do the heads right now." With that great news, we took the heads and all the other parts they needed over to them.

We had lunch, then went back to the maintenance depot for more work on the motorcycle. Late in the afternoon, we went back for the cylinder heads, waiting another half hour for them to finish - about 17:30. When they gave the cylinder heads back to us, the man refused to charge me. Of course, I thanked him, and shared with him some photos of the trip, and showed him the map.

That night, in the police car taking me home, the driver showed me his paycheck - about $155.00 a month. He told me he had three children. As we drove, he kept saying, "You are a brave man to be doing what you are doing." I thought to myself, "Who is the brave one? My major concern in life is keeping my old motorcycle running. He has the tougher job - feeding three kids and a wife! He explained that housing was his major expense; affordable housing was almost nonexistent. Living conditions were terrible. I don't feel brave or much like a hero, knowing that Zulato and so many others are pitching in to help me get this motorcycle and the trip back on the road. The worries to their daily life - the problems they face - the meager salary they receive - are major challenges. It amazes me how they survive; to my thinking, they are the brave ones.

The next day we stopped at John Thornton's house and picked up my outer primary which he had repaired himself; he'd put a metal sheet on to the side of the primary with the initials, "IBM."

"What do you mean by that?" I asked him.

"Intrepid Birdman," he replied. John Thornton was an avid hang glider enthusiast.

Although it is Saturday and his day off, Zulato meets me at the garage with Vadimer. We put the cylinder heads on, and now everything is ready. We started it up, and it didn't sound bad, although the timing was off. When we revved the engine up, it made a lifter clicking noise which we thought would work itself out. We put the gas tanks on and fueled it up. By now, it was 16:30 in the afternoon.

A fellow named Mark Anthony shows up on his Harley Davidson. We are not happy to see him because it seems like things just seem to go wrong when he comes around.

My plan is to ride the motorcycle back to the apartment, despite the heavy rain this particular day. Rain is rough on the man, but good for the motorcycle because, for a brand new engine, it helps keep the motor cool. When I hit my first corner just outside the garage, the motor stalls, and it is extremely difficult to get started again. From there, I go to the freeway where it is raining so hard that I miss my turnoff and end up in a favella area of Sao Paulo. I go around in circles for almost an hour before I find my way back to the freeway and out to Tapeula and the police garage.

Zulato, Mark Anthony and Valdimer are still there; perhaps they suspected I wouldn't make it to the apartment. The lifter is clicking so badly by now that I feared it would damage the motor. I parked the motorcycle and Valdimer called for a car to take me home where I was grateful to have Sandy there - she is a good shoulder to cry on!

Sunday I had all to myself to recover from my sneezing and coughing cold. I thought about Patagonia and Tierra del Fuego, and the terrible cold I'd be facing in those areas.

Monday was pressure from start to finish. I didn't even get to finish my coffee before the police car arrived a half hour early. Down at the police station, we rolled the motorcycle out and fueled it up. Lieutenant Dante said, "I'll give you an escort to see how the thing is running. I'll send a backup vehicle with Valdimer and Zulato." Then, he called ten policeman who weren't doing anything, every one on a Honda, and onto the highway we went. In the few blocks, we never had to stop because the escort went ahead to block traffic so we could just ride through. It was quite exciting!

After only ten miles, my primary belt broke. As I pulled over, we listened to the engine and could tell there was a problem with a lifter. We loaded the motorcycle onto the back of the pickup truck, and drove back to the garage where we got the lifter out. A piece of toilet paper we had used to clean out the sockets had caught right at the bottom of the lifter. We put the thing back together, installed a new primary belt, and were then interrupted by a TV crew that had come down to see the motorcycle and do an interview.

Once we completed the interview, they wanted me to ride the motorcycle. So, the police escort was again assembled to take me around the block a few times. A camera man was mounted on a police motorcycle facing backwards. It worked out fine. Back in the garage, we finished the interview.

Next enters a very lovely young Brazilian girl from the magazine *Marie Claire*. She interviewed me for another hour; by now it is about 19:00. The unmarked police car that would take me back also took the young lady from *Marie Claire* to her destination. So, instead of an hour and half getting back to the apartment, it was two. She didn't seem to mind the driver going down the street on the wrong side of the road on narrow streets, sometimes blocking traffic. He'd dart down the oncoming lane, puffing on his cigarette, then push his way in when cars came on the opposite direction. I never had a driver like this. The young woman in the back was talking calmly to me, and here I was on the edge of my seat! It took everything I could do to concentrate on her remarks as I braced myself for the inevitable impact.

Somehow it just didn't happen.

The next day, before I tested the motorcycle some more, Zulato came out with a plaque that said, "Crank Cases Donated by the Policia Militar Escort Platoon - São Paulo, Brazil - April 1992." I was very proud of that plaque. When I asked Lieutenant Dante how much all the repairs would cost, he said, "No problem, don't worry about it."

At lunch we had a great laugh. Lieutenant Ricardo had a doctor friend he called "a commodore," and I thought a commodore was a rank usually given to a Naval Commander. He explained that "commodore" meant "a lady's man."

"What does it mean in English?" he asked.

"It means a stud" I answered, and raised my right hand up like a hard pecker; everybody just roared with laugher.

That afternoon, Lieutenant Dante, Lieutenant Cladio, and Zulato all rode motorcycles with me out on the highway, about 35 miles out of town and back. The motorcycle noise was gone, and it seemed all right for the moment.

The following day was to be a long one in the saddle. I had an escort over to the Cheshire Home for a news interview. The Cheshire Home was about 25 miles from the police garage in horrendous traffic. As we rode through the lanes, with police sirens blaring away, the intersections were all blocked off. The speeds kept getting faster and faster. I managed to keep up with them all the way, sometimes going between lanes of stop and go traffic at 40 and 50 miles per hour. When we arrived at the Cheshire home, I did a newspaper interview and photographs were taken. I hoped this would get exposure for the Cheshire Home in the newspaper.

After the interviews, we took another 25 hair raising mile ride back to the garage where the police all patted me on the back. I was shaking from "Post Traumatic Stress" while they're all complimenting my riding skills. They never knew how scared I was.

Bad information was still coming back from Marilyn Dear in Hong Kong about a permit to get into China. Despite the news, I felt that I must go on ahead and at least stage whatever I am going to do in Asia out of Hong Kong. My feeling was that I would reroute the balance of the trip if I couldn't get into China. What bothered me most was my promise to Lord Cheshire to visit the home in China. I made up my mind I would keep that promise - even if it meant I had to go there on a train!

Then a break! To my delight, I received news that somebody in China had told Marilyn it should be "NO PROBLEM" to get me in...unescorted! That lightened my mood a bit.

Richard Stevens then informed me that South African airways had agreed to fly me and the motorcycle to Hong Kong for $3,100.00, $1,900 less than the cheapest quote I had so far. While that was good news, it was still too expensive for my blood, and I decided that I would send it over by ship.

Guilherme invited me to attend a barbecue for the official opening ceremony of his maintenance shop in Leme, about 120 miles (200 kilometers) north from São Paulo. He gave me directions, and I agreed to go thinking it would be a good test for the motorcycle.

When I rode the motorcycle from the garage to the apartment in Campo Belo (about 20 miles), Ray found a place for me to park the machine downstairs. His mother and father were newly arrived from England the day before. That afternoon we all talked about England, about the problems between the conservative and liberal parities, and the weather in England - always an acceptable subject.

The next morning I went down to the motorcycle where there was a yellow ribbon, with a note saying "Good luck, Dave, in your endeavors." "I'll surely need it with this pig," I thought.

Farewells and Tributes from True Friends

As I traveled that day, people were waiving to me, recognizing me from all the news media coverage. Somehow, this attention helped me forget my heavy chest cold, sneezing and coughing. Over a dozen articles had been printed in magazines and newspapers, plus the television coverage. I felt a close camaraderie with the Brazilian people as I rode the 120 miles without incident out to Leme where I arrived at a huge warehouse that had been turned into a massive workshop by Guilherme for Harley Davidsons.

Guilherme and I had a nice lunch, talking about the Harley Davidson's factory treatment of dealers. In the late afternoon, factory men from Milwaukee, Wisconsin, arrived to inspect the premise. As they walked through the inspection, Guilherme shared that his main problem was getting parts on time. When Guilherme had to go take care of some other business, he invited me to show Wayne and Lou some photographs and the map of my trip. Frankly, I was very reluctant to do so because they didn't seem the slightest bit interested. To this time, there was only one person I found in the Harley Davidson Motor Company who seemed to care anything about this journey, and was willing to help - Dan Klemencic. The other executives just did not seem to understand what I was doing, or why I was doing it. They only focused on dollars and cents. Of course, in all fairness to them, attending to the business at hand is what saved the company from going out of business all together.

I spent the night at a sugar estate belonging to Guilherme's family for two generations; it sat on top a hill, with sugar cane fields surrounding it in all directions. I stayed in a little cottage across a lawn with a veranda; what a place for peace and solitude!

The following morning, Guilherme took me to a private sugar estate that adjoined their land. We visited a huge mansion, over a 100 years old, which must have hosted many gala parties and balls over the years. He also showed me a church near a lake; I wondered, "How many weddings and funerals have been performed here?"

Next, we went into the rain forest and I saw a little tin shack built to house the "caretakers of the forest." I learned that it was a privately owned rain forest! The owner was a wealthy sugar mill owner. The forest was full of monkeys running up and down the trees and vines that abounded. How relaxing that time was.

Back in his jeep, we drove to Leme for the barbecue and opening ceremony. It had rained during the night. so the grounds around the big maintenance center were very muddy. About 12:00, the policia militar came rolling in, about 20 motorcycles in all. When they hit the mud, everybody was fishtailing but nobody fell off. If it had been me, I would have gone down right there for everybody to see.

The wonderful barbecue was a side of beef put onto a spit and cooking since early morning. After we ate, there were lots of speeches. I tried to give a slide show, but it was interrupted by other activities. Frankly, in the context of the day, not many were really interested in my speech besides the Escort Riders.

At the end of the celebration, the Escort Riders asked me if I wanted to ride back with them, and I readily agreed, careful not to slip on the mud on the way out.

The ride home was something I will never forget as we traveled in a tight formation at about 60 mph (100 kph). The two lead motorcycles had their headlights on. We rode in the fast lane, myself right next to the meridian. The eventual darkness and rain did not slow down our pace. In Campinas, we stopped at a petrol station that catered to the police and filled up. Even here, quite a crowd surrounded my motorcycle as the other policemen told them about this world traveler they had befriended. On the way again, I remember thinking, "How many foreigners would ever do anything like this? What a great privilege and experience." These men looked straight forward, sitting at attention on their machines; I tried to emulate them as best I could. Riding in tight formation, I found my concentration must be total. Any mistake by any one person could easily result in a major accident since we are following only inches from each other.

In São Paulo, they were all patting me on the back for staying in formation with them. I really appreciated the compliments coming from these masters of motorcycle formation riding. What I didn't tell them was that I was right at my limits. To say the least, we were riding the edge.

In a big book that documents the history of this platoon, I discovered that this police escort unit had a relationship with Harley Davidson that went back 60 years! One of the photographs that stuck out in my mind was of a man on a knucklehead Harley Davidson (made between 1936 and 1947) jumping off a ramp over 15 human bodies. I asked, "Zulato, how did you get fifteen volunteers?"

"No problem, Davidey," he replied. "CONVITA."

The "volunteers" were convicts! They figured that if the motorcyclist made a mistake and ended up landing on the convicts and killing a few of them, it didn't really matter. I wondered if your place in the line is determined by the seriousness of your crime. Would a petty thief get the number one spot, with number fifteen reserved for a rapist or murderer?

They had a photo in the book of the largest motorcycle pyramid stack - forty men moving on Harley Davidsons; it was a Guinness book world record.

On Monday we serviced the motorcycle, doing final preparations for resumption of the trip, and conducted a final newspaper interview.

Tuesday, May 5th: The day for leaving São Paulo. At 06:30 the police car was out front waiting; I took all my bags with me. It felt strange leaving the apartment which had been my home for a number of weeks. At the police station, as I was loading the machine, Sandy Smith arrives with Claudio and Eliana. Claudio is also a resident of the home, a paraplegic from polio. Marisa, the director of the film crew there that day, did an interview with me and some of the policia militar, and photographed Eliana giving me a necklace and a kiss.

I was escorted out of town, the escort consisting of half a dozen motorcycles, one with a television camera mounted on the back. Sandy Smith, Eliana and Claudio rode in a Volkswagen station wagon, and I trailed just behind the police. After good-byes to Captain Rooie, Lieutenant Ricardo, and a few others, we rode out of the police station into the traffic and another hair raising ride for 35 miles across São Paulo. Intersections were again blocked off so I could just cruise right through!

At the outskirts of São Paulo, I said good-bye to Lieutenant Dande, Lieutenant Claudio, and the rest of the policia militar. Merisa completed her interview, then asked, "Dave if you had one wish right now, what would you wish for?"

I looked her straight in the eye and said, "To finish, to go the distance."

I got on the motorcycle and left the escort; only Bruno was with me as we rode down the road about a mile before he waived good-bye and for the first time in seven weeks I was alone again and on the road.

As I rode out that day, I thought about the trials and tribulations I had experienced coming down through the Amazon, and how the motorcycle finally gave up in Salvador. I reflected on the trip to São Paulo, my weeks working with Zulato, the police, all the new challenges to solve.

I remembered the pleasure I had sharing with the Cultura, the children, and other groups, and the good done for the Cheshire Home and for the policia militar's reputation as they assisted this rag-tag world traveler. I remembered the ride through the streets of São Paulo and in tight formation on the freeway, and the great privileges given to me by the Cheshire Home. Even breakdowns were part of the journey, I realized, and vowed they were never to discourage me again. It was because of the mechanical problems that I was able to experience all of these wonderful things instead of just breezing through São Paulo. My stay was a time to repair the motorcycle, but also to spread good to others. All the frustration and work on my part certainly had been worth everything I gained from this period!

Chapter Twenty-Six

Awe-Inspiring Agony!

The road was known as the "highway of death" because there were more accidents along this stretch than anywhere else in Brazil. On my first day, I passed a truck that had plowed into the side of the hill. Other than that, the road was accident free and traffic seemed to move well on the double laned highway.

As I journeyed up hills and through mountains, the landscape was rain forest and jungle. The sun was out in between the clouds. In the late afternoon, I found a massive parking lot where trucks stay at night, so I decided to spend the night there after covering about 150 miles that day.

The following morning I was still coughing and hacking from my cold, and the mist and rain did not promise a great day. I put on my rain gear, loaded the motorcycle, and took off. The terrain was now pine trees and small villages as I made my way south through pastures and cattle lands. Despite the rain, I made good time. At one service station, the man, out of respect for the trip I was making, wouldn't take any money. Thank you very much!

At day's end, I had traveled 360 miles before I spotted a little dirt road, made my way back into the bush, and found a place to sleep high above the Rio Jaquarna River.

The third day out I made it into Porto Alegre, a seaport town on the Atlantic Coast. I called the Cultura English School, and a lady came and guided me to the school where I was greeted by Allen Fear, who heard about me through the Barnsley Warriors. That night, I gave a talk and slide show which went over very well. Questions were asked, and afterwards we drove back to Allen's house where we ate some sandwiches and closed our day.

The following day I did a television interview at the school before heading out.

Allen had served in the British Royal Signaling Corp for ten years, and I could sense that his heart was really with me. He'd have given almost anything to carry on down the road on a motorcycle himself, but those days were behind him. Now, he was a responsible person, married to a lovely Brazilian girl, and the father of a new baby.

At 09:00, the TV people were there to film me riding out of town; they waived good-bye at the outskirts.

On a winding road not too far out of Porto Alegre I got careless and nearly ended up getting hit by a bus coming around a corner. Once again, I grew to appreciate my maker. It seems that my life is always only a fraction of an inch from having my candle pissed on.

The road out of Porto Alegre was fairly well maintained as I traveled through cattle and ranching country, and farming areas. Finally, about 30 miles (50 kilometers) from the border, I stopped at a petrol station in the late afternoon. After 300 miles, I was going to call it a day. The station owner told me, "You can park around back and put up your tent there."

Chicken and bread was my dinner on this night, devoured in a drenching rain storm that thundered an end to my day.

Tomorrow I'll cross into Uruguay.

One of the first things that struck me in Uruguay were the gauchos - cowboys gallantly galloping along on their horses with their pantaloons and little flat hats. They always carried a big machete knife, and sometimes had dogs running beside them. What majestic men and animals - like something you'd see in a travel log, only this travel log was in a cold rain. Nothing is to good for me.

The countryside was either forested or ranching country; the automobiles were two extremes - modern or very old. I saw a refrigerated van on the road where the chassis and cab dated back to the thirties. Hopefully, the refrigeration unit was from a newer era. I also found gasoline to be twice as expensive.

When I arrived in Montevideo, the capital city of Uruguay, I asked directions down to the port where I will take the ferry across to Buenos Aires. At the port, I hit mud and fell down. Stevedores nearby helped me pick up the motorcycle, and told me "You'll need to go into town to buy a ticket for this ferry." This didn't make much sense to me, but who would know better than the locals?

When I parked my motorcycle, I met two young men, George and Marcello, who said they would help me find the ticketing office in town. We went to the gate guard and asked the guard if we could park the motorcycle near his guard kiosk, and he said "Fine."

Ticket Trauma, Barn Beds, and Wicked Weather

We caught a taxi to the ticketing office, and George and Marcello did all the interpretation. "He wants a ticket to Buenos Aires leaving tonight," they said. "How much will that be?" When they told me the amount, I needed to walk a few more blocks to a place where I could change some travelers checks. When I returned, they told me, "We have made a mistake on the cost of the ticket. You will need more money." Just another routine boat ride!

Back at the port, I waited for two and a half hours, then went through Customs and Immigrations. When I was ready to board the boat, I showed them my ticket, and the man says, "This ticket is for a town 90 miles north up the Rio Plata." I couldn't believe it.

"But I told them I wanted a ticket for Buenos Aires."

"Well, this is not enough."

"Can I pay the difference and get another ticket?"

"No, you must buy a whole ticket."

I was numb! The shipping line was called "Buquebus" Lines; I now dubbed them the "Blue Balls Line." I must admit I became horribly upset at the young fellow behind the counter (it really wasn't his fault).

"What can I do now?"

"You can buy another ticket here."

"You mean I could have just waited and bought a ticket right on the spot?"

Naturally, that made me even angrier. I went to the toilet area, took off my right leg where I keep all my extra money, and gave him a $100.00 cash so he would issue me a new ticket.

"Can you tell me how I get my money back on the other ticket?" I asked.

"You will have to take it to the office in Buenos Aires," he replied. "After they approve the refund, there will be a two week wait before they send it to you."

I tore up my $80.00 ticket and threw it away. "Blue Balls Line" number one had won the first fight!

I've heard it said that when something bad happens to you, something good will happen the very same day - so I'm due for something good.

We embark onto the ship, and the crew immediately takes an interest in the motorcycle. "We will look after it with extra care," they tell me. I took my bag off of the back for the night and ascended a couple of flights of stairs up to the cabin area where one of the crew showed me to my cabin. "I'll get in here and take a real quick shower before anybody else comes and uses it," I thought.

I jumped into the shower and cleaned up, and was ready as the ferry was then casting off by that time and heading across the Rio Plata. It takes all night for some reason to get to the other side. I was still contemplating why my ticket had been messed up. What was the problem? Had George and Marcello played a very nasty joke on me or in fact had there just been a mistake made in communications?

At the ship's duty free store I shopped for a spoon for Mom. Because my clothes were rather ragged looking, I couldn't get any of the sale's people to even acknowledge me. Finally, I just gave up and went back to my room to relax. It is now clear that I have the room to myself tonight - that's at least some consolation for getting screwed on the cost of the ticket.

Prices on the boat were outrageous. A simple cup of coffee was about $4.00 American. "Forget it, I said." The fellow working at the counter told me, "Please, go ahead and sit down," then served me coffee, some rolls, and a ham sandwich at no charge! I ate the feast with gusto. Naturally, I thanked this man very graciously. What a kind gesture!

As we came near Buenos Aires, one of the stewards came up and handed me a big tin foil parcel loaded with cheese, ham and bread rolls - luxuries I couldn't afford to buy. Then, he shook my hand. Bad people, good people; bad experiences, good experiences - on this trip, the latter outweighs the former by far!

I met Richard on the boat, and he volunteered to show me to my destination. He told me, "You'll need to go all the way across town, and I'm going that way, so it won't be any problem." When we got to Customs and Immigration, Richard just rode right on past me, waiving. That's the last I ever saw of my guide. Thank you, Richard. Welcome to Buenos Aires.

Buenos Aires is much like any big city in Europe, with sculptures and gargoiles on the buildings, and statues in the parks. Rain came down like a cow peeing on a flat rock, and traffic was heavy. Despite asking directions, I ended up getting turned around. Finally, I did the thing I hate to do, but is the safest thing - I hailed a taxi cab! I showed the driver a written address to the Harley Davidson shop, and he said "Follow me." We drove about 20 kilometers across town and when we got there, he charged me $25.00! I paid him off with great pain in my heart at the cost.

The owner of the shop and his mechanic greeted me - both were named Juan. They knew I was coming since I had called them from Porto Alegre. They wheeled my motorcycle inside and I immediately started changing oil and doing a service on the machine. At lunch time, Juan bought me a very nice steak.

When I finished working on the motorcycle, I offered to pay for the use of the shop, but Juan replied, "No way. That is on the house. Just promise me you'll be careful. The way is very cold and difficult to Tierra del Fuego. Especially be careful of the ice." This was to be an understatement.

Juan brought in a projector, so I showed both of the Juans the slides of the journey. When I finished, Juan (the owner) took me to an inexpensive hotel for the night. When I tried to pay, he said, "No. This is on me. I will see you in the morning at about 09:00."

The next day at 09:00, Juan picked me up and took me to his shop where I loaded the motorcycle, then followed JoJo, an apprentice mechanic, 20 miles (35 km) out of town on his little Honda scooter through several slum areas to the Number 3 Highway that runs all the way to the bottom of the continent where Tierra del Fuego, my destination, is located.

Once out of Buenos Aires, I bucked head winds and rain for about 100 miles to yet another station. "No gas." On another 12 miles (20 kilometers) - and "Si, senor, we have gas." How I made it that far I honestly don't know, but I needed to fill up my two and a half gallon spare gas can also.

May 12: I came to a park and playground and asked if I could camp there. The fellow said, "Sure, pull into the park. That's fine." I found a place to shield me from the wind, then I unloaded. There was an open garage on the grounds, so I quickly decided to stay in here for the night to avoid the rain and 50 mph winds. As I rested in a dry place, ready for sleep, I thought about Juan's summary of geography. He said, "Everything from the Mexican border, down through Central America, Northern South America to the southern edge of Brazil, meaning above Rio De Janeiro, is Indo-South America (Indian, South American). Everything south of Rio De Janeiro was Euro-South American (Uruguay, Argentina, Chile, and the rest of Brazil)." His analysis rang true to my experience. Here, the people were like Europeans, and the cities were cosmopolitan. Work attitudes were different, as were the attitudes of people towards one another.

In the northern part of Brazil, people were nasty with each other, especially on the roads. In southern part, attitudes were far more positive. As I moved further south, cities like Montevideo and Buenos Aires had a very European look.

The roads in Argentina are by far the best in South America. The area I'd come through this afternoon out of Buenos Aires was all cattle ranching country.

The next day I battled a gusting head wind of about 50 miles per hour that blew me around on the road, making it difficult and unpleasant to ride, especially in the rain. I put on my rain suit and my spare helmet with a face shield given to me by Allen Fear.

At one service station, three local young beauties spoke to me while I was sipping on my coffee. I communicated as best I could with these lovely girls. It is my opinion that the most beautiful girls in South America are either Brazilian or Argentinean.

By the time I made it to Bahia Blanca, the temperature during the day was almost freezing. I thought of Ace Martin's travels in Patagonia. Bruno and Juan's weather predictions were absolutely accurate.

In Bahia Blanca, I got lost. While looking for the road to take me out of town, I did not pay attention to the traffic, and nearly got hit by a truck as I ventured into a one way street - the wrong way! Luckily, the truck driver saw me; his attitude was not nasty, but more like, "Hey, fellow, be careful."

I stopped that night in an empty campground. The police in the town checked my identification and asked "What happened to my legs." To avoid being provocative (by mentioning that I served in the South African Army), I just told them "my legs were hurt in a bad car accident." I'd say a light infantry vehicle hitting a land mine is a bad car accident, wouldn't you?

I spent a very quiet night in the campground, exceptionally fatigued, and slept for ten hours, dreaming of snakes. "I hope this dream's not a bad omen," I thought.

The main event in my journey through South America was riding to the bottom of Tierra del Fuego in this terrible weather. I don't particularly like battling elements like this, but Tierra del Fuego is my target area - the place I must go, so nothing will turn me away - not bad weather, or any other hardships.

Outside Bahia Blanca, I enter Patagonia - a semi-arid, very beautiful desert. The skies are either overcast, clear or cloudy, but without rain. Along the road were many frozen mud puddles; it had rained recently. When mud puddles are frozen, that means the temperature is zero centigrade or lower. The roads were good, so each day I ride between 300 and 350 miles (500 to 580 km).

At one place, I planned to camp behind a hotel, but because the wind had been blowing so terribly all day long that I just wanted to get out - no matter what the weather would be that night. When I knocked on a couple of doors of the shut-down hotel, a lady answered. I motioned to her that I wanted to park around the side and sleep, and she said, "Go ahead."

I pushed the motorcycle around to the side of the building, planning to use the outside back of the barn for shelter. When I was about to cook my dinner, a gaucho approaches wearing pantaloons, a big knife in a saddle boot, and a rifle. Two dogs were at his side, barking at me.

"Shut up," he told them.

I explained, "Senor, I am sleeping here to get out of the wind."

"No problem," he told me.

The ground was frozen around me, and the kind man said, "Senor, do you want to sleep in the barn?"

I figured the horse and dogs inside might make it tough to sleep, but decided to accept his offer for the motorcycle, since it would be easier to start in the morning. This fellow had been out trapping, foxes, and other small animals. In the garage he had pelts stretched out drying; I could only surmise that this was a winter source of income, since the hotel looked as though it hadn't been in use for quite some time.

During the night, while laying back and reflecting on the day, I became worried that the dogs in the garage might grab my gloves and chew them up. What could I do on the motorcycle without a proper set of gloves? The idea was unthinkable; in the morning, I was greatly relieved to discover that my gloves had not been mauled.

Preparing to leave, I knocked on the motel door and asked for a cup of coffee. The man motioned for me to enter, and gave me a basket of sliced bread pieces and a big mug of coffee! When I finished the first cup, he filled it again. What luxury - breakfast and coffee at the same time - and actually served to me!

"Senor, mucho gracious," I said as we shook hands and I headed out into the cold and up the road.

As soon as the gray hour of dawn started, I stopped to put in some petrol and watch the sunrise. For thirty minutes I stood in the absolute silence of Patagonia - with no wind blowing on this morning. I watched a magnificent sunrise in ice cold air over a distant mountain. It was awe inspiring

Later that same day I came through a pass that stretched for about 15 miles (25 km). The scenery was magnificent, looking out across Patagonia from on high.

Eventually I arrived at Rio Gallegos after traveling on roads with ice, and temperatures below zero centigrade. I don't know how low. In Rio Gallegos, I fueled up again and headed for Tierra del Fuego.

Out of Rio Gallegos, I hit a potholed dirt road full of mud, rocks and gravel. I was okay on the rocky gravel, but I had to be especially careful of the mud. There were big ruts - sort of an icy version of Zaire or the Amazon. I made very slow progress in first and second gear all the way down to the Chilean/Argentinean Customs and Immigration offices at the border.

I crossed out of Argentina into Chile. I'd do it again the following day because the tip of South America is cut in half by Argentina on the east and Chile on the west. The wind was blowing fiercely, the ground was hard, and the water puddles were frozen.

From Rio Gallegos it was about 60 miles to the Magellan Straits, with twenty miles on a concrete road, the balance on gravel. When I arrived at the ferry landing that goes across from the mainland of South America to Tierra del Fuego, the wind was howling and there was a bit of snow in the air.

I rolled my motorcycle down the ramp and onto the ferry. When I went to pay the man, he refused my money. Then, that rusty old ferry hauled a truck, a few cars, and my motorcycle **across the Magellan Straits** (about a 20 minute ride).

On the other side, traveling down a dirt road I hit a big rock and bent my rear rim; then, I hit another rock and bent the front rim. It just seems I can go for periods of time with no problems, then blam, a new problem TWICE in a matter of minutes.

Chicken Shit, Black Teeth, and Frozen Fingers

I located a tire shop, and spoke to the owner about my rim problem. He handed me an iron bar and a big hammer, and I knocked out bends in the rear and front rims. The man didn't like the way I had formed the rear rim, so he took the hammer and really hit it *hard*. I would hate to mess with this guy. He wasn't as tall as I am, but he was wide as a doorway.

"Do you mind if I spend the night here?" I asked him.

"No problem," he replied. "You can leave your motorcycle in the garage."

"And myself?" I asked.

He pointed over to a fence in a chicken run about a 150 meters away. I carried my tent and sleeping bag the 150 meters to the chicken run where I erected my tent. I had to keep the tent closed so the chickens would not wander inside and shit all over the place.

God it was cold! I thought to myself, "If the temperature drops any lower, even those chickens will look good."

I talked to a truck driver who had been driving from Buenos Aires to Tierra del Fuego for 20 years. Painted on the side of his trailer were the words, "Buenos Aires to Tierra del Fuego - 80 hours." Since the trip is 2,000 miles, that's really something, especially since trucks are govenored at 50 mph (80 km). I was amazed at this driver who had no teeth.

Teeth were different in this region. I noticed that most people had severely stained teeth, some almost black. This was the case right down through Patagonia. I eventually discovered it was from the very strong tea they drink.

That night I treated myself to a hot, home cooked dinner in the local restaurant, then went out to the chicken run to go to sleep. In the middle of the night, I had a hell of a scare when a cat managed to crawl inside my tent - obviously looking for shelter from the terrible cold. I jumped and scared the cat so badly that he scrambled back out and was gone. Poor kitty! Poor Davy. My heart was thumping away just as fast as his was!

Now awake, I thought about my trip down through Patagonia, and the four freezing nights I had spent along the way. One night I slept underneath a truck/trailer, trying to shelter myself from the weather. Would I be able to carry on? Some reports in Caleta Olivia and Fritz Roy had Highway 3 closed up ahead. I spent one night at a police station where I met Mario, a policeman with rotten teeth.

In the cold mornings, it is very difficult to motivate myself to climb out of the semi-warm sleeping bag and into the cold to put on my legs. My sleeping bag is very thin, and is rated as a two-season bag. I also carry a waterproof bivy bag which fits over the sleeping bag and raises it a season - but it is not really suitable for subzero temperatures. I carry this thin bag because when it gets wet, it dries out very quickly. To keep warm, I sleep with my jackets and a pair of pants over my stumps. In the morning, I get up, take off the pants, and put on my *ice cold legs*!

It was Monday.

Mondays are a bad day for me.

I got up, put my legs on, gathered my gear, broke down the tent, said good-bye to my companions - the chickens - and hauled everything in two trips over to the garage. By the time I finished my breakfast of eggs, toast and coffee, the garage was open, so I wheeled the motorcycle out, I loaded it up, then pushed it over to the pumps. After filling up the machine up with gas, and paying the attendant, I noticed that one of my gloves is missing. I couldn't believe it. No one was around. Could the wind have blown it? I looked around, but I couldn't see it anywhere. I remembered seeing a dog around, and now I'm starting to sweat and get irritable. I checked around the corner, and sure enough, there's a dog chewing on my glove! Fortunately, I caught him before he chewed a whole in it. Now this might not sound like much to you, but think of yourself in **subzero** weather centigrade riding along with just one glove. Believe me, that is not a pleasant prospect.

Oh, yes, I can now guarantee you that there's at least one bloody dog in this world who will never again go for a glove that smells like motorcycle oil.

After retrieving my glove, I started the machine up. It was running rough, but I push on, hoping it will sort itself out when it gets good and hot. About three miles down the road, the engine starts coughing, cutting out and sputtering. What now?

I stop and take the carburetor apart - about a 15 minute job; the fuel bowl is full of water. I drain the gas from the gas tank, but find no more water. However, I do notice that my fuel line has got ice on it. I put it all back together, and the motorcycle starts and runs fine.

Driving down the road, my hands are freezing. Sometimes gasoline gets on them, which increases the torture of the ice cold and high winds. I'm on a rough dirt road, putting along in second gear for about three miles, when the engine starts cutting out, coughing again. I stop, find water in the carburetor, repeat repair sequence. This happens two more times; about 10:00, I stop, with the thing coughing again, in front of a frozen water puddle. I take the carburetor apart, by now plenty angry. Just as I stand to grab a tool, a gust of wind hits me and the motorcycle and knocks us both into the large, icy puddle! I climb out soaked with ice water, staring at a motorcycle upside down in about a foot and a half of water and ice. I manage to get it over on its side, but not much else. Two vehicles see my problem, stop, and two men - true to this area - get down in the water puddle with their boots, helping me lift the motorcycle up and out of the puddle.

One of the men then gets back into his car and takes off. The other hangs around while I collect the parts. All of my bags - everything had been submerged in the wet and miserable, freezing water. What else could go wrong?

Bad question to ask, right?

When I looked at the fuel bowl, it was cracked! In disgust, I showed it to this stranger who had "E.N.A.P." (the initials for a natural gas plant about 10 miles [16 km. up the road) painted on the side of his pickup. He looked at the fuel bowl and said, "Maybe I can help." He then climbs into his pickup and off, back in the direction of E.N.A.P..

"He will either be able to fix it," I thought, "or he'll be back in an hour or so."

Well, I stood along side that road, freezing cold, soaking wet, in the wind, for the next six hours! Many thoughts went through my mind. I wondered if my late grandparents or dad would be proud of me right now, or just think I was an idiot? One thing this journey has taught me - if you can't take constant hammering, don't try it.

As I waited, I meditated, looking across the land while slowly freezing to death. I noticed lamas out on the hillsides of this barren area. Tierra del Fuego has been rolling hills, very rocky, devoid of any major forest or trees - very cold and inhospitable. How ironic. Tierra del Fuego means "land of fire" in Spanish... what an absolute, utter lie, or perhaps it was the product of some twisted sense of humor.

"Do I really want to carry on with the trip?" I questioned. Naturally, the clear answer back to me was that there's no stopping! Even though this day had been a real shitter, I would not let myself get down. I knew there must be a reason why I was slowed up, although it might not be apparent for quite some time.

Finally, after six hours, the fellow comes back and says, "Maybe," handing me back the fuel bowl. It now has some type of bizarre looking compound on it. I put the fuel bowl and the rest of the parts back together. Believe it or not... it held gasoline! It didn't leak! It started up!

"Go to E.N.A.P. plant," the man told me, "and they will put you up for he night." That sounded grand to me. Of course, during the 10 mile (16 km) ride to the plant, the motorcycle continued cutting out, coughing and sputtering.

When I rode into the welding shop at the gas plant, things were much warmer and the bike started idling okay. I realized then that part of my problem had to do with the low temperature. I introduced myself to the foreman who was busy on a major project, repairing a manifold that was about 20 meters long and had half a dozen huge flanges welded onto it.

I met Thomas, the man who had invited me to spend the night. He took me over to his house where we had beans for dinner. Thomas was a very devout Christian, and I certainly appreciated his hospitality and the much-needed shower. The rest of my gear needed to be dried out, including my wet slides, my wet camera, and my wet sleeping bag. About 21:30, I was finally able to lay down on the floor of this man's humble living room and go to sleep.

The next day at the shop, the men were still working on the flange. They had worked all night. Thomas told me, "I'll assist you when I can on the motorcycle, but I must first work on the flange." He left me to work on the bike. When I took it apart, I couldn't find anything wrong. When I started it up, it idled fine. To test it, I took it outside in the cold (well below zero) and banged along the road for a couple of miles. After only a few miles, it started missing.

Back at the shop, more water in the carburetor, but none in the gasoline. Yet, the fuel line and valve were frozen. I just couldn't understand this.

Finally, on the morning of the next day, the welders said, "Dave try this. Let's cut off the cooling to the front of the engine by placing a shield around the front of the motor."

This seemed to cure the problem. The shield protected the front cylinder from being hit by the cold air, and allowed more heat to be created. I would never have thought of that myself

I spent one more night with Thomas, but we only talked briefly since he was physically exhausted; his crew had just worked 48 hours straight!

The following morning, on ground frozen so solid I slip all over the surface as I walk, we went to the plant. When they opened the shop, I loaded the motorcycle, had a cup of coffee with these fine fellows, then rode away. They could not believe I was venturing out again into this wicked weather. Even inside the welding shop, with heaters going, the men were wearing sky suits to try and keep warm.

As I took off, dodging patches of ice, it took all my skill to just maneuver around the frozen obstacles and keep on a straight coarse on this narrow little dirt road with on-coming trucks. Caution must be used at all times.

By late morning, **I hit the Chilean border and cleared customs again and back into Argentina.** I enjoyed a nice little run along the Atlantic Ocean into Rio Grande where I purchased gasoline. The ocean was a deep, dark blue seemingly touching the blue, light colored sky - what a magnificent contrast in the same color. I've never seen anything like it.

As I moved inland, the Rio Grande River was frozen as I started moving up into the mountains. I made about 90 more miles (150 km.) through light snows. Suddenly, the entire road dirt road transformed into solid ice and snow - with no patches to maneuver around. The snow was at least two feet deep along the sides of the road. When I hit the ice - need I say it? - the motorcycle went down and I went flying along on my side right behind it for about 50 meters, my body speed at about 35 mph (50 km).

In Argentina, the roads had been in good condition, and I was usually able to get traction and find ways around the ice patches. Not here! I'm looking at solid snow and ice.

Cold - Cold - Cold

At this point, I'm close to one of my main goals - Bahia Lapitia, the bottom tip of South America. Whenever I'm close to a goal, Dave Barr's Law takes effect. That law simply states: the closer I get to a goal, the more problems I'll have. This law has been proven conclusively. Remember the problems I encountered near Bezert, the Northern most city of Africa? How about the weather problems and mechanical breakdowns at the North Cape? Or the challenges getting to Prudhoe Bay in North America?

Well, once again Dave Barr's Law strikes!

I'm close to Bahia Lapitia - so solid ice welcomes my machine!

Just yesterday the welders solved one cold-weather problem that plagued me for three days with the shield to raise the temperature of the engine and stop the motor from missing. What magic do I have left now to conquer frozen roads?

The motorcycle rested on its side on the icy road for about 10 minutes when a bus full of people stopped for me...after about a 50 meter slide on the ice. Six passengers came over to help; I only wish we had a video camera to replay the scene on one of those funny video programs. You should have seen them trying to get the motorcycle up onto its wheels. They were slip-sliding around, falling over each other and the motorcycle. It would start to come up, then fall back down again. I just hoped they wouldn't get grease on their pants. After wildly hollering at each other, they finally got it up and to the side of the road.

Next, they got me up. You see, I was down and unable to get myself up. On this ice, my artificial legs are almost useless for walking or even standing. They helped me over to the side of the road next to the snow bank where I was able to get some traction and stand up. As you can well imagine, I deeply thanked these fellows for their help.

An hour passed before a vehicle passed and asked if they could help.

"I need to load the motorcycle onto a truck and get to Ushuaia," I explained, having no clue if he understood me. He just said "Okay," jumped back into his truck, and was gone.

About 20 minutes later, he came back with two large policemen who introduced themselves as Jeraldo and Juan. They were mountain police and carried submachine guns and pistols, looking more like soldiers in their blue uniforms. These three men then stopped another vehicle and recruited that driver to help us. Now, we had five men, and together we managed to lift the motorcycle up into the back of the truck of the original fellow who had stopped for me. I rode in the back of the truck for the next eight miles, looking at the snow covered hills and trees, at little villages along the way, at a logging camp, and at my numb hands. The scene was all so picturesque and cozy with these buildings in the snow, yet I'm sitting here freezing my ass off, wondering how I'm going to get to Ushuaia, then to the bottom, and out again.

As we were driving, I wondered if the fellow on the motor Guzzie I passed this morning managed to get down all the way to Ushuaia, or if he had to turn around. I would never know. One thing I did know - I felt like a blooming idiot being down here this time of the year!

At the police station, we off-loaded the motorcycle and my gear and put it against the wall of the building. I thanked this very kind Samaritan and off he went outside to the falling snow.

Jeraldo and Juan had just killed a sheep that day, so they had some big steaks. Before you could say "snowman" or "frost bite," they were frying up steaks and potatoes and onions. What a feast! We ate and talked for the next hour with the aide of my broken Spanish and well-worn dictionary. We talked about the problems in South Africa, and about the problems we have in the United States. I was somewhat amused that they believed America is the land with gold at the end of the rainbow. They had no concept of how hard it can be to cope in American society, or of the inherent pressures that go with it.

I was invited to stay in the sleeping quarters of this little log police station. When it came time to retire, they hung their submachine guns up next to their beds. I put my sleeping bag out on the floor, soon to be entertained by the snoring of these two men. The glow from the wood stove in the other room shed a warm and comfortable light into our room, but it brought no peace of mind to me as I wondered, "What am I going to go through tomorrow to get the motorcycle down to Ushuaia?" I knew one thing - I would carry on south. I had no intention of turning around or going back.

The following day, the policemen took turns going outside and flagging down vehicles, searching for prospective helpers to load the motorcycle on the back of someone's truck to take it to Ushuaia. By now, the motorcycle is buried in snow. Apparently it had snowed all night, and the crunching of the snow indicated that the temperature was somewhere around 20 minus. Horribly cold!

Finally, at about 09:30 in the morning, they managed to stop a Chevrolet pickup with a driver who said he'd be "happy" to take me and the motorcycle into Ushuaia. And, it had a king cab! "This is a wealthy rancher," I thought to myself.

Now, the driver, the passengers in the pickup, the two police and I picked up the machine and plopped it in the back of the pickup with all my gear. I climbed in, and off we went on a rather hair-raising ride (this fellow had no chains on his tires). We traveled very slowly, 10 to 15 miles per hour, for about 15 miles, winding around maintain corners with some very steep cliffs. It was wonderfully beautifully and fatally dangerous. Since there were no guard rails on the road, it was easy for me to visualize us slipping right over one of these beautiful cliffs to a very ugly death.

Eventually, we came down the mountain to a sign that said, **"Ushuaia," the most southern city in the world that is inhabited all year round.** We stopped there and they very patiently took a photo of me standing next to the pickup with the motorcycle and the sign of Ushuaia in the background. Then, we went on.

The driver knew of a little motorcycle shop in the area called "Falcon Negros" meaning "Black Falcon" Cycles. Richard was the owner of the place; he took a look at the motorcycle and said "No problem."

I bid my benefactor good-bye and thank you. He would take no money.

Richard took about thirty minutes finishing what he was doing, then we rolled my motorcycle inside. The primary had a big hole torn in it from the fall, so I pulled the primary off and gave it to Richard to fix. I serviced the motorcycle, changing the oil.

Richard had a friend come by that afternoon who brought us a big lunch of meat and potatoes. As we sat at a little table, we passed around the tea pipe - a little tiny tea pot with a silver straw that's used to suck out a very, very strong, concoction of tea made with a small measure of water over some sugar and tea leaves. It is because of this brown gunk that is sucked through that silver straw that these people have such black teeth. They reminded me of the Vietnamese with beetle teeth.

When the tea ceremony was done, Richard took me to a commune house where I was charged $9.00 a night. Tito owned the house, and he told me, "In the morning I will take you down to Bahia Lapitia," supposedly the geographical bottom tip of South America.

The little commune was full of very friendly, poor people. I fit right in! They were mainly young and middle aged, easy to enjoy. We all huddled next to the hot stove - commune fashion. Once again, I did my best I could to communicate with everybody with my dictionary. There was one older lady who called me "Chico" in an affectionate way. There was four of us in the room that I was sharing.

The following day, Tito picked me up about 09:30 and we started driving the last 12 miles (20 km) down to Bahia Lapitia. He had a four wheel drive Subura pickup, a necessity since the snow was quite deep in some places, and there were little semi-frozen streams to go across. It would have been a battle even in the summer to ride my motorcycle all the way down here, especially across some of these creeks.

Finally, we reach a sign that says "Fin Highway No. 3." At that point, I was 3,202 kilometers (about 2,000 plus miles) from Buenos Aires, and at the end of Highway 3 in Tierra del Fuego. I stood next to the sign a little downhearted because I didn't ride my motorcycle all the way to the bottom. I remembered as I stood there that in Prudhoe Bay, my thoughts had not been of conquering the world, or of being grateful for making it to the top. Instead, I could only think that I had to get back down that stupid road!

Now, here I am in Bahia Lapitia, at the bottom tip of South America, 17,000 miles (27,200 km) from Prudhoe Bay, thinking "How in the hell am I going to get out of here?"

After a few photographs, we went back to the pick up and started back. Tito was a real hot rodder. (Why I always attack these hot rodders, I will never know.) He scared the hell out of me on the way back, shooting around the corners; he nearly rolled the vehicle once. I have the darndest luck with these guys. It was a miracle we survived getting back to Ushuaia.

The next challenge was to find a vehicle that could take the Harley Davidson back to the mainland. There were trucks running in and out all the time, as Ushuaia is supplied both by sea and truck. The seaport was an especially picturesque place with a number of ships out in the black water, and snow right down to the waters edge. This created a gorgeous contrast of black and white. All the time I was there, it continued snowing.

I'm having a hard time making the people here understand why I have come down to their place in the world; they think there is something wrong with me.

Tito and I went from place to place looking for a truck. We eventually found a truck that would take me and motorcycle the following day, so we drove back and loaded the motorcycle onto his pick up, then took it back to the truck depot.

Leo, the driver, had a crew to load the motorcycle onto his semi-tractor/ trailor, a big Mercedes rig. I was to meet him the next morning at the outskirts of town and he'd take me back to Punta Arenas, which suited me just fine. "It is snowing all over the island of Tierra del Fuego," they told me. I knew that whatever I had been through would be worse in other places.

Back at the commune that afternoon, I enjoyed talking with the residents. We

287

chatted, cooked dinner, passed the tea urn around, and eventually called it a night.

The next morning I caught a cab down to the truck stop and waited for an hour for Leo to wake up; he was sleeping in the truck. When Leo woke up, we had some coffee and he started to warm up the motor. The snow was coming down quite hard by now, and Leo had chains on all the wheels of the truck, guaranteeing me that my motorcycle was "No problem."

He was right. We conquered the mountains with "no problem" because of the traction from the chains. The Rio Grande River was still frozen solid, and we saw ranch lands full of sheep who wandered freely with the cattle. The road was full of ice, but the truck handled that nicely.

We saw an incredible sunset. The whole horizon was on fire - maybe that's how they got the name Tierra del Fuego.

At Bahia Azul, we waited an hour and a half for the ferry to come back across. We loaded on in the dark, and went across the Magellan Strait in a very stormy sea. If we capsized, we would certainly all drown in those cold, frigid waters. Finally, safe on the other side, Leo celebrated with some Coca Cola mixed with some very strong coffee. That and cigarettes is what this guy lives on. He's going to kill himself; I just pray it's not tonight.

More very large patches of ice, but now the road is half concrete on the way to Punta Arenas for the last 80 kilometers; sometimes, the ice spans hundreds of meters. I am thinking to myself, "How the hell am I going to get out of here tomorrow when I attempt to get over to Puerto Natales?"

At midnight we arrive in Punta Arenas. At the truck yard, Leo says to me, "Tranquil, David," meaning "Relax." Leo then tells me, "You can stay in the truck sleeper tonight," which is very good news to me. I am not reassured by that stupid word "Tranquil." It keeps appearing every time I start getting uptight. Tito was saying it all the time. They don't understand the frustration that comes with not being able to speak the language.

Monday, about 07:30, people started coming into the truck yard. The snow was still coming down, the wind was blowing, and the ground was frozen solid. I thought, "Oh, here we go again. Another beautiful Monday."

About 09:00 they took the motorcycle off. One fellow there was openly antagonistic towards me...why, I don't know. The motorcycle started up, and I rode out of the yard into the snow and wind.

Slipping and Sliding Past Death's Door

Punta Arenas had roads in good shape; there was no ice on them, though it was terribly cold. For the first 5 miles (8 km.) out of Punta Arenas, things are going fine. My speed is up to about 50 mph (80 kph) when, All of the sudden, the motorcycle is sliding out from underneath me, and I'm sliding on the ground right next to it! I reach over and shut the ignition off while sliding to stop the motor from racing, and look up to see a big Mercedes tractor and trailer rig coming, bearing down on me, the driver's eyes as big as saucers. I imagine mine were too!

Time stood still.

We passed each other within arms length. I could have touched that truck's wheels. If that driver had not been a cool head, knowing to leave his controls alone, instead of braking, that would have been it; fortunately, he steered a straight path. I must have slid about a 100 meters, right off into the gravel at the road side.

When I finally stood up, there wasn't even a hole in my pants. Other people witnessed the spectacle and stopped to help me get the motorcycle up, asking "Are

288

you all right?" Then, I hear that word again. "Tranquil. Tranquil."

I am thinking "Fuck tranquil." All I want to do is get moving and get out of this bloody weather!

I said "Thank you for your help," and decided not to fight the roads anymore today. Instead, I backtracked to the truck yard, and hoped that this weather might be a bit warmer tomorrow.

Back at the yard, I asked, "Does anyone know of any trucks that are going north to Puerto Natales that I could pay to have the motorcycle put on?"

"No" they said "we don't. But we'll ask around."

In the afternoon, Leo came back. His faced dropped when he saw me (probably didn't want anything more to do with me). I explained my problem, and he nodded. He introduced me to Post, a little short fellow. The two made quite a contrast since Leo was quite big. When I asked Leo if I could put my tent up out in back for the night, he seemed astounded that I would sleep out in this weather.

Post motioned that I could go with him and stay at his house that night. We caught a cab to the waterfront on the Magellan Straits where you could see the Strait and the island of Tierra del Fuego from his back door. Mrs. Post was a very Indian looking woman who gave me a big hug and introduced me to her two little ninos (children). She made us a very nice dinner.

When I inquired about a shower, I learned these people did not have hot water! In a frigid climate, no hot water heater! Water was heated in a huge pan and they took spit baths. They did have a flush toilet, but other than that, there were no amenities. The place was heated by an old wood stove; the house was literally made from clapboard. Again, I was amazed at the contrast. Post had a million-dollar view and lived in a pauper's home.

We communicated as best we could. He invited his mother-in-law over along with many kids in the neighborhood. We all sat and talked and took some photographs. Eventually, it was time for bed. Fortunately, my bed had about 10 pounds of blankets, and I needed them all it was so cold inside their little house.

The following day at the truck yard I try to state my case again about finding a vehicle that will take the motorcycle. I wait all morning, sitting out on a wood pile reading my book. It is freezing cold, and there's a light snow coming down. "It doesn't look like the weather is going to abate," I think to myself.

That afternoon, with nothing developing concerning a ride, I start to think, "Maybe I will give the roads a try again tomorrow. Perhaps I can ride down the shoulder of the road. If I get flat tires, so what? I now have a jack." Puerto Natales is 160 miles from here, so if I ride, it will be extremely difficult.

That evening I went back home with Mr. Post. Although we could barely communicate, he and his family displayed the universal language of kindness and understanding. Mrs. Post insists that I bathe. Maybe I stink! She makes me, right there in front of her husband, take off everything down to my waist. I had a very good spit bath in their sink where they wash their dishes and bathe themselves. She then took all my dirty clothes and hand washed them.

The following morning when we got up, everything was dry. I put my clothes back away in my bag and very gratefully gave her a big kiss. As I was leaving, she put a parcel in my hand - full of sandwiches and home baked bread that her mother had made for me. The kindness from these very poor people deeply touched my heart.

The morning started out quite warm at Post's house. By warm, I mean about minus 9 degrees. But, by the time we arrived at the truck yard, there were snow flurries and the wind was blowing so hard that I had to hold onto Post to walk over to the warehouse. It was there we said good-bye to one another. What a kind man;

"God drive with you my friend," he said.

I loaded the motorcycle, wheeled it out, thanked all the office personnel for doing basically nothing, and started up. Once the motor was warm enough, I rode out of town. The wind was very, very high, and snow was blowing in flurries. There was no ice on the road until about 9 kilometers out of town. This time I saw the ice coming, and was ready for it. I got off the side of the highway and rode where there was snow and gravel, but no ice, averaging about 30 miles per hour. I had to especially watch for frozen patches of water, rocks, hidden bottles, or broken glass, hidden in the snow. The motorcycle seemed to be running well, in no small way thanks to the shroud around the front of the engine that cut all cooling to the front cylinder.

After about 50 miles, I realized I needed gas; in the concentration on the weather, I hadn't thought about petrol, and was now down on reserve. I saw a man along the side of the road and asked, "Do you need any help?"

"No, senor," he replied.

"How many kilometers to gasoline?" I asked.

"Puerto Natales, senor, para gasolina."

"Oh God, I'll never make that," I thought to myself, but I will not turn back again. So, I went forward, coming to a little village that was all snowed in. I was very fortunate that the roads were gravel under the snow, so they were not all iced up. I managed to get back off the main highway and asked, "Is there was anybody with gasoline here?"

"Try a little store at the edge of town," I was told, and sure enough, a man who sold black market gasoline brought out a jerry can and I fueled up with enough gas to take me all the way to Puerto Natales.

From the time I turned off the main highway, the road was half concrete, half gravel; I stayed on the gravel side. Sometimes, the gravel side was on the oncoming lane which was fine until an oncoming vehicle loomed into sight. I would try to get over to the side of the road and slow up without panicking the oncoming vehicle and let him pass me in the same lane. As long as I could stay on top of the gravel, my traction was good. If I spotted a patch of ice coming with no gravel sticking up from it, I'd give it a bit of throttle, speed up and then hit the ice. At that moment, I'd pull in the clutch and rev the motor, then majestically glide across the ice. The engine fly wheels on a Harley Davidson run vertically, so they help steady the motorcycle's center of gravity. One must be completely relaxed and ready to catch it when it takes traction again on the other side. If there's torque going to the rear wheel, the motorcycle would go down on its left side, sliding right out from underneath me with the rear wheel coming around, forward.

Even with my shield, the weather is now so cold that the motor is once again starting to cut out as I go up in altitude. "Please, you son of a bitch, just give me a break today," I thought, carefully staying on the gravel part of the road. There were a few times I thought I was going down, but somehow I managed to stay up. Eventually, I came down out of the mountains, leaving the green forests and beautiful, snow-covered hill sides. Unfortunately, it was hard to appreciate some of the most beautiful scenery in the world because I had to concentrate so hard on negotiating that ice-covered road. I am so sick of snow I could spit.

Below the snow line, I saw a gaucho riding along across the pastures with a pack of dogs around and behind his horse. What a beautiful thing to see, his pantaloons blowing in the wind, his big knife bouncing on his hip, and a little tiny hat that seemed cemented to his head. I waived at him, and he waived back at me as he sat proud in the saddle, seeming to say, "Hey, senor, here is your reward. You made it."

That was the longest 160 miles I have ever ridden.

My heart was in my throat the whole time.

Chapter Twenty-Seven

Iceless Paradise!

Coming down out of the mountains into Puerto Natales, the fjords of the southern hemisphere are in front of me. Puerto Natales is right on the inland sea that runs between Puerto Natales and Puerto Montt, and is full of islands and fjords; most of the islands are uninhabited, with the snow often coming right down to the waters edge. The sea itself is black, and the rest of the area is beautiful green pasture land.

At the ferry office, they tell me it will be another two days before the ship sails. I make arrangements to come back and get my ticket in the morning (they won't change any money that evening). A man looking at the motorcycle comes out of the office and introduces himself as Conrade. I ask him, "Where can I find a cheap place to spend a couple of nights?"

"Follow me," he replies, leading me to a run down hostel. After I stow my stuff away, he says, "Why don't you come over to my house and have some fresh bread and coffee?" That sounded wonderful, so I followed him to his place, where he served me hot bread, and I met his wife and two sons. We talked for the next hour or so about his charter business out to the islands.

Back at the little hostel, I enjoyed a very needed shower then climbed into bed about 21:00, making sure to thank God for bringing me through these last few days.

The next day, I bought my ferry ticket. They told me the ship would sail north on the following night. I rode over to Conrade's house, and made an arrangement with Conrade, Jr. to help me wash my motorcycle down. We spent the rest of the morning and early afternoon washing it down with hot water and soap, getting A BIT of the grease off. The thing actually looked like a motorcycle when we were done!

On the way back to the little guest house, I spotted a Yamaha Enduro with a sidecar in front of a cafe; I pulled in and met Agnes and Christian, two people from France, who were traveling throughout South America. I introduced myself to them and said that I was a world traveler. We got to talking and had some coffee. They were very amicable people, and could speak English!

"Do you have a place to stay?" I asked.

I told them where I was, and that it was only a few dollars a night.

"Fine, we will go there," they decided.

That evening, they emptied out their sidecar and the three of us went on their motorcycle to downtown Puerto Natales. We stopped at a cafe and had tea and hot dogs for dinner. I was surprised at how much power their machine had.

Boat Battering Continues

The following day we went and got their ferry ticket, and spent the rest of time working on the motorcycles, getting them ready for whatever was to come.

In the evening, when we went down to the shipping office to put the motorcycles on the boat. They informed us that we couldn't load them until 04:00 next morning, and to go ahead on the ship with our valuables. My bag weighed about 40 pounds; I put it on my shoulder and followed Christian and Agnes out to the ship... quite a walk, almost half a kilometer. We climbed a couple of flights of stairs which was murder on my stumps. I was very fortunate that it was freezing cold out; had it been hot, my pain would have been double. We were all shown to a room and told to wait there until about 03:30 when they would wake us up to load our motorcycles.

I wrote in my dairy, took off my legs, and had just fallen asleep when there was a knock on my door; someone was demanding to get in. "Wait a minute," I told them, but the banging continued. I banged on the door myself and shouted, "Wait a fuckin minute!" The man kept banging, so finally I just opened the thing without taking the time to put on my legs.

"You horrible cretin, you fucking idiot" I screamed at him. I'm sure he didn't know what to make of this passenger shouting at him with no legs. He calmed down, and asked for my ticket. I felt horribly humiliated, sitting there with my legs off. I retrieved my ticket, and then he told me in broken English and Spanish, "There's a mistake about you being in this berth."

"Wait here a minute," he said.

"No shit," was my intelligent reply as I went to put on my legs.

I waited; he never returned.

At a quarter after three, they came to wake me up, and I went over and woke up Christian to bring the motorcycles on board. We went down to a lower deck where a crewman rudely told us to go back up. By now, I've had enough of these assholes and started shouting at this guy, telling him exactly what he was, "to get a life and some manners while you're at it."

The jerk looked dumbfounded at me as Christian grabbed me by the arm and said, "Come on Dave." We went back upstairs and waited a full hour in the freezing cold before they called us back down the two flights of stairs to the shipping office to start the motorcycles up and bring them onto the ship.

Once they were secured, we went back up where I met the Steward who had been banging on my door. He apologized and I apologized. It was obviously a mistake in communications; he told me, "You can keep the cabin and be by yourself and not have anybody else in it." I thought that was a very nice gesture. My ticket for me and the motorcycle for four days was $200.00 - a pretty good price since it included food.

About 06:30, we put out of Puerto Natales and start up through the fjords. When the sun comes up, it just turns gray. We are battered by gale force winds, so the ship is in horribly rough seas, with snow coming down on top of that! Although it was terrible weather, in its own way it was very beautiful from inside the cabin where I could see it without riding my motorcycle. I was amazed at all the little islands with trees and rocks. It was fascinating to me to know that there are still places like this still in the world where there are no people, roads, automobiles, trash or anything else that goes with the ravishes of modern man.

The ship I'm on comes with cows, horses and sheep. During our four day trek, only the horses were fed. I don't know why. This is certainly not America!

The second morning we came to a picturesque little tiny village located on one of the small islands. "What do these people do for a living here?" I wondered. I got a good look at the fjords as we traveled in and out of the various islands. What a sight! Mountains covered with pine trees and snow came right down to the water's edge where rock or dirt showed through, as black as the water itself. It was shockingly beautiful!

The passengers on the boat were from Germany, France, South America, and various other places, including me from the United States. It is rare to encounter another American in the places I go. Many French, Germans, Swedes and British, but not Americans. Have we lost our pioneering, adventurous spirit?

The ship broke into the Pacific ocean on the afternoon of the second day, entering into rough seas and sea sickness began. Part of my entertainment during this time was watching having liquid laughs over the side. The sound of retching would go on for two more days.

We entered a huge, natural bay headed for Puerto Montt. I stood on the bow and saw the sun rise under the clouds - incredible, beautifully red. Suddenly, it was gone up above the clouds, and the sea, once gleaming with a red tinsel, was now black. Later, the sunlight shot down through the clouds. It seemed almost sacred.

There was a rumor circulating as we were coming into Puerto Montt that they wouldn't off load anything until 16:00, and that a boat would come across for the passengers. That was a bit of an irritation for Christian, Agnes and me. It turned out to be just that - a rumor, second shitter on the right information. We came into port and never slowed up as we made our approach to the dock. The back of the ship was open, and we were told to take our stuff down. I loaded up the Harley Davidson, and when the ramp was dropped, I rode it right off with Christian and Agnes behind me. After a quick police check, we rode out of town and parted company with the rest of the passengers.

We purchased gasoline and headed in the same direction out of town. After about 20 kilometers, it was time to waive good-bye to my friends; I never saw them again.

Sputtering Carbs in Sorry Santiago

Alone once more, I headed north to Santiago, a little over 600 miles (1000 km). I made about 100 miles that day. I pulled in to buy some bread and noodles. I was directed to a place for the evening where it was strikingly beautiful under the trees, and if it rained, I knew the branches would help shield me from the storm. After a fairly restless night's sleep, listening to trucks whiz past on the main rode, I awoke to a dense fog and a breakfast of a scrumptious salami sandwich, it was time to go.

As soon as I started up, the carburetor flooded out and I had to stop, take it apart, and try to adjust the float level. Once I got going, the thing was starving for fuel and started flooding again. Pulling into a service station, I'm thinking to myself, "Good morning, here we go, what a wonderful day this is going to be." Same procedure, but this time, when I'm back out and moving, there's no flooding. "Well I win one, what do you know?"

The dense fog destroyed visibility, and my headlight wasn't working, making the ride doubly dangerous in this forested, mountainous area, loaded with road curves. After about 100 miles (160 km), the fog started to clear as I bounced along the rough, concrete, washboard road.

To the west of me, heading from south to north, up Highway 1 was a beautiful area of rolling hills and forests, and to the east, agricultural lands. Off in the distance I could see the snowcapped Andes mountains rising out of the horizon, majestic and beautiful.

I made about 300 miles that day, stopping at a truck stop to endure yet another restless night's sleep. No bread to buy, so I purchased crackers in a restaurant at the truck stop. Salami can be found at little stands along the road through Argentina and Chile; it is the best salami I've found anywhere, and, conforms to the ultimate Dave Barr food test... it is quite cheap.

Late that afternoon, I managed to get a telephone line through to the head of the Cheshire Home, a Mrs. Lucy Pee Wonka, and told her, "I'm on my way." I had sent her letters and post cards when I was in the United States, and along the way. People connected with the home from Brazil had promised me they'd communicate with her, so she knew I was coming. On the phone, she seemed very hesitant about seeing me, but finally agreed that I could go to the home in Santiago the next day and contact her.

The next morning I made Santiago, immense in size, and strange enough, a city where bicyclist are allowed on the freeway, hooking along at about 40 to 50 kilometers per hour. I couldn't believe it. "What were bicyclist in big groups doing on the freeway?" No one seemed to mind, least of all the police.

At a service station a young girl gave me very good directions to the Home, sheltered behind an iron gate and fence. The nurses wouldn't let me in. I tried to explain to them in my lousy Spanish about Lucy Pee Wonka, but that didn't work. I located a pay phone and asked to speak to Lucy, but was told she wasn't in (she told me she would be there). Obviously, I was dealing with someone who did not take me very seriously and had caused me a lot of trouble. Why didn't she just write me a letter saying, "Sorry, Dave, we do not want you to come to the Home as there is nothing you can do for us?" I was so angry I could spit. In retrospect, I could see where the staff might have been reluctant to let me enter. After all, I was pretty dirty, and the motorcycle might have scared them. At the same time, they were not willing to do anything, even though I kept using Lucy Pee Wonka's name.

In the end, I simply got on my motorcycle and said, "Fuck Santiago," heading out of the city. Naturally, I got turned around and became lost trying to exit the city. On the outskirts of nowhere, I asked somebody for directions in broken Spanish and, to my delight, he answered me in English!

"Follow me," he said, "I'm headed out of town."

I followed this man for the next 60 miles as he was headed straight north through Chile. Since I was to turn east and head for Mendoza, we finally parted, waiving to each other. What a kind man.

I found an empty campground off the road, feeling a bit depressed. It had been raining for the past hour, and I was still a bit angry at the Santiago home. Once in the campground, there was a spring nearby where I was able to get fresh water; that felt good. I closed my day around 19:30 due to the terrible weather.

The Andes were ahead, and I didn't know what to expect. It hurt the way the Santiago home turned me away with no communication after I had traveled many miles to get there. I could have gone out of Chile through Bariloche after I departed from the boat in Puerto Montt, and headed back across Argentina with better roads.

The following morning, I noticed my gold ring, hand made by a friend of mine in South Africa and given to me before I started this trip, was missing off of my finger. I looked all over. I went back to the brook where I had drawn water. I looked in my gear. I looked on the ground... all to no avail. With very low morale, I realized the ring was lost. It is the old domino effect - when things are going bad they just stay bad. With me it runs in streaks that can last for days.

The Andes Adventure

It rained hard all the way to Los Andes where I fueled up and headed into the Andes Mountains. The higher up I went, the rain changed to snow, and the motor started cutting out again. "Lets just keep pushing on," I thought to myself. Finally, up ahead, there was an Army road block and a line of cars trailing back a few hundred meters. The snow along the side of the road was about a foot deep. The concrete road had huge ridges in it for traction in icy conditions When I came to the Army outpost, the man tried to tell me "There have been avalanches, so we are not passing traffic right now." Everybody stood in the snow and the cold for the next hour, waiting for the Army's decision. Finally, the group was informed, "It will be five to seven days before the pass is open."

"Fuck, what now?" I thought in my usual, tranquil manner. "Does my miserable luck just stay with me?" I questioned. "This is all I need...to be stuck here for 7 days."

The traffic started to turn around and head back down the mountain; I was no exception. We traveled about 40 kilometers (25 miles) back to the town of Los Andes where I asked a fellow if he knew "any cheap place to stay" in the town. He took me to a little flop house hotel where they charged me $7.00 a night; believe me, this was the cheapest place in town. They had a storage area behind the hotel for the motorcycle, so I unloaded my gear from the machine and put it away.

I was now stuck in the cold and rainy town of Los Andes, watching the snow keep piling higher up in the Andes. I met a guy named Pepe who had a little motorcycle shop; he couldn't speak any English. I kept trying to pry information out of him about what was happening concerning avalanches up in the pass, but he wasn't able to tell me. I met his friend, Juan, who had just come from the United States and spoke

English very well. Juan took me to the office of the company clearing the pass, and we asked, "How much longer will the pass be closed?"

"Another five days," they replied.

It was always "another five days."

I couldn't get real answers to anything. No one seemed to know.

In this town, no one understood me. I wandered around and gradually learned what the locals were thinking. One told me, "I thought you were a drunk who had just drifted in and was staying over at the hotel." When he learned that was not the case, he invited me over to his house to meet his family and enjoy a meal - although the communication part of it was terrible.

By the end of seven days, I couldn't stand it any longer! I wanted to turn around and head for Bariloche which was 700 miles (1200 km) south, a place I had passed on my way to Santiago. "I can attempt to get over the pass there," I reasoned. Pepe insisted that I stay. He talked to Juan who said, "I will speak to my father. He knows somebody who might be able to help with information."

The next day I learned that Bariloche was closed as well, so it would have been futile for me to turn around and head the opposite direction.

After nine days, word came that the pass was open, so I hurried out of town heading north up and over the pass towards Mendoza. The motorcycle ran better; Pepe had given me a couple of pointers. "The altitude may have something to do with it," he told me, "so take the air cleaner filter off." I did, and it ran much better. Up and up I went until I was in the snow line. When I came to the Army post, the soldier said, "No senor, pass no aberto."

The face shield on my helmet fogged up instantly! You couldn't see my head. I went insane with anger, and was hollering and shouting. The poor soldier jumped from fear of this wild looking character with the fogged face shield.

He opened the gate and let me pass.

No more than a kilometer had passed before I hit the first avalanche tunnel. There was ice everywhere ahead of me. These tunnels were open on one side so light could get in. There's a massive road grader backing up towards me, about 100 meters away. I shut the motorcycle off and started backing it up, trying to get off the ice patch. Before I knew it, the road grader was almost on top of me. Fortunately, the grader driver was trying to light a cigarette, and had to turn around to shield himself from the wind to cup the flame. When he did, I caught the corner of his eye and he stopped the grader about 10 meters (10 yards) from me. It would have been impossible for me to have jumped off the bike and get out of his way.

It was a close call!

I managed to get the motorcycle out of the way slowly by backing up, turning around, and heading back with my tail between my legs towards the Army post and Los Andes. As I passed the soldier at the post, I just waived to him; he waived back with an "I told you so" smug look on his face.

Back at Los Andes, I settled into the hotel again, then went for a little walk around town where I met a young American couple. They didn't know where to go to find a cheap place for the night, so I invited them over to the hostel. They settled in, explaining that "We're here to snow cki for the rest of the season. Tomorrow, we plan to go to the top of the pass to find out if snow skiing is in season." They promised me they would also make inquiries as to how things were coming on the Argentinean side of the pass.

I wandered around for another two days. The skiing couple had gone to the top, and discovered no new information. On the 12th day of my stay in Los Andes, Pepe greeted me with a huge smile, saying, "The pass is open, senor."

"Right," I replied sarcastically.

"No, senor, it is true," Pepe insisted.

The following morning I gathered my gear while it was still dark and left the hotel, driving once again to that now very familiar Army post. The soldier there just opened the gate and saluted as I went flying by. I saluted him back.

I made my way through the first avalanche tunnel, noticing and avoiding patches of ice inside the tunnel. The road continued to climb at a very steep angle - at one point, a few thousand feet. The road would go half a mile and do a U-turn, going up another half a mile, then another U-turn going up... like a colossal stairwell. The road was often very narrow so only one vehicle could get by. Since the avalanche was not totally cleared, huge blocks of snow sometimes littered the road. I managed to ride between them. I didn't stop to photograph anything for fear of another avalanche. As I rode along, I could see vehicles that had been swept over the side of the mountain by the avalanche. These colored dots in the snow were a very grim reality of the dangers of travel at this time of year in the Andes.

Upward, the road carried me through a series of avalanche tunnels. Fortunately, they always had a bit of light in them so I could spot the ice, mainly at the entrance and exit.

Up over more switch back roads. The motorcycle seemed to be running very well; at one point, at the top of the switch back, I was going around a bend where an avalanche was still being cleared by bulldozers and graders. I hit ice and went down. Of course, I couldn't upright the motorcycle by myself. Some passing soldiers helped me. Many other cars had gone past before the soldiers stopped; I guess the others were afraid to get out and help - a disappointment, and certainly out of spirit to what I had previously experienced. Perhaps it was the ever-present threat of an avalanche.

I sliced open the back of my hand on this fall, so the soldiers insisted I wait for an Army medic to come up; within ten minutes I had field dressing applied to my hand.

Onward, I came to and cleared Chilean customs and immigration. Up ahead, I encountered two long tunnels, each over a mile in length; they would prove to be a nightmare. I saw this black hole in the side of the mountain and realized I was going into a long dark tube. There were no lights inside of the tunnels, and entering the first one I noticed about 20 meters of ice. I sped up and pulled in the clutch and glided gracefully across the ice and into the tunnel.

There were patches of ice periodically through the tunnel which stood at about 12,000 plus feet. I cannot possibly describe to you the cold in that tunnel. Fortunately, the ice was only in very short patches; a large patch would take me down for sure. When the motorcycle hits a pocket of ice, it always jumps, then starts a sideways movement until it can catch traction again. I had to relax while holding on tight to the handlebars.

My headlight, now repaired, would only reflect so far in front of me, so it was difficult to make out the dividing line. I kept my speed about 30 miles per hour so if another vehicle entered the tunnel, I would have a bit of time to decide what to do. Often, the lights from oncoming traffic would blind me so I couldn't see the dividing line. I just moved to the right of the narrow road, hoping that the oncoming truck or bus would miss me.

A couple of times I felt like I was getting vertigo; I didn't know whether I was moving forward, up, down, right or left. I remembered a mission we were on in Vietnam, and a pilot who had a recon team on the ladder. We were covering him in our gunships when he got vertigo in some clouds and crashed into the side of a mountain, killing the helicopter crew and the recon team. 15 good Marines lost their lives because of vertigo. Another time, we nearly crashed into a mountain at night because the pilot got vertigo.

I just held on tight and prayed to God that I didn't wreck inside this seemingly endless tunnel.

Out one tunnel - what a blessed relief - and traveled no more than a mile before sighting the nightmarish entrance to the second. Once again, I glided over the ice. In the oncoming lane I spotted a bus emerging out of tunnel. I stayed totally relaxed, trying to keep my heart out of my throat, leaving my fate in the hands of the good Lord. The grill of the bus loomed bigger as we went gliding past one another, only inches apart! I felt the hand of God Himself was there to intervene or I would have hit that bus. I slid another 20 meters before the motorcycle took traction.

When I came out of the last tunnel and headed downhill, **I realized I was in Argentina.** Somehow, a great burden lifted from my shoulders, and I said a prayer of thanks. I stopped at a police post and asked "Are there any more tunnels?"

"No, there are no more," was the wonderful news.

Now on the Argentinean side, the road is much straighter with fewer curves. Whoopee! But, there are massive, long patches of ice I must glide across, and plenty of truck and bus traffic since the pass has been closed for 12 days. Down the far side I went about 10 miles (16 km) to the customs and immigration post, a very crowded place to be sure. Travelers had been waiting in Mendoza for days to get across.

Customs cleared rapidly, so I was on my way once again. Gradually, the road became actually dry, with snow piled about three feet deep along its side; it started to become warm!

At Uspallata I fueled up and found water, taking off my rain gear for the first time since south of Buenos Aires (seemed like a lifetime ago). I made my way into the Patagonia countryside where I saw a small dirt road leading back off into the distance where I could shut the machine down and rest in the total silence of the semi desert area I was now in.

June 16: That night in the gathering dusk I watched a giant condor take off from a mountain, silhouetted in the setting sunlight for a good 10 minutes before he flew off into the distance, That was my reward, my wonderful sense of peace after having fought a nerve-wracking, dangerous battle of crossing over the Andes Mountains in the middle of the winter.

Under the evening stars, I remembered the 12 days I sat in Los Andes, not really having any meaningful communication with another human being, full of irritation and apprehension about trying to get over the Andes, but unable to vent it. I remembered those weeks in São Paulo, busy from before dawn until after dark, working on the motorcycle. Then, I thought about those expecting me in Hong Kong - the head of the Harley owner's group, and Marilyn Dear who had been working so hard to find a way for me to get into China. Now, in the peacefulness on the eastern side of the Andes in Patagonia, I had my first real hope in quite awhile of making some real progress. I felt fairly comfortable - mentally and physically, as I closed the day by climbing into my sleeping bag, dead to the world for my first full night's sleep in weeks.

$60 for Gasoline and Oil?

The following morning the motorcycle was running fairly well in that mountainous area with rough roads. Soon I was in Mendoza where I stopped to fuel up and take off again. The roads improved, so I made very good time. It started to cloud over and rain; back into my rain suit. Oh well, I'd had a break!

I went through San Luis and at the end of the day ended up in Rio Cuarto, 320 miles (510 km) from my starting point that morning. I stopped and bought some bread and salami to go with my noodles, and inquired about a place to stay.

"There's a campground that's not used at this time of the year," the store clerk replied, giving me directions. She told me her father was an English teacher, and when she heard what I was doing, asked me, "May I interview you with my tape recorder. I would like to put you on our little radio station."

"Indeed," I replied, giving her a brief history of the trip and the reasons for doing it. At the campground, I barely finished my dinner when a television crew and another young woman showed up for a brief interview with a crowd of about 20 people. In the evening, everyone went their way and I was able to rest that night without being disturbed.

I woke up to fog - always a worry. I never know the roads, so poor visibility is an ever-present danger. After I loaded my motorcycle, it fell over. I had to unload it, upright it, then reload it. "Good morning" I said. The day was starting out with a bang.

My first stop was in Villa Maria. The fog had not let up. But I could still see some things, such as a cemetery where there were many statues of angels and large grave crypts. As I passed it, I longed for the time to stop and study the history in the graveyard in more detail. "I could go around the world on a brand new motorcycle for what some people spend on a grave crypt," I think.

In Villa Maria, after buying gasoline, I asked where I could get a cup of coffee. "No, senor, no coffee." Wouldn't you know it!

Off I go again into a head wind for the next 110 miles (175 km). I honestly don't know how I made it. There's no spare can of gasoline - it had been stolen in Los Andes. Eventually, I made my way to a place called San Francisco where I stopped for a sandwich. A nearby old man asked me, "Where are you headed?"

"To Paraguay, and then to Brazil," I reply.

"Don't go Paraguay," he says. "Much rain has fallen. It is flooded. Impossible. Roads are bad. Mud."

I understood his concern very clearly, and took his warning to heart. I'd had enough bad weather and miserable roads with ice and mud to last three lifetimes! If I could re-route and avoid these conditions, I will.

About 100 miles later I come to Santa Fe where I learned that the Rio Parana had flooded homes, and put many businesses under water. People were living in tin shacks along the road. I stopped to photograph at one place, and appreciated the people's attitude of allowing me to document their misery. I waived to them and they waived back. In some places, the water is almost a foot deep in the road. I carefully followed the rest of the traffic, and had no problem drowning out the motor. Eventually, I came to the far side of Santa Fe and spotted a grassy lot behind a service station where I secured permission to park.

That day I covered 325 miles (510 km). As I inspected the bike, I noticed an oil leak on the base of the front cylinder. Even with new cases I am being plagued with this same horrible problem. Doesn't anything ever fix the first time?

The following day I rode across beautiful cattle country, eventually hitting a head wind. I relaxed while riding through these beautiful forested and cattle ranching areas. The motorcycle seems to be running pretty good for two days in a row - rare for this old Dog. I secured an extra gas can at a service station, but they were out of gas. I was low, so this was not welcome news!

Towards the latter part of the day, in Poiso de los Libres, a town on the river that separates the city of Uruguaiana in Brazil from Argentina, I found gas and serviced my motorcycle, changing the oil, getting it ready for the last 1,500 miles across Brazil to Sao Paulo and Rio De Janeiro. I drew quite a crowd while I was working on the machine, and when I asked "Are there any stores where I can buy bread," they motioned to me to stay. Within minutes, a loaf of bread appeared for which they would accept no money. When I fueled up the machine, and went to pay the man, I was shocked! He charged me nearly $60.00! The oil, 8 liters of it, was about $8.00 a quart, and that, combined with gasoline, made the bill about $60.00. After paying,

I rode out of town to a truck stop and found an area off in a corner where no one would bother me and set up camp for that night.

The next morning, the dawn was coming up **as I crossed the bridge going over to the Brazilian side of the river.** The sun broke over the city of Uruguaiana and it was beautiful. I cleared customs and immigration quite quickly, and was able to change money at the border, getting enough to take me all the way back to São Paulo so I wouldn't have any exchange hassles like I did with Sagi and Omer.

The Brazilian roads were terribly rough, so it was hard to travel over 35 miles an hour because of the constant potholes that ran up to a 100 meters and were on both sides of the road. I was constantly dodging them while watching for trucks that thought nothing of driving on my side of the road to avoid a pothole.

At about 100 miles, I stopped to fuel up and once again experienced that lousy, low-octane Brazilian gasoline, laced with alcohol. I drew a crowd, and chatted for about 10 minutes, answering their questions as best I could in my totally pathetic Portuguese.

Near the end of the afternoon, I arrive at a gas station and truck stop. I've ridden about 340 miles (530 km), and am ready to stop. As I am paying for my gasoline, a guy comes to me and says, "Is this you?" He had been reading the magazine, *Dose Rohdas*, which carried an article about my adventure.

"Si, that is me," I told him, shaking his hand and giving him an autograph. He told me he was the owner's son.

"Do you know a place I can sleep around here?" I asked.

He pointed to a grassy knoll just up behind the service station and restaurant. I sat up my camp there, and soon a crowd and television camera appeared. Late in the afternoon, they all left and I was able to cook my dinner and be alone, thinking to myself, "I'm on the home stretch."

The next morning, the sun once again greeted me, and for the second day in a row I would not be wearing my rain suit. Unbelievable. The roads were good all the way to Porto Alegre.

Then, back on to the "Highway of Death" where I went up mountains and wound around curves with numerous white memorial crosses. Although the sun was out, many curves were dark and had water condensation, making it easy to slide. All in all, I covered over 300 miles (500 km) that day. When I came to my last service of the day, I went to start the motorcycle only to hear nothing but a clicking sound. "What, a problem with the starter?" I thought. A crowd started to gather, and one fellow spoke a little English.

"I'm a motorcycle mechanic," he told me, inspecting my machine. "Here, this battery bracket is broken. The bolt holding it is right up against the starter wire. It is shorting out the whole system."

"It is a wonder that I didn't burn out all the wires," I think to myself.

We wheeled the motorcycle back over to a grassy patch where I repaired the damage, made my dinner and closed my day.

The following day I was up and moving at dawn, once again through heavy fog. This seems to be the norm for this area and one must be very careful of an accident because the truck drivers here in Brazil don't have governored trucks such as they do in Argentina and Chile, so they go a lot faster.

In the afternoon I stopped at a service area, but there were no telephone tokens for sale; tokens are needed to operate the telephones. I walked into the service area office and offered to pay the owner cash so I can call ahead to São Paulo and let Sandy Smith know I'm coming so she could meet me at the outskirts of town and show me the way in.

The owner agreed.

First, I kept getting a busy signal; all lines into São Paulo were taken. After three quarters of an hour, we actually get through to Sandy's maid, who hangs up before I can say three words. I am so mad I could spit! Why do I have so much trouble with telephones? I offered the man about $2.00, but he refused my money. I then asked, "Could you please take it and call this lady. Tell her I will call her again between 09:00 & 10:00 tomorrow." He agreed.

Further down the road, I found a dirt trail back off into a banana grove. I rode back about 500 meters, found an open field, and set up my camp. That night, I looked up at the stars, realizing this would be the last night out on the road for a long time.

Final Reunions

The next morning, fog greeted me again as usual. This day I saw a couple of very grizzly accidents from the night before. Finally, I was able to speak with Sandy on the phone, and she said, "Yes, I received the message from a young fellow." She agreed to meet me in about an hour's time.

As I sat along side the road waiting for Sandy, a Japanese fellow on a Honda pulls up, saying "I know who you are. I've seen you in *Easy Rider* magazine." He took out of his pocket a picture of a 1951 Panhead Harley Davidson done up like the *Easy Rider* bike Peter Fonda rode in the movie. I admired it. We spoke to each other for about a half an hour until Sandy Smith showed up.

It was great to see Sandy again, although I felt bad about trying to give her a hug - I stank and had black all over my face from days worth of diesel exhaust. I had not taken a shower in a week, and had traveled 2,500 miles from Los Andes to São Paulo. I smelt like the south bound end of a north bound mule.

I followed Sandy across the western side of São Paulo, a city that is massive and confusing, all the way across to the police maintenance depot garage of the Policia militar. They waived me right through to the back. I rode to where the escort platoon is housed, and met up again with Lieutenant Claudio, Lieutenant Dante, Zulato, and Valdimar. They were all patting me on the back even before I could get the motorcycle engine shut off. What a wonderful feeling to be back among these good men! I had climbed a very great mountain, and there was such a great feeling of satisfaction and pride, and none of it would have been possible without the help I'd received from all of these kind people who lived the adventure through me. We put the motorcycle out of the way, and made arrangements with Lieutenant Claudio to let me and Zulato work on it tomorrow.

Sandy drove me back to her place where we had tea and I took a much-needed shower, being clean for the first time in a week. That evening, Richard Stevens and Vicki came around and we all went to our favorite restaurant for a wonderful dinner. They congratulated me on my 6,500 mi. (10,000 km) round trip to Tierra del Fuego and back.

That night, I realized I was going to put things in overdrive because Richard had given me the news that SAA flies once a week, on Sundays via Johannesburg, then there's a five day layover before flying on to Hong Kong. It was important to be on the plane this Sunday so as not to lose another week. Since it is Thursday, I realized my last night with these people is tonight. I must move full steam ahead to make the plane; it will be pressure until the bitter end.

The next morning, the faithful police car was waiting for me to drive me back to the garage. Zulato and I got stuck in. The first thing that we did was to wash all the dirt and grim off of the motorcycle. When that was done we started repairing odds and ends.

Of course, the carburetor was giving me trouble again. It started leaking right there in the shop, so we took it apart a half a dozen times. In the afternoon, two very lovely girls from the school of motoring safety ask me if I would come back to their school and meet the faculty and some of the kids. That is the last thing I wanted to do right now, but being wonderful and polite as I am, I agreed. They waited about thirty minutes for us to frantically try and get the carburetor working, when finally Zulato said, "Just go with them and leave it to me."

We drove across town in a police car, and at the school I met the staff; they immediately showed me a video (I was screaming inside to get back and work on the bike). Next, they showed me the different phases of training they give to the kids, who mobbed me on the way out for autographs. The school was very comprehensive, and made kids aware of the dangers of being out on the road.

Finally, the driver and I bolted for the car, heading back to the garage where Zulato had solved the carburetor problem; Good on you friend! We performed a few other minor repairs like the battery bracket. Then, it was back to Sandy's for a very nice shower and a pizza dinner before saying good-bye to Sandy, one of the most giving, helpful people I met in all of South America!

By this time it was late enough, so the traffic was fairly light. The driver took me back to the garage of the policia militar with all my gear. I would stay in a little room with a bed in the back this night. I slept fitfully, knowing the next day would be my last on the road in South America.

The next morning I'm up about 03:00 and start loading the motorcycle. To my great surprise, Zulato appears so we shared a piece of pizza for breakfast, realizing that this is our last moment together. He climbed into his Volkswagen and motioned for me to follow him to the freeway.

It was now 04:00, and still very dark. At the bottom of the freeway ramp, we stopped to hug each other for a full minute; we both had tears in our eyes. How do you say good-bye to someone who had so little but gave so much? We had worked together hand in hand for six weeks without understanding each other's words. With a heavy heart, I turned away from my friend, started the motorcycle, and rode down the highway towards Rio De Janeiro.

Gradually, the clear night gave way to 100 miles in the fog. At my first fuel stop, the man asked, "Aren't you the man on television?" This happened regularly throughout Brazil. He gave me some coffee and would not take any money. How I will miss these people.

The motorcycle stopped my sentimental musings as the carburetor once again started giving me trouble. "You son of a bitch," I thought, "you will just make my life miserable until the very end. You will give me no relief."

I covered 250 miles that day on rough roads and several hours of fog. Riding into Rio De Janeiro was like riding through mile after mile of favella. The roads were full of trash, with kids darting out onto the highway. It was dangerous riding. Eventually, after getting turned around, I found my way to the McDonald's. I parked next to the building, planning to get a cup of coffee, when a manager comes out and asks, "Are you the fellow traveling around the world? We have read about you. Please, come inside."

Before I know it, there are two Big Macs, fries and a coke served to me. For some reason, McDonald's meat in Brazil seemed far better than anywhere else in the world!

At about 10:30, I meet up with Maria Elaine, a friend of Sandy Smith's. Maria Elaine guides me over to the airport. We go from place to place, trying to find the proper office. Eventually, we located Varig who said they control all freight coming in and out, and could help us.

Unexpectedly, we were told that the motorcycle needed to be boxed up. I nearly threw my arms up in fits. Does it ever work out the way people say it is supposed to work out? Just straight forward, simple and easy.

"Where can we go to do this?" I ask.

"Try the other hanger."

There we meet a few fellows who told me, "You need a photocopy of your ticket." I hadn't yet bought the ticket from SAA, so we took the motorcycle over to the warehouse where it would be loaded onto a pallet (not boxed up). We left the motorcycle in the care of a guy named Avon, then raced back across Rio De Janeiro.

Thank you, Marie Elana. I would never have found any of these places without you and your ability to speak the language!

At the SAA office we met Philip Van Reinsburg, a very helpful and kind young man who told me what I needed. After the ticket was ready, I was informed, "We cannot accept traveler's checks."

Next, we had to go to the government bank about a half mile down the road. We walked through the crowded sidewalks to the bank where we were told we were "too late," that the foreign exchange office had closed. We walked back to Philip and begged him to accept our checks. He called and received permission.

While issuing the ticket, he stopped and said "There's a problem here. You do not have your permanent residence book. I can't give you the ticket."

"Well why?" I asked. "I've never had a problem before."

"You have got to have a Visa."

"No, I don't need one. I am a permanent resident."

Now we get on the phone immediately to Don Hornsby in South Africa. Philip spoke to him, and Don agreed to fax him a letter saying they were going to meet me at the airport with my book of life. Good enough.

He gave me the ticket. We then made a photocopy of it and raced it back across town to the air freight terminal where they took the ticket and cleared the motorcycle for loading. I would come back the following day and prep it for the actual trip.

Finally, with a bit of relief, we were able to drive back to the very beautiful garden apartment Marie Elana and her husband, Rob, had overlooking a lagoon. Their apartment was full of plants flowing out on to the veranda that overlooks the lagoon and the ocean in the distance. What a magic, million dollar view!

When Rob came home, we sat and talked on the veranda in the very peaceful evening. I was able to start relaxing, winding down from the day. In bed that night, I thought to myself, "I have made my last ride in South America this day. The adventure here is over."

The following morning Philip Van Reinsburg called, saying he still hadn't received the fax. I called Don Hornsby who told me "We're having trouble getting the fax through." Pressure right down to the last moment. Finally, Philip did receive the fax just before he quit for the day.

We went to the top of Rio De Janeiro, the highest peak where a famous statute of Jesus Christ overlooks the city. We drove up and up through a very narrow road in the mountains - at least a hundred stairs to get up on top to see this amazing statue. It was majestic and enthralling, made from mosaics.

We visited Copacabano Beach where all the roads had been repaved for an ecology conference held there the year before. Rod spoke of that conference, saying, "I hope that it wasn't just a lot of flag waiving and false hype. I pray something will actually come from it."

That evening we drove along the waterfront, and observed the beautiful people sitting in cafes enjoying coffee and conversation while viewing the ocean. There were transvestites and prostitutes plying their trade nearby. I have never seen so many beautiful girls (or boys) in one area in my life.

Back at the apartment, I flopped into bed and closed my last full day in South America.

The following morning we took a drive down the coast. I was amazed to see all the islands, and imagined it would be fun to be on one of these islands, alone, for a week, just camping and relaxing with no pressure. We had lunch at a wonderful barbecue restaurant; the best meat I have ever had anywhere in the world is in Brazil.

Back at the apartment we all took a short nap, I took a shower, we had a cup of tea, then off we drove to the airport through the series of tunnels with lots of light and no ice! As we drove along the statute of Christ, at the bottom of His feet was a golden cloud encircling the whole mountain top. Right at the base of the statue, where His feet were, the light shined up on the statute and also down on the cloud. It radiated the warmth and love of Jesus Christ. Rob said he had never ever seen it like that ever in all his time in Rio. I thought about how Jesus called Himself "the light of the world." This evening, looking at that statute, I felt it was so.

At the airport I said good-bye to my last two friends in Brazil, Rob and Maria Elaina, and thanked them for all the help. I went to the departure lounge where Philip gave me the fax from Don Hornsby and bade me farewell. He also told me that "You will have to clear the motorcycle in and out of customs again in South Africa, then pay for its onward voyage to Hong Kong."

I boarded the plane for takeoff at 23:00 that night of June 28th.

As the plane gathered momentum moving down the runway, the city of Rio and eventually the continent of South America faded quickly out of site. It is always a moving moment to think back on all the adventures I had come through, some better than others, and to remember all the incredible people who had helped me experience this journey I was living. I said a small prayer of thanks.

The feeling of triumph never lasts very long.

As South America disappeared below the aircraft, and we winged out over the Atlantic Ocean, my mind was already focused forward to Hong Kong, the gateway to Asia, and continent Number 5 on this incredible journey to the ends of the earth.

After fall on ice.
The Bulldozers Clearing an Avalanche, 12,000 Ft. On Chilean side of Andes Mts.
June 16, 1992 Caili

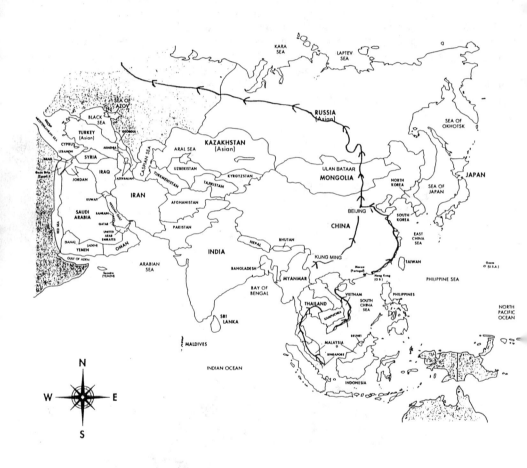

Stage Five: Asia

Chapter Twenty-Eight

Beating the Bureaucratic Beast

The flight across the Atlantic to South Africa was a very painful one because my left stump was giving me a lot of grief. On the plus side, I witnessed a wonderful sunrise - brilliant red reflecting on the clouds - as the sun cleared the horizon at 37,000 feet. Absolutely magnificent!

We put down at Jan Smuts Airport in South Africa where I cleared Customs and Immigration, then met Peter Manderson and Felicity Hornsby. After quick greetings, she whisked me off for a quick radio interview with John Burks, at 702 Radio, one of the main radio stations in Johannesburg. While waiting to be interviewed, reports came over the news wire that there had been 36 deaths in one of the townships surrounding Johannesburg. A massive "stay away" was in effect, explaining the lack of traffic on highways as the plane was coming down. The morale of the nation was low, even at the radio station. One woman came up to me after my interview and asked, "Why did you bother to come back?"

That evening, after dinner, we drove to the Cheshire Home where I saw Luke in his bed - in virtually the same place I had left him almost two years before. Of course, the main subject we discussed that night concerned the future of South Africa, what with all the problems arising since Mandela had been released from jail. Everybody seemed to know somebody who had been killed, robbed, mugged, or had their car stolen.

Don Hornsby tried to be optimistic about the future, but the underlying current of feeling for most was a feeling of hopelessness. An uptight, apprehensive attitude in both blacks and whites seemed to cover South Africa during my few days there. When I spoke to Elliot, Don's black foreman of many years, and the other employees I had worked with in the past, they all said the same thing: "People in the townships are afraid. It is not true," they maintained, "that the townships are pro ANC. Intimidation runs rife, with young comrades running about burning, looting and killing those opposed to the thoughts and ideologies of the ANC." A very dim picture indeed. "We hope the world will come to understand the political monster they helped create with their sanctions and economic pressure."

Prices had changed drastically since I left due to the devalued rand. When I went to buy a couple of hamburgers one afternoon, the incredible prices shocked me. The rand had devalued to a ratio of almost 3 rand to a $1; when I left, it had been about 2.4 rand to $1.

Don gave me a couple of faxes from Marilyn Dear in Hong Kong. She told me that the Leonard Cheshire Foundation could offer no support for a trip into China. In fact, they did not want me to go because they were afraid I would be hurt. In my heart, I didn't sense that China would be any more dangerous than the rest of my adventure. It irritated me that they were treating me and this trip as though I were helpless, instead of an experienced world traveler.

One evening, when having dinner out with Monty Brett, a real help with my journey from the very beginning, and also with Peter Manderson, our conversation came around to the Cheshire Foundation's stand on China. Monty said, "Why don't you throw in the towel and quit the whole thing. What's the point of carrying on?"

That night I climbed into bed feeling rather grim about my future in China, yet I knew I must push forward until every avenue was exhausted.

Hong Kong's Hassles, Highways and Harbors

I spent a full day at the custom's office getting my motorcycle transferred from the import level of a main warehouse to the export level upstairs. The Customs people bent over backwards to help me, and hand carried my paperwork right through the channels. We did in one day what would normally take three weeks. At the end of the day, my stumps were straining, but I was in good spirits when I saw a ribbon on my motorcycle with a note saying, "Good luck, Dave." It was from the Brazilians at the air terminal in Rio De Janeiro. Those three words helped me not to get discouraged, and made me more determined than ever to keep pushing forward.

My last night in the country, I met Nevil Morit, a fellow I had counseled in the hospital two years ago; he had one leg off above the knee, one off below. He showed up riding a Sportster with a side car he had built. Well done Nevil! The man had suffered an incalculable amount of operations over almost two years until he finally got his final amputations and started walking, getting on with his life again. Now he is riding his motorcycle. Good for you!

As I went to bed that night, I thought, "Tomorrow on to Hong Kong and the start of the fifth continent." I knew a major battle with bureaucracy was about to begin.

The next morning I went to the Cheshire Home and said good-bye to Luke with a most heavy heart. I hugged him; of course, he couldn't hug me in return. We both had tears in our eyes as we parted once again.

At the airport, after sadly saying good-bye to Don and Felicity, dear friends, I carried my 40 pound saddle bags down stairs to security checks. At 17:30 we boarded the plane and took off. Soon, we were over the Indian Ocean as I contemplated the adventure that was about to unfold in front of me.

The flight was uneventful except for when we flew over Vietnam. When we crossed over the country just north of Da Nang, I tried to locate familiar landmarks. From that altitude, I was unable to spot Marble Mountain, but did locate Monkey Mountain where we used to fly on our helicopter test flights.

About an hour later, we landed at Hong Kong airport where I was greeted by Avel, Robert Simpson's driver. Robert was Marilyn's friend. When we inquired where to go to claim the motorcycle, we were run from one office to the next, up and down stairs, to the point where I was on the verge of a catatonic rage...I was THAT upset! Finally, we located the motorcycle at the Jardine Air Freight Terminal on the far side of the airport.

When we started to go over there, Avel's parking ticket wouldn't work in the machine, so we had to call a policeman to clear the machine and open the boom; traffic was backing up behind us, and people were honking, making general tits of themselves. Welcome to Hong Kong!

Free of the parking monster, we went to the other side of the airport, going from one office to the next, filling out forms but receiving no action. When one fellow said, "Now you must go back to the other side of the airport for a document you need from Customs," I went wild and started shouting! Finally, they took my papers, left for about ten minutes, then returned saying, "We will release the motorcycle if you sign these papers."

After retrieving the motorcycle, we called William Chan, owner of the "All Motorcycles" Harley Davidson shop; William was to become a very dear friend during my time in Hong Kong, and he gave me a place to store and work on the motorcycle. "I'll send a truck over," he said. One half hour later, a truck arrived, and we loaded the motorcycle on and drove across Hong Kong to Jaffe Street in Wan Chi where we unloaded the motorcycle and wheeled it inside the shop.

Next, Avel and I drove in this wonderful air conditioned car across steamy, hot Hong Kong to a three story apartment building in Midlevels where I greeted Marilyn with a big hug. I realized that I would be in Hong Kong for awhile when she told me, "You'll be staying at Robert's apartment," a very luxurious place.

Marilyn lived on the 19th floor of an apartment building in Causeway Bay. I also met Robert Simpson, a middle aged man of medium build with light colored hair, impeccably combed. He was a cultured man, and a very high-powered operator in the business world. The three of us sat down with a couple of Marilyn's friends and talked for hours. First, we talked about the proposed 1997 takeover by the People's Republic of China (PRC), and of the lack of confidence in how things would work out. If the Chinese started interfering with the way business ass run in Hong Kong, they felt the economy would start to collapse, and that most Europeans and wealthy Chinese would leave. I shared about South Africa's problems, and the lack of morale in the country.

Late that afternoon, we sat down to dinner on the balcony of Robert's apartment, viewing a jungle of concrete skyscrapers. One under construction was planned to be one of the highest apartment skyscrapers in the world - 65 stories high. I was amazed at this concrete mass before me. "Only a few years ago I could look out onto Hong Kong harbor," Robert told me. "But no more. My 3 story apartment is now rare, and is just too small to see over the skyscrapers. They are building so fast, Hong Kong uses more plywood than any other city in the world. It's a city constantly under construction."

That night after a welcome shower, I laid back, thinking, "The first day of Stage 5 is over."

The next day at the motorcycle shop in Wan Chi I met Noro, the head mechanic. As we talked, I learned that this little workshop on Jaffe Street costs William Chan thousands of dollars a month to keep open. I was amazed at the cost of renting in Hong Kong.

July 5: After looking the motorcycle over and running a couple of errands, Avel took me back to the apartment. That evening, Marilyn joined us. She was in great physical pain; she could only work half a day before the pain would become too great; by midday; she would usually come home in incredible pain. I was amazed at her efforts to help me in the midst of her own suffering with slipped discs in both her neck and back.

Marilyn is a tall, slender and eloquent woman, ever so graceful when she walks and moves. Her hair is jet black with just a bit of gray invading it. Her skin is a creamy white, and her intelligent hazel eyes are set in a face with lovely and delicate features. Of all the women I've met, she is the most dynamic female I've ever had the privilege of calling "friend." Without her help, her searching to find somebody inside of mainland China interested in the journey, I would have never been allowed to enter. From February until July she had been the motivating force working to get me inside China.

Avel drove me down to the China Resources Building where I was greeted by huge, mythical animals in front of the building, put there to ward off evil spirits and invaders from a bygone age. Inside I found the Visa Application Center where I paid 90 Hong Kong dollars, and left my passport with them for 24 hours.

The Hong Kong weather in July and August is terribly hot, and frequent rain produces humidity which makes it even more unbearable.

One day Avel picked me up to meet Marilyn at a very exclusive shopping center. Picture this in your mind... a very eloquent, graceful woman striding along next to a clacking, banging, squeaking man with artificial legs. We went from place to place, me carrying the basket, Marilyn making decisions about the various foods we were going to eat. Of course, she never let me pay for a thing! And she didn't buy beans!

One afternoon, after sweating away in the motorcycle shop, I met the president of the Harley owner's group of Hong Kong, Peter Stoessel. We chatted for a few minutes, then he invited me out to dinner on one of the islands. That evening a car picked me up and took me down to a junk (a Chinese boat) that belonged to a corporation. Booze was flowing from the bar as the captain maneuvered the junk out into the Hong Kong harbor. I was amazed at the amount of boat traffic in the harbor - as busy as the Hong Kong streets. The Chinese always seem to be on the move - on land and on water - always going somewhere, doing something. People with purpose.

We observed Kai Tac Airport from the harbor, watching planes land and take off, then eventually arrived at one of the islands just around sunset. We departed from the boat, and went to a restaurant with a huge table on a circular platform. Food was heaped on the platform. There were prawns, clams, fish, chicken, noodles, and varied vegetables. What a feast!

On the way back, in the midst of all the boat traffic, I thought, "Millions and millions of dollars worth of junks and yachts in such a small area. It is a wonder they aren't crashing and colliding into each other." The skill of the captains was amazing.

We took a different route home to Aberdeen Harbor where we saw the huge, floating Jumbo Palace Restaurant - one of the biggest, if not the biggest restaurant in the world! It is a multi-storied affair, all lit up like a Christmas tree. It was stupendous! The colored lights reflected in the night, and off the water's surface in the harbor. We went into a nightclub adjacent to the floating Jumbo Palace, had a few drinks, then went home.

I never got used to Hong Kong at night. It was incredible, what a place! It never slows down or stops. In Las Vegas, Nevada, that's also the case, but in Las Vegas people are there to gamble and have a good time. In Hong Kong, people plan and work non-stop to make money! Any businessman making a success of his company in Hong Kong must be among the super elite of the business world.

In observing these people, I felt like a fish out of water, although they were very kind and respectful to me. There were vast differences between their world and mine. Many of my problems were so small and petty compared to these men who made decisions that could topple empires and effect the lives of hundreds of people. Whatever I do usually effects only me.

In Hong Kong, Peter Stoessel introduced me to the PRO (Public Relations Officer) of Esso, saying, "Why don't you give Dave a thousand dollars?"

He replied, "Dave, you wouldn't mind putting some stickers on your motorcycle would you?"

"Indeed not," I replied quickly.

The man then handed me a thousand American dollars and a few Esso stickers. Later, in Beijing, ESSO got their money's worth when one photograph of the motorcycle ended up going out on the wire services all over the world.

I made a couple of rides with the HOG club in Hong Kong; one place we traveled to was the top of a mountain over looking Kowloon on one side and the PRC on the other. Chris Pedder, who's family lineage went all the way back to the opium wars, pointed out to me Shenzen, a huge sprawling city on the other side of the border.

"You will be going there when you cross the border," he told me.

"If I cross the border," I thought to myself, still having no confirmation that I could go.

Training Schools, Traffic Schools, and Obstacle Courses

Chris was an Irishman who spoke Cantonese, had a black belt in Kung Fu, and was an inspector of the special task force department of the Royal Hong Kong police. He told me, "We have one of the most efficient anti-terrorist units in the world." By what he told me, it was certainly the one that was most experienced in actual practical application!

Chris later took me through their training school where I was allowed to go through the obstacle course with 9 mm pistols and later, a Hecker and Cock submachine gun, doing house clearing with hostages in them. It was a full days worth of shooting, and an incredible experience for me - the most shooting I had done since leaving the South African Army.

I constantly sent faxes to Lin Xu Chang in Fuzhou, 500 miles (800 km) north of Hong Kong right along the South China Sea. Lin ultimately was the person instrumental in getting me into Mainland China without an escort. He moved major bureaucratic mountains to get the Chinese government to allow me in on a tourist visa to ride my motorcycle unescorted across Mainland China. To anyone's knowledge, it had never been done before! Only a Britisher who entered China illegally, and was chased by the Chinese police, had ridden for any distance, unescorted, through China. This fellow who had come in illegally from Nepal had been chased by the Chinese police all the way across China to Hong Kong where he exited. Another man, a German, who worked in Mainland China, had himself made a motorcycle trip to Pakistan, Afghanistan, and on to Germany from Beijing on a Chinese motorcycle.

Lin had been working on my entrance for months with Marilyn, along with Sung Ping Michael in Shenzen; we were faxing each other in a three way triangle. Shenzen would be my first stop in the PRC if I was allowed to enter.

Peter Solly, the head of the Cheshire Foundation in Hong Kong, had a total lack of interest in having me do anything - even speak to the residents of the Home. I did meet Diana Koo, a very dynamic lady based in Pen Nang, Malaysia, who said she would "let me know" if I could do anything for the Foundation in Southeast Asia. At least she was positive, although nothing ever worked out. Diana was the author of different training manuals used by staff to train people with disabilities, and was constantly on the move throughout Southeast Asia to over 40 homes, training staff and working with the residents.

During my time in Hong Kong, there was a lot of trouble with the Vietnamese that were in camps there. The North and South Vietnamese fought among one another regularly, but neither group wanted to go back to Vietnam, and the Hong Kong authorities didn't want to keep them. They were truly a misplaced people. They were offered $300.00 and a plane ride back to Vietnam if they would repatriate, but none were interested, so they kept them in internment camps.

I kept getting reports from people that there was no petrol in China. This confirmed what I had been told by the Leonard Cheshire Foundation. Naturally, this was another big worry. As a precaution, I welded a rack to the back of my motorcycle that would hold 30 liters (7 1/2 gallons) of fuel. Others reassured me, saying, "Dave, there's plenty of trucks and buses on the road, and they've got to get petrol from somewhere." At any rate, at least I was prepared.

During my time of waiting, I gave a few slide shows and interviews. One of my memorable times was organized by Peter Stoessel. We visited the Duchess of Kent Hospital for Disabled Children where there was media on hand, a couple of newspapers and a radio station. We did interviews and photographs with three Harleys there, and with kids climbing all over them. Later, I showed some slides of my trip to the kids; my comments were translated by one of the nurses. We were deeply taken by these kids, a happy go lucky group of children despite their massive disabilities.

Running around the surface streets of Hong Kong on the motorcycle got the engine very hot. Surface streets had to be ridden in first and second gear with lots of stopping at traffic lights; sometimes, the lanes were so narrow I couldn't go between the cars.

One time, during a promotion at the Federation of Handicap Youth, there was a television crew filming various members from the Harley owner's group while we rode disabled people around in the parking lot. There I met Jane Perini, a dynamic young English woman about 25 years old who lived out on Lan Tau Island, and worked for the Hong Kong Federation of Handicap Youth as an organizer and interpreter. She spoke and wrote Mandarin fluently. Jane and I became friends, and she made up some language flash cards for me which proved invaluable during the trip across China to Beijing.

Reed Resnick, a fellow from New York, also gave me an invaluable tip. "Dave, get a horn," he told me.

"I have a horn," I replied.

"No, Dave, get a **BIG** horn," he advised. Fortunately, I had the good sense to listen to his wisdom, and that horn probably saved my life on more than one occasion.

During my wait, Hurricane Gary was heading towards us, so the "red flag" went up, and all of Hong Kong shut down, going home until the red flag came down. "Gary" veered in another direction and missed us; by late afternoon, the town was hustling once again.

Week three: I still had no confirmation on entering Mainland China, and I was really getting anxious. I refused to consider any alternatives. I had to get across China. Faxes to Sung Ping Michael and Lin Xu Chang were sent almost daily. Each fax would say, "Don't worry," then they would ask for some new requirement.

The Motorcycle Shop started each day with a morning meeting led by William Chan. All bowed, talked about the day's work, then bowed again. Now Noro is Japanese, and the rest of the boys in the shop are Chinese, yet they all get along fine, with no animosity from the time of war when the Japanese occupied Hong Kong.

Once at lunch, Noro told me that, "The Japanese people are not taught anything about the war. As far as they are concerned, the war didn't happen for the younger generation."

I was asked to one of the biggest Cheshire Homes in the world - the Sha Tin Cheshire Home. The dining area was large enough for me to speak to about 150 residents. They were a very cheerful lot, and my little talk went over very well.

In my travels, I noted that Hong Kong has more Mercedes, BMWs, luxury cars, especially Rolls Royces, than any place in the world. This is definitely the decadence capital of the world. Very rarely do people get over 50 miles an hour, and that's only on the freeways. Generally it is stop and go driving on city streets.

Crowds are everywhere. It is crowded on the subways and the buses. It is crowded on the sidewalks.

By now, I feel I am over-staying my welcome at Robert's apartment. Looking beyond China, I am also concerned about the permits it will take for me to cross Mongolia and Russia and ride back to Europe before the snow is flying in Europe and Siberia. There are no Russian or Mongolian embassies in Hong Kong.

I heard about a big strike in South Africa from Don Hornsby, and no one was very optimistic about the immediate future. I wanted to be with my friends during their hard times, but there was nothing I could do.

In late July, I read in the obituary column that Lord Leonard Cheshire had died. Truly, the passing of a giant of a man. I don't think in this modern day anyone will ever be as close to sainthood, and do more for the disabled, than Lord Cheshire.

Leo Lamb at the Hong Kong Federation of Handicapped youth asked me to help create a video for the benefit of people with disabilities who want to get a license to ride a motorcycle. "The courts deny people the chance to train and take a license on a motorcycle if they have a disability," he told me. "Yet, most people with disabilities here are not able to fight the havoc of the subways and the buses, and the cost of a car is just way out of line to their income. The best way for them to get around would be a motorcycle. Without this, their lives become very limited."

How could I refuse when he asked, "Dave, would you come down to the Hong Kong School of Motoring and ride one of their motorcycles through their obstacle course and let us film it?" He then told me, "We will turn this film in as part of a package of arguments that we have had going for some time with the court. Hopefully, they will overturn their decision and let people with disabilities ride motorcycles."

That's exactly what this trip was and is for.

Leo picked me up from the motorcycle shop and we drove to the New Territories in Sha Tin where I was taken to the Hong Kong School of Motoring. There I met the managing director, Mr. Peter Smith, an Australian. He gave me a helmet and Yamaha 125 motorcycle to ride on. I felt like an ape on a football, and honestly do not know how I managed to get through the obstacles, successfully negotiating the thing from both directions. At the end, everyone thanked me. Later, Peter Smith asked me to his office and presented me with $10,000 Hong Kong dollars ($1,200 American dollars). I was flabbergasted, and said, "Thank you very much. This is much needed." It seemed funny to me that in Hong Kong I was finding the sponsorship I had been looking for all over the world, and had been unable to find.

Many newspaper articles appeared about the trip in Hong Kong, the best one by the famous Kevin Sinclair. Kevin had a huge hole in his throat because his voice box had been removed due to cancer. A young Chinese girl came with him as his voice. We also talked about fighting to live, and he related to that, saying, "I saw people all around me in my war that just accepted their fate and were ready to die, to be put in the box. Well, I wasn't prepared to accept that, so I endured three major operations and chemotherapy to be alive today." I didn't realize his incredible skill as a writer until the newspaper article came out, "Champion of the Disabled," one of the strongest, most forthright articles I have ever read on the journey.

The most incredible person I met in Hong Kong was Simon Murry, managing director of Hutchison Whom-Poa, a conglomerate. His only boss was Lee Kai Shing - probably the wealthiest man in Asia. When I met Simon at his office, I was shocked to see a middle-aged man with glasses, gray eyes and a very firm handshake. His office was up 22 floors, and overlooked Hong Kong harbor. It was decorated with flowers and bookcases around the whole room, with a huge desk near the window, I thought to myself, "I would hate to have the responsibility that goes

311

with this office." We talked about our military lives; Simon had served five years in the French Foreign Legion and wrote a very good book called "Legionnaire." He signed a copy, and gave it to me. As I read about his life, it was clear he had worked himself up from the bottom.

I still had no confirmation from China.

August 14: I spoke to the very exclusive Rotary of Hong Kong Island East. My audience consisted of very high rung business people, both European and Chinese. We met at the splendid Excelsior Hotel in a banquet room. After eating, the President introduced me and I spoke for the next 25 minutes. It turned out to be one of the better keynote speeches I've ever done! It flowed and had power and intensity. People were standing up clapping at the end.

One evening I received a fax stating that my Chinese driver's license and temporary registration had been approved! What wonderful news! Soon I would be rolling!

Now, my next hurdle was with the Hong Kong authorities for my Immigration and Customs on the motorcycle. I needed a "closed road permit" that would allow me to go to the border on the motorcycle. Over the next few days, I hassled with the authorities, back and forth, from office to office. At one point I lost it, screaming at a Customs Department officer, "I just want my permit to get out of Hong Kong and be on my way. I've never experienced this type of bureaucratic bullshit anywhere in the world." The poor woman was on the verge of tears, and it was wrong that I took this attitude towards her - she had sincerely been trying to help.

Without insurance, neither the Customs permit for the motorcycle to exit through the Lo Wu border or the closed road permit would be issued to me. Of course, I didn't have insurance because no one would insure me. William Chan volunteered to act as my insurance agent, and wrote what could have very well been a bogus insurance contract. When I then took my policy to the vehicle department, they said, "We need all of your Customs papers." Next, I went to the Customs office and secured the release document from South African Airways. It wasn't enough. I was told, "We need the flight papers of the motorcycle as well." When I came back with the flight papers, they finally issued the release for the motorcycle to go through the Lo Wu border!

I was not finished yet. I now went on to the traffic department where they told me, "We will need more time." I was beside myself since my plans were to leave the next day, the 19th. "We will do everything in our power to enable you to pick up your permit by tomorrow, but we can give no guarantees."

Ms. Wu at Customs told me, "You need to get your visa renewed," so I did.

August 19: Ms. Wu called and said, "Your permit is ready. Come and pick it up."

That was it!

Robert and I said good-bye to each other, gave each other a big hug, and I thanked this very kind man for allowing me to use his wonderful apartment for the preceding six weeks. After I said good-bye to Marilyn, Avel took me down to the traffic department to pick up my closed road permit, then on to All Motorcycles where Peter Stoessel and William Chan joined me. After some photographs with the staff, I said good-bye to all, then was escorted out by William Chan, Chris Pedder, Peter Stoessel, Stanly Ho with Jane Perini on the back of his motorcycle, to the border at Lo Wu - about a 32 mile trip. At the first check point, the others said good-bye, and with a heavy heart, I watched them ride away.

Chris escorted me to the second border check, then the third check where I actually exited the Hong Kong territories. Here we parted. I will always respect Chris not only as a soldier and policeman but as a real man. We gave each other a big hug, he took a photograph, I turned in my "Closed Road" permit, showed them my exit permits from Immigration and Customs for the motorcycle, then looked across the bridge into Mainland China where I could see the red, Chinese flag flying in the distance. It was with great apprehension, and soaked with sweat from the heat, that **I left Hong Kong and the free world behind, crossing into China.**

Crawling, Crashing and Honking Through China

Quickly I cleared Immigration and Customs. I was surprised! They called Sung Ping Michael for me, and took me to an air conditioned room where I was served tea! Then, reporters and a television crew appeared, along with Sung Ping Michael, a young fellow about 30 years old. He worked with the Shenzen Workers Travel Service.

After introductions, I gave a short interview, rode the motorcycle around in a few circles, then was released. I followed Michael's bus to the motor vehicle department where my motorcycle was inspected and, to my very great relief, cleared.

Inside the vehicle department, I got my first taste of Chinese interpreters. A government interpreter gave me his card while the head of the vehicle department stood speaking to me for about half an hour, waiving my driver's license in front of me. After thirty minutes of understanding nothing, the interpreter looks at me and says, "This man say Chinese drivers very bad drivers. Be careful." What an understatement that would prove to be! Next, he handed me back my driver's license and shook my hand. Sung Ping Michael said nothing, obviously not wanting to upset the government interpreter.

Finally, I was cleared to be on my way through China!

To everyone's knowledge, I was the first person on a "Tourist" Visa to be allowed legally into China to ride alone to my destination of Beijing. This was a very great privilege, especially since Beijing was 2500 miles (3900 Km.) from Hong Kong.

When I started to follow the bus, full of reporters, on the motorcycle, we had been on the road just a few minutes when a young boy darted out in front of me. I had to lay the motorcycle down to prevent running over the kid. The reporters all jumped out of the bus, some taking pictures with a TV camera and crew in attendance. What a great beginning, fall on my ass in front of a great crowd and give a story for all of China's reading public!

That evening, I stayed at the Far Eastern Hotel, and went out with Michael to a typical Chinese restaurant where we had a lovely dinner with his two secretaries. Back at the hotel he changed some money for me, then I laid back in my room and tried to go to sleep.

I was up at 04:00, I took my gear back down to the motorcycle and loaded the machine. At 07:30, Michael joined me after sleeping in his office that night. He explained to me how to get out of town.

At about 08:30, I said good-bye to Michael and his office people, then was on my way, almost immediately hitting huge lines of traffic backed up to the signal lights. I would have to maneuver through towering trucks and great walls of rolling metal to get to the front of the line. Sometimes my saddlebags would actually hit the tires of a truck. Eventually, I found my way out of Shenzen - a very dirty city. As I entered the countryside, I would no longer see any road signs with English subtitles; from now on, everything was in Chinese.

As I was poking along in second gear, a truck in front of me suddenly came to a stop. I pulled around him to avoid skidding into his back, and almost hit an oncoming truck. Fortunately, the driver of the oncoming truck was alert (which is rare) and dodged off to the right of the road. Even more fortunate, there was no bicycle traffic at the spot where he veered over. One thing I would learn quickly on this trip: drivers in China don't seem to get upset at each other when somebody does something wrong and endangers their life. They seem to be understanding and forgiving, or just complacent.

The roads soon went from not so good and very narrow to very bad and, at times, dirt roads full of holes, sometimes filled in with broken rocks. I breathed a lot of dust and the diesel exhausts of thousands of trucks poured into my face. Trucks are the main motor vehicle traffic on the road. There are a few private cars, plenty of over-loaded buses, and one cylinder diesel tractors that have two wheels pulling a cart behind them, usually crammed beyond capacity with bricks, hay, dirt, or anything else you can imagine.

Construction is almost always a constant as the roads are in a constant state of repair, meaning long traffic lines where it sometimes backs up for miles on a single lane road. My strategy was to ride in the oncoming lane until a truck appeared, then to dart back into the right lane to keep from getting hit. It was all very hair raising. Generally, my motorcycle never got over 30 to 35 miles per hour.

In the first few hours, I saw more bicycles than I have ever seen in my entire life. Traffic is a kaleidoscope of people moving along the main artery up the east coast of China on the main mode of transportation in China - the bicycle.

When I needed fuel, I often used the gas I carried in the drum of gas on the back of the motorcycle. Gas stations were usually located on the outskirts of every town. Since I could only make about 200 miles (300 km) a day, from morning to evening, gas was not a major concern.

Outside Hui Zhou, I stopped at a small, country restaurant where I showed my flash card asking for something to eat. A price was decided upon, then I sat down to a huge bowl of noodles and shrimp. A crowd of about 10 people gathered, sitting around my table, watching me eat. Unlike Africans or Brazilians, they were very quiet.

The late afternoon rain created mud and slick roads, so about 17:00 I flashed my card that read on the English side, "Can I sleep?" - the same message was written in Mandarin on the other. I pointed to a big pile of bricks and my host nodded. I pushed the motorcycle under the awning of a brick factory next to the restaurant. So instead of putting up the tent, I just laid my tarp out on the ground. I completed a few evening chores on the motorcycle with a crowd of about 15 people standing around. At 20:00, not caring whether they looked or not, I took my legs off and made the sign of sleep. The crowd nodded its collective head and walked off, leaving me to my myself. Sometimes, I must admit, it gets on my nerves having these crowds stare at me every time I stop.

I had been looking closely at my compass all day, going roughly northeast along the coastal road so as not to lose my way. I soon learned the safest course for not getting lost was to follow the main flow of trucks. The real problem for me is the big cities, when traffic is going in every direction.

The following morning, it was still raining, so I banged along at about 30 miles an hour in third gear. Even when the road was asphalt, if there was a huge hole, they would crush rock and fill it. When I ride by a rock quarry, I invariably see an army of Chinese there with hammers, breaking rock to make gravel. I couldn't believe it!

314

Then the gravel is put into these big pans they carry on their backs, or in front of them, to a one cylinder tractor with a trailer bed on the back. They fill up the bed, then the tractor takes off to a construction area. As a Westerner, it is inconceivable to imagine hundreds of people busting rocks with sledge hammers to make gravel, but that's a typical scene in China. The abundance of people becomes a substitute for machines in many areas of life.

Horns are going off all the time on the road. When vehicles pass each other, there are horns - *loud* horns blasting my only eardrum to nothing. There are truck and bus horns, plus motorcycles beeping along with their horns. Occasionally, a private car blasts me out of the way as well. The rule of the road in China is simple: whether driving a bicycle, a motorcycle, a tractor, a truck, a bus, or a private car... go where you want to go, when you want to go, and honk your horn to get there!

Drivers in trucks sometimes stand outside their trucks on their running boards, looking around behind them for whatever reason, totally away from the controls of the truck other than their one hand on the steering wheel. Trucks drive right in the center of the road. When two encounter each other, they turn and miss each other at the last second; buses do the same thing. It is a constant game of chicken, and the debris from these chicken contests spills on the road when the drivers collide. I saw at least three to four truck or bus accidents a day, and bicycles are constantly hit.

Little motorcycles are in frequent accidents, but that is not the case with most which are the larger Chinese motorcycles created from a 1939 BMW design with side cars added. They take up more room, so they travel more or less at the pace of cars or trucks.

On these roads I listened very carefully at corners for horns that might be sounding. If I heard one horn, that means one vehicle is trying to pass another around that blind corner, so the horn means "Get out of the way." If I heard pandemonium, two vehicles are trying to pass another vehicle on a blind corner, and the horn means "Every man for himself." Most countries have a method to their traffic, but in China it is just, "go for it."

I'm overwhelmed by the amount of bicycles. Each big city I enter presents an array of bicycles, trucks, buses, and whatnot. Often, the main road to the city is torn up, so I'm riding and blasting through holes full of water or gravel, not knowing how deep they are or how big the rocks they tossed in the hole may be. It is a real rough ride. If traffic is moving slowly, and I can't get around the truck in front of me, I inhale the diesel exhaust and it paints my face black as I do my best to hold the motorcycle up. Many times my feet are down on the ground while I'm straining with my gut to control the 800 pound (390 kg) machine loaded, not counting the extra gasoline.

The people working out in the rice paddies reminded me of Vietnam. In between the rice paddies, banana trees are growing. No space is wasted. Farming is even tiered up the sides of the mountain. It seems everything is under cultivation or populated, and the whole country seems busy doing something!

One time, as I was riding along, a one cylinder tractor never looked, but simply made a U-turn without signaling. The driver had no mirror on his tractor, and I just barely missed him. How any of these people live to experience old age I don't know. Later, I discovered there were 150 million disabled people in China. My guess - the majority were from road related accidents.

Truck Tire Tea and Chicky Babes

In the country areas, tea is put out on the road to dry. The roads are narrow in the best of times, with most vehicles driving right down the middle. So, with tea drying along the road, there's another few feet of road taken up. They put rocks around the tea to keep you from running over it. There were times, I confess, when I had to dodge between the rocks, right into the tea, to avoid being hit by an oncoming truck or bus.

The larger vehicles almost stop and sneak around one another to keep from driving on the tea. Sometimes, drivers disregard the rocks and drive over the tea anyway. If you drink Chinese tea, you should know it was probably dried out on road and probably had a few sets of truck tires on it before it found its way into the bag that eventually finds its way into your cup.

One area that really irritated me... when the truck drivers stop to fix a flat tire, or some other repair, they put large rocks on the road to ward off other drivers. When they finished, they just leave the rocks in the road and drive off! What an attitude.

The third day in China, in the late afternoon, I entered the city of Fuzhou. My stumps are killing me, my ass was hurting, and my back was in pain. It had been a rough ride indeed. Fuzhou was the most modern city I saw anywhere in the southern part of China, and is the capital city of the Fujian province. A big crowd gathered, with many people shaking my hand. Nobody spoke English. . When I showed my flash card with an address to the Fujian Workers Travel Service, one young man came forward on a little motorbike and motioned for me to follow him. He took me across the city, then back down an alley behind a building where he pointed to the travel service office. I had to force him to accept 10 RMB (about $1.50) for his service. He didn't want to take it.

I entered the office and introduced myself to the people at the front desk; they had been notified of my coming, and were expecting me. Almost immediately, the cup of Chinese tea appeared. Early in the trip I acquired a taste for Chinese tea which remains with me to this day. About 20 minutes after my arrival, Lin Xu Chang appears and tells me to follow his little motorcycle over to the Dong Hu Hotel where I will stay. It was an all Chinese hotel as opposed to a hotel for foreigners. An all-Chinese hotel looks very nice on the outside but is extremely dirty on the inside, frequently with holes burnt in the carpet, and no hot water. At the Dong Hu Hotel, the motorcycle was taken over to a private area and unloaded, with all my baggage carried inside. Unfortunately, the porter came away with a shoulder full of grease after taking my tool bag off of the back. Once in the hotel, I took a cold shower, had dinner with Lin, then went to bed.

The next day was full, complete with television and newspaper interviews about the trip. Next, I pushed the motorcycle 50 meters down the street to a wash rack for bicycles and motorbikes. With a helper and some detergent, we cleaned all the mud off the motorcycle. When we were done, I was ringing wet from sweat because of the fiery hot, humid day.

That afternoon Lin took me to his house on the back of his little Yamaha 80 motorcycle. I met his family, and we all had a lovely meal in his very tiny apartment in the old section of Fuzhou.

Fuzhou is a big and prosperous city that wears its age well - it is over four thousand years old! It is a diroot trading partner with Taiwan. Lin's area was unique because it was sandwiched back in little alleys and narrow streets. I was amazed how he maneuvered his little Yamaha with me on the back. I was scared to death as we whizzed through this maze of humanity, bicycles, people and carts.

On the way back to the hotel, we stopped on a side street where a puppet show was going on. The crowd watching was enthralled. There's no charge for these shows; coins are voluntarily put into a cup for the performers. Lin explained, "It is an escape from reality, and a Chinese tradition of many centuries to watch these shows." I found it interesting to see the puppets dancing around, all chanting in Chinese, then singing songs. The crowd was composed of all ages - all in absolute wonder and amazement, totally lost to the world around them, absorbed into watching the puppets and their antics.

Lin stayed at the hotel with me, sleeping in the other bed rather than driving home that night. We received a couple of phone calls, and Lin said, "They are prostitutes - chicky girls - wanting to know if we want any action up here." Of course, we declined. Prostitution is illegal in China, yet it flourishes in places where the authorities look the other way.

In the four days it took me to get to Fuzhou, I had averaged about 125 miles per day. What a slow journey! I have never been on such dangerous roads anywhere in the world.

The following day I met with the Disabled Federation of Fuzhou where I met a number of young, dynamic Chinese people. One blind man was a well-known composer of music in China. Another was a social science professor, another a poet, another a singer known throughout the country.

That evening I was the guest of honor at a dinner in the hotel at a very ethnic Chinese restaurant with antique, hand-carved partitions in wood and painted with different murals. The hotel manager and a high ranking Army officer sat at my table as we enjoyed a fifteen course dinner. The food just kept coming on a round saucer that rotated. The Chinese are not at all inhibited in their eating habits. They eat with chopsticks, and if something is really good, they'd pick it up off the table and put it into my bowl. If they really liked something, they would smack with their mouths open. If they ate fish with bones in it, they'd spit the bones on the table next to their plate, not worrying about table etiquette. I could just imagine my mother hollering if wine or bones were tossed on her tablecloth!

After about an hour of eating, drinking, and smoking, many were getting quite drunk and loud, really losing their inhibitions, shouting above the old style Chinese music in the background. Being a non-drinker, I'd lift my glass to my lips, acting as if I had drunk the contents. Sometimes they would refill it, spilling it all over the table.

The following morning, Lin showed me out of town at 06:00 in the morning - the streets were already horribly crowded with bicycle traffic, people going to their factories and various places of business.

We beeped and honked all the way. A truck came by me on my left, then an old man turned left in front of me, forcing me to slam on my brakes and slide, hitting him. There was nothing else I could do. He was tossed from his bicycle, and me from my motorcycle. A crowd gathered immediately, and I had help in moving the motorcycle off to the side of the road.

Traffic stopped. Truck horns started blaring. People were shouting and hollering at one another, grabbing the old man. I pushed into the middle of the crowd, trying to determine if the old man had fractured his spine. I couldn't find anything that felt wrong as I checked his bones, legs and arms for breakages. The old fellow was hollering bloody murder! The crowd showed no animosity towards me as a foreigner who had just hit one of their fellow Chinese. Lin advised me, "Give him 50 RMD (about $8.50) to ease his pain." I dug into my pocket and stuck some money in the old man's pocket.

In the meantime, we moved to a chair at the side of the road so traffic could pass. The noise level was still high, what with people hollering and shouting and horns blaring - just absolute pandemonium and pressure. When the old man looked into his pocket and saw only 50 RMB's, he started shouting even louder. A man said something to Lin, and Lin suggested, "Perhaps we should go now...before the police come."

I didn't need a second invitation!

I jumped on the motorcycle and Lin showed me the rest of the way out of town where I carried on alone over a mountain range, thinking to myself, "Well good morning, Dave Barr. This day has certainly started out right."

As I rode through the winding roads up a very steep mountain, I stayed on the alert for trucks passing each other on blind corners, listened for horns, and watched for trucks in the middle of the road. There were no guard rails on these roads, so if I went over the side, I would be gone!

Every now and again I spot a little turnout along the side of the road. Up in a tree there would be a 55 gallon drum and hose. Occasionally I would see a truck parked there, pouring water on the brake drums. When drivers felt their brakes were too hot, they would pull into one of these places, pay the attendant, and pour out the water to cool the drums. What a mammoth task it must have been to find the streams or wells to carry water in buckets up to these barrels up in the trees. Sometimes there were no rivers or wells within a mile. The challenge was incredible.

Coming down the other side of the mountain, I entered many small agricultural villages. In one, I saw a whole battalion of the Chinese Army carrying hoes and picks instead of rifles on their shoulders, working in the field in full uniform. They were waging a war against weeds and helping to grow food.

About three that afternoon I felt my back end whishy, washying around - a flat tire. Fortunately, there are compressors along side of the road throughout China. I spotted a little building like a cafe with a compressor out in front, and pulled in next to the compressor. A man came over, and I pointed at my rear tire with no words spoken. I unloaded the motorcycle, jacked it up and rolled the wheel out from behind it. We worked together, breaking the tire down in the rain. Not very far away, I noticed five very lovely Chinese women, all dressed up and painted in this open-faced building that was part of a dirt lot. One of the girls in a wonderfully short mini skirt came over with an umbrella to shield me. Since I tend to be a very single minded person, my mind focused on the tire. As she squatted down next to us to try to keep the rain off of us, I must admit I was a bit distracted, my eyes wandering up her dress in a very discrete way. She noticed what I was doing and laughed, as did the fellow helping me. I turned red with embarrassment, even though I was laughing with them. Back to work Dave.

By the time the tire was fixed, it was 17:30, so I made the sign of sleep, pointing just across the lot to a little shed. They nodded "yes" to my request, so we pushed the motorcycle over to the spot. After I put my tent up, I went over to the so-called restaurant to have my dinner - less than 50 cents for a large bowl of noodles and prawns. As I ate, the girls asked me questions and I would answer as best I could with my flash cards.

After dinner, the normal crowd of about 15 to 20 people gathered, finally leaving about 20:00. About this time, trucks started pulling into the parking lot, and it finally dawned on me that I was at a roadside bordello, complete with laughter, drinking, hooting and hollering that lasted through the night.

What a wonderful night! Noise, heat, humidity and plentiful mosquitoes! When I finally took my legs off, somebody squatted at the front of my tent and stared at me.

By now, I'd had enough, and lost it, hitting the poor fellow square in the face, knocking him away from me. It had been a long, hot, miserable day, and I was exhausted. I drew down the flap of the tent, and outside I kept hearing the word "gweilo" which means "foreign devil." I noticed lighters being lit near the tent. "Perhaps they are going to try something with me," I thought, knowing it would be impossible to put on my legs inside the tent in an emergency. I took out my protective gas which has a range of 15 feet. Then, I opened the tent flap in aggressive anger, coming out with the gas to do the lot of them if necessary. To my astonishment, I saw a beautiful young Chinese girl who squatted down in front of me and said, "Can I help you" in broken English.

That was the first English I had heard in two days! I looked at her and said, "Please, tell these people to go away to let me sleep in privacy. It is not nice to stand and stare." She nodded her head and started shouting at the crowd. When the crowd dispersed, I told this young angel of mercy, "Thank you very much." What a wonderful sight and help she was. She smiled and left. Though I never saw her again, she just may have saved my journey through China.

About 05:30, I loaded the motorcycle and looked across a small ravine between me and the open restaurant, ready to leave. I spotted all the young chicky girls brushing their teeth outside. I wondered to myself what they had in their mouths the night before. I waived good-bye to them and they smiled, waiving good-bye to me.

The one thing I will never do again is to pull into a major city to have anything to eat, due to the crowds that would surround me. At one place, when I ordered some sugar rice and hard boiled eggs, as I sat down to eat ALL the chairs around my table were occupied with people staring at me, climbing on the backs of one another. It was so cramped I didn't even have enough room to use my chopsticks. The bowl I was holding in my hand was right in front of my face. It was virtually impossible for me to eat, but I finished my breakfast. I paid the proprietor and forced my way out through the crowd to the motorcycle where people were spilling over into the streets. I felt like Moses parting the Red Sea of humanity, shoving aside these black eyes and black heads of hair, dressed in Maoist jackets.

In one small village, a small boy darted out in front of me; I swerved, narrowly missing him. I must be absolutely absorbed with the road ahead, or disaster will strike. Market places often spilled out into the roads, and I had to carefully push my way through, being cautious not to hit someone.

In heavy road construction areas with huge lines, many times I went around on the right, like the Chinese did on bicycles. If the Chinese see a pedestrian in front of them, they beep on the horn. If the person doesn't move, they hit them with the motorcycle and knock them out of the way (which I had to do myself on a number of occasions). I was always able to make my way to the front of the line where the road construction people would stop traffic or make an effort to get me across the constructed area in front of everybody else.

Once, in the late afternoon, I came to a traffic line and couldn't get around on either side - there was a drop on the right, and on the left it was raised two feet for the oncoming lane. As I sat there, some drivers started looking at the motorcycle, and said, "You should go ahead on the left side." I indicated to them that I couldn't because the motorcycle was too heavy to lift up the two feet. Immediately, eight people joined together and lifted the motorcycle up that two-foot shear embankment to the oncoming lane. I thanked them and headed down the newly paved area, leaving them to wipe grease from their hands.

I spotted a patch of mud a few hundred meters in front of me. Since there was

319

now some oncoming traffic - they were letting one direction of traffic go, and when that group passed, they let the other go. That traffic was now coming at me as I tried to negotiate my way out of this mud. Unfortunately, I hit a rock underneath the mud's surface, knocking me off my course and into an oncoming truck, knocking me from the motorcycle to the side of the road, into even deeper mud, stuck under the motorcycle.

Traffic stopped. Drivers waded into the mud and took out the motorcycle. My right thumb was badly sprained and was now virtually useless. It had been caught between the throttle and the front brake.

On my way again, I was now in great pain from my thumb, and my stumps were also killing me after miles and miles of having to hold the motorcycle up over rough ground and through holes, straining every inch of the way at low speeds. Naturally, in the midst of this agony, the rear end of the motorcycle started to get wishy washy under me again.

Another flat. Within seconds, I spotted another compressor and pulled in. The crowd appeared, and a fellow came over and helped me work on the motorcycle. This crowd was FAR more aggressive than most. They pressed together in the heat, so close to me that I literally could not see - the leering heads were blocking out the sun. Somehow, in the midst of this crowd and blistering heat, we managed to get the wheel out, fix the flat, and remount the tire.

To get the compressor to work, he flagged down a one cylinder tractor with a pulley on the motor. They put a fan belt across from the tractor to the pulley on the compressor. Then, a couple of fellows took the compressor and started pulling it away until the belt had enough tension to turn the compressor and pump air into the compressor tank to fill my tire. This was a "tug of war" with machines. After this workout, I felt dehydrated from the heat, with sweat pouring off me. They started handing me bottles of water - I probably drank about a half a gallon. After paying for the water, I went to pay the compressor owner for his help with the tire and he said, "Meiyo," waiving his hand in a "No" motion. I found this type of generosity very typical of rural Chinese.

Roach Restaurants and Throbbing Thumb

On my way again, I was famished, so I stopped at a roadside restaurant in the country. Now, in the best of times a Chinese restaurant is usually dirty, but in the country, they seem even worse. I walked into the kitchen area and showed my flash card indicating "I would like something to eat." I noticed garbage piled up in the corner and under the sink. I pointed at some eggs and noodles, then showed my flash card asking "How much." We agreed on the price, and she cooked the meal in what I can only describe as filthy conditions far beyond the comprehension of most Westerners.

On my way again, I took a short cut out of Wenzhou and the road improved for a bit. "If I take this road around Hangzhou to Shanghai," I thought, "I'll miss the road construction." It worked that way for a short time.

When I stopped for gasoline, the man wouldn't take any money, saying "Welcome to China." Many others who refused my money told me the same thing. This is especially touching since these people don't make very much money to begin with - the average wage is only about $30.00 per month.

Just when I was congratulating myself on my good road decision, I encountered more road construction, hitting holes with a foot and a half of water in them. I plowed through these very quickly as they were usually no more than 10 yards across (so I wouldn't drown out the exhaust).

About 17:30, I pulled off to a quite place where there were no people. As I manipulated a rocky road, wouldn't you know it, I fell over on the motorcycle. Within a minute, two men appeared out of thin air on bicycles and helped me upright the motorcycle. I pitched my tent in this rocky area, and suddenly about 15 people were standing around and staring. This went on for hours! They offered me cigarettes. They tried to ask me questions. I had my mechanical translator, but it is not doing the job it should. However, the hand-held machine was of great interest to them. They passed it around and pushed on the buttons. Then, I showed them my flash cards. One said, "I'm going around the world for the disabled." Since many of these people are unable to read, they passed it around until one person could tell them what I was doing, while the others nodded their heads.

At 19:30, I took out my dictionary and show them the word "privacy," indicating I'd like to sleep. They nod, and leave me alone so I can take off my legs and start to relax with the mosquitoes and heat, sweating through the night.

Suddenly, a flashlight shines into my tent! I opened my tent and showed them the word "privacy" in my dictionary. They left, and at last I was alone with my thoughts of the day.

The following morning at 05:30 they were back again, ready to watch this crazy foreigner put all his stuff back on the motorcycle and ride out. In my exit, I nearly ran over their bicycles as I tried to control my machine over this rough rock. I could just imagine their reaction if I hit about six bicycles!

I rode along the river with pain still shooting through my right hand. It had swollen up during the night and kept me awake with its throbbing. Now, the vibration in the handlebars intensified the pain, making it extremely difficult to put any pressure on the front brake lever. I could only travel about 30 to 35 miles per hour along the river road, although it wasn't really crowded. It was quite a beautiful ride, and at one point I came across an ancient dam, and at another, I passed a three-story high statute cut in one piece out of the rock. I've never seen anything like it in my life. I just stood there, waiting for transport to some unknown destination.

The city of Hangzhou is known as "the garden city," and has an island out on a lake where the local royalty used to live. It is an old city, and very beautiful in the tourist area where I saw Europeans for the first time in a week.

The road out to Shanghai started badly. When I stopped for gas at one point, a woman on the steps outside a cafe screamed loudly at the sight of me, then ran inside when I came up the steps. The owner came out and shouted at me, and I shouted back, going down the stairs and heading for the cafe next door where a gentleman served me tea, a cake, and we tried to converse with my flash cards. Again, he would not take money.

Meet a bad person, meet a good person. In fairness to the "bad" person who screamed, I had huge rips in my pants, mud all over me, and I probably stank like a dead skunk.

On the road again, I was actually able to put the motorcycle in fourth gear and get up to 50 miles an hour for the first time in over a week! Still, it was dangerous as bicycles would unpredictably dart out onto the road. It was amazing that I missed a couple of them; all I needed was another Fuzhou incident. After traveling over 50 kilometers (30 miles) in fourth gear, I felt like I was traveling over 100 miles an hour. What a major difference! I saw three major accidents in that time, showing that even the Chinese don't know how to handle speed on their roads. I saw many broken down trucks, including one pulling the rear axle out while sitting stationary in the fast lane of a double-laned road.

Coming into Shanghai on a nicely paved, modern freeway, I saw subtitles in English on all the road signs - the first I'd seen in days.

At the Quang Hu Hotel, a lovely young woman named Lillian came out to greet me, directing me to a security area for the motorcycle, and then leading me to a room reserved for me costing about $8.50 for the night. The rate was more than I could really afford, but so as not to let my friends lose face who made the arrangements, I paid, staying in the cleanest Chinese hotel I ever occupied.

The following day the Disabled Federation of Shanghai came over and picked me up. Due to traffic, it took us an hour and a half to go four miles (6 km) across Shanghai to a meeting area in one of the old concession quarters, places reserved for various foreign countries with business interests in China before 1949.

There I met with a group of people who stood up at different times, telling me what they were and what they did. Frankly, it sounded like a lot of communist rhetoric. Shanghai suffered terribly during the cultural revolution.

When they asked, "Is there anything we can do for you?" I explained that I needed volunteer work to get through the winter while I haggled with the Russians and Mongolians about entry into their countries. They just shook their heads as if to say, "There is nothing we can do." I found that was the attitude of most people in government organizations. They would always present a very warm welcome, and even ask how they could help. But, if I made a request of them, they immediately became non committal, and did nothing. Overall, the women seemed easier to deal with than the men.

Joe, our interpreter told me, "During the cultural revolution, I was placed in exile out in a farm commune for reeducation. It created great hardships on me and my family. We could not communicate with one another for years."

People who had education and professional positions were the main targets of the cultural revolution started by Mao in June of 1966, and lasting until his death 10 years later. During that decade, the persecution was terrible for millions.

The following day a television crew appeared, but the producer didn't believe I was going around the world. "Where's your proof?" he demanded. I showed him pictures, my map and passport. After going through it with amazement, he profusely apologized to me and started our interview with Lillian interpreting the affair; her English was impeccable.

August 29: That night I laid back, thinking that this is precisely eleven years to the day since we had hit the land mine and my life changed forever. Looking back to where I was then and where I was today, I could never have imagined my life would have taken this path.

The following morning rain came down hard, flooding Shanghai's streets in about six inches of water. I carefully sloshed my way through the mini-river out to the main highway which is above the water. I was able to travel at about 45 miles per hour on this double laned road. Nevertheless, I still saw six accidents in about 75 miles, accidents with trucks, cars and a bus.

When I stopped to get fuel, a man pulled in behind me and said, "I saw you on television yesterday!" He was so excited that he gave me two moon cakes and some hot tea to drink (the tea is usually in a glass jar originally used for something else). One drinks directly out of the jar, and it is frequently passed around to many drinkers. A moon cake is very popular in China, and is made up of pecans and other goodies - more like a pie than a cake.

I made it to Nanjing, a major city, about midday, and went to a phone to call the

Amity Foundation. Of course, nobody spoke English, so a nearby fellow got on the phone for me and told them, "There's a foreigner with a motorcycle here." From that, Amity knew who I was and gave directions to their office.

Enabling the Disabled and Sewer Breath Bo

Now, this man climbs on the back of the fully loaded machine. We are so packed that I am virtually sitting on top of the gas tank! Off we go in the rain through the city, dodging bicycles, carts and all the other unmotorized traffic. When we rode through the foundation's gates, I was stunned to see old British buildings - like in England about 80 years ago, a step into the British past right here in China! We hailed a cab for my new friend, then went inside where I met Mrs. Tan, head of the office. "Welcome Dave," she said. "You'll be meeting some people from the Disabled Federation later, but for now, let me show you to your room." She led me upstairs to a huge dormitory. Once that was taken care of, I wheeled the motorcycle around back and unloaded it, carrying my baggage up to the room.

Ms. Gu was my interpreter, and over the next couple days there were many activities. Mrs. Gu introduced me to the head of the Disabled Federation, to two women who would accompany us. Mrs. Gu introduced me to Wu Ann Ann, and Cow Bin Bin, and them to each other. I chuckled to myself, thinking "I get such a charge out of the names, particularly several people in sequence." Mrs. Wu Ann Ann worked for the Foundation in another department.

We visited a prosthetics factory opened up during the Korean War. They told me, "We've treated over 20,000 veterans from the Korean War." Since Nanjing is a city of five million people, they figure there's one hundred and seventy thousand disabled people. China's government is very progressive, offering incentives to businesses that employ people with disabilities. At the factory, I was amazed at the technology that the Chinese had invented, including a three-wheel drive bicycle, chairs and combinations of various wheel chairs.

In one section, they showed me a hand-actuating arm that could pull up to 60 pounds of pressure. I believe it was a nerve impulse arm, and it reminded me of the joke about a guy who had a voice controlled arm. He would say, "drink," and the arm would bring a cup to his mouth. He'd say, "smoke," and the arm would light up a cigarette. One day, he went to take a pee and said, "Shake it off, arm." It felt so good he said, "Go ahead and jerk it off." When the arm jerked it off, he screamed, "Oh no, fuck me," so the arm took what was left of his tattered dick and shoved it up his ass. I couldn't help but cackle as I thought about this, although it was not a joke I was inclined to tell my Chinese friends, especially with a female interpreter.

We also toured the Jing Ling Piston Factory with over 1,000 employees, 400 of them with a disability. Because of the high noise level in the factory, most of the people with disabilities were deaf. They placed them in the extremely noisy areas and did not need to be concerned about hearing loss or ear protection. "What a practical solution," I thought.

At the naval hospital, the Amity Foundation's hearing section created custom made hearing aides. They trained people in the medical field there and in agricultural and languages as well, providing teachers in these fields.

We visited one place where they held what is called "free discussion" with the Disabled Federation, a lovely group of young people. I was impressed by their aggressive attitude towards life. They asked me about the disabled in America, which I don't know anything about, so I told them about South Africa and England where I have a fair grasp of what goes on. After our meeting, they told me,

"Tomorrow you must be a tourist for a day and see some of Nanjing. We will take you around in our three wheel scooters." I agreed. This was to be a decision I would later regret.

The following day, one of the first places we went was to the tomb of Sun Yat Xian, known as "The Father of the Republic." Sun Yat Xian was a progressive thinking man who wanted to modernize industry, the military and the government. He was in cahoots with Mao Zedong and Zhou En Li in the early days of the Communist party, but died in the early twenties. His tomb has 392 steps to the top. It was decided I would walk to the top without stopping, accompanied by two others, Li Xiang Guang, a disabled Vietnam Veteran from the PLA (People's Liberation Army) with a leg off just above the knee, and one off just below the knee; he wore only one prosthesis and was on crutches. Together with a massive polio victim on crutches, we went to the top where we met with reporters, thus raising the profile of the disabled in Nanjing.

We made it to the top non-stop; I was stunned, wandering around like a dazed idiot. All three of us were sweating like whores on pay day. Anyway, we met the reporters, did short interviews with photographs, saw the tomb of Sun Yat Xian, then went back down the 392 steps! These actions served as a motivation for other disabled people, and there was plenty of positive press in the newspapers from the experience.

After our climb, we went on a bit of a tour around the city. The ride was a nightmare! The drivers simply didn't look. They would just zoom out into the traffic with trucks and buses everywhere. I rode in the back of Li Xiang Guang's three-wheeled scooter as he raced through traffic, saying to myself as we passed the tour buses, "You boys will never know what you are missing." At the day's end, we attended a "banquet" in my honor where a huge meal was consumed by all. There was so much I became distressed by the amount of food that would be wasted. When I mentioned this later, I was told, "It is not wasted. The kitchen staff receive the remains, and split it up." It is a tradition that if nothing remains on the table, and you are still hungry, the host loses face. After the banquet, we went to a park and sang songs such as "The Red Sun Rising While Mao Leads Us." Of course, the songs were from the Cultural Revolution.

While we toured, we stopped so I could purchase a new horn... mine had worn out!

The next day, I was on my way north. Just out of Nanjing was the mighty Yang Ze river where statues of armed Chinese soldiers stood along the guard rails. The river was crowded with various kinds of craft, and appeared horribly polluted. The bridge itself was very rough, and most crowded. I continued to be shocked at the awesome displays of humanity at virtually every location.

My next stop was Xuzhou, where Billy Graham, the great preacher and man of God, was born. Zhou En Li, one of the founders of the Chinese nation, was also born here.

Further north, a valve hung up in the front Cylinder. After letting it cool down, it apparently freed up because it started again.

Next, a primary drive belt broke. I pulled along the road and started working. The inevitable crowd gathered, and soon they were bearing down on me. I had to use my flashlight to see what I was doing! After thirty minutes, the crowd spilled out onto the road, blocking traffic. The police came and started to forcefully disperse the crowd. What a relief when I finished and could take off once again. I can't describe the personal pressure I feel in these situations.

In Jinan, I made contact with the Disabled Federation, most of whom were deaf mutes. I've never run into a livelier bunch of people so full of energy and life. The interpreter assigned to me had breath like a sewer. Bo unfortunately felt compelled to get right in my face when he interpreted. A few times, his sewer breath nearly made me sick. As my special blessing, Bo was with me constantly during the next twenty-four hours. At a meeting with the Disabled Federation, shit breath reeked from three feet away. Even the disabled stayed six feet from this fellow. As he translated my words to them, they would read his lips - from a safe distance of course, then put the conversation into hand language. Quite an interesting interaction.

Just when I thought Bo was gone for the night (he left for home about 21:30), he appeared at my dirty hotel room with another fellow, and the conversation lasted for another hour. When they left, I had to open the windows to mellow the smell he so generously left.

When I entered Tianjin, a port city just 75 miles east of Beijing, many people seemed to know who I was. In this crowded, huge city my next challenge was to locate the Disabled Federation. I spotted a motorcycle parked along the road, so I pulled up and showed the address to him. Within two minutes, a crowd gathered, and the Chinese started shoving pieces of paper at me with pens, not asking, but more like DEMANDING my autograph. For the next thirty minutes I signed my name, and tried to write something for each person. As I did, a pot of tea and some rice cookies appeared on the back of the motorcycle. When the cookies, tea and autographs were completed, the man with the motorcycle led me across town through the crowded streets to the Disabled Federation. Well done!

The Disabled Federation arranged to house me in a University dormitory that night, and the following day we went to a Disabled School where they taught kids different skills; it was a combination high school, trade school institution for children from twelve through seventeen years of age. Their disabilities ranged from paraplegics, to polio, to deafness. They sang songs for me, and asked about my journey. At my visit's end, I received a gigantic five-pound moon cake - the biggest I saw in my entire trip through China. Mind you, this to a man who is constantly conscious about the weight on his motorcycle.

The date was **September 10**: The beginning of the Autumn Festival. As I prepared to leave, the staff invited me for a "quick, simple meal." Knowing it would hurt their feelings if I declined, and also knowing there is no such thing as a "simple meal," I agreed. For the next two hours I sat eating from 15 to 18 different courses. I could not believe the huge mountain of food on the rotating table. It seemed that the Chinese eat virtually anything. One of the dishes was fish stomach and it looked like snot. It shimmied all over the chop sticks and slinked down your throat. Disgusting! Of course, they plop this food into my bowl with great glee. "Try this, Try that," they seem to say, although no one speaks English. Fortunately, my interpreter for this banquet had pleasant breath (I had caught a cold from Bo). At the end of this feast, they took me back to the Disabled Federation School to pick up the motorcycle and wave to the kids who had come to the windows.

Out of Tianjin, the expressway was a toll road, double-laned, enabling me to travel the last 70 miles of my journey across China to Beijing at 55 miles per hour. I was able to enjoy the flat, agricultural countryside, dotted with little villages (not developments) and farms, with many family housing units that must have dated back at least a century. They had survived the ravages of World War II, the coming of the Communist's, the Cultural Revolution, and all the different periods of Chinese history.

September 11, Friday: Arriving in Beijing, I flagged down a motorcyclist, a Mr.

Fong, who took me to Liang Mau Towers, meaning "landmark towers" in English. There I located the offices of Deguessa, the company managed by Peter Stoessel, the President of the Harley Owner's Group in Hong Kong. I met a young Chinese lady named Juliana who spoke impeccable English. Mr. Fong then left, giving me a big hug, rare for a Chinese person.

Juliana had been expecting me, and took me to a hotel near Deguesa's office. Again, it was too expensive for me, but I agreed to stay there over the weekend.

In Beijing, my first journey across China had finished.

Two Years to Beijing

Instantly, a new set of problems start. It is too late to cross Siberia unless my permits are issued immediately, which would be a minor miracle. If they do not come through, what will I do for the winter? I have only one month left on my visa, then I'll be forced to leave China.

In a trip like this, all you do is change problems.

No longer am I faced with the major road hazards and severe weather problems. Instead, I'm faced with "What will I do for the next six or seven months to get through the winter? How will I get the permits to cross Mongolia and Russia?" I have been warned it could be difficult. That warning was an understatement.

I met some people in the parking lot at Liang Mau Towers who knew of a cheaper place for me to stay. That night I called one of them and asked, "Do you know where there's a room to rent on a long-term basis?" "I may know of a cheap hotel," he said. The man made some inquiries and called me back later, saying, "Let me take you to the other side of Beijing and see about a room."

September 12: We took a cab to a hotel called the Long Tan Hotel, where many "low-end" tourists stayed. They charged $6.00 a day for a room with a shower. It is a very basic room. I decided to move, and went back across town to get my motorcycle and then ride it back to this place.

Today marked two years on the road. I thought about that September 12th, 1990, and how I felt inside when I said good-bye to Don and headed up Africa; I thought about September 12th of 1991 when I was in Anchorage; now on September 12th, 1992, I am in Beijing, thinking to myself, "What am I going to do now that I'm here?" After traveling across four continents, as usual, I'm very unsure about the immediate future.

The next day, Monday, I go to Liang Mau Towers to Degussa's office where I would get my first taste of the public transport system in Beijing. First of all, it is very aggressive! If you don't push and shove your way on, you are not going to get on that bus. Often, when I didn't move quick enough for fear of stepping on people's feet and hurting them with my steel foot, I would get pushed out of the way by others.

The system works like this: when a bus pulls up to stop, the people wanting to get off are like a stick of paratroopers. Everybody is bunched up behind one another... "Ready, set, go!!!" The doors open and you jump out into the crowd that is coming the other way, fighting to get on. If the first man can get out okay, you've got no problems. But, if that man hesitates at the door, count on a real battle.

Of course, the buses are always packed to overflowing! And there's always that odd individual who will have his ass stuck out, blocking the doorway, and they can't close the doors! If the doors can't shut, the bus won't go. So, when this happens, some big hulking Chinese monitor (in the north of China, the Chinese are as big as Westerners) with a red arm band and a little red flag will start bashing into the butt of

326

this person until he is finally packed onto the bus. I've seen this go on for as long as five minutes before the bus was packed enough so the door could close! Amazingly, no one ever seems to get irritated about this. Of course, once the packed bus would depart, invariably, the next bus would arrive - empty.

It took me three hours to travel six miles across town, stopping to change buses three times, and taking long walks in between the bus stops.

Once, in my early days in Beijing, I tried to get on the No. 28 bus and everybody is yelling "No"..."Meiyo." I didn't understand their protest, thinking they were trying to make trouble for me because I was a foreigner; few foreigners use buses. "Piss on you people," I thought, jumping on the bus anyway. Well, the bus never stopped when it should have. It continued miles beyond the normal stop, me frantically shouting at the driver as it passed my destination. This caused me to walk a good mile to catch another bus to take me back to my correct stop. The people sat with smug smiles on their faces. This smelly foreign idiot had failed to listen to their warning.

At the office, I wrote some letters to various people; Peter Stoessel said I could write letters, mail, and use the fax machine - whatever I needed in the office. This place was a wonderful island of tranquillity, a virtual oasis in this sea of aggressive humanity called Beijing.

In the afternoon, the battle with the buses resumed once again.

I contacted John Leicester, a United Press International (UPI) correspondent, referred to me by Jane Perini (my Chinese flash card creator!). John and I had lunch, and he told me, "The manager of the agency here in Beijing is going on leave for a few weeks, so why don't you come and stay with us?"

"That would be great," I replied.

"Your motorcycle can be put safely away in the UPI garage, and can stay there as long as you like."

UPI has an office in an old diplomatic compound now used mainly for the different news agencies from all over the world. The old buildings were built in the fifties by the Russians for the Chinese, and used to house Russians who lived and worked in China. Russian media still occupy a portion of these buildings.

My motorcycle was moved into a secure lockup garage, away from the public eye. During the next two weeks, John introduced me to Han Wei, who was so taken with the trip that he wanted to do some type of filming with me. I told him I'd be happy to accommodate any need he had.

Lawrence Wong worked in the Degussa office, and I asked him to make inquiries about working over the winter doing volunteer work. My hope was to stop the constant outflow of my money. Larence told me, "I might be able to find you a job that actually pays. I know a Professor Jin at the Language Institute who has a Language School to teach basic English. Perhaps you can help there."

The Professor agreed to try me out. On the night I taught my first lesson in Basic American English, I worked out of a simple little text book speaking to young school kids, a few college students, and a few professional people. In this class I met one of the most refreshing people I'd come to know in China: a friend and benefactor named Huang Ze-Qing, a lovely 21-year-old girl. Ze-Qing was a student at People's University, and an honor student in philosophy and physics. She just kind of attached herself to me, and we would have a long term relationship on a very friendly basis.

Professor Jin liked my teaching, and said that he could use me in the future. Unfortunately, after I taught a few more English lessons, he canceled my contract because I could not secure a visa that would guarantee my stay in China. He needed a teacher who could teach the entire two month class, and I could not give him assurance that the authorities would renew my visa. This experience left me in a rather low mood because I felt my options were slipping away.

During my evening teaching, I learned to mistrust China's taxi system. After class, I would take a little mini-taxi back to my room for a charge of one RMB per Kilometer. (then, about .15 cents a mile). I found these drivers to be legalized, scheming thieves. I constantly had to watch my wallet to make sure they were not overcharging this foreigner.

The Chinese economy consists of a three-part price system: one price is for the average Chinese in the street, the second price is much higher, and reserved for the wealthy Chinese; the third, and most costly price, is reserved for the foreigners.

Spitting is the national sport in China. I've never seen a race of people spit more than the Chinese. Trash receptacles always had goop dripping off of them. The ground is dotted big yellow lumps of phlegm, and walkers must constantly dodge mounds of mucus. I've even seen people spitting on buses, then squish around on it... the spitter's shuffle! Even restaurants are not exempt from this symphony of saliva. The Chinese freely spit bones on the floor and table while eating, then lob a big goober on the floor. I was shocked and appalled by these demonstrations of salivary excretion.

John Leicester was a big help to me my entire time in China. He acted as a social anchor, and always welcomed me into his apartment. At times when I longed just to hear English again, I'd go visit John. During my travels, I'd come to appreciate the very small things. Once, at Johns, I enjoyed the first bread I'd eaten in a month!

I never mastered the bus system, so I constantly took the wrong buses. Somehow, buses with the right number always took me to the wrong stops. Then, I'd get off and usually have a mile or more walk to another connection. This was a constant source of frustration.

Communication, or more precisely, non-communication was the other major aggravation of daily life. Try to ask directions when no one understands English. Try to say what you want to eat. It is a war of non-words. At times, I'd just scream, looking like a babbling idiot. As this long-nosed foreigner vented his frustration, the Chinese would calmly look on without ever as much as batting an eye...ever inscrutable.

Great Expectations...Great Wall!

I asked Ze-Qing to guide me to the Great Wall, and she agreed. We mounted the motorcycle and took off, almost immediately encountering stalled traffic, with the police motioning us to the side of the road. The Paris-Moscow-Beijing Rally was coming into town, so the roads were cleared for these 4x4 road vehicles. All splattered with mud, they shot past us with drivers sitting up proudly behind the wheels with their crews, followed by support and logistics vehicles. At the end of the flurry, the motorcycles came charging in, the most popular being the Yamaha Tenente. I understand the total race covered about 10,000 miles (16,000 km) - about 12% of the distance I'd ultimately traveled - without support or logistics vehicles.

Once they passed, we continued to the Great Wall where I was absolutely enthralled with the immense and incredible wonder. It amazed me how it flowed, following the crest of the hills as far as I could see. We were not able to go up on the wall because, once again, we drew a big crowd, and I felt insecure about leaving the motorcycle on its own.

After leaving the Great Wall, we stopped at an empty corn field, pulled off the road, and enjoyed a lovely little picnic Ze-Qing's mother had prepared for us - chicken with all the goodies that go with it! I was touched by the mother's gesture, and by this young girl's unspoiled disposition and feelings about the world and people around her. Ze-Qing was a slender young woman standing about 5' 4", with a short, jet-black hair style, and black, penetrating eyes that radiated intelligence when they looked at you.

A meeting was set up by Han Wei for me to meet Yin Le, a producer for the Beijing Youth TV Film Producing center. Yin Le was an impeccably dressed fellow who couldn't speak any English. Through John as an interpreter, Yin Le asked, "Would you be willing to make a trip across China in the name of the Hope Project for children whose parents cannot afford to send them to school? We will raise money for them, and also raise the profile of the disabled in China."

"Yes, I'd be happy to help your group if you would be willing to pay the expenses," I replied.

"Good," he answered. "We will talk later." By his expressions, I could see he was very excited about the prospects. I too was excited. "Maybe they can even help with my visa," I thought, "giving me more time to work on the Russian and Mongolian problems."

The Mongolian Embassy told me to "Come back 30 days before you leave for Mongolia," but were noncommittal about what they were going to do.

My first day back in the Long Tan Hotel my right leg was its usual noisy self - squeaking, clanging, and banging on each step. I sound like a tank with a rod missing as I walk down the road with my funny looking square, iron foot. This day, when I got off the elevator, I walked into my room where the girl was cleaning. When she saw this grungy foreigner enter the room with the clop, bang squeak of my leg, her mouth dropped opened, her eyes wide with fear. When I saw her fear, I said "sorry," turned around and walked out, only then realizing I was in the wrong room. What that poor girl must have thought I'll never know.

I killed a lot of waiting hours in my room reading, waiting for the telephone to ring. I always seem to be waiting to hear from somebody about something.

On October 1, 19:49, Mao Zedong at Tianamen Square announced the founding of the Peoples Republic of China at the end of the Great March. Now, in 1992, it is a holiday, and I am out wandering around looking for bolts. I frequently wear out the heads of the bolts on the sole of my right foot - they last about three weeks per bolt before it breaks. So, I'm out looking for anyone who might sell bolts when I come upon a shoe repairman who told me to "Sit down." This fellow works on a street corner with a little box where he sets the shoe and puts on new heels. He takes off, and his wife offers me a little bit of tea from a quart thermos. Her little two-year-old daughter is gawking at this strange-looking foreigner, and I stared back, wondering "What does the future hold for this poor family?"

The shoemaker ran back and forth until he finally found a bolt that fit, so he made one final trip to bring me back several of these bolts and nuts. As poor as he was, he absolutely refused to accept any money! I was coming to understand there were two types of entrepreneurs in China: the people who will do anything to help you out, and then not charge, or charge only a fair amount, and those who will rip you off.

On my way home, I stopped to get a gembee - a big, thin pancake cooked on a stove with an egg and some vegetables broken onto it, then rolled up. I stopped at this one place because they charged me the "Chinese" price - not the tourist price - for the gembee. This day the stand had a different fellow, who overcharged me. When I challenged him, a shouting match started, and a huge crowd gathered. I let the man know that he was a thief; my appetite was spoiled.

Meet a good person, meet a bad person.

Ze-Qing invited me to her parent's flat one day; she and her mother cooked a wonderful meal. Her father was a chemical engineer who at one time was quite high in his work unit as a supervisor. His life reversed when he received a little gift from Japan from somebody who had worked with him. This gift arrived during the Cultural Revolution, and because of that gift and a letter he sent to the person, he was persecuted terribly. Her father was removed from his position, they lost their apartment, and were moved into a one room flat with no toilet, no running water or any other convenience that we Westerners consider necessities. He was reduced to shoveling coal into a wheelbarrow, then pushing it from the coal yard to the furnaces.

Mr. Huang was a very despondent individual, as were most of the adults who lived through that period of Chinese history. The Cultural Revolution started in June of 1966 and lasted for ten years until Mao died. During that time, Mr. Huang had to write confessions in newspapers about his "crime," as did millions of other Chinese people. These confessions were tacked to walls in various parts of the city. His said, "I was wrong and decadent to have received that gift."

"At least with Dung Xeou Ping at the helm, China is progressing in its free markets society," he told me. "A man may be rewarded for his hard work and endeavor, so things are better." Mr. Huang had also moved back up the ladder in his work unit in the chemical industry. They now lived in a little two bedroom apartment with a tiny bathroom, an even smaller kitchen, and a tiny dining room - considered a great luxury for a middle class Chinese family.

China Documentary - Fact or Fiction?

Yin Le asked me to attend a meeting with a group interested in doing the documentary of my journey across China. John had to translate everything. I was always amused how the Chinese could speak for ten minutes, then John would follow it with a thirty-second explanation. Obviously, I missed a lot! One thing I did know - these people were putting together a proposal for another trip across China!

The amount they were talking about to do the trip was $90,000 American dollars. "So much for the trip!" I thought.

They asked me, "What do you need?"

"I cannot continue to stay at the Long Tan Hotel paying $5.50 each day (that was even with a manager's discount!)," I told them.

"We will move you to another hotel, a better one," they replied. "We think that a hotel will pick up your tab in return for the media exposure."

"That would be wonderful," I said. "Do you think you can do anything about my visa?"

Within the next few days, Han Wei got my visa extended for two more months!

Next, at Yin Le's flat, I was introduced to a young lady who would be helping with the translations. Mona's English centered around the tourist trade, and she was competent in this field, but I found her very lacking in her English dealing with the disabled, Chinese education, and problems related to the motorcycle. I requested they find somebody with English as a first language to assist Mona. Mona would be the "official" Chinese translator for "FACE," but I wanted an English speaking translator for keeping me informed.

Yin Le's flat was one room with one light bulb hanging from the ceiling, and one little window. What a depressing place for a 35 year-old man to live! It had no running water or toilet. The toilet was down the end of the hall - a stinking affair which you could smell all over the floor. Yin Le's flat was jammed packed with a

VCR, a television, a stereo, a bookcase and a fax machine. Plus, he crammed in a bed, a table and a couch. There was no room for anything else.

Ze-Qing found a job for me that would provide a room. It seemed the production group was dragging. The $90,000 budget had inflated to $140,000 for the documentary (who were they trying to bullshit). That seemed ridiculously high to me. I held out no hope of them ever finding that much money. When the group heard about my proposed job, they said, "David, please don't take it. It will mess everything up." In the end, I agreed not to take the job which caused Ze-Qing to lose face over the entire matter. However, she never showed me any animosity. I took the risk of not accepting the job even though I had no faith in the group being able to find the needed money. I knew they were working terribly long hours to make this documentary happen, so I decided to show solidarity with them.

It was decided that we needed some media hype to give me a higher profile in the country. We evolved a plan to take some photographs for newspapers and magazines throughout China in a very special place. So, on **October 10th**, we made **our first trip to Tianamen Square**. I was to pose under Mao Ze Dong's portrait for the various newspapers and magazines in attendance. Normally, no one is allowed to approach Mao's portrait from Jen Guo Men, the boulevard of Heavenly Peace that goes right through the middle of Tianamen Square. Instead, we must approach it from inside the "forbidden city" which is roughly about three quarters of a mile ride, parting the seas of thousands of tourists from every place in the world, ending up under an archway directly below Mao's portrait.

The photography session was a very powerful moment as I realized that no one had ever done this before on a motorcycle. They had to go very high up the governmental ladder to enable me to be photographed there. You must understand that it was just above this portrait that Mao announced the Peoples Republic of China on October 1, 1949! He also started the Cultural Revolution from that spot. It is a very sacred spot to Asian Communism.

As I was posing there, I was amazed at the crowd. The square was swarming with security police, making sure all went well. At the end of the session, I rode back under the arch and to the back part of the forbidden city of the emperors. I honestly doubt if many people have ridden their motorcycles through this route. On my way, Ze-Qing was on the back of the motorcycle; I could tell she was thrilled about the opportunity.

After this event, they moved me to the Beijing International - probably the finest government hotel in Beijing. By Western standards, it is not very fancy, but it was far better than the Long Tan, plus it was on the main bus routes and near a subway station. And, the food was free! I was thrilled until the group told me that the hotel room was also to serve as an office for the production team.

In China, I feel like I am always about a step behind whatever is happening. When told about the "office" that was to be my room, I thought, "There's no way I'm going to have them coming in and out all day long, using the telephone and smoking like steam engines. I simply won't put up with it."

They had to learn to communicate better with me; that's why I asked for an English speaking interpreter to keep me properly informed. Mona was not doing a good job, and it was a constant source of friction between us. In the end they respected my wishes and got an "office" in the Quang Hu Hotel; that news brought me great delight.

They had a gymnasium at the Beijing International Hotel so I started working out again with music; it reminded me of my morning workouts in South Africa.

When I took breakfast in the morning I'd often see the tourists talking amongst themselves in English or French or German, preparing for the day's tour. I thought to myself, "How little I have in common with these people."

I was still waiting by the phone to hear some information from the group about what we were doing...what is going on. I hate being in the dark, and I hate surprises even more - such as my room suddenly becoming their "office." Being who I am, I was very open about showing my displeasure, which caused friction.

One afternoon while working on the motorcycle, a Russian fellow who was living right across from the garage came up to me and introduced himself as Igor Surickov. We chatted, and I told him about my desire to cross Russia.

"You will encounter many problems," he replied. "If I were you, I'd start working on them now."

The more we chatted, the more he took an interest in my trip. In future days, whenever he saw me working on the machine, he would come down and chat. Finally, he said "I am going to approach my brother on your behalf. He was a policeman in Moscow. Perhaps something could be arranged."

I have learned that somebody would have to agree to sign and take responsibility for me as I traveled through Russia. Igor told me, "It is very rare that people travel from eastern Siberia to the west. I'm not real optimistic about the whole thing."

More worry.

In America, I learn that the presidential race is at the height of mud slinging. In Israel, historic peace talks are taking place with the PLO, but the Hezbolla are firing rockets at the Israelis from north of the demilitarized zone in Lebanon. In Beijing, Dave Barr is stuck, always waiting on a telephone.

One day, while working on the machine, I noticed play in the rear wheel. I took the wheel off, checked it out, and discovered that the bearing was shifting around again inside the spoke-bearing hub spindle. Another major problem! I had last fixed this problem in England; over 40,000 miles (60,000 km) had been ridden since then, and the problem was back.

Now, with the help of some foreigners in the Diplomat compound, we ran around town trying to find a solution to the problem. We could not find a person who could understand what was needed to repair the machine.

Nobody understood the way the Englishmen had fixed it. Han Wei told me, "I know of a shop called the Beijing Emergency Motorcycle Repair Works." We took the rear wheel over there, and a woman measured it with the help of a supervisor. While they were making a new part, they hard-chromed a bearing oversize to fit into the wheel hub just to keep us going.

The following day we met with Hope Project heads from various provinces. Han Wei and I rode up on the motorcycle with Jin Lei and Yin Le in a taxi cab behind us. My machine can't sit and idle for long periods in traffic, so I was cutting down the right side in the bicycle lane when somebody once again didn't look and turned - I hit another bicyclist! We pulled over. The man was very understanding when he was told what the group was about, and what I was doing. We shook hands, and with great relief we went on our way, very grateful that no payoff had to be made, and that the man appeared to have no serious injury.

At the Hope Project office the leaders pledged to give us a hand as we took the journey across China promoting their cause. Of course, they stand to financially benefit from our project, but as yet there is no money in the bank. It was up to Jin Lei to find a company or companies that would sponsor our group. Jin Lei was the most dynamic person in our group, and the motivating force behind the whole project. Without her persistence and drive, it never would have happened.

About a week later, I received a call saying, "Your parts are ready on the motorcycle." What unfolds next is a typical example of Chinese non-communication. I took the rear wheel off the motorcycle, broke the tire down and took it off. Next, Mona and I jumped into a cab and drove to the Beijing Emergency Motorcycle Repair Works. When we arrived, reporters and photographers were there waiting for me to appear on the motorcycle! Instead, they got a rear wheel and my greasy hands. The incident was horribly embarrassing for Yin Le and Jin Lei.

"You must communicate with me," I told them. This problem kept coming up the entire time we worked together. "If you talk to me, and tell me what is going on, we won't have these problems." The shop leader was very distraught that I didn't show up on the motorcycle. He presented me with a spindle perfectly made to hold the bearings and the spokes. They then took the wheel, and within an hour it was laced up and true. A woman had made the spindle on her milling machine. I gave her a box of candy in appreciation, but before she took it, she had to get permission from the factory foreman. This woman made about $30.00, yet she was so skilled that the spindle is on the motorcycle to this day!

I attended a meeting with Jin Lei and the PC Brand Computer people. They are an American based company that builds their machinery in Taiwan, and have an office in Beijing. We spoke to Andy Tam, the managing director, who recognized me from the Good Morning Show I did while in Hong Kong. After the meeting, Jin Lei told me "I have a very positive feeling."

"Well, don't get your hopes up too much," I responded, putting a damper on her high feelings. Ironically, in the end it was PC Brand Computers that virtually bankrolled the majority of the trip! So much for my instincts!

Hong Kong School of Motoring
Dave on Yamaha 125 going through test for camera.
August 1992 Hong Kong.

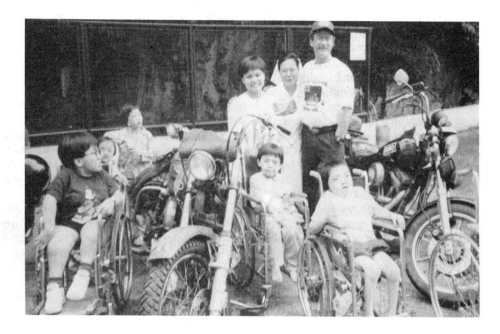

Duchess of York Hospital for disabled children
July 1992

Boat City on the Road to Beijing
August 1992 China
(Note: 1 cycle and a diesel tractor on right)

Chapter Twenty-Nine

Misinterpreting Our Way Through China

One morning when I was walking out of the hotel, I gave a woman beggar some money. Immediately others moved in. One woman had a little child who now ran along side of me, and I accidentally stepped on his foot. He screamed and leaped through the air. It left me with a terrible feeling in my heart, knowing I had caused pain to people already living in utter misery.

There was another beggar I encountered outside the Diplomat Apartments who had no legs below the knee. His wore two prosthesis he had made himself - very crude. I gave him some money one day, and when I saw him again, I started to give him some more, but he wouldn't take it. Instead, he gave me a pear! I was very touched by this gesture. From that time forward, we just nodded at each other on the street in respectful recognition. One day, I gave him a photograph with my name on the back. We would run into each other in some of the most bizarre places in the city, and he always carried that photograph with him.

Ze-Qing told me, "Never give money to beggars. It only encourages them. I have heard that they take unwanted children and deliberately maim them, cutting off arms or legs, just so they can beg for the family." I was never able to confirm this assertion, but I do know that most Chinese live very hard lives. Some of the disfigured kids I saw in Beijing and other places in China were in desperate need of help.

My first meeting with the Beijing Federation of Disabled was very negative, so a second meeting was called. Jeffrey Shin was short and arrogant, acting as though he had no time for us. We dubbed him Jeffrey SHIT. In our second meeting with Yin Le and Jin Lei about our intended ride across China for the disabled, and Hope Project, they now indicated that "We would like to get involved."

I learned one day that Dong Xueo Pings' son, Dung Poo Fong, is a paraplegic, thrown out of a second story window in Shanghai during the Cultural Revolution by the red guards. It is through Dung Poo Fong's valiant efforts that the disabled of China have made progress. Only ten years ago, the Chinese disabled could not even go to college; now they can. They are moving more into mainstream society, and the government offers incentives for companies who hire the disabled as workers in factories.

November 4th: Heard election results from the United States. Very depressing for me - Clinton was ahead. Saw film clips of Barbara Boxer and Diane Feinstein, shouting, "Californians will all live together - gay, black, Mexican, and white, in a utopian society." I thought, "Yeah, and you will make sure that you never personally live in that utopian mess with the rest of us."

November 6th: We made a second trip to the Forbidden City to pose beneath Mao Zedong's portrait. This time I am less euphoric about this "great moment" because it is my second GREAT moment. As I am posing for photographs, I think to myself, "Mao's portrait is the very symbol of Communist oppression. A Harley Davidson motorcycle is the symbol of freedom of the road, I wonder what Mao would think to see this legless, foreign devil posing under his portrait? He'd probably turn over in his grave."

November 7th: The first day of winter by the Chinese lunar calendar. As if on cue, snow fell. They told me, "That's a positive sign." What it was a positive sign of, I was never too clear on. I was positive it was cold!

Bald, Blind, and Other Hair-Raising Adventures

In China, I met Dr. Zhang, the creator of something called "101 Hair Products," a very expensive formula that supposedly grows hair on bald people. In China, it is the fountain of youth for the hair industry. Dr. Zhang invited me to his factory to watch his product being made. Of course, I never saw any of the guarded secrets. Dr. Zhang was a kind man, and he gave us a donation of 5,000 RMB ($650.00). "I cannot justify going to my Board of Directors for more money, but perhaps this 5,000 RMB will keep you operating until you find the needed money for the trip." During our tour, there were over 100 photographers, reporters, people with disabilities and factory workers gathered in a big conference room located on top of the factory. I spoke to them for 45 minutes through a real interpreter - Mona's boyfriend, Cheng, who spoke English like a Oxford gentlemen. He did a wonderful job.

While I'm speaking, my audience is digging into bowls of fruit and nuts, throwing the peelings on the floor or on the tables; the room looked like a garbage bin by the time I finished. In contrast to the gold lettering on red banners in the room, it resembled a high class pig sty.

Next came the factory tour, though we didn't see much because the formula is actually mixed behind curtains by blind people! Once again, it was a case of the disabled being used in a very positive manner. Over 400 workers with disabilities were at the factory, and Dr. Zhang provided living quarters for them all.

In my spare time, I taught English to a Russian girl named Oxana, the daughter of Valdimar Federuk of TASS Radio. I found her to be an articulate and lovely young woman, deeply interested in Chinese art. She spoke English quite well, and had a working grasp of Chinese as well. She was preparing to go to university in Moscow the following year.

Beijing, a gray concrete city, is getting colder and colder. There is little greenery anywhere, so it is dusty when it is not raining or snowing. The dust comes from the Gobi Desert. Beijing is a dreary, cold, depressing place.

Jin Lei is still searching for the golden egg that will get us on the road. We visited the PLA - People's Liberation Army - Factory No. 3603 where they built Jeeps. They had national serviceman working on the assembly lines, building a Jeep more or less comparable to a Toyota Land Cruiser. We met the directors and high-ranking officers, and they pledged one of their vehicles for our trip. Jin Lei had hoped for more. Well, something is better than nothing.

At a party given by the Disabled Federation of Beijing, I gave a speech which Mona dutifully misinterpreted. Then, I witnessed demonstrations of classic calligraphy by a man who had no arms. When he was done with his calligraphy, it read, "To succeed in your journey for the disabled." Next, I saw a wheel chair ping-pong match. A man with one arm played the champion of Beijing (not disabled). The one-armed man only lost by a few points.

Jin Lei and Yin Le are beginning to look haggard. They are going for the gold day in and day out, not sleeping much. My heart goes out to them, and at the same time, it is difficult to trust them because they never communicate what is really happening. I want to believe in them, but my guard is always up.

Sundays are my day with Ze-Qing. She always comes over to the hotel and we watch CNN together. It helps her learn English. Sometimes we visit other people and places in the diplomatic compound; I always enjoy having her around.

I met a unique person named Andrew Head who has been living in China for nearly ten years. He spoke and read Chinese, although he is a white Anglo Saxon

American. He also spoke French fluently, and a bit of Russian. He had learned Ti Chi from one of the great masters of China. If I understood the story properly, one of the prerequisites to learning Ti Chi was that every morning, rain or shine, for three years he was to stand and watch the group in the area where they worked out, whether or not the group was there! The Ti Chi master supposedly told him, "If you miss one day, I will not teach you." Andrew was also a student of traditional Chinese medicine, and was soon to receive his doctor's degree. Andrew was married to a beautiful Chinese girl named Shirto from Taiwan. She worked seasonally as a ballerina in the Taiwan Ballet.

I told Andrew about my getting depressed and not sleeping properly. "It is nothing, Dave," he told me. "Very normal. After ten years in China, I still have trouble sleeping." He called my depression "the foreigner blues," explaining that "people from the west often have to go back overseas for a few weeks break every now and then. The African students and students from other third world countries come to China to get an education because it is inexpensive, and then go stark raving mad because they cannot afford to go home for a break."

Andrew continued his sharing. "The group will tell you what they want you to know, when they want you to know it. You can complain about it all you want, but you will never get the full story." Andrew went on to tell me, "Dave, I understand your feelings, worry and apprehension. You are at a crucial point with the group. It will be difficult to achieve what they want to do, but when it is over, you'll be glad you did it!"

To my way of thinking, I keep hearing the words, "Don't worry Dave, no problem." In Chinese, its "May vin Ti." Whenever I recognize those words, I immediately worry.

The group informed me that sponsors had been located, a date had been set to go, although I was never told how much money had been found. Never getting a definitive answer caused great dissension between Yin Le and me. Finally, one day I was informed that our trucks were on their way south to Kunming. I rode the motorcycle over to an air freight packaging company with poor Mona freezing her ass off on the back. A Mr. Wong boxed it up to send it down to Kunming by air freight. I was told that Yin Le and I would leave the next day.

November 28, 1992: At 04:00 I got up and packed the rest of my bags, taking everything downstairs. My back was killing me as I had strained my muscles from lifting heavy things in the cold. What a great trip beginning - terrible pain in my back. We took a cab to the airport, got on our plane, and a new adventure began.

I was amazed to see people in the bloody plane spitting into bags, Yin Le being one of them. If we crashed we'd have goober flying everywhere! I looked out the window to see snow covered mountains in the distance; they were particularly beautiful as we flew over Yunan Providence. On approach to Kunming, in southwest China just north of Vietnam, we landed and were met by Jin Lei and taken to a government hotel.

Naturally, in the true spirit of my trip, this hotel set the world record for filth! On tho outside it looked shiny and beautiful, but the inside was a horrible mess. Spittoons were everywhere, and the Chinese are not known for their spitting accuracy.

The rest of the group arrived by train in the following two days, followed by the trucks. I remember that first night we went out to a meal in the old quarter of Kunming. We had a big hot pot dinner where we put the vegetables and meat into a huge boiling pot that eventually makes its own soup; everybody eats out of the communal pot.

We came upon a karaoke shop - which has bed sheet partitions and an opening to the street. The shop contains a few chairs, a VCR and a television. They put a karaoke video in, a song comes on, and then someone stands up and makes a colossal ass of himself or herself trying to sing with the music, with the public in the street watching.

Kunming is a very crowded city with plenty of dirt and rubbish in the streets. There are more bicycles here than any place in China, except Shanghai. I saw huge intersections jammed with bicycles and thousands of shouting Chinese - all rather amusing if you are not condemned to live in it.

December 1: I called this T-1 - for "training day one," a code I had use in the Marines. I had another 29 days to go before the whole thing was over.

We visited the Leonard Cheshire Foundation home in Kunming. At the time, it was the only home they had in China. It was primarily a school for training people with various disabilities. As we rode through the gates of the home, I was fulfilling half of my promise to Lord Cheshire. The other half would be completed if I made it to the Moscow home, about 8,500 miles from Kunming.

I visited the various classrooms, including an economics class. Kids five to six years old were learning to speak with headphones to amplify their poor hearing.

We had lunch in their communal cafeteria, where the teachers doubled as cooks and cleanup crew. I wondered if the meal they served was special just for us - rice with a few little bits of meat and vegetables.

I asked Mona, "Why are there so many who need prosthetic limbs but don't have them?" Of course, she gave me one of those half-assed answers. The only reason I could summarize was that "they don't have enough money."

A very lovely young woman with a leg missing (she had a prosthesis) gave me a haircut. At the home, I saw calligraphy by a person with both of his arms out at the shoulders. He too had been an electrician, and knew the electrician who gave me calligraphy in Beijing. This man was also a marathon runner. I could only imagine he must have been a real powerful runner because he didn't have to carry the upper weight of his arms.

Next, we were treated to dancers who were deaf. When they dance, somebody off to the side is making sign language to them to go through certain moves since they can't hear the music. They tell them when to start, what to do and when to stop; it's amazing to watch. If the instructor is ever out of their line of sight, everything goes wrong. The music is for the spectators.

In Yunan Province, there are 32 different ethnic groups; in China, there are 52. As Westerners, we see them all as "Chinese," but they are frequently drastically different.

The day before we start our journey across China, we go to Dung Fong Square to lay out where we would place the table for all the dignitaries scheduled to give speeches, where the motorcycle would sit, and where the camera crews would station themselves.

The Orphan Beggar and Group Blow-Ups

As Jin Lei and I were speaking to one another, a beggar came up to us and gave me 10 RMB - the equivalent of a $1.50. He had tears in his eyes. Jin Lei, with a tear in her eye, explained that "This man says he is an orphan, an outcast all his life. He knows how hard it is to be alone. He is giving you this money to show how much he cares about your trip. It is kind of a solidarity with you as you travel around the world for the disabled."

I was deeply touched by this man, and thought of the biblical saying that says there's no greater gift than a gift from the poor, for it is a gift from the heart. 10 RMB would have kept this beggar for a week or more, yet he gave it to me. For a moment, I felt this was all staged for my benefit. God forgive me for having such suspicious feelings, but I just couldn't help it.

I had a big blow out with Jin Lei and Yin Le at dinner that afternoon. The head of the Communist Youth League suggested that I ride all the way to the Stone Forest, about a 120 kilometers (75 miles), with the Disabled Federation of Kunming. Now, their scooters only travel about 20 miles an hour, and it is very hard on my engine to ride that slow for that long. Going up hills, they slow to about 5 miles per hour. They volunteered me to do it without speaking to me about it. When I heard about it at the dinner table, I threw a fit, getting up and leaving the dinning hall.

Yin Le and Jin Le lost big FACE over this whole affair. After lunch, they came to my room, shouting and hollering; I hollered back. Remember, it is very intimidating to be alone with this group. I haven't seen a foreigner in days, and they are really very angry at me. I got upset and angry back. I told them, "Don't you volunteer that motorcycle for anything without talking to me first. You may control the group, but you don't control that machine. If that is a problem, then let's put the motorcycle on the truck and send it back to Hong Kong and call it a day." I knew I couldn't really just take off by myself; the Chinese security police would have something to say about that. So, I was in a really sensitive position! They later told me, "We felt like beating you."

In the end, we agreed they would speak to me on matters concerning the motorcycle. Then, we reached a compromise. For the sake of the cameras, I agree to ride out of Kunming with the scooters. Once we hit the country, we will go on and the scooters can meet us at our destination.

It was indeed a very brave act for these folks to travel on these little tiny 80 CC three-wheeled scooters to show solidarity with my trip. But, I couldn't jeopardize the entire project by risking a major break down from the slow speeds. They had put thousands and thousands of dollars and a great deal of work into this plan, placing their trust squarely on a 20-year-old motorcycle with 200,000 miles on it at the time. They don't know what I know about my old dog. Ultimately, our heated meeting split up with a better understanding. "Yes, we will keep you informed," they promised me.

It was very rare that they did.

December 3: A very rough, long day, starting with Jin Lei and Yin Le being down in the dumps because the Hope Project of the Yunan Province had let us down. They had backed out of accommodating us while we were in the province - which they had agreed to do. This was a big shock!

Next, on our way to Dung Fong Square, one of our vehicles hits a bicyclist. A huge crowd gathers, and the man is very belligerent. In the end, Yin Le soothes things over by giving the guy 50 RMB (the magic amount).

At Dung Fong Square, the motorcycle was set up in front of the speakers table. There was a red flag put on it with some Chinese writing. I could only imagine it said something like, "Look out! Long-nose fool on the motorcycle." Then we had to disperse a big Ti Chi group of approximately 200 people, all with swords and double long knifes, going through their morning Ti Chi. They had a look in their eyes that said, "We'd like to use these weapons on you for disturbing our practice."

A crowd of over 5,000 people gathered around us and the all-Chinese girl's school band. They had me posing with them. The crowd was a sea of black hair and black eyes, staring in utter amazement at all the television cameras.

Then, the ceremony started, the band played, the mayor of Kunming gave a speech which was misinterpreted back to me, then the head of the Communist Youth League gave his misinterpreted speech. I gave a speech for 10 minutes which was misinterpreted back to everybody else. This went on for the next hour. Communist rhetoric is a necessary part of the procedure for us to start our trip for the Hope Project and the Disabled Federations. After I received flowers from a young school girl and received the communist salute, it was time to start our journey across China.

Here's the highlight of the day! With the entire crowd looking on, the motorcycle would not start! "Oh no, what is the problem this time?" I wonder. After examination, I discovered the problem was in the carburetor. The battery was so low it had to be jump started. As you might imagine, the pressure I was under was absolutely indescribable.

Finally, the old thing starts and I jump on it, shaking hands and the sea of thousands parts down a lane maybe 3 feet wide. "Don't hit the little kids darting around," I think to myself. It was amazing trying to ride between these people. The Disabled of Kunming were waiting on the street in their scooters, and our film crew was right in front of me with the security police leading them. I figured, "we will go real slow so we can get all of this on film." Instead, after all our discussions from the previous day, they took off like bats out of hell, leaving the disabled behind instead of riding slowly out of Kunming and filming them with me. I had tried to lag back, but they kept motioning me forward. Once again, misinterpretation reigns supreme!

Rock Legends and Chinese Culture

Out of Kunming, the road was fairly open, so we rode along at 35 to 40 mph (50 to 60 kph), all the way to the Stone Forest in the mountain. The Stone Forest is a massive area of incredible rock formations with tunnels through rocks and spires. We took some photos at the entrance of the Stone Forest with the river running along side of it, then Jin Lei and myself made quite a tour in and out, over and through, for the next hour or so. We then relocated all the vehicles and our equipment back at the place where we would spend the night. Of course, the location did not have any hot water.

We had dinner in a very crowded restaurant with the security police and local dignitaries. I thought to myself as everybody was smiling, "How kind these people are, yet at one time we considered each other enemies. I hope that time never comes again."

That evening, we saw the highest rock in the Stone Forest called Aushuma. Legend has it that Aushuma was a young girl who had a boyfriend. She was separated from the boyfriend by her father who sold her to a wealthy landlord to be his concubine. She pined for this young man, and when he tried to steal her away, he was killed. She then climbed to the top of the rock and jumped off into a pool of water that surrounds it and killed herself. It is said that her soul emanates from the rock itself. Quite a beautiful rock indeed.

Later, we saw dancing by the Han Klan, one of the many different ethnic groups. One danoo was a wedding dance. I was sitting with the disabled who had finally arrived on their scooters an hour or so before. They threw a small bag, something that represents a future marriage for the recipient. I remember that my finger caught the handle of the bag, then all the disabled jumped in like a pack of wild dogs and wrestled the thing away from me. After that, one of the dancers came up to me and handed me one of these little hand-woven, very decorative bags. I looked at the rest of the disabled and growled like a mad dog, and everybody howled with laughter.

They invited me to come out and dance with them. I was pushed up onto my feet and out into the dancing, circling around a bon fire. I was doing my best not to step on somebody's foot, but failed. I came down very hard on one fellows foot as we were kicking out in front of us. He howled like a coyote and jumped up like a screaming mortar bomb. He hobbled away from the dancing looking at me sideways with malice.

By the time we got back to our rooms, it was 24:30. So ended the first day of our trip back to Beijing.

The following day was spent going through small villages. The road was bad, full of holes. The villages were dirty, mud brick; the more official buildings were constructed from cement, and the market place overflowed right into the main road. We had the first of our close calls on this road when our police escort almost had a head on collision with a truck. We saw three very grim accidents in the first 65 miles (100 km.) we covered. The police vehicle in front of us had it's siren on constantly, and I thought "Holy mackerel - another three and a half weeks of listening to this and my head will be splitting." I was also breathing in the exhaust fumes from the trucks we're passing. Though the sirens were blaring, these trucks were not interested in moving over. That was a constant point of irritation for all concerned.

The first school we came to was a school for the disabled in a town called Gui Yang, a dirty cement city, very crowded, with no particular personality, quite depressing for a westerner who enjoys seeing a bit of architecture. We located a good hotel by Chinese standards, and parked the motorcycle safely in the hotel foyer. Later, we went to a school for deaf children where I met the various school leaders. We were shown the different skills they learn, some seamers or seamstresses, and some weavers. Interestingly enough, there was a massive brewing still for a very famous Chinese wine - quite potent! We were also shown the kid's living quarters - 8 children in a room, very crowded, on hardboard beds. When I met these kids where they play basketball and other sports, they mobbed me. It seemed to me they were just starved for affection since they didn't live with their families. I was impressed by their energy and forthrightness, trying to communicate with their hands.

Next, we drove across town to meet the mayor. I climbed five flights of stairs to a big room where we met. There were bananas and tangerines in front us, plus plenty of peanuts. The mayor stood up and gave about a half hour speech, boring everybody to tears. Then Jin Lei gave a talk about our trip. I was sitting behind the mayor, off to one side, making funny faces at Jin Lei. The rest of our group could see what I was doing, so could Jin Lei; it was everything she could do to keep from laughing. When we left the room, it was a garbage heap of peanut shells and peelings. Thanks for the bananas!

Back at the hotel we were treated to a big banquet and karaoke where various members of our group got up and made asses of themselves by singing to the music. It was about 21:00 before we closed the day.

The next day we pushed on - up through highland areas. Because of the climb, I was constantly shifting between first and second gear. Following another vehicle is already starting to get on my nerves, and my nose is always breathing the exhaust of the jeep. My face is constantly black, and my lungs are hurting. As we traveled down into the dusty low lands, I was eating dirt as well. Finally we came to the Yunan, on the Gui Zhou border, where we changed security police.

341

One security policeman was having a birthday. A cake was produced, and we all sang, in Chinese, "Happy Birthday" to inspector Wong. As we posed for photographs, I noticed a tear in some of the women's eyes, including Jin Lei's. I still wonder why they were so emotional - it was only a bloody birthday. Perhaps Inspector Wong was dying - I don't know.

We visited another Hope Project School later that day. This one was really primitive - no electricity in the school, and the construction consisted of crumbling brick walls and rotting timbers.

The kids were out with tambourines and drums, all beating on them, wishing us a very warm welcome. Jin Lei and I walked around the whole courtyard of the school which was lined with children. I said to Jin Lei, "Well what next Jin Lei? Do they start stoning us?" Jin Lei looked at me with a very worried look in her eye and said, "No make joke!" So, I carried on with a straight face.

After this visit, we headed on to Quing Long in Pan County of Gui Zhou Province, one of the poorest in China. Our hotel had no hot water, all the toilets were stopped up and stinking, and we couldn't take cold water from the tap and flush toilets at the same time!

After food and entertainment, it is now 23:30, time to start working on the motorcycle. Suddenly, a shadow appears; it is Chung Wei, a fellow I rather like, although we can't communicate with each other. Chung Wei is a Vietnam Veteran from the PLA who was in a special reconnaissance unit. Once, he became separated from his unit on a deep penetration into North Vietnam. He ended up navigating his way back to China on his own, having a couple of shoot outs along the way with the Vietnamese hot on his tail. He had a part of his thigh shot out.

I get along with Chung Wei better than anyone else in our group. The name "Wei" means "great," and he was indeed a great person, one I was proud to call friend.

"No, please, don't help!"

The following day the escort was going so slow I hollered at them to "speed up." In the end, I just passed them, taking off. I could see their heads turning and shouting as they tried to catch up with me. All I did was move at a steady 50 kph (roughly 35 mph), just gliding around the corners. The group's mini bus brakes were overheating, but I wasn't going to stop constantly for them. Finally, on the downhill side of the mountain I pulled over, and they pulled up behind me. They were very irate. Yin Li was losing face by me doing my own thing. He soothed the situation over, and said nothing to me about it.

Although it irritated everybody, I kept telling them to go a certain speed, and during the entire trip was at loggerheads with the security police and the group over this problem.

The mountain villages we passed had dwellings made of stone, quite primitive yet very lovely. They were neater villages than the ones down in the low-lying areas.

There always seems to be a haze in the distance in China. To have a truly clear day is something I don't really remember. Unfortunately, this haze spoils the land.

At Yellow Tree Falls I saw an incredibly beautiful waterfall. Many hotels and businesses display giant photographs of Yellow Tree Falls, it is such a famous place in China. We spent an hour or so there, did some filming, had our lunch and were on our way over a pretty good highway.

Once I ran out of gas before I could get the reserve on and get the motor turned over again. People from the buses rushed over with a can of gas. I tried to tell them

"No, please, don't help," but they did not understand my point. In the end, they were so aggressive (though they meant well), that they ended up spilling gasoline all over the gas tank, down onto a hot engine, creating a fire hazard, instead of just letting me take care of the problem myself.

At the hotel that night, I worked until 22:00 on the motorcycle. The rest of the group didn't go off to bed either - they edited the day's film, planned for the next day, and **hopefully** would tell me through Mona what was going to happen.

The following day, we were supposed to visit a factory in the city when I noticed they were carrying all my bags downstairs. I demanded to know what was going on, but no one seemed to know. When Yin Li showed up, I started shouting at him, saying, "Why am I never informed as to changes in plans? What am I, just a roust-a-bout?" Quickly, we were both shouting; others joined in. Later, I learned there was a great deal of tension within the group. It is no wonder - we are traveling and working 20 hours a day.

We drove to Gui Yang and saw a factory that produces light bulbs, and then listened to speeches and rhetoric that I could not understand. Some are in the local dialect, not Mandarin. At times, Mona doesn't even know what they are saying. She just whispers in my ear, "Sorry, don't understand."

December 7: We arrive at another hotel - fancy on the outside, seedy and miserable on the inside. My bed didn't even have a mattress on it. As usual, the shower and toilet area are absolutely despicable by our Western standards.

The following morning we had a meeting with the local officials and I was told that "The fellow you are about to meet is a very powerful man in the provincial government." I was told his name was "CHAIRMAN" Go. He was a very big, hulking fellow - friendly in a non-official way.

In our meeting room, I saw my first and only "No Smoking" sign in China! I never saw another. In the meeting, I was given a beautiful embroidered cloth with a very serene scene in China. Jin Lei spoke strongly about the Hope Project, and how it only supports 750 children in the Gui Zhou Province where there are roughly 100 million people! She also speaks forcefully about so few little girls in the program. She was speaking truly from her heart; a tear could be seen in her eye.

Toys, Boys, and Joys

After speeches, talks and reporters, Chairman Go took us all to a big lunch. It was one of the finest meals I have ever had in China. We were then escorted by a blind fellow, the head of the Disabled Federation, to a toy factory where I was greeted by the disabled people working there. One was a girl midget who guided us to a very dirty, dingy sweat shop where all these poor disabled people were working to make ends meet by making toys. There was truly a warm feeling of welcome and identification within this group - a family atmosphere. They have so little, yet accept their lot in life with incredible fortitude and dignity.

Next, a visit to a school for the disabled - 13 were blind and the rest were deaf. I went through the classrooms and was shown how they learn sign language. I was very grateful when they gave me a book of sign language so in the future I might communicate with these people a little bit better. Afterwards, out in the courtyard of the school, we saw more dancing in various costumes. Once again, we heard the music but the dancers didn't.

The following day before breakfast Chairman Go appeared. I had passingly offered, the day before, to give him a ride on the motorcycle through town. He showed up early this day, ready to leave. Now, this was a big fellow - over 200 pounds. I was very grateful that my extra helmet fit on his head. He climbed on the back, and we rode out behind our escort vehicles through a very crowded city full of vendors, bicycles, hand and donkey drawn carts, trucks - the usual. Then, we went out into the country for another 15 miles. As we traveled, I realized I had a very powerful communist figure on the back of my machine. China is certainly changing. When we finally came to a stop, everybody shook hands. Chairman Go was all smiles; perhaps it was a relief to just survive the ride. Chairman Go struck me as the most sincere official I met in China, not because he mounted the motorcycle, but because he seemed to have an outward eye towards the future, and a positive outlook.

Our group rode through the rest of the morning, stopping for lunch. In the afternoon, we traveled on a dirt road...something I've repeatedly asked them to avoid if at all possible. This road led to a very primitive village made of mud, brick and wood buildings. There was no electricity or running water that I could see.

We were met by the entire village. Drums were beating, and an air of festivity prevailed. Then, two little girls, ages about 12 to 15, grabbed my hands and led me over to the Hope School. One grabbed my hand so tightly that the ring on my finger was crushed into another finger. Her grip was like an iron vice! I couldn't believe it. Pain shot up my arm! I was virtually on my tippy toes, and that's saying something for not having any toes! With young iron-fist leading the way, we walked along and painful couple hundred meters to a building in the school.

A young girl stood and spoke about how grateful she was to the Hope Project. She said, "I am an orphan, and yet I am able to receive an education." She had tears running down her face as she spoke. I walked over and gave her a big hug to show some solidarity with this poor young girl (and at the same time wondering if the event wasn't staged).

That evening, after all the filming and ceremonies were over, I told Jin Lei, "I am tired of eating dust. From now on, I'll ride in front of the group."

That evening, as I was moving down the road, I hit a hole full of dust on a corner and fell off the motorcycle at about 15 miles an hour. Luckily, there was no damage done to the machine. When we got the motorcycle up, I started shouting at Yin Li, "Stay off these fucking dirt roads." You guessed it..."May vin ti" he replied.

On to Kai Li where there's more terrible rooms and bad speeches. The food was great, though we sat on the floor to eat at little small tables. It was a very scrumptious affair, but I had a hell of a backache!

After dinner, I went to work on the motorcycle, but people were constantly hovering around me. I really got upset. "Please leave me alone! Go the fuck away so that I can do what I want to do!" Chung Wei held the flashlight for me, and I enjoyed his company since he's never in the way - a silent partner. I put a new voltage regulator on, praying the old one did not burn up my battery.

I lugged my gear up four stories to my room! By the time I cleaned up and crawled into bed, it was just short of 02:00. This was a very typical for us.

Bridal Suite Surprise!

In the morning, after taking my gear downstairs, I took the motorcycle out of the room where it was stored. None of the locals would come near me after last nights ranting and raving at them to stay away. After a small breakfast, our group was underway. Jin Lei told me, "Last night you insulted all the local dignitaries."

In the afternoon, slip sliding around on dirt roads in the rain, we moved into Hunan Province where we were met at the border by some young girls and officials from the Hope Project. These young ladies were dressed in silver head dresses, the same as the hand crushers of the day before! I nodded, but did not shake their hands! We received hot tea on the border, and it tasted especially good after riding for hours in the ice cold rain.

We spent the evening at Feng Huang. Get this...I was put into the bridal suite! I couldn't believe it when I saw a chamber pot made of wood in the corner. Even the bridal suite had no running water or toilets! There was a big communal toilet and huge sink to wash in, but no showers or other amenities.

I thought of all the young couples who had started the first night of marriage in this room, and thought, "If this is the height of luxury in this city, according to our standards as Westerners, they aren't going to experience too many luxuries in life."

I was told, "It is good luck to be in the bridal chambers." I thought to myself, "Well, isn't that just great. I seem to have all the luck. Will it never cease?" No sarcasm here.

Another big meal that night. I was astonished to discover that we are paying for all these feasts out of our fund. The city does not pay for anything, even though we are doing something for the charity in that city. In China, the group coming into the city is the one responsible for the meal, the wining and dining. The entertainment is the responsibility of the officials.

The next morning my sleep was shattered about 04:00 by thousands of fire crackers; it sounded like a fire fight was going on outside. I found out later that there was a wedding on that day, and the bride was on her way to the groom's house before anybody could see her. The firecrackers were to herald her arrival!

That morning the whole square was filled with school bands playing, and officials on stage above the square giving speeches. I gave a 5 minute speech. When it was all done, the band played a tune while they marched and we followed, soon finding our way out of the city once again. I kept pressing the police to go faster so I didn't have to continue shifting between second and third gear. Finally, I passed the police again, creating a problem for Yin Li who was in the car with the police. He didn't like losing face like this, and I didn't like to put him in that position, but I had told them repeatedly the problem it created. Of course, this problem is compounded by an interpreter with English limited to the tourist trade; try as she might, we were totally out of her league.

We were still out on the roads as the night descended on us. The police continue with sirens wailing and lights flashing, and the oncoming trucks still refused to pull over. The truck drivers are offensive people who just don't seem to care. Finally, we came into Dai Yang and find a hotel quite nice by Chinese standards.

We were up early and out to see a couple of Hope Project Schools. As we travel, I noticed that there were fewer bicycles compared to most Chinese cities. "That's because the area is exceptionally poor. People cannot afford a bicycle." Mind you, a "Flying Pigeon" bicycle, brand new, is only about $20.00 in American money.

Dai Yang, like many Chinese cities, was dirty and under construction; it had no particular personality, just drab, square cement buildings. The people dressed Maoist style, very bland.

We came to the first of two schools where they had Hope Project children. I was introduced to Hong Bo, another one of China's misinterpreters, a real "Ya, ya, ya" guy. After an hour of him showing me around, saying "Ya, ya, ya" to my every question, I told him just to "Fuck off and stay away from me." This was a big loss of face, but I kept saying "Don't ya, ya, ya. If you don't understand me, please say so." He wouldn't do it, so I just didn't want him around. Even Mona was far more preferable.

In each of the schools the kids were singing; the Hope Project students showed me their grade books. I kept seeing a 100 percent marks, though I didn't understand what I was seeing. I was always receiving the Communist salute from the young pioneers.

We were then escorted out of town and up through some mountains. Funny enough, the police were now doing a fine job of keeping speed up through the hills and even the winding corners! At Zhang Ja Jei, I saw massive rock pillars spiral up to the sky. It is a very beautiful area, a place that Mao Zedong used to come to for retreat and rest. Some of these pillars go up as high as 350 meters (yards) straight. They are like marble columns of rock reaching into the sky.

Saving Face and Amazing Feats

"Do you think you could climb to the top of one of these pillars?" I was asked.

"Yes, indeed," I quickly responded.

"There is a stairwell with 1,045 steps," they told me. We took a bit of a drive up a mountain path to the base of this one particular column which was on top of a mountain. On the way up, our group bus got stuck and needed to be pushed. They allowed Mona and I to take the Jeep and go on ahead. When we got to the base of the steps, I said, "Come on, Mona," and we started up.

Once I got a rhythm going, I made pretty good time. About 15 minutes into our climb, without stopping, Mona wanted to sit down and rest. I said, "No, let's just keep going." She looked at me with a look on her face that said "You fornicating, smelly foreign devil." I just smiled and kept going. She had to force herself to keep up. My walking stick made it much easier, and sometimes there were hand rails. Most of the time, there was nothing to grab onto. The stairs were very rough cut stones. After about 25 minutes, I was up on top where there was a little tea garden restaurant! "How did they get all the building materials up to this place?" I wondered. There was also a pagoda. We waited for about 20 minutes before our huffing and puffing group appeared with their camera equipment. Of course, they were angry at me for leaving them behind. "You see, you have to tell me what you are doing. If you don't communicate, you have problems." It was something they never learned.

Our group was accompanied by Mr. Wu, the governor of Hunan Province, an extremely powerful man. He had climbed up to the top because I was climbing up. The mayor of Dai Yang climbed up because the governor had climbed. Everybody was saving face.

We went up to a pagoda about another 60 steps; the view from on top was absolutely magnificent! It was late afternoon and some clouds were below us. Adding to the beauty of the blue in the distance, white clouds were scattered above and below the pillars. We went to various landings on top of this massive rock pillar - about 200 meters across the middle. In this gorgeous setting, I gave a little talk for our film. I shared that "When you are climbing a mountain, it seems like you will never get to the top. But once you arrive at the top, and you see that you've gained the whole world, thinking back on the climb, you realize it wasn't so difficult after all."

On our way down the stairs, I met a man with shoulder poles on, with tea in one of the buckets and cabbages in the other. He was hauling them up for the little tea garden restaurant on top. "So that is how they got all the building materials up to the top," I thought. "People like this man carrying supplies on their shoulder poles." Then I told Mona, "That man must have a heart like a elephant. He must be one of

346

the strongest men in the world to be able to climb up and down, day in and day out with weights on his shoulders." And for what? Probably the equivalent of about $30.00 per month. It is inconceivable!

That evening we enjoyed some really incredible entertainment after the mayor gave his mandatory speech to about 200 people in the auditorium. Some lovely girls came out and did a harvest dance. It was very beautiful, them in their costumes dancing about. Next, I saw the most incredible demonstration of the martial arts. One man got himself all psyched up and then was put on a 6 foot spike. He was striped down to the waist, and as the spike poked into his abdomen, they spun him around in circles! I couldn't believe what I saw. When they took him down off the spike, there was no sign of blood anywhere. Another man pierced his breasts with some needles and hooked a couple of strings onto the needles, with bricks at the end of the strings which were down around his knees. He then started turning in circles, and as he spun about, the bricks, through centrifugal force, came out level with his shoulders. When it was done, and he took the needles out of his breast, there was no blood.

Next, 3 people worked themselves up a frenzy, then one laid down on a bed of glass, another on four razor sharp swords, and the third on a bed of spikes. It took three people to place a cement slab on top of the last man. Another man came along with a sledge hammer and started smashing the slab until it finally broke and fell away. Then, they took each one of the individuals off one at a time; again, no blood.

The most impressive performance was by a man who came in and handed me a stone about 8 inches long by 4 inches across and 4 inches deep. It was a granite rock - not glued together. They sat it down on the edge of a small table (not between two tables). The man then worked himself up, higher and higher, until finally he was at such a peak that I could feel the energy coming off of him. My heart was pounding like a sledge hammer. I couldn't believe what I felt from this man. When he finally moved at the rock and hit it, he didn't just break it, he scattered it! Pieces flew all over the room. I don't expect anyone to believe this; I would of had trouble even conceiving of it had I not seen it with my own eyes.

Afterwards, he came over and shook my hand. He was stripped down to the waist the same as the others had been, so there was no trickery. I realized this day, more than most, that I was in a part of China where few foreigners ever go, and was seeing things such as these martial art forms that were not polluted by outside influences.

That night, I finished working on the motorcycle by 24:00 and wearily poured myself into bed.

The Disabled Federation of Nanjing
August 1992 Nanjing, China

Jin Lei and Yin Lee on January 10, 1993
Our last day of filming on the edge of the Gobi Desert. China

Chapter Thirty

"Live Your Dreams!"

On the road, it is freezing cold, and sometimes I spot patches of ice up in the higher areas. I'm growing weary of our security people...tired of trying to tell them to speed up so I don't have to constantly shift back and forth. Finally, I pass them again as we shout and holler at each other.

We changed our security police later that afternoon! The new bunch were the best we'd ever have. As we move forward, they keep a steady pace of 30 to 35 miles an hour. In one village, a truck in front of us would not move over. The security pulled up around him, pushing him off the road! One of the policeman pulled the driver out of the truck and started beating him soundly about the head and shoulders. The security man looked over at me, perhaps worried about what I would say. I stuck my thumb up and said "How," meaning "Good" in Chinese. Reassured, he resumed the painful lesson to the driver's head with renewed vigor. During my trip I've endured tremendous trouble because of Chinese truck drivers, being run off the road and even clipped by them because they don't want to yield. This certainly taught at least one truck driver a much-needed lesson.

After the beating, it was off again.

We came into one city where hundreds of people lined the streets waiving little flags in the rain that said, "Welcome Mr. Dave Ball." I picked up a motorcycle escort of two motorcycles with side cars on them, the BMW type, with two lovely girls in the side cars. We were all waiving to one another and the crowd as we go by. All in a *freezing* rain. I was very taken by their efforts except for calling me "Dave Ball." Another Chinese misinterpretation!

After a huge banquet with speeches, we hit the road again in the pouring rain, traveling the rest of the afternoon and evening. By the end of the day, my clutch hand is killing me, and I'm soaked. Finally we arrive at Changsha, a major city in southern China, following our escort to the Lui Fang Hotel where the motorcycle was stored in a tea room at about 22:00. When I walk to one of the vehicles to get my bags, one is missing. I try to locate someone in the group, but nobody at the hotel speaks English. How do I get a hold of Yin Li or Jin Lei? All I can do is fart around on the various hotel floors until I finally bump into one of our group who can lead me to help. My 45 minute search finally ended when my bag was discovered sitting in one of the rooms. "I'm so fed up with them doing things and not telling me what they are doing," I thought to myself as I wearily drug myself down to the tea room to prepare my motorcycle for the next day. There was a poor girl, one of the hotel staff, sleeping on the couch. I felt very sorry for her, but I had to get my work done. I spent the next hour preparing the machine with Chung Wei standing quietly nearby with the flashlight. When all this was done, I went to a very lovely room with only ice cold water for cleaning. The day ended at 02:00, with me still greasy.

The following day we went to the Number One Teacher's University where Mao Zedong studied between the years 1916 and 1918. At the entrance of the school, a band was playing on one side, and hundreds of students in different colored track suits were on the other (each color a grade level?). Speeches were given, and I was presented with a beautifully brocaded silk cloth with a lovely, serene scene on it, then given a tour of the school, even sitting down at Mao Zedong's old desk and taking some photographs while security police patrolled the area in black leather coats - Asiatic versions of Gestapo or KGB men.

When we came out, all these kids wanted to have there photos taken with us. So they all pressed in and with arms around one another we took photos. I looked at their fresh, bright, expectant faces which were so full of hope for the future and could only wish them well in a half-hearted manner (my reasons will be given later).

Next, we visited a school for deaf children. Through Cheng, I told them that "We are all part of a family, the disabled, and though it is not a family by choice, it is a good, strong family." The talk was translated into Mandarin, then into sign language, and seemed to go over well. Once again, these little ones were so full of affection that they mobbed me. When I selected one little girl to stand next to me, a plain girl with one eye drooping, a teacher shoved her away in a rude manner and placed a cute little girl next to me. When the photographs were over, I found that rejected little girl with a look of disappointment on her face and with my own camera had pictures taken with us standing side by side. Although she couldn't hear me, I whispered in her ear, "God loves all His little children," hoping my message got through by depth of feeling.

In one room where they teach the art of massage, they had me lay down on the table as a bit of a joke. The blind masseuse started working on my back, and when he got to my legs, his unseeing eyes liked to have shot out of his head. He'd never encountered a prosthesis, and didn't know what to do. We all had a good laugh.

During a factory visit, we were stuck in an elevator between floors for 15 minutes before we reached our destination just in time to hear the factory manager give a boring speech. "I'd rather be stuck in the elevator," I thought to myself. We were shown a room that holds a machine to measure earthquakes (numerous in China).

That evening, we hit a drunken pedestrian - his head broke out the windshield of the bus as we knocked him flying. We checked him over and could not find any broken bones; people inside the bus had been thrown around, but no one was hurt seriously.

Jin Lei and I jumped into a cab back to the hotel, leaving the rest of the crew to sort out the mess. At the hotel, I washed once again with cold water, put on a shirt and tie, and went down to our evening's entertainment where a young girl, about 8, sang us a song, while a 12-year-old girl danced, and a 10-year-old played the harp. Another young girl of 12 created some classic calligraphy for me.

The Vice Mayor of Changsha, Mrs. Zhong, made her speech and presented me with honorary citizenship of Changsha. With a bit of the devil in my eye, I thought to myself, "What would Mrs. Zhong and the rest of the Changsha hierarchy think if I came back here and requested welfare benefits? Would I be so warmly welcomed then?"

The following day we installed a new windscreen, absolutely necessary in this cold weather with patches of ice on the road and in the rivers. In the late morning, we crossed over to Hubei Providence where we said good-bye to one group of security police and Hope Project officials and welcomed their replacements. I was introduced to Alece Waldo, a lovely French girl who spoke Chinese. It was the first time in two weeks I had met another European person! She was assigned to do the interpretations for me during the rest of the trip for unofficial matters. Mona was quitting, but her boyfriend, Cheng, who joined us in Changsha, would travel with us to Wuhan in central China.

My Hysterical Highlight

We took the next day to settle in a big hostel where I secured some diesel fuel and with Alece we started cleaning up the motorcycle, getting the machine ready for the next half of the journey. About 11:00, Yin Li arrives and wants me to go somewhere with them; I reluctantly comply. Dressed in a dirty blue sweat shirt and pants with wholes in the knees, covered with dirt, dust and grease, hair uncombed... they take me to the Wuhan Agricultural University and hustle me inside a massive auditorium where over 2,000 Chinese students are standing in silence, intently waiting to hear this greasy looking foreigner speak to them!

Jin Lei said pointedly, "You make speech!"

With Cheng standing right next to me, I started speaking, encouraging them to "Live your dreams. When you look around in the morning on your way to school or work, you see people on the bus or in the subway with heads hanging down, waiting to go through another miserable day of their life. These people awoke that morning, putting their dreams aside just to waste another day. I challenge you to wake up tomorrow morning and instead of putting your dreams aside, open your eyes and live your dreams. Thank you!"

Cheng stood right next to me. When I emphasized something, he emphasized it. It was as if my voice and thoughts flowed from me through him to be delivered to this massive crowd of expectant young faces. In the end, when I said "Thank you," these kids came down over the parapets as a single wall of humanity moving in our direction. The security police grabbed me and Cheng; we were hustled out of the hall through a backdoor where we were placed inside a police-controlled area, quarantined off to hold back the crowd. I don't know if they wanted to kill me or what.

Quickly signing the school log book, we jumped into the car waiting for us and were whisked away from throng of pushing young people. Cheng later said to me, "Dave, that went wonderful. It really took hold. Those young people loved it." Of course, the security police didn't care for my message - it was exactly what a communist government doesn't want students to hear...but they did. "Cheng, you never know, this may be a turning point in some young person's life," I said. "You may have helped shape the future of China by the words you translated." He mulled this over, then cautiously replied, "Yes...maybe."

"Chen, the greatest moment of this whole trip has just passed us," I continued.

"Yes, you are right. I am very glad to have shared it with you."

Cheng is a bright fellow who spoke English like a British public school boy; he also spoke fluent German. His job in Beijing was to analyze the black boxes of various aircraft during maintenance periods, a most exacting job; later, he went into business for himself, and I'm sure, to make a smashing success of his life.

Back to the motorcycle and work, I was served hot tea by an old lady who lived there as a caretaker - the best tea I ever drank. As I worked on my motorcycle, she kept filling my cup as I tried to mentally come down from the morning's adrenaline rush.

We had dinner in the dark since all the electricity was out. Back in my room, I thought, "It is nice to have Alece around, keeping me informed about things, avoiding any unpleasant surprises."

The next day, not far out of Wuhan we crossed the Yangze River on a ferry, then traveled about 30 miles down a dirt road to a very impressive Hope Project School where we met the teachers and the kids. We were shown the living quarters of the children and teachers, located about 1 mile (1 1/2 km) from the school. The kids had little mats on huge beds and they all slept together on the bed. The teachers - young, bright university graduates - slept on straw mats placed on top of hard board beds! Their other furnishing is a table and a chair in a tiny room. There is no light, no electricity, no toilet! The walls and floor are earthen. I couldn't help but think back to Changsha where those bright, expectant faces excitedly prepared for their future - the barest of rooms in a remote school. Shocking.

The following day, we came to another dirt road. "Hey, what have I said about dirt roads?" I asked Jin Lei. "Don't you understand? If I slip and fall and break something, your whole trip is shot."

"Only few miles, short time on road," she replied. We then traveled about a hundred kilometers (65 miles) down this dirt road in the rain and mud. So much for "few miles."

We stopped at a farm out in the country for a prearranged visit, since you just don't decide to stop at a farm in China. We were greeted by a woman with 3 children. When one little girl climbed on my lap, I asked Chung Wei for some candy, and gave the little girl one piece. She ate the candy with a look of delighted surprise on her dirty little face; I gave her another piece. Immediately, the little girl jumped off my lap and ran over to her brother, giving him this piece of candy. I couldn't believe it. This child, in her poverty, had probably never had a piece of candy before, yet she rushed over to give her second piece away to her brother. "Most kids I know would have fought over the candy before sharing it!" I thought.

The following day, we came to a proposed Hope Project School where I probably insulted some of the officials. As I was going up some stairs, they kept trying to help me, hovering around my every step. Finally, I told them to "Get the fuck away from me. I can get up the stairs on my own." They looked at me in surprise and shock that I would speak to them that way. I just get so tired of being treated like I can't even walk up stairs when I'm in the process of man-handling an 800 pound motorcycle around the world! Don't they see the contradiction?

The officials showed us land in front of a building where hundreds of people were chopping and digging. "This land and the labor was donated to build the Hope Project School." I thought to myself, "What bullshit! People don't give land and their time away in China. It was probably taken from them by the government to build a Hope Project School."

Down the road to Xin Yang, a small city, we were greeted, had lunch, then taken to another Hope School in the country. This unique school was neat and clean; the classrooms were all in one story brick buildings. When we arrived, the kids were singing in Chinese, "Welcome, friend, welcome."

On a walk through town later, I see the humble dwellings of the people. When they have electricity, it is carried through wires wrapped around nails in the rafters, attached to light bulbs that hang down from the ceiling. Sometimes, I see little plug in boxes with huge junctions and with many plugs in them. "Holy mackerel," I caution them, "Be careful. This is likely to short out and cause a fire."

The response is always the same..."Ma vin ti."

On our way out of town, I saw buildings once used to house the Communist Eighth Route Army Commanders and political leaders; Mao Zedong, Zhou En Li, Dung Xueo Ping, and Lui Shouaqi all lived in this area before the great march, and during World War II.

In a little town of Xin Xiang, we came to a school for children who are blind or retarded, the atmosphere was incredibly depressing; the school doubled as a sanitarium. "To work in this atmosphere must take some very special people indeed," I thought to myself while walking through the cold, gray cement buildings without grass or trees around.

The following morning, a caliper on my front disk brake lost a bolt. I decided to wire it up against the lower fork tube, while the entire group stood around trying to tell me what to do instead of just letting me do it. One of them, Chunnie, a driver, was very forth right in his advice to this dumb motorcyclist. I just turned around and shouted "Shut the fuck up. Leave me alone!" About this time, everybody understood my gentle message and backed away, leaving me to wire it up. The repair held all the way to Beijing.

The temperature is below freezing; rivers have ice covering them, especially in the early mornings. Driving is quite dangerous, especially in small villages where they throw their waste water on the road; during the night, it freezes up, creating a hazard.

Hotel Hostility and Jen Lei's Stand

We hit the pearl of capitalism, Zhen Zhou, where I put my motorcycle away in the hotel foyer. A cleaning woman near where the motorcycle was standing just threw a fit, squawking like a chicken gone psycho. "You move motorcycle," the hotel manager said.

"If I have to move the motorcycle, then the entire group will leave your hotel," I told him. Jin Lei and the rest of the group backed me up. We rolled the motorcycle out of this dirty place with spit all over the floor (they had the gall to worry about my motorcycle being in there), started it up and we left, finding a cleaner hotel. Yeah Gang!!

The following day, we were greeted by a Chinese Women's Motor Scooter Exhibition Team, a dozen very lovely girls who came to escort me to Two Point Seven Square located right in the middle of the city, surrounded by modern department stores. Two Point Seven Square reflects the history of the location. I was told, "On the second day of the second month of the year 1927 there was a general strike in the factories in Zhen Zhou. The British killed many striking factory workers." When I asked how many people were killed, the only answer I ever received was "Many Chinese killed." Seldom do the Chinese give a direct answer to a direct question.

At Two Point Seven Square bands were playing, and the mayor of Zhen Zhou gave his speech, then I gave one. There was clapping and slapping each other on the back. Next, I was taken on a tour of some of the department stores; I was amazed at the amount of western merchandise they contained (made in China).

In the late afternoon, Jin Lei and I sat talking with each other. She told me she had been an emergency room surgeon for six years, making about $40.00 a month! One of the reasons she was working with our film group was, "To find some type of a better future, perhaps in the film industry." I believe she was the most dynamic woman I met in China.

That afternoon, a young boy with one arm came and spoke with us. He said, "I want to make a trip across China for the disabled on a bicycle by myself." We wished the young lad "Good luck." There wasn't much that I could tell him except to describe some of the hardships he would face. He told me, "There might be a lot of trouble with the government. At one time, two fellows in wheel chairs went from Tinjin to Boijing - about 75 miles (120 kilometers) to support the Special Olympics. Unfortunately, when they arrived in Beijing, they were put on a train and sent right back to Tinjin, and admonished not to do anything like that again." The government had forbidden any news media coverage of these two brave young fellows' patriotic endeavor. China does not encourage any special interest group to stand out and do something unusual. The young man feared he would receive the same treatment.

On our way out of Zhen Zhou, we bought gasoline at a service station run by the army (I was never clear on why). When Jin Lei realized we had been cheated on the cost of the gasoline, she challenged the soldier, then his lieutenant who came out of the office. My hat is off to Jin Lei, she faced this officer down, telling him exactly what she thought of him. By this time, the soldiers were on one side, and all the men in our group were on the other, ready to do battle with each other if necessary. Chung Wei took out a television camera and started filming the whole event. Finally, the lieutenant, losing big face, backed down, inviting Jin Lei into his office where they talked for the next thirty minutes! Ultimately, he gave her a refund on the cost of the fuel. Well done Jin Lei! What a lady! It is virtually unheard of for a woman to do these things in China.

Once we were on the road again, my clutch cable broke. I sat down on the side of the road to replace it (I always carry extra). A huge crowd gathered, but the group kept them far enough back from me that I didn't need a flash light in my mouth to see in broad daylight!

December 24: We made it into the city of Handan that afternoon where it was very cold, 5 minus centigrade (1 + - degrees F) in the daytime...we are back up in the north of China again. Alece and I ate dinner that evening with the group, and were greeted with "Merry Christmas." We were very touched by the group and the hotel staff singing to us.

December 25: On Christmas morning, we depart in weather about 8 minus in centigrade (15+ - degrees F). We must be very careful of ice on the road as we wind through a maze of traffic - trucks, bicycles and carts, heading towards Shi Jai Zhuang, a military town housing the PLA's Army's Officers Academy. Our hotel rooms were on the 18th floor, with an elevator ride of roughly 10 minutes; two of the four elevators were functional. Once the two good ones come, you can imagine the panic among the people to get on.

That afternoon I was taken over to the Army Officer's Academy to give a speech. There were two companies formed, ready to listen to what I had to say. I was introduced by major Hu, and the speech was interpreted by a young lady, Sun Lei, who didn't speak any English! (Cheng had gone back to Beijing to resume his job, and Alece couldn't interpret anything official). Just for fun, I spoke for five minutes about my times as a young marine. When I was done, Sun Lei stepped up to the microphone and this is what I think she said: "All right you bastards, now that this long nose fool is done yammering to you, this is what you are going to do: 1. Step up to this red box on the table, 2. Put money in it for the Hope Project, and 3. Sign your names. If you don't, when you get back to the barracks your ass is grass, and we are the lawn mowers!"

Through her inspiring interpretation, the soldiers now stepped up, put their money in the box, signed their names, and marched off. Merry Christmas!

That evening, I had a televised interview with the Deputy Chairman of the Province. For ten minutes we told each other how glad we were to be in each other's presence, with a fairly competent woman interpreter as the go-between for our praises. I might add that women interpreters usually won't say "Ya, ya, ya" if they don't understand. Instead, they ask me to repeat myself or explain better.

At the hotel, the elevators had stopped completely; the power in the building was down. I climbed 18 floors to my room where my reward was a hot cup of tea and cold water to wash in. What a wonderful Christmas day in China!

The following day we visited Mr. Shin's paint factory, and then were taken to a school where he personally supports 100 kids in the Hope Project. He helped build the school, and many other things around the area, such as dams and water reservoirs. I was given a red scarf, and then received the Young Pioneers Salute.

After a sumptuous lunch, we drove to the Bethume International Peace Hospital where they train military doctors. We visit the Doctor Norman Bethume Museum, named after a Canadian idealist and martyr who worked himself to death caring for the wounded during the war of independence.

After dinner, were are sitting around the table with the Army doctors in their uniforms; Jin Lei, a doctor herself, was in her element. One lieutenant said to me in broken English, "We know you soldier. You appreciate that all soldiers are same family." He had a very good point indeed. We are the ones who patch up the mistakes of the politicians and diplomats.

December 27: We move on to Zhou Zhou where the daytime temperature is between 8 and 10 degrees minus centigrade (12 -15 degrees Fahrenheit). It is flat, agricultural country that is frozen - the rivers, the dams, the streams - all frozen! Very cold!

We stayed in a hostel, and Alece and I dug in and cleaned up that greasy, horrible motorcycle that had been out on mud roads. When that was done, we enjoyed the first of a few "real" simple meals on the trip. I couldn't taste much due to a bad cold; everybody in our group was worn down or sick, even though spirits were high with only two days to go!

The next day we toured China's equivalent of Universal City. We entered a massive area built in Ming Dynasty architecture, and were given a tour through the whole movie complex. There was a mock up of the Great Wall - quite impressive. Alece said something to me that really rang home. "All these kids can't afford school, yet they have spent tens of millions of RMB out here on this so-called Universal City for the sake of entertainment."

What a GREAT Ending!

December 29th: The last day of our journey across China! We started out long before dawn from Zhou Zhou, heading north to Beijing, arriving in the cold, gray dawn. There's ice on the road in various places, so we all must be careful. We travel up through the mountains, over the snow line, then to Badaling and the Great Wall of China. There our group is very warmly greeted by Mr. Jin and Mr. Lee of the Disabled Federation of Beijing, accompanied by other people with disabilities.

We go up on the Great Wall where they show me various places of interest. Then, I climb up hundreds of steps to the high points as the group is filming. The huge sheet - about 100 yards long by a yard and a half wide - that individual donors have been signing as we travel across China is impressively laid out, talking about the Hope Project and our journey of the Loving Hearts across China. Jin Lei's goal was to bring it back with 100,000 signatures. Tourists from various places in the world came up and put money in a box, then signed their names alongside all the Chinese names.

Once I am down from the high points, we took our final ride to the Beijing International Hotel. At the last minute, I was informed that, "You must ride motorcycle inside the hotel." That must be accomplished by approaching on a taxi ramp, then making a 90 degree turn over a curb, then driving through double doors into the main lobby of the hotel to greet the awaiting local dignitaries! No problem!

The ride back from Badaling to Beijing is freezing cold. I ride through the middle of Tianamen Square on Jen Guo Men Boulevard - the Boulevard of Heavenly Peace - to the Beijing International Hotel. As I come up the ramp, I spot the band at the end of the ramp near the entrance of the hotel and swing out all the way over to the left, then turn as sharp as I can without dropping the motorcycle 90 degrees to the right. I hit the curb and gave it a bit of power and bounced over, managing to keep this thing on its wheels and ride through the double doors into the main lobby of the hotel to be greeted by Mr. Mau, the head of the advisory committee, and still a personal advisor to the great leader of China, Dung Xeio Ping. I climbed off the motorcycle, relieved I did not fall in front of everyone. Will wonders never cease!

I take off a few of my jackets, and was handed a cloth to wipe my dirty face. There was still grease on my hands as Mr. Mau gave his speech, followed by Jin Lei's speech, followed by a speech from an official of the PC Brand Computer Company, followed by my own speech after Mr. Lui, managing director of the hotel, presents me with the Emperor's cup, a great honor.

The band played while we went upstairs to a press conference. For thirty minutes, we were drilled by over 50 reporters from the newspapers, magazines, television and radio. After that, was the customary wonderful banquet. I couldn't get near much food because people kept wanting to take photographs with me. I'd put in a few mouthfuls of food, stand up, take a photograph, sit down and try again. The food was incredible; it hurt when I saw massive portions taken away, maybe to be thrown out. I certainly hoped not.

After the festivities, I ride the motorcycle back over to the Diplomatic Compound, going back to the room that had been assigned to me for the next month. After a good, hot shower, I reflected on the past month and thought to myself, "Of all the hard work and hassles we endured as a group, it only served to bring us closer together." We had our problems throughout this very pressurized month where we suffered each other's company for as much as 20 hours a day, but in the end, it was worth it. I don't know what they thought of me, but I came out of the experience with at least one good friend - Chung Wei. I also acquired a great respect in my heart for the Chinese people who work so hard for so little. I wondered if all of our group shouldn't have received the Emperor's cup.

December 31: Jin Lei insisted I go to a New Year's Eve Party with her and Yin Li. I didn't really want to, preferring just to relax and close the year as quietly as possible. Instead, I ended up going to the Beijing International Hotel's gigantic entertainment hall. We sat at the table of the managing director of the hotel, Mr. Lui, and more speeches were given, along with entertainment, including dancing, gymnastics and balancing acts. Frankly, the incredible entertainment was lost on me because this is the time of year that I like to reflect and be alone. At the stroke of 24:00, everybody stood up, shaking hands. There was no warmth or affection in it at all. I wished everybody goodnight, and fled out of there as quickly as I could to my room.

That night, Jin Lei informed me she would be taking a job with PC Brand computers, starting on March 1. Congratulations to Jin Lei, the new marketing/Public Relations person for that company!

At last I could, in my solitude, think about the year past. What a month - what a year it had been. I thought of last year at this time when I was in the quiet of my mother's home in Bodfish, California. How far I had come since then. Since I left my mother, I had traveled over 20,000 miles (32,000 km) in third world countries. I thought about the various weather conditions and the kaleidoscope of people I'd encountered. I thought ahead to 1993 and all the new trials, tribulations, and challenging miles still to be faced. With these thoughts, I closed the year of 1992.

January 1, 1993: New Years Day was spent with Ze Qing's family. I remember meeting her after I left the bus station, her holding firmly onto my hand as a simple gesture of warmth and genuine friendship. I appreciated it ever so much. Ze Qing and her mother laughed at me as I tried to help them make dumplings to prepare for the dinner.

Back at the hotel, Jin Lei told me, "We are going to have to hustle. They want to use you further in the future to do motivational talks. She also told me that the Hope Project would not help in the cost of editing the film. I thought "Well done boys. You have received all this effort and help from us, and you don't want to help with the cost of editing our film?"

Later, they booked me with various companies to give motivational talks about our trip, and share what we had tried to accomplish through it. At one of these talks in a company that was going to make a contribution for editing the film, they had a song come up on a large karoake screen; no one sang along. The song was "I am sailing, I am sailing." I was very touched by it for some unexplainable reason. Jin Lei was watching me, and noticed my reaction. She later used that song for the ending of the film we had made. Whenever I show the film, I'm always reminded of the incredible, beautiful Jin Lei.

January 10: Jin Lei asked me to ride the motorcycle to the other side of Badaling to do some ride filming on the edge of the Gobi Desert. Of course I agreed. "Parts of the film didn't come out well," she told me, "and we need to re-shoot some things." They also wanted to create the ending of the film out in the countryside. We rode and drove to a place about 65 miles (100 km) from Beijing; once again I rode through the Great Wall. The temperature at Badaling was about 15 minus centigrade (8 degrees Fahrenheit) that day, with snow on the sides of the road (luckily, no ice). Way up on a mountain I stopped and asked Jin Lei to put some more jackets on, to cover her face, and to put on a helmet so she could ride the remaining 20 miles (32 km) on the back of the motorcycle. I wanted her to feel what I had been feeling (minus the feet) right through China .

When we got to a little hostel, we unloaded our gear, then scouted out the area where we would film - right on the edge of a frozen lake. They took one of the vehicles out on the lake and spun donuts with it, doing all kinds of crazy, goofy things. We rode horses that afternoon to scout the land and decide on tomorrow's operations.

That evening, as we sat around with our chopsticks eating dinner, laughing and carrying on as only the Chinese can do at meal time, I sadly thought, "This is the last time we will all be together."

The following morning, we were up before the sun, started up the motorcycle and rode out to the edge of the frozen lake; snow started coming down. The one thing I had asked is that we "set up and start the motorcycle one time so I don't warm up and cool the engine off, then warm it up again."

"Yes, yes, may vin ti," I'm told. After I started it up for the third time, and warmed it up, they told me, "Shut it off." Naturally, I then got mad, started hollering at Jin Lei, and unfortunately made her cry. The whole group seemed equally tense, with people shouting at one another in the extreme cold, with high winds and snow coming down. As we continued our filming, the snow was about 6 inches deep, powdery, crunching under our feet.

I managed to ride the motorcycle over the fields for the last bit of filming, then straight on to our living quarters where we put the thing away. By this time, ice was forming on the roads, so I couldn't ride it home. We checked the weather reports and learned that "No vehicles are allowed past Badaling."

So, we drove to Badaling, then took a train. The motorcycle was left behind, locked up in the little hostel where we had stayed. On the train, I was shocked at the filth - rubbish and spit were tossed into a bucket which was unceremoniously lifted up and its contents were then dumped out a lowered window onto the train tracks. There is plenty of trash along side of the railroad tracks as well. By the time we made it to Beijing, my lungs were on fire from all the cigarette smoke in the train cars. To end our day, we took a half mile walk back to the Beijing International Hotel where I went straight to bed.

There was snow and ice on the streets of Beijing for the rest of January, making it terribly difficult for me to walk without slipping and falling. Towards the end of January, we went back out to Badaling to pick up the motorcycle. On the way back, I had many scares, dodging patches of ice and big snow drifts still on the road.

I decided to send home all the gifts I had accumulated, but there is only one post office in all of Beijing where you can send packages overseas because everything must be checked out by Customs. Fortunately, Ze Qing helped me post off these momentos.

January 20: President Clinton gave his inaugural speech. It all sounded beautiful, full of liberal stupidity urging more control and less freedom - at least that's how I interpreted it.

My English lessons with Oxana Fedrouk continue through January.

January 28: I was invited to Yin Li's house for the Chinese New Year, to usher in the Year of the Rooster. We had a jovial meal with his family, with Jin Lei there to interpret.

One Sunday, Ze Qing and I went to visit Scott. Ze Qing and Scott told me that "The Chinese way of doing things, especially in the generation that grew up during the Cultural Revolution, is to never tell the truth - it will only get you in trouble. Say no more than what you need to say."

"That's why I was always only half informed," I thought to myself.

I am still waiting on the Mongolian and Russian visas. On the Russian side, Igor had posted my letter to Moscow, but as yet we didn't have any word back. It was decided that we would call a meeting of the Russian media at Vildimar Fedrouk's apartment on Friday.

The Mongolians didn't know what to do with me, and I never spoke to anyone who spoke good English. I sat on the edge of my seat about these matters; they didn't seem to be going anywhere, and time was running out. One day, I finally got to meet the Mongolian representative and state my case.

"No problem," he replied, so I know I'm in trouble.

On the world news scene, South African President De Klerk was telling the nation to get their house in order and stop all the political violence. Multi-party talks were to start in March, a transitional government was to be in place by June, with elections by April of 1994.

In America, one of President Clinton's first official acts is to push for gays in the military.

At home, I have word that Mom is suffering from a slight touch of pneumonia. This is very frustrating and disturbing to me, since I'm too far away and can't help.

The Russian Run-A-Round and Budding Hemorrhoids!

One day Igor said, "We have an appointment at the Russian Consulate." We went there, but they never even let me in! Igor entered and spoke on my behalf. When he came out, the Consulate General came with him, asking me very bluntly,

"What do you want?"

"I would like to travel across Russia."

"You can't."

"Why?"

"Because there are no hotels in the Siberia's."

"I don't need hotels."

"No, you can't go," he said, turning around and walking away, displaying a typical communist mentality. Igor said, "We are going to have to find some organization to sign responsibility for you. I will work on it."

I was looking for a place to live because in February I must move out of the hotel. I always seem to be waiting by the phone for a call that has something to do with permits for Mongolia and Russia, or for a place to live.

One day I had a hemorrhoid sprout. I went to Jin Lei to see if she knew of any place that I could go. We first tried a Chinese hospital, and they sent me to the foreigner hospital where they told me an operation would cost $400.00 and I would have to be in the hospital a week. I couldn't afford to do this. "$400.00 just to get my ass fixed," I thought. "That's just another way to ream a guy!" Remember, a month's wages for a doctor was about $40!

I was in horrible pain, and it was now even **more** difficult to walk. The thing was big enough that it felt like it would burst any moment, causing me incredible embarrassment and physical damage. Ze Qing, ever resourceful, suggested, "We go to another hospital." We went across Beijing to Er Long Lu, a hospital just for hemorrhoids! I soon dubbed it "the House of a Thousand Assholes." We arrived about 11:30, and the admission window closed in our face for lunch break. We sat around for the next hour and a half until we caught a nurse who took us upstairs to meet a Doctor Wu and Doctor Ma. The doctors told Ze Qing to translate as Doctor Wu leaned me over a table with my pants down. This so-called operating room resembled a butcher shop; blood was all over the walls. Suddenly, in terror, I realized that Doctor Wu was approaching my backside with a pair of forceps and a huge syringe in his hands! He didn't wear any sanitary gloves! An incredible pain hit me in my ass, and I nearly went up the wall hollering and shouting. Out of the corner of my eye I could see Ze Qing facing into the corner of the room, jumping up and down. They were telling her something, and she was trying to translate it back to me. Poor dear! In the end, the doctor cut out the hemorrhoid and kept it in the forceps to show me. "Judas fucken priest, get it away!" I thought. He then patched my painful, throbbing backside, and allowed me to pull up my pants. While all this had been going on, the nurse at the door was trying to hold it closed while patients in the hallway tried to push it open to have a look at this long nose in the operating room getting surgery.

After all this pain and humiliation, the doctors refused to accept any money. Ze Qing told me, "Operation normally ten American dollars. If it doesn't work, then do again for you."

"Don't worry," I replied, "it will work. It has to work!"

After an hour of recovering from shock and pain, we walked out, relieved that I had finally received treatment. About a week later, I took a box of candy to the administrative ladies, and Doctors Wu and Ma. They told me, "We had read about you in the newspaper, and that's why we were willing to do something. Normally, it is illegal for a foreigner to be in this hospital."

Ze Qing continued to be an invaluable, wonderful companion, and I looked forward to our times together on Sundays. She asked me, "Do you want work again?" I did, so she contacted Professor Jin who had an English class. I agreed to teach a two month class of basic American English. When I was introduced to my class, I expected a bunch of kids, but instead found very mature adults from many different walks of life. There was an Army Colonel, a woman high in the police department, a professor, a doctor, an economist, among others - all wanting a grasp of English. If you ever run into a mainland Chinese that says such words as "bullshit," you'll know where he received his grounding in English!

One Friday I was supposed to go over and speak with Oxona, and was surprised to find at her apartment, her father Valdimar Surgeo from Radio Moscow, and Andri Kabinikov from Konsomolka Pravada. They had called a meeting. These kind Russians were interested in what I was doing, and wanted to plan a strategy with the media to help find somebody to sign responsibility for me in Russia. They took comprehensive notes about my trip, and Surgeo agreed to broadcast information over Radio Moscow. Vladamir also was involved in nation-wide radio, and Andri was with one of the biggest newspapers in the country. What great news - the media people were trying to make something happen. "This obviously is going to be my ticket in," I thought to myself.

A few days later, my friend, Chung Wei, gave me very depressing news. He said, "There is no permit you can acquire to go through inner Mongolia, a Chinese military area. It is all just for the army."

Next, I received a phone call from Valdimar Karlikov of Russian TASS television. He said, "I want to do an insert for Russian TV with you."

"Thank you," I replied. "I am at your service."

We met one Friday morning by the garage where I keep the motorcycle, and he followed me out into traffic. They were filming as I rode along. They were very surprised to see the reception that I received from Chinese passing in cars - people waiving to me, sticking up their thumbs. At the end of the interview, I was pushing the motorcycle when my right foot slipped out from underneath me. Down I went with the motorcycle! I quickly got the thing back up on its wheels, very embarrassed; I hadn't dropped the thing in months, then dropped it right in front of a television camera. Mr. Karlikov very kindly waived it off.

A fax from the Cheshire Foundation in London said, "We will not be able to help you enter into Russia. We prefer that you do not cross Russia on your own. It is very dangerous."

You can imagine my reaction - anger. "Why should they worry?"

One evening I was invited to the diplomatic compound at John's apartment to meet a friend of his from Mongolia named Amanda Ling. Ze Qing came with me since she loves to meet foreigners. Amanda was very informative about Mongolia, and confirmed what I had suspected when she told me, "There is no proper road between the border and Ulan-Baatar," a distance of 400 miles (600 km).

When talking with Igor Surikoff one day, he told me he was eight years as a pianist and composer; he spoke Chinese, English and German, and worked for a company that dealt with Chinese imports and exports.

"I never tell the Chinese that I can speak Chinese. I let them use interpreters, and then I listen to their conversations amongst themselves. It is a very effective advantage in the business world." Igor also told me that "I am being called back to Moscow, and I don't know when I'll be back in Beijing." I'm saddened to hear he's leaving since he is my one contacts within the Russian community.

I'm uptight a lot, and don't sleep much. All I want to do is to go. Though much good has come from my stay in this country, I just want to be on my way.

February 24: I attempt to see Mr. Surenjev of the Mongolian Embassy. In the lobby, the receptionist tells me that "Mr. Surenjev is not here." One day, I visited the office with a bottle of vodka and Mr. Surenjev came out. Unfortunately, we cannot communicate since he doesn't speak any English. He just motioned to me with his hand to wait. He went away and came back with a Mr. Ghankuyagh who spoke English. We chatted about what I hoped to do in Mongolia, and he told me, "We worry about you and your safety."

"Don't worry about me," I responded. "I have traveled across the Sahara," I continued, showing them a whole series of photographs and the world map. I said, "If I die in the Gobi Desert, that is my responsibility, and I will write a letter to you to that effect."

"No, that is not necessary," they said. "We've just never had a foreigner by himself on a motorcycle cross the Gobi." I reiterated that I have already been over most of the world on my own. They conferred, and Mr. Ghankuyagh said, "The ambassador is not here right now, but he will be later this afternoon. Call back tomorrow morning and we will let you know." They did NOT take the bottle of vodka.

The following day the Mongolians agreed to issue my visa and let me cross their country on the motorcycle. Yea, Mongolians - well done fellows!

I called Alece at the Beijing Film Academy, and she reported that, "They are going to let you come and stay here." Well done, Alece, thank you very much! A great day for news.

There must be an epidemic of flu going around because I notice an extreme about of vomit on the street. It is not uncommon to walk along and have to dodge both globs of spit and piles of vomit within a short distance. It always makes for pleasant strolling.

I am trying to find the motorcycle parts I ordered from Scott at Lancaster Harley Davidson. They seem to have disappeared.

Bus Stop Strategies and Constipated Corny

Everyday is a fight on the buses in the streets of Beijing. I often use a mini- bus to get to my destination since they are only a couple of RMB, about 20 cents, and are far less crowded than the big buses. Unfortunately, they don't go to as many destinations as the large buses and subway system, which I fight two nights a week to get to the southwest side of Beijing. The subway doors are twice as wide as buses when they open, and slide straight backwards. Of course, you don't step up when you enter, so the people exiting the subway have to force their way directly into the crowd instead of jumping down into the morass of humanity like a stick of paratroopers would from a plane.

Just imagine in your mind that the subway platform, sometimes a quarter of a mile long, is crowded with one through tens of thousands of Chinese, and they are all waiting for the subway to stop and for those doors to open so they can force their way onto the train as quickly as possible. Once inside, packed like anorexic sardines, the crowd now has one new objective in mind - get off the train at the right stop. Two antagonistic forces clash at every stop - one wants on, one wants off. When those doors open, it is bang, clang, clunk - the clash of the titans! Lift your elbows, push, shove and bully your way in or out as quickly as possible. Instead of just politely entering and exiting as it is done in most of the world, Chinese people make the subways a brutal collision of bodies and wills.

Pity the one poor devil who comes in from the country with a large parcel. That package will always get snagged by all the incoming people. I've seen people stand

and scream and shout as they unwillingly get forced back onto the subway car as the doors close and the car is on its way to the next stop. When someone gives me an elbow, I quietly try to come down hard on his foot with my right foot - mostly made of steel. If my aim is good, that person usually comes out of the crowd like a piece of screaming popcorn. Inwardly, I smile; outwardly, I act like I have no cue to what all the commotion is about.

At the end of February I moved over to the Beijing Film Academy, a university to teach youngsters who want to get into the media industry how to handle cameras and various occupations dealing with the production of films. It is located north of Beijing, miles from where I was, but convenient to the bus routes and subways. My new quarters were not as nice as the room I had; I moved into a dorm for the equivalent of a dollar a day. In our dorm room there were two other guys. David Jung Westler was a sculptor of some high reputation, now trying to locate people interested in doing sculpturing for him. He would let them do the rough sculpturing, then he would come and finish the work. The other fellow was Andri Drelau, a scholarly young man, very religious, from Rumania. Over the next two months I learned much from this wise person.

I managed to buy food tickets to eat at the student's cafeteria, a dirty place. The food wasn't bad, but I immediately noticed that everybody had one bowl and one spoon; I took my wooden spoon and my bowl that I used when traveling. Of course, crowding and shoving prevail; there's no such thing as lines. As you walk past the servers, various items are slopped into your food bowl, one on top the other. Then, you sit down and gobble it up while listening to the noise from all the babbling voices.

At one of these meals I met Peng Jing - Quan, a student from the south of China, and a self-educated man. He didn't know how to read or write at the age of 14, but taught himself, went through school, and somehow became quite well known as a film producer in the southern part of China. He attended university to take some brush up courses.

One day he took me over to the student's dormitories; I was shocked to find they live four to six students in a room! The toilets were blocked up, stinking up the end of the hallway. Food was throw out into the hall instead of into trash cans - a real bit of Paradise.

My Sundays with Ze Qing were to end since we would no longer enjoy the privacy of my room for talking on our own without people listening. Ze Qing during this time also met her future husband, a young French fellow named Sebastian, a philosophy major. Instead of going into the Army to do his national service, because he had a good education he went and did his two years of national service in the diplomatic corps for France, stationed in Beijing doing administrative work. I was very happy to see that Ze Qing had met somebody her own age with her own kind of ideas, and to see how taken she was with this young man.

I must admit to being a bit hurt as this relationship evolved, although I personally never had any designs on her. Even though we saw less of each other, Ze Qing was always there if I needed anything. She never let me down.

After the Russian media began their campaign, I'm told It was "well received in Russia, but no one has yet come forward to sign responsibility, though some seem to be interested." Alex Chulitsky, whom I had been writing to since July the year before, had been trying in conjunction with the Cheshire Home in Moscow for disabled Russian veterans to find a way to get me in. Of course, they could not sign responsibility for me, especially in view of the home office concerns about my safety.

I found a place near the academy to get a haircut for 15 cents. This little hole in the wall beauty salon housed a beauty of a woman barber.

I finally found my motorcycle parts were at UPS after being held up out at the airport. My paperwork was sent to Beijing International after I left. I managed to get a hold of the paperwork from the hotel. I found the UPS from an address written in Chinese; I got on a mini-bus and showed them the address. They then motioned when I should get off; no English exchanged. For the next 45 minutes, I wandered around showing people this address, and they pointed me in various directions; no one will ever admit that they don't know. Eventually, I came upon an old man who took me the last 50 meters to a small building where the office of UPS was located.

Once in the office, a man told me "You will need to go out to the airport and get a Customs declaration."

"Where do I go for that?"

"Down on Gen Guo Man Blvd., about 10 miles away," he told me.

Next, I battled my way on the public transport system down to Gen Guo Man and the Customs Building. After waiting in line, a Customs official recognized me from the media coverage as he took my paperwork back to his supervisor who stamped his permission to let my parts in duty free, saving me about $125.00 with the stroke of a pen. I thanked this kind public servant, shook hands, then headed back to UPS.

Now, I had to wait about two days until they eventually delivered the parts to Degussa.

The people at the dormitory are all very liberal, and I tend to be middle of the road, the odd man out. I appreciate how David Jung, Andri, and I get along; none of us are extremely liberal or conservative, and David is 42 , my age.

March 9: I woke up this morning and I felt something had shifted in my favor with the Russians; my gut feeling was based on nothing tangible. Though I still had some apprehension right up to the time I actually received my permit to cross Russia, it was a feeling that things were going to go right.

Andri Kabinikov got a hold of me that day, saying "I would like to do another article." We met on Friday, did the article and took some photographs. He told me that "in the next week or so, if nobody comes forward to sign responsibility, the newspaper is going to do so on your behalf." What incredible, incredible news!

March 15: Signs are all over Beijing declaring a new, more open, freer China. I had a day with Ze Qing at Andrew's house where we had a big hotpot meal and talked about these signs popping up all over the place. I remarked that "The air quality seems much better the last couple of days." They told me that was because "The Olympic committee is in town, so they shut down all the polluting factories."

I still get very down and depressed, experiencing the foreigner blues. Within 6 weeks, on April 25, my visa will expire and I am going to go forward into Mongolia regardless of whether I have a Russian visa or not. My thinking is "If I can't get this visa while I am in China, then I'll try to get it in Ulan-bataar, a little bit closer to Russia."

I always seem to be replacing bolts and working on my right foot and leg. It is just as noisy and squeaky as ever; it is impossible for me to walk down the street without people looking and gawking at me.

David Jung and I now realize that Andri is a crude. We have never seen him take his toothbrush to brush his teeth, or take a towel and go to the shower downstairs. When I shower, I must take a chair downstairs, take myself apart, bounce and shuffle the chair along into the shower stall, take my shower, back out, put myself together, and head back upstairs. Andri just doesn't do it, and smells like a giant armpit. You can smell him before he arrives and long after he leaves. We've never even seen him change the sheets on his bed! Oh well, it takes all kinds to make up the world, even armpits. At least he is an informative stinker!

I received a phone call from a lady in the citizen services of the American Embassy asking, "Would you like to live in somebody's apartment and look after their 14-year-old dog?"

"Yes, I will do it," I told her, thinking "This will give me privacy and maybe even a bit of luxury and help save some money." So, I agreed to stay in the American embassy doctor's apartment for the next few weeks while they made a trip to Thailand and Vietnam, looking after Corny, an ancient, long-haired sausage dog.

Whenever Ze Qing would help me out with something special, I tried to do something in reciprocation. One time after she helped me find and purchase some particular difficult-to-find items, I took her to the multi-storied McDonald's on Wong Fu Jing Street - supposedly the biggest McDonald's in the world. She had never even had a hamburger before. I will always remember the look on her face when she sat down with a cheeseburger, french fries and a strawberry milk shake, absolutely wild with glee.

In the doctor's flat I was able to watch CNN news again. I saw that Yeltsin was under pressure for his rule by decree, and heard that there were opposing forces in the parliament which were the old guard communist. These forces wanted to impeach Yeltsin and remove him from office. In America, I was very happy to see that President Clinton and other western leaders were supporting Yeltsin, especially Helmut Kole in Germany. At this time, Yeltsin's mother died. I couldn't help but worry selfishly as to how this would effect me crossing Russia. Yeltsin must be a very tough guy what with his mother dying and all the other things he was facing at the same time. How he is holding up, I don't know.

It was only two kilometers (1 1/2 miles) to Degussa's office, so I walked over there every morning to take care of faxes and correspondence. This office was invaluable to me in my communications and organizing with the outside world.

In a meeting with Andri Kabinikov, he told me that "Konsomolka Pravda will sign responsibility for you." That secured my permit to pass through Russia on the motorcycle! In return, I agreed to do a motivational media promotion for disabled veterans and people with disabilities across Russia, stopping in ten major Russian cities.

When I instructed Oxana on Fridays, she would always tell me how bad Russia was. "There's many robberies and crime, and the economy is rapidly deteriorating with the political situation." She was informative in a negative way. I noticed other Russians I spoke to also never said anything positive about Russia. Oxana told me that "You must be very careful when crossing Russia, especially in the Siberia's, because there are many bad people roaming about."

I was summoned to a meeting with Jin Lei and Yin Li at the Beijing International Hotel. On the way, another cab driver tried to cheat me, going a longer way to the hotel to run up the meter. I reached over to stop the meter at a stop sign, and started choking the cretin, vigorously shook his head back and forth as I throttled him. He didn't know what to think. This was not normal behavior for a tourist. Climbing out, I slammed the door and walked off, leaving him to gasp and wonder.

In early April, the political scene in Russia had calmed down, and I was reassured by Andri that there would be no problem with my visa. While looking after Corny, of course he had to get constipated. Joyfully, I got to put on a rubber glove and literally pull the shit out of him. It amazes me the things I will do to keep body and soul together on this trip.

Andri Drelau had traveled extensively in Russia, and talked to me about the changes. "They still have a very socialist mentality. Anything that looks like trouble or is different, is 'Nayet' in Russian, meaning 'no.' If you say 'no' that solves the problem. Russia, like China, wants foreign money and investments, but they still don't want to open up. They are a very closed up country."

In my last class, which everyone passed whether he or she spoke a word of English, we spent an hour and a half in free discussion, speaking of many things, including the handing over of Hong Kong in 1997. The Army Colonel said "China must have Hong Kong." I asked him, "What if it is done wrong and all the big money makers of Hong Kong take their money and flee to various other places in the world? What will be left in Hong Kong?" The class agreed it must all be done diplomatically, with FACE for everyone.

Others spoke about education in the states, and freedom of speech in China. I was amazed at their willingness to learn about the western ways of doing things. I said good-bye to a wonderful group of Chinese people with fairly bright futures. To my great relief there will be no more subway battles an hour each way, twice a week.

The apartment owners came back to find a happy Corny. I'm glad the dog didn't die on me, although I admit I'm sick of the damned dog by this time. As I left I thought, "You can die now, Corny." This was April Fool's Day.

Good-bye, My Friends

I went to Degessa on my way back to the film academy to pick up my mail, and discovered a letter from a company called "Writgen" in Germany. The letter had been passed on to me by my mother, saying that they had sent a check. Writgen was a friend of the late Jurgen Schultz; they knew each other from business. When Writgen was down in South Africa, Jurgen showed him my written material.

I wrote Writgen a letter saying "When I get back to Europe, if I get back to Europe, I will contact you about doing some type of media promotion to give you something back for your help."

In the diplomatic compound I met a French woman named Ilana, the correspondent for the Mexican news agency. I told her how, at the end of the month, I needed a few days at the compound, and she said "You are welcome to stay with me for a few days. My roommate doesn't live in her bedroom, so she won't have a problem with you staying here."

One night, David Jung talked me in to going to a discotheque with some other people in the dormitory. I was surprised that the place we visited was so modern inside with several videos up on the wall and music blaring away. Much of it was rap which I think is crap. There were girls dancing, and the black fellows there seemed to be having a great time. The Chinese people were standing in the corners just trying to act cool. I spotted a couple of Marines who were all puffed up and muscle bound. They didn't want to talk to me. Finally, after about an hour of noise and crowds, I slipped away from my friends, getting the hell of there and catching a taxi back to the room. I'm so sick of crowds by this time, it would be impossible to express how much I hated the crowding and pushing everywhere.

I was told that April is not the most pleasant month to travel across Mongolia because it is "the month of wind and sand." Daytime temperatures reach 60 degrees, but with the wind chill factor it can come down to about 30 in the day, and at night, even though the wind may drop, it goes down to as low as zero Fahrenheit (15 degrees minus centigrade). This is all bad news for me. I think, "If I have to travel at very low speeds across this stretch of desert - about 750 miles - it will be just as well that the temperature is low so I don't overheat the motor."

One night, about two weeks before I left the country, Jin Lei and Yin Li came and gave me a video tape of our trip across China. We watched the tape, then Yin Li and I gave each other a big hug and said good-bye (rare for a Chinese man). I said good-bye to Jin Lei with a heavy heart, knowing I'd never see either one of these incredible people again. We had come through many trials together, and we had come away from them as friends with respect for one another. I wish them success in the future.

There was a lot of dust and wind in Beijing. "The wind is coming off the Gobi Desert," I was told. Combined with the dust and air pollution in Beijing, the weather was mucho dreary.

April 10: David Jung Wesler said good-bye to me and Andri. Our laughter and low humor jokes are coming to a halt. Now it will just be me and Andri in the room. People seem to be moving everywhere. John Leciester is on his way to Hong Kong to take a position as a correspondent with Associated Press International. He'll be leaving on the 19th.

Andri Kabinikov told me, "We have an appointment at the Russian Consulate General to get your visa - it has been granted. We will report on the 13th of April. There will also be a briefing." Whoopee!!!

At the consulate, I met some ladies behind the counter who told me "The roads will be very bad during May in Siberia. They are full of mud, is very cold and it snows a lot." They were all cackling amongst themselves. After that bit of cheer, I was motioned into a room where I sat in front of a big fellow with Asian features, looking as though he were from Eastern Siberia. He sat me down and said, "Do you know you are going to be going through places that are liberated gulags? These people have never had freedom, and now, all of the sudden they are turned loose on the world. They still have no place to go. You mustn't talk to anyone, you mustn't make friends with anyone. You must be careful of everyone."

I answered, "Yes, I will, I will!

"Are you sure you want to do this?"

"Yes, I am sure I want to do this. Please give me the BLOODY visa!"

He was holding my visa in his hand, finally turning it over to me. They stapled it into my passport and I walked out of there a very relieved person with a clear knowledge that the trip could now continue. To get to Russia, all I had to do was cross the Gobi Desert.

A stranger on the street told me, "I saw your film aired on television, and I really liked it." Thanks to the people of my group for not telling me when it was aired.

Andrew and Shirto Head treated me to an Easter Dinner at the China World Hotel. We dined with some friends visiting from California, sitting on the 37th floor with an incredible view of polluted Beijing. The food was great, and plentiful.

A friend staying at the Film Academy had just returned from Ulan-bataar and reported that "Ulan-bataar was 16 degrees Fahrenheit at night and 60 in the day. There was no wind in Ulan-bataar, but the wind was blowing in the desert south, so the temperatures are going to be much lower there."

April 12. Armed with my visa to cross Russia, I set the date to start the journey again on April 20th - the same day I started my journey across China. On April 17th, the Harley Owner Group of Hong Kong had just finished a run along the Great Wall, and they invited me to attend a dinner at a hotel in the south of Beijing. I brought Ze Qing with me; she was thrilled to mingle with all these high-powered foreigners. I felt a pain in my heart that evening as I watched her, realizing that in a few days I would say good-bye to her, and probably never see her again. That same day I said good-bye to Andri. The last thing I remember was my friend, Andri the crude, walking away picking his nose as my taxi drove away. The same day was also my last lesson with Oxana. I wished her well.

There was definitely spring in the air. You could feel it. I could feel the spring fever in my veins. I had moved over and was staying with Ilana.

One day, Andrew took me to Doctor Shen, a man held 23 years in prison under Mao because he would not renounce his views of traditional Chinese medicine. We also visited a Professor Wong, who's grandpa taught him traditional Chinese medicine when we was a child. He was able to write in ancient Chinese calligraphy. I met another of Andrew's friends, a young fellow named Floyd, destined to be expelled from the country in the next couple of weeks because he had been intimate with a Chinese girl from Taiwan, an area the Chinese still consider part of China. They had warned the couple to split, they didn't, so he was being sent back home. After spending five years trying to get his gymnastics degree, Floyd was leaving China with no degree at all. He told me "The gymnastics they teach to foreigners are very basic. The real advanced techniques of Chinese gymnastics are kept a secret among the Chinese themselves." So much for a free and open China.

I also met a high ranking Lama through some friends staying in Beijing. This man was returning to Tibet after 20 years of exile in Switzerland. I was impressed with his serenity. Of course, he wasn't dressed in the normal monk's clothing, but in the clothes of a westerner. I would have liked to sat longer with this man. When we parted, he took from his breast pocket a little blue piece of material with a loop on top, and a little tail on the other end. There was something inside - a piece of cardboard. He told me "Wear this in your left breast pocket and keep the loop turned up. It will protect you." I thanked this very kind man for giving me his personal protection.

On April 18, while with Scott waiting for Ze Qing and Chung Wei, we met the old man with no legs. He came up to us and showed us the picture I had given him, rumpled by now. It was at this time that I bade this person of the streets good-bye.

When Ze Qing and Chung Wei arrived, we had lunch, then sat talking in the garage while I took care of a few things on the motorcycle. At the end of our time together, Chung Wei gave me a big hug. I told him, "I consider you my Chinese brother and respect you very much." He pulled from his pocket a compass that he had used to navigate his way out of Vietnam when he was a soldier. He gave that compass to me; I was so touched that I nearly cried.

Ze Qing and I went to visit some Americans working for the embassy. We enjoyed a pizza dinner, then watched a video documentary on Mongolia. My fears were confirmed - there were no proper roads from the border north, and I saw a lot of soft sand around the border. Oh well! I will tackle those problems when I arrive in Mongolia. After saying good-bye to our hosts, we walk a few blocks, holding hands, sharing a warm feeling for each other. On a street corner, I hailed a cab, gave her a big hug, and wished her God's love and long life. We pledged to write one another, then parted I asked her not to come and see me off - I didn't trust my emotions. As she left, an empty feeling echoed in my heart, one like I haven't felt for many years. It brought back the memory of when I was leaving for Vietnam and said good-bye to my girlfriend, Chris.

I'm numb by this time as I walked through the Diplomatic Compound to John's apartment. John was leaving the following day for Hong Kong, and has been very instrumental in bringing about the contacts through Han Wei that eventually enabled us to make the film.

In bed that night I hurt inside as I reflected on the happenings and emotions of this day: meeting the beggar, saying good-bye to Chung Wei and Ze Qing, preparing to leave the country, and the anticipation of the renewal of the journey were all heavy on my shoulders and heart.

April 19: I went to the Degussa office to say good-bye to Juliana and Lawrence, then retrieved a fax from the London Cheshire Foundation, asking if I wanted "an armed escort across Russia." With great anger, I faxed back, saying "No. Don't bother." I couldn't believe how psyched out these people had gotten. Uncertainty was part of the journey.

I called Don to say that I was going to be on the road, and for him to take care of himself. He told me, "Dave, obviously you didn't get our letter. We were in another shooting in March with two Africans. I killed one and got myself wounded in the arm. Dave, it was a very close call. The bullet went through my arm and lodged in the sack of my heart."

I was so hurt that I lost control for the next minute or so and cried. I didn't know if it was just the fact that Don had been hurt, or the emotional accumulation of all the good-byes to so many people who had been so helpful to me, plus the buildup of putting the trip back into motion into the unknown. For a full minute I cried like a baby. Don finally said, "Come on, Dave, get a grip!" I said "Yeah, okay," and we continued with our conversation. He told me "I am now out of danger and life is as usual at the Petrol station. We are rebuilding the whole thing so there will be more security." I wished him, Felicity and the rest of the family God's love and to BE AWARE! His parting shot to me was, "Don't get clever."

Andrew had picked me up in his jeep and we drove to a big department store in the area, a Japanese consortium where they were friendly. I bought cigarettes, salami, cheese and bread. That afternoon I finished loading the motorcycle and said good-bye to Andrew Head, wishing him well. I will forever prize the things he taught me. That evening, I cooked dinner for Ilana and her cousin visiting from France. My mind is definitely not on the conversation. In bed that night, my mind relives the past seven months since August 19, 1992, when I crossed the border at Lo Wu.

After a restless night's sleep, which is usual for me before I start a major journey, I awoke to the traffic noise out on Gen Guo Men at 03:52 in the morning, got up and had breakfast - some bread, cheese, and a cup of coffee. On my way out, I looked at the peacefully sleeping cousin of Ilana out in the front room and thought to myself, "What a difference between their lives and mine. In their future, they go forward with the known, I venture into the unknown." I took the elevator down and walked through the quiet courtyard to the garage. Once again, the machine is sitting loaded and ready for the next stage of the adventure to begin. I feel that gnawing feeling in the pit of my stomach as I roll it out with great difficulty (it now has 10 1/2 extra gallons of gasoline, and weighs about 900 pounds). It has been seven months since I carried a full load on the back. By now, Scott, Valdimar, Oxana and Andri have come to wish me well and good-bye.

After shaking hands and a few photos, I hit the starter at 05:10 that morning, bringing the machine to life. After it is warmed up, I say good-bye to these very fine people who are responsible for opening doors for me in Russia. Now, my challenge is to get to Russia and carry on with the ground work that they had prepared for me.

I gingerly wind my way down the alley between the garage and apartment buildings, nearly hitting one of the buildings trying to adjust to the increased weight on the motorcycle. Once out of the diplomatic compound and onto the road, then the expressway heading out of Beijing, it was a cool, sunny spring morning as the journey resumed and I headed north.

Tianamen Square, Beijing China
November 6, 1992

Dung Fung Sq. Kunming, China
December 3, 1992. Start of Documentary

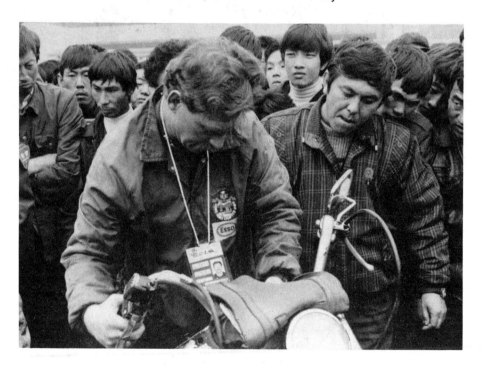

Huge crowd and motor cycle won't start. What pressure!
Kunming, China December 3, 1992

Chapter Thirty-One

Surviving the Gobi

Within the hour I hit my first traffic jam; trucks were backed up for miles. I cut down the oncoming lane, darting in as opposing vehicles come by. I spot the problem - somebody broke down on a corner right in the middle of the road, making it was virtually impossible to get around without having a head on collision with an oncoming vehicle. Once through this mess, I went to Zhong Jia Kou, the last major city in China by my route. I battled my way through the traffic, the market place crowds, the bicycles. Once I was out of the city I was stopped by police just outside of Hau Da, the last pavement. When I left Hau Da, I was truly in the Gobi Desert!

It was quite cool, though sunny, and the road very rough. After 40 miles, the road petered out, and I was now on a small dirt track. I noticed dirt tracks going everywhere, so I took out my compass and started watching it very carefully, making sure to head north west.

About 3 in the afternoon, I see this huge brown cloud coming at me from the distance. It goes from the desert floor right on up into the sky like an impenetrable brown wall. The realization hits me that I am in for a whopper of a sand storm! It hit me full blast, head on with about 60 to 70 knots of wind, the sand blasting my body. I covered my face with a bandanna, and pulled my helmet down over my forehead as much as I could. Pushing on, I tried to blink the sand out of my eyes. Even though the ground was hard enough to be stable, my speed from the time I left Hau Da was down to about 15 miles an hour. This is not a problem because of the cold; the temperature was about 30 degrees Fahrenheit. At night, it drops down to about 10 degrees as I move over the low and rolling hills, watching the compass, always moving in a north west direction, knowing sooner or later I'll hit the railhead (I'm not sure of the exact distance - around 200 miles).

I ride this way for the next few hours, occasionally seeing Mongolian writing on home - made signs. The writing goes from top to bottom in a spiral, almost like a barber poll; what it says is anybody's guess. Probably "What in the hell are you doing out here?"

About 18:00 I see some buildings off in the storm and head towards them, thinking "At least I can get behind a wall to shield myself from the flying sand." One of the buildings is a sheep's pen, and I pull up beside it. As I do, I notice a head in the window of one of the other buildings. I battled to stay upright while walking over to the building, making the sign for sleeping to the two other faces now in the window. As I walk back to my motorcycle, a man comes out and I show him my flash card that says "I am traveling around the world for the disabled and would like to sleep here." He motions for me to come with him. I ride the motorcycle over to the main buildings, and took off what baggage I needed. We went inside their very humble dwelling of mud and brick with a earth floor; there's no electricity or running water

I sat down and the woman of the house, a hunch back who moved sideways, prepared tea. The man of the house was a polio victim and used crutches. Only the son, about 20, appeared to be healthy. As we drank our tea and looked at one another, I realized that these are Chinese and not Mongols. About 19:00, just before sunset, we ate dinner. Lord knows what it was. When it was time for bed, everybody - mom, dad, and son - slept on a cement slab heated by draft from the heater/stove that was fueled by dried animal dung. The stove is homemade, not manufactured. It contains a concrete base with a metal sheet over the top of it. The exhaust is drawn through the cement slab, heating the slab they sleep on. They put my bed right against the slab, next to the heater; it was a frame with a chain link across the bottom to support me. Putting my sleeping bag down on that, they started taking their clothes off to get into bed. When I take my pants down, they have a good look at my prosthesis. We all had a disability, and shared that in common. As we get undressed, they start cackling and laughing amongst themselves. I think to myself, "These people must be very cool by accepting this astronaut from a foreign world into their front yard, then inviting him to come in, eat, and go to bed with them." People never cease to amaze me.

We all crawled into bed to listen to a little radio with tinny sounding Chinese music for the next hour. As I listened to the wind roaring outside, and the sand blowing, I thought to myself, "I truly left China behind. I've covered 298 miles, of which 140 were on dirt, into another dimension this day. Last night's sounds of city are gone; tonight, the sounds of the Gobi.

The next morning, after some tea I took my gear out to the motorcycle, loaded it, and gave the father a pack of Marlboro cigarettes. I knew he would have been insulted had I offered him money. Marlboros are something that he had probably only heard about; now, he truly had his own pack! There was a look of absolute delight on this man's face. The poor mom didn't get anything except a nod of thanks from me.

Off again into the wind and dust that was still howling and blowing at the same force of yesterday. It is all I can do to keep from being knocked off the motorcycle. Mind you, I am in second gear and not going any faster than 15 mph (25 kph), and constantly watching the compass. I am not on any proper roads - just tracks, and they go every which direction. I know sooner or later I will hit the rail head.

About 09:00 I come onto the railhead and follow it north into a small town where I fueled up at a petrol station, not knowing what to expect up ahead. The wind was freezing cold, and the temperature was down to about 20 or 25 degrees with the wind chill factor. Before I left that station, I experienced Chinese hospitality in the form of rice cakes and tea served to me; it helped get the sand out of my mouth.

The Dastardly Desert Attacks

The only feature I've seen in this desert so far was a cemetery before I came into the town, and a single power line. I had the railway to my right side as I went north, and soon came upon unexpected soft sand and went down. The sand storm is even worse now in this area of sand dunes, the first I've hit, and the sand is flying around while I do my best to keep my face covered and shield my swollen lips. What do I do now? The only thing I can do - unload the motorcycle to upright it! Ahead of me I see that the dunes gets worse, so I decide to turn around, but am unable to do it because my motorcycle is down inside a track which is about 2 feet deep.

I wait patiently, for what I don't know. After about thirty minutes, believe it or not, along comes a tractor with three Chinese on it. They jump off and they help me get the motorcycle up onto level ground above the track so I can turn it around. They jump back into the tractor and take off, waiving. I thought to myself, "I don't blame you for going." I tried to make my way out of this sand and fell off another half dozen times in the next half an hour just going a mere 150 meters back to hard ground. Each time I fall I must pick up the motorcycle with no load on it. In soft sand, once going forward, my right foot often slides from underneath me. Down goes the motorcycle again. My other problem is the right side where my mechanical knee doesn't have the strength I need to hold the motorcycle as I walk it through the sand with the motor running.

Finally back on hard track, I walk back 150 meters and pick up the 7 1/2 gallon drum of gas, all my tools, all the other baggage and carry them back to the motorcycle - about 250 pounds of gear in 4 different trips. On the way back, the wind knocks me off my feet at least six times. I refuse to let it unnerve me; I'm numb to it. I don't curse, I don't bitch, I simply get up, pick it up, and walk as far as I can go until I get knocked off my feet again.

When the motorcycle is loaded, I search for another way out. I ride back down the railway line, spotting where the dirt track crossed the railway. As I go across, somehow I get on a wrong track again, one that leads deeper into the dunes. I manage to turn around, but still fall off. Same exercise again.

Finally, I spot high ground and think "Maybe it is a road under construction with a hard base underneath it. In the meantime, I'm still being blasted by sand and wind howling at 60 or 70 knots, maybe faster. The noise was so loud that you would have to scream to be heard by a person standing directly in front of you. It is like being next to a jet engine or in a massive wind tunnel. As I beat along this high ground, I start north again along the western side of the railway. After going along about a half mile, the wind knocks me completely off of the motorcycle, right on the edge of an embankment.

The motorcycle is laying on top, and I roll down a 2 foot embankment. I get up and once again start the exercise - unload the motorcycle, etc. One problem: for the next half hour I can't get the machine up any higher than my chest. When I step forward, because the embankment was as high as it was, and I was standing on the small beveled slope, I was never able to get a good footing. The left foot kept sliding out from under me, and the motorcycle would fall back down.

No way I was going to get this thing up by myself. So, I turned around and covered myself with a pancho in this icy sand blaster to wait out the storm, however long it would be. My gasoline and the battery water leaking. Alone in the sand, I thought about when my father and grandparents were alive, about the holidays when the whole family was together sharing food and a warm family atmosphere. I thought about women, and about the past difficulties in my life, the things I've lived through. I tried to think about anything but that "BASTARD" motorcycle that I couldn't pick up, or about being in the frozen Gobi Desert, thousands of miles from home.

At times like these it brings home to me the cheap and shallow symbols we westerners hold onto that have absolutely no meaning in the Gobi. This is a place of survival, not of big egos or materialism. People who live here exist by a different code.

For hours I sit through this storm, reflecting over the years of my life. The struggle of serving in four different armies. The hundreds of faces of soldiers that I had struggled through so much with. The 9 1/2 months in the hospital in South Africa. The operations, the amputations, the pain, the disappointment, the depression, and the conquering of all these things, culminating in me sitting in this frozen desert weathering this terrible storm.

Suddenly, about 19:00, the wind stopped as if someone threw a switch. It didn't die down - it just stopped. The desert went from horrific noise to absolute silence. I came out from underneath the tarp, and saw half the stuff on the motorcycle was buried, and looked around me as the dust is settling. With my heart palpitating, I stagger around. I'm not the steadiest person on my feet normally, and less so in sand like this, trying to come to grips with the sudden silence.

Surveying the world around me, I realized that I hadn't been so totally alone. Off in the distance was a shepherd on a mule. I waived to him and he came over to help me lift the motorcycle up and turn it around. I would go no further on this day. After giving this man a handful of cigarettes, which he gratefully accepted, he was on his way and I was alone once more. I rolled out my sleeping bag, sat back with some sandy bread and cheese, my mouth full of sand anyway, crunching away at dinner, Gobi style. My water bottle was a block of ice. Darkness comes while I'm eating a very humble meal. I realized that there was no moon this night, and the stars were so bright at this elevation of about 6,000 feet in a unpolluted land that they seemed so close I could reach up and touch them. The silence was so complete that I could hear my heart beating. "How wonderful it is to lie here totally alone," I thought, "to be as one with God and not have people standing around looking at me." For the first time in months and months I was really alone.

After a peaceful night, I awoke around 05:30 to a little bird twittering very close to me. I climbed out of the sleeping bag and put on my legs. When I went to take a drink of water to wash some of the sand out of my mouth, the water was still frozen. The biggest question of the day is whether or not the motorcycle will start. There's no help within miles. I hit the starter button and it groans, but then fires - the day begins. As I straddle the thing and start moving, I decide to get back over to the other side of the railway tracks. The shepherd of the night before had kept pointing over there, so I figured he was trying to tell me there was a main track.

As I made it to the railway tracks, I realized that I had turned north too soon yesterday. I followed a track and found a main thoroughfare, just sand and dirt, but it was bigger than anything I had been on; this was the most traveled route.

As I started, I noticed three Chinese tractors in front of me running in tandem; I figured if "I can get in front of these guys, if I fall off, I know they will stop and help me." I rode a little faster than normal to pass the tractors, waiving "Hello, hello." They smile as I pass them. It wasn't two minutes after that I hit a deep sand drift and go down, trapped under the motorcycle. As I make a feeble effort to dig myself out, the tractors arrive. The men jump off and pick up the motorcycle. In sign language, I tell them that "I am willing to pay them to take the baggage and allow me to ride in front of them so they can pick up the motorcycle if I fall." Everybody agrees. So, my baggage comes off of the machine and on we go. I fell off the motorcycle time and time again during the rest of that morning as we went another 80 miles (130 km) through these sand drifts where the track constantly switches back on itself. I can't get up enough speed to hit the drift quick enough to get over it. These guys repeatedly stop, pick the motorcycle up, and take off again.

We come into a little village in the late morning. On the way into the village, I take my last dump of the day, and they pick it up. To thank them, I paid them 50 RMB each, maybe a bit much, but they had worked hard, were very poor, needed the money, and what would I have done without them?

Around 09:00, the wind started up again, so we had beat our way through the sand storm and out onto hard ground by the time we made it to this little village. I put my baggage back onto the motorcycle and started north for Erhot, about another 15 miles (25 km) on a very rough but beautiful paved road. My rear shock absorbers were finished, so the back of the motorcycle was bouncing constantly.

Perturbed Police and Welding Wonders

In Erhot, I fueled up then moved into the city proper where a policeman started motioning me to go towards a building where I saw soldiers standing outside. I went over and the soldiers motioned me to stop. As I got off the motorcycle, they took my passport and are shouting to each other. They brought somebody forward who could speak a bit of English, and he asked me, "What are you doing up here coming through a restricted area?" I explained, "I am on an around the world trip and am on my way to Mongolia."

"How did you get here?"

"I crossed the desert from Zhang Jai Kou."

Again, they chattered amongst themselves in disbelief that I had come across alone. I then produced a stack of newspaper articles and the letter that Yin Li had given me. It was a very strong letter of all my virtues, and told how much I had helped Chinese disabled and the Hope Project. They looked at this letter, plus all the newspaper articles. Now they face a bit of a quandary. If they sent me back, I could go to the newspapers and embarrass them terribly with the fact that I had beaten their security system. More chatting. I look out the window and heard a big commotion, then see the motorcycle on it's side. There had been a big crowd around it, and the Chinese like to touch and fondle, never malicious, just extremely inquisitive. As I ran outside with my so called interpreter behind me yelling, I realized the kick stand had broken. We uprighted the machine and wheeled it over to a building and left it standing there.

Now what? As I despaired, the interpreter has a rat-faced grin on his face. He tells me, "You are going to go to a hotel until arrangements can be made for you to travel across the border, or not travel across." Now, my heart is in my throat. "What will happen now?"

"We will only know by tomorrow." he says with his rat grin.

Two security police in a jeep escort me over to a hotel where the motorcycle is secured, and I take my baggage piece by piece upstairs. This hotel is a real shithole. As usual, the toilets are plugged up and stinking, and the halls are covered with spit. The overall smell is of rot, and my room smelled like someone had shit in the corner the night before.

Once settled into my little corner of paradise, somebody told me through the interpreter, "I can have your kick stand welded." As I take it apart, I realize how difficult it is to weld, and explain to them how the edges will need to be beveled down. I hear that familiar "Ma vin ti," - "no problem" - so I start to worry. An hour later he returns, but the kick stand is not like I wanted it. I put it back on and test it; it seems to hold.

That evening some people come over and invite me to dinner. The man is disabled, and so is his daughter; these Mongolians own a little restaurant in a gher (a giant tent). With my so called interpreter, Ho from the Army, I ride on the back of his motorbike over to the gher where we have a huge dinner placed before us. Once again, a "simple meal" turns into a massive banquet. Then, they want to take photographs for the next 45 fucking minutes; photographing and toasting. In the meantime, I feel like I am literally going to shit in my pants! There was no polite way for me to say I needed to get out of there, and every time we were ready to leave, somebody else would produce a camera.

Finally we get away. I have got a death's head grin on my face from squeezing my cheeks together to try and hold off Mother Nature's onslaught. We go to the hotel and I very quickly say goodnight to the misinterpreter, racing up stairs to find one of the least plugged up toilets to relieve myself. I closed my day in suspense, not knowing what tomorrow would bring.

In the morning the interpreter said, "You will have to wait a few hours as a Chinese official has gone over to the Mongolians to see if it is okay for you to come across." Mind you, they have my passport. I haven't seen it since the day before.

It is a big worry. I sit in suspense for the next few hours in this miserable, concrete military city full of dust and debris. Finally, the word comes down that "You are going to be allowed to pass. Please follow us."

I follow the security police on my motorcycle, but their jeep stalls and they have a hand crank to start it up again when the battery fails; it is a Beijing Jeep. We finally arrive at a massive supply depot. I think, "Man, no wonder they don't want anybody up here." At the border outpost, I am not allowed to even get off the motorcycle. A Chinese Army officer takes my passport, picks through the pages, stamps it, hands it back to me, and says, "Zoa Mongo" meaning "Go Mongolia." I put that motorcycle into gear and got out of there before they could change their minds! "Good by, rat face," I thought, "enjoy your lovely world."

Money, Monks and Mercedes

As I rode through this new land, a bus load of Mongolians were standing outside their bus. I waived my hand as I passed, and they all started jumping up and down saying what I hoped was "Welcome to Mongolia." About 30 seconds later, I almost fell on my ass going through a sand drift, but luckily I was going fast enough to overcome it.

At the gates entering Mongolia, the guards come out and shake my hands. They are armed with AK 47s, dressed in full military uniforms, and they start handing me money! "What a wonderful bunch of guys," I thought. Later, I learned the stack of money they had given to me was the equivalent of about ten cents; Mongolian money was virtually worthless. The portrait on the bills was of Comrade Choybulson, one of the most vicious butchers Mongolia ever knew. In the 30's he had approximately 30,000 Buddhist monks executed; Choybulson was the Stalin of Mongolia. After their independence, the Mongolians still hadn't bothered to take his ugly face off of their currency.

After the guards stamped my passport, they motioned me to sit. "What's up now?" I thought to myself. After about 15 minutes, a Mercedes no headlights, no hubcaps, and with all the windows broken out drives up. The vehicle was beat up beyond recognition except for the hood ornament, still shinny. Out steps the mayor of Zimun Un, a Mongolian border city. He walks over to me, flanked by his bodyguards, shakes my hand, and utters something totally incomprehensible to me. Then, he gets back into his Mercedes and motions for me to follow him. We purr along for a few minutes, then they suddenly make a sharp stop at a checkpoint; the guard seemed to appear out of no where. As I hit my brake, my foot slips off the rear brake on this gravel road. Mind you, I don't have a front brake because the brake line had broke a few days ago. The only thing I can do besides run into the back of the mayor's Mercedes is drive over an embankment in the road and onto a sand drift with concertina wire on top of it.

Into the concertina wire I go, bogging down into the sand. I do not move, knowing that if I start trying to move around, this razor wire will cut me to pieces. The mayor and his five guards get out of the Mercedes, roaring with laughter at this crazy foreigner. They come over and start cutting the wire away, then we push the motorcycle back out of the sand and up onto the road where I proceed to follow the mayor into the city.

He pulls into a big open yard outside of the train station where there's a crowd of about fifty people. Again, he stops before I expect it; I hit the brake, but can't make a full and quick stop with just the rear brake. Again, two options: lay the motorcycle down, or hit the Mercedes. Down I went. I got up off the ground, bowed to the crowd standing there awe struck, mouths open. They are probably thinking, "This clown thinks he is going to cross the rest of the Gobi desert on his own? How did he get this far?"

We lifted up the motorcycle, then I was invited inside for a simple lunch of lamb and rice. One person in the town spoke about six words of English, so Oaucher became the interpreter, stammering and shouting intensively as the same six words kept coming out of his mouth. At least he didn't "Ya, ya, ya" me. He had mastered "I don't understand," then would turn and tell the others whatever he thought they wanted to hear.

After lunch, I asked "Is anybody is going north?"

They did not know of anyone.

"Well, I go Ulan UI," I told them, preparing to leave. Ulan UI was about 75 miles (120 km) away, so I still had time to make it that day. They nod, then lead me in a jeep out of town, watching me fall off the motorcycle three more times! Mind you, the wind is howling, so huge sand drifts have formed amongst the town's buildings on the road. Some are two feet deep, and you can't ride over them - or through them. Of course, I fall off. As people help me up, I'm sure they are asking themselves as they shake their heads, "How is this fool ever going to do it?"

When we arrive at the north side of Zimun Un, we shake hands and nod good-bye as I take off alone, trying to keep the machine in second gear, at about 20 mph (32 kph), as long as I can, along with the ground, the gravel, the sand and the wind.

Watching my compass, my path towards the northwest is moving away from the railway tracks and telephone line, so I don't see much for a landmark except an occasional gher, a Mongolian tent, usually with camels and sheep poking around. For the next 75 miles (120 km), there are no other signs of civilization.

In a series of dips and potholes, I get tossed off the motorcycle. My drill is always the same: unload, lift up, get out of hole, go back and fetch the gear, reload, start motorcycle, get going. After a few hours of this routine, I finally hit a rise, and spot Ulan UI in the distance. I thought to myself, "Perhaps I should just spend the night out here and avoid a leering crowd." Then I think, "Maybe the mayor called ahead and told them I was coming. If I don't come, they'll probably start worrying and send out a search party. After all, my performance was less than confidence inspiring in Zimun Un."

I opted to deal with crowds gawking at me all night rather than worry others unnecessarily. Riding down into Ulan UI just before sunset, the wind quiets down, and the freezing cold of the Gobi desert at night starts to set in.

In town, I locate an abandoned official building and pulled in. Soon, a policeman with one eye appears; in my mind, I dub him "evil eye" because when he took my passport, he turned his head to one side and glared down on it with his beady eye. After examination, he returns my passport and he points in another direction. I know he probably wants me to stay somewhere else, but I tell him, "No problem. I'll sleep here...on the ground."

As we talk, here comes the crowd! People are everywhere.

He is nodding, saying "Nayet," speaking to me in Russian, the Mongolian's second language. It was clear that I must follow so he does not lose face. Finally, I nodded and started to load my motorcycle. "Nayet, nayet," he tells me, instructing the crowd to grab my stuff and bring it on their shoulders. They start walking, and the policeman climbs on the back of motorcycle with me and guides me through this little village with no paved road - just sand and gravel, and very dreary looking buildings.

We arrive at a set of these buildings where we stop and he orders a few of the hardier boys to push the motorcycle up 3 or 4 steps into a kind of a kitchen area. He leads me into another room where the crowd drops my gear.

Very quickly I'm learning that Mongolians are very aggressive helpers. I think to myself, "I've got to watch them so they don't grab the wrong stuff and break a lever or some sensitive piece of equipment." They want to help so badly, and I'm just concerned that they might unwittingly break something. I'm prepared to yell at them to "stop," because I've learned you must shock them before they realize there's a problem.

Once the motorcycle is secure, I'm brought another meal of lamb, rice, boiled fat, and excellent Mongolian bread, plus fried balls of dough, simple and tasty. The top village official, Mr. Tazserin, entered while I was eating, and introduced himself. The crowd around me was now drinking vodka, and they offered me some. I refused. Later that evening, about 22:30, two Mongolian girls who are trying to learn English made an effort to speak a few words; we talked broken English back and forth for the next hour. Finally, I signaled that I wanted to sleep. Mr. Tazsernin started shouting, and the crowd disappears.

Settling back into quiet and comfort of a hard bed with plenty of blankets, in this very humble surrounding, I closed the day.

The next morning as I started to carry my bags outside, the crowds again appeared and started helping me. As I tried to load the motorcycle, it took everything I could do to keep them from helping me; they were more of a problem than a solution. In the chaos, I heard a "crack" and the motorcycle fell; the kick stand had broken again. "Man, it is a good thing I didn't sleep out last night!" I thought. "How would I have gotten the thing up and loaded out in the desert on my own?" Mr. Tazsernin looked at the kick stand and said "Nayet problem," making the sound of a welding machine.

They bring up a motorbike, and I am told to follow him on my motorcycle. In the freezing cold, with wind howling, we rode down a hard gravel track, heading directly east for about 25 miles (40 km). At one point, they stop for everybody to smoke a cigarette. I took a photograph of a featureless landscape high above the beautiful desert - magnificent if you like desert.

We finally entered a little village and stopped at a maintenance depot for heavy equipment. Obviously, by the looks of the machines, there were mines in the area (what they mined, I don't know). Some Russians looked at the kick stand while I tried to explain what I wanted - beveled edges, then weld it - which they did. They also welded my rear brake pedal which was ready to break (then I would have had no brakes!). Once done, we ate a simple meal. The Mongolians diet seems far less complicated than that of the Chinese. Mongolians eat to live; Chinese live to eat.

After we had something to eat, they bag the leftovers and present them to me. Every body shakes hands. One man gives me a Buddhist bible, and another pins a little metal on my chest with a figure out of their mystical past. In the midst of these ceremonies, I ask "Ulan-Bataar?", and they point to the north west. I nod "Thank you," knowing I have about 300 miles (500 km) ahead of me before I see the capital city.

Off I go, and in about 50 miles (80 km) I hit the town of Saynshand. Luckily, I came directly upon the tank farm which housed the only two gasoline pumps in the area. Saynshand is an abandoned Russian mining area or military base (I was never clear which).

I carry 9 extra gallons of gasoline to cover emergencies, including the possibility of getting lost. Towns are often 130 miles (200 km) apart, and when you get to that town, they might not have gasoline. My top speed on these roads is about 20 mph (32 kph), so fuel consumption is higher than normal.

Since my shock absorbers are shot, the ride is extremely rough as I'm beaten and bounced off the seat regularly. My ass and back are just taking a whale of a pounding.

Out of Saynshand, I continue north the rest of the afternoon. At about 17:00, I just stop for the night. If you want to stop in the desert, just stop. No one will come along. There will be no one to hassle you or gawk at you.

I stop the motorcycle, shut it off, and spend the next hour working on it. Next, I spread out my tarp and my sleeping bag, eat some of the leftovers and wait for the starry, beautiful night to come. About 19:00 the wind stops.

Gobi nights are the quietest I have ever experienced. At times like these I become very much one with God and Jesus Christ; I can feel their presence since there's nothing around to distract me from spiritual feelings.

After a peaceful night, I wake up to a frozen world. Temperatures are falling drastically. When the weather is this cold, putting on my legs sure shrivels the old dinky right up. Of course, my main worry is "Will the motorcycle start?" After more leftovers, I load the machine then hit the starter button - the moment of truth. It fires right up!

Leftover Lenins and Vodka Victories

The sand and wind are flying in flurries, and I battle through it, carefully watching my compass since there are no landmarks, and visibility is often down to just a few hundred meters. As I bounce my way along, I start to enter the city of Choy. On the outskirts of the city I discover an abandoned Russian Army Base; the scene felt very eerie as the sand and wind blew through the abandoned buildings. There were painted logos on the cement walls of the different armored units - soldiers in tanks, holding AK 47s, the hammer and sickle in the back ground. These were the power symbols of a now crumbled empire, left to be consumed by the merciless Gobi desert.

In Choy, I saw the biggest statute of Lenin I was ever to personally see. It stood about 45 yards (meters) high; unfortunately, I couldn't get a photograph of it because it was surrounded by flying sand. At one point, the wind was so fierce that it knocked me off of the motorcycle; some Mongols nearby helped me upright the machine. Once up and away, I started searching for a petrol station.

Eventually, I came to another tank farm. I had navigated the last 40 miles (60 km) on compass alone. When I pull up to the pump, I take my gas cap off as quickly as I can to get the least amount of sand in the tank as possible. Wouldn't you know it - there was no electricity! I left the motorcycle in front of the pump and the lady points at the lights as if to say "We have no electricity." She then motioned for me to sit down on the couch; I sit for the next two hours.

Two Mongols show up on a little motorcycle. What they were doing out in that kind of weather is anybody's guess. They had a camera, and wanted to take photographs, so we pushed the motorcycle to the side of the building, out of the wind and sand, and took photographs. As we talked, the electricity came back on, and I fueled up.

One Mongol motions for me to come with him, and I realize I am trapped. Since it is late in the afternoon, I thought, "Well, I can't really turn away from this man's kindness; it will hurt his feelings." So, I follow him across town to his front yard where I am promptly knocked over by the wind. We pick up the motorcycle and move it inside his house! There's no running water, but the house was meticulously clean. The man is a huge Mongol, about 6 feet, 6 inches, and real broad. As is often the case, he was gentle. Somehow, his friends know I'm here, and start coming over. Soon, the room is packed with people, all drinking vodka and talking to each other. They keep offering me a drink and I keep saying, "No, no."

For the next six hours this goes on! Drinking. Eating. Talking. Finally, the crowd left and we closed the day.

The next morning, very early, I rolled the motorcycle out, started it up, and followed this fellow out of town as he pointed northwest, saying "Ulan-bataar" pointing again to the northwest.

As I rode through the icy cold morning, the wind and the sand were merciless. About midday, I discovered another abandoned Russian Army Base, and couldn't find my way around it. Finally, I see a road across some tracks going up the side of a hill, and follow them up some very steep grades. From there, there was no track at all, except animal tracks which followed the contour of the huge hill. I think to myself, "If it had rained, I would never be able to manipulate this terrain in the mud." Even though the ground was firm, it was still difficult on some of these ledges which empty into steep valleys. Some tracks appear to be from camel caravans pulling wagons.

Once, I came upon a caravan, and motioned the guys over to the motorcycle so we could take a few photographs.

Eventually, I realized I was no longer in the Gobi Desert, and must be getting very near to Ulan-bataar. I was right. Over a rise in the distance I spot a concrete road which led into Ulan-bataar. I headed toward the road, but ended up in a bog area, going in circles. Finally, I realized that the only way to get to the road was through a stream. I searched for shallow areas, and discovered a place where it was only 3 meters across, and about 1 1/2 feet deep.

Getting a flying start, I hit the water. Fortunately, it was clear enough that I could see the bottom, avoiding big rocks and managing to get across without stalling the motorcycle. At last, I hit my well-earned reward - the concrete road. I brought the machine up into third gear. It felt like I was flying! When I shifted to fourth gear at 50 mph, I felt like I was getting ready to take off for the moon!!! What a joy to experience this very rough concrete road for the last 10 miles (16 km) into Ulan-bataar.

Once there, I approached some soldiers and asked directions to the Disabled Federation by displaying a small note I had written in Mongolia by the embassy in China. The Lieutenant instructed one of his soldiers to show me the way. For the next mile, this soldier ran in front of me with his tongue hanging out. We finally came to a dilapidated building with a gher in the back. He pointed at the building, saluted, and took off running back to his detachment.

People started pouring out of the building. A massive burn victim came up to me and shook my hand, babbling away as he handed me his card; one side is written in Mongolian, the other in English. Mr. Batachulaan took me to the gher where I would be staying for the next few days.

I was amazed at the inside of this gher. The frame and structure of this massive tent was all hand painted very ornately with different Mongolian designs in red and gold. The scenes had something to do with past battles and glories of the Mongolian Empire. There was a stove, a big table and two beds with satin covers on them. "What an incredible place," I thought. "I never had a tent like this when I was in the Army."

The man now places a call to the American Embassy, and the lady on the phone who could speak English acted as our translator! One thing I asked for was a shower; in the six days since I left China, I'd not had one opportunity to clean up. Upon hearing my request, we all piled into a Mercedes and drove across town to where they had a shower (the tent had no shower, no toilet, no running water). What a wonderful treat! A hot shower! As it turns out, that was the only one I'd get during my five days in Ulan-bataar.

Feeling fresh, we headed back to the gher where I met a young Mongolian girl named Lamsaren, and she served as the interpreter, introducing me to the fellows who owned the Mercedes. We were able to communicate thanks to Lamsaren. She told me, "You stay here for five days. Many people want meet you. We hold ceremony. You meet many disabled people. Be on television."

"I need to do repairs on the motorcycle," I told her.

"In the morning," she replied.

We sat down to a meal with plenty of vodka. These fellows were fairly aggressive, insisting that I drink. I had to tip the glass up to my lips, pretending to drink. When I put it down, they would try and pour more vodka in, and of course, it would always spill over. Somehow, this solution seemed to make them happy. Naturally, everyone but me was roaring drunk before the evening party ended. As I settled in for the night, I realized that I was possibly **the first westerner to cross the Gobi Desert alone, south to north, on a motorcycle.**

The next morning, as soon as I was up, people came in from the kitchen in the building next door to the gher. The women started preparing the table as Mr. Batachulaan arrived with Lamsaren. We sat down to a breakfast of fat, rice and lamb - a cardiologist's nightmare. They eat this way to ward the cold off. After eating, they wheeled my motorcycle out, a major concern. All I need is for them to break something that cannot be replaced.

I followed them across the city to a garage. As I ride, I notice that this city is very spread out, not nearly as crowded as the cities in China. The civilian buildings are mundane blocks of cement; government buildings are quite grand in their designs. I often pass Mongolians on ponies riding through the streets. Others lead camels, There are some cars and bicycles, but certainly nothing like China.

Mechanical Marvels and Purification Folly

At the garage, I spend the rest of the day repairing the front brake. The rear brake linings have come off, scaring the inside of the brake drum. Mechanics put a new lining on, cutting it to measure; how they did it, I don't know. To get the fit right, they'd just grind off a little here and there until it worked. Also, the rear fender and rack was repaired. I needed brake fluid, but they only had a little bit left - but just enough. I said, "No, you keep it," but they insisted I use what they had left.

At the end of the day, we went to the American Embassy where I met the staff. One man was a Vietnam Veteran now working for the State Department; he had part of his foot missing from the war. We chatted about our military experiences. When we started to leave, I noticed a case of brake fluid on the floor. "Would it be possible to get a bottle?" I asked. Another fellow pipes up, "You can **buy** one." I tried to explain to that cheap prick that my intent was to buy one all along.

My veteran friend saw the conflict, and said "You will not buy one." I explained about the Mongolian mechanics who had given me their last bit of brake fluid, and how they accepted no money after helping me all day. "It would be a nice gesture if I could give them a bottle of brake fluid in return."

"Here, you take it."

The dick head looks on, red with embarrassment. Again, I offer to pay, but the veteran says, "No. I won't hear of it."

In my tour of the city, I saw a monastery built in the sixteen hundreds. Of course, we traveled everywhere in the black Mercedes; Moenang was the driver, and stood about six foot four, and was as wide as a house. He could have been Genghis Khan's bodyguard. His flat, beat-up face reflected a mean looking character.

Before we entered the monastery, we marched around the building spinning brass and steel drums that were to bring us good luck. In the temple, I saw ceramic, painted Buddha's - gold Buddha's - all behind glass cases. Everywhere, monks were chanting. The scene was very mystical!

We visited the vice-mayor of Ulan-bataar, the head of finance, the head of the armed forces, and countless other dignitaries. They presented me with books, gifts and other things I can never carry with me. After awhile, it dawns on me that Batachulaan and the other people escorting me around are all Army Officers. Batachulaan, a major burn case, was caught in an office fire as he tried to save the furniture.

When he was recuperating, the doctors did not want him out in public, so he told me he used to tie bed sheets into a rope and scurry down the four story building to go see his friends. This with burns and bandages! Now I understand why he is the head of the Disabled Federation.

The following day was spent with the media at a big hall where I met more officials and was entertained by a Mongolian dance team consisting of both men and women. Naturally, speeches were given, and I gave my usual speech. Next, I was awarded the Genghis Khan metal for having crossed the Gobi Desert.

I met a young soldier who had shot himself in the leg; he begged me to take him to America where he could have an operation done to repair the leg. There was nothing I could do, and felt so disappointed with my own inability to help him. I ran into this problem on numerous occasions, but sadly, these problems are out of my financial league. I vowed that someday, if ever I receive enough money, I will form a foundation to assist disabled people like this poor man.

The next day, they held a ceremony with another crowd of people. Women chanted and sang, throwing goats milk all over the motorcycle. Lamsaren said, "This will purify motorcycle." "You will never purify that greasy son of a bitch," I think to myself. That done, an old lady presents me with a Buddhist ring with a very peculiar red stone on it. I've never seen one like it. It is red right in the middle. The lady tells me, "Give this to your mother at the end of journey. It will protect you." Next, I receive a scarf called a "hataok"; they put it on the handlebars of the motorcycle to purify and protect the machine.

Finally, the ceremony ended with hugs and kisses. Moenang, Batachulaan, and a few others then led me out of Ulann-baatar where it was lightly snowing and horribly cold. This wretched weather reminded me that I am now on the edge of the Siberia's.

Once again, my escorts climbed out of their car and performed yet another ceremony, throwing vodka to the west, then taking another glass of vodka and throwing it up into the wind and snow. Everybody then gave everyone else a kiss on the lips. Batachulaan was crying. It was with my usual heavy heart that I started the motorcycle and left Ulan-bataar and these very kind people behind.

I journeyed north over a horribly rough tar road where my maximum speed was between 30 to 35 mph (50 kph). I am bounced and hammered up and down on this rough road; often, the wind is knocked right out of me. About mid morning, my motor starts missing, so I pull off the road and discover that the points are burnt. I clean them, and put on a new condenser. A man in a tractor stops, motioning that he saw me on television. He shakes my hand, and I'm on my way.

The landscape is rolling hills and mountains snow covered in the distance. I ride through my last miserable looking city at the border in Mongolia, all gray cement and square corners, with broken up concrete streets covered with mud.

4,500 Miles to Moscow!

At the border I change into my Konsamolka Pravda T-shirt, as Andri told me to do, and **crossed over to Russia** where those I passed seemed to be saying, "Who is this foreigner - this JERK - who is coming into our territory dressed like a fool with this T-shirt on?" They examine my papers and see my official visa, but cannot believe what they see. The sponsoring newspaper is supposed to meet me at the border, and bring me money to change into rubbles, plus a dictionary and a road map. However, the Konsamolka correspondent is nowhere to be seen. The soldiers take three hours to place a phone call through to Moscow to determine if I am authentic or not. As they try to place the call, I think, "No wonder their empire fell apart. They can't communicate."

When they finally do make a connection, it is too late in the day for me to go on, so the soldiers carry my motorcycle up a flight of stairs to a patch of grass between two Russian Army Barracks. There, I put up my tent for the night! The soldiers bring me dinner - a white porridge, hard bread and tea. After my meal, I retire, grateful that the Russian soldiers didn't stand around gawking.

A man in a black leather long coat walked up to my tent and stared at me. I thought, "Maybe this guy is going to flash me." I assume he is some sort of security man. The man spoke no English, but indicated that he wanted me to stay in a hotel. I made it clear that I did not want to leave the motorcycle or my gear behind. He looked quite perplexed, obviously not accustomed to hearing "No."

He went away and I closed my day.

The next morning I moved all my gear back downstairs; the soldiers moved the motorcycle for me. About this time, the base commander shows up and drives me over to the main armor corps base where we have a very welcome breakfast in the officer's mess. I imagine the man's rank was that of at least a Colonel (little did he know that he was eating with a corporal).

After breakfast, he took my gas can and filled it up. I wanted to ask him about a map, but I didn't know the Russian word for it, and had no dictionary. I also didn't know the Russian words for changing dollars to rubbles. Clearly, my contact, the correspondent with the newspaper, was not going to show up.

Back at the motorcycle, I loaded and started up with the Russian commander standing there with his troops behind him in formation. As I warmed up the motorcycle, he salutes me and says something. I can only imagine he was saying. "The word in Russia, my boy, is tuff shitsky!" With the thought of that salutation ringing in my ear, I put the motorcycle in gear and started across Russia with no Russian money, no road map, no dictionary and no means to communicate...and Moscow is only 4500 miles (6300 km) away.

Oh yes, I do have a map - a 1964 National Geographic Map of Asia.

What else could I possibly want?

Ze Qing - A True Friend
April 1993

L to R - unknown, Lesia, André, Dave and Ze Qing
Taken at Beijing Film Academy
April 1993

Chapter Thirty-Two

American Disappears in Russia!

Mayday, May 1st: In the bitter cold I watched the sun disappear as it started to snow on this reasonably good road through the mountains. Lakes and rivers with ice were lined by plush forests. Soon I was on a dirt road, and by late morning I entered Ulan-Ude, the capital of Balaute.

I journeyed west along the southeast side of Lake Baykal - the deepest fresh water lake in the world; it appeared to be frozen. The road was extremely rough. I mean rough! I was bouncing off the seat regularly. No potholes, just lots of rough road. Despite the banging and beating of the road, I made about 300 miles (500 km) that day before entering the small town of Bikalisk where I began looking for gasoline.

At the fire station I stop and say, "Beninze," meaning "gasoline." They answer "da," and take off my big gas can, filling it and my main tank by siphoning gas from one of the fire trucks. They make the sign of sleep and invite me to stay with them. I realize it would insult them if I did not accept their gesture. I agree to spend the night.

We wheeled the motorcycle around to the garage where I do some minor maintenance, then am led into the main barracks room where all the other firemen sleep. Most of them seem to be very jolly fellows, trying to communicate with me although there was no real communication. After dinner, everybody left me alone for the rest of the evening. They tried to get a phone line through to Irkutsk, the next major city in eastern Siberia on my way North West, but failed. It is hard for a westerner to imagine the communication difficulties. In Mongolia, it took two days to book a call to China, their neighbor.

After restless night's sleep (firemen kept coming in and out of the barracks's room), I rolled the motorcycle out and loaded it. They rolled out their biggest fire engine - it looked like a dinosaur compared to the equipment we have in the West. These men were very proud of that engine, and we took a photograph of the firemen, my motorcycle, and me. Next, they took a collection for me because I had mentioned "rubbles." I now had 2,000 rubbles, the equivalent of about $2.00 in American money. They would not accept any dollars in return.

The firemen led me out of town, shook hands, and saluted as I rode out on my 200 mile trip to Irkutsk, a major city on the southwest side of Lake Baykal. It was quite beautiful riding through the mountains and looking down onto the lake from 3,000 feet above. I passed huge logging operations on the side of this majestic, calm and peaceful lake.

What I didn't know was that this was the middle of a holiday weekend. It was Sunday, and as I moved into Irkutsk, I stopped and tried to ask directions to an address that I had received from the Pravda Correspondent. People kept pointing. Once, when I stopped to ask directions, two drunks, a man and a woman, tried to climb onto the back of the motorcycle. I had shove them away, and got the hell out of there before I had any more trouble with them.

I find my way out of Irkutsk, and ask if there is a telephone anywhere. "No. No working telephone." I spot a phone booth, but both phones were smashed, and the sides of the booth were shattered. It was very depressing. I decided to spend the night out of town, somewhere in the hills, and search again tomorrow.

I found a dirt road about 5 miles out of town, leading back into the forest, where I came to a rock quarry. I placed my motorcycle in the back of the rock quarry, out of sight, and put up the tent, relaxing and reading the rest of the afternoon, enjoying the peace, and being alone, not having to try and communicate.

The following morning on my way back to Irkutsk, I stopped at the police box on the outskirts of the city and showed the policeman the letter from the correspondent. He didn't really know what to do with the letter. About this time, a Mongolian came driving by and saw the motorcycle. He stopped, turned around and came back with his book for an autograph. The policeman must have thought I was somebody special.

The policeman then got on his radio and called for a police car to escort me down to the newspaper office in Irkutsk. The office was closed for the holiday; of course, I'm unaware that it is a three day weekend. The policeman then makes another phone call, motioning for me to just wait. He leaves. After about forty-five minutes, I go into the building to try and discover what happened to the policeman. I try to communicate, but the lady keeps pointing at the building next door. I show her my piece of paper with the Irkutsk phone number, and ask if she would try the number. "Nayet," she replies.

After waiting a full hour, I say "Piss on this place" and head out of town, finding the main road, and head for Krasnoyarsk, roughly 600 miles (1,000 km) from where I am in Irkutsk. At one point I stop to help a fellow motorcycle rider on a Ural with a sidecar. I tried to assist him, but he was too drunk; there was nothing I could do for him. I felt sorry for his wife and kids who were with him; what a terrible life they must have.

Later, I saw another motorcyclist pulled over to the side of the road with his wife - he needed gasoline, and was sober, so I put some gasoline into his tank.

The sun actually came out for awhile, making it pleasant, even though it was still quite cold. By the afternoon, I crossed through a farm community, and got a drink of water from a well that had a windup crank with a rope and a bucket on the bottom of the rope. I filled my water bottles to overflowing with this most wonderful tasting water! Kids were playing nearby, and gazed at me and my motorcycle in amazement. Later, I found a place in the woods on the edge of a pasture to I spend the night.

Rubbles, Bandits and Snowstorms

The following morning, snow was starting to come down as I traveled down a very rough dirt road. There's no warning when the dirt road starts. I'll be on pavement, then without warning, I hit dirt. As you can imagine, I am constantly knocked out of the seat, and find myself frequently gasping for air, the wind knocked out of me. My big problem is keeping my right leg on the brake because it keeps bouncing off. There are ice patches on the road, but they're not a big problem because they are usually mixed with rocks and gravel for traction.

The snow increases in intensity. When it stopped, rain would follow, creating mud. My speed is down to 15 mph (25 kph) or less. In a small village, I try to buy some bread for the night. When I stop and ask where I can buy bread, I somehow think that if I pronounced the word "b r e a d" slowly, they will understand. It doesn't work. Finally, one man says "Magazina, magazina." I don't know what "magazina" is, but as I ride along, I think to myself, "Now wait a minute. A magazine holds things, such as ammunition, so maybe he is talking about a store." Soon, I saw what I thought was a "Magazina." I stop. Sure enough, it was a store! I buy a loaf of bread there for the equivalent of about 2 cents. It is a hard, grainy, dark bread, but quite tasty if you are very hungry.

That afternoon, as I was riding along, two Toyota cars pass me with right hand drives. I think to myself, "Maybe they were stolen from Hong Kong and have been brought overland. They're probably on their way to be sold on the black market." The drivers waive to me as we pass each other off and on during the day since they traveled faster on the paved roads, and I'd pass them on the dirt and mud sections. In the middle of a horrific snow storm late that afternoon, they flagged me down. I could see they were a couple of criminals.

One took a big knife out, and I instinctively grabbed both his hands, and to his disbelief, I shoved the knife back into the scabbard that was in his other hand. They told me they were from Valdivostock; I knew then that the cars must be stolen from Kong Hong.

I said "Dollars, rubbles," and they must have thought they were dealing with a crazy man; I had an advantage in that they were not dressed like I was. I was dressed for the cold, and they were standing out there shivering their asses off. We worked out a price with pen and paper, after the knife was put away. They realized they weren't going to rob me. I also had my gas out and was ready; they knew I wasn't defenseless. We came up with a price that was good for them and good for me. I changed 60 American dollars for Russian rubbles; in the end, everyone was happy. A policeman stopped and tried to question us; the criminal conduct took over, and we all acted as if nothing was wrong. The policeman shook his head, then left. So did we.

I stopped to get some water for cooking that evening, enjoying the change in scenery. I have been traveling through very forested areas, viewing gorgeous little farming communities where everything is built out of wood instead of the cement in a normal city. The houses are very homey.

It struck me as strange that even in these little communities I'd often see a statute of Lenin - never a very big one, but his face or figure were always present. Outside this one village I found a little track off into the forest, and took it back away from the road to where I couldn't be seen. A couple inches of snow were on the ground as I put up my tent and prepared for the evening. My camping ground was right next to the Trans-Siberian Railway. In the distance, I spotted a cemetery, and decided to go explore it a bit. One of the things I noticed over many of the graves was the hammer and sickle; on others, there were stars - some white, but most red. I wondered what these people had done with their lives in this remote area of Eastern Siberia.

My dinner consisted of bread, noodles, salami and onions. When I finished, I just bundled up in my sleeping bag, praying my motorcycle would start the next day.

To my great relief, the next morning, it started, firing up quite quickly, bellowing smoke everywhere (it is using a quart - liter of oil a day). When I had warmed up properly, I slip/slidded out of there in about 4 inches of snow to the main road. Eventually I came to a tarred road and had to ride off on the shoulder to keep from sliding.

At the next gas station, I went down on some ice. Truckers at the station came over and helped me get the motorcycle up and over to the pumps. When I went to the window to pre-pay for the gas, the Russian woman behind the bars in her kiosk - office - motioned for me to come in. I entered and stood in front of the heater for the next half hour. She gave me tea and cookies as I warmed up. Finally, I paid for my gasoline, went out and fueled up, and with the help of more truckers, pushed the motorcycle back onto the gravel where I could now ride. Later that day, the snow finally stopped and the wind blew. I don't know the exact temperature, but it was "Colder than a well-diggers ass in January."

I approach a police check and the policeman motioned me over and indicated that I am to enter his little hut. "What now?" I think. To my delight, the policeman makes me a sandwich and some tea. What a relief! I thought there was going to be trouble with something.

Back out into the cold, the snow starts falling again, and the wind continues to kick up. Extremely miserable! Finally, I enter Krasnoyarsk, a city that separates eastern and western Siberia. I go directly to the police box where the policeman reads my letter and then gets on the telephone. Shortly, a car arrives to escort me into Krasnoyarsk proper to the apartment block where Vasseli, the correspondent, and his wife, ELeana, live. We put the motorcycle in the police parking area where it will be safe, then return to their small apartment where Eleana immediately shows me the shower.

Late that afternoon, Vasseli makes a few phone calls to assure everybody that I am okay (obviously, nobody had known where I was). They knew I had entered Russia, but from there, I had virtually disappeared from their information network. Apparently, the correspondent in Ulan-Ude had let them down. The one in Irkutsk had been on his long week end, and did not expect me to arrive that soon. In fact, I learned that in the newspaper they had a headline that said, "Be on the look out for Dave Barr, an American who has disappeared in Russia!"

Paraplegic Racer and Hospital Drunks

In the early evening, a man named Leukum pulled up in a car; he was a paraplegic due to a motorcycle accident he had while serving in the Russian army, and was now paralyzed from just below his chest on down. Despite his handicap, Leukum was one of the most positive people I met in all of Russia. We went over to his house for dinner and conversation (Vasseli translated). One of Vasseli's friends, a man named Prophet, believe it or not, gave me a Russian-English dictionary to help me communicate. At Leukum's apartment, he had installed a motor to lift the garage door. He also had hand controls for his car, even though it had manual transmission. He looked like a helicopter pilot out of control, arms moving in every direction trying to shift, put the clutch in and out, then accelerate, all by hand! What a contraption. Leukum had built the apartment up for himself, including the ramp leading to the front door.

His mother and sister lived with him, and waited on us, serving the most mundane diet I've found anywhere in the world - basically potatoes, some salami, some bologna, cucumbers (always) and bread.

Leukum then took Vasseli and me on a tour in his hot rod around Krasnoyarsk. He took us to the river that flows through Krasnoyarsk, the river that separates east and west Siberia. We went helter skelter through the city; he scared the hell out of me as he dodged potholes, pedestrians, buses and other traffic. "Leukum has missed his calling in life," I told Vassel. "He should have been a rally driver!"

Back at Vasseli's apartment, we closed our day.

One thing I notice about Russians: when you go into their house, everybody takes off their shoes. No matter how old or beat up the apartment is, you take off your shoes. I also notice a strong stench of urine in the elevators, the hallways and stairwells leading to the apartments. Vasseli told me it is because "People take dogs out. Dogs piss in elevators. Sometimes drunks piss as well." Also, the clocks are different; I have traveled into my second time zone since leaving China.

The following day, I work on the motorcycle, changing the oil after being led by two fellows, Valodia and Victor, across Krasnoyarsk to a heavy equipment service depot. I was shocked at the amount of junk that was laying around the place. They assigned somebody to help me if I needed it. The depot was dark and dingy; I had found this is often the case with factories and other work places - both in China and in Russia.

As I worked, I was served lunch with the rest of the crew working there. When Valodia and Victor came back for me that afternoon, I kept saying "oil." showing them oil. They bring me 30 weight oil; I cannot use that in my engine since it is too light, and the engine will tear itself apart. I'd also heard that Russian oil is not noted for it's great quality. So, I made the sign for 50 weight oil.

"Oh, nayet," I hear, "that is not in Russia." Next, I make the sound of an airplane - blurrrrrrrrrrr - sticking my arms out like wings. They don't understand. I cannot ever begin to convey how difficult and frustrating it can be to try to get my point across in these situations, especially if the topic is the least bit technical. There are times I actually get headaches over these communication problems. It is like beating my head against a wall. Unfortunately, I had forgotten my dictionary on this day, so I keep saying "oil" and make like an airplane. They must have thought I was out of my mind! In the end, we called Vasseli and I explained to him what I needed.

Next, the men bring me jet oil, which won't work either since it is a synthetic oil and will not perform properly. It is still too light. Now I pretend to be a piston engine, making sputtering sounds. Finally, a light seems to go on and they bring me to an old airport where they gave me 10 liters of aircraft oil - roughly 55 or 60 weight. It was like glue, but thick enough to go into the older Harley Davidson and not hurt the lower part of the motor. Finally, I finished my service of the motorcycle and rode it back across town to the police barracks.

That evening we went to a meeting with the disabled. It was my first time to actually meet a disabled group in Russia. Though they treated me kindly, their attitude seemed very negative. They seemed to say, "Our life in Russia is very hard, and there's nothing we can do about it."

And their life is difficult here. For example, it is not uncommon for a paraplegic to be stuck up many stories in a building with no elevator. He is literally at other people's mercy to get down the stairs if the wants to go shopping. He becomes a prisoner in his own apartment. Further, the cities in Russia are often spread out, with long distances between various facilities. The equipment, such as their wheelchairs, are not like our racing wheelchairs, very lightweight. They are heavy and cumbersome - if they have a chair at all! Many disabled are missing limbs, and don't have a prosthesis. They are told, "Government have no money for prosthesis." So, I grew to understand why many of those I meet seem to have a depressed mentality.

The following day I planned to leave, but couldn't because the snow was about 8 inches deep. Vaselli and ELeana provided a bit of family entertainment through their son, Sasha, who played on the piano and started singing. Although only 9, he was very talented, and enjoyable to hear. Next, we watched a 1965 Russian War movie about "the Great Patriotic War," which is World War II. This movie was clearly a propaganda film. I was surprised that during the commercial breaks, I saw ads for Snickers Candy Bars and American made toys. So much for the Russian propaganda of a bygone era. I hope that the Russians don't lose their sense of humanity through this mad onslaught of the free market society.

May 9 - V.J. Day: The snow melted off, and it was time for me to go. We went down to the garage to get the motorcycle, and I discover that the police had stuck a pocket knife with about a 6 inch blade in a hole in the middle of the dashboard. This gift was meant as a sign of respect for what I was doing. I was very touched by this gesture. After loading the motorcycle, I followed Leukum out onto the main street where we watched a pathetic Victory Day parade celebrating W.W.II.

Once out of town, we made very good time in the bitter cold. I thought, "Well, how can I lose? Kemerovo is just a little over 200 miles away, so it shouldn't take me too long to get there on a road and weather like this." Believe it or not, Leukum led the way for 100 miles! In the end, when we parted he had a tear in his eye as he pressed a bore's tooth into my hand as a charm to protect me. I added this to my many charms already collected on the journey.

Now on my way to Kemerovo, within an hour the sky clouded up, the wind began to blow in force, and suddenly, it was snowing! It wasn't long before there was packed snow on the ground and I was starting to fall off the motorcycle. When trucks passed me, their tires would throw snow up on me and blind me completely. It hurts when I get hit by flying snow from an oncoming truck. Once, as I fell off the motorcycle, a man pulled up behind me in a Jeep and helped me up. When we entered a small village, the man drove in front of me and motioned me to stop at a sign for a hospital. He went inside the hospital and spoke to somebody there, then came out and motioned to me that I could sleep there tonight.

He helps me push the motorcycle through about a foot of snow into the back area of the hospital where some people come out and help me unloaded the machine, taking my gear into the hospital, and putting the motorcycle away into a garage.

The three people who helped then motioned for me to go with them to their little house about fifty meters away. They kept saying, "Doucha, doucha" which I now learned meant "wash." Once inside their house, I was shocked! It was full of drunken Russians all hollering and shouting at each other! One woman comes up to me and starts grabbing at me. I dub her "fang" because she has one tooth sticking out of the front of her mouth, breath like a dragon, and a face that looked like a wet fart. She was pulling me towards her. I don't know where she wants to go, and I don't want to find out. In the end I think to myself, "I've got to get away from here," and started saying, "Accidenta, accidenta. Doctor. Doctor." They are all so drunk they just start pointing back to the hospital, screaming, "Hospitala, Hospitala." I somehow managed to escape their clutches, cross the snowy ground and approach the hospital on a dead run (which is impossible for me). Once there, I looked for a place to hide.

The hospital has no running water or flush toilets. Most of the patients look like they are dead already. It was primitive, but extremely clean. Dinner that night was boiled milk, noodles and bread. At about 22:00, with snow still falling outside, I closed our day and experienced a hot nights sleep next to a radiator.

The following morning, I spoke by telephone to Alex Chezkazov, the correspondent. He said "I come to bring you to Komorovo." "It isn't necessary," I told him. "When the snow melts, I can get there."

"I come," he insisted. The distance was about 65 miles (100 kilometers).

About 14:00 in the afternoon, Alex and a driver shows up. They tell me the road conditions west of here are terrible. Alex tries to speak English, but his is not very good; we communicate mainly through sign language, by looking at each other real hard, and by using the dictionary. We roll the motorcycle out to the main street and then carry out my gear. I notice the asphalt is devoid of any ice or snow. "Maybe it will be an easy ride," I think. When we take off, the good road conditions lasted for about half an hour, then we hit packed snow and ice; I went down, and within the next hour, repeated that joyful event four more times. I ride mostly in first and second gear, eating the snow of passing trucks, and hitting mud, holes, rocky roads and gravel.

It took four hours to travel the 65 miles into Kemerovo. Once there, we took the motorcycle to a police garage, then they drove me to a small hotel that was astoundingly clean inside; much better than anything in China.

They left me alone at the hotel to clean up, then came later in the evening to bring me to Alex's apartment where I was introduced to his mother-in-law, his wife, Tanya, his son, Gleb, and their little daughter, Dasha. We sat down to a sumptuous meal and stumbled through the communication process. Despite our lack of words, I could tell this was a very close family. After dinner, Tanya sat down at the piano which occupied a major portion of the living room, with Gleb standing next to her. With Dasha on her lap, she started playing and Gleb and Dasha started singing. What a trio! As I traveled throughout Russia, I discovered that most middle class Russians have some sort of musical or arts background. Culture has a high premium here; unfortunately, it seems to be lacking in the United States.

When the evening is over, Alex was going to take me back to the hotel. But, when we hit the main road, he flagged down a car. I said "Alex, this is pretty nice of this guy to stop for us."

"Dave, he is a pirate taxi. He works a regular a job during the day, and drives at night. You flag him down, and he takes you where you want to go for a fee."

Capitalism has arrived.

The following day, I work on the motorcycle, and meet an interpreter named Valentine; his father had been in exile in Australia for most of this fellow's childhood. He spoke English with an Australian accent! After a news interview, I went to his house where we had a nice dinner of chicken - the only time I was served it in Russia.

The next day, Alex takes me to the police garage where the media film me loading the motorcycle and heading out of town. Since the sun was out, they assured me that going to Novosibirsk should be a trip with "No problem." I've heard that before. We stop at least six times for photographs on the way out of Kemerovo.

Broken Bridges, Horse Milk and Caviar

Finally on the road by myself, I start to make good time - 45 to 50 miles an hour. When I saw a bridge coming up, I said to myself "Slow down, Dave. Slow up." I don't know why I did, but it was a good thing because I was forced to make a sudden, sharp stop about six feet from the edge of the bridge. You see, the bridge over the river wasn't complete! Although there were no warning signs, the bridge had about a 15 foot gap right in the middle. Imagine what would have happened if I went flying into the far side of that bridge at 50 miles an hour, and then drop into the river. Instead, I had to go across a flay (wet, muddy field). The river was deep enough that the motorcycle had to be pushed through the water and out the other side. A couple of boys nearby helped me, and I rewarded them with a pack of Marlboro cigarettes; joy radiated on their faces. Unmarked road construction is a real problem throughout Russia, and it is something I must watch for all the time to stay alive.

Almost without warning, it started snowing again. I got lost in one city, found my way again, and finally ended up in Novosibirsk, the biggest city of both the Siberia's. I went directly to the police box and showed them my letter; they knew who I was, and called Andre Chelnikoff. Andre soon shows up in a Volga car; he's wearing a long coat, and has a mustache; his hair combed back. "This is Stalin's reincarnation," I think to myself. Andre acted like a Communist; his attitude was dour and miserable. I learned later he came from Tzekastan, which is right next to Gruzia (Georgia), where Stalin came from. I followed Andrew to a police garage where the ground was wet, and the cement surface inside the garage was slicker than diarrhea; I fell down in front of everybody - NATURALLY. We lift the motorcycle up and put it away. As I gracefully crawl - slink - slither away, they take me to the Octoberski Hotel, a communist party hotel.

In the evening, Andri came by and took me to a sauna. The Russians all go into the sauna to open up the pores of the skin and get all the toxins removed from the body, and to relax; it is an ancient tradition to treat a guest to the sauna. Afterwards, we shower, eat; and the others again consume major amounts of vodka.

One fellow, a doctor, had been in the Olympics (never learned what event). Another, Sasha, was a happy fellow who enjoyed the reputation of a shrewd businessman. The gym proprietor had been the number one weight lifter in the Siberia's some years ago, but was now a paraplegic from a weight lifting accident.

The following day I was introduced to Lena, Sasha's daughter, a very lovely 18-year-old Russian girl who spoke very good English. She would serve as translator while we toured a bit of the city. The first place that they took me to was the tomb of the unknown soldier. Now, I have been to "the Wall" in Washington, D.C., and seen the 58,000+ names of the American Veterans that died in the Vietnam War, but the tomb of the unknown soldier with all the names of the Russians from just the Novosibirsk area alone that died in the Great Patriotic War staggers my imagination. It is pinnacle upon pinnacle upon pinnacle with names on four sides going up to the top - maybe 20' high 10' across, and down.

Next, on the outskirts of town, they show me these places that look like cemeteries along the road with little round tubes as headstones. "What are those?" I ask. They explain that there are dugout cellars underneath, and that the round tubes are for ventilation. "People grow vegetables and fruit, then put them into their personal cellar and lock it up for winter. Then they remove the food as they need it."

In the afternoon, we meet the Disabled of Novosibirsk - a much different group of young and middle aged people. This particular group seemed well educated, and they seemed receptive to my message about helping themselves. In Russia, the disabled are always complaining about the government. "You can't depend on the government to give you a helping hand." We discussed how to get their lives going again, and to make their lives more meaningful. "You must do it yourself." I hope our discussion plants a spark in them about how they can decide to improve their own lot.

Next, I'm whisked off to meet Evon Evonovich, the mayor of Novosibirsk; he strikes me as an easy going politician without too big of a head. I was later told that he receives a great amount of flack from the old guard mentality because he is a more moderate politician.

When we enjoyed dinner that night in a communal dining room which also served as an office building to various government agencies. A heated discussion erupted about the statue of Lenin which is in front of the main theater, and stands about 25 meters tall; it was the biggest surviving statue of Lenin in Russia at the time. The protesters said, "We should tear it down." Andri told me "There's still much hard feeling towards the government for persecution." Later, I believe Lenin finally came down in that town.

Just down the street, an old church was being reconstructed; it had been destroyed after the Bolshevik revolution.

I was warned about the road to Omsk on the trans Siberia highway - 400 kilometers of very bad road. "You take a detour," they told me, and described a route 200 kilometers (125 miles) out of my way. "Better for motorcycle, better for you." I agreed to heed their advice.

Next they wanted to show me a liberated gulag. "Would you like to spend the night?" they asked. I sensed that I had to say "yes" to this request because they wanted to get away from their wives and go out for a HOOT. So, the following morning we loaded the motorcycle; on our way out of town I took a photo of the motorcycle with the threatened statute of Lenin. We traveled about a 120 miles through open farming countryside until we came to the liberated gulag of Krasnozerskoye. There we were greeted by the mayor. The police here were different looking; they wore caps and long black leather coats. I didn't like the looks of these guys at all. Once greetings and handshakes were done, the motorcycle was put away.

Lunch lasted for four hours! The Mayor, Valdimar, Andri, Sasha, and a local correspondent put away about five bottles of vodka! I am bored sick, and just want to get away from these characters. Please understand, I am not a prude. If people want to drink, fine, but I don't appreciate being the only non-drinker in the crowd when they decide to go on a four hour binge in the middle of the day.

The main claim to fame of this gulag was their horse milk! I don't know what medicinal purposes this horse milk is supposed to have, but the very thought of it makes me sick. We visited a health spa that featured this wonderful concoction, and I couldn't believe how dirty and miserable the place was . Of course, the rates were cheap too - the equivalent of a couple of dollars a day.

The next morning, when we sat down to breakfast, the correspondent was missing - probably too hung over from the night before, or simply not invited to attend after his inappropriate behavior the night before. Caviar was served - at breakfast! Disgusting stuff in my opinion. As it is wolfed down, I wonder "Where do these guys get their appetites?" Of course, vodka was served; four more bottles were consumed.

By noon, all I want to do is get the hell out of this place! Finally, we bring the motorcycle around so the mayor can show us the way out of town. He told me, with Andri translating in his drunken state, that "We have too much freedom to move around now."

About five minutes out of town, they pull off on the side of the road for more vodka and caviar on the hood of the jeep. By this time I was sick of these guys. Everybody is trying to grab me and hug and shake hands - all the expressions of eternal friendship!! I finally make like horse shit and hit the trail. I was never more happy to be on the road on my own again.

I rode 65 miles (100 km) in the direction the party animals had told me to go when I hit a very rough dirt road for another 40 miles until coming back onto a rough asphalt road at Kachery. Then, I headed northwest like I thought I was supposed to, but apparently I had jumped the gun. After 33 miles (50 km) of not seeing anything, I realized something was wrong and stopped when I saw a tractor. With a Russian flash card I asked "What direction to Omsk?" The driver pointed back down the road and makes a sign to turn around. I had to double back, so by the time I hit Kachery I've traveled about 66 miles (100 km) out of my way. But, it did not spoil my good mood. I was just delighted to get away from the funny farm at Krasozerskoye.

Outside of Kachery, I pitched my tent off in the woods, especially enjoying the silence and solitude.

On the road again at 06:30, I was baptized by a heavy rain. I made my way towards Omsk, about 120 miles (200 kilometers) away. There, I stopped at the police station and showed them my letter. They shook my hand and took me to a little trailer with a stove - like a little canteen - and a cook immediately dumps a can of horrible looking corn beef into a pan and throws in an egg as his cigarette ash drops into this meal he is cooking up just for me. Oh well, it is the thought that counts! Once I completed my sulfuric-seasoned breakfast, a police car arrives and the men motion for me to follow them. With sirens blazing, they escort me right through the city of Omsk. At the entrance to a mundane looking apartment block is the KP correspondent, Vadum, waiting for me. He has a beard and long hair, and gives me a hug. We put the motorcycle in a boiler room, then go up to his apartment where I meet his wife, Larisa, and their little daughters, Natalie and Lena; again, I notice the closeness of this family unit.

We spent the balance of the day trying to communicate with each other. By now, I've learned some key Russian words, and with the help of my dictionary I am getting along better. Of all the languages I have come across on this trip, it seems I have a better ear for Russian than the other languages.

The following day we went across town to visit a building that used to be the white Russian government headquarters after the Bolshevik Revolution; now, it was the office of KP and the New Review Newspapers. I did an interview there for both papers.

About midday, I met Alex and Andri, both Afghan veterans. We start to talk, and out comes the vodka. Andre was a doctor, and asked me, "Would you like visit hospital?" "Yes, I would," I told him.

"First lunch," he replied, taking us to a restaurant called "The Fantasy." For the next four hours, I sat inside this nightmare of a place while my hosts boozed it up. After the lunch, Andre said, "Too late for hospital."

The following morning as I loaded to leave, Larisa has tears in her eyes and Vadum can't hardly look me in the eye. I follow their car out of town, and a film crew captures part of my journey out of their city. After our good-bye - a big hug - I'm on my way. For the next 350 miles (550 kilometers) it rained. As I entered Kurgan, the petrol station charged me for more petrol than the motorcycle could hold. When I asked for change, the lady refused. "What a nasty person you are," I told her, sure she could not understand.

Now I ventured into a forest area on the edge of the mountains. Eventually I found a trail back into the woods and set up my tent in the pouring rain,. No hot dinner tonight, since I can't light my stove. As I entered my tent for the night, I wasn't thinking, and closed the tent because of the rain. The rain sealed the tent, and I woke up in the middle of the night gasping for air and with a terrible headache, nearly asphyxiated. Quickly I opened the tent and stuck my head out to breathe good clean air.

The following morning the motorcycle wouldn't start. I open up the points and see they are burnt. I replace the condenser, clean the points, and fortunately, just barely get the machine to kick over before the battery wears down. In this cold, the battery wears down very quickly, so I was greatly relieved when the motor finally fired.

Courageous Veterans and Mafia Madness

At midday I come into the city of Etkatrinaburg (under the old Soviet empire it was called Sevidalosk). Same procedure. The police read my letter, call for the KP correspondent, car comes quickly, I follow car where I'm greeted by my hosts. In this town, their names were Valodia, the KP correspondent, and his lovely wife, Marina, who spoke English reasonably well. At their apartment, she heated water for me, and I cleaned up the best I could before dinner was served.

Later in the evening, I met two Afghan disabled veterans, Dimmar and Reef. Reef had his jaw and all of his teeth shot out, and received a pension of $21.00 a month, and a free room from the government. Reef emphasized "One room" that contained one light bulb. I could just imagine his horribly dim room, much like Yin Li's in China. Reef had a wife and two children who shared the tiny flat. "Afghan veterans are very bitter towards government," he told me. Not surprisingly, they told me most Russian veterans die from alcoholism.

Dimar was a very serious shell shock victim with needle-like eyes. Both men had finally stopped drinking, but I noticed their fingernails chewed off down to nubs; both seemed very nervous. Dimar had a wild look in his eye; I could tell he suffered severe mental damage.

They told me about life in the Afghan war. "First, we were loaded onto planes and trucks and shipped out - not even time to tell families. Three months before we can write home. Our mail is screened. Sixteen soldiers in one tent. Freezing cold. Our food is only bread. Many soldiers kill themselves. Some shoot themselves in foot to get out. Officers did not care."

As I listened, I thought about how easily these men could be defeated in a conventional war. "Just drop some leaflets," I thought, "and say - 'Come on and surrender, men. We've got a hot steak dinner and a trip to Disneyland waiting for you." That would end the war.

Most Russians I talked to seemed "proud" to be Russian, but spit on their government - be it the old communist government or the new reformed government. Throughout Russia, the people seemed very depressed, and had no faith in their government.

The next day I visited a place with crosses where I was told that this is the spot that the Czar Nicoli, his wife and daughters were all shot by the Bolsheviks in 1917. Their pictures were posted on these crosses.

I was also taken to the edge of the Ural Mountains to a back area where, between 1930 and 1940, the Russian officers who were purged out of the army by Stalin were taken and murdered. Only a small sign marked the murders.

Next, we drove to a monument that separates Europe from Asia. In Asia, it is the Siberia's; to the west, eastern Europe.

The following morning there's about 8 inches of snow on the ground, and I realize I'll be going nowhere today. Marina, a school teacher, says "Please, come to my school and speak to the kids." I agreed. One little bastard in the class asks me, "Hey, where are your dollars?" I wondered, "Who has been teaching you, boy?" The rest of the children were respectful.

In the midst of the snow, the entire city of Etkatrinaberg has no hot water! Apparently, Etkatrinaberg's hot water is supplied through a central system from another city, and their boilers are down for maintenance. What a system.

The following day as I prepare to leave, Marina gives me a big hug, and I can see the sadness in her eyes. I don't think it was because I'm leaving, but because she will no longer have the opportunity to speak English, and to talk about world affairs. Frankly, Valodia didn't seem to care much about the world, and his wife seemed to have a keen, inquisitive mind.

Riding into the Urals, I crossed into Europe, leaving Asia, my fifth continent, behind. The Ural roads are covered with mud, so when a truck passes, I enjoy a wonderful mud shower! My glasses constantly cloud, so it is easy to miss the potholes that knock the wind out of me when I hit them. Just another pleasant ride through the country!

As I moved out the other side of the Urals, which really are more like low foothills with pine trees and green pastures than mountains, I hit a fork in the road and can't decipher the writing on the sign. I pull up to a car parked along side the road to ask, "What road to Perm." As I pull alongside of him, I put my right foot down on a piece of gravel, the gravel gives way, and the motorcycle crashes into his car door, pushing it right inside!

The poor guy had been sitting peacefully with his wife and daughter in the back of the car, when this motorcyclist pulls up next to him and crashes into his car. Fortunately, the man handled it well. I immediately got off the motorcycle and removed it from the man's car. He climbed out his good door and came over to help me. He wasn't hollering or shouting, but his wife is chirping like a bird; I realize where the trouble is going to come from.

Immediately, I take out my wallet where I always carry about $30.00 in one dollar bills. I start putting them, one by one, in his hand. when I counted out $25.00 and closed his hand, he says "Nayet problem."

By this time, the police pull in behind us; one asked me "Vodka?" and I answered, "Nayet alcohol." I motioned that I was willing to take a breathalyzer test, and they said "Nayet." In all the commotion, I still did not know whether I was on the right road to Perm.

I continued on for about 20 miles, and sure enough, came to Perm. The first thing I notice immediately is the number of drunks staggering around in the streets. I tried to locate a sober person so I could ask directions. Finally, a driver pulled alongside me in a car and said, "Follow me." He leads me to a sign that reads "Kazan," and points in the direction I need to go for my next stop.

When I am ready to stop for the day, I always look behind me to make sure there are no cars. If I see a car behind me, I ride on at a low speed and let the car get around me, then double back to where I see a reasonable dirt road heading back into the forest. I do this as a safety precaution, and to hopefully be alone and undisturbed. Of course, there are guest houses everywhere along the road in Russia, but these places are often full of drunks, so it is easy to get into more trouble at these houses than if I stay alone in the country.

This day, as I turned into a side road, my front wheel hit a rock and down I went. After unloading it, I managed to lift the thing up and get my block underneath it, then set up camp. After dinner I enjoyed a very peaceful night, my first back in Europe.

The following day I rode over 350 miles, bringing me to Kazan', the capital city of Tatarstan, about 500 miles east of Moscow. In Kazan' I find my way to the Army barracks where a soldier gives me tea, then gets on the phone and calls the correspondent, Boris, who comes out to greet me with his friend, Irene. I follow them across town, and put the motorcycle away at a police garage. At Boris's apartment, I drop off my bags and then we head off for a sauna, a shower, then return to his house for dinner. Boris asks, "Would you like to stay in hotel?", and Irene pops up and says, You can stay at my apartment." I agree.

Irene is a very outspoken, anti-government woman. When we are alone, she starts telling me about the corrupt government. She has a major disability in her back, and uses a cane for walking, with great pain.

The following day we drive to the government building and meet the minister of social maintenance, a woman named Galina, who had the gall to ask me if there was some organization that I could refer her to that could help her go overseas so she could learn more about disabled people. Of course, I told her I could not help her.

We visited a driving school which teaches three classes of 25 students a year how to drive a car to people who have just received a disability. It is also a daycare center for mentally handicapped people, although I didn't see one mentally handicapped person. We had lunch with the administrator of this establishment with plenty of vodka; they seemed disappointed that I would not drink.

Later, at Irene's apartment, she told me "The biggest criminals are in the government. Most are still old guard communists. Many are Mafia." It seems anyone with money or a nice home or a good business in Russia is "part of Mafia." Irene got a pension of $11.00 a month. "Don't spend it all in one place," I thought.

The following morning I was led out of town by Boris and Irene to the Volga River on the western side of Kazan. I asked Boris, "Is everything all right in Nizneogorev for my arrival?" "Yes," he replied, "I have spoken to Anton Fortonov and he is expecting you." With that reassurance, I say good-bye and board the ferry across the Volga River.

It didn't rain or snow all the way to Nizneogorev. There was still plenty of farm lands and forested areas, but I am also starting to notice more industry along the road, and memorial markers are making a comeback. I haven't seen them since South America. In Russia, these unfortunates, who are perpetuated by memorials, often have their pictures pasted on these little memorial plaques.

On the outskirts of Nizneogorev, (once called Gorkiy), I stop at a police station. They weren't interested in me or my letter, and just motioned me in the direction of downtown. I leave there, and stop a police car a bit later, showing him my letter. He brings me to yet another police station where I'm greeted by three drunken policemen. Then I try to call the correspondent, but there's no answer. I left hurriedly, anxious to get away from these men who reeked with booze.

As I drive through town, again, I see more drunks. Obviously, this national affliction for vodka and drunkenness is a reflection of a horribly depressed people. This town seems to have even more drunks than any other city I've been through yet. Finally, I spot a hopefully sober policeman named Nick who told me to follow him to yet another police station where we put the motorcycle away. He then takes me to his very humble apartment shared by him, his wife, son and daughter. Erna, Nick's wife, fed us potatoes, baloney, bread and cheese; the meal was spiced up a bit with a wild berry jam Erna had made. Nick told me he had served ten years in the Army and six years as a policeman; in four years, he could retire. He tried to speak English but with little success. We used the dictionary, and our communication was extremely strained.

The next day we sat around the house. When I suggested we walk outside, he shouted "Nayet." Instead, we got into a little car and drove out to the countryside where they owned a tiny "dacha" - a tiny hut about 10 feet by 10 feet; it held farm implements for their vegetable garden.

On the way back home, he points to a factory and goes "Volga, Volga" meaning the Volga car, one of the leading Russian cars.

After another strained night at his apartment, the next day he got on the phone to somebody. When he finished his conversation, we jumped in his car and went to a television station where I did a television interview, interpreted by Leoind, a very competent translator.

A city government official was in attendance, and said, "We will put you in a government hotel. I thought, "That should help take the edge off of everything." The policeman had been very kind to me, and I am thankful he took up where the KP correspondent had failed.

I managed to reach my friend Alex Chulitsky by phone in Moscow. Alex said, "Do not come into Moscow until June 1." That was two days away. I told him, "No problem, I'll just camp in the hillsides for a few days." Alex had a fit! "No. No. You can't do that. Too dangerous." Finally, I agreed to stay in the hotel for the next two days.

At the hotel, I met a foreigner, a German working for Wirtgen, a man who helped sponsor me. I wrote him a note to take to Reinhard Wirtgen back in Germany.

Another fellow I met during my two days at the hotel was Bob Carlson, a retired member of the board of directors of Case. He was over doing volunteer work in Russia, helping to change their factories from war industry manufacturing to civil production.

Leonid invited me to attend a arts and crafts show by disabled children that was taking place there in the city on the following day. I agreed.

The arts and crafts we saw the next day included a ballet performance by a deaf young woman who was ever so graceful, beautiful, and impressive.

Servarda - The Vanishing Beauty!

Finally, on June 1, still about 250 miles east of Moscow, Nick escorts me to the edge of town where we say our tearful "good-byes and I head down a very typical rough Russian road from Nizneogev to Moscow. About midday I approach Moscow and notice vendors along the road becoming more numerous. They are selling sandwiches and cool drinks. About 12:00, I saw a sign saying "Moscow" in the distance, and stop to take a photograph. About a half mile down from there, I find the police box and report in, showing them my letter and the phone numbers to call. They motion for me to sit down and wait.

After about two hours, Alex Chulitski, the person who had been trying to help me ever since I was in Hong Kong the year before, arrived. There were camera people, and General Yuri Nauman, the head of the Leonard Cheshire Home for disabled Russian war veterans. After some filming, I met the chief editor, Volari, of Kosamolka Provda, who presented me with a giant electric teapot, in the old Russian style and tradition. "What am I going to do this on a motorcycle?" I wonder to myself. I also met a young woman named Sevarda, a very beautiful blond Russian girl. She too was a correspondent.

After the handshakes and filming, with dreams of lovely Sevarda in my head, I followed General Nauman about 25 miles, bouncing along on my shot suspension system, to the Cheshire Home. As I rode through the gate, I realized that I had now fulfilled my promise to Lord Group Captain Cheshire to visit the home in Kunming, China, and the other one in Moscow. I was warmly greeted by the staff and some of the residents of the home - young men with arms and legs missing from the Afghan War.

That night in my room, I reflected back on the events of the day, feeling great joy in my heart that I had made it Moscow and the Cheshire Home.

The following morning I met Andri, once in the naval infantry, and my interpreter for the day. Alex and Oxana arrived in a car and drove us all down to the KP office where we were met by a swarm of reporters. For the next hour, I was grilled in a conference room by reporters from different newspapers, including one from the Moscow Times, an English newspaper. As I answered questions, my eyes kept focusing on luscious Sevarda, and I contemplated discretely wonderful, joyous scenarios in my mind, fluttering with thoughts of love at first sight.

After the conference, questions just keep coming as I try to attract Sevarda's attention; unfortunately, in the chaos she disappeared, and much to my deep regret, I never saw her again. Paradise lost! Not the first time for me.

Back in the car, I ask Andri about the different landmarks and things I've seen. "What about the tanker trucks along the road filling up cars and Jerry cans with gas?"

"Black market petrol trucks," he replies. "The petrol costs more, but there's no waiting in a long line. Black market gas is quick, but you pay double or triple the cost of government gas."

I also saw foreign oil being sold out on the street. I was doing quite well with the aircraft oil I had been using ever since Krasnoyarsk, so I stuck with it. The motorcycle was using two liters every 300 mile (500 km).

Andri and I talked about the problems in western society. "Too many women out in the workplace, in government. They should be home taking care of children," he told me. I thought to myself, "You'd never get along with American girls with ideas like that, my boy!"

We visited a home where children with learning disabilities are taught to speak, and other learning skills. These kids were very warm and affectionate, but were separated from their families like the kids in China.

On our way home, Andri pointed out the KGB training school and headquarters. It was a huge square cement building with a very imposing manner about it. He told me, "It is no longer called KGB, but they still do the same job."

I was amazed at Moscow's grand architecture. I saw what Andri called "an ice cake" on top of Moscow University - a star with an oak leaf around it. He told me, "It weighs 53 tons and is 28 stories up to the top of building." In 1928, when this building was constructed, there were no skyscraper cranes; everything was carried up ladders and hoists! He told me "Six engineers were in reeducation labor, working on this building. They somehow got word to Stalin that they could put the ice cake up on top of the building if he would let them follow their plan. Stalin told them, 'If you can get it up, I will let you go.' So, they somehow put that star and oak leaf on top, and Stalin set them free."

Moscow is a hustling, bustling, massively big city with a personality. I found it to be quite clean and tidy, although Andri claimed "It is actually dirty compared to what it used to be." I was amazed at the amount of BMW's, Volvos and other foreign cars running about the streets. But of course, Mafia.

The motorcycle was running okay; the main problem was oil consumption. It was smoking like a steam engine, and starting hard. Alex managed find a can of ether I could use to start the thing a little quicker. We decided it would be best for me to not do anything major on the motor, but just attempt to get to Sweden.

During my two weeks in Moscow, Alex Chulitski and I became friends. He was a deep, sensitive person. When we talked, if I made a positive remark about something, he would, in typical Russian fashion, make a negative remark. Alex too was ill at ease about the reformed government. Most Russians seemed to favor reform, but had no faith in how things were unfolding. They especially hated the horrible inflation (anybody would). Alex told me, "We are not like the Chinese. They take the shortest route, the most practical to do a thing. They are very pragmatic. Not so Russians. If we can make it difficult, we will." As a country, Russians seem very fatalistic. "In this new push to make money," Alex said, "I hope we don't sacrifice our qualities as a people in the mad and crazy struggle."

Alex also agreed with what others had told me. "The biggest criminals were the old communists. They created Russia's current problems. Yeltsin has inherited a big bag of rotten worms."

My motorcycle had not been washed since Zhou Zhou, in China, in December, 1992. Six months and 6,000 miles later, after traveling through every type of weather, it was time to clean up the roaring mess. I took a full day to clean it, and that night was invited to a talent show of young theater performers. As I watched this troupe of singers and actors perform, I was especially enthralled with the beautiful women. The piano player spoke very good English. Unfortunately, instead of just letting me enjoy the entertainment, Alex insists on translating everything, and this day he has horrible onion breath. Nightmarish thoughts of Bo, the sewer mouth from China, ran through my head.

Lack of motivation seems to be a common problem with Russia's disabled veterans. There's plenty of depression as well. In many, their eyes appear as if they were shell shocked or mentally damaged. The other thing I notice is that some would be fitted for legs, and others not. Later, I would learn that money is a major factor. There's not enough money provided to buy even a basic leg.

One boy told me his story. "I not an army veteran, but they let me stay at the home. In Uzbeckistan, a stray mortar round exploded in my house. Blow up whole family. Sister. Brother. Mother. Father. I lost leg below knee." The Cheshire foundation let him temporarily stay at the home. As I think back, I was so distracted with the media from morning until evening that it never occurred to me that for a few hundred dollars I could have bought this kid an artificial leg. That thought still hounds me to this day. I stand guilty of complacency. This trip was for the disabled, and I could have helped him.

Russian Veterans, Past and Present Problems

I gave a talk to the 27th Motorized Guard Brigade, an elite armored Brigade, without my slides. As we drove on base, I spotted on a pinnacle, two stories high, a huge head of Lenin (the size of a double-car garage). It was very imposing.

Once inside the gate, I was greeted by a Colonel and taken on a tour of the military museum; it depicted how this brigade fought valiantly during World War II, and gave more of its history. In the auditorium, about 60 junior grade officers sat in attention. Yuri Nauman, a retired Major General, was there with me, along with General Stephonivsh, second in charge at the home. I spoke for the next hour about the journey around the world, and when they asked questions, the conversation shifted to my being a veteran in Angola. Apparently, some of their members served in Angola when I was there. The South African forces had taken prisoner a Sergeant Major; a friend of mine who spoke Russia took care of him for the next two years, and they had become close friends. The Sergeant Major was ultimately repatriated.

At the end of the talks, they presented me with a left boot for my artificial foot; it fit perfectly! I told them "I'll wear this boot until the trip is finished," and I did. The boot is now retired at my home in California. One irony on the boot. The sole I made out of a boot that bolted to the bottom of my steel right foot was the sole from an American Army Jungle boot. So now, on one foot I have the boot of the Soviet Army, and on the other, the sole of an American army boot. The cold war is over!

A few days later, we went to the headquarters of the air borne division to give another talk about my journey and past military experiences to the commanders of the airborne division. Present at this talk were officers from Lieutenant Colonel right up to Major General - two active Major Generals were in the crowd. After my talk, they presented me with a medallion with their logo of the airborne division on it, something I am very proud to own to this day.

These officers were different from the ones I spoke to a few days earlier. Clearly, they were on Yeltsin's side. One of the problems during the early April, 1993 strife that took place within the Russian government was that the different sections of the army took conflicting political positions. Had the armies clashed, Russia could have collapsed into a major civil war.

I have been asking General Nauman if he could arrange for me to ride up in front of Lenin's Tomb in Red Square to take some photographs. "I don't think it is possible," he told me, "but I'll try." Fortunately, German National Television wanted to do an interview with me, so pressure just started to build towards doing the story in Red Square. Finally, approval was given, and the government granted permission for me to ride into Red Square on June 12 with two motorcyclists from the Technicians Motorcycle Club.

Red Square History and Political Cemetery Games

June 12: We meet on the far side of Saint Basil's the blessed, the church with the spiral domed edifice you see in so many news reels. When everything was ready, the two other motorcyclists and myself form up behind the RTL's TV car; by now, the entire square has been cleared of thousands of tourists. They film us moving from Saint Basil's towards Lenin's Tomb. The sky is gray and overcast, but it didn't stop me from savoring this great moment. As I near the square, I realize that I'm the only man alive who has ridden through the forbidden city of China to pose in front of Mao Zedong's portrait in Tianamen Square, and now, I'm riding into Red Square to pose in front of Lenin's Tomb. This has never been done before.

Oxana and Boris Demchenko take photographs for the Russian Motorcycle magazine known as *Moto*. We ride around in a circle filming, then posing again in front of the tomb. Finally, we retreat back to Saint Basil's and around back to the parking lot as a very special moment in the history of this journey comes to an end.

Afterwards, we ride to a park to celebrate with the Technicians Motorcycle Club. Interesting enough, there's only one Harley Davidson in the group; the rest ride Eural Motorcycles. They were all happy about the filming, and celebrate with copious amounts of beer, as good bikers often do. A hawker came up to me to try and sell a little medallion encased in some plastic as a paper weight. It was less than a dollar, so I bought it. My buddies get upset at this fellow for trying to sell me something to me, and they lean on him very hard with a hang dog look. He gave me back my money, and said, "Thank you for traveling across Russia for the sake of the disabled." He let me keep the paper weight.

Next, they presented me with a video tape of one of their parties that they had out in the woods, and signed the cover. After that, I rode back to the home.

Nellie Fedorinko, the secretary and interpreter, came to my meetings to do interpreting. She was a very unique lady who spoke very good English in a high pitched voice. At the home, she told me, "Wow, I am glad we are finally away from the rockers," meaning the motorcycle club.

That night, as I thought about Red Square, I remembered Alex Chulitsky showing me a sculptured stone edifice that was flat across the top, with sculpturing all around it. It was the length of a human body, and had about five stairs leading up to it. Alex explained that "They would take criminals up there, and lay them across the flat table. Then, they cut their heads off." As I thought about the day's events, it struck me hard that today I saw all of these tourists from various nations sitting there on the steps of the chopping block, eating ice cream, resting their feet. Somehow, it seemed like a sacrilege. If the ghosts of the past could come back and see that, I am sure they would have a fit.

In Moscow, two unique people I grew to know were Boris and his daughter, Oxana. He was editor of *Moto Magazine*, and had personally covered 6,000 kilometers (4,000 miles) on his motorcycle on the Trans-Siberian Highway when it was all dirt. He told me that often bridges were down, and the machine had to be either ferried or ridden through fairly deep water to get them to the other side. He accomplished the journey in three weeks.

Another trip he took was through the Siberias. His group traveled in snow mobiles in temperatures of 55 minus, camping up in the Arctic area during the winter. He showed me photographs and diaries of these amazing journeys.

At one time, Boris had worked in industry, and at another, he earned his living as a singer. He had the spirit of an adventurer, very rare to find in people from socialist countries.

I enjoyed one lovely afternoon with Alex Chulitski's family out in their country dacha - a two story, five bedroom wood home with everything beautifully kept inside and out. Alex proudly showed me the Harley Davidson he was overhauling; he owned it eight years at the time. It was an old World War II WLA flathead, the only kind of Harley Davidson I ever saw in Russia.

The itch to be moving is starting to grow strong. The one thing I am trying to do is avoid making any contact with the media North of me, so the last part of the run can be done without any media pressures.

Nellie suggested that I take a day and tour Moscow. I told her, "I would like to see the Kremlin, and walk through Red Square. So Alex Chulitski, Oxana, his wife, Nellie, and a fellow named Alex, a psychiatrist at the home, joined me as we wandered around the Kremlin. I noticed a cannon with a bore of 849 millimeters; the cannon balls were one ton, and the cannon barrel weighed 15 tons, and sat on an 8 ton carriage! We saw a bell that had fallen from the belfry tower during a fire in the Kremlin centuries before. As the firemen poured water on it, the bell cracked, reminding me of its counterpart, the liberty bell. In one of the Kremlin churches, we saw the caskets of some of the past Czars.

Nellie and I drove a couple miles to one of the most unique cemeteries I have ever seen - for the very elite of Russia. Stalin and Ivan the Terrible are not buried here. Where the top leaders are buried, tourists are not allowed into this cemetery. We walked around for a couple of hours, especially admiring the incredible sculpturing. Some of the statutes seemed to be alive. On one grave, they had part of an aircraft engine and a propeller on the headstone; the dead man was an aeronautical engineer.

We also saw Kruschev's grave. When he backed down to Kennedy, and pulled the missiles out of Cuba, he became a doomed man in Russia. The proof of his lack of stature was his grave - far away from that of Stalin and the other criminals who have controlled Russia. The fact that Kruschev was buried here was an eternal reminder of the ultimate and final insult bestowed upon him.

I saw the grave of Mrs. Joseph Stalin, who committed suicide after being married to one of the biggest monsters in all of history. Perhaps because of the suicide, she too was buried in this cemetery, far away from her husband, probably as a punishment for her deed.

Next to Mrs. Stalin's grave was the grave of Nellie Fedorinko's father. As I understood it, Field Marshal Fedorinko was commander of all the armored forces of the Soviet army during World War II. This man somehow survived all of Stalin's purges of his officer corps during the 30's and early 40's, and during the war answered only to Stalin. There was the head of the infantry, the armor, the navy and the air force - so he was one of four very powerful men. Fedorinko died in 1947. Nellie told me, "When my father died, my mother, at great risk, grabbed us kids and took us to get baptized." She also remembered casually meeting Stalin's daughter. I realized that Nellie, as a child, actually had contact with one of the biggest pricks in all of history.

The Western World Via a Russian Submarine Base

June 16: It is time to hit the road. After a restless night's sleep (usual for me before a new phase of the trip) I prepare for the final run back to the western world. Nellie and a few others show up to lead me out of town. A big bag of sandwiches was given to me, and I told Nellie "I don't have room to carry these." She told me, "Just take them!" Not wanting to hurt feelings, I crammed the sandwiches inside one of my saddle bags, flattening them. As I start up, the staff and residents of the Home come out, choking on the motorcycle's billowing smoke as they shake my hand good-bye.

I had become close with a resident of the home named Nickoli, although we could not communicate. He was the epitome of the old, tough soviet soldier. In World War II, part of his arm was shot away. Later, in the Afghan war, part of a foot was shot away. He clearly understood what the sharp end of war was all about during his career in the army. When we passed each other in the home's hallways, I'd say, "Nickoliiiii," and he'd reply "Davvvvvvid." We'd always shake hands, but today, as I prepared to leave, he just stood there with tears in his eyes. Finally, we give each other a hug, then I follow General Nauman and Nellie out of town to the edge of Moscow.

We stopped on the road leading north towards Saint Petersburg, got out of the car, took some photos, and exchanged hugs. Then General Nauman stood back from me, stuck out his jaw, and said "In Russia, I am your father!" I stood back, thinking to myself, "Okay, Dad," and we saluted one another as I headed north on a rather typical rough Russian road.

The countryside was farming and agricultural, with sometime forests and rolling hills. After about 250 miles (400 km), I hung a valve in the head, my valve guides being loose. I stopped and let the motor cool down and then turned it over; it pulled itself back into the cylinder head again. The resident psychologist in the home, Alexi, had predicted a series of things going to happen to me over the next few years. This breakdown was one of them. He had told me that when I hit this area, I would have "Motor trouble. Nothing serious. You will be on your way in ten minutes." Indeed, I was.

I rode another 150 miles, and located a place off the road amongst some abandoned buildings; I put my tent up there the night. It felt so good not to have people or media around me. Thinking about Norway, my next destination, I really relaxed for the first time in a couple of weeks as I closed my day.

The following morning, instead of going to St. Petersburg, I cut directly north, heading for the Arctic Circle. As the day progressed, the road became less and less crowded. Thankfully, there were still plenty of services along the road. I enjoyed the forests, lakes and beautiful rivers I saw along the way. It was nice to be removed from the pollution of the lower part of Russia. As I moved forward, I was running out of fuel. I spotted a couple in a car who were standing alongside the road eating something. I stopped, asking them if they could sell me some gasoline. They gave me some gas and a couple of hard boiled eggs, bread, salami and a cup of very strong Russian coffee. We tried to communicate by using the dictionary, but without much luck.

As I resume my journey, the sun is out in full force and I am especially enjoying the day. I haven't felt this good in a long time. The motorcycle, though it is leaking oil and smoking like a steam engine, seems to be running pretty good. As I move northward, I see some little dirt tracks off into the forest. I decide to follow them, calling it a day. Heading about a mile back into the forest, I set up my camp, have my dinner, and work on the motorcycle. How grand it is to listen to the sounds of nature around me and really relax! Funny, you might think I should be more tense on the road because of the uncertainty of things, but I am geared better for that than I am for all the hassle of the media and fulfilling other people's expectations in the different cities I travel through. I deeply enjoy sitting back and listening to nature without seeing or hearing another human being. That day, I had covered 415 miles (600 km) on a rough road, so I was physically very tired. I ached all over. Not only are the shock absorbers on the motorcycle gone, but so too is the rear wheel swing arm that actuates everything. It has over an inch and a half of sideways play. All the bearings are shot. Yet, it was with peace in my heart that I closed the day.

The following morning, out on the highway again, hoping that with some luck I'll make Murmansk today. The scenery changes from beautiful to incredible. The sky is absolutely blue and clear, and serve as a lovely backdrop for the pine trees and the rock formations. I often spot Russians off on the side of the road camping in areas near streams; this is the first time I've seen this. I even saw some brave souls in bathing suits...only a couple hundred miles south of the Arctic Circle. It is colder than a witches tit up here, yet these people are out in bathing suits in the stream, swimming. I think to myself, "These people must have fish blood."

As I pressed north, I traveled about 250 miles without seeing a petrol station, and again was running low. I saw a Lada car parked alongside the road and pulled behind the fellow, knowing every Russian carries two or three jerry cans of extra fuel in the back of the car. I say "Ti, benzine?" meaning "You have gasoline?" in my horrible broken Russian. He answers "Da," meaning "Yes." He gave me 5 liters, and refuses my money when I try to pay him. His name was Boris, and I did not notice any vodka bottles inside his car. He seemed like a nice, sensitive man. At the next town, when I was getting gas, he stopped just to make sure I was okay. He spoke no English, but motioned to me through signs that he had seen me on television.

About 100 miles (160 km) later, **I came to the Arctic Circle, my third and last crossing.** The sign was in Russian, but I still knew where I was. As I took a photograph, Boris pulls in and takes a photograph of me standing in front of the monument to the Arctic Circle, a monument larger than those in Norway, Finland, or Alaska. During the rest of the day, we pass each other a few more times.

I rode another 200 miles or so into an area that just experienced a major fire. The area was charred for miles. Then, it started to rain. It was horribly cold, although not cold enough for ice to form on the ground. I came to a sign that **said "Murmansk," signifying that I had now traveled to the most northern city in the world.** I thought of the time I had the motorcycle in the back of a truck when I came into Ushuaia in Tierra Del Fuego, the most southern city in the world. I had just completed another milestone in the journey. To my knowledge, no one has ever gone to the southern most and northern most cities in the world on a motorcycle.

Boris pulls in behind me again, taking more photographs. Then he says, "David, ya dorma?" and makes the sign of sleep. I answer "Da." thinking to myself that it would be nice to spend my last night in Russia with a Russian family. I say "Motorcickla" and he says "Garagea nayet problem." Off we go, but Boris doesn't head into Murmansk, but instead goes around the bottom of Murmansk on the western side, right out of town! He then takes a paved side road off to what I believe was the Cola Inlet. I stop him to take some photographs as I realize this is the shipyard where all the Arctic convoys had come during World War II to keep the Russians in the war. A very historic place. As I am taking pictures, I hear a loud "craccck" - the kick stand broke again, and the motorcycle is down. Boris helps me pick it up, looks at the kick stand, and says, "Nayet problem." He then makes a motion that it can be welded.

Since we've stopped, I ask, "Boris, Murmanska that direction?" he goes "Da" and I say "Ti dorma?" meaning "Your house?" When I ask about his house, he points north away from Murmanska. I take out my Russian road map which I've had since Krasnoyarsk, but there is nothing on this very detailed map to the north. He then points right up to the edge of the Barents Sea and says "Murmanska." I have a good feeling about this guy, so we continue on. I've got to follow him now - he has my kick stand!

We travel another 40 miles over a horribly rough road along the Cola Inlet. As we go over a sharp rise, I look down and see some revetments (bomb-proof walls) in a small harbor. Then I see a sign saying "Murmansk 60," but I'm too tired and in too much pain to take notice. I have ridden over 500 miles today on a terrible road, and Boris was still going!

Finally, he stops near a horrible little cement block lockup where they keep cars and other things. There I meet Ivan, Slava, Victor, and Alexi. Boris explains the problem with the motorcycle kick stand, and I hear the familiar "Nayet problem." Somehow, I'm not worried when I hear these Russians say it.

They bring out a big box covered in rust - a welder. Victor takes two bare wires coming out of the welder's rusty housing, walks over to a junction box where there are other bare wires, and in his most professional manner, hooks these wires to one another, then welds up the kick stand in no time flat, doing a professional job. I was shocked! When the welding was done, we put the motorcycle away in one of the lockups, and they gave me the key for good faith.

We next went to the most miserable apartment village I have ever seen. There was no grass; cement, rocks or mud were on the ground. The apartment buildings were cold and square, some as high as twenty stories. Some actually appeared to be splitting apart from the weather conditions. These prefabbed apartment blocks of cement were extremely cold, and the halls stunk of urine.

We take the elevator up to Boris's apartment along with Ivan and Slava. Inside, I am given a chance to clean up before sitting down to a dinner of salami, bread, potatoes and a cup of tea. Out came the vodka, and I thought "Oh no, here we go again. I've been 19 1/2 hours on the road, I'm tired and beaten stupid from the roads. I've had it. I just want to relax. Put the damn bottle of vodka away." Well, they must have read my thoughts because, surprise, surprise, they have just two shots, drinking to their health and to my health, then put the bottle away! Afterwards, Ivan and Slava go home. I ask Boris about his wife, and he looks up the words, "Work at night." I go to sleep in the living room of his small apartment.

The following morning we have bread and tea. When Ivan and Slava show up, we go ahead and get into Boris' Lada. He puts on the windshield wipers. I've learned that Russians must take them off every night or somebody will steal them. When we get to the motorcycle, I start it up and sounds really rough. This fulfills the third of the prophecies given to me by Alex. The first was that I would have motor trouble outside of Moscow; I did. The second that I would break something; my kick stand had broken. The third that there would be fog, and the motorcycle would run rough; it was.

I shut it off and looked at the points; they were burnt, so I cleaned them up and put on another condenser. It started right up. Ivan and Slava ask me "Benzine, David, benzine?" and I said "Da." They told me to shut it off. They leave, then come back with 20 liters (about 5 gallons) of fuel - enough to see me handsomely to the border. I try to pay them but they refuse. I try to explain, "I am going to Norway where rubbles are not worth anything. Here, take my rubbles."

When I ask what they do for work, they draw a picture on the ground of a submarine, and the penny dropped. "Da submarina offizer, submarina," they say in unison. I only then realized that I had spent the night the nuclear submarine base in the Arctic! The village was where the personnel lived who serviced the base we had passed on our way over the rise where I saw the revetments.

They were officers in the Soviet Navy! Career men. To think that just three years before they could have been the ones sitting off the coast of New York, Miami, or California in a Russian boomer with their finger on the button of a nuclear missile launcher. They were our enemies. And now, look at all they had done for me! Amazing. It was very touching. I was beside myself.

We loaded the motorcycle, and I followed them 45 miles (70 km) back out to the main road. There we stop, take photographs, and share an emotional good-bye with these fine men and sailors.

I bounce and bound along for the next 150 miles until I come to a boom across the road. I could see in the distance a huge Russian Army Base. At the gate were both Army and Naval personnel who seemed absolutely astounded to see a foreigner. "What are you doing here?" they babble in Russian. I take out my letter from General Nauman, and they get on the phone and start hollering. Finally, a soldier came over to me, handed me my passport and letter back, then stood and saluted. They all shook my hand, opened the gate, and motioned for me to go. Obviously, I was passing through a highly restricted area.

From the time I had left Murmansk 60, I had been traveling through a miserable, bleak area, one of the worst I've seen anywhere in the world. It was just gray, seeming devoid of any real vegetation. There were war memorials everywhere, and memorials to the October Revolution, but not much else. After going through the army base, I eventually traveled another 100 miles (160 km) and came to the town of Nickol, one of the most polluted cities anywhere in the world. A yellowish brown pawl hung over the place, and industrial smoke stacks billowed unfiltered pollution into the air. How do people live here?

The main street of Nickol consisted of coal dust. At the petrol pumps, I went to the back of the line, and people started saying, "Nayet, nayet," motioning me forward. They allowed me to fuel up in front of everybody else. Gasoline here costs only .20 cents a gallon, inconceivably cheap by our standard, although expensive to Russians. When I left, gasoline was coming out of my pockets. In Norway, fuel runs about $4.50 a gallon.

On my way out of town I saw perhaps the most miserable funeral in my life. In the back of a 5 ton dump truck was a plastic coffin, with two little Lada cars following. In the on-coming lane was a wedding procession, with a little doll on the front of a Lada, with two other Lada cars following...the wedding limos! As they passed, and realizing the terrible, depressing aspect of this town, I wondered, "Who is the lucky one, the guy who is done, or the couple just starting?"

I continued on to the border post where I met the Army once again. They took my loose leaf Visa out of my passport altogether, and pointed down the road. I rode another 5 miles on a very narrow, tarred rough road in the pissing rain until I arrived at the next check point. Again, an Army officer came out and checked my passport, then pointed for me to continue to the last check point which was right along a river area where it was very swampy. At this place, I stopped the motorcycle by the gate, got off, and I was getting out my passport when a Russian officer came out, waiving his hand and shouting "Nayet," telling me to stop. He takes off his unit badge, walks over and pins it on me, then stands back with tears in his eyes and salutes me. I can only surmise that he has seen me on television, or read about the journey in one of the national newspapers. It is with an incredible heavy feeling in my own heart (my emotions were running really high) that I started the motorcycle and saluted this man.

He lifted the boom, and 10 months from the very day I entered China, and the Socialist world, I moved back into the Western world again, leaving the gray crumbling cement of socialism, with its incredible but depressed people behind.

Down in a Sandstorm in Inner Mongolia
April 21, 1993. Gobi Desert.

*Dave on motorcycle outside garage in Diplomatic Compound. April 1993
Posing with Konsomolna T'shirt on for André Kabanikov. Beijing, China.*

*In the Gobi Desert, Mongolia
Encountered a camel train. April 1993*

Chapter Thirty-Three

European Ecstasy, Completed Dream!

All of the sudden the road seemed smooth, even though it was still raining. There were lines down the middle, dividing it. I rode to Norway Customs outside of Kirkens, and saw a bus full of Russian Christians coming to Norway for a seminar. They recognized me, got out of the bus, and asked me to write something profound in one of their books, I'm not very profound, but I wrote: "He who believes with all their heart, for them there will always be strength and light to do His will." The power of my emotions almost over came me.

When I entered the Customs and Immigration office, the man sees this soaking wet fellow. Upon viewing my American passport, he says, "My God, man, where have you come from?" The question really gripped me at that particular moment. "I have come all the way across from Hong Kong," I said, "from a very far land. I have traveled about 8,000 miles (13,000 km) since I left Beijing in China.

"Where are you headed?" he asks.

"I am going through Karosk to get to Finland."

"No, don't do that," he says. "Take this road into Finland. It is only about 40 km (25 miles) from here. You will save 300 km (190 miles)."

"It looks like a dirt road," I observed.

"It is for about 20 kilometers. It is a narrow but good road."

As I rode through this beautiful country, I think to myself, "Okay, that's another prophecy coming true. He told me I wouldn't take the route into Finland that I had planned, and that I would not change money in Norway."

With feelings of sorrow and elation I rode on through Kirkens and across the border into Finland on a dirt road. Now, my idea of a dirt road was that I was in for a rough and muddy time. Instead, this was like an autobahn. Even in the rain, I am flying down this dirt and gravel road at 50 miles an hour. It is smoother than anything I have been on in Russia, pavement or otherwise (perhaps that's not saying much). When I hit the paved road, it wasn't long before I came into a little village along the river in northern Lapland (Finland). I located a church, pulled into the yard, and a Father Yari came out.

"Can I put up my tent here for the night?" I ask. He agreed, and invited me to come in and take a hot shower, my first one since I left Moscow! I was in an especially good mood because I hadn't heard a single word of English in days until I arrived at the border on this day.

After my shower, the light of day waned only a little because it is not true night here. The area is about 200 miles (320 km) north of the Arctic Circle. Later in June, the sun is shining all the time. I relaxed for the next nine hours, reflecting on what I have come through from the time I looked at the Red flag at the bridge at Lo Wu, in Hong Kong. I remember how I felt that day, ten months ago, crossing into Communist China. I thought about all the miles, the roads, the weather, the trials, the sand, the mud, the snow, the heat, the millions of faces, of people striving just to live, the difficulties, the triumphs, Tianamen Square, Red Square, the Cheshire Homes, the disabled.

It all came home to me in a flood.

With these emotions crashing through me, I couldn't even begin to sleep. I was high on emotion, now safe with no worry about anyone creeping up on me in the woods, or any of the other myriad problems that could happen in the areas I had come through. It was with great peace that I closed my day, my first back in the Western world.

I Did It!

The following morning, Father Yari came out and opened the front gate to a sunny beautiful morning. As I rode about 55 miles (90 km) on wonderfully smooth road along lakes, rivers and beautiful trees on both sides of the road, I was so elated it felt like heaven. The motorcycle had started easily, and was running really well (although still smoking like a bastard).

About 10:00, I came to the junction of the E4 Highway, about 40 miles (60 km) north of Ivalow...at this point that I had circumnavigated planet Earth! I parked the motorcycle next to one of the signs and took a couple of photographs. There were no crowds to welcome me, no celebrations, no speeches. Nothing but the quiet of an Arctic morning. I said a prayer of thanks to God and Jesus Christ for bringing me through so much since that incredible morning on September 12 when I hit the starter button and started this epic journey. Always being a man who knows how to celebrate and party down, I opened up a can of cold beans I'd been carrying for thousands of miles - baked beans never tasted so good! When finished, I straddled the motorcycle, started it, and said "Okay old Dog, we still have a long way to go."

Indeed, there were still 20,000 miles (32,000 km) left to ride before this journey would be over.

I headed south for Sweden.

The road during the day was beautiful along wonderful wooded country with lakes and rivers. Although the weather was still a miserable cold, in my mind it was probably the best ride of the entire trip. The motorcycle never ran better than it is doing right now. It probably realizes it is close to receiving the love and attention it needs. When I stop at Santa's Village, right at the Arctic Circle in Finland, people come over and take photos of the motorcycle. Only then was I able to tell someone that "I have just completed the circumnavigation of the world this morning." I could see their faces light up as they shared my own radiant joy. My enthusiasm must have rubbed off on them.

In Torno I went southwest. Torno and Kemi are right at the top of the Gulf of Botinviken (the Baltic Sea). There I went around the west side and down to Lulea in Sweden, asking directions here and there, riding finally into the huge yard that surrounds the clubhouse of the Aurora Choppers Motorcycle Club. There were Svend and Ingmar, two of the club members, still trying to start Svend's Panhead. This was the same scene I remember when I left two years before - Svend trying to start his Panhead, with Ingmar looking on. He's probably still trying to get it started!

After greetings, I told them about my maintenance problems. They told me to wheel in the motorcycle, and "When you're ready, have at it. Stay here as long as you want."

The Aurora Choppers have a nice, three story clubhouse, so I had a place to stay. It wasn't long before I was in the kitchen having some coffee and once again talking with my dear friend, Kenta, the man who had helped me so much with mechanical problems in May-June of 1991.

For the next three weeks, I work on the motorcycle. Not since Brazil has it had such major maintenance done on it. It had done a hell of a good job running from extremely low temperatures to extremely high temperatures, using all kinds of oils, through all types of weather and roads. It literally needed everything from shock absorbers to wheel bearings to the upper end of the motor being overhauled. Kenta was right there to help me all the way. Thankfully, he and Johnna have a distribution dealer license for motorcycle parts so they provided all parts at their costs.

The day we got the machine running again, they held a motorcycle show in Lulea sponsored by the Labbia Skogen's Motorcycle Club - "Labbia Skogen" means "Wolves in the Forest." I entered the motorcycle as most "unusual motorcycle." It was amazing to see all these incredible machines on display. Make no mistake about it, the Swedes are some of the most incredible custom bike builders anywhere in the world. Of course, they will all tell you the same thing, "We have a lots of time to work on them with the long winter."

It was surprising the amount of interest my machine drew. It always had a crowd around it; I taped my world map up on a shop front window. At the end of the show, Johnna won the most nostalgic motorcycle award. The prize was 1,000 krowns (about $150.00). Later that day, I felt something being pushed into my pocket and realized he had just given me his prize money. I was very touched. The attitude of bikers in Sweden was extremely unique - a brotherhood beyond just Harley Davidson's - it was a brotherhood of the motorcycle.

At the end of my three weeks, Kenta and his wife, Lotta, on the back of their chopper, escorted me out of town. While riding along the highway, we waived to one another and I headed south toward Germany to visit a sponsor. The ride would be about 1,200 miles (2000 km) south of Lulea. It rained every day, all the way to Germany.

Broken Leg and Gracious Germans

My first night out was miserable, but I was very pleased that the motorcycle seemed to be running with no major problems. When I got to Orebro, I stopped at the Midguard Motorcycle Club once again, spending a couple of days with these folks where I gave a talk and slide show. Eric, the same fellow I stayed with in 1991, took me around the town to show me some of the sites, including a castle over 700 years old, and some of the old restaurants in their cozy, antiquated settings. We don't see much antiquity in the United States. What a lovely town!

The same as when I left two years before, it is raining as I carried on South, sleeping out in the woods next to a big lake that night. All was quiet and peaceful, except for my private battle with the mosquitoes.

The following morning I rode into Heisingborg where I caught the ferry to Helsingor in Denmark. Across Denmark it was rainy and windy, the same as in 1991. On the far side of the island I caught a ferry to Puttgarden in Germany. I knew I was back in mainland Europe as soon as I hit Germany because, upon leaving the port, I was caught up in traffic that backed up for about 20 miles (32 km). I had to cut lanes along the main route, and outside of Bremen, I cut lanes again for about 30 miles (48 km). On the far side of Bremen, I found a campground in a secluded area.

The next day I headed towards Banhoniff, just southeast of Bohn in the northern part of Germany. I was due for one of those times on a journey that tells me I only change problems from one moment to the next. Be it bad roads, bad people or bad weather, I am always riding the edge!

In Germany, it was bad weather and heavy, heavy traffic. I was cutting along the fast lane, while passing an accident off to the side, when I hit an oil slick and flew off of the motorcycle. I could hear the engine screaming as it powered up on its side. As we flew along, I felt my right leg collide with something - I don't know what it was. As we came to rest about 30 feet from where we went down, I scooted over and shut off the motorcycle. My right leg had been torn in half. The police ran over from the other wreck. I started hollering, "Hey, there is oil on the asphalt. You ought to do something. Block the lanes off or something.' The police captain replied, "Don't shout, don't shout." "I'm shouting because you have neglected to pick up that oil, and that's the reason I crashed. Get the motorcycle up," I snapped. They hurriedly pick it up; it was leaking gasoline.

There in the pissing rain, people are zooming past me. I feel incredibly fortunate that I didn't collide with a car, especially since I don't have insurance. There was no need for the ambulance that had been summoned to the accident, but the policeman insisted that "You must be taken away in the ambulance."

"I am not paying for an ambulance!" I shouted. "I am not paying for it, fuck you all!" They couldn't believe my belligerent attitude towards them. I'm sure the German police are not used to being yelled at. They also couldn't believe I wasn't in great pain, what with my right leg dangling as it was as I tried to support myself on the motorcycle. They were even more astonished when they found out that both legs were gone!

The ambulance driver soothed the situation, saying "Money is no problem. We will take you for free." "What about the motorcycle?" I asked. "I can ride the thing with one leg." The policeman shouted, putting his hands to his head as if I was mad.

"No, you are not riding it with one leg!"

I eventually had to capitulate because I realized these guys had experienced enough shocks for one day. They called in a tow truck and promised the motorcycle would all be handled very delicately. They realized it was a Harley Davidson, and worth a lot of money.

The policeman asked me, "What are you doing here?" and I told him how I'd been around the world on this motorcycle. He started to tell me to "be more careful," and I blew up again. "Fuck being more careful! There's oil on the road."

"No, you are going too fast."

"No, I am NOT going too fast. There's oil on the road."

Anyway, the paramedics picked me up and carted me away to the ambulance, stopping the heated debate. In the ambulance, they assured me that they wouldn't charge any money for the ride. They were good fellows. At the hospital I said, "I don't want to be here. All I want to do is to have the prosthetist repair my right leg."

The staff are beside themselves. "You don't want a checkup?"

"No, I don't want nothing. I am not paying for nothing." Finally, a doctor comes out - a very beautiful tall blond, blue eyed German woman who says, "We won't charge you for anything. We just want to look you over."

Mind you, I've been on the road for a few days and smell like the south bound end of a north bound skunk. I haven't showered in days. I took my dirty clothes off and she looked at me with disgust. Of course, I had a couple of scrapes. She asks me, "Do you have any pain?" and I answered, "Yes, I have a pain in the ass from this whole bloody affair." That brought a smile of sadistic delight as she administered a painful tetanus shot to my withered, smelly posterior.

After putting my clothes back on, I once again said, "All I want now is a taxi to the prosthetist so that I can get my leg fixed."

"We will arrange to have you taken there by the hospital driver," the doctor told me. The driver took me across town, and after some hassle in finding the place, he came to the prosthetist. I explained the problem, and he took off my right leg. After inspecting the leg, the staff bursts out in laughter, as if my leg were the joke of the week. They told me they had authorization from the hospital to do whatever was needed to repair this leg, and the state would pay for it.

"I don't want that," I snapped. "The German people are not responsible for me."

When I was in Moscow, I bought two mechanical knees made of titanium. I gave the staff one of the knees because the leg was broken in half right through the knee. "Just remount this new knee in the old socket," I tell them.

"Don't you want a foot?"

"No foot. That's too much money, and the Germans are not responsible for me. Just repair the leg so I can get going."

With a look of amazement, they told me "It should be ready by tomorrow morning. Come back then."

That was a disappointment. Where would I stay? It was decided I could go stay at a half way house for recovering alcoholics and drug addicts - just the place for a party animal like me! Some days the chicken shit is endless.

At the half way house, one of the hospital staff shows up, a woman named Karol, and she says, "My husband and I own a Harley Davidson. We have been thinking that perhaps you would prefer to spend the night with us."

"Boy, you bet I would," I answered. She went to fetch her husband, Michael, and they took me back across town to their very neat little apartment where I spent the night. As I rested in bed, I reflected back on the day. I had covered about 350 miles in the rain, and ended the day with the accident, an ambulance ride, and a visit to the hospital and the prosthetist. I had been in a wheelchair and on crutches for the first time in 11 years. With a feeling of being fortunate to be alive, I closed this day with a humble prayer of thanks.

The following morning they took me back to the prosthetist who had worked late on the leg doing some adjustments. By 10:00 it was ready; I put it on and started walking; these two guys couldn't believe how I was able to get around. They were very gracious, and said, "no charge." I asked them to call a taxi to take me to the garage where the motorcycle is, but one said, "I will take you."

Thankful, the motorcycle was in good shape, and I only had to pay for the towing of the machine. Fair enough.

Once I loaded the machine, I started on my way again, back out on the highway, passing the very spot where I had the accident. There was still oil on the pavement. Obviously, no other motorcycles had come to grief in Leverkusen. In the Banhonif area, I located Reinhard Wirtgen, and spent the next three days with one of the more unique people I've met on the entire journey (by his own request, I can say no more).

Three days later I was on my way to Zeeberg in Belgium, where I caught a ferry that set sail that evening for England. I realized as it set sail that **I had now come overland from the South China Sea to the Barents Sea to the North Sea.**

That night, I looked for quiet spot where I could read. Since I was booked on what they called "deck class," I was entitled to collapse anyplace I could find a spot. An unused couch ended up being my "room" for the night. I took off my legs and fell into a fitful sleep.

Tho next morning, in the calm North Sea, I went outside and watched a wonderful sunrise. Along about 11:00, the ship put into port at Harwhich where everybody debarked and I was back in good ole Blighty again.

The Most Courageous People on Earth

At the port I was met by Judith Walker, the head of the Cheshire Home. When I was in Sweden, I volunteered to do a speaking, media tour for the Cheshire

Foundation. It was agreed that on July 18 I would arrive in England and start the tour the next day. I followed Judith to the home, put the motorcycle away, and relaxed with the residents.

The following day I met with media, did a slide show, then took off on my way around England, visiting 17 homes in various places throughout England during the next three weeks, trying to do my part to work with the disabled. A few times I helped with the feeding of those who could not feed themselves. I met many with extremely lucid minds, yet because of muscular sclerosis, they are so disabled they cannot speak. They have lost all their teeth, and are strapped down in their chairs so they won't fall out. Most cannot feed themselves. I try to help, but I must admit I can handle a world-wide trip better than trying to put food into their mouths. They often spit all over the place, and drool on themselves, with snot coming out of their noses. God forgive me - but I am not very good at this. I am very thankful that we each have our own ministry in life. Meeting these so unable to help themselves makes me appreciate how wonderful and easy my life is compared to their challenges. I think to myself, "Lord, these must be the most courageous people on earth!"

One home I stayed in was haunted - the Sandbatch Home. One staff member told me, before my slide show, not to go into the TV room and mess with any of the books. I examined the room, and found volumes of books about the family that had owned that Home since 1600. Looking at these volumes, I noticed they were out of order. Since I was warned not to touch them, because absolutely bizarre things would happen, I left them alone. The Home had had two exorcisms, and during the construction of an extension wing, supposedly the construction materials were constantly being moved around or lost. They also claimed that in the laundry room a person will sometimes hear the door slam shut, and then it gets icy cold inside. 200 years ago the butler hung himself in that room.

There's also a spiral metal staircase that goes up into the attic of the Home. I went up it one morning; there are some offices up there; they say there is one room that they could never convert to an office, and to this day it remains barren and empty. Ice cold. The staff claim the place is riddled with ghosts.

I met a fellow named Super Tim, a tetraplegia - he had slight use of one hand, but his body was bent way out of shape. In his electric chair he used to ride 7 miles to the train station, get one of the cars and head for London. There, he would work as a high-powered computer programmer, troubleshooting programs for a company. After work, he'd go back to the train station, back to Sandbach, then ride another 7 miles in the chair back to the Home. Only then could the staff take him out of the chair, clean him up, and get him ready for the evening. Quite a guy! Super Tim, indeed!

I did a slide show at New Melton, right on the English Channel, for the smallest Cheshire Home in the world - only 6 residents. There I met Sammy Miller, one of the world's top motorcycle racers. He invited me to come and see his museum, an incredible collection of motorcycles dating from the time motorcycles were first created until the present day. I saw a Honda 4 cylinder, with dual overhead cams, that dated back to 1963. His trophy case went from the floor to 6 feet high, and covered an area of three walls in his huge shop. I've never seen a trophy case so full of trophies and awards for road racing, flat track (speedway), for enduro racing, you name it.

Sammy taught seminars in various places in the world, and restores motorcycles in a shop behind this place. He had ridden over to the home on a 1928, V-Twin

Brome Motorcycle. It looks much like a Harley Davidson, but is English. It is the same make of motorcycle that Lawrence of Arabia rode when he was killed.

I asked Sammy, "If the Harley factory doesn't want it, would you like to put my motorcycle in your museum, seeing how you don't have any Harley Davidsons?"

He answered a flat "No." It wasn't hard to see that he was very anti-Harley Davidson...there wasn't one Harley in his whole collection. What a shame.

In another Home I again was reminded of the very grim realities. As I was having lunch with some residents, one of the jolliest fellows asked me, Dave, do you realize how lucky you are?"

"Yes, I do," I replied.

"For many of us, we are just sitting, waiting for the grim reaper."

And I knew it was true. Many have massive disabilities and diseases. They have done all they can do, and are just waiting for their lives to end. He did not say to this make me feel sorry for him, but to remind me to appreciate the great gift of my health and life.

Brothers and Sisters of the Wind

August 10, 1993: I rode back into London and went straight to Tiger Cycles where I hadn't been since June, 1991. I was greeted 10 minutes later by big, fat, mean Tigger who rode up on his Harley. He's so big it is hard to put my arms around this guy, like trying to hug a big beer barrel. After our reunion, we put the motorcycle away. The shop was no longer operative. We talked about the past two years and everywhere I've been, plus what I needed to do now on the motorcycle.

The next day I rode 200 miles north up to Barnsley, and reunited with the Barnsley Warriors. Over the next two days, I got new names painted onto my gas tank by Trosky, who originally did the paint job. I hit Barnsley just when they were having their annual party. It was good to be around my old friends. At the end of that weekend, I was very sad as I said "good-bye" to these brothers and sisters of the wind. I'll always remember the Barnsley Warriors as the first motorcycle club in the world to lend me a helping hand.

After riding back down to London, I steam-cleaned the motorcycle.

The following morning I rode to the east end of London, to Barking, about 30 miles (45 km) away, to do some photography for P&O Containers and Shipping. They had agreed, through the help of the Cheshire Foundation, to ship my motorcycle to Australia for free if I would pose for some pictures for their quarterly newsletter.

The following day Tigger and I went to the Barking container depot again. This was my last ride on the motorcycle in Europe. On top of Tigger's Jaguar we carried a packing crate, in pieces, for the motorcycle. Once at the terminal we put the motorcycle in the crate and packaged it for its trip to Australia. Then, it was stored away for shipping; I was told it would arrive in Australia in about a month.

I felt relief because I would no longer be riding in Europe. Believe it or not, to ride around the streets of London is an absolute and utter nightmare; the average speed is about 6 miles an hour. I must cut mile after mile of traffic in very narrow lanes (compared to the United States and other European countries).

I had made it! The riding part of Stage Five was over. It was with great relief that I left the machine in the very capable hands of my new sponsor, P&O.

I spent the next few days wandering about on subways and buses, getting my visa for Australia. My stumps just kill me from walking the long distances.

August 27: I say good-bye to all and head for the London airport where Tigger and I exchanged an emotion-charged, but quick good-bye, then parted company. Tigger is a bizarre kind of underworld character, but he's also extremely unique. He's been a wonderful benefactor to me and the journey. Without him, I honestly don't know what I would have done.

After checking my baggage, I soon found myself on the aircraft, then up in the air. As England shrunk away, and we flew over Europe, I realized that Stage Five of this continuing journey was behind me.

I said a prayer of thanks.

60 miles/95 Km out Kemerov in Western Siberia Russia.
I stayed in the hospital and hid from a family of drunks.
May 1993

European Ecstasy, Completed Dream!

Statue of Lenin in Novosibirsk Western Siberia.
Russia May 1993

Red Square in front of Lenin's Tomb.
June 12, 1993. Moscow, Russia

Red Square. Moscow, Russia.
June 12, 1993

Murmansk 200 miles North of Arctic Circle.
June 18, 1993 Russia.
Picture taken by Boris.

Stage Six: Australia

Chapter Thirty-Four

"No Problem, Mate!"

The plane landed in Johannesburg, I cleared Customs and Immigration, and was met by Don Hornsby. Our conversation immediately turned to all the crime going on in South Africa, especially with black on black violence. As Don is sharing, I stare out the car window and see the brown winter bushveld near Johannesburg, the city I first saw in 1979. Then, it was clean and orderly; today, trash was blowing everywhere, and there are many people just loitering in the streets. "The people are very depressed, Don told me. I notice that there's not much traffic out on the road...even less than when I had came here for five days on my way to Hong Kong.

We spend the rest of the afternoon at Don's service station, then his home. Late in the evening, I finally settle back and close the day.

August 29: Today marks twelve years to the day that we ran over the land mine, and here I was, back in South Africa.

Today Don and I head for the Cheshire Home where I surprise Luke. After giving him a big hug, we visit the other residences of the home. "The country is in bad shape, Dave," they all tell me. "The Home is not worth a damn," some others say. This is very unfortunate since these people need constant care.

I learn that there is a 46 percent unemployment rate among the black population. Rent, water and electricity are being paid by 20 percent of the population, i.e. the white population is paying for the black population. There's a terrible problem with immigrants coming illegally into South Africa from Mozambique, Zimbabwe, Angola, Zambia and the entire subcontinent as far north as Zaire.

The government had just imposed a tax on businesses downtown to clean up after street vendors. There was an uproar about that. There was also an uproar in the University of Witswaterstand around exam time. The black students are holding demonstrations, trying to keep other students from going to class. I think to myself, "Here these people are going to college for nothing, yet they are causing trouble. They don't deserve an education." Most of the trouble makers are political science majors. How many politicians do we need in Africa? Africa needs engineers and technical skills, not more politicians.

September 2, 1993: A day of peace was organized by 702 Radio, and something incredible happened that had never happened before in South Africa. At 12:00 noon, for five minutes, the trains stop, people stop on the freeways, businesses shut down, and both black and white people hold hands and form circles all over South Africa, praying for peace. It was a touching moment!

Don got all of his employees and customers together in a big circle in the middle of his service station. He said, "Come on. Lets all hold hands and get together before we murder each other tomorrow."

The main problem that I noticed was the black on black violence. There seemed to be better good will between blacks and whites - more than I had seen in previous years. It seemed much easier to talk to black people about their political views as they openly shared how dire the situation was in the townships with all the political and factional violence.

I notice that the expressions on people's faces at night in the bars seem to indicate that they hope things will be better in the near future. The false sense of optimism often wears off quickly with the morning violence, bringing home the stark reality of the difficult situation. The sound of emergency vehicles and sirens always seems present.

My friend in Germany, Norbert Hine, told me by phone that he wanted me to go to Hamburg on September 11 to do a television interview with Premier TV. "Of course," he told me, "they will pay you for your trip." Well done, Norbert!

John Burks at 702 Radio invites me to do a radio interview, live on the air, and I happily obliged him. I was scheduled for 45 minutes, but the interview lasted an hour and a half. By the end of the interview, I was drained mentally.

On September 11, I told Luke I was going to Hamburg for an interview. I gave him a hug, and thought, "Three years ago on this very night I said good-bye to you in the same bed you are in tonight." I thought about the fear and apprehension in my heart at that time. Of course, I still have some fear and apprehension as I look forward to Australia, and getting to the top of Cape York.

I flew up to Hamburg and was taken to the Grand Hotel, one of the finest in Hamburg. That evening I had an interview with Premeir Television; it lasted about 12 minutes. The interviewer was a beautiful, red haired woman named Sabrina. The interview went well until she asked, "Dave, what do you call your motorcycle?"

"Well, I call it an old dog because it runs like a dog sometimes."

"You don't ever call it a bitch, do you?" she asked.

I was taken aback and couldn't believe the question. "I sometimes call it worse things than a bitch when it won't run right," I finally stammered.

After my trip to Hamburg, I gave one of my most positive talks and slide shows ever to a group of 75 people. The original people were there: Don Hornsby, Monty Brett, Mike Calendar, Mike McWilliams - people who helped with the original Namib trip. I was so gratified that they could come and watch it.

September 19: The day I am scheduled to fly to Australia, I feel a deep sense of peace and tranquillity come over me as I write my diary at about 08:00. I went to the hospital to say good-bye to Luke (he was taken from the home a few days earlier because of pneumonia). He was in intensive care ward. There I met Cheryl, his wife, and his mother, Mrs. Kotze, and they informed me that Luke had died at 08:00. I smiled at them, and frankly felt absolute joy for my friend. He had finally been released from the terrible burden of life that he had carried so gallantly over the past seven years. I kissed his forehead, I prayed to God his soul to keep, and walked out of the room, saying good-bye to his family.

I drove to Cheshire Home and told them the sad news. I didn't want it to come from somebody else. There was a strong look of hurt on all the faces of those who carried burdens similar to that of Luke. These people who life had treated so cruelly just looked down with tears in their eyes. With that, I said good-bye to Gary, Sandy and Steve and walked away. Don and I drove in silence to the airport. His last words to me once again were "Don't get clever."

After Customs and Immigration, I boarded the plane which almost immediately departed, flying over Africa, and eventually the Indian Ocean. I thought to myself "This has been another terrible day of very painful good-byes," one of them permanent.

I was on my way. Stage Six was about to unfold

Watch for Roos and the Big Wet!

Eight hours later at 05:12 in the morning the plane touched down in Perth. I cleared Customs, and was met by Brad Wood, the manager of Exclusive Motorcycles, and a biker's biker. We went down to Exclusive Motorcycles to meet the rest of the group. My machine had already arrived, and over the next couple of days we went back and forth because of all the bureaucratic problems getting the motorcycle into the country. Finally, we retrieved it and brought it back to the shop.

Brad had good contacts in the Department of Transport in Cambera. He contacted the Harley Davidson shop in Cambera, who paid $50.00 to somebody in the DOT of Cambera to pass a form back to us in 24 hours; the form normally takes 3 weeks. Things are flowing very well.

I give a slide show - my first in Australia, attended by about 45 people, and received a welcome $100.00 check from Paul and Max of the Vietnam Vets Motorcycle Club.

September 24: What a jubilant mood in Perth today! It has just been announced that Sydney will host the Olympics in the year 2,000. At the motorcycle shop, there was a bit of black humor, the guys joking amongst themselves that the rest of the students from the Tianamen Square protest will now be taken out and shot after the Chinese failed to win the Olympics; after all, the Chinese government has nothing to lose now.

"Look out for roos, mate," meaning, watch for kangaroos and emus, animals that hang around the side of the road. They are hit all time. I notice that most cars, especially the ones from the countryside, all have "bung bars" on the front of them; trucks too. These bung bars serve as protectors for the front of the vehicle from when kangaroos or emus jump out in front of them. The animals hit the bar and go "BUNG," tossed off to the side of the road, dead.

I'm always making inquiries of those who might know anything about Cape York at this time of year. I'm told that this time of year "It is not bad to go up," but if I don't get there soon, it will be a problem because of "the big wet" - the rainy season in the north of Australia. In November, the place apparently becomes a definite "no go." I am thinking, "I will not get there before November" as it is thousands of miles away from me by the route I am going to take around the country.

September 25: I am ready to roll. I take the motorcycle out of the shop, say good-bye to everyone, climb on the motorcycle, and what do you know, it won't start. Bruce, the head mechanic, comes over. After a bit of investigation, we discover that there is a problem with the ignition which he sorts out rather quickly.

While making the repairs, I get a call to "hold on" because a television crew is coming to film me riding out. Once again, trouble with the motorcycle turns out to be beneficial for the purpose of my trip. After TV interviews and filming, the group follows me out of town. Brad's last words to me are, "Look out for the roos, mate!"

I follow a fellow named Charlie, an older guy, a biker of many years with a craggy face and buck teeth. Charlie is good with a joke anytime, and a master of low humor. I follow him out of Perth until he stops about 20 kilometers (12 miles) outside of the central part of Perth, pointing me in the right direction. Charlie's final words to me are, "Dave, life is like a shit sandwich. The more bread you have, the less shit you eat." With laughter in our hearts, we shake hands and I head south towards Agusta Bay.

The countryside is not very populated, but there are many ranches, gum and oak trees, and green pastures. How good it feels to be alone and out on the road! It is a one lane road, but in very good condition without much traffic. By late afternoon, I come in to Agusta Bay and decide to spend the night at a campground since I am having a bit of carburetor trouble, and don't want to be stuck out in the middle of nowhere if the thing does not start.

As I work on the motorcycle, a fellow named Peter Duncan walks over and asks, "Can I give you a hand?" The carburetor intake manifold is the problem - a pinched manifold sealing band. "Yes, hold this," I said, and he helped me put it back on. I think to myself, "It is a good thing I stopped in the campground." Peter invited me to share dinner with him and his wife; they had just caught some fresh fish.

At dinner, Peter tells me about his World War II experiences as a gunner in the Royal Navy. "I was on the Murmansk Run in the North Atlantic and the Barents Sea during the war." He knew Murmansk from a distance, so we had something in common.

The following morning the motorcycle starts very easy and I head off down to the corner of Australia **where the Indian and Southern Oceans meet and I arrive at Agusta Bay, another landmark in my trip around the world.** I can't get down to the lighthouse as it is closed, and won't be open for a another few hours yet. I take some photographs of the sign and the ocean on both sides, then head out on countryside with rolling hills and woodlands. There are fields of yellow flowers, and I can almost smell the freshness in the air as I roll on, making miles very quickly. I see my first sign warning of kangaroos.

Late in the afternoon, I pull into a petrol station in the small town of Jerramungup. As I put fuel in, a fellow comes out and hands me a note. I worry when I see someone carrying a piece of paper to me since that's almost exactly how I was told about my father's passing in a service station in Southwest Africa. This note, believe it or not, is from my friend Paul Hogan! I have not seen him in eleven years! I used to stay with him when I had leave in the Zimbabwe/Rhodesian Army. The attendant gives me a phone number, so after fueling up, I walk over to the phone booth and call Paul. He was a little over 300 miles (500 km) from where I was in a place called Norsman, right on the edge of the Nullabore. We agreed to meet the following day.

What an incredible surprise! Although I must admit that I did have a feeling that I would run into some of my old African Army mates who are Australians, especially Paul Hogan, it turns out Paul read about me in an article printed in a National Newspaper.

I ride into the countryside and find a small dirt road off into the bush. I stay on this road a mile or two, off the main road, and find a secluded area in a field of flowers. It is nice and cool. I put up my tent and lay back after cooking my dinner and working on the motorcycle. As I was sitting back with a cup of Ze Qing's green Chinese tea, I watch an incredible sunset, feeling a wonderful sense of peace and happiness that I was out on the road alone in these beautiful surroundings - a true sense of freedom and peace. When the stars come out, I see the southern cross for the first time in years. It is so bright, but in a different position from the last time I saw it in Africa or South America. This day I had covered 400 miles without too much trouble, and the motorcycle seems to be running reasonably well.

The following morning is more country, only there seems to be more bushes. I ride on about 300 miles (500 km) to Norsman where I call Paul's house; his wife, Ann, comes over to guide me to their small house where they live with their two daughters. Paul has been a miner for a number of years down in the pits. He had worked in South African gold mines at one time, and was an officer at the parachute jump school at Newserum in Harare, Zimbabwe/Rhodesia, where we first met. We enjoy a night of reminiscing about old friends and parties, and skydiving at Dellport Farm, just outside Harare. At 23:00, we turn in and close the day.

The next morning up early, Paul, on his little motorcycle, leads me out of town. At an intersection where the road goes north to Kalgoorlie, or east to Adelaide, I looked east and the sign says Adelaide 1,986 kilometers (about 1,200 miles). Paul and I shake hands, our very short time together is over, and I ride off into the Nullabore.

Almost immediately I see kangaroo road kills, sometimes 3 or 4 in a very short distance; the smell from the side of road, although not overbearing, is that of dead animals. Sometimes I pass a hundred or more in an hour! I later learn that even though there are so many road kills, they still have to cull to keep the numbers of kangaroos in proportion with what the countryside can handle.

The weather is semi-arid with plenty of low scrub; the road is straight. I go in one stretch for 110 km (70 miles) without a bend. There is a side wind running, but nothing terrible, and it is cool all day. Again, the motorcycle seems to be running very well! Sometimes I ride 75 to 80 miles in between little villages which serve as service areas for the cattle and sheep stations, which are farther in the outback away from the road.

At the end of the day I find a dirt road off towards a relay beacon, ride on it a couple of miles, and find a path back into the sticks used by animals. Then, in a little clearing, I establish my camp, never seeing or hearing another man.

The following morning I decide to photograph the road kill of a kangaroo, so I stop the motorcycle and photograph this thing from different angles. I took a good 5 minutes. Of course, there is virtually no other traffic on the road. I thought, "I'll never get a photograph of a live kangaroo, so this is what I must resort to for a photograph with a Roo."

I next cross into Southern Australia where I get a few roo pictures, take a photo of the border sign, and push on. Miraculously, I do not see anymore dead kangaroos along the road. I was told later that they have a regular patrol to come and pick them up. I stopped to take a photograph of the Southern Ocean, thinking to myself, "How many Oceans in various places of the world have I rode along?"

Later that day I start seeing trees again, and even some farms off in the distance that are sheep stations. It starts to get much hotter as well. Outside of a place called Wurilla, I find a cluster of old buildings back off the road and pull in amongst them. The flies are incredible! I naturally go into the Aussie salute mode, constantly flicking my hand in front of my face, waiving flies away. As I look around these old buildings, the one I am next to has a stage - maybe an old community theater. Now it is all torn up inside, a mere memory of a bygone day and a simpler age. Again, I see no one out here. It's just me and my hay fever, which had been bothering me all day. Flies and hay fever - what a joy! I wait until dark to cook my dinner since I did not want to eat flies at the same time. That night, I welcome the darkness for the relief from flies, and for sleep.

When I wake up the next morning at 04:00, it is a wonderful gray hour; the sun is not yet over the horizon, but my pesky friends are back as I eat my "fly sandwich" wearing a scarf around my face, under my eyes, to keep the flies away.

I am sneezing so badly when I finally hit the road around 05:00 that I can't see the road and almost have an accident! I decide to double up on my allergy medicine, making me groggy while on the motorcycle; not a good combination.

I see some road trains, but never the big ones like I had expected -the big three trailer rigs; most I pass are exceptionally big two trailer rigs. It will make the American truck manufacturers happy to know that virtually all of them were pulled by American trucks, the most popular being the Kenworth.

I hit a head wind all day as I travel through a terrain of farming, sheep and cattle stations. For some reason, my left stump is killing me. At times I take it off the crash bar and try to move it around, hoping to ease the throbbing. When I put it down when I stop the motorcycle, it virtually takes my breath away it hurts so bad. On my right side, my belts are pinching and making me miserable. Situation normal. Towards the end of this day I ride into Adelaide, heading for the Harley Davidson shop.

"You are welcome to work on the motorcycle here," the shop owner told me. One of his customers owned a nearby body shop, and said, "You are welcome to spend a night or two with us. However long you need to stay."

After two days in Adelaide, servicing the motorcycle with Penright Oil, my first oil sponsor. I say this not because they sponsored me, but because I honestly believe they have the most incredible oil my machine has ever used. I used their oil all the way around Australia and right up through Southeast Asia and still had their oil in the motorcycle when I arrived home here in the United States.

When I leave Adelaide, I am escorted out of town by one of the HOG members of Adelaide. I immediately see rolling green hills and forests with lush pine trees, much as are found in North America. Along the coast, the weather starts to change, and so does the scenery. The road is rough, and the countryside becomes marshy, flat and very stony.

Towards the end of the day I speak with a lady in a store who was upset about Paul Keating. She told me that "The arrogant bastard wants to separate from the Crown. All he wants is to become the first President of Australia." I think to myself, "The people in Russia and China struggle to live and South Africans oftentimes face death on a daily basis, while people here are worrying about separating from the crown?"

Flies, Friends, and Soggy Sandwiches

About 40 miles (60 km) out of this little town, I find a dirt road that goes back through an incredible countryside with pine forest on one side and green pasture lands with cows and sheep grazing on the other. I put up my tent in the cow pasture, cook my dinner and wait for the evening to come.

The cows, getting used to my presence, start wandering closer to me as I listened to the breeze gently blow through the pine trees, a very soothing, lovely sound. A full moon comes out, and for some reason I think about the group that made our little documentary in China, wondering what they were doing now. The melody of the song "Blame It on Midnight, Blame It on the Moon" rolls around in my mind as I close my day. Sure enough, about midnight it started pissing rain, continuing through the rest of the night and into the next day. So much for paradise.

The next morning, I load up and enjoy a soggy peanut butter sandwich for breakfast (at least there are no flies). On the dirt road out to the main highway, I slip and slide quite a few times, but manage to stay on the machine. I made good time on the paved road into the province of Victoria where I once again enjoyed beautiful green rolling farmlands with lots of trees. It was wonderful. Only the rain dampened the enjoyment of this ride.

In Mt. Gambier, two young fellows working in a service station give me a cup of coffee. We chat for a while, and they seem taken with my trip and why I am doing it. They ask, "Will you write to us?" I agree, and get a post card out, saying, "Put your address on this. IF I make it to the top of Cape York, I'll send you this card from there."

The next town was Arat, and there I was supposed to catch up with the Harley owners group of Melbourne the following day. I find a campground and put up my tent. The wind was howling through the gum trees as a fellow named Jack comes over and says, "Would you like a hot cup of tea with my wife and I?" "Sure I would," I answer, and for the next two hours we sit sipping tea and talking. I learn that Jack was a tail gunner who had flown 50 missions on Lancaster bombers (25 more than was required during World War II). He and his wife are now retired and travel all over Australia. After our visit, I go back to my tent with water on the floor and enjoy a couple of cold salami sandwiches, falling asleep listening to the wind and rain.

The following morning I go into town, hoping to thaw off with a hot cup of tea. It is freezing cold, and quite windy. At a designated location, I wait for the Harley owners group of Melbourne to show up. About 09:30, here comes 5 Harley Davidsons with 7 members from the HOG of Melbourne! It is wonderful that these people had rode so far out of their way - about 125 miles - to escort me into Melbourne through the howling wind and cold. Alex Version, the leader, and I had been writing to each other since *The Enthusiast* article in the summer of 92 had been published.

426

Our ride into Melbourne was very rough. On the outskirts of the city we stopped and I did an interview with Channel 7 News and a newspaper, then we went on to meet the owner of one of the Harley Davidson shops, a man who restores and races old Harleys from a bygone era.

Next, on to Lower Templestowe. I realize these guys do not cut lanes, but I can't sit in slow traffic with the old shovel head. I tell them, "I've got to cut through the lanes," which I did, with them following. They have big wide buckhorn or drag bars on their motorcycles, so their fingers come a lot closer to hitting the cars than mine do. We go to the house of Dennis and Rosemary Williams in Lower Templestowe; he runs a plumbing business out of their home. I put the motorcycle away, and enjoy a very welcome shower.

The following day a fellow named Stacks, Dennis and I get on the motorcycles and ride to Wilson Promentary, the southern most point of the continent of Australia. Unfortunately, we cannot go the last 10 kilometers since they refused to allow any motor vehicles down the foot path. It is with a bit of a feeling of disappointment that we ride the 120 or so miles back to Melbourne on this very overcast, cool day. It rains on us off and on, although the countryside is quite beautiful. "There's a lot of flooding in eastern Victoria this time of year," according to Alex.

That night I meet Alex's father, Sergio, and he shows me the most incredible collection of military firearms I have ever seen. He was a partisan with Teto's forces in Czechoslovakia during World War II - a man with a very rich history.

The following night I give a talk and slide show, one of the best I present in all of Australia, to the Melbourne HOG. They were a very attentive audience thanks to excellent projector equipment loaned to the group by one of the members.

I spoke on the phone to Felicity Hornsby back in South Africa. She had been robbed again since I left. Although she was armed, she decided not to shoot it out with the robbers. When they frisked her, she kept rolling around on the spot where she kept her fire arm, so they never found it. Well done Felicity! What a cool head!

October 7: Stacks and Dennis show me the way out of Melbourne and I'm on my way north again in the wind and cold, but on a good concrete highway. I ride along incredibly green pastures as the sun comes out and the wind stops. It is some of the most beautiful motorcycling I have experienced anywhere in the world. The hills are gentle rolling hills with big and small trees. I go through some flooded areas, and am happy to see that none of the buildings have actually been washed away. However, it is clear there's plenty of cleanup work for these poor people!

That afternoon late I pull off the road after riding about 350 miles (550 km) and locate a gravel quarry next to a beautiful lake where I pull in and pitch my tent. I am isolated for the evening.

That night, I think about many things. I am grateful for not having to worry in Australia about wild animals or criminals. My mind wanders to thoughts of Cape York, and what my life will be like when the trip comes to an end. I think about writing a book, but then say, "Hey, don't count the chickens before they hatch. There's a lot more miles to go and many dangers to face before you make the final grade." I also feel good knowing that I had crossed into New South Wales that day.

The next morning, swatting flies, I start on another beautiful ride on a sunny day over a wonderful concrete highway, way ahead of my schedule for getting into Sydney. I was told not to come in before a certain date because the Harley's Owner Group of Black Town and New South Wales want to come out and greet me. So, I only ride about 150 miles or so then find a little hide away where I can be totally alone and set up camp. I spend the rest of the day reading, writing post cards, and just relaxing with nature.

The following morning I come into the outskirts of Sydney and locate the bar and grill where I was told to wait for the Harley group. I sit back for the next couple of hours sneezing and miserable, waiting for them to come. When they start arriving, it was 4 or 5 bikes - about what I expected. But over the next thirty minutes, 30 Harley Davidsons appear. What a wonderful surprise!

After greetings, we caravaned down to the harbor. Since it was now noontime, and very hot, I had to cut lanes because my engine was heating up. Once in the harbor area, we pulled under a bridge - a very big tourist area. The tourists gawk at our motorcycles.

We are supposed to conduct a TV interview at this location, but the TV crew never shows up. We call to ask why and they tell us, "There was a murder we had to cover." Well, I guess that is what the news thrives on - murder, politics and sex. In this sense, Australia is not much different from the United States.

That afternoon, I go with Dave and Beverly Collins, two English people living in Australia, to their modest home in a place called New Town. The following day we ride to meet a group at Black Town Harley Davidson, and from there we ride up into the Blue Mountains to see incredibly beautiful pine trees and rock formations, plus many small villages. The ride is hard for me since I have the old four speed transmission, and the group members all have five speeds, giving them all the power in the world. It is a fun ride none the less, and at the end we visit a drug and alcohol rehab center where they are having a party...a dry party. A band is playing, and hamburgers and hot dogs were being barbecued. Lots of coffee!

We ride back to Black Town Harley Davidson where the owner's son opened the shop for me to safely store my Harley Davidson away. I then ride on the back of Ron's bike, a full-dressed Harley Davidson, blaring Roy Orbinson songs along the freeways back to New Town.

Tom Brown is one of those unique characters in the Harley Davidson world, and the owner of Black Town Harley Davidson. He raced a 1958 Pan Head Harley Davidson with a sidecar as he had a stiff fused hip from a bad motorcycle accident. This sidecar was clocked at speeds of a 129 miles an hour on the straights! Mind you, Tom is a very big boy, standing about 6 foot 3 inches, and weighing about 230 pounds, so his machine must pull an incredible amount of weigh besides the sidecar and its passenger.

Acrobatics, Barbecues, and Sticky Valves

A fellow named Michael took me down to the Bankstown Airport to see the School of Acrobatics. I met a pilot named Paul there who took me up in a monoplane. We flew over Sydney Harbor, spotting landmarks around the Sydney area until he burned enough fuel to start tossing the plane around. He then started doing some incredible acrobatics. I think Paul was trying to get me to blackout; to my great relief, I didn't. What a magical experience! Once back on the ground, "People frequently throw up in my plane," Paul told me gratefully.

My next stop is back over the Blue Mountains and down the other side at a town called Dubbo where I knew Ian and Betty Ann McArthur since the *Easy Rider* article published in March 1992. These two kind people had written and offered a helping hand, so we had been writing to each other for the past year and a half. They arranged for me to do a talk and slide show to benefit the disabled in Dubbo. So it was with great anticipation that I rode over the Blue Mountains and down into the rolling hills and farming areas of Dubbo, a town of about 35,000 people.

I meet Ian, a machinist, and his wife, Betty Ann. We take the motorcycle over to the clubhouse of the Rebels Motorcycle Club where it will stay for the next couple of days. I met the president, Steve Tolmie, and we spend the next few hours talking about various aspects of my trip, and what would happen over the next few days. When we leave the clubhouse about 21:00, we drive down a small country lane for about 20 miles until we come to some mailboxes on the side of the road. One was the frame of a Bonneville Triumph motorcycle - that was the mailbox for the homestead of Ian and Betty Ann, known as "Bonneville." We drive a few more miles to a beautiful brick home that they had built themselves.

Inside, I was amazed at the very tasteful decorations they had accomplished, building the house both inside and out - all the cabinets and all the furnishings. They remind me of my own mother and father who were always remodeling and working around the house, doing additions, always working together.

Ian owned some amazing motorcycles: a 1906 Triumph, a 1915 Big Wheel bicycle, some BMW's and other Triumphs. He had rode one Triumph all the way up Cape York and circumnavigated the whole country as well. He also had a 1975 Harley Davidson he bought and rode all over the United States. Naturally, their house also had a huge workshop full of motorcycle parts from various years and for different kinds of motorcycles.

The following day I am to give a talk and slide show. We go to the club house of the Rebels where I meet Mayor McGain who introduces me to the crowd that was there. The program was to benefit the disabled, and had been advertised in the paper and announced on the radio the day before I arrived in Dubbo. As I presented my talk, I was surprised that there were only two people with disabilities out of the whole town in attendance. When it was all over, of course we had a barbecue. In the end, Steve, the president, walked up to me and said, "Dave, here's half of the money - about $250 - that was supposed to go to the disabled, but since only two of them showed up, piss on them. You take it." Far be it from me to argue with the president of a 1% motorcycle club. I readily accepted.

The following day we go to retrieve the motorcycle and bring it to Ian and Betty Ann's; I would leave on Monday. As I ride back, my machine suddenly starts running on one cylinder; the front cylinder valves had seized. Ian goes on home and brings back his Holden car and his wife. We tow the motorcycle with him on it, and me sitting in the car with Betty Ann. I remember her looking back in the mirror and saying, "Gee, I married a wonderful, handsome man." I said to her, "Betty Ann, be careful. Protect and cherish that love because it so fragile and unpredictable, and can be taken away from you so quickly." She looks at me and smiles as if to agree.

This was to be a problem that would plague me throughout the rest of Australia due to the combination of heat and bad gasoline. The Swedes, when they did the cylinder heads, had done them according to their very cool climate, and far better grade of gasoline.

In Ian's shop, we pull off the front cylinder head off and sure enough the valve is stuck open in the cylinder head. We decide to pull the rear head off as well, in case there are problems with the rear cylinder valves. These events are disappointing, since I had a valve job done on the machine in Sweden. Ian said, "Dave, don't worry. It will be no problem getting everything sorted out and back together tomorrow." That's good news. In my heart I knew that any delay could effect my arriving in Cape York before the Big Wet. Any delays could effect my chances of making it to the top.

Then it came back to me. This was the area that Alex in the Moscow Cheshire Home predicted I would start having trouble with the engine. I just wondered how much trouble I was going to have.

The following day I link up with Steve Tolmie who takes me to the engineers who receive the cylinder heads and do the valve job. Steve and I had already broke them down and bead-blasted them. Late that afternoon we pick them up and drive back to Ian's place where the three of us take about 2 hours to complete the repair. It won't start. We can't get the lifters to pump up. We then pull the lifters out of Ian's Harley Davidson and put them in mine. When we try again, it works!

The following morning we wheel the motorcycle down to the flag pole and take some photos with the house and motorcycle. I'm thinking, "How nice it would be to just spend a day quietly here." I am very tired physically. My days have been running from 05:00 in the morning to 24:00 at night. Rejecting that thought, I decide "Dave, you must go forward." I start the motorcycle and follow Ian down the country lane away from this bit of paradise and on into Dubbo; we say good-bye to one another and I ride off in the direction of Tamworth, through rolling hills with lots of trees and rock formations.

Tamworth is known as the "country music capital" of Australia; I spend the night with some friends of Ian's, then move onward the next morning quite early towards the coast. The hills become higher and steeper, and far more forested - looking like rain forest in some areas. The heat was tremendous and wore on me thanks to the humidity which was up and intensifying everything.

I become turned around somehow in a place called Tenterfield, and go the wrong way, costing me about 50 miles (80 km). Finally, I pass through Lismore and the coast where I see the South Pacific Ocean. I ride along the coast to Bryran Bay, and there, just below the Light House, I hit the most eastern point of Australia and take some photographs of the Light House with the bay and ocean in the background.

My final destination this day is Cleveland where I plan to meet up with an old friend, Rusty Clark, from South Africa. As I ride up the coast the last 150 miles, it starts to rain; also, a valve starts seizing again. I just cannot believe it! Why can't I ever fix anything just once? Why does it have to be a repeat? As I come into Cleveland, I call Rusty and he meets me. After a big hug and "How are you doing?", I follow him over to his shop.

We put the motorcycle away and I tell him about my problems. "We'll sort it out tomorrow," he tells me. I am reassured by his comment, since Rusty is one of the better men in the world as far as restoring old motorcycles. He has the masters touch in his soul.

I spend the next few days working on the motorcycle and suffering in the humidity and heat of Cleveland, a suburb on the edge of Brisbane. We run a compression test, and it confirms that the front valve is sticking. We pull both cylinder heads off and send them out to be repaired. Rusty looks at some other things, and tells me, Dave, your cam shaft is no good." Rusty re-worked all that needed to be done, and in the end, he would not accept any money for his labor. I only paid for the parts; mind you, in Australia they are very expensive.

Over the next few days the motorcycle was up and running. I immediately say good-bye to Rusty, not because I don't enjoy his company, but because I must get to Cape York quickly. Virtually everyone I talks to keeps telling me, "In November, you are going to have trouble with the Big Wet." Also, heat is a serious problem up there. If you think it is hot here, just wait!" So, it is with this concern for the very near future that I push on North.

The motorcycle seems to be running good for the first day. The second day as I near Townsville, the valve nipped up again as I make my way to Townsville Custom Cycles, an after market Harley Davidson dealer. The shop is owned by Yowie, a big rough looking biker with a peg leg. So, we immediately have something in common! He welcomes me to the shop and says, "Do you have any problems?"

"Indeed I do," I answered. "I feel like I'm nipping a valve". We run a compression test, and the motorcycle passes. I knew I was going to have trouble ahead, even though everything seemed okay now. I decided to just push on after taking care of a few odds and ends.

At the clubhouse of the Renegades Motorcycle Club, I greet one of the members who lets me in and shows me a place where I can bunk down for the night. Here I meet Red, one of the members, who has no use of his left arm as the result of a motorcycle accident. The Renegades have a cemetery on their premises! Each headstone has their logo - a death-head, frontal view, with a knife through the mouth and two tomahawks beside it, and feathers behind it all. The saying underneath each grave says, "We are as you will be, you are as we were."

I didn't get much sleep that night as I was bunked down very close to their pub; the guys were partying down most of the evening. Oh well, at least I wasn't in the rain getting soaked. The following morning I head towards Cairns, up the coast. I ride through sugarcane fields and very tropical areas with the torrid heat to go with it. In Cairns, I ask directions to a good place to sleep off on the roadside. "Try the Mulgrave River" I was told. Backtracking a bit, I find a trail along the river, and locate a little place right on top of the embankment of the river, out of sight. Laying back, relaxing, I enjoyed seeing the occasional boat come down the river. I sat real still as they passed since it was illegal to be in there camping.

The following day I return to the Renegades Motorcycle Club in Cairns to meet Prong. He tells me, "Dave, there's been a bit of trouble. I can't put you up at my place. Would you mind staying at the campground?" I agree, and we decide to meet when the motorcycle shop opens on Monday at 07:30. I then leave Prong and ride to the campground - one of the most beautiful I've ever seen! After the reception lady talks to me about my trip, she says, "You can stay here for nothing. We are just happy to have you!" I was deeply touched by her kindness.

That evening I meet a young couple who travel all around Australia. They had just been to Cape York, so they are a great source of information (although their trip had been a month before). They tell me what I don't want to hear: "Dave, be careful. This is NOT the time to go up there because of the Big Wet."

The following day Prong greets me with this wonderfully encouraging comment: "You're not really considering riding this thing up to Cape York are you?" Before I can answer, he continues. "Dave, the roads are sandy and corrugated - like a terrible washboard. There's bull dust - that powdery stuff - all over the place!"

As I listen, in my heart I believe I have a fighting chance.

"Then there's the rivers," he continues. "They're going to be swollen because of rain. The Big Wet is coming."

I was told it had been raining here off and on for the past two weeks, so the Big Wet was definitely on the way. During the rest of the day I work on the motorcycle, changing oil and doing other jobs. One much-needed item was to take off the rear tire and replace it with a knobby tire for better traction on the sand roads. Next, I take off all my excess gear and leave it with Prong. No tent. Nothing with weight unless it was absolutely necessary to operating the motorcycle. The lighter the load, the better my chances. With that, Prong says, "Be careful mate. I'm really worried about you getting caught up in the Big Wet." I nod good-bye to him, then ride over to the campground for the night.

In the evening I get a bit of a briefing from a reserve major in the Army that I had been corresponding with since England about what to expect on the run up. Finally, about 22:00, as I lay back (minus tent) under the open, sure enough, it starts pissing rain! I spend this night out in the rain, wide awake, waiting for tomorrow's ordeal to begin.

About 05:00 I roll up my soggy sleeping bag, enjoy a sandwich and a cup of hot tea given to me by a couple in the camp, then start the long awaited attempt to get to the top of Australia.

Bouncing and Banging to Cape York

Riding up the coast, it rained off and on through Mossman where I cut east into the mountains and journey up through the rain forest that was shrouded in clouds. Very wet. When I come over the top and down the other side, suddenly I am in a very dry bushveld area. Like night and day. The bushveld is more like Africa than I have seen anywhere. Soon, I am going through Mt. Carbine and then out onto a dirt road which would continue for the next 600 miles (1000 km) - right to the top! As I move along, I discover that Prong was right...it is very rough with washboard corrugations!

I travel over a rise with more mountains, then down the other side. The road is very dusty, and I'd eat plenty of dirt whenever another vehicle passes. This part was not wet like on the other side of the mountain. It was as if a line had been drawn, and God declared: "One side of this mountain will be tropical rain forest, and the other side will be dry bush savannas like Africa."

As I come to Lakeland and notice new problems with the engine - it is starving for fuel. Since it is hotter than blue blazes, I decide to remove the fuel filter; that takes care of the problem. While I am repairing the machine, a woman came up to me and wanted to talk. Truthfully, I didn't feel like carrying on chit chat at the time. My vision is very focused right now on what I am doing; I've got a mind set and don't want to be disturbed. She told me, I wish I had the nerve to do what you are doing." Instead of saying "Thank you" or some other nice answer, I replied, "Lady, if you did have the nerve, right now you'd be sitting here in the dirt and heat with greasy hands fixing your motorcycle as well." She smiled and just went on her way.

Once out of Lakeland, there are only two ways to go. Somehow, I missed the sign and went on towards Cooktown. For the next 32 miles (50 km) I bound and bounce over a very rough road - the wrong way! I turn around, very angry with myself, and ride back towards Lakeland where I catch the right road, heading northwest instead of just north. As the miles bound and bounce along, my speed grows up to 50 mph (80 kph) - a stupid mistake. Suddenly, I hit soft sand and the motorcycle starts fishtailing wildly. I battle to keep it on it's wheels, and as I struggle, my mind flashes back to the accident in the Namib Dessert where I cracked my pelvic and ribs. I thought to myself, "Don't repeat that mistake" and I thought of Don's words now ringing through my mind, "Dave, don't get clever." I slow up and put the machine down into third gear, now stable in the sand. I remain in third gear for the rest of the trip as I move through the sand. When I come into the small outback settlement of Laurel, I fuel up and let some air out of the tires for better traction.

At Han River I pull off back into the bush for the evening. My left stump has been giving me nothing but agony all day long. The heat aggravates it, and the heat aggravates me as well. Once I settle in, I do a bit of work on the motorcycle, then open my sleeping bag; it dries quickly in the heat, and there will be no problem with rain tonight. I lay back to enjoy a cup of Ze Qing's tea, and to witness an incredible red sunset, because of dust in the air. Today I traveled 320 miles (520 km), 200 miles (320 km) of it on dirt. No wonder I'm so beat! As I prepare for sleep, I could only wish I had the energy of the different birds I hear singing throughout the evening. Thankfully, there was a wonderful evening breeze to cool and soothe my hot stumps and lower my body temperature. I have a problem throwing off heat, so when I pull my legs off and let that cool air get to the stumps, I can feel the pain flowing out of them.

The following morning I am up at about 04:30, and crank the bike up at 05:10. It is still quite nice and cool. As the battle begins, the road progressively gets worse with washboards and corrugations sticking up as much as 6 inches high at times. They rattle my teeth and blur my vision. The front end is not only working up and down like the pistons in the motor, but the wheel is gyrating from left to right as well. It is very difficult to keep the motorcycle under control at certain speeds. I move along at about 35 mph (50 km) to keep control of it, and to keep the vibrations from rattling my teeth loose in my mouth. Of course, I'm hitting more and more bull dust that often conceals a hole maybe a foot across, or even twenty meters long. These holes are **bone-jarring** when I hit them! Naturally, the dust then flies up and blurs my vision. Finally, there's the odd vehicle that comes by on the road that leaves me blind, completely choking on and eating dust.

Out of Musgrave, I start my first long stretch of soft sand. The technique here is to get into a rut in the sand and hold the throttle and keep my speed no slower or faster than about 35 mph (50 kph). The biggest problem in these ruts is maneuvering around gentle bends and staying in them. If I start coming out of the rut, I'll fall off the motorcycle. Quite often, there are bushes near the ruts, right next to me. If I hit a bush or tree out here, obviously I am in big trouble.

At other times, I hit a hole in the sand where the sand is covering over hard ground. There's nothing I can do. Sometimes is throws me off the motorcycle. Other times, these road hazards throw me up off the seat and almost over the handlebars. Coming back down on my ass is really painful. Clearly, the wedding tackle is going to take a real beating this trip.

Struggling to keep my right foot on the break peddle, I come into a series of dips. At the bottom of these dips are dry creeks. These creeks generally have concrete at the bottom of them for water to flow over and they were amazing steep dips, maybe going down 20 meters, then back up the other side. It is exciting riding; luckily, the road going down to them and coming back up is not eroded away. These roads felt like being on a roller coaster at low speeds.

Total Concentration or Total Disaster

In Coen, I try to get information on the road up ahead. I am always asking, "What are the conditions of the road up to Cape York?" Most people can't tell me anything. They don't know. "Oh, we fly if we go," or "I don't know, I haven't been up that far." It is amazing to me how so many people can live such confined lives out here in this vast country.

While buying some fuel, I spot some aborigines and decided to approach them. As I walk up, they turn their heads down and away from me. "Do I look like a derelict?" I thought. "Do I really smell that bad?" I wondered. Later, I learned from an aborigine woman that "When you radiate much energy, they won't look at you." Thinking back to the time, I not only felt nervous, but very aggressive...I had to be to handle that 700 pounds of motorcycle in dangerous riding conditions. It is either total concentration or total disaster!

From Coen to Archer is a distance of only 60 miles, but I needed to refuel again because there's no gasoline for another 250 miles (400 km), all the way to Bamaga. I carry an extra 3 gallon can on the back of the motorcycle as well. From the Archer River, I ride for 120 miles and see no other vehicles. I realize I am getting farther and farther into "the Outback" as I head north up the peninsula. Finally, late in the afternoon, after traveling through a barren area, I arrive at Wenlock River - the first major river crossing. The river is about 30 meters across, and there's some Australian Army personal camped on the other side. A couple of them are watching me. I go down the river and spot tire ruts going through the river, and realize that they cross it quite often here. The road looks quite well worn. Carefully riding along the top of the rut over on the far side to where the water is less than a foot deep, I prepare to venture in. Mind you, these rivers are supposed to be full of crocodiles! All along I've heard, "Don't go near any rivers mate when you're up there. They've got crocodiles in them."

I let the motorcycle cool down, figuring it wouldn't be too good to hit the water with a fiery hot engine and seize a piston. Finally, I start up and move forward, doing fine. About three quarters of the way across I slipped off the rut and down into about 2 feet of water. That was that. The exhaust drowned out and the engine stalled. Some of the soldiers saw this and came down. One of them took my camera and got some photographs. They push me and the motorcycle out. It starts right up with no problem. I ride over and decide that it was enough for this day. "I will spend the night here above the river banks and prepare for tomorrow morning to get up to the top, if possible."

The Air Force personnel tell me, "We come up here once a year to do mapping and navigation with helicopters, and on foot." They tell me they are still looking for a pilot who crashed somewhere in the area a number of years ago in his F16 and has never been found. Later, in Perth, I learned they did locate pieces of the plane, but no pilot. Persistence will pay out.

The fork oil is all over me! I use 140 weight gear oil in the front forks. It is very thick; it is the only oil that will stay in the forks because the tubes are more or less worn out. It works its way up the tubes to the top, and can't drain down, so it sprays out through the vent caps on the top of the tubes. When it does, it blows all over me! So, I'm covered not only with dirt and dust but with fork oil as well.

There are times during the day when I feel the front forks and they are extremely hot, especially over areas where there are corrugations, since they are pumping up and down constantly. That night on the river banks I am virtually exhausted, and the worse is yet to come.

The following morning I got up at 04:30, did my pushups, and prepared for a rough day. The starter motor makes a grinding noise as I crank up, and the clutch is sticky. Most likely it is a bit of rust from yesterdays dunking. The first thing that hits me on the other side of the Australian Army camp is deep sand. There are sand ruts for miles! I run through about 80 miles of these ruts, with only an occasional break of hard ground with terrible corrugations.

As I head for the Jardine River, it is white knuckle riding. Total concentration in the tremendous heat. By 10:00 it is up around 110 degrees. The road is no more than a small sand track through the bush. The trees come right down to the track, sometimes forming a canopy over the path itself. Keep the speed up or fall.

It gets very hairy on some of the corners. If I fall and hit a tree up here, the chances if I hurt myself badly, I will die. There's just no one else up here. I have not seen one car during the course of the day to the Jardine River, which is a distance of over 200 miles (320 km) from my morning start.

Eventually, I hit a road quite a bit wider. This road is full of terrible corrugations and deep sand. As I move on towards the Jardine River, I arrive about 11:30 and the heat is sweltering. I wait for about an half hour for the ferry to come across. When it does arrive, a big fat fellow named Max, the ferry operator, charges me $15.00 for about a 2 minute ferry ride.

We start across about a 75 meter wide river that is quite deep. There is no way to cross this by vehicle; apparently, it is full of crocodiles, although I don't see any. On the other side, Max serves us some tea and some cookies.

Now I'm on my way to Bamaga, another 40 miles (60 km), through soft sand all the way. The motorcycle is running quite well for all the stress, strain, bouncing, and sand that it has gone through in the last few days.

Bamaga is on the northwest side of the tip of Cape York Peninsula, and as I ride to a service station, virtually out of gasoline, I hear a voice call out "You made it. You bloody well made it. I don't believe it. You bloody made it!" I turn to see a fellow at the entrance to the garage, a fellow named Ron. He repeats his statement again, then shakes my hands. There were a few other fellows there as well - all shaking my hand and saying "You made it. Well done. Is there anything we can do for you?"

I asked if I could make a few phone calls. Once that was done, and the fuel paid for, I walk over to a grocery store where I buy some groceries for the night.

According to the locals, I still had about another hour's ride to get to the tip. So, off I go into some rain forest type areas. It was so dark I had to turn my headlight on. The road for the most part is good, with only a few short stretches of sand; the rest is hard-packed dirt and quite wet. I worry about the mud as I cut through the rain forest tunnels where it is virtually black inside, like in Zaire (that brought back unpleasant memories). Fortunately, the road through these tunnels is excellent.

Finally, about 15:30, after covering 300 miles (500 km) that day, I come to a sign saying, **"You have made it to the top of Australia."** With great pride I pull the motorcycle next to that sign, take out my tripod and shoot some photographs. Frankly, I feel no sense of relief because I know I've still got a 600 mile (1000 km) ride back down the same yellow brick road! Oh me, oh my!

I went up into a campground, and then realized that I still had a 2 kilometer (1 1/2 mile) walk to get to the very tip. There is no way to get a motorcycle on the little path that goes through the rain forest. It is just a little path, and I have to duck down a lot. It is very difficult for me to walk bent over. On through the rain forest I went until I came out to a big hill of rock. For the next kilometer I climbed up and down rocks and ledges until I arrived at a sign that was anchored in the Ocean. It says, **"You have arrived at the northern most tip of Australia."**

Unfortunately, I couldn't ride up there.

I took a few photographs, then came back over this very treacherous and difficult terrain. Walking on a pair of stilts is dangerous near ledges, over rocks, and climbing hills. I came to a cement pillar about 3 feet high, and on it is a dial with compass bearings for Los Angeles, Honolulu, Paris, London, Johannesburg. Very interesting! Go this direction another 10,000 miles and I can arrive in Los Angeles, California.

At the camp ground I started to cook my dinner and nearly caused a forest fire. I always clear an area around my gas stove which burns petrol. For some reason, it starts leaking and blows up with fire. Good thing I had the area cleared out around it, as no amount of dirt will put it out. I finally take off my jacket and suffocate it. After doing that, the state of my jacket wasn't very good. As soon as it was dark, I laid back and closed the day.

The following day I clean out the starter drive and regrease the whole assembly, then head back to Bamaga. As I was buying fuel, a fellow named Robert comes over and says, "Hey, would you like to spend a few days with us?" I said "I can't, but thank you." Well, Robert insisted on buying me lunch at the local restaurant with his family. As I was ready to leave, his mother stuck a $100.00 bill in my hand. What nice people!

By this time it was almost noon, on Friday, as I ride out towards the Jardine Ferry through the sandy ruts. I see Max going the other way about 5 miles (8 km) from the river. When I get there, no one is attending the ferry; it is locked up. I just blow my cork. "How dare you charge people that much money and just leave whenever you feel like it and leave everybody stranded!" Being a survivor, I ride my motorcycle on to the ferry, then take out my trusty old hammer and smash the lock off of the wheel house, start the diesel engine up, and shanghai the ferry across to the other side where I leave it. "Fuck you, Max! If you want the ferry, swim for it boy!"

Off I go down the road.

I took a "short cut" Ron suggested, not going the way I had come. When I come to a river, I get stuck at the bottom of a creek but manage to get started and out to the other side. Very lucky! This is a much more difficult track than I had been on the day before. As I go through the sand ruts, my speed is about 20 mph (32 kph) because of the sharp turns and stability problems. When I hit the McDonald River, it isn't very deep, but has lots of rocks along the bottom. Thankfully, an old white man living among the aborigines gives me instructions on how to cross. I make it across, but as I go up the other side of the embankment, it is too steep so the motorcycle digs in and that's it - I fall over.

I try to move the thing, but end up falling again. After getting it up, I just waited there for an hour until, around dusk, a Toyota Land Cruiser comes along with a family having a bit of an adventure vacation. They help me - the whole family pushing and groaning to bring the motorcycle up to the top of the river ravine. Then, we push it off into the bushes where I decide to spend the night. After thanking the people very graciously, they went on their way and I made camp.

The next morning, I had only gone about 500 meters down the sand track when I went down. The road winds too much, so it is tough to even get out of first gear. Since the sand is very deep, I was going to fall over repeatedly. This time, my right leg is caught underneath the motorcycle. I must dig myself out; it takes about thirty minutes. Next, I must unload, lift the motorcycle up, reload and then get going again. To make matters more challenging, I am also having throttle problems.

Down again. Same routine.

Mosquito Net Miracle

As I move forward, falling off and digging myself out is becoming all too regular a happening. Every time I hit a corner, I go down because of problems with the throttle and not being able to get enough power. I decide to take the throttle apart, but fail to put out my tarp. As I take the throttle apart, there's a small round bushing with a hole in it about 5/16" across, a tiny steel ring. Naturally, I drop it in the sand! Without this ring. the throttle simply will not work. I look at the sand for the next 10 minutes, not daring to move, trying to spot where the thing might have fallen.

Finally, I get down on my knees and start picking through that sand. As I am searching, a vehicle comes along. Peter and Craig work with the park service and water conservation. They are out checking streams in the area, and stop to discover my ridiculous situation. As we talk, I get an idea.

"Do you have a mosquito net?" I ask.

"Yes, we do," they reply.

So, out comes the net and we start shoveling sand into it. After 15 minutes, a tiny little o-ring steel bushing miraculously appears in the net. Peter holds it high above his head like a trophy. We are so giddy that we actually take a picture of this "event." I finish my repair, and triumph over impossible odds, and ride down the road to the ranger station just a few miles from our spot.

"Why don't you spend the rest of the afternoon here?" they ask

I agree. It will give me time to properly service the throttle, then push on in the morning. Since I have already made it to the top, I have no pressing time limit to get down. I am no longer worried about getting caught in the Wet. In this area, they say "It arrives only later in December."

After a good lunch, I spoke with a fellow named Dave. He had been an electrician until one day he was working on a power line and was electrocuted. It flung him off the pole. He told me, "I saw light at the end of a long dark tunnel, and a very dark figure standing in the tunnel reaching out to me. I knew if I took the hand in that tunnel, I would have left this world behind." In the end, he decided to stay where he was and carry on in life. As he told me this story, I thought about the two electricians I had met in China with no arms. This man did not know how lucky he was.

The following morning I battle on down through the sand, mile after mile, back towards the Wenlock River, going through a couple of ravines. As I let off the throttle, I hear a valve sticking again. My heart sinks to my knees. "No. Not again. Not here of all places. Please don't let me down now."

Pushing on about another 20 miles, sure enough - bang - I seize a valve in the front cylinder head. I pull over and try in vain to free up the valve. No dice! It is stuck solid. What now? I wait for 3 1/2 hours, and not a single vehicles comes by. In fact, I have not seen a vehicle all morning! Finally, an Australian Army truck stops. I tell them of my situation, and of course, like all true Australians, they tell me, "No problem, mate." We load the motorcycle on the back of a 2 1/2 ton truck, tie it down, and drive back to the camp.

The commander at the camp ordered the truck to Wepia which is right on the coast, about midway up the Cape on the west side. He instructed his men "To pick up some supplies, and take this pig of a motorcycle and dirty Dave into Wepia with you." I thank him for the help.

We ride through very rough bushveld. As we travel, I sit in the truck, watching the miles go by, feeling heartbroken that I can't cover this territory on the motorcycle. I feel as though something is being stolen from me. I think to myself, "How much easier this trip around the world would have been had I rode a "purpose built motorcycle" instead of my old, worn and tired Harley Davidson."

In the late afternoon, we arrive in Wepia and the soldiers put me down in a field across from a little housing project. I ask some strangers, "Is there anybody around here that by chance owns a Harley Davidson?"

"Sure," they reply. "The guy right across from where you parked your motorcycle."

I wait for about 2 hours until it gets dark. Suddenly, here comes a fellow down the road on a Harley. I couldn't believe it. As he pulls into the shed where he stores his motorcycle, I come up behind him and say "Hello" very timidly. He turns around and looks at this dirty apparition and says, "Yes, what can I do for you?"

I tell him my problem, and when I'm done, he says, "No problem, mate. We'll get your motorcycle over here, and in the morning we'll sort you out."

Greeni had heard about me, so that helped.

"Your motorcycle looks fantastic," I told him. "Sure you don't ride it all the way up from Caimes every time you make a trip down."

"Oh, no," he laughed. "I put it inside a truck and send it down, or it goes out on the boat to Darwin from here. We have about 20 miles (32 km) of paved roads right in the Weipa area, so I tool around on them just to keep the thing limbered up."

That night I laid, dejectedly thinking about all the miles I had come over that day, and how cheated I felt not to ride them.

The next morning we push the motorcycle over to a garage that Greeni shares. He is a painter, and shares the garage with John Gilmore, a mechanic who works on Marine diesels and fishing boats. Once the motorcycle is there, Greeni goes about getting ready for work, and I discuss my problem with John.

"There's a transport going down to Caimes. Do you want to put the motorcycle in the back of a truck?" That thought to me was absolutely depressing. I knew I could take the easy route and nobody would ever doubt what I did. But somehow, that just didn't sit right.

I called Prong down in Caimes, asking, "Can you turn a head around if I send it to you?" "No problem, mate" he told me. "We can get it done in 24 hours." So, I opted to put the cylinder head on an airplane and send it out. I immediately start to work, taking off the gas tanks, the carburetor, the front cylinder head, and put the parts in a bag. It flew to Caimes that afternoon. I clean up the parts, and with nothing else left to do, go back over to Greeni's for the evening.

The following day I piddled around on the motorcycle doing various little jobs.

The next day the cylinder head comes back! It is short work putting it back on. By the afternoon I am done, and the thing starts fine! I am very relieved, although I know there is much more to go - I am still about 450 miles (650 km) from the closest asphalt to Weipa.

The following morning I am up just after 04:00 and do my pushups. Shortly after, a fellow named Robert who runs a travel agency comes in with his wife. Together with John Gilmore and Greeni, and his boss, Bruce, we all share coffee. John gives me a long-sleeved shirt to wear since my jacket is a charred mess, and Robert sticks a $100.00 in my pocket. After our good-byes, Greeni starts up his motorcycle and shows me to the edge of town.

The whole trip up the Cape I saw a lot of Wallabies, but this morning it just seems like they are out in full force! I must be very careful because they love to dart out in front of me. Obviously, if I hit one, I'm going down. I ride over 120 miles that morning to Archer without seeing another vehicle. Once in Archer, I get fuel then head to Coen where I enjoy a sandwich and a cup of coffee. Next, I battle sand, ruts and corrugations all the way. When I am south of Musgrave, most of the heavy sand is now behind me. Now, I only face bull dust and corrugations.

I beat and bounce through the fiery hot day with a temperature about 110 degrees, to Laura where I fuel up again, get water and move down the road until I find a secluded spot to rest and relax.

After my cup of Chinese tea, I receive two new visitors - little lizards. One crawls right up on my leg; I am able to pet him. What a nice interlude. Eventually, as I stir a bit, they scurry off under a log as I enjoy the stars.

The following morning, the road has improved. I am past the last of the sandy areas, and can now put the machine in fourth gear, increasing my speed to about 45 miles an hour. I have one close call with a wallaby (small kangaroo) that jumps out in front of me. "Look out for those roos, mate." At Lakeland, I turn south, going the right direction this time. In Lake Palmer, I get fuel and a cup of coffee. About 10 kilometers south of Lake Palmer, I come into the Mount Carbine area and hit pavement again. What a wonderful feeling! At this moment I feel my greatest sense of pride and accomplishment for having made it to the top and back.

The rest of the trip back to Caimes is breathtaking scenery I can now appreciate. When I arrive, I go directly to the motorcycle shop where I am greeted by Peg and Prong. I thank them profusely for helping me out with the cylinder head. The rest of that day is spent cleaning the motorcycle and putting my normal rear tire back on.

The next day I finish up all the work on the motorcycle, get my gear together, and move on south to Townsville where I spend a day with Red. Yowie comes down, and comments, "There ain't a good one between the three of us." He's right. Red's arm is gone, my two legs are gone, and Yowie has only one leg.

That evening I reunite with an old friend I haven't seen since Zimbabwe/Rhodesia in

1980 - 13 years ago! Dick Gledhill was also a parachute jump instructor, and had been in the Zimbabwe/Rhodesian Light Infantry before that. We chat for a while, then I give a talk and slide show to the Club members and a few people from the outside.

That evening I think about what I had just come through, and about the adventure to come: 1,500 miles (2500 km) to Mt. Isa, my next stop. A frog jumped onto my left stump as I was laying there. I let out a yell and nearly go through the roof. So much for quietly falling asleep.

Run up Cape York Peninsula to the top. It was hard going.
November 1993. Australian Outback.

On the road in the Land of Oz.
October 1993

Top of Australia. 600 miles from pavement.
It was necessary to walk to the tip, 1 mile.
November 4, 1993. Now to return.

Chapter Thirty-Five

Shooting Stars and Aussie Salutes

The following morning I head towards Mt. Isa. The first sight I see is a big red kangaroo. I have installed what they call a "Shu Roo" - a deer whistle - on the motorcycle. It works! That kangaroo looks up startled, then scurries off in the proper direction, away from the road! This is reassuring to know, since I'll be hitting a lot of range land with no fences. Cattle, horses, sheep and kangaroo carcasses litter these roads, and I would just as soon not contribute to the carnage. It is deadly for them, and definitely dangerous for me!

The heat soars to at least 110 degrees this day as I travel through very flat bush countryside in northern Queensland. After traveling about 420 miles (630 km) that day, I decide to pull off into the bush and spend the night. With the sounds of birds and nature around me, I fall asleep gazing up at the magnificent stars.

The next morning I'm up very early, wanting to get moving before it gets too hot, and before the flies start targeting me for breakfast. The area I go through today is almost total desert, with long tracks of land where there are absolutely no trees growing at all. I see low scrub and ant heaps in the thousands. Cows and sheep are also along the road, and I am constantly alert to the threat of one jumping out in front of me. That would certainly be the end of the trip.

After two more days of riding through the seemingly endless expanses of northern Queensland, smelling dead carcasses of animals along the way, I finally come upon Mt. Isa.

Just outside of Mt. Isa, things start to get a bit more hilly; I see a few mesas along the road, and more curves. It is not uncommon for me to go 100 miles without seeing a single building. The heat is horrendous, and I detect a valve is starting to nip up again.

I call Gillian Portegys; I've been writing to her husband, Shane, ever since *The Enthusiast* article had been published in the summer of '92. She had Mick, a jolly fat fellow on a shovel head like mine, ride out to meet me and guide me to the house. I tell Mick about the valve problem, so we take the machine to a motorcycle shop for a compression test; there's even compression on both cylinders.

At Shane and Gilly's place, I settle in for the evening. In the background on TV, I heard the announcer asking, "What were you doing thirty years ago today?" I was just a kid on that November 17, but I could still remember it was the day President John F. Kennedy was shot.

The next few days I work on the motorcycle and give a talk and slide show. One fellow says to me after the show, "Anybody can do that." I didn't answer him, but I thought to myself, "Mate, you just try it." Now I don't say this to compliment myself, or to make myself look big, but the trip is extremely difficult, a dangerous adventure. Any long-range motorcycle trip is always a big and unsure undertaking.

That night I see a shooting star and quickly make a wish to just complete the rest of the trip. I am starting to think about the future, when the journey is over, although I always remind myself that there are thousands of miles ahead just to finish Australia. Then, I face Southeast Asia and all the problems and dangers of the roads there.

The following morning, Mick guided me out of town on his shovel head. About 20 kilometers out we see an incredible red orb rise out of the desert. In the sunrise, we pull over and bid each other good-bye.

Road Trains, Crocodiles and Giant Bats?

I rode on alone, making forward progress through these very flat lands once again. I never dreamed I'd ever see so much scrub on semi-arid land, virtually desert. This day I see my first three-trailer road train, and pull over to take a photograph of this huge latvian. It has 60 wheels! The driver tells me "I am pulling about 120 tons." Road train indeed! I found this driver and every other to be absolute gentlemen of the road. I never saw any of them go above 80 kph (about 55 mph). They were good drivers.

On I travel through the day until I come to a T junction at Tennant Creek that goes north to Katherine. By the end of this day, I cover another 400 miles (600 km) in the still stifling heat. I felt a valve nip during this day, and think to myself, "Oh, please, no, not again." My target for this night was a place I'd heard about along the Edith River, about 30 miles (45 km) north of Katherine. So, I fuel up and make my way north to the lazy Edith River where I ride to a fairly shady, secluded spot and stop for the day...swatting flies.

The following morning as I move north I ask to use the phone at a gas station. The man insists I use his personal phone. "Well, thank you. I'm calling a fellow named Slim in Darwin."

"Oh yeah," the man replies, "Slim Walker. I know him." Funny enough, I had the wrong number, but this man has Slim's correct phone number! It seems everybody knows everybody in the Northern Territories. When I reach Slim, he tells me to, "Give me a call from the service station at Noonamah" - only a mere 200 miles (320 km) north of my current location.

One thing that strikes me as I head closer to Darwin is all the abandoned World War II airstrips that Americans had occupied during the war.

When I arrive at Noonamah, I call Slim and within ten minutes a red Chevrolet appears, and a woman gets out and introduces herself as Linda, Slim's wife. Slim stayed in the car. I walk over and introduce myself to Slim, then follow them to their house in a place called Humpty Doo, out in the country. When we pull in, I am struck by the house being surrounded by a virtual palm tree jungle, an oasis inside a rain forest; Linda collects palm trees.

Slim had a big workshop where he keeps his Harley Davidson. When he gets out of the car, I notice he's on crutches. Inside the house, with a beer in his hand, he tells me how he'd been hit by a drunk and had broken his right foot quite badly. His left knee had needed surgery. When the surgery was complete, it somehow became infected. As a result, he has been laid up for nearly a year and a half.

In the afternoon, a fellow named Trevor appears and volunteers to, "Show you some sights." The next morning, we hop on the motorcycles and journey to the north part of Darwin on the eastern side where they have huge gun emplacements put in during the war, but that were never used. Then, we ride around to a harbor and a sea plane ramp. Trevor shows me an area where they scuba dive on sunken American ships. "There are 23 American ships sunk in this harbor during World War II. When the USS Perry went down, it had 69 crew members still aboard, and her guns were blazing. She was fighting the Japanese planes till the time that she went under."

Trevor went on to explain that "In the '50s the ships were sold by the U.S. Government to the Japanese for scrap metal. They came in and took all the siding off of the ships." As I heard this story, I thought "How sacrilegious of our leaders to do something like that."

It is terribly hot and humid in Darwin, hotter and more humid than anyplace I've stayed in Australia - very much a tropical rain forest area.

We ride over to the Harley Davidson shop where I service the motorcycle with Penrite oil. After that, we take an easy ride back to Slim and Linda's.

The following evening I meet with the Vietnam veterans motorcycle club, and one man from the Disabled Association. By the time the meeting is over, I agree to give a slide show the following night. The Viet Vets round up some people, locate me a slide projector, but we have excitement right down to the wire because the bulb went bad. Richard, the President of the Vietnam Veterans Motorcycle Club, saved the day by finding another bulb. The show was given to an audience of about 50 people, and they listened very intently. Unfortunately, only one person from the Disabled Association came to the show.

We run another compression test on the motorcycle the following day, and it still registers good compression. I know a valve is seizing up, and it is just a matter of time. My next destination is Kunanarra, well over a thousand miles away.

The following morning, I head south back along the rolling hills and the airstrips to Katherine where I turn West. The terrain now becomes far more rugged. All day I hear music rolling through my head as I sometimes do, thinking of the future. I also think of my friend, Luke, and hope he is riding with me.

As I come into the Barkley Road House, the terrain starts to change. By now I have covered about 450 miles (700 km), and I notice the distances are getting longer and longer between petrol stops and any civilization. At the Barkley Road House, I fuel up, get water, then move down the road. When I see a slip road, I take it back towards the Victoria River and pull into a secluded area to put up my tent. I am close to heat exhaustion, soaking wet with sweat, so I keep pouring water down my gullet. As fast as I pour it in, it comes out.

The flies are terrible. My face is all covered up, and I am swatting the flies with the little energy I have left. My head hurts, and I feel like my entire body is on fire. Finally, about 05:30, the heat of the day breaks and I start to cool down. I think this is only the second time on my journey that I have come so very close to heat stroke. Sitting all day long, covered up on the motorcycle, takes its toll. I sometimes drink nearly a full quart - liter of water a stop, still not enough as the heat builds up for the Big Wet.

As evening comes on, the flies do a shift change with the mosquitoes. In the distance, I can hear the trickle of the Victoria River. I've been told "Don't sleep too close to the banks of the river because of the crocodiles."

Off in the distance I suddenly hear a whooshing sound! Not one I recognize. I look up and am shocked to see the vanguard of what are legions upon legions of HUGE, giant bats - bats far bigger than any I've seen before! They block out the moonlight and stars completely. The whooshing of their wings shatters the peaceful stillness of the night. I'm enthralled. I've never seen anything like these millions of flying mammals all on their way to various places to execute whatever tasks nature created them for. After about 10 minutes of this phenomenon, their numbers started to trickle, and finally, there is only the occasional bat flying around.

Once again, the panorama of stars, shooting stars, satellites, and the Southern Cross all silhouette against the mesas around me. With all this incredible wonder, I close my day.

The following morning I am rather listless and lazy from the previous day's heat. Thankfully, the cool wind in my face serves as a morning reviver. Eventually, the sun started to shine down through the canyons I am now moving through. There are trees in the distance, so I am no longer in pure desert, but semi-arid land with mesas all around, rugged, but very beautiful.

Hypnotic Hazards and Aboriginal Dreams

During this day I am having trouble staying awake. Once, I wake up in the oncoming lane on a course heading for a bunch of trees; I just barely manage to get the motorcycle under control without going off the road and killing myself. That really was a shocker and something that greatly upsets me. I sometimes travel distances of 170 miles (270 km) - thanks to my extra fuel - without seeing a single building, and the sameness of the scenery tends to lull me into an almost hypnotic stupor.

In what seems like no time at all, I'm in Western Australia again. Two things strike me: the numerous Boabab trees along the road (a touch of Africa), and the tremendous infestation of flies. My first stop in Western Australia is in the town of Kunnarra. At the service station, somebody pulls up next to me on a Harley Davidson and says, "Hey, I know who you are. Peter Saint said you were coming." This man takes me over to a garage and calls Peter Saint, who comes to pick me up.

At Peter's house, I meet his wife, Rasidah, a mixture of Malaysian and Aborigine. A kinship is formed almost immediately between us. Pete is the fire chief of the area, responsible for 400,000 square km (250,000 miles) in Western Australia. He was also a judge. Imagine that...how many guys do you know with tattoos on both arms who are judges or fire chiefs?

Rasidah told me about the rural Aborigines, and did not want anything to do with Mabo - a movement to take back lands that the Aborigines feel they were forced to give away a century earlier. There's an air of racial tension as a result of this very hot issue. She also showed me her medicine stick, and shared her dreams of this medicine stick being handed down from her tribe as far back as her grandfather. She received possession of the stick when an old lady came to her house and handed it to her, fulfilling the dream.

We discuss my trip, and I share my concern that one day, God Willing, I'll make it home and the journey will be over. "No, Dave," she said, "your journey will never finish." As if to punctuate this point, at 14:30 in the afternoon the rains just starts pouring down - the sky opened with a torrent that was unimaginable. Peter tells me, "This is the first rain we have had this season. That's a sign the Big Wet will be here soon."

My first day out of Kunnarra, I move in a westerly direction, traveling 200 km (125 miles), and never seeing anything. I enter a town, fuel up and am back on my way. The countryside is still desert, semi-arid, with almost out of place Boabab trees.

November 29: Another day struggling to stay awake. On one stretch of 290 km (180 miles), I only see the road and the bushveld around me. I almost fall asleep again. The temperature is up around a 115 degrees, and by the end of the day, I've traveled 460 miles (700 km). Off the main road, I follow an animal trail back into the woods and shut the machine down. The immediate silence is wonderful after a full day of wind, engine noise and vibrations. I enjoy sitting quietly on the suddenly still and silent machine, savoring the peacefulness of my home for the night. Later, as I lay in the stillness, I see a cloud formation with the profile of an aboriginal head, it's hard staring eyes looking off across the white, fluffy, sculptured horizon. It is awe inspiring. Even though the trip is arduous and often extremely dangerous, Australia is the closest I've experienced to a vacation land for me. It is the best and easiest part of the entire ride around the world. I realize, too, that when I arrive in Perth, it would be over, and Southeast Asia looms heavy on the horizon.

In the morning, the flies are up before the sun. It is back to the Aussie salute, trying to keep these things out of my nose. I must eat my food underneath a scarf or some kind of protection to keep the flies out of my meal and my mouth. As I move west towards Karratha, the landscape is very flat with barren, rolling hills and bush. The temperature by 07:30 in the morning is already up to 105 degrees as I enter into Reobuck. My next stop is 170 miles (about 260 km) up the road. Of course, along the way I must stop to put petrol in out of my can. I'm always amazed that when I pull off the road and shut the machine down, normally no one ever passes me! Even if I take a fifteen minute break, not a single car will pass! My only company on these stops are the flies, which descend from absolutely nowhere in seconds.

My next stop is Sandfire Flats. I fuel up there, and speak with a lady for about ten minutes; she seems to be searching for something. We share a very intimate conversation, then I bid her farewell.

I feel my valves starting to nip up again; trouble is coming with the motorcycle.

The people are always friendly at the little gas stations along the way. Many offer me places to stay, free of charge. Of course, I decline, wanting to be out on my own. I realize it is so easy to find places here in Australia as opposed to places in Asia. There's no crowding in Australia at all. As I stop for the night, I'd traveled another 470 miles (770 km).

The next morning I received a visit from two kangaroos, bouncing along about 50 meters from me, watching me and flicking their ears back and forth, doing their Aussie salute to keep the flies off of their heads. They watched this silly human interloper until I start up the machine, breaking nature's silence. My two friends bounded off for their inevitable date with a diesel.

As I come into Port Headland, my valves are seizing up again. I can hear the front cylinder leaking. My heart is now down in my knees. "Why, oh why, do I have so much trouble with the same thing reoccurring?" I stop for gas and a cup of coffee, and try to call Pilbara Motorcycles, and Smithy, the owner. The phone wouldn't work. I wanted to alert him that if I did not arrive by a certain time, to come look for me since a valve probably had seized up.

Feeling very uncertain about the next part of my ride, I get onto the motorcycle and head out of town - for better or worse. I still face a stretch of desert. The temperature is now about 115 degrees at 11:00 o'clock in the morning! As I go down the road, I realize after about 4 miles (6 km) that I hadn't paid for the cup of coffee, so I turn around and go back to the restaurant. After paying for the coffee, I come out and notice a big truck that says "Harley Davidson" on the side, painted up in big letters. I go over and find out that it is the service vehicle for Frazier's Harley Davidson in Perth! Once a month these guys go out on the road and service their customer's motorcycles - people who live hundreds of miles away from the Harley Davidson shop.

What an impressive operation! I speak to the two fellows with the truck and get on their cellular phone and call Pilbara Cycles to let them know I am inward bound, and that I might have trouble getting there. Thanking these men, I push on another 140 miles (230 km) to Karratha, stopping for fuel. As I turn on the exit off the main highway, I am met by a vehicle from Pilbara Cycles. "Follow us," they said, leading me to the shop where I was greeted by a rolly-polly, short jolly fellow named Smithy. He takes care of the retail side of the shop. The maintenance side is managed by Mick Bellie.

Once greetings are over, I explain my compression problem. We take a compression test, and wouldn't you know it, the bastard thing has a 100 pounds on each cylinder! It is not doing it now. I just hope this thing will get me to Perth where I can fix it once and for all!

In the evening, Smithy takes me to his house to clean up, then we take off to a wonderful restaurant overlooking a harbor where ore ships are filled from the very big mines in the area. The other big operation in the area is a giant natural gas plant. With a cool sea breeze and no flies to bother us, we ate Cray fish, shrimp, scallops, various fish, salads and french fries! I finally collapsed into bed about 24:00.

Nipping and Limping Back to Perth

The following day I work with Mick repairing various things on the motorcycle, getting it ready for the final run back to Perth - about 650 miles (1100 km) away. In the evening, I was taken down to the University by Smithy's son where I gave a slide show to about 25 people. Unfortunately, no one from the Disabled Association showed up. In all fairness, they are having their Christmas dinner.

The following morning I start out again; by 05:30 in the morning it is already blazing hot. I say my good-byes and go my way down the road through desert country. I ride for mile after mile, eventually coming out onto the coastal road where the terrain changes dramatically to coastal scrub brush growing up out of sandy areas. The wind is terrible, and of course, in the true Dave Barr spirit, it had to be a head wind. My valves are nipping up again, and I experience compression and power losses regularly. I am just thinking to myself, "Please, Old Dog, hold on till we can get to Perth. Don't let me down now!"

I make my way down to Geraldton, spending a couple nights with Derrick and his wife, Linde, a friend of mine from the army in South Africa. Derrick meets me at the outskirts of town and takes me to their humble but happy home where a warm family atmosphere prevails. After settling in the following day, I go to a small church with Derrick and Linde. I am amazed at the very close feeling in this church. During communion, Derrick drops the plate, scattering the contents all over the floor. He handled it very well, and we both struggled to keep from laughing. Oh well, you can't have the bull in the china shop.

After church that afternoon, we talk about the church and the world around us...the coming of the new age, a one-world government, a one-world religion. If the world sees the fulfillment of all the different scenarios we discussed that afternoon, the future would look very bleak and frightening for Christians.

The following day it is time to leave again, but the motorcycle will not start. There's virtually no compression. Finally, it turns and fires, and off I go down the highway, hoping to cover the last 250 miles (400 km) to Perth. Naturally, about 100 miles (160 km) out, as I fight a head wind, both of the exhaust valves seize. I try to loosen them up by shooting WD 40 into the cylinders. No dice. So, I sit along side the road, crest fallen. The thought of burning this bastard machine even crossed my mind.

After about an hour, a truck pulls up with a trailer on the back. I ask the fellows, "Are you heading towards Perth?"

"Yep, we are," they reply.

We put the motorcycle on the back, and they take me all the way to Exclusive Motorcycle where we off load it and wheel it around back. Wouldn't you know it! The last 135 miles (215 km) in the circuit around Australia and the old dog just wouldn't run.

December 7: On Pearl Harbor Day, I get up and take the cylinder heads off the motorcycle for the fifth time so George, the engineer, could work his magic.

Next, I try to call some of the embassies. The Cambodian Embassy does not exist in Australia, I'm told. I did locate the Vietnam Embassy, but "Sorry, we have no information for you. But don't worry, everything should be okay. No problem."

Coming from someone other than an Australian, those words struck fear into my heart once again!

For Singapore, they told me, "You will only need the Carnet Passage." To secure that in Australia, I call a horribly boring bureaucrat with a set of rules that was incredible. He told me, "Why you've been riding illegally all around Australia." Of course, this little man is one of those who always tries to stop others from doing things that are different or adventurous. For him it is better to live life in a rut.

George, the engineer at Exclusive Motorcycle, gets my cylinders apart and confirms that both exhaust valves are seized. He works them over and does his super dooper magic on them. Generally, the fee for such a job is over a thousand dollars, but he refuses any money. He says, "Well, if you have to do something, clean up my shop every morning."

"You've got it," I reply. I was there to clean that shop every morning from that time on.

After George repaired the cylinder heads, I've had no problems. I've put another 10,000 miles on the motorcycle at the time of this writing, and the old dog is still going great. No problem at all! Well done George!

Exclusive Motorcycles is the most professional shop I've experienced - in attitude and workmanship - throughout the entire world.

December 11: After four days of intense work, the motorcycle is ready for a test ride.

I decide to go visit the Harley Owner's Group of Hong Kong who are now on vacation in Australia. I am anxious to say "hello" to people I have not seen or heard from in sometime. So, I roll the motorcycle out, but there's a problem with the throttle. Although I am in nice, clean clothes, I get dirty while fixing the throttle. Starting up again, the oil light comes on. Again, I work on that and get dirty.

Finally, I get away and ride over to Frazier's Harley Davidson where I meet up with the Harley Owner's Group of Hong Kong. It is great to see these people again! They have been so helpful and interested in the journey.

Motorcycle Records and Skydiving Surprise

That same weekend, Bruce was racing his dragster and set a West Australian record of 177 miles per hour! On Monday I ask him, "What does it feel like to go that fast on a motorcycle?" He says, "It feels like you are having your ass rammed up around your shoulders when it takes off." Bruce always has a poetic way with words. His single engine Sportster Harley Davidson develops over 300 horsepower; Bruce and George were the ones who built it up.

December 14: Election results were on the news from Russia - Yeltsin had won. I was very pleased to hear that. I also received confirmation from P&O that I could go on the ship to Singapore around the 6th of January. I had already given my word to Graham Hickman, managing director of P & O, to be the guest speaker on the January 12th annual general meeting of the Fremantle Rotary; there's no way I will let him down, not after all the help P & O has given to me. They will box up and ship my motorcycle to Singapore for me, and then assist me in the landing, offering logistical support when I arrive.

December 16: I speak to the Vietnam Veterans Motorcycle Club on one of the Army bases in the Perth area; my talk is very warmly received. Though I didn't want any money, they insisted I take $240.00 which I thought was incredible. On top of that, they went out to my motorcycle and put a Vietnam Veterans Motorcycle Club sticker on it. Their motto is "Together forever." It is with great pride that this sticker is on the machine to this day.

I want to put at least 350 or 400 miles on the motorcycle before I prepare it for shipment to get the upper end loosened up properly. So, I get up early in the mornings and take the motorcycle out for about 30 miles (45 km) down the highway, then back again to the shop. I figure the cool of the morning is a good time to break in the upper end.

December 17: My friend, Paul Hogan, arrives at Brad and Kathy's house. We drive out to the drop zone. Now, I don't figure to be doing any skydiving right now, but Paul introduces me to a very unique fellow, Ken Taylor, one of the owners of the drop zone at Clifton Lake. Paul says, "I know Dave from many years back in Zimbabwe/Rhodesia. Why don't you let him skydive with us? Let's clear up some students today, and he can jump tomorrow." Ken has a leg off below the knee from a motorcycle accident.

I think, "Well done, Ken and Paul." So I help pack parachutes for the rest of the day to help pay for the skydiving. That afternoon and evening were spent in laughter with Dick Gledhill, Paul Hogan and myself. It felt like old times at Delfort Farm.

December 18: I kited up, took my right foot off, and took the shoe off the left foot. Having done this, I am able to walk sideways with very great difficulty, very out of balance. In walking to the plane, I fall down a number of times. Once in the aircraft, we go up to 10,000 feet on the first jump. The plane is a little single engine Cessna that goes down a rough dirt runway flying out over the Indian Ocean and back around on the jump run. It feels so good to be up in the plane as it has been a little over two years since I have done any skydiving.

We come in on jump run, with final directional adjustments given to the pilot. Then the count.

"Ready. Set. Go!"

Everybody jumps leaping into the sky. It takes us only a few seconds to make a five man formation. There was Dick Gledhill's face - I hadn't seen it in 13 years in the sky. Paul Hogan's - the same. Of course, there's my new friend, Ken Taylor, and a couple of others. It is an incredible thrill indeed. We do two formations before breaking off.

Back on the ground, everyone is elated and happy to have been up in the air together. Later that day we do another skydive.

Barbie Dolls, Road Wrecks, and Stolen Joy

In the week to come, I try to get information on Cambodia. Finally, through a very dynamic fellow at the head office of P&O in Singapore, David Cross, I learn that "There will be no problem getting you into Cambodia." That is good news. Then he says, "As far as Vietnam is concerned, all you need to get is your visa and everything should be no problem."

My days are filled doing odd jobs for Exclusive Motorcycle, and trying to gather information on the next stage, Asia.

Christmas Day, 1993: Listen to the news...there's trouble in the Middle East with the Hesbolla, the Syrians and the PLO. The talks are not going well. South Africa is experiencing black on black violence, yet Mandela and De Klerk are scheduled to receive Nobel Peace Prizes. North Korea is refusing to allow inspectors to look into the nuclear reactors to determine if they are making or using nuclear fuels for bombs. The whole world seems to be the jolliest place in the universe. Merry Christmas.

On the lighter side, Barbie Dolls and GI Joes make the news. Some body is taking the voice boxes from GI Joes and putting them in Barbie Dolls, and vice versa, then putting them back on the shelf!

December 31, New Years Eve, 1993: I sit in the backyard listening to the traffic go by. At the stroke of midnight, my meditations are interrupted by the sounds of fire crackers off in the distance and people partying down. I think about this night a year ago. We had completed our trip through China a few days before, followed by the empty New Year's celebration in the Beijing International Hotel - without emotion. The permits to enter Russia and Mongolia were the only things on my mind. Looking back, I saw the Gobi Desert, the cold, the sand storms. I saw Siberia and snow, Europe and rain, Australia and heat. The battle up and down Cape York. Most of all, I saw a rainstorm, a Russian officer, a badge being pinned to my chest, a salute, a gate opening and reentering back into the Western World. I saw a signpost that said the "E4 Highway," telling me I have gone around the world. I see incredible people and thousands of miles behind me. I wonder to myself, "Who am I really promoting - Harley Davidson, the disabled, or myself?"

At 24:20, I go back into the house and very quietly thank God for all He has brought me through, asking Him to take me through even more.

During the days to come, I acquire some maps of Southeast Asia. I look at the maps, plan my route, and scheme, especially thinking about Vietnam and whether I will be able to even go through the country. Lord knows, out of all of Southeast Asia, I feel a real yearning to go back to Vietnam.

The big news in Australia is that fires are raging through New South Wales around the Sydney area and the Blue Mountains. Remembering how beautiful the Blue Mountains were, I was saddened to hear they are now ablaze, and feel compassion for the people living in that area.

I set a date to go. I arrange it with David Cross and the P & O office in Singapore, and with the office here in Perth. My motorcycle is to be boxed up on January 11 and prepared for it's voyage.

One morning Charlie asked me to drive his one-ton Ford meat truck back to the house from the depot where he had parked it. We drove out to the depot 40 miles (60 km) east of Perth. We said good-bye there, then I climbed into his Ford and headed back to Perth. About 45 kilometers (25 miles) east of Perth on the Wannerroo Road, a 7 ton dump truck suddenly pulled out in front of the two cars in front me. I thought to myself "Here we go. We will be held down in speed with this guy." We hadn't traveled too far when I saw a car in the on-coming lane. It appeared to be speeding up. Then, he turned directly into the on-coming dump truck, hitting it full force, head on. Their combined speed must have been about 130 kph (80 mph).

The impact crumpled the whole front up; the car lifted in the air as if by magic, up and over the cab of the truck, somersaulting end over end, landing on it's roof right next to where I had pulled off of the road when I witnessed all of this happening. The car had literally somersaulted over 3 car lengths - one being the truck, plus the other 2 cars in front of me, landing directly in the oncoming lane on its roof.

Quite shaken by the sudden violence of the wreck, I stopped, got out of the truck, and walked over to look through the window of the car to see the steering column pushed into the face of the occupant. I was baffled as to what had happened; the only scenario I could come up with was that perhaps the guy had fallen asleep at the wheel, or had committed suicide.

Later, I learned that it was indeed a suicide. I thought to myself, "Holy mackerel, what would it have been like if the car had landed on the top of Charlie's truck, or one of the other two cars in front of me? If I had been on a motorcycle, with large pieces of the car all over the road, the scenario would have been grim indeed. Life is so uncertain. Here one second, gone in another."

I carried on down the road, arriving at the P & O shipping terminal, delivering oil and a few other things to be packed with the motorcycle. Since I had ridden it over a day before, the box was already made; it was a top notch, professional job of packing indeed.

Brad and Kathy had a bit of good luck and a lot of bad luck.

On January 17, the day before I am scheduled to leave the country, Brad and Kathy suggest we go out to dinner. Earlier in the day, Brad had sold his pickup truck and is quite jubilant because he received a good price for it. So, we went out to celebrate the sale and my leaving the next day. We park their Ford Fairlane and go in to have dinner at the Sizzler (we spare no expense when celebrating). When we come out of the restaurant, somebody has stolen their car! In one day they had gone from a two car family to a no car family!

January 18: (the 17th in America): We hear news about the earthquake damage in Los Angeles - very distressing. I immediately call mom - she has been rattled, but is okay.

I go down to the shop with Brad and say fare-thee-well to all the professional people working there; they have been so kind to me over the past couple of months. Then Brad takes me to the airport where I bid this true biker and benefactor good-bye. I carry my saddlebags on my shoulder from place to place in the airport, then walk on through Customs and security to the departure lounge.

At 13:00, the plane takes off out of Perth and heads up over Western Australia. Two hours later, at 15:00, we fly over the coast of Northern Australia, across the Timor sea, in the direction of Singapore. I mutter a prayer for guidance and strength.

Stage Six of the journey is over, and Stage Seven is about to begin.

I am turning for home!

Shanghai Jardine Ferry
November 5, 1993. Cape York Peninsula, Australia.

Finding the 'O' Ring. The needle in the hay stack!
November 5, 1993. Cape York Peninsula, Australia

Camels in Western Australia.
November 1993.

L to R. George, Dave, Bruce, at Exclusive Motorcycles.
Perth, Australia. January 1994.

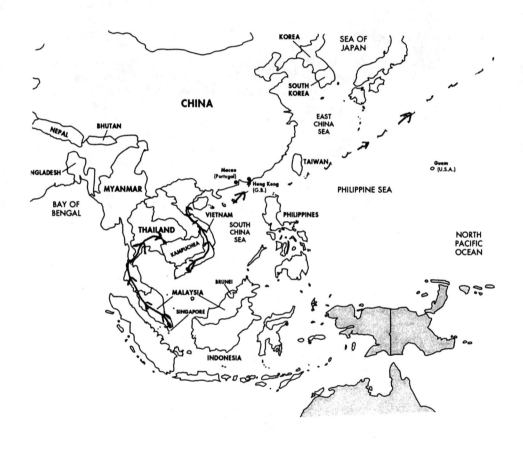

Stage Six: South East Asia

Chapter Thirty-Six

Turning for Home

The plane flew into Singapore at about 21:00 in the evening, and after clearing Customs and Immigration, I took a cab down to Bencoolin Street and the Phillip Choo Hostel. The room assigned to me was as big as my thumb, and cost 25 Singapore dollars a day (about 17 American dollars), far too much for my budget! I'd been told that this rate was "very cheap" for a "room" in Singapore. Well, pardon me for not being grateful! My cubicle measured maybe one foot longer than the bed and three foot wider.

Singapore heat and humidity, even at night, stifles me in my room as I lay down on a bed that immediately sinks down in the middle, giving me a back ache. Free entertainment is provided by some giggling idiots in the next cubical, obviously a communal room; of course, they cackled all night long.

One of the first things I do the next day is go down to the Chinese Embassy and show them my letter from Yin Li. It worked! They expedited my visa immediately. Usually, visas take five days if you want the cheap price. If you want it right on the spot, it takes a premium price - about $40. Instead, they processed mine for nothing! "Well done!" to the Chinese. I ask the embassy about reentering China again on my own, and they reply, "We don't know." Better the honest answer than the usual "No problem" "Mei vin ti."

The cab drivers in Singapore never cheated me, and were very kind, usually speaking enough English to get me to my destination. The cabs themselves were thankfully air conditioned - a big plus.

The cheapest places to eat were the massive eating halls which sometimes offered dozens of restaurants under one roof. You pick out your food, then sit at little plastic tables. My favorite breakfast is a pancake with an egg cooked into it, and curry sauce on the side. Look out for the coffee...it is strong - strong - strong!

The atmosphere in Singapore is festive; decorations are going up everywhere, preparing for the soon-coming Chinese New Year.

Subway cars are air conditioned, and the system is neat, clean and very functional. The Chinese people here are very well mannered; the "push and shove" aggressiveness of the mainland Chinese or the Hong Kong Chinese, for that matter, is not present in Singapore.

I called Mr. Deong, an elder in the Foochow Methodist Church, on the recommendation of his daughter, Mei Ling. He told me, "I have received word from Mei Ling that you would be coming." Mr. Deong told me that "I would like for you meet the pastor of our church." A meeting was arranged for the following night.

At about 19:00, a car arrives with Mr. Deong in the back; Pastor Ding Bing Ho was the driver, and he took us over to the church where we sat for the next thirty minutes. Pastor Ding Bing Ho questioned me about my trip, and mostly, about my religious convictions. "I am a Christian," I told him. At that time, however, I did not belong to any denomination in particular.

After our conversation, Pastor Ding said, "If you would like to move into the room we have available on the other side of the building, you are very welcome. Unfortunately everything around here is under construction, and is often quite noisy."

"Thank you very much," I replied. "Anything is better than where I am at right now." Of course, they were also very well aware that the Phillip Choo Hostel doubled as a house of prostitution as well as a hostel. I thought to myself, "Great, I'm finally getting away from the giggling idiots in the room next door."

The following morning I move over to the church and was given a room that had a bed and a table- much more spacious than my pathetic cubicle! Unfortunately, Pastor Ding was woefully accurate about the construction noise. As if these men knew Dave Barr's lucky laws of travel, they always seemed to station the air compressors, the jack hammers and their loudest conferences right outside my window. Although my new room had no air conditioning, the ceiling fan provided relief from the heat. The best feature of my new living accommodations was the cost- it was free! These very kind people generously provided the room to me, refusing to take any money.

After securing a bus schedule, I make my way down to the bus stop, catch a bus, get off, then walk to a subway terminal that took me to Tanijong Pagar Station. I then walked about a kilometer to Hoe Chiang Street where I located Keppel Towers Building and the P & O's offices. There I finally met David Cross, a very tall, astute looking fellow who had taken quite an interest in my trip from my time in Perth. We've been communicating off and on by telephone and fax for the last 1 1/2 months.

"My main concern right now, David, is getting the information I need to get a visa from Vietnam."

He assured me that it could be done. However, all was not smooth. He told me, "Dave, the motorcycle is here in Singapore, but there is a small problem. There is some paperwork we need to take care of, and when that is done, we can take delivery."

"Here we go again with the age-old Asian bureaucracy problem," I thought to myself.

It would have been so easy had I been on the ship with the motorcycle. When we landed, I could have just off loaded and checked the "camet passage." That document had already arrived at the Singapore office thanks to my cousin. Well done, Mindy! Without this document, the motorcycle would not be allowed into Singapore.

Laws, Spikes and Vanishing Birds

After our meeting, I am walking back across to the subway station and notice that no one spits on the streets in Singapore. Remember what a huge problem that was in China and Hong Kong? Later, I discover that Singapore has a law against spitting! If you get caught launching a loogie, you pay a $75.00 fine.

It doesn't stop there! Singapore also has a law against chewing gum, and that's a $500.00 fine. Small wonder that Singapore has non-slimy, non-sticky sidewalks. Overall, it appears to be a very orderly, clean and well run city. Of all the cities in Asia, Singapore and Hong Kong are the two that really stick out in my mind as very organized, thriving metropolises with a very First World mentality.

The first Sunday at the church I planned on attending the service. I discovered there were two congregations at the Foo Chow Methodist Church. One service being Fujian, the ethnic background of most of the Chinese in Singapore; Fujian is a providence in Eastern China, on the South China Sea just below Shanghai, and just above what used to be known as Canton. It is in the capital city of Fu Zhoou where I had stopped and met my benefactor, Lin Xu Chang.

I attended service in the English speaking congregation with over 300 Chinese; I was the only long nose, and stuck out like a "Dog's Balls." The congregation smiled and shook my hand, asking me questions about the trip. At tea time after the service, I sat with a group of young people, answering their questions. One young man came up to me and asked, "Would you like to come to my house for tea?" I said, "That would be nice."

We then rode buses all the way up Serangoon Road to the north part of Singapore where we came to a massive apartment block; his apartment was quite large and very well kept. As we enjoyed tea, he explained to me that he had been in the Army for his national service, and turned to Christianity after his mother had died. "I live now with my father, and want to become a missionary and do the Lord's work." This created conflicts with his father, who believed he should seek a "good job with a good future." I encouraged the young man to be true to what is in his heart, and to live his dreams.

In making the move to my new room, I thought I had escaped the giggling idiots.

Unfortunately, that was not the case.

After the noise from construction would stop about 19:00 each day, I'd enjoy a time of grace until about 24:00. At that point, the cafe that was right across the street from my window had apparently served enough alcohol to trigger giggling idiots and boisterous drunks; my window acted as a sound conduit to relay directly to my ears their festive celebrations. The noises seemed to crescendo until they'd always wake up about 03:00, and I'd lie awake in bed, forced to hear these characters carry on.

Within a few hundred meters of the church was a Hindu Temple on Serangoon Road. The church itself was located in a place called "Little Indian." There were open fields on the eastern side, and I'd often see thousands of Indians in these lots. I asked the pastor about them, and he told me, "They are illegal immigrants from Sri Lanka and India. The police turn a blind eye to them as long as there is no trouble. They are over here looking for work."

Singapore struck me as a melting pot city. I saw Indians from different religious sects, mostly Hindu, and Chinese, and Europeans - and all seem to live and work together rather well. Now, I am sure there are undercurrents of tension that as a foreigner I could not detect, but the city, on the surface, seemed to be a melting pot that worked. Businesses were mixed - Chinese and Indian business on the same block. Everything seemed to be fairly harmonious.

Singapore's streets are wider, so it is a much more open city than Hong Kong, with definitely fewer high skyscrapers. The people are friendlier than in Hong Kong, and still maintain a dynamic quality.

During this time, I become much closer to the Lord. I appreciated more and more the help He had given me on this trip. At this time in my life I took all the various charms I had been given - a scale from the dragon's back, a terrible mask to frighten evil spirits away, a fist that had been given from a Brazilian girl to ward off evil spirits, a Buddhist ring I wore on my little finger (from the ceremony to purify the motorcycle in Mongolia) - and put them away! I determined to put my faith in the Lord, no matter what happened, even though I was going up through some very "Buddhist territory" on my way back to China. I just felt myself coming back, closer to the Lord, ever since my weekend with Dereck Andrews in Geralton, Australia. This was just a natural progression.

David Cross was very helpful trying to work out the details to release the Harley Davidson from Customs. In the end, we waited eight days before we could get the thing out of the terminal building. We broke down the packing crate right there on the spot, and I rode the motorcycle back over to P & O's offices, then on to the church.

At night in my bed, as I listen to the giggling idiots across the way, and hear the rush of traffic outside on the race course road, I long for the open night skies out on the open road.

A freight forwarding company is right across the street. One morning, I come downstairs in the dark to do my exercises. I look across the road, and the freight forwarders were open. They had a guru in the corner who was chanting, with all the staff standing around. The Hindu workers bowed down in prayer while the others who were not Chinese stood back and watched in silence. Incense was burning, and there were Hindu decorations around the inside of the office. I ultimately learned that the elaborate ceremony I witnessed was to bring prosperity to the new business.

Normally I eat bread and beans for breakfast. Same for lunch. My hot meal at night, and usually at one of the food halls.

I call the Singapore Cheshire Home and speak to Mrs. Hickely. Lord Cheshire's cousin; she has been involved with the Home ever since 1957 when it opened. We agreed it would help the Home for me to do some media, plus a talk and slide show. Dates were established. I work with P & O to set up the media out at the Home, so both benefit.

One day, while riding in the Pastor's Dings car, I'm holding on for dear life as he tells me, "Dave, you must be careful on the roads. If you have an accident, well too bad." I think to myself, I hope this is not one of those. "Well too bads!" I always seem to find the worst drivers.

To keep myself distracted away from his driving, I kept our conversation going. We spoke about the Chinese community in Singapore. He told me, "Most Chinese have two families. They have the family here in Singapore, and the other one back in China. Some even have three. Many are immigrants from Malaysia, and Malaysians are very strict about their religion. Malaysia is a mainly a Moslem country, although other religions are there. Moslems do not tolerate other religions the same as we do in Singapore."

January 27: Pastor Ding suggests that I take a walk down Serangoon Road to witness the ceremony in progress. So, I go across the dirt lots, pass the Hindu Temple, working my way through the crowd to the street. The sight that greets me is bazaar. There are people coming along in precessions who have these big frames mounted off of their shoulders. On these frames are flowers and sometimes, feathers. There are chains coming off all the different sides of the frame. At the end of the chains are hooks through the skins of these various participants! Sometimes, great big spikes go through their cheeks - horizontally. These spikes often go vertically through their lips and tongues as well. Some would have a spike stick out of their mouth. When these marches came to the front of the temple, they would turn towards it, stomp their feet, chant something and smash a coconut. Then, ashes were tossed up in the air.

"What does all of this symbolize," I asked later.

An Indian man told me, "For two months before the ceremony these people must forego any type of sex. They also starve themselves, and eventually raise themselves to a different mental plain. They do this as a kind of recompense to the Gods. Perhaps they have somebody who is sick or in bad health. They endure this suffering so the Hindu Gods may smile down on this other person. Perhaps they want to do better in business, or have a better life, but first they must make recompense."

Sometimes I feel that the people in the church just put up with me out of Christian kindness; I am a real alien in their midst, and I know they don't really understand me. Although I was never treated badly or disrespectfully, there's a bit of standoffishness since they do not quite understand the concept of a "world traveler." I also think my disability baffles them, and they just aren't sure how to act around me.

Simon Lee, a representative for Meta Building Supplies, was instructed by his boss, Uwe, in Germany, to put some money towards the journey. One evening, Simon Lee and Amlin See, his girlfriend, come over and take me to a nice restaurant, then to a channel area full of restaurants, ice cream parlors and tea houses. The setting along the water with lights reflecting was most majestic as massive numbers of foreign and Chinese people sat around eating, drinking, and enjoying one another's company, and life in general.

A few days later, I rode behind Simon to a parking lot in a big sports arena where he took some photos of me wearing a Meta Building Supplies logo. Later, I had that logo painted on the motorcycle.

While I was in Singapore, I had a few bad dreams. In one, I saw myself riding down narrow roads in Southeast Asia, with the grill of a big truck looming up, out of the road. I could not make room for the truck, and ran right into it. A frightening scenario, and one I constantly had faced in China and other places. Now, I was about to re-enter that world again. My date was set for February 7.

On the Saturday before the 7th, I met with the television and newspaper media out at the Cheshire Home. Later, I gave a talk and slide show to the residents.

My visa came in for Vietnam, but at a cost of one hundred and fifty Singapore dollars (about $100.00 American). I couldn't believe it. That was the most expensive visa I ever purchased. The word back from the Embassy is "No problem with the motorcycle." I fear these words.

The hotels in Vietnam are reputed to be very expensive, so David Cross says he will speak to Thien, their representative in Ho Chi Min City, to ask him to locate cheaper places to stay.

On the Sunday before I resume my journey, I go into the bathroom to clean up for church and find the bird cage where Pastor Ding usually keeps his bird is knocked down on the floor; I couldn't locate the bird. When pastor arrives a bit later, I tell him about the missing bird. Of course, the bird constantly made a mess, and Lim, the caretaker, was responsible for cleaning up each of those messes. Well, the pastor comes down after checking matters out, but says nothing more about the bird. When I go back upstairs and see Lim, he is sweeping things up. He looks at me and smiles and says, "BIRD DEAD." We both had a laugh.

Bridges, Bars and Banter!

On my last visit to the Cheshire Home, I meet two girls who had seen my slide show. Both had spina-bifada, and both were in wheelchairs. Mary and Elizabeth were twin sisters, but didn't know about each other in their early years. When they were babies, they were separated from their mother and placed into two different families; ultimately, they both ended up in the home where they discovered they were twins. The closeness of these two, after re-discovering each other, was touching.

February 7: Get up at 04:30 to the sounds of the giggling idiots. I carry my gear down to the motorcycle and load it up. I do my pushups and say a prayer. At 06:30, I wake Lim up and bid him good-bye with a big hug. He unlocks the gate and I'm on my merry way onto the freeway, headed for the Jahor Bridge.

On my way to the border, the motorcycle cuts out on me a few times. I keep my fingers crossed that it won't be too bad of a day. After clearing Customs in Singapore, I cross the Jahor Bridge and the motorcycle quits. This Bridge carries a lot of traffic, and there's no place to really pull off. I manage to re-start the motorcycle, and frantically get across the Bridge before I am flattened. On the Malaysian side, I tap on the carburetor and check that the accelerator pump is working. Something is definitely wrong, but I'm not sure what it is. I decide to push on and see how things go.

Breezing through Malaysian Customs, I ride through Jahor, an incredibly built up city. I certainly wasn't prepared for what I saw in Malaysia - a very modern country with a first world mentality. I didn't expect it because most of the people I had spoken to in Singapore didn't speak very highly about Malaysia. I ride along on the best two lane highway I saw anywhere in Asia, making very good time, flying along at 60 mph (95 kph). This blessing was unexpected.

On this super highway I was passed by another Harley Davidson. The rider looks at me, I look at him, then he slows down and we shout greetings. He shouts, "I am going to the Harley shop in Kuala Lumpur." "Can I follow you?" I asked, and he nodded "Yes."

Shortly, my motorcycle starts cutting out again, and I realize it is a fuel starvation problem. We pull off, I buy gas, then we move forward through farm lands and rain forest. The machine would run okay for the first 60 miles (95 km), then would start giving me problems again. We would pull off and get gas.

As we come into the Kuala Lumpur area, there was massive road construction which translated into massive traffic jams. We cut lanes in the tremendous heat for about 20 miles (32 km). Every now and again we would pull off into a little niche in the cars to let all the little motorcycles go by. It was unbelievable how fast these guys were whipping down between the lanes.

Once in Kuala Lumpur, as I was cutting down the lanes at about 5 miles an hour, a truck moved over and hit me, knocking me into the car on my right side. I went down right in front of the car! The truck continued on, but before I know it, a large group of little motorcycles had stopped to help. The owner of the car, an Indian fellow, got out to help me, getting the motorcycle up and pulling it over to the side of the road so we could assess the damage. "I will pay you," he told me in English. "No, don't worry about it," I said. "Just go on and be careful."

Further into the city, my motorcycle quit on a bridge. There was nothing I could do. Ed, my new friend, told me "I'll go on to the motorcycle shop and tell them to come and pick you up."

A dispatch rider stopped to help, using his cellular phone to call the Harley Davidson shop. He handed me the phone, but they do not understand what I am saying. Finally, Stanley Ambrose from Harley Davidson International came on the line. He said, "We will send a service vehicle out to pick you up." By then, Ed had arrived and gave them my exact location.

When the service van arrived, we blocked traffic in the tremendous heat, as we put the Harley Davidson inside. We drove back down to the shop in this wonderful, air conditioned vehicle. The managing director of Harley Davidson in Singapore was Mao, a thin fellow, who greeted me and introduced Stanley Ambrose. "I'm having carburetor problems," I explained to them, "and I didn't feel like fixing it on the road in case there's something more serious. Can I work on the motorcycle here?"

Of course, they agreed.

As I investigated, I discovered that the rubber bit on the needle had come away from the top of the metal piece, so it wasn't seating properly. So, I replaced it with a new needle. Interestingly enough, the dealer didn't have one, but I carried one in my kit. I put it in, and everything worked fine! Mao suggested, "Why don't you spend the evening with me?"

"Champion idea," I replied.

That evening I am taken to dinner with Mao and the head of the Ibex Group, a fellow named Yiya. They presented me with a few gifts. I couldn't carry them on the motorcycle, so Mao very politely says, "Don't worry, Dave, I'll post them to you in the United States." Back at Mao's apartment, I finally got to bed about 24:00. It had been a very long day indeed; of course, I had experienced "the magic of the road" as Ace Martin put it in his book, *Live the Good Life*.

The following day we drive back down to the Harley Davidson shop. On the way,

I was struck by the very middle class neighborhood where Mao lived. The houses and offices all had ornamental iron bars over windows and doors. He explained, "Crime here is very bad." These compounds remind me of the Chinese living areas outside Hong Kong.

I meet a reporter named Mime, a Malaysian girl dressed in Moslem garb. She asks some of the most irritating questions! I think to myself, "This girl is going to get the story all messed up." When the story was posted to me later, I was surprised to see that she had done a very good job.

Television people came down to the shop, and I did a short interview for them. After that, Mao agreed to show me the way out of town. When we hit the outskirts of Kuala Lumpur, Mao stopped and we shook hands. I said good-bye to this very kind man and was on my way.

I push forward through very mountainous areas, enjoying a countryside with rubber plantations and tall palm trees. I spotted buildings that were obviously for the caretakers and workers, back inside the palm trees. There were little villages in rain forested areas as I blissfully rode along on this wonderful highway.

There were giant tall rock formations covered in rain forest type vegetation rising up right out of the flat lands. About 50 miles (80 km) outside of Pen Nang, the rain starts to come down with a vengeance, cooling me and my machine. I traveled over a massive long bridge that spanned the distance between the mainland and Pen Nang Island. Of course, when I arrived at the Island I took the Dave Barr special - a wrong turn, heading in a wrong direction, through a crowded island packed with traffic.

I called Diana Koo, a lady I'd met a couple of years earlier in Hong Kong. She arrived about 30 minutes later, and I followed her across the island to her place - two houses, back to back. One house was an office for the Cheshire Foundation of Southeast Asia, and the other was her living quarters. Diana is a very dynamic English lady who is responsible for setting up Homes in Mainland China, and is the driving force behind the training of staff. She also helps train residents for new occupations.

The first evening I spent with Diana, she held a party for some adult Chinese whom she called "her kids." When they were children, they had polio and she trained them to be able to take care of themselves as they grew into adulthood. They all show up in scooters with wheel chairs or crutches in the back. They cook on a barbecue set up in the front yard as they banter back and forth. Diana speaks the local Chinese dialect. At about 22:00 the day is done for Dave Barr, and I go to bed, leaving these young people chattering away into the wee hours.

The following morning, Diana and I went to pick up two people, one from a Cheshire Home and one from a private residence. The girl at the Cheshire Home has stunted growth, and the other, Ivy, has no feet, deformed hands and no teeth - but she speaks English quite well. We took these two girls and the odd little things they had to sell down to the Holiday Inn Hotel, right on the coast of the north part of the Island. They set up their stall and we left them there for the rest of the day.

As we drove back, Diana told me that she had "written several books and pamphlets on the training of staff and people with disabilities," and that she had "overcome many problems with politics within the Homes. Many times I just have to swallow my pride and carry on for the good of the residents in the Home." What a great lady you are indeed.

I noticed many Hindu Shrines along the way, we stop for photos.

Year Of The Dog

Next, we drove through the largest cemetery I have ever seen - miles upon miles on both sides of the road, graves stretching as far as the eye could see. In this

Chinese cemetery there were no regular rows. The graves were just everywhere. "This place dates back a couple of hundred years," Diana explained. It contained many beautiful family burial shrines.

A funny thing about the Chinese I have met in both Singapore and Malaysia. They all will say, "I am Chinese from Malaysia," but they are Chinese first. This was to be true in Thailand as well.

Diana owned a car called the Proton; this car was everywhere, and was manufactured in Malaysia, and had a very good reputation, and was quite cheap compared to the Japanese cars and other automobile manufactures.

February 10: The Chinese celebration of the Year of the Dog began. Alex told me to be very careful because the sign of the Dog is very antagonistic to the dragon - the sign I'm born under. One thing I do know, however, is that when Alex predicts something, his prediction comes true.

On this day I bid Diana good-bye, load the motorcycle and head back along the waterfront, taking a ferry across to the Mainland. From there, I'm about an hour's ride to the border where I cleared out of Malaysia with no problem, waived through quickly after stamping my passport and taking my Customs and Immigration card from me.

Thailand was not so fast.

I was told to walk the motorcycle forward in a line, and that took thirty minutes. Then, checking out the papers for the motorcycle took another half an hour. About this time, a group of riders from Singapore recognize me from the newspaper articles and want photographs; more congestion.

The Thai's didn't like the commotion, so they finally gave me the import permit. I didn't appreciate their arrogant attitudes.

Immediately across the border in Thailand, I notice the towns were much dirtier and the countryside dryer looking, very brown, not nearly as neat or clean as Malaysia. The road was a single lane, and the Thai drivers are not the same skill level as are the Malaysians. "Welcome back to the Third World, Dave Barr."

Motorcyclists in Thailand scream along on their 125 cc Hondas and Yamaha's at speeds in excess of 60 mph (95 kph). Many ride small racing bikes, and zoom between the cars far faster than is safe, scaring the hell out of me.

At one gas station, a girl offers me some ice cold water and bread, which I gratefully accept, eating while she and her friends gather around, touching my legs and smiling; communication is impossible. The Thai seem very warm and hospitable, though I already have strong negative feelings about their governmental officials.

At the end of the day, I had covered 330 miles (540 km) - a good roll. I spot a rock quarry in the distance, and pull in, getting out of sight. I spend a wonderful night out under the stars, locating the big dipper, and realizing how much I missed seeing the Southern Cross and the solitude of the Australian outback.

The following day, I am forced off the road four times onto the dirt shoulder! When cars want to pass a motorcycle, they simply flash their lights and get into the oncoming lane and go for it. They don't care about the rider getting hurt. Sometimes, the drop from the road to the shoulder is up to 4 inches, and at 50 mph (80 kph), that is extremely dangerous. The results can be frightening! It takes all my strength to control the motorcycle, then dodge bicycles or animal-drawn carts.

Many Buddhist temples dot the roadside. At one place, I took a photo of the motorcycle - inside the temple - in front of the Buddha. Another time, I saw a painted Buddha over six stories high, rising up out of the jungle. Many artifacts along the road are majestic and religiously powerful. I'll never forget seeing the monks walking along the roadside in their robes with their food bowls, living off the charity of others in a very benign fashion.

At one stop, a young girl running the gas pumps lets me use her phone to call Elena Erig, telling her "I am inward bound for tomorrow." She invites me "to stay a few days," and gives me an address and basic directions. She did not warn me about what I would encounter when I entered Bangkok the next morning.

That night, I locate a small dirt road and ride off into a farming area where I find a cow paddock that is surrounded by vegetation. I pull in, hoping to conceal myself. I set out my tent and lay back, relaxing with a hearty tin of beans.

About 19:00, here come the cows! The young woman herding these bovines is holding a little baby in her arms. I get up and kowtowed to her, and she kowtowed back to me. I made the sign of sleep, pointing to my tent. She points at the cows and I go "Moo, moo, okay." She looks at me kind of funny then walks away, seemingly unalarmed by this foreign stranger. Within minutes, four or five men and a woman show up. Again, I say, "Moo, moo, okay," holding my thumbs up, pointing at the cows. They all nod after kowtowing.

They motion, "Do you want to eat?" I said, "No," and show them that I had eaten.

They invite me to sleep in their village, but I think better of the idea. I could just imagine an entire night with curious people crowding around looking at me, and me not being able to communicate or sleep.

Every time I say "Moo" and point at the cows, they look at me strangely. Later, I find out that "Moo" means "Pig"! They must have thought I was the stupidest foreigner they ever met. Imagine, I couldn't even tell the difference between a cow and a pig!

In the end, they took the cows out of the paddock, probably wanting to keep them safe from this demented foreigner. I don't know where the cows stayed that night.

The rest of my evening is peaceful except for the snake that crawled right over my face, causing me to jump up in fright. After searching for it extensively in my sleeping bag, I finally give up, just grateful that it didn't bite me.

The following morning, I was on the road before the sun was up. The smell of cooking fires surrounded me, reminding me of my military days in Vietnam and Africa. As I headed towards Bangkok, the sun rose over a massive Buddha in the distance out of the jungle on a hilltop, silhouetting the giant Buddha in black against the blazing red-gold ball of the sun.

Miles before I arrive in Bangkok, the traffic becomes heavier and heavier. Out of all the cities in the world that I have ever traveled through, Bangkok has the worst traffic and the dirtiest air - it wins the Dave Barr Award for the most polluted city in the world!

After cutting lanes for miles, it takes me about two hours to finally locate Thomas and Elena's address at Crystal Court on Soi 7. As I pull in, the guard calls up to Thomas' apartment, then tells me, "Wait for the man to come down." As a passing comment, he then says, "A year ago a fellow from South America on a black Honda Goldwing stayed here with some people." I think to myself, "Could this be Amelio Scotto, probably the greatest overall traveler on a motorcycle ever to live?" How birds of a feather do flock together.

Once inside the apartment, I immediately take a shower and put on clean clothes. Thomas is from Germany, we had met casually once in South Africa when he was working for Bosch. His Italian wife is from South Africa, and Elena and he met and married there. Now, Thomas is manager of the Bangkok office for Bosch. Thomas is an avid motorcyclist, and has traveled all over the sub continent of Africa on a BMW. Currently, he rides a Honda Enduro to work. He tells me what I've already discovered, "You cannot make any headway in the traffic. My office is only about two miles away, yet it takes me two hours to get there by car."

As I look around their apartment, I think, "Not bad, Dave Barr. You've gone from sleeping in a cow paddock to staying in a luxury apartment - virtually overnight."

February 12, 1994: That evening we go to a very nice restaurant and enjoy a tasty dinner, stopping at a tropical beer garden on the way back. We see several prostitutes come in and sit in an area that the management had reserved for these women of the night. The men from foreign lands radiate lustful looks as they gaze at these women whose own eyes reflect their hunger for money. I am told, "This is one of the few bars where you can pick up a prostitute without having to pay the house." Another fun place to tell Mom about when I get back home!

Public Relations, Polluted Nations

After we leave the bar, Thomas takes us on a drive through the city. It is so glittery and brightly lit up, I was amazed. Motorcyclists race one another from street light to street light through the heavy traffic at tremendous speeds, testing their daring and precise riding skills. I saw a few accidents where these motorcyclists failed the test. I think to myself, "Look after yourselves, fellows. You get a disability in a place like Thailand and you are really in trouble!"

On Monday I call P & O and speak to Mr. Suwat, the managing director of the office. He tells me to come through. When we meet, I am greeted by a big, very easy going Chinese fellow. He leads me to a conference room with a banner saying "Welcome Mr. Dave Barr, World Traveler." We take some photos in front of the banner, then set up media appointments for their benefit, and the benefit of the Leonard Cheshire Foundation.

Mr. Suwat took me and 8 staff members to a wonderful lunch at a very exclusive restaurant where I feel on display, answering questions all through lunch. They also present me with 10 liters - quarts of Penrite oil that had been sent especially from Australia for me so I could do my first oil change of the trip.

Back at Thomas' office, his secretary has located the address of the Cambodian Embassy. I take a cab in that direction, and the cabby drops me off in the "general vicinity," leaving me with a long walk. As I start to walk, every few blocks I stop to ask directions. I come upon a group of young men sitting on their motorcycles, and ask directions again. One points to the back of his motorcycle, motioning for me to get on. He then takes me about two miles, directly to the Cambodian Embassy. I force 10 bhat on him (about $.50).

Inside, the Cambodian Embassy tells me that there's "No problem" for me to travel in Cambodia on a motorcycle.

The following day, Mr. Suwat schedules us to meet some media people and go to the Cheshire Home north of Bangkok. We fight our way through traffic until we come to the grounds of the home - well kept, with a peaceful little pond, a green lawn, some trees and a new addition to the home.

We are greeted by Puangpet Boonsai, one of the directors of the Home. We have a tour, then listen to some songs the residents sing for us. There is a Buddhist shrine in one location of the home, and a place to worship Christ on a cross in another.

We have a sumptuous lunch - with ice cream no less - which I am sure is as big a treat for the residents as it is for me. After lunch, Mr. Suwat puts a check in my hand, and I pass it on to Puangpet. It is gratifying that P & O, a sponsor that has helped me so much, is also willing to give something to the home.

I notice there are no televisions in the individual rooms, only one TV. This helps create a family atmosphere which was definitely missing in other homes I have seen throughout the world. In those homes, the residents tend to have their meals together, then go to their individual rooms to watch TV, failing to interact with the rest of the group. With one TV, this is a very close group of people.

On our way home, I once again see the ghettos and slums alongside the highway, sometimes built up under the bridges; it reminds me of Brazil. I think of all the people living over the channel and near the rivers, the stench of polluted water all around them. "How this city glitters so at night, yet in the day it is a very grim, dirty place."

I have never seen traffic this heavy in any city, anywhere. The air quality is dreary and depressing; I've heard that Beijing is worse, but having been there, I don't believe it for a minute. And oh yes, there's a drought, with temperatures near 100 degrees F (38 c) during the day.

I made a call to the Vietnamese Embassy to try and learn what I would need for the motorcycle. "Yes, you will need a permit to ride the motorcycle through Vietnam," they tell me, "but you can only secure that permit from Phnom Penh" - the capital city of Cambodia. Next, I contact the Vietnam Veteran's Affairs Organization in Phnom Penh and they tell me, "Dave, it is no problem for you to park the motorcycle in our compound. It is guarded."

I was invited to lunch by Roy Comings in the P & O office, and said yes, figuring we would enjoy a bowl of noodles together.

Roy had other ideas.

He drove down along the river until we arrived at a huge restaurant. As we were walking through the entrance, I realize that the restaurant was actually suspended over a huge, trashy bog. When we were seated, we could look out onto the polluted river and the harbor beyond. I imagine it all looked pretty at night, but during the day it was definitely an eye sore. The food was great, but due to the river location, it was quite expensive - for Roy. I must admit, I was not a good conversationalist on this day, as my mind was thinking about the trip ahead.

At 04:30 the next morning, I carry all my gear downstairs out of this wonderful, large apartment where I have been spending the last few days, taking it all down to the motorcycle in preparation for the day's adventure. Aruathai, the public relations girl from P & O, arrives about 06:00, and by 06:30, the TV people arrive. After an interview and a bit of a riding demonstration, it was finally time to go!

Thomas guided me out of the central area to the north of the city on his Honda. We waived good-bye to one another and I was on my way, heading north of the city with no problem, turning at the intersection that would take me east to Ayronyapetet on the border.

The road was a very crowded one; it felt as if there were a cloud of smoke hanging over it. The countryside was very scrub brush and miserable looking brown. There hadn't been any rain in weeks. On this road I see some of the most incredible Buddhist temples I have seen anywhere. They all display gold-painted, huge Buddha's sitting up in a compound away from the highway. Amazing!

I notice on my first petrol stop that I had sprung an oil leak, but decide to carry on. Arriving at the border, I make my way up to the concertina wire. A lieutenant standing there said in broken English, "You need special permit." All of a sudden I have this horrible feeling of impending disaster. I ask him, "Where do I go?"

He gave me directions to a building miles away. After about thirty minutes of riding around in circles, I finally find the place, and go in. The official inside gave me a cup of tea, made a few calls, and then said, "I am sorry. There is nothing I can do." He then tells me I must go back in another direction to yet another set of offices.

I follow my new instructions, and meet a head inspector, a Mr. Thaw Suk; I'll call him "The Suck" for short. This man had a very condescending attitude. I would have appreciated it if he had asked me for a bribe and just got it over with, but he didn't. Instead, he just kept saying, "No, you cannot pass. The border is closed to third countries." I plead with him, saying "I've been all over the world. Please let me pass."

"No, you can't."

He looks at my Cambodian visa and says, "This visa is for airport only. The only way you can go to Cambodia is by plane."

I knew he was lying. In the end, I turn away, giving him a piece of my mind. I am sick of bureaucrats, especially those who lie and have arrogant attitudes, men like "The Suck."

With a very depressed feeling in my heart, I ride backwards through traffic for another 250 miles (400 km), passing hundreds of slow trucks, to the Cheshire Home located right near the intersection at the north end of Bangkok; the residents and staff very happily open the gate for me. The boy in charge, Bumrung, then calls Puangpet, and I tell her my problem. She tells me I can spend the night at the home, or however much time I need to sort things out. Thomas also invites me to come back to his apartment. I'm not quite sure what I'll do, but I am thankful for my options.

The following morning I'm up early and hit terrible traffic at - can you believe it? - 05:00 in the morning! It is high speed chaos on the freeway going into the city. Buses stop out in the middle of the freeway to pick up passengers who are dodging traffic to get to the buses. The pall of smoke is terrible; my lungs always hurt after a ride. Finally, I arrive in the area of Thomas' apartment building, and fall over at a stop sign. Another fellow on a motorcycle helps me lift the Harley up. Eventually I make my way back to Soi 7 where I wait. At 07:00 Thomas is on his way out, and opens the door for me (I didn't want to wake him up). I take my gear inside and greet Elena, telling her "I apologize for having to impose on you like this." She says "Don't you worry about it."

After I store my gear, I head back to the P & O office to see Mr. Suwat. "Dave, you are more than welcome to use any of the communications equipment we have," he told me. I thank him, then call David Cross in Singapore, asking him "What would be the chance of getting on a ship from Singapore to Vietnam?" He was encouraging. "Dave, I don't see any problem with it. Let me check on it and I'll know more later."

Aurithai later tells me about something called a "Friendship Rally" going from Bangkok to Ankerwat in Cambodia. It sounds like a bit of fun, with an underlying theme of promoting peace between the two countries. I call the ministry of immigration, and he advises me that "The Adventure Travel Company is organizing the rally up to Cambodia."

The following morning I receive a call from "Ed," a woman who tells me to come down to her office and complete some papers. She also said, "It will cost $350.00, plus $100.00 to cover any 'unforeseen' expenses." I take this to mean that bribes must be paid. I catch a cab and meet Ed in her office. She tells me, "There's no guarantee I can get you in. Do you still want me to try?"

"Yes, indeed," I tell her. The Rally was to leave the following day.

While I was walking back to the apartment, feeling worried and depressed about the last few days, and unsure of the near future, I see a man sitting at the foot of an overpass, begging. He has two tiny hands growing out of his shoulders, and no arms at all. I think to myself, "What do I have to feel sorry about? I have good health, and the motorcycle is running okay. So what if I have finally hit a border I can't cross? It is not the end of the world."

The following morning I wake up and ride to the Rally address given to me - an Isuzi Dealer in Bangkok, meeting in the parking lot. The Harley was lifted into the back of a pickup truck. I wasn't totally sure what Ed had worked out for me, but I was game to try anything to get into Cambodia. Once the motorcycle was loaded, I answered questions from many people who were curious about the trip.

The people traveling in the so called "Friendship Convoy" were on a high level in the Thai society, and extremely curious about my trip. In the end, we left Bangkok about 10:30 in the morning heading to Aranyapethet, once again battling through traffic. It seems like it takes us forever just to get out of Bangkok on our way to the border.

It takes the convoy four hours to arrive at the border, and we stay at a medium grade hotel for the evening. Ed is in charge of making all the final arrangements for us to cross the border the next day. When people in the convoy ask "Are you going all the way with us?", I answer, "Well, I am going in with you, then I splinter off on my own." Ed had warned me about talking about my intentions, but I misunderstood her to say, "Don't talk about this with anybody who is an official, or outside the group." In the end, I feel my openness was probably my downfall. Ed came to me later in the evening; I shared a room with her brother, an amputee with a leg off below the knee. She tells me, "Dave, there is a problem. The man who was to take care of the Immigration process out of the country is not here." Then she adds, "Don't be saying things to anybody about not coming back with the group. This may have already caused problems."

The next morning, we off loaded the motorcycle from the truck, and I loaded on my gear. By 09:00, everybody was on their way up to the border; I was told to wait. I wait about thirty minutes with no word. Finally, I start the motorcycle and I ride to the border. I go to the head of the cue where I see Ed standing, chatting with other people. I wait, feeling very apprehensive, sensing things are not working out the way they should be. Finally, Ed came to me and says, "Dave, please, we are not going to be able to get you across. I shouldn't even be talking to you."

"Well, just give me my money back and I'll be on my way."

Ed dug into her purse and gave me 9,000 bhat in Thai money - all I gave her plus a $100.00 bill! I put the money in my pocket and thanked her, then waived to the others and headed back with a low feeling in my heart. I think to myself, "I will not let this depress me. I will not be discouraged. Sooner or later I was bound to find a border I couldn't cross."

I ride back the 250 miles (400 km) in the blistering heat and smog that always seems to hang over the road to Bangkok, returning to the Cheshire Home where I put the motorcycle away and take a nice, welcome shower. After relaxing, I call David Cross in Singapore and explain my predicament, telling him, "I'm heading back," - the distance to Singapore from Aranyapethet was roughly 1,300 miles (2100 km). "I'll start working on a ship to go out on," David replied.

Next, I call Mao, my friend at the Harley Davidson shop in Malaysia. Mao immediately tells me, "Come and spend whatever time you want." "Would your group like a slide show?" I ask. "Indeed we would," he answered.

The die was cast; I'm on my way back to Singapore, once again getting to battle the roads back down through Thailand. That late afternoon, Bumrung and I go out to the marketplace, heavy with the smell of various foods cooking, roasting peanuts, rotting garbage, and smog. Late that evening, I study the maps of Bangkok because I was going ride out on my own - a good 35 miles (50 km) across the city from where I was. I memorized the names of all the different roads I needed to take to get out of the city.

The following morning I am up at a little after 03:00, pushing my motorcycle down to the front gate. From there, I look up to the balcony of the main living area and see an old man sitting there in a wheel chair, watching me. We waive to each other, then I start the machine, let the engine warm up, then move on down the road, finding the ramp on to the chaotic highway through Bangkok. Even at 04:00, there's smoke over the roads and traffic is already unbelievable. As I make my way from one street to the next, I see the full moon, a big round orb covered by the dark brown smoke coming up from the city.

About 35 miles (50 km) later, I come to the outskirts of the city and stop at a petrol station for gas and a cup of coffee, then head out into the cool morning and the sunrise soon to follow, dodging trucks, being run off the road a few times, and breathing diesel exhausts for the rest of the day, covering about 600 miles (1000 km) in my mad dash for the border.

Gum Tree Hoodlums

Outside Thung Song I take a little path off into some gum trees and ride back off the road about a kilometer. I must admit I got a bit sloppy because I usually try to hide myself. In this case, I was not able to do so. It wasn't long before two Hondas come along the path with 5 young men on them. They get off the Hondas, and sure enough, when they see the motorcycle, they try to communicate with me. No dice. As soon as they stop, I took my protective gas out and slipped it into my right pocket, standing with my back up against the tree near where the motorcycle stood.

The fellows came over and smiled, then talked amongst themselves, acting a little bit smart aleck. One says to me, "You money?"

"No," I said firmly, not showing any fear. Then he sits down on the Harley Davidson. When he puts his foot on the kick stand, I say, "Enough. Get off," and stop him from trying to turn the motor over with the crank. I did this firmly, but not insultingly. I knew he must not loose face. I stood ready to pull the gas and use it on him. In the end, one offered me a cigarette. I declined, but reached into my shirt pocket and gave the guy a pack of Marlboro cigarettes which they passed around. They try to communicate with me for the next 40 minutes, and I never act arrogant or indignant. I always remain respectful, not insulting, but firm. I did not want the situation to turn ugly. They warned me about snakes, and I said, "No problem." In the end, they decide to move on, probably thinking there was something wrong with this foreigner they found in the woods. They climbed on their motorcycles and left. When they were gone, I think to myself, "Dave, you'd better get out of here." I load the machine, start it up, and raced out of those woods as quickly as possible.

This time I find another little dirt road that comes to a little hollow against the side of a mountain, completely out of sight! I put up here for the night, never seeing or hearing another person. I think to myself that night under the stars with no smog and a full, bright moon, "How long will it be before I sleep out under the stars again?"

The following morning I was up early, after enjoying a luscious can of cold beans for breakfast, I'm on my way! The road's a good one, though narrow, and takes me through pattie fields, which have steam coming off them around sunrise - very majestic. I see rock formations that jettison up 200 feet, right out of the fields. Further along, I hit some fog, and am enthralled by this sunrise over a very beautiful, rural setting. Around 09:00, I make it to the border, coming to Customs. After waiting in line, they see my import permit for the motorcycle is three days overdue, costing me $13.00 American (300 bhat).

When I go back to the office where the man has my passport, he looks at me and said, "Maybe a little consideration?" and I give him my best "Fuck you" stare. I've had enough of Thai officials. "You aren't getting one penny out of me." He gives my back my passport with a frown, and I head off.

On the Malaysian side of the border, an official looks at me and says, "I don't like Bill Clinton," to which I reply, "That's good. I don't like the son of a bitch either!." He says "Great," stamps my passport, salutes, and I'm on my way down a beautiful two lane highway. After about 50 miles, I stop for fuel, and the owner of the service station and I chat. He says, "You know, we are in the middle of Ramadon right now." That's 30 days of footing from 05:00 in the morning until 19:00 at night, with no smoking, eating, drinking of any kind. I suggest, "You must be losing weight." "No," he replies, "I have gained five kilograms. At night, I just stuff myself like a pig." We both have a good laugh.

I am making very good time, covering about 300 miles (50 km) on this fiery hot day full of humidity. The motorcycle is handling well. I'm thinking, "Great work by my friends at Exclusive Motorcycle." As I push on south, at about 17:15 I come to the outskirts of Kuala Lumpur and call Mao on the telephone; thirty minutes later Mao appears, and I follow him to his apartment. Just as I'm inside the front door, the skies open up and it starts to rain - the first I've seen in two weeks! Thailand had been bleak and dry except for the extreme southern part. At 19:00 the fast broke, and we enjoyed a nice meal, sitting on the floor, in customary Malaysian tradition. We turned in about 01:00; I fell immediately to sleep.

The following day I was able to steam clean the motorcycle, and repair some oil leaks and perform other general maintenance. About 18:00, everybody cleans up and we head down to an exclusive Malaysian restaurant. I've been fasting all day in solidarity with Mao and his friends, so it is with great delight that we all tucked into a very traditional Malaysian food served for the Ramadon holiday, enjoying live ceremonial dancing and a martial arts display. Back at the apartment, we all quickly hit the rack.

The following day I met with some media, and about 20:00 I gave a talk and slide show that went over well.

March 2, 1994: I take all my gear out and load the machine, then Mao gets on his motorcycle and I follow him through the city up to the freeway. Instead of entering the freeway, we go on a little road next to the freeway that's just for motorcycles! We ride along for about 9 miles, passing all the smaller machines, going through miniature tunnels and over tiny little bridges and under trees. It was fun - our Harleys were gargantuan compared to the little motorbikes.

We cut between lanes to get out of the city, and near an off ramp, Mao stops, we give each other a final hug, then I'm on my way, riding into the last dawn for quite sometime, making my way south on the highway back to Jahor. Of course, it only took me a few moments to clear Customs out of Malaysia.

On the Singapore side, a different kettle of fish is cooking. First, I'm stuck in line, pushing the motorcycle forward as people are checked through Customs and Immigration. When they get to me, they tell me "Push motorcycle over to side." An inspector comes along and says, "You will need to clear the motorcycle through with the "carnet passage," and you will need to secure insurance." I ask, "Can I buy that insurance here?" My heart starts to sink, knowing they are going to hit me with some obscure rule, creating a big problem. He answers, "No, you can't. You can only buy it at the automobile association." However, he did write me a permit, so it was great relief that I cleared through Customs and was on my way.

I call Pastor Ding from Malaysia and ask, "Can I come back to the church?" and he replied, "No problem." I then make my way directly back to the Foo Chow Methodist Church and into the courtyard, greeted by construction noise. Upon unloading the motorcycle, I report to the Pastor's office that "I have arrived."

Next, I'm off to P & O's office to meet with David Cross. We discuss my problem, and he turns me over to Michael Damschmit who informs me that "P & O doesn't have any ships going to Vietnam," but that they "might be able to take you on board a Maersk Lines vessel. We've spoken to some people at Maersk, and they've agreed to give you a hand." I am amazed how the different shipping agencies work with each other. Michael told me "I will try to get you on a ship for Saturday, but I'm not optimistic."

Leslie Quahe is a minister, and one of the directors of the YMCA. I offer to give a talk and slide show, and he was delighted. We meet at the Foo Chow Methodist church where I hop on the back of his motorcycle and head through town to the YMCA. He shows me around, and then offers me a room "for nothing." "I appreciate that," I tell him, "but I don't want to hurt any feelings over at the Foo Chow Methodist Church." He understood, and offered me the opportunity to "use the gym every day as much as you want." Now that was an offer I could accept!

We decide that I'll give a talk to the staff the next day, and at that show I met a very lovely young woman, Lee Gek Mui, who came to be a very appreciated and special friend during my time in Singapore.

Michael Damschmit calls and tells me "There's a problem about you leaving on Saturday, and there's also a problem about your visa. It is an "airport only" visa - the only type issued to a tourist. I'll keep checking, and let you know."

I had a sinking feeling that I was in for another major hassle. Later, Michael called back and said, "The Vietnamese said 'No problem. Just go.' It looks like it will be a week or more before I can arrange for you to get on a ship."

On Friday evening, Leslie Quahe came over on his Honda Goldwing. We ride out to dinner with a group of local motorcyclists. I met many different peoples - Europeans and Chinese - we all went into to a nightclub. Leslie is a very safe rider, and he handled his motorcycle well in the rain, and in street traffic, never scaring me. The nightclub was overbearing - the music, the noise, the smoke. I excused myself and walked a few blocks in a pouring rain, finally catching a cab back to the church where I wearily closed the day.

That evening I have one of those feelings come through my heart that I would not just be allowed to ride the motorcycle through Vietnam. The last time a feeling like this hit me was just before I received my permit to cross Russia. All I want to do is get on the road and get moving. I'm so tired of being cooped up here in Singapore.

The bearing in my left leg caliper went bad, so I go to the Tan Toc Sing Limb Center. They've never seen a leg with such an old design. They say, "There's nothing we can do for you." So I go out to a bearing shop and buy some bearings that will fit the caliper. Trying unsuccessfully to get the screw out of the bearings in the caliper. I decide to go to a motorcycle repair shop and tell them my problem. They know me from a newspaper article. Before you know it, the proper tools come out, we get the leg apart and I was able to insert the new bearings!

I do a lot of walking whenever I am in a city such as Singapore, using buses and subways. I also use the cabs, but I always seem to be out in the street or walking along when the rain comes down. In Singapore, there's never much warning. It just starts pouring!

The Harley Davidson dealer, Edwin Cho, asks me, "Why didn't we know you were coming? How come we had to find out through a newspaper article?" I told him, "I met one of the executives of Harley Davidson International in Perth and asked him to send me information on Southeast Asia. He promised to do so the following week, when he returned to the United States, he never did. So, I had no way of giving dealers advance notice."

I learned later, it was only sent on February 14 to Perth, a month after I had left. I received it in Hong Kong in April.

Edwin seemed hurt that he had not been informed, as though he had somehow lost face.

One Sunday after church I met with Lee Gek Mui and went to her church. I am getting quite a bit of religious training lately. After church, we enjoy a nice lunch, then go to the botanical gardens. There are 100's upon 100's of Filipino domestic servants here in Singapore, just like in Hong Kong. In Singapore, they gather around the botanical gardens, and in Hong Kong they congregate around the ferry terminal on Sundays. We walk around the garden and come to a secluded spot where there's a rose garden with a canopy. When we hit that spot, it starts to rain.

We duck under the canopy, and only a few odd drops get through to us. We chat for over an hour.

What a lovely girl. She had worked when she graduated from high school, saved her money, then put herself through college in New Zealand, getting an English literature degree. She was also scuba qualified. Very different! She told me that "My mother and father had a fit when I decided to turn to Christianity and break away from the traditional ancestral worship of my family."

Lee Gek Mui is very active in the gym; I see her there almost every morning. It gets lonely living the way I do; most days I have no real contact with any one, so I especially appreciate our time together.

In the gym, I'm slowly improving, raising the number of repetitions and also the lengths of the workouts. It makes me feel very good. Soon, I am doing about an hour and fifteen minute morning workout, and feeling in tip top shape. I get all sweaty and hot, then go comb my hair and wash my face, then walk out around 11:30 every morning. As I walked to the soup kitchen where I could get a bowl of soup or noodles, the skies would open up and it would just start pouring rain - that took care of the shower.

I received word from David Cross at P & O that I will be boarding a Maersk Line ship on March 18th, Friday, for Vietnam. This was very good news indeed.

In the next few days I went out with Gek a few times to various places around Singapore.

I learn that the process of buying a car in Singapore is outrageous! To get a permit just to buy a car costs $20,000 American dollars. Next, there's the cost of the car - often three times what the normal cost of a car is in the United States. It is phenomenal to think that a person buying a mid-sized Toyota might pay as much as a hundred thousand dollars for that car! And that's not all. There are road permits to be purchased every day when a person wants to go into the city center. Better to use the public transport.

I need to renew my visa to get out of Singapore, so I go down to the Immigration office in an incredible place called the Pidemco Building. I took a number, then filled out forms. When I finally got my number to get my visa, there were 250 people in front of me! I go into a huge waiting room just for the people with numbers to be called. There were people from all over the world in this room. It seemed like hours before my number was finally called. I get up, give them my passport, and they say, "Yes, we will take care of this. Come back tomorrow." As I am on my way out, a bit angry because I didn't get my visa after all that hassle, I tripped on something and fell down. Of course, there were the inevitable giggles when I got up. When I got up I gave the person a stare, and they shut their mouth. It is so embarrassing to fall down in public like that. The anger and meanness it brings on doesn't make me the most pleasant person to be around.

The following day I enjoyed the company of Gek; she went with me to the Pidemco Building. At least I had somebody to talk to during my long wait. I was very intrigued by this young woman's outlook on life, which I can appreciate. She's a lovely girl. One of her ambitions is to start a trading company.

The day before I leave, we go to the movies. I meet her outside a huge movie complex in a very commorcial area. As I was sitting on a bench out in the sun, a young lady of pleasure sat down next to me and tried to sell her wares. I thought, "You poor dear girl. You have to be out here in this heat trying to sell your ass. What type of a miserable life do you live?" Soon, Gek popped out of the entrance to the subway station and we went on to one of the biggest movie complexes I have ever seen. There were thousands of people in it. Of course, I being the one that is always dressed to kill was wearing one of my old T-shirts with holes in it. Gek, being a tidy girl, gave me a new T-shirt. I looked at her and no more words needed to be said. I then marched right on over to the men's room, went in, combed my hair and put on the new T-shirt, throwing the old one away.

Somehow , Gek managed to get up to the front of the line. The movie we wanted to see was *Schindler's List*. We went into the theater, found our seats, and for the next two and a half hours both of us were enthralled by this incredible movie. Gek grabbed my arm at times and leaned against me. It brought on the feeling of how empty my life is in that respect. I felt very gratified to have these few moments and few days with this lovely person. After the movie was over, we said a very rushed good-bye for my bus had arrived. I thought, as the bus pulled away, "God speed you on the way to your dreams."

Back at the church that evening, I packed and got ready to go. The following day would be a full one indeed. I close my day late in the evening listening to the giggling idiots over in the cafe across from me. I think to myself, "I hope I never have to listen to those dopes again."

The following morning I'm up at 04:30 and the idiots at the Cafe are still going. I go down to the bus stop, catch a bus downtown, then a subway train to the offices of P & O to say good-bye to David Cross and Michael Damschmit, thanking them for all their great help. From there I go to the YMCA to say good-bye to Leslie Qauhe. Next, back to Foo Chow Methodist Church, taking my gear downstairs. The rain starts to come down. At about 11:00 a truck arrives along with a car holding Michael Koh and K.C. Lim from the Maersk Line offices.

The motorcycle is lifted on the truck with a cherry picker, then secured. I ride with the truck driver, and the other fellows tell me, "We'll meet you down at the port." I was not allowed to ride the motorcycle into the port - that's why it was put on the truck.

We drive across town in a driving rain to the gates of the port, then to Customs. At Customs I show my carnet passage. They check the motorcycle out, then Immigration took my passport and stamped it. I am to go directly to the ship. We went down to the dockside and off loaded the motorcycle. About this time, we see the ship coming into port, "The Saigon Concord."

Once the "The Saigon Concord" was alongside the dock and tied up, I waived to the sailors and take a ride around the dock area for a few minutes, carrying the driver of the truck who brought me down. The reason: I was trying to get the battery charged up by running it for about 10 minutes. When that is done, the motorcycle is lifted by crane and put between the rear hold and the bridge of the ship. With containers up in front of it, it is strapped down. The ship had 4 officers who were Danes, and the rest of the crew was Filipino. Good old Filipinos - the international workers, going anywhere, doing anything.

Once the motorcycle is stored on board, I carry my gear up the gang plank with the help of one of the crewmen, who showed me to a clean little room at the back of the ship. I have an elated feeling because I was moving again. At about 18:00, K.C. Lim and Michael Koh bid me farewell. I thank these kind young fellows for all their help, and tell them "I'll be in touch by mail."

I was told that I would eat with the officers! Dinner that night is a delight with quality salami and things I hadn't experienced in quite a while after eating in the food halls at night, and beans and bread during the day. What a treat. That evening about 22:00 I close the day.

The following morning at 05:30 I was up early and could hear the preparations being made to shove off. At 06:30 the ship got underway. Now, Singapore Harbor is said to be one of the busiest harbors in the world, and I believe it. Ships galore lined up along the dock.

Soon we were out of the harbor and heading for the open sea, passing incoming ships of all kinds, including a huge cruise ship. I think to myself, "Here are these people eating, drinking and dining, enjoying all the luxuries, and I'm having an adventure that is fairly rare - on a cargo vessel - that doesn't happen much anymore."

The morning breakfast was eggs over-easy, freshly baked bread, bacon and strong coffee. This was all a great treat to me.

During the day I read *News Week* and catch up on all the news and events going on around the world. The days pass quietly at sea. I go up to the bow of the ship periodically to get a bit of exercise and move around. I then go down to the engine room which was spic and span clean. The noise level was incredible. It reminds me of when I worked on the offshore pumping platform in the Gulf of Suez.

In the evening we talk about various aspects of the trip. I am especially excited since tomorrow we will finally arrive in Vietnam - almost 24 years from the time I landed there as a young marine.

The following morning, March 21, 1994, I was up and on the bow of the ship watching flying fish - good luck. Dolphins were cutting across in front of the bow of the ship. The sunrise was magnificent! It comes up red below the clouds. As it rises above the clouds on the horizon, shafts of red brilliant light shine down on the ocean. It is enthralling.

We move towards the mouth of the Saigon River, and I see Vung Tau in the distance, and the statute of Jesus Christ on the top of the finger of land that comes out to the ocean. There were many ships and different types of coaster craft in this protected area. One ship especially struck me - an old LST dating back to the time of the Vietnam War. Now it was a derelict, a rustic relic of the past.

We sit at the mouth of the river for about an hour and a half until a boat comes along with a pilot, a policeman and a Customs and Immigration officer. Now we can continue up the Saigon River. The heat of the day is mounting, and there's no wind.

We wind along as if we are on a giant water snake. The swamp lands seemed endless, occasionally broken by little fishing villages on islands. I notice the fishing boats have little eyes painted on the bows. We also pass barges and outdated Russian freighters in Saigon Harbor. American Navy warehouses and docks line the way into the harbor; they look unkept. There are numerous little river craft and sampans scurrying back and forth. What an incredible setting! It reminds me of the pictures you see in an expensive book on the Far East.

Finally, we tie up along the dock and Captain Keld tells me, "You have been cleared to go ashore." That is wonderful news. I'm introduced to Bui Van, the representative of the Maersk office, who tells me "They will take the motorcycle off in about 2 hours, but apparently there's a problem."

My heart sank.

When they unload the motorcycle, they tell me to "ride it over to a Container box." As I prepare to do that, the ship's cook comes over and gives me a sack of food. I waive to the crew and start the motorcycle up with a big crowd around. Now I really realize I am back in the Third World - with all it's attention to my every movement. I ride the motorcycle over to the container box, it is pushed up inside, and the box is closed and locked.

A Budda on Route.
February 1994. Thailand.

Riding in the streets of Saigon. (Ho Chi Minh City)
March 1994. Vietnam

Chapter Thirty-Seven

Good Morning Vietnam

I go on the back of the Honda motorcycle with the P & O representative, Thien, and from there we ride out of the port. I am struck immediately by the amount of small motorcycle traffic, the most popular being the Honda 55 or Honda 90. We ride down Dien Bien Phu Street where a pall of smoke is hanging over the street. I notice immediately that nobody has a rear view mirror. They just signal with their arms or turn as they please, very much like the Chinese.

We ride a few miles across town to the Maersk Line offices and I speak again with Bui Van. "I don't think it will be a terribly big problem getting the motorcycle out," he tries to reassure me. Thein then takes me to a hotel that is very cheap for Ho Chi Minh City, costing me 12 dollars a night compared to prices I've heard that start about 95 dollars a night. I feel very fortunate. They show me to a very large, spacious room with 2 beds in it, and it's own bathroom! Thein tells me, "I'll be back in the morning."

I settle in that evening, walking down the street to find a place to get something to eat. Dinner cost me about 75 cents. On the way back, I pass some of the tea houses and young ladies of the evening who say to me, "Hey Joe, how are you? Hey Joe, why don't you come in for a drink?" "Some things never change," I think.

The following morning I order my first cup of Vietnamese coffee from a young girl in front of the hotel. It came in a small glass with a little aluminum pot to put on top the glass. At the bottom of the pot where the coffee was are small holes. You put the water in the top, and as the coffee drips into the cup, it is very strong stuff. I have never had coffee anywhere in the world, and that includes Brazil and Scandinavia, that was stronger. I have to request a cup of hot water to go with it to dilute it as I drink.

Thien picks me up on the back of his motorcycle and we go to the Vietnam Disabled Veterans Federation where we speak to some low-level officials who show absolutely no interest in what I am doing. Thien later explains that "There are many disabled veterans coming back, and coming to the building, so you are no novelty." Understandable enough.

He then takes me to the Maersk Line office where I am introduced to Nhat, who will serve as my mentor in the coming week. During the day we are together much of the time. There were always problems, and Nhat was the one responsible for trying to solve them. "The motorcycle is over 175 CC's - that's why it is not clearing." I would hear this excuse so often I wanted to puke! Nhat told me he has a special friend, very high in the Customs, who has been directing him from place to place.

One day we were asked to come down to the port. We walk up a few flights of stairs, and meet a man dressed in the uniform of a custom's officer - this was Nhat's friend. He couldn't speak any English, but through Nhat we communicated. Nhat says to me, "This man wants to know if you were in the war?" "Yes," I answered. "What service were you in?" "The marines," I answered. "What did you do in the marines?" "I was a crew chief and a gunner in a helicopter gun ship," I reply.

All this time the man is sitting behind the desk, nodding. After a half an hour and a cup of tea, he gave Nhat some orders and we shook hands. From there, we continue to run around the city doing other chores.

In the afternoons I go back to the hotel, usually uptight from the day's uncertainties. I'm just sitting on the edge, never knowing whether I am going to be moving on through Vietnam or going back to Singapore. To relieve the boredom, I'd sometimes get in a sickaloo and ride around.

One evening I was out in a sickaloo and was amazed at all the sweat shops as the driver traveled through the back streets. Saigon is definitely a thriving city. There is always the roar of small motors of the Hondas and other little motorized vehicles zipping around helter skelter. There seemed to be a higher standard of living in South Vietnam than in China or in Thailand.

As we move through the back streets and all these small businesses, I notice welding shops grinding away, and hammers banging in little carpenter shops. Lord knows what they are creating. There are sewing shops where women sit behind sewing machines, and little tiny restaurants and tea houses. People were running about with shoulder poles, maneuvering their way through the bicycle and moped traffic. Of course, there are the ever-present sickaloos - three wheeled bicycles. The rear part looks like the back end of a bicycle. Where the front wheel of the bicycle should be is mounted a basket for a person to sit in, with 2 wheels, one on each side of this basket area. There's usually a cushion with a back to it where the passenger sits, and a place to put your feet.

I was astounded at the good condition of many of the old American military trucks that were still in use. They come blasting through the streets spreading the traffic the same as someone running along down a country lane and shooing chickens in every direction.

The city was thriving and alive! I could smell various foods cooking and garbage rotting. As we come down one street, I see a beggar. Now, there are beggars all around Vietnam, but this fellow has both of his legs off above the knee, and is laying on his stomach on a little short board about 2 feet long. It has little wheels on it, and he pulls himself along with pieces of tire over the knuckles of his hands.

I asked the sickaloo driver to stop, thinking I would give him something because he looked right up at me. As I got down, I gave him a dollar. Before I know it, beggars were all around me. They were all my age or slightly older, and all of them were missing an arm or a leg, or two limbs - perhaps war veterans.

I gave each man a dollar, and shake hands with them, then get back in the sickaloo. As we pull away, I look right into the eyes of the fellow down on the ground and something passed between us at that moment that was unique - an unspoken understanding of the suffering and misery of soldiers who fight a war and get caught in the middle of its horror.

I feel like it is no good to try to go back to Cambodia since I've had all my paperwork taken from me, and am not able to get back into Vietnam. When I am asked which direction I want to go, I say "North and cross into China at Mong kai." They talk, then say, "Fine. You go north."

The die is cast.

I stop at the old American Embassy, remembering how it looked from some of the films I have seen in the past. I try to visualize the ending days of the war - all the panic, anticipation and apprehension that must have been in the hearts of the thousands of people trying to get through that gate to the helicopters that were flying people to the ships, and eventual salvation. There was desperation in their hearts as they tried to get out of Vietnam, knowing their world was collapsing around them. It must have been a horrible time.

Later that day, I speak briefly to the President of the Vietnam Veterans Restoration Committee, and he gives me an address up in Danang of the East Meets West Foundation, I read about this Foundation in the book *Heaven and Earth*.

I am struck by the women who traditionally wear "adhoi" (Vietnamese clothing), with big hats and long gloves coming up their arms - a real touch of elegance as they seem to glide along on their little Honda motorcycles.

Later that afternoon I go to the Ton Duc Thang Museum - he was the second

President of Vietnam. As I went through the museum, my guide spoke in broken English, telling me that "You first American in long to go through museum." I feel gratified, and hope for a good feeling between America and Vietnam.

On the fourth day, I receive permission to remove the motorcycle from the docks to P & O's compound. We go down and roll it out of the connex box, drawing quite a crowd as I start it up, then follow Nhat out the front gate and through the very crowded streets of the docks back to P & O's office. I ride the motorcycle directly to the basement and put it away. I am not to ride it around until it is fully cleared from Customs, but I am able to work on and service it. In the meantime, I can only hope the paperwork is being resolved.

One Saturday evening just after I had taken my legs off and settled back with a book, I hear a knock on my door. The lady who runs the hotel says, "You have a visitor downstairs." Never fails. Legs off, have a visitor. Now I must put them on and go downstairs. It is Nhat, who says, "How about we go on motorcycle and I show you around Ho Chi Minh City at night?"

Champion Idea!

We rode the motorcycle down to China Town and eat. Nhat tells me in a conspiracy tone, "Be careful of the Chinese. They make fake Rolex watches and many other illegal things."

On this Saturday evening, the crowds were dressed to kill, looking quite smart. I often saw the Vietnamese drinking beer - something I had not seen anywhere else in Asia. It must have come from their time with the French and the Americans.

Riding through the streets, I was staggered by the number of people on motorcycles. Some morons were actually racing through the crowds, barely missing other motorcyclists or the crowds. Nhat explained this crazy attitude of motorcycle drivers is the main reason the government has declared, "No more motorcycles over a 175 CCs."

Nhat explains that "My average work day for Maersk, is from 08:00 in the morning to 21:00 in the evening, " about 13 hours a day, 6 days a week. "We make good money compared to most people, and work for a joint venture company. Viscon shipping is the government side of Maersk Lines." He made about $150.00 a month. Nhat told me "As a student, I protested during the Vietnam War against the American presence here, and was put in jail for a few years before the end of the War." By the way he treated me, I never detected any animosity; he was very attentive to my needs, and very kind and informative. When I ask him about things, he's always forthcoming with the answer.

"When I was released from jail, I was inducted into the Army and within a few years was fighting in Cambodia. I could only imagine that the management of the office was very sympathetic to the Viet Cong cause.

I met a driver who said "I was in the South Vietnamese army. At the end of the War I spent 5 years in an reeducation camp. I could only imagine the horrors he suffered.

March 28: The custom's officer who handled our paperwork and gave permission for the motorcycle to be imported on a temporary basis wanted to see the machine. I ride it across town with Nhat on the back. The officer looks at the motorcycle, taking photographs, then gives it the final okay, stamping some of the papers, and saying, "Welcome back Vietnam. Go in peace." It was a touching moment. His attitude was not phony, as I often found in China, but a very genuine feeling between veterans. Later I learned the inspector had been a Viet Cong officer during the war,

Back at the office, I speak for about thirty minutes with a gray haired man named Mr. Tan about Vietnam, the Vietnamese, America and the future. He seemed to be the boss of the office, with Bui Van underneath him. They held a little ceremony this day, presenting me with about $150.00 as a gift from the staff. What a touching gesture from

475

the 25 people working in the office. One woman named Bui Kim Qui did the translating as I give a speech of thanks. Tears were in many eyes - both men and women's. I am almost overwhelmed by this emotion. The warmth and kindness of these Vietnamese was undeniable. They had nothing to gain by helping me - I did not represent a company, and I sure didn't have much money. This gift was a gesture from the heart, and that made it unique.

March 29, 1994: This morning I'm up at 05:00, pay my bill, and have my coffee at Mamasans little stand out in front of the hotel. About 07:00 Nhat arrives and we put my gear all on the back of his Honda. He stops and buys me breakfast, then we head to the P & O garage. As I was loading, I notice my front tire is flat. I take out my air compressor and air it up. The journey through Vietnam starts with a bang! With air in the tire, I notice the valve is leaking. Nhat says "No problem." He pulls the valve out, gets some grease, and puts a small amount on the valve; it held air. We say our good-byes as I shake hands with the people who had gathered around inside the P & O compound. I give Nhat a big hug, and as I start up, I look at the faces around me, full of smiles and kindness. Nhat is now standing next to a wall with his hand up in a gesture of fare-the-well; a tear is in his eye, I felt the same pain of good-bye once again in my heart as I ride out onto to Dien Bien Phu Avenue. There's a pall of smoke over the road this day as the "morning rush" is underway.

Countryside Cemeteries and Dead Dogs

Moving out of Saigon and heading north, the road is strangled by the smog, thanks mainly to the incredible amount of truck and bus traffic. I see many ever-present Hondas as I bounce along a rough road, full of holes. I have been told on a number of occasions that "The road gets worse north of Hue." I was just grateful and relieved to be allowed to finally travel through this country alone.

I bang and bound along, dodging trucks, buses, mopeds, Hondas, bicycles with big baskets, and the multitudes of people moving along the road with shoulder poles on foot. I'm not long out of the Saigon area when I see my first major Viet Cong/NVA (North Vietnamese Army) cemetery. I was to see these things continuously through the country all the way to Haiphong. They were everywhere, and generally very well kept up. I felt very privileged to be finally on the road, and wonder "How many people have ridden a motorcycle through Vietnam on their own?"

The countryside is under cultivation with rice pattie fields or palm trees growing. Sometimes, it is just low scrub brush. I came over a rise and suddenly see the South China Sea, riding along it for a number of miles. I pass through a fishing village that is tropical and beautiful, a well kept village with palm trees lining both sides of the road. Out the other side of the village, and going up over a low mountain pass, I stop to photograph the boats down in a little harbor, some as large as 3 tons, and all with little eyes painted on their fronts.

If I stop to take photographs, I must get off the motorcycle, get my camera out and take the photographs quickly or a crowd forms around the machine before I know it.

Most of the time I travel in third gear, going about 35 mph maximum through the country, often going 85 to 100 miles nonstop, then pulling off for gasoline or a photo. Fuel is absolutely no problem - very inexpensive.

In the late afternoon as I am move along the road, I see a rock quarry off to the side of the road, and go back a 1/2 mile where the brush and trees have been cut away. I stop under a massive shadow so it will be very difficult to see me. Once the motorcycle is covered with the tarp Ken Taylor had given me in Australia, I get out some sardines and a piece of bread - homemade by good bakers - the best of anywhere in Asia.

I enjoy watching the waning light of the day down below as the village went about its business. I wondered, "How many times did American soldiers ambush that village?" I really was having a great experience just being on the road by myself, especially enjoying the stars. It feels so good to be out on the road again, to finally get the trip moving in a positive direction, putting behind me the bureaucratic bullshit that comes with traveling in these areas of the world and just be moving again. It is with these thoughts that I close the day.

I awaken in the pre-dawn. After a sandwich, I load the motorcycle and quietly watch the village come to life. People with various farm instruments move out into the rice patties in the distance to start the day's labor. Vehicles travel along the road - bicycles, Hondas, trucks and buses go on to their destinations. About 06:00 I fire up. The sun is just coming up, and the day begins in earnest as I ride out to route 1 heading north.

I say to myself, "Good morning, Vietnam," thinking back to the times when we would be flying in from night medivacs and listening to the ADF (aerial directional finder) in the back, myself and the gunner - all listening to the music from armed forces radio. I am speeding up on route 1 in a fresh new day, bringing back incredible feelings from days long past. A shiver shoots up my spine.

I go through some more fishing villages during the day. Enthralled, I take photos of people working in the rice patties. This is a time of peace, not danger. I stop at one village in the late morning where they are spreading the rice out to dry in the sun, taking up a couple of feet on each side of what is already a narrow road. I stop to take a photo and a crowd starts to form; within 2 minutes 50 people are gawking. One lady puts her baby on the seat of the motorcycle, but he cries before I can take a photograph of him. I feel no animosity from this crowd, only curiosity as to what I was doing.

Another time I stop and buy a sandwich for the equivalent of about 10 seconds at one of the little roadside vendors who makes his living out of a little push cart selling sandwiches and sodas.

More cemeteries - not only NVA/VC military cemeteries but cemeteries for the general population. I would see them in the villages and out in the countryside; they are everywhere. When I was a serviceman flying in the war, I also noticed cemeteries everywhere; it sometimes felt like Vietnam was just one big cemetery.

Late in the afternoon I hit a rainstorm for about 20 miles; the roads become very slick and dangerous. About 16:00 I see a church and decide to pull in there for the night - an interesting mistake. A small crowd gathers, and the pastor comes out, introducing himself as Pastor X. He says, "I must report your presence to the security office." I said, "Oh, no, I will just go." He says, "Please stay." So, I figure that perhaps the reporting is just a routine. After I stand around for about 45 minutes, a security man comes, looks at my passport and smiles. He says, "You must take the motorcycle inside." We push it up into a sitting room outside the main church building. As people stood around outside watching, I did odd jobs on the motorcycle, and wrote in my dairy with kids standing all around me. By the time I was done with my dairy, the kids had already lost interest in smelly old horseface, and had gone on their way.

The security man comes back and speaks with the Pastor. He says, "There's a slight problem." I say, "Well, listen, if there is going to be a problem (even though it was getting dark) I will be on my way." I never imagined it would be such a hassle to spend a night in a church. But this is Vietnam - a communist country.

The pastor invites me to dinner, and we sit down to a simple meal of fish, mushrooms, rice and soup. He introduces me to his mother, 82 years old with beetle teeth. This is something I notice that isn't as common as when I was here 24 years ago. Then, it was very common to see people with blackened out teeth from chewing beetlenut. I didn't see much of that now. I also meet his wife and two daughters. In broken English, he speaks about the hardships he's suffered since 1975 when Vietnam was liberated. "Many churches burned. My family persecuted for years. NEVER give up faith," he said.

I thought, "This is one of the few men I have met who has truly suffered for his belief in God." He told me that "In my congregation, only 30 percent have Bibles." The government has become more liberal, and now allows religions of all kinds - Buddhist, Catholic and other denominations. "I am able to remodel the church. Get it in shape. Many new Christians here - one a day in my church. Future will be better. Security problems with you because they still hate the church."

At about a 22:45 the security man comes again, this time with his boss! I don't like the looks of this little guy. He was short, wearing sandals, a uniform, and had a head full of cowlicks and rotten rat-like teeth set in a dark round face. His fingernails were very long, and he looked like what he turned out to be - a prize prick.

We banter back and forth. He tells me, "You must move on for your own security." I now realize that he just doesn't want me there because it is something different. "I can't ride at night," I tell him. He didn't like me challenging authority. I could see it made him uneasy. We banter back and forth, getting nowhere. I see that the Pastor is starting to get uneasy, and realize I did not have any right to endanger this man.

I finally say, "Okay, I'll go. But you must help me move the motorcycle out." I show the pastor where to put his hands so as not to get them greasy. For the security man, I point to the front forks, indicating he should push against them to prevent the machine from going down the stairs too fast. When we are finished, he has hands full of black grease! I smile and roll the motorcycle out to the street and start up.

I say good-bye to this wonderful man of God, and ride away into the night, leaving dick head to wander around to find something to wipe off his hands. For roughly 30 km (19 miles) I dodge trucks that are all over the road, although there was no non-motorized traffic or Hondas out, these people obviously having more sense than I did. I hit a full sized dog with the front wheel. The crash bar hit him and knocked him away from the motorcycle, saving the day.

Eventually I make it into a small town, and see a hotel along side the road. I pull into the forecourt of the hotel; the person in charge comes out and shows me a room, but I beg off, motioning I want to sleep near the motorcycle. He understands, and we push it over to a corner of the forecourt under a roof just in case it rains that night. I put out my sleeping gear. When I was ready to go to sleep, the crowd moved away so I was able to have a bit of privacy to take my legs off and get into my sleeping bag. The hotel did not charge me anything.

Tracing the Past, Finding the Future

The following morning I'm up early and put my legs on before the crowd shows up. Breakfast is a bagel and some coffee, then I'm on my way down a very foggy road, grateful there's not much traffic at this time of the morning. It wasn't uncommon to have a big truck come looming out of the fog in the middle of the road and be forced to dodge him. Many of these encounters were within inches of disaster.

The road was up above the rice patty dikes. As the fog burns off, I look off to the west and see not only rice patty dikes but mountains in the distance - probably the Quaoon Mountains. I come over a bridge at One Core River, thinking about the hundreds of times I had flown north out of Marble Mountain to turn west and come right down this river, only a few feet above the water, and over this very bridge! It sent a shiver up my spine as I had yet another sharp glimpse of the past.

I ride on the main street running through Da Nang and head eastward towards the coast. After a mile or so of not knowing where I was, a couple of young fellows on a motorcycle stop. I show them the address of Viscon Ship, and follow them down the main street and up along the waterfront. The waterfront is an outlet to China Beach and the ocean. It is different now - there's just fishing vessels tied up along the wharf; no more Naval patrol boats like so many years ago. We found the Viscon Ship office, where two people greet me, Mr. Tan and Mr. Dia. After greetings, we roll the motorcycle inside the compound, and I remove the gear I'll need at the hotel. Dia took me over to a hotel that was quite cheap - $6.00 a night - with a shower. The quality and cleanliness of the hotel was weak, but it was cheap - and that's the bottom line! After cleaning up, I go back to Viscon Ship where I meet Vin Quyen of the Lao Dong national newspaper and we make arrangements to do an interview on the following day.

We then go down the office of East Meets West, and I meet a young American Vietnamese fellow named Julian Do, the managing director. I speak to him about going out to Marble Mountain and Peace Village. I also ask him "Do you know where the helicopter base was?" He didn't.

I had heard from people who have been up on Marble Mountain that the base has been all turned under and that there isn't anything there now. Somehow, in my heart I knew this wasn't right. After a nice lunch with Dai, I spend the rest of the evening back at the hotel.

The following morning Dia comes by and takes me to Viscon Ship's office where I meet Vin Quyen and we ride out to Marble Mountain. I recognize the roads we were riding on, and see Monkey Mountain in the distance. Just out of the Da Nang area, we come to a tank farm that wasn't there before. There was a wall along the tank farm, so I couldn't see out to the ocean. Finally, when we come to Marble Mountain, I think, "We have gone too far and somehow have missed the base."

On the south side of Marble Mountain, we took some pictures for the newspaper article, then went to Peace Village. I notice some back roads as we ride north along China Beach, and I duck into one of them, weaving through a village, coming up on a rise. Sure enough, there was the helicopter base along the ocean front running from north to south! I immediately notice that there has been construction done since I was last there - obviously, it had to do with turning the base over to the South Vietnamese Air Force. The taxi way and runway are still there as they were, except for the weeds growing. I look around as quickly as I can, then take some photographs of myself next to the Harley with the helio base in background.

A crowd is closing in, and I think to myself as Vin is taking photographs, "The only thing missing now is the machines of war to come pounding out of the sky and land at the base." How many hundreds of times I had left behind this haven to fly out to the uncertainties of the war, always fortunate to be welcomed back into it's comforting fold. No more had these thoughts of the past gone through my mind when a military jeep comes racing toward us. Out of it pops two Vietnamese Naval Security Officers. They start shouting and carrying on. Vin ran over to them and introduces himself, showing his press card and giving them a newspaper article to read from the Lao Dong that had been done down in Saigon. They read this article and look at me. They give me back my camera, shake my hand, then make it very clear that we must go.

Well, at least I got a glimpse of the old base!

I mount the Harley and take one last look at the place where I had been stationed 24 years ago for one year. We rode away back Da Nang.

Once the Harley is put away, I ride on the back of Vin's Honda to his little apartment and meet his wife, Vung, and his young daughter, Dong Ann. She was very excited since she had just found out she passed all her examinations to get into university; obviously, this was an extremely intelligent young woman because thousands apply and only a few can go - there's no room.

During the evening we enjoy a dinner of prawns, rice, and vegetables. Vin told me that "I was a student activist against the war when the Americans were here so many years ago." When I ask him "What is your feeling about the government and communism now?" he was very evasive.

Vin was quite a writer. He had written six novels, and his daughter, Dong Ann, was doing well with her English. "She wants to be part of the diplomatic corps and travel overseas," he told me. After a fun and informative evening with these people, I was taken back to the hotel and closed my day.

While laying back in the nether world between sleep and being awake, I saw and heard in my mind's eye the machines of war coming and going to and from their missions of destruction. Their blades pounded a fearful path through the skies, 24 hours a day. I heard once again the dreadful noise of their rockets and machine-guns, delivering their deadly energy upon the enemy, or anyone unfortunate enough to be caught within their horrible grasp. It was with these dreams of a bygone day of misery and destruction that I eventually found passage into restless sleep.

The following day I make my way to Viscon Ship's office on my own, get the motorcycle out and ride down to the office of East Meets West and meet Gene Powers, a contractor from San Francisco. He is going over to Hope Village and is waiting for a ride that hasn't shown up. Julian suggests that I put him on the back of the Harley Davidson and take him over. Gene didn't realize I was missing two legs at the time. I said "Hop on." We put him on the back and follow another motorcycle that was on its way over there through the back streets and out to the main street of Da Nang for a good few miles until we eventually wound our way to "Hope Village" - a village for Vietnamese children who are orphans.

There were a few disabled children here with hearing, speech and sight problems. This is also an East Meets West project through Mrs. Ly Le Hayslip, the author of the book *Heaven and Earth*. When Gene found out I didn't have any legs, he was quietly shocked. We had a tour of the Peace Village. I noticed Gene dropped $100.00 in the donation box, and I dropped in about $5.00. We took some photos with all the kids around the motorcycle.

I made my way back to the main office of East Meets West, leaving Gene to meet with the rest of the Vietnam's Vet Restoration Committee. Julian Do asked me if I would take him out to Peace Village; I was happy to help.

Along about this time a group of motorcyclists on machines bigger than 175 cc's pulled up in front of the office. Julian explained, "They are a motorcycle club here in the Da Nang area." Unfortunately, none of them spoke any English. We all shake hands, and Julian says, "They want to ride with us out to Peace Village," so we all rode together through the streets to Peace Village at the base of Marble Mountain.

We took some photographs at the entrance. But before I could go on, Julian said "The bikers want to take you to lunch," so I follow them into town to a very ethnic looking restaurant with great food. They keep trying to get me to drink. I say "Thank you, but I don't drink." They couldn't believe that they an American biker on a Harley Davidson didn't drink! One kept saying "boom boom girls" to me, and I kept saying, "No, no thank you." I think they were astounded by my lack of desire to do all the things that Americans were into during the war (including myself).

Eventually, I ride back to Peace Village on my own and take more photographs with kids all over the motorcycle, then take Julian back to the head office. As we ride back, he tells me "Those bikers are very well-to-do people to own such large motorcycles."

Frankly, I was relieved to get away from them.

Later that day, I took a sickaloo back to the hotel, cleaned up, then went looking for a place to get a bowl of noodles. Back at the hotel, I took off my legs and started to read when I hear a knock on the door. The porter tells me, "There's a bunch of guys on motorcycles here to visit you." It is the "boom boom" boys I think to myself. "Please tell these people that I am in bed, sleeping, and cannot be disturbed." I certainly hope that didn't hurt their feelings, but I was no longer into boom boom!

I'm having problems with my rear brake, so I pull the wheel and find the wheel cylinder had leaked. I clean it out with some sand paper. Dia got me some brake fluid, and I was going to put it back together, Dia says, "No." A couple of fellows in the group of about 10 people who were standing around watching. It needed new inner seals, so they ran off. I couldn't imagine where they would find them. In ten minutes, they came back with seals that matched exactly. I put them in the wheel cylinder. It seemed okay after cleaning off the brake shoes and all the fluid that leaked on them.

Di took me out to lunch, then to his brother and sister-in-laws house. He showed me a shrine to his mother and father, both passed away. We took some photographs; I was very touched by their very humble abode.

I was repeatedly warned by people in the south part of Vietnam to be careful in the north. "There are many cowboys, so don't sleep out on the road." They gasp when I tell them I had spent a night out by myself south of Da Nang. "Don't do that. Much trouble with the police." After their strong advice, I decided to stay with hotels on the rest of the journey. "People in the north are very primitive. Be careful. They are aggressive and ill-mannered," I was warned. Apparently, there's great antagonism throughout the south for the people of the north, and in the north they say nothing about the southerners!

A little girl hung around the office. She was always silent, always watching, standing off to the side. She belonged to a lady who worked from a little push cart in front of the office, selling potato chips, cigarettes and nick knack's. I think to myself, "What type of a future does this poor little child have?" I feel sorry for both mother and child.

That evening Dai says, "I'm going to take you out and show you all over Da Nang at night." So, on this Sunday evening, we take off with the building guard and get something to eat - a bowl of noodles. While we are eating, a child comes up begging. As I start to give the child a bit of money, an old man pushes the child aside and tries to take the money. I withdraw it. Dia and the guard push the old man back and tell him to get away. After this incident, I felt guilty about eating a bowl of noodles. When finished, I decide it was so good that I have another bowl (the guilt wasn't that deep!). Dia and the guard were drinking a beer, and the guard appears a bit tipsy.

When we complete dinner, the kids come back over, and I give them about a dollar. The old man is gone. As we leave, Dia tells me, "Don't do that. It encourages the kids to beg." I had to agree. "Dia, I know you are right, but I feel so bad sitting here and eating while these children are hungry."...He nodded and didn't say anything. I had disappointed him.

As we ride around the city that night, it is alive with so many lights. It seems as though there are millions of motorcycles on the street. Of course, there are the usual idiots racing with one another between the motorcycles. Dia told me, "They race, and maybe the winner gets a beer or something like this. Unfortunately, they cause many accidents."

As we ride along, we pass 3 girls on a Honda, all dressed up and looking lovely. They come racing by and the guard makes a sudden maneuver on his bike, hitting the girls. Both motorcycles go down with all occupants flying through the air. Dia pulls over, and tells me to "Go across the street over by the channel."

As I watch from the distance, there's plenty of shouting and hollering. In the end, the girls want money from the guard. Dia later told me, "The crowds will always side with the women, but the guard had turned around and started shouting, "Call the police. You are riding three on a motorcycle." That did the trick. The girls jumped on their motorcycle and took off. We go back to the compound. So much for this evening's festivities.

It is common to see three, four or five people on a motorcycle. A sickaloo can hold as many as six Vietnamese - a whole family sometimes. I have seen four people on bicycles. Of course, in the country I'd seen two pigs strapped down on the back of a little Honda, obviously being taken to slaughter.

Everything is vibrant and alive. I enjoy all the cooking smells, and it is interesting to see Vietnam now as compared to war time. No more military vehicles charging through the streets, no more uniforms, and no noise from the constant pounding of helicopters in the distance.

On Sunday morning, it is time for me to go. As the guard opens the gate, here comes Dia, Mr. Tan and a couple of other fellows on a motorcycles, ready to escort me out of the city. This was comforting, since I had been warned about the pass I was going to go up and over, and had been bracing myself mentally during the night. Since there weren't many motorcycles out at 06:00 in the morning, we had a peaceful ride as we turned north up Highway One and rode about 10 miles (16 km), stopping at the base of the pass that I was to go over. We exchanged hugs and shook hands. I could see emotion on the faces of both Dia and Tan. With no more said, we bid each other farewell.

I followed another motorcyclist on the road, and he led the way. We went up and up, and before you know it, I could see the South China Sea far below. Unfortunately, there was no sun out. We were under the clouds; it was quite gray. I could see the base of Monkey Mountain off in the distance.

At the bottom of the pass, my new found friend said good-bye and went back up. Only then did I realize he was not with our original group, and had traveled with me just to make sure I made it safely to the other side. I rode on through rice patty fields, noticing far more buffalo out in the fields than before.

As I ride, I see a little girl dressed in rags, with matted hair, standing with her arms out for balance, on the back of a water buffalo that was emerged in the rice patty field all the way up to it's back, with its head just out of the water. Her tiny feet were planted squarely on its broad back as it slowly slogged through the mire of the field. It was a scene as old as time, and it will be forever imprinted in my mind. Unfortunately I was not able to stop and take any photographs.

Poster Power Lives!

Around noon I come into Hue and stop at the citadel where so many people were killed during the Tet offensive of January, 1968, by the North Vietnamese Army. Hue was a major battle ground during the Tet offensive between the U.S. Marines and the NVA. It was out of Hue too that I thought of one of the most incredible "DAVE MAN" posters that appear in every issue of "Easy Rider." That poster showed a man on a Harley Davidson Panhead wearing jungle fatigue pants, boots, and a regulation green T-shirt, riding out of the jungle up Route One with helicopter gunships firing into the jungle, with explosions and fire coming up behind him.

This picture and its powerful message of remembrance for the 58,000 brothers that were killed during the war really struck home with its emotional power. All of the sudden, I realized that I was the man in the painting, on my mighty iron steed, riding free for all of them to Hanoi. God rest their souls. I am one of the very few, if not the only one, who has ever traveled on a Harley Davidson from south to north, from Saigon to Hanoi, alone.

Later that morning of April 3, 1994, I stop and get a piece of bread for lunch. This will be the last time I stop at a roadside food stall in North Vietnam. A crowd forms very quickly as I go into this little shack on the side of the road. A lady brings me some tea and I select a piece of bread off a table covered with flies. As I was eating it, a man behind me started to grab at my knife that was on my belt. I turned around and slapped his hand, then grab it saying, "Cam on ban," meaning "Thank you friend" so that he doesn't lose face. He nods, and there was no scene.

All the time people are hovering near me, they are trying to touch my legs and arms, inspecting every little thing. It is very unnerving. Finally, I get on my motorcycle after paying and ride on through the afternoon, bouncing along, dodging traffic.

In late afternoon I come into Vinh, the most miserable looking city that I have seen anywhere in Vietnam. It was a proper shithole. I managed to find a hotel for the night, and the proprietor was very kind. He put my motorcycle near the main entrance so it could be watched all night. My gear was carried up to the elevator and I went up 16 floors. The room was clean, but unfortunately there was no running water. All water was brought in by buckets. Here I experienced the three price system: one for foreigners, one for people from Cambodia, and one for normal Vietnamese. Dinner cost me $1.00, and that was with the extra bread I planned to take along so I did not have to stop again for food at a road stand.

About 05:30 the next morning, I'm on my way in the fog; it is just barely light. The road conditions were difficult, especially when oncoming vehicles loom suddenly out of the fog and I am forced to dodge them and avoid hitting bicyclists at the same time. In the north of Vietnam, there are many more people riding bicycles than in the south. It seems to me that the average man in south of Vietnam is far better off than the average man in the north.

In the late morning I approach a rusted old ferry that loads on vehicles, then we start across the river. Of course, people are touching my legs, arms, and shirt with aggressive inquisitiveness, talking excitedly amongst themselves in awe. How weary I grow of this routine.

I come to a couple of bridges during this day. On the first one, the guard on the bridge tells me to, "Go around on the walkway where the little motorcycles and people with bicycles walk." As I was move along this bridge, my right leg gets caught underneath me and I fall over to the right. Two men immediately help. One helps me push the Harley Davidson the next 150 yards. I was sweating blood. I am also having problems with my brakes again, so I start working on them after crossing the bridge. A large crowd gathers around me. It is so difficult to see because the crowd blocks out the light; it feels like China all over again.

With that accomplished, I see the two friends from the bridge. I take out a pack of cigarettes and give it to them. They seem very happy. After this experience, when I come to a bridge I negotiate it the same as a car. Unfortunately, these bridges weren't built with boards laying across the bridge. The boards lay long way, so as you ride along, it is very difficult to keep from falling into a rut between the boards. These ruts cause you to fall, and can possibly ruin tires. I learn to criss cross back and forth to keep from falling, timing it to avoid any oncoming vehicles. Also, sometimes the bridges are shared with the railroad, and have tracks on them to make things a bit more interesting.

I come to another NVA/VC cemetery and take photographs. As I stop, two couples on little Hondas stop, both waiving the peace sign to me. I thought back to the time I went to the Wall in Washington D.C. with Lang Price in June of 1991. I remembered how upset I was at the Vietnamese woman selling umbrellas in the rain, and how I asked to park police to remove her, which they did. And now, here I am at one of their sacred places taking photos. Instead of removing me, they greet me with peace signs and hand shakes. I think, "Dave, perhaps you have a lesson to learn about forgiveness and reconciliation." I realize too that all of these war cemeteries, all the bodies in them are transplanted. None of them were there before 1975. It must have been a monumental and enormously grim task of locating, exhuming and reburying.

While it is still quite foggy, a big truck comes roaring towards me. I had to dodge him quickly, hitting a bicyclist with two big baskets on the back of his bicycle. I caught one of the baskets and knocked the guy off into the rice patty dike. Sorry fellow, but I felt it prudent to keep going, knowing you were not hurt.

Later, I run over another dog. The front wheel hit him and he crashed into the crash bar and was knocked aside, a flat dog. I NO STOP!

That afternoon I enter Hanoi. The last 30 miles were really hectic since the roads become far more crowded with bicycles and non-motorized traffic, plus the Hondas, the trucks and buses. There was a passenger train that stopped at various intervals along this road leading into Hanoi, and I noticed Europeans hanging out the window and I waived to them as I went by. I could hear shouts of encouragement coming from these people. It made me feel REAL good!

On one of the main streets of Hanoi, I managed to flag down a motorcycle, show him an address, and then follow two young fellows across Hanoi to the Viscon Ship office where I waited for about a half an hour. Finally, along comes a Nissan 4 x 4 vehicle, and out climbs Jimmy, a young Danish fellow, the office manager of Maersk Lines in Hanoi.

I introduce myself, and he replies, "Yes, we are expecting you." I met two of his staff, a young woman named Henna and a young fellow named Phong, both Vietnamese. I immediately take a dislike to Phong. I went upstairs, telling him of my need to rest a bit. Instead of listening to me, he immediately calls a reporter who appears and makes me roll the motorcycle out of the reception area and push it out into the street. Of course, everybody starts to help, and they always seem to pull it away from me instead of leaning it towards me. I lose my balance and over it goes!

I get very upset! I lift it up and continue to push it to where the photographer suggests we can get some good photos. We made the Army mad at that point because some of the photos were near the main gate of the Army base at the end of the street.

After the interview, one of a few I would do while in Hanoi, I take my gear across the street to a small hotel and get a room for only $15.00 a night. It was a small, old French Provincial room, clean and very well decorated. I felt fortunate to get it for that price - including breakfast and hot water with a shower!

The following morning I got a lift on the back of a Honda motorcycle over to the Chinese Embassy, a huge compound not far from Viscon Ship. I show them Yin Li's letter, my media, and of course my video tape. The fellow behind the desk said "I don't think there's anything I can do," but he called a young woman. Very nicely after reading my letter, she said, "Well, what can we do for you?" I said, "I'd like to cross the border into China from Mong Cai and ride back to Hong Kong."

"Oh," she said, "that might be a problem." I had a sinking feeling that things weren't going to work out. She said, "First of all there is a problem with your license. We cannot issue any permit for you to go on without taking care of the license, and we can't do that here. Mong Cai also is closed to Third Countries."

Enemy - Foreigner - Friend

I think to myself, "Oh, no," because all my Vietnamese paperwork for the motorcycle is for Mong Cai or Haiphong. Bui Van must have been thinking I might have problems with the Chinese, and so he gave me an out by the seaport. This turned out to be very,

very wise on his part. The lady then said, "You can go through the other border which is about 200 kilometers northeast of here. The permit to ride the motorcycle is your main problem."

I realized it would be a major feat to get all my paperwork changed for the motorcycle to go through the other border. Now, I was in a bit of a quandary with what to do. I could get stuck here for weeks, and maybe still not get into China. When I ask the girl if she could try to do something quickly, to get some information, she replied, "No, meiyo."

The man behind the counter was obviously in charge of the place, but he didn't speak very good English, and was a little more direct in his answer. He just didn't want to know anything about it.

With a down feeling, I got a sickaloo back to the hotel, realizing all the problems and bureaucracy that faced me. I think, "I have ridden 6,000 miles in China and I feel that I would be better off, and it would be easier on everyone and fairer by far to Maersk, and Viscon Ship management, not to try to change all the paperwork. I will just take a ship to Hong Kong where I can get the motorcycle ready to go back to the United States."

Jimmy, of course, agreed with me.

April 5: Some of the local newspapers want to do an article on the trip. They want me to ride into Ho Chi Minh Square, which is what I've been asking to do right along.

About 11:00, I ride the motorcycle across town following Phong to the edge of Ho Chi Minh Square . A huge crowd gathers. It is very difficult to keep them away as they take photographs. Within 15 minutes, we are finished. I think to myself, "This is a crowning grace to the trip. **I have now ridden into the three squares of communism - Tiananmen Square, Red Square and Ho Chi Minh Square.**

As I ride back to the office, there's only a few moments to reflect on my little bit of motorcycle history. Bringing me back to reality, I discover the rear brake is dragging again. It has been giving me problems since Vinh. The following day, I bring it over to an Army base, believe it or not, where I work with another fellow for half of the morning taking care of small repairs, once again putting seals in the rear wheel cylinder. This time they hold. Thankfully, my friends in Da Nang had bought extras. I must have put them in wrong the first time.

That afternoon I was surprised by a visit with Gene Powers again. What a gratifying time to see this man. We spent the rest of the afternoon chatting, and in the evening, he invited me to a dinner where I was introduced to a North Vietnamese Army Colonel from the war who was looking after this group. They sat us down at a long table. To my left was a lady named Ann and at the end of the table was a fellow named Wippel who had a tracheotomy. I'm hard of hearing, so when Wippel spoke, Ann would then relay his statement to me. We all laughed because poor Ann was sitting between Whispering Wippel and Deaf Dave!

The following day I took care of a few things with Viscon ship that they wanted me to do with media. I met a very bitter man who told me that he'd been an airplane pilot for a number of years. During the Cambodian War he had flown air to ground attack planes and then later, when he got out of the Army, he had flown other various aircraft that had been captured from the South Vietnamese Army after the liberation. He said he had known of pilots that had stolen their planes and took off, flying to Taiwan.

"I never considered anything like that," he told me. But one day they found him with a few cartons of cigarettes after flying down to Saigon, and informed him, "You are no longer a pilot." They yanked his license, and he's never flown since. He's a very bittor man indeed. He did say he felt "lucky" in one sense because he had friends who were just "suspected" of bringing things up from Saigon who were put away into reeducation camps for very extended periods. I thought, "What a brutal government you live under."

"Things are getting better," He told me. "The new President is a southerner, and when southerners rule the country, things are far more liberal and better for the people." This spoken by a northerner.

He said, "The government had to change to bring foreign investment into the country. The country was going broke, but now it is starting to change."

Many times people told me, "Three years ago the shops were empty. Now, the shops are full of merchandise. You see people riding on motorcycles, neon signs on buildings - all signs of growing economy."

Jimmy told me that he felt the combination for turning the nation around was the "combination of intelligence, the willingness to work HARD, and belief in the family unit!" All that I speak with say the same thing: "Socialism doesn't work."

April 8: I start up and ride through very slick streets in the morning drizzle. I haven't slept since 02:00, worrying about this last ride down to Haiphong Harbor, about 60 miles (95 km) away. A muddy, gray, misty road led me out of the city.

Not far out of Hanoi, I see another military cemetery under construction. The bridges I go over are hair-raising as I manipulate the big gaps from the missing boards. I ride along with a death grip on the handle bars, doing everything I can to keep from falling into one of the ruts. On the dodge, I see a couple of very nasty accidents. The truck traffic is extremely heavy as they go back and forth from Haiphong Port to Hanoi.

After about 2 1/2 hours, I arrive in Haiphong, a dismal city that had been heavily bombed during the war. Two fellows on a little Honda showed me to the office of Viscon Ship, Maersk lines.

Arman Gonzales, a Filipino, and Mr. Khan, the head Vietnamese, and a fellow named Quan all greet me. I notice immediately that the atmosphere here is far lighter and happier than Hanoi. I was quickly surrounded by lovely Vietnamese women who worked for the two companies, enjoying tea and describing some of my adventures around the world. One spoke English quite well.

Quan asked me for my passport and visa so he could go get the motorcycle cleared to exit on one of ships, either the Saigon Concord or the Mekong Venture. When he came back a few hours later, he told me "the motorcycle cleared with no problem, but there's a problem with your visa. It is an airport visa. It is illegal for any tourist to exit the country on a ship."

My heart just fell. The sense of impending disaster once again loomed up in front of my eyes. Quan continued. "You will have to return to Hanoi to get this sorted out."

Now I hit the roof! I had shown my visa to Phong in the other office, and the answer there was always "No problem. Don't worry."

I was in a rage! Quan suggested that Jimmy would soon arrive, and maybe he could help sort something out. When Jimmy arrives, I explain my dire situation to him, and he told me to "Give us a bit of time to sort this out with Hanoi."

This is Friday, and I learn that the following Tuesday the Mekong Venture will be in port and then leave again for Taiwan and Hong Kong. What made me so angry is that I could have been "sorting this out" while I sat on my ass for days in Hanoi! "No fucken problem!"

That evening we run some errands with Jimmy around Haiphong Harbor before returning to Hanoi. The driver told me "My father went down the Ho Chi Min Trail in 1959. He also fought from the iron triangle, living in the tunnels under ground for 13 years. In 1070, he was taken prisoner by the Americans. They sent him out to an island just off the coast from Vung Tau. After liberation, they brought him back from the islands, setting him free. He walked all the way back home and surprised my mother. He had not been able to contact her in 16 years, then one day, just shows up!"

Can you imagine? I thought to myself, "How much anxiety this woman must have suffered, never really knowing about her husband, and then, suddenly, he walks back in her life and the family is united once again." What a shock!

"My father never said anything derogatory about the Americans, or how they fought the war," he continued. "He always had good things to say, especially about their conduct as soldiers."

It was gratifying to hear this. This young fellow had been a captain in the army and fought against the Chinese in the north as recently as 1985. He also fought the Cambodians in the late 70's. He was a well experienced soldier.

After all the errands are run, we drive 60 miles (95 km) back to Hanoi. On the way, we pass a 100 plus convoy of cars that had been made in Korea. Jimmy told me, "These are cars on their way into Mainland China." As we passed them, I thought "It is nice to be in this air conditioned vehicle, not have to breathe diesel exhaust."

We arrived back in Hanoi at about 23:30. Jimmy invites me to share his huge two story apartment, very French Provincial, and I accept. I gratefully take a shower and then collapse, exhausted, but am unable to sleep because of the anxiety over what the next few days will bring.

The following day, Jimmy and I go down to the office. It was to be an incredibly stressful day of waiting, sitting on pins and needles. Jimmy introduced me to Mr. Hoa on the Viscon Ship side of the office, and told him my problem. Mr. Hoa could speak a bit of English, and seemed to be a very knowledgeable man. The reader should remember that all of these people I deal with are Vietnamese, and are my age or older. Virtually every one of them had fought in the war. The areas around here - mainly Haiphong and Hanoi - had been bombed fairly regularly by the Americans. These people had personally suffered much at the hands of Americans - both in combat and by bombing. Yet now, they were so gracious, and anxious to help me!

Mr. Hoa nodded, but didn't say much except "Come with me." We got on the back of his little Honda and rode down to the police station. He explains my problem to one of the policemen, who says "It is impossible for foreigner on a tourist visa to exit the country on a ship. You will have to fly back to Tong Son nuit Airport in Saigon, and then take a flight to your destination."

That will cost a fortune, and I will be separated from the motorcycle! I was filled with apprehension and worry until he told me, "Maybe we can do something. You need a letter." So, we drive back to the Viscon Ship Office and he orders Henna what to write in a letter. Henna is not a typist, so she pecks away agonizingly slow. My heart is in my throat, thinking, "Please Henna, get on with it girl!"

When the letter is finally finished, we ride back over to the police station. The police then say, "We need another letter." So, back again. This time, Mr. Hoa tells me to stay at the office while he goes back to the station. When he arrives back, he tells me, "The police are away for lunch. We won't know anything until about 14:00."

It was 11:00 in the morning.

For the next few hours, I wait, worrying about what the verdict would be. There's always a snag, it seems, even in the simple stuff.

14:00 came and went, but Mr. Hoa never came down from his office. Mr. Dung, his associate came in, obviously just returning from the police station at 15:00. I looked at him with an expectant look on my face. He just looked away, and my heart sank, almost stopping. I realized right then that I would have to return to Saigon on the motorcycle and try again from there, which meant back-tracking 1,300 miles (2,100 km).

Mr. Dung went upstairs to Mr. Hoa's office, and I was soon called up. Mr. Hoa looked at me and says, "Visa okay. Okay." He gave me back my passport. I looked at the visa and it had a special stamp in the back of it saying that I was to exit on the Mekong Venture, a ship due in today.

Suddenly, I would leave the following day! I was jubilant! Dancing around the office! I gave Mr. Hoa and Mr. Dung hugs. After my spontaneous show of affection, Mr. Dung rather hurriedly left the office.

I offered money to Mr. Hoa, not knowing if he had to pay bribes to swing this deal. I thought of him as incredible, and wanted to give him some sort of reward.

"No. No money," he told me.

"Thank you Mr. Hoa!"

And then, in a very touching tone, he said, "David welcome back Vietnam." I was overwhelmed. I had been receiving this kind attitude throughout the country. Only once did I ever experience any animosity.

As you can well imagine, it was with an upbeat mood that I rode back in the air conditioned vehicle to Haiphong that evening. When we arrived, we drive down to the port. I was given permission to sleep on the Saigon Concord which was loading up at this particular moment. On the ship, I sat back and relaxed in the ward room, reading a magazine, when some policemen come in and ask for my passport. They ask, "Are you a passenger or crew member."

"I am neither," I reply. This conversation was not in English. Arman and Quan were there, and act as translators, telling the police my situation, and explaining that they wanted me to sleep on the ship that night. "We don't know," they respond, calling their superior. Another policeman came down, and he wasn't sure either. So, he called somebody else. As in any communist country, the rule is, "If you are not sure what to do, just say no."

That's what they did in a very polite way. "You no stay here," they told me.

A man on the ship with a big scar running from his forehead right around the side of his head, told me that he'd been in the NVA for years, fighting in the war. This man gave me a big hug and said, "Welcome American back to Vietnam. The time of war is over, and now is for peace. Let us be friends." This was the second time this had happened to me. A few days earlier, a disabled veteran with one arm missing said virtually the same words to me.

I gathered my gear and they took me to an office where I spent the night. Before I go to sleep, I show many of the workers pictures of my journey, and a map. The interest was incredible since most of these men had never traveled beyond Vietnam. They were hungry to know more about the outside world.

The following day I go into town and locate a hotel; we agree on a price. When I am ready to move in, they up the price, so I tell them "Get stuffed." Once again, the three price system strikes. We find another hotel room, and once again the same game is played. This time, I shout at the lady and she backs down to the original $12.00 a night.

I'm still very apprehensive about tomorrow; it just seems that there's always a "no problem." I walk out to get a bowl of noodles, and once again, people stare at me wherever I go. I am growing very weary of the comments and attention.

April 12: My birthday, and I'm up very early, heading down to the Maersk, Viscon Ship Office; there, I work on my dairy in peace without crowds of onlookers. By 07:00, the staff starts to arrive. Quan comes along, and I can tell by the look on his face that there's a problem, He tells me, "Dave, there is a problem with immersion suits. There are only 8 immersion suits on the ship for the eight crew and officers. It is against regulations for you to go on the ship."

I nearly went screaming wild. What now? Every time every thing appears to be going well, we hit some unforeseen obscure little regulation and there is a major problem. I told him, "Listen Quan, let's go down and see the captain."

He very reluctantly agreed.

We get in the van and drive down to the port. There on the rail watching the loading was a very big heavy-set fellow. I ask permission to come aboard The Mekong Venture, and ask to see the captain, who turns out to be the fellow watching the loading.

I introduce myself, shake his hand, and start to talk. I plead my case with him. I say, "Captain, if there's any fine for you having me on this ship, I will pay those fines. I will put up a deposit of whatever amount you want for those fines that you might incur, or for any other problems you might incur."

He was taken by my boldness, I am sure. He didn't expect to hear what he heard.

"Okay," he said. "I will okay you going onto the ship. It shouldn't be a problem (No problem, oh no!). You can get your gear and bring your motorcycle down. We will load it on the ship in the afternoon."

What a great relief! Wonderful! So why do I have this feeling of uncertainty?

Quan and I raced back across town. We fly through traffic with the horn blaring, slamming on the brakes, dodging people, nearly killing and just missing hundreds of people! What a ride!

Back at the office compound, I get the motorcycle loaded up and say good-bye to all the people who worked there, especially to the really sweet girls. After some photos, I ride out behind Quan who is now on his little motorcycle. We ride through the very crowded streets of Haiphong out to the ship, thinking to myself, "This is my last tidbit of a ride I will have in the Third World - probably ever." I waive to the crowds who look up in wonder at the sound of the Harley. I imagine some of them also recognize me from the newspaper articles.

I arrive at the ship, and policemen immediately come down to see what the crowd is doing, gathering around the motorcycle. I recognize the major of police, and a captain I had already had dealings with earlier. They are shaking hands, and everybody is nodding to each other. They want to sit on the motorcycle and take photographs. Of course, I oblige them. My gear is taken up the ladder to the room I will occupy on the second story, above the fantail.

Within an hour the captain authorizes the crane to lift the motorcycle and put it down on the fantail just outside of my room. The crew then lashes the motorcycle down to the fantail railing. At last, the motorcycle was on the ship, and so was I! I felt semi-relaxed, although I still couldn't let down. By this time, I have learned that you can be certain of absolutely nothing.

I spent most of the rest of the day up on the bridge watching the loading of the ship by the cranes, all Russian, and very slow. It was gray and miserable outside, normal for this time of year. In the late afternoon, at about 17:00, dinner was served. The crew consisted of 4 Filipino and 4 Polish officers. There were as many chiefs as Indians on the ship.

By 19:00 I saw a vehicle pull up next to the dock and out steps officials from Customs and Immigration, the police department, the harbor master, and Quan.

The ominous precession proceeds up the gangway, and my spirits start to sink.

The captain tells me to "Go to my state room."

I did.

As these fellows enter, all smile and nod their heads except one, the harbor master. He's a gray-haired man, and by the look of him, I felt there was going to be trouble. I sit back and listen to the dealings that now take place between the captain and the rest of the officials. The harbor master says, "There is a problem with the immersion suits. You cannot go."

I nearly fainted. The feeling of impending disaster was upon me. All the negative scenarios I could possibly imagine were now happening. I could just imagine my motorcycle landing in Hong Kong without me there. I was on the verge of a catatonic breakdown. The only thing I could think to say was, "Please, sir, don't put me off this ship. Please let me go."

I dare say I would have got down on my knees and begged to stay on that ship. The ship captain, Captain Gumneniuk, and Quan start doing some fast talking in Russian, both being fluent in the language. Then, the discussion includes the others. As they talk, my fate hangs in the balance. Finally, Quan motions to the harbor master to follow him, and they went outside, speaking to one another for the next 20 minutes, while I sat waiting.

When they come back in, the harbor master has a different look on his face; he nods to me. My passport is stamped, all the papers for the motorcycle are stamped, some papers are extracted from my folder, and my passport with the visa removed is handed back to me.

At that moment I realized we had won!

Quan and Captain Gumneniuk had so vigorously pressed home their argument, and saved the day. My entire body was shaking (and it takes a lot to get me to that point). I don't know if I was shaking from relief, or from fear that something else could go wrong.

The group then stood up and filed out. As they did, I knew that each one of them had experienced injury or affliction on them or their families by Americans during the war. If not by bombing, then in actual combat. For this man to change his mind and allow me to travel on the ship against regulations, no matter how obscure, was a very great thing. I will be forever grateful.

As he left, he shook my hand, as did the other officials leaving the room. As they drove off, Quan stayed on the dock for a while until a company van came along.

By 20:30, we are ready to cast off. When the ropes are hauled back onto the ship, and the ship starts to pull away from the dock, I waive to Quan who yelled, "You write."

"You bet I will write," I yelled back. "Thank you, Quan, thank you."

In truth, I couldn't thank him enough, and never will be able to.

As the ship moves away from the dock, I think to myself, "At last I am on my way to Hong Kong, and back to the world of plenty. Quan is on his way back to his world of government imposed limitations and struggle."

It was now 20:30; Quan had met me at the office at 07:00 that morning. His hours are long, his pay is short, and the bullshit he puts up with on a daily basis is incomprehensible. Arman Gonzales had told me, when I was complaining about having an ass full of bureaucratic bullshit, "Dave, I live through this every day."

My sincerest sympathy to all.

I could not breathe easy until after the ship cleared the harbor, and the pilot and police were taken off of the ship by boat. It was only then, as their vessel faded in the distance, and our ship drew away from the lights on the coast, that I started to relax on our way to Hong Kong. I remember my exit from Russia. This was a feeling of similar relief - as though a giant weight of uncertainty had just fallen off of my shoulders.

My mind now was free to remember that today I am 42 years old. 23 years ago, this month, I had left Vietnam with pain in my heart, knowing I was leaving fellow Marines and friends behind. I had flown and fought with these men, and it hurt to leave them.

Now, I was again leaving Vietnam with a heavy heart - but for the Vietnamese who had once been our enemies. Their help made it possible for me to leave for the fabled lands of freedom and plenty, while they remained behind, living their lives out in difficulty and hardship. I soon laid back and closed my day, and the last adventure of the journey.

Happy Birthday, Dave.

Chapter Thirty-Eight

Rolling Thunder

The following morning at 06:00, after a restless night's sleep, I go up on the bridge and find Captain Gumneniuk, sincerely thanking him for his intervention.

"Ya, it is no problem." My heart skipped a beat with the utterance of these most feared words.

As we sail on, I ask about his career as a sailor. "I've been 30 years at sea, 10 of those fishing in the North Atlantic above the Arctic Circle. I could tell you a few stories! This is a German ship, and we stay out at sea six months at a time. My time off is less than my time on."

The day was overcast; not much of a sunrise. By afternoon, we were coming into the Hainan Straits. Hainan is an island off the east coast of China, and the Captain told me "I am very apprehensive about going through Hainan at night because of all the fishing trollers and nets. Those nets can get caught in the prop."

"There's also a problem with pirates," he continued.

Naturally, I was surprised to hear that.

"People now a days don't think much about pirates," he continued. "Most Westerners think of them as a bygone day, but apparently they still attack ships and loot them."

When I traveled on the Saigon Concord with a Danish crew, we ate prime rib, french fries, and other fancy meals. The crew of this ship was eating rice, fried fish, beef and chicken as tough as shoe leather. I'm not complaining about the food, mind you. It is just great to be on this ship - period! If they fed me out of cold cans and confined me to my quarters, I'd still be a very happy person. It's just that I couldn't help but make comparisons between the two ships. Both ships were neat and clean, and the crews were both very professional. The main difference - this crew had a far harder life, serving longer periods at sea.

Little Ships, BIG Men

Finally, my body could relax, and I probably established the Dave Barr sleeping record - the longest night's sleep since the adventure began - TEN hours! I especially enjoyed the relaxing roll of the ship when I hit the rack. If I wanted, I could leave my door open and actually see the motorcycle strapped securely down to the hand rail at the fan tail, from my bunk.

We came into some pretty heavy seas, but this proud little ship of 2500 tons handled the swells quite nicely. Days pass. On April 18, at 14:00, I spot the high rise buildings and smog of Hong Kong on the horizon.

As we sail closer to the harbor, I see more and more ships at anchor. Once into the harbor, I am astounded at how busy Hong Kong harbor is. Mighty ships with luxurious names - President Grant, Cho Yong Glory, UniGlory - stand at proud attention, and dwarf the Mekong Venture.

We tie up to a mooring buoy and wait a few hours until a pilot comes along. Once the pilot is on board, we go into the harbor proper and tie up to another buoy and waited for the container barge to come out.

There are no proper docks for unloading. Barges come out with cranes on them and take off the containers, then put on more containers; it is all done out in the harbor.

Along about 18:00, a container barge comes alongside and starts the cargo transfer. By 22:00, it is done.

Now it is time to take the motorcycle and put it on the barge. It is lifted over with ease by crane. The baggage is then carried across, and I go across to the barge after saying good-bye and shaking hands with Captain Gumneunik and Andrzej, the engineer. Once on the barge, I notice the Captain has a tear in his eye, as I did in mine. I was leaving behind very good men. As we pull away, I waive to the engineer, Andrzej, and he waives back. We keep waiving until the BIG men on the proud little ship are too small to see, swallowed up in the lights of hundreds of vessels and the malaise that is Hong Kong Harbor. Oh God, I beg of You to give them calm seas and long life.

The Chinese stevedores are all hollering and shouting at one another as I turn back to reality. They are serving a meal, and invite me to sit down and eat with them. It wasn't a request; it was something I must do. We had a pot full of macaroni with boiled, tough meat. With bowls to our mouths, we shoveled it in with chop sticks.

After dinner, I watch as the barge is pulled passed the skyscrapers right down, almost to the edge of the water. Gradually, Hong Kong drifted out of sight.

Where we went, I don't know, but I remember seeing Marlin's apartment building in Cause Way Bay. About 24:00, the barge pulls alongside a dock somewhere on the other side of the island. Everybody settles in for the night. I sleep restlessly on the floor.

The next morning, in the light, I try to spot landmarks. Nothing doing. When the crew gets up, they waste no time in shoving the motorcycle into an empty container, bringing it level to the rail of the hold. I toss my gear inside, then me and two crew members climb inside the container which was promptly planted out in an open dirt field. Everywhere around me the dirt was all turned as it was all under construction. We then took the motorcycle and my gear out of the container.

As I was loading my motorcycle, I said to the crew, "Fang shan Hong Kong?" They looked at one another and laughed. "Hong Kong," I repeated, and they point off in the distance. I couldn't see anything familiar in that direction.

After thanking them in my few words of Mandarin, which they probably didn't understand, I started up and rode away, soon coming to a gate and street in a built up area. At the street I ask some taxi drivers for directions. "Not interested. Don't bother me," they seemed to say.

Reunions and Encores

I decided to get on the street and follow the signs to Hong Kong, which couldn't be too far. I eventually found my way to one of the freeways, and it was easy from there to ride to Wan Chi and the All Motorcycles shop on Jaffe Street. By this time, it was only 07:30 in the morning; I waited a few hours before anyone shows up. At this point, I still hadn't checked in with Customs, and I hadn't had any of my motorcycle papers cleared yet.

About 09:30, Danny, one of the managers of All Motorcycles, arrives and opens up. We push the Harley Davidson inside; one of his assistants, Tony, goes with me to the Customs office. We go from office to office, floor to floor, window to window, getting turned around, spending $16.00 for a book of import permits, then found out at another window that I didn't need them.

After all the running around for no purpose at all, I now need to change some money. This proves to be difficult since I want to change Deutsche Marks. We went to one bank and they refused to change them because the corners were torn. Finally, I took out $20.00 and said, "Well, change this," and they told me, "That will be 30.00 Hong Kong dollars," which amounted to about $3.75 American

I hit the roof and told them to go to hell. Now I knew I was back in the First World.

We go back to the shop and Danny says, "Here, take these 500 Hong Kong dollars. You can pay me back when you get your money changed."

From there, I to say "hello" in Northpoint to William Chan, the owner and manager of the shop. William gave me a big hug, then we sat and chatted. He introduces me to his staff, and shows me around the Northpoint shop which has grown since I was last there. The Jaffe street shop no longer had a work shop; it had become a boutique for Harley Davidson paraphernalia.

By late afternoon, I was ready to go to Marilyn's apartment. How great it was to see her. It's been almost a year and a half since the last time we'd seen one another before I left for Mainland China. My gear inside, I take a very welcome shower as a relief from the Hong Kong heat and humidity. We all turn in early that evening.

April 20: Tomorrow it will be one year from the day I left Beijing behind to head out into the Gobi desert, Mongolia and Russia. So much has transpired in that time. I call Ze Qing and catch her at home. She is "very busy," and will graduate from University in a few months with honors. She asks, "When can I see you? Are you coming?"

"I am sorry," I answer, "but there is no way I can come all the way back to Beijing. I cannot spend the money." She understood.

I make an appointment to visit with Maersk Line and offer to do media promotion for them. They decline, saying that "Maersk was just very happy to help." I then ask about sending the motorcycle on to the states. "How much would it cost?" John says, "We may be able to do it for nothing. Let us know the dates and we will see what ships are available."

When I went to P & O, they offered me the same thing! I told their public relations officer that "I would be happy to do any media for them. Just let me know how I can help."

I meet with the President of the Harley Owner's Club, and we make arrangements for me to give a talk and slide show, and about 50 people attended. We enjoyed a great meal, and the slide show and talk went over very well. It is one of the better talks I have given on the trip, although I admit to being a bit nervous since I haven't given a talk in quite sometime.

I also gave an encore talk and slide show to the Hong Kong East Rotary Club. They told me that "This is only the second time we've ever had a person back for a second talk." I felt very complimented.

One Sunday, I ride with Little Joe, a Japanese fellow from All Motorcycles, on the back of my motorcycle with the Harley Owner's Group of Hong Kong. I was glad they stayed out on the highways since my motorcycle needed a good run at proper speed to loosen it up a little bit. The ride was 1,300 miles (2100 km) through Vietnam at speeds of anywhere from 25 to 30 miles an hour (35-45 km), in second and third gear.

My time in Hong Kong did have one major damper.

After giving the talk for the Harley Owner's Group, I mentioned an incident in China where I hit an old man on a bicycle. He was hollering and shouting and carrying on, and I thought he was bullshiting. When I put 50 RMB in his pocket, he stopped, looked at it, then shouted louder. The following day Marilyn told me, "Dave, there's is something I should tell you."

"What, Marilyn?" I replied, not liking the tone of her voice.

"Well, when Lin was here we chatted about your time in China. As we talked, I sensed something was wrong. I finally managed to get it out of him that the old man that you hit was disabled, and is now bedridden, and in a lot of pain. His back had been broken."

What a shock!

A sick feeling hit me right in the guts.

I thought, "Oh my God, the journey around the world was for the disabled, and I have disabled somebody on that journey! Oh God, forgive me. What an ass I have been,

493

making a joke of it in my talks. Oh, how terrible of me!"

As Marilyn looked at me, it was everything I could do to keep from breaking down. I managed to control myself, saying, "What happened? How did Lin handle it?"

"Apparently he went back and the crowd was very angry, wanting to go to the police. Lin was very brave. He somehow managed to settle the crowd down, and negotiated, over a period of time, a settlement with the family. How much he gave them I don't know. Since the old man had been the bread winner of the family, he also got the son a very good job in a factory."

"What a great guy," I think as I hear the story. Lin Xu Chang is what I call an incredible man.

I spent the next few days trying to get a hold of Lin on the phone. Finally, when I did, I explained how high in regard I hold him. "You are responsible solely for saving the trip. Had the authorities caught me, they would have put me on a truck and shuffled me out of the country. You saved everything."

I then shared with him all of the good that had come from my time in China. He accepted this very graciously, trying to be modest, saying "You would have done the same for me."

On the media scene, bombs are exploding all over South Africa. One day there were 19 deaths. Elections are only days away.

Chris Pedder, my guide to the border at Lo Wu, asks me to give a talk and slide show at the police academy, and it went very well. Most of the policemen were Chinese officers, although many were Europeans. When I was finished, one of the officers, a Chinese inspector, took off his tie and carefully placed it in the hat being passed around. The tie displayed the Chinese colors of courage. I proudly wear that tie to this day whenever I give a talk and slide show.

How Do You Close a Dream?

April 29: I saw a glimpse of Mandela giving a speech on CNN. He was winning the election by a landslide. Mandela was saying, "It is not the outcome of the election that is important, but the fact that all people, all South Africans, could vote their hopes and dreams for the political party of their choice." I thought to myself "Bullshit, Mandela. If you guys lose the election, you will go back to bombing and murdering the same as before."

William Chan got in 3 brand new Harley Davidsons, so we brought my motorcycle down and boxed it up in one of the new crates. William has a friend take the motorcycle down to the warehouse of Marsk Lines, who has made arrangements for the motorcycle to be shipped in the coming week, free of charge! It was scheduled to leave Hong Kong on May 5, heading back to the United States.

The evening of May 4, I am invited out to dinner with Marilyn by friends of ours, Holger Gossmann, a German fellow, and Julie, his Chinese-American wife. We met at the Regents Hotel, the finest in Hong Kong. We walk up the forecourt of the Regents Hotel, strolling in the midst of Mercedes, Rolls Royce's, and a few Daimlers. The whole forecourt is lit up and elegant indeed. Inside, covered with rich furnishings, the atmosphere proclaims immense wealth and luxury. We meet Holger and Julie and go to the fish restaurant where there's an aquarium the full length of one wall, with fish swimming serenely back and forth, oblivious to the watching humans. In this famous fish restaurant, Holger has reserved a window seat looking out on Hong Kong Harbor. We could see all the high skyscraper buildings in the distance. The malaise of ships, Junks and ferries run helter skelter across the harbor, their lights blaring against the blackness of the night, and reflecting off the water.

Our conversation was light, and the meal was just as delightful. I think, "How

494

incredible and lucky I am to be sitting in all this elegance with these fine people." Looking out at the harbor, I wonder, "What will it be like tomorrow when I arrive back in the United States?" I have this impending feeling of anti-climax, as if the world were closing in on me.

"What are you going to do when you get home, Dave?" they ask me.

"Well, the first thing I've got to do is get the motorcycle back from the shippers. It should be there in two weeks. As I understand the plan right now, I will then take it for one last ride back to the factory, and there turn it over to them to be put in the Hall of Fame, which should be open by now. Then, I'll get started on the book."

In the midst of all the uncertainties of tomorrow, one thing I knew for sure: there'd be no more nights out in places like the Regent Hotel.

After dinner, we walk along towards the ferry boat terminal in an area of beautiful rock gardens where young Chinese couples are laughing and talking to themselves. I think to myself, "How I will miss Asia. I've become very accustomed to the ways of the people of Southeast Asia and China. I will miss the hustle and bustle of Hong Kong and China where people move with purpose and direction - towards success."

On the ferry, a cool breeze blows through the seating area. Marilyn and I chatted lightly about Hong Kong's future. There is still apprehension about what life will be after 1997. Many Chinese tell me they will go to Canada. My friends on the police force who are Europeans will lose their jobs. There will be no white police inspectors - only Chinese. It is with these thoughts on our minds that we cross Hong Kong Harbor.

At the ferry terminal, we take a cab to Marilyn's apartment building, go up to our separate rooms and close our day about 24:00, my last abroad.

May 5, 1994: This morning I say good-bye to Marilyn. What a benefactor you have been to this journey!

After packing, Patrick Ho from the motorcycle shop picks me up in his Audi, and we drive to the airport where he gives me a watch and a box of good Chinese tea.

About 11:00, I walk through the departure lounge, and through Customs and Immigration, boarding the plane about noon. Soon, we were off.

As the plane flew out, I viewed Causeway Bay and Hong Kong Harbor for the last time. We flew over Mainland China and I visualized many of the roads and close calls I had there in the past. After leaving the coast and flying over the ocean for about three hours, we landed at Kimpo Airport.

"These last three and half years feel like one endless day," I think, "since each day starts so early and finishes so late; one moment flows into the next. Now, here I am flying from one day back into the same day - crossing the international date line. I've experienced, literally, a day without end."

Before entering the departure lounge for the connecting flight, I saw a young Chinese girl singled out and rudely pushed off to the side. When I walked passed her, I said "I hope you are able to go on." There had been a problem with her passport and visa. She said, "Yes," and not much else. I could feel the terrible tension and apprehension she felt at that moment.

I sat down and waited. Soon, we boarded the plane and took off over the Pacific Ocean. Another 10 hours went by, then we touched down in Los Angeles International. After clearing Customs and Immigration, and being welcomed back into the United States, I went up to the reception lounge and spotted my Uncle Harvey and my dear old Mom, Lucille Barr. We all give each other big hugs! There are no tears of joy, for we have done this too many times before. Tears only come when we part.

We throw my gear into my Uncle's vehicle, and drive to his house.

All very anti-climatic.

Welcome home boy! Back in freeway traffic.

The following day we visit some relatives. Nobody really asks about the trip. Instead, they talk about all the immediate things in their surroundings. Of course, I feel like the odd man out. How can I even begin to relate what I've been through in these past few months, in the past few years, to my family?

Later that day, Mom and I drive on to her home up in Bodfish, California, resting on the side of a mountain in a rural area about 160 miles (250 km) from Los Angeles. In the quiet nights of this country place, I would lay back and think about all the miles I had put behind me. I knew there was still one more ride - or so I thought at the moment - to take the motorcycle back to the factory. That should be enjoyable, riding in America.

May 9, 1994: I call the factory and speak to Dan Klemencic, telling him I am back in the States. He said, "Great, Dave, when are we going to see you so we can have a ceremony and give you a brand new motorcycle and take yours over?"

"Well, I don't know. I guess that depends on you folks. Is the Hall of Fame finished?"

"No," he said.

"When will it be finished?"

"I don't know right now," he answered.

"Well, what are you going to do with my motorcycle?"

He said, "We will store it away."

"No Dan. I didn't do this to get a new motorcycle, and I am not throwing this back to you in an arrogant sense. I appreciate that you would give me a new motorcycle, that was not part of our deal."

Without that offer, I probably wouldn't ride one again what with the cost of them today.

"Dan, I want to keep my motorcycle until you are ready to put it into a museum. It is not meant to be just stored away."

He kind of mulled this over quietly on the other end of the phone. I continued.

"If you are ready to display it at any time, please let me know. If that is not satisfactory, I will give the $2,500.00 back to the company that they gave me for overhaul of the motorcycle."

May 10: Dan called me today and said, "Well, there's no place where they can display it. You should just keep the motorcycle until such time as the Hall of Fame is built, and then we will take it."

With that phone call, I realized my journey around the world was over.

I put the phone down and wander, in a dazed state, out to the garage to collect my thoughts and get myself together. I spent the next week sorting out all the media, and the various gifts I have received from wonderful people the world over. I got a phone call indicating that "the motorcycle has arrived at Maersk Lines, and is being cleared through. You can come down and pick it up." I did, with the help of my Uncle Harvey. We took it to my cousin Allen's body shop where I cleaned it up and serviced it.

Then I ride it back to Bodfish where it now spends most of its time in the garage, not out on the roads of the world. It is not ridden that often any more. I would hate to see something happen to it, for it to become a piece of junk.

I spend many hours out in the garage working on the various aspects of my book about this incredible journey around the world, and the things I have learned from it. I have come to realize that no man is a rock or an island. We all need help sooner or later. I have been so fortunate to receive that help from people who were hungry and in rags, right up the ladder to the very high and mighty, all to make the journey happen. I have received help and guidance, strength and wisdom from God and Jesus Christ, or I wouldn't have survived. Too often my fate was totally in God's hands.

Looking upon the motorcycle as I work in the garage, sometimes my mind begins to wander to far off lands, to incredible people I have met along the way, and to the seemingly impossible situations we have come through. I often think about the worry, the work, the dangers, the roads, the countries, the people, the uncertainty and the million and one things it took to make this journey. In my mind's eye, I see people standing in villages or along a road in some far off place, turning to man and machine with eyes wide and mouth agape, looking on in wonder at the ROLLING THUNDER!

The end.

A Picture of Uncle Ho Chi Minh
Da Nang, Vietnam. March 31, 1994

Heading up Route 1.
It doesn't take long to draw a friendly crowd.
Vietnam. March 1994

Vietcong/North Vietnamese Army Cemetery.
One of many along Route 1.
April 1994

Remnants of Marble Mt. Helicopter Base
where Dave was stationed 24 years ago - April 1970 to April 1971
As it appears now March 31, 1994.

Ho Chi Minh Square, Hanoi.
April 5, 1994 Hanoi, Vietnam.

On the South China Sea.
Aboard the Mekong Venture.
L to R - Captain Gumuniek, Engineer Andrzej, 1st Officer Joseph.
April 1994.
Great Big Men on a Proud Little Ship!

ABOUT THE AUTHOR

Dave Barr is a 43-year-old native of Los Angeles, California.

At the age of 17, in June, 1969, Dave joined the U.S. Marine Corps, serving a three year enlistment; he served one year in Vietnam as a helicopter crew chief and door gunner on a Huey gun ship, and received 57 air medals for missions flown in Vietnam.

In 1972, he separated from the marines, but could never comfortably settle into civilian life, instead feeling an inner-call to seek adventure, to fight for an ideal.

In 1974, Dave went to Israel, and within a year joined the Israeli paratroopers where he served from 1975 to 1977.

Upon returning to the U.S., Dave fell into the routine of living from day to day. Determined to once again pursue the call to adventure and far away places, Dave took off to the Mid East, and then to Zimbabwe, Rhodesia, where he served in the Rhodesian Light Infantry, One Commando, for one year. When the unit was disbanded after the liberation, and Zanu PF came to power, Dave, like many soldiers of the day, went south and joined the South African Army on January 15, 1981, serving two years in the Pathfinder Company of the 44 th Parachute Brigade under the leadership of Colonel Breytenbach.

Dave has now formed the **Dave Barr Foundation** (see next page) to assist the disabled, particularly war veterans throughout the world where their governments fail to help in their rehabilitation. The Foundation's primary purpose is to provide artificial limbs for those who would not otherwise have them. He also continues to assist the Leonard Cheshire Foundation whenever possible. Much of the profits from *Riding the Edge* will go towards enabling the disabled in distant lands to live better lives.

Dave enjoys skydiving, and has been in and out of the sport for twenty-one years. He has made over 500 jumps, 200 as a double-amputee at the time of this writing. His greatest love will always be a ride through the open country, early in the morning, on his motorcycle.

IF YOU ARE THANKFUL FOR YOUR GOOD HEALTH, WHY NOT GIVE A GIFT TO HELP THOSE LESS FORTUNATE?

As Dave Barr travels around the world, He constantly meets many disabled people who cannot walk - simply because there is no money available to equip them with artificial limbs. After seeing a pattern around the world of deficient care for the disabled, Dave decided to launch a world-wide effort to equip them with the limbs they need to live their lives as fully and completely as possible.

To assist the disabled, Dave continues to support *The Leonard Cheshire Foundation*, a world-wide organization for the betterment of the disabled.

Further, he has established *The Dave Barr Foundation*, a non-profit organization dedicated to encouraging the disabled and war veterans, primarily in Third World countries where the care is usually less than adequate, and to provide them with whatever they need.

For some, it is providing an artificial limb.

For others, it may be counseling.

For still others, it may be providing information on how to best modify machinery to adjust to the disability.

Currently, there is an overwhelming need for artificial limbs!

Because of our contacts in Third World countries, we can provide a basic artificial limb to most disabled for around $500 - that's a fraction of the cost of a limb in the United States. Of course, our limbs are not as sophisticated as the high-priced versions, but they still represent FREEDOM and INDEPENDENCE to those who receive them!

Won't you help us with your tax-deductible donation today?

Kindly send your gift to:

**THE DAVE BARR FOUNDATION
P.O. BOX 8633
BODFISH, CA 93205**

On their behalf...THANK YOU!

502